SOCIOLOGY

SOCIOLO

JAMES W. VANDER ZANDEN
The Ohio State University

FOURTH EDITION

JOHN WILEY & SONS

New York
Chichester
Brisbane
Toronto

Production was supervised by Rose Mary Hirsch

Copyright © 1965, 1970, 1975, 1979, by John Wiley & Sons, Inc.

All rights reserved. Published simultaneously in Canada.

Reproduction or translation of any part of
this work beyond that permitted by Sections
107 and 108 of the 1976 United States Copyright
Act without the permission of the copyright
owner is unlawful. Requests for permission
or further information should be addressed to
the Permissions Department, John Wiley & Sons.

Library of Congress Cataloging in Publication Data:

Vander Zanden, James Wilfrid.
   Sociology.

  Includes bibliographical references and indexes.
  1. Sociology. I. Title.

HM51.V35   1979   301   78-14447
ISBN 0-471-04341-9

Printed in the United States of America

10 9 8 7 6 5 4 3 2

TO MY SONS,
NELS AND BRAD

PREFACE

No other academic discipline touches the human condition as closely as sociology. As a science of society and human interaction, it develops our understanding of how we, as social beings, are woven into the fabric of our society. Sociology aids us in understanding what is happening about us and what social forces are coming to bear on us. Armed with such understanding, we should be able to act more directly, consciously, and deliberately to shape our lives in a constructive manner.

This book aims to achieve these goals by providing students with a firm foundation in basic sociological principles. It seeks to make sociology come alive as a vital and exciting field, to relate principles to real-world circumstances and events, and to attune students to the dynamic processes of our rapidly changing contemporary society. In this way the study of a science comes to captivate student interest and excite student imagination.

In keeping with this perspective, I have again included in this edition Excerpts from Student Sociology Journals. The journal entries contain students' recordings of observations or events which they then interpret with a sociological concept or principle. These Excerpts are provided to answer student complaints that college introductory courses are often little more than concepts—so many words that they have to learn and recall in definition form on examinations. All too often, students mechanically learn the concepts, at least well enough to pass their exams; when the course is over, if not earlier, they forget them.

I would like to avoid this condition in sociology. I have sought to provide students not only with a comfortable, genuine, and firm grasp of key sociological concepts, but with a visceral understanding of them. The Excerpts offer the advantage of being very readable—of bringing the full drama, color, and richness of the human experience to bear in the learning process. In a very real sense, *student teaches student*.

I would also like to help students to begin thinking like sociologists. Since much of modern sociological research is highly technical, instructors find it easy to slip into the habit of merely *telling* students that "Sociologists have found . . ." or that "Studies have been done. . . ." Yet we certainly do not want to contribute to the production of robots who mechanically recite facts with little or no insight or creativity. To do so is to belie the ethos of science — a spirit characterized by rationality and skepticism.

Accordingly, I have also included Research Studies in this edition. Introductory students commonly find that many of the most important papers in professional sociological journals are "too heavy" for them — they cannot handle the complicated methodological and statistical procedures. Hence, each Study contains a significant piece of sociological research presented in a form understandable to the neophyte. The Studies are related to the subject matter of their respective chapters and are divided step-by-step into problem, hypothesis, method, findings, and conclusions.

I have made a number of changes in this edition. A chapter has been added dealing with gender roles and inequality. The chapters dealing with the economic and political institutions have been combined within one chapter. The previous edition undertook to interweave material from the symbolic interactionist, structure-function, and conflict schools. This edition expands the treatment of the symbolic interactionist and conflict perspectives while adding material from the ethnomethodological and social exchange orientations. Finally, a variety of new topics are considered including ethics in scientific research, the definition of the situation, negotiated order, sociobiology, language, Jean Piaget's approach to socialization, socialization across the life span, role-taking and role-making, impression management, groupthink, the status attainment process, and major institutional trends.

JAMES W. VANDER ZANDEN

CONTENTS

1 INTRODUCTION — 3

WHAT IS UNIQUE ABOUT SOCIOLOGY? — 7
- Sociology as a Science — 8
- The Subject Matter of Sociology — 12

SOCIOLOGICAL THEORY — 13
- Structure-Function Theory — 14
- Conflict Theory — 15
- Social Exchange Theory — 16
- Symbolic Interactionist Theory — 17
- Ethnomethodology — 18

THE NATURE OF SOCIAL RESEARCH — 19
- Selecting and Defining a Problem — 21
- Techniques of Data Collection — 22
- The Experiment — 27
- Analysis — 30
- Ethics in Research — 31

PRACTICAL USES OF SOCIOLOGY — 32
- The Pure Science Orientation — 34
- The Applied Science Orientation — 36
- The Critical Science Orientation — 37
- Enlightenment and Engineering — 38

RESEARCH STUDY 1 — 24
- Street Corner Society — William Foote Whyte

RESEARCH STUDY 2 — 28
- Ethnic Prejudice and Susceptibility to Persuasion — Russell Middleton

PART ONE: CULTURE — 41

2
CULTURE: AN OVERVIEW — 43

THE NATURE OF CULTURE — 45
- What Is Culture? — 45
- The Definition of the Situation — 51
NORMS — 53
- Folkways and Mores — 53
- Law — 56
- Negotiated Order — 56
VALUES — 60
SYMBOLS AND LANGUAGE — 63
- The Importance of Symbols — 64
- Language — 66
SUBCULTURE AND COUNTERCULTURE — 67
- Subculture — 67
- Counterculture — 69
RESEARCH STUDY 3 — 49
- Cultural Components in Responses to Pain
  Mark Zborowski
RESEARCH STUDY 4 — 58
- Negotiated Order in Psychiatric Hospitals
  Anselm Strauss

3
SOCIALIZATION — 75

NATURE AND NURTURE — 77
- The Relationship Between Heredity and Environment — 77
- Sociobiology — 80
- The Inadequacy of Human Environment Alone — 82
- The Inadequacy of Human Heredity Alone — 84
- The Dynamic Interplay of Heredity and Environment — 87
THE SELF — 92
- The "Looking-Glass Self" — 92
- Self-Appraisals — 94
- Mead's Theory of the Development of the Self — 97
- Socialization Across the Life Span — 102
RESEARCH STUDY 5 — 90
- Cognitive Development—Jean Piaget
RESEARCH STUDY 6 — 96
- "Born Losers" Jeanne Marecek and David R. Mettee

4
ROLES: THE FASHIONING OF EVERYDAY LIFE   109

BASIC CONCEPTS   111
- Roles   111
- The Role-Set   114
- Social Structure   116
- Role-Taking and Role-Making   117
- Impression Management   120

ROLES AND IDENTITY   122
- "Who Am I?"   123
- Valid Identity   124

ROLE STRAIN   127
- Role Conflict   127
- Mechanisms for Dealing with Role Conflict   132
- Role Ambiguity   136

RESEARCH STUDY 7   126
Face-Saving at the Singles Dance — Bernard Berk

RESEARCH STUDY 8   135
Becoming an Ex-Priest — Frances A. DellaCava

PART TWO: GROUP BEHAVIOR   145

5
GROUPS AND FORMAL ORGANIZATIONS   147

THE NATURE OF GROUPS   149
STATISTICAL CATEGORIES   151
SOCIAL CATEGORIES   152
SOCIAL GROUPS   153
- Primary and Secondary Groups   153
- In-Groups and Out-Groups   158
- Reference Groups   161

FORMAL ORGANIZATIONS   164
- The Nature of Bureaucracy   165
- Weber's Conception of Bureaucracy   166
- Social Consequences of Bureaucracy   168
- Alternative Formulations Regarding Formal Organizations   170
- Informal Organization   174

RESEARCH STUDY 9   159
Experiment in Group Conflict — Muzafer Sherif

RESEARCH STUDY 10   173
The Practicalities of Rule Use — Don H. Zimmerman

6
CONFORMITY AND DEVIANCE — 181

CONFORMITY — 183
- Factors Producing Conformity — 183
- Group Forces and Conformity in Judgment — 186

DEVIANCE — 188
- Social Definitions of Deviance: Drug Use — 190
- Deviance and Social Life — 191
- The Prevalence of Deviance — 193
- Rehabilitation Versus Deterrence — 198

THEORIES OF DEVIANCE — 201
- Anomie and Deviance — 201
- Conflict and Deviance — 205
- Differential Association and Deviance — 208
- Labeling and Deviance — 209

RESEARCH STUDY 11 — 196
- The Professional Fence — Carl B. Klockars

RESEARCH STUDY 12 — 211
- Societal Reaction as an Explanation of Mental Illness: An Evaluation — Walter R. Gove

7
COLLECTIVE BEHAVIOR AND SOCIAL MOVEMENTS — 215

DETERMINANTS OF COLLECTIVE BEHAVIOR — 219
- Structural Conduciveness — 220
- Structural Strain — 221
- The Growth of a Generalized Belief — 222
- Precipitating Factors — 223
- The Mobilization of Participants for Action — 223
- The Operation of Social Control — 224

CROWD BEHAVIOR — 225
- Contagion Theories — 225
- The Convergence Theory — 227
- The Emergent Norm Theory — 228
- Crowd Selection of Targets — 230

THE MASS — 231
- Mass Communication — 232
- The Significance and Effects of Mass Communication — 233

THE PUBLIC — 236
- Public Opinion — 237
- Public Conceptions of Social Problems — 238

Contents

SOCIAL MOVEMENTS	243
The Nature of Social Movements	244
Elements of Social Movements	244
RESEARCH STUDY 13	240
Accidental News: The Great Oil Spill	
Harvey Molotch and Marilyn Lester	
PART THREE: SOCIAL INEQUALITY	253

8 SOCIAL STRATIFICATION   255

INEQUALITY	257
Power Hierarchies	257
Privilege Hierarchies	259
Status Hierarchies	261
SOURCES OF SOCIAL STRATIFICATION	263
Functionalist Theories	264
Conflict Theories	265
APPROACHES FOR STUDYING STRATIFICATION	267
The Objective Approach	269
The Subjective Approach	269
The Reputational Approach	270
THE SIGNIFICANCE OF SOCIAL CLASSES	274
Health	274
Child-Rearing Practices	275
Marital and Family Relations	275
Religious Life	277
Political Behavior	278
SOCIAL MOBILITY	279
Caste and Class Systems	279
Social Mobility in the United States	281
The Status Attainment Process	283
RESEARCH STUDY 14	286
The Status Attainment Process—William H. Sewell and Robert M. Hauser	

9 RACE AND ETHNIC RELATIONS   291

RACIAL AND ETHNIC INEQUALITY	293
Dominant and Minority Group Relations	293
Ethnocentrism	294
Prejudice and Discrimination	296
Institutionalism Racism	299

xiv Contents

SOURCES OF RACISM	302
Diversity and Categorization	303
Competition	304
Unequal Power	308
SOCIAL UNITY AND DISUNITY	310
Consensus	311
Functional Reciprocity	312
Coercion	315
Assimilation, Segregation, and Pluralism	316
MINORITY RESPONSES TO DOMINATION	318
A Typology of Responses	318
The Black Protest	320
RESEARCH STUDY 15	306
An Example of Culture Contact Without Conflict Ethel John Lindgren	

10
GENDER ROLES AND INEQUALITY 327

GENDER ROLES	328
Gender Roles and Culture	330
Gender Roles and Biology	333
Acquiring Gender Behaviors and Identities	336
Gender and Achievement Motivations and Expectations	341
SEX STRATIFICATION	345
Homemaking and Childcare	346
The Wage Economy	348
Sexual Inequality, Exploitation, and Abuse	352
GENDER ROLES AND CHANGE	354
The Women's Movement	354
Androgynous Roles	356
RESEARCH STUDY 16	343
Skewed Sex Ratios and Token Women—Rosabeth Moss Kanter	

PART FOUR: INSTITUTIONS 363

11
INSTITUTIONAL PROCESSES AND CHANGE 365

INSTITUTIONS IN EVERYDAY LIFE	367
The Importance of Institutions: The Case of the Pitcairn Islanders	367
Interrelationships Among Institutions	370
Systems	371

Contents

Functions and Dysfunctions	373
Manifest and Latent Functions	375
INSTITUTIONAL CHANGE	376
Rate of Change	377
Processes of Institutional Change	380
Innovation	381
Diffusion	390
Reworking and Reinterpretation	394
Social Change Under Pressure	396
Resistance to Change	398
RESEARCH STUDY 17	387
Competition in Science—Warren O. Hagstrom	
RESEARCH STUDY 18	392
The Diffusion of an Innovation Among Physicians James Coleman, Elihu Katz, and Herbert Menzel	

12 THE FAMILY 403

FUNCTIONS	406
Sexual Regulation	406
Reproduction	407
Socialization	408
Maintenance	409
Social Placement	409
Personal Needs	410
FAMILY AND MARRIAGE PATTERNS	412
Cross-Cultural Variation in Family Organization	412
Advantages and Disadvantages of Consanguine and Conjugal Patterns	414
Forms of Marriage	416
MATE SELECTION	417
Social Aspects of Love	417
The Social Regulation of Mate Selection	419
Factors in Mate Selection	421
MARITAL SATISFACTION	423
SOCIAL CHANGE: SOME RECENT TRENDS	427
One-Person Households	428
Unmarried Cohabitation	429
Single-Parent Families	431
Communes	433
Homosexual Relationships	434
RESEARCH STUDY 19	425
Marital Satisfaction over the Family Life Cycle Boyd C. Rollins and Harold Feldman	

13 RELIGION   439

THE NATURE OF RELIGION   441
- Secular and Humanistic Religions   443
- Religion and Magic   445

FUNCTIONS   447
- Dealing with the "Breaking Points"   447
- An Integrator of Society   449
- Opiate or Inspiration?   450

TYPES OF RELIGIOUS ORGANIZATION   453
- Church   453
- Sect   455
- Denomination   458
- Cult   458
- The Emergence of Sects: The Black Muslims   459
- Critique of the Church-Sect Typology   461

THE PROTESTANT ETHIC   462
- The Weber Thesis   463
- Critique of the Weber Thesis   465
- Religious Preference and Worldly Success   467

SOCIAL CHANGE: SOME RECENT TRENDS   471
- Secularization   472
- Countercultural Religions   473
- Catholic Pentecostalism   474

RESEARCH STUDY 20   469
The Socioeconomic Achievement of White Religio-Ethnic Subgroups: Social and Psychological Explanations—David L. Featherman

14 THE ECONOMY AND THE STATE   479

THE ECONOMY   480
- Functions   480
- Work   484
- National Development   494

THE STATE   497
- Functions   499
- Power and Authority   502
- Power in America   504
- Democracy   509

SOCIAL CHANGE: SOME RECENT TRENDS   512
- Poverty   512
- American Voting Behavior   514

Contents

RESEARCH STUDY 21	493
Occupational Structure and Alienation	
Melvin L. Kohn	

15 EDUCATION   521

FUNCTIONS	523
Completing Socialization	524
Transmission of Specialized Skills	524
Reproducing the Social Relations of Production	526
Research and Development	527
A "Sorting and Sifting" Agency	528
Latent Functions	530
THE SCHOOL AS A SOCIAL SYSTEM	530
Classroom Life	531
Bureaucratic Organization	533
Informal Organization	534
School Effectiveness	536
SOCIAL CLASS AND EDUCATION	539
Alienation of Inner-City Children	541
Subcultural Differences	542
Educational Self-Fulfilling Prophecies	544
SOCIAL CHANGE: SOME RECENT TRENDS	547
School Desegregation	547
The "Back to Basics" Movement	549
RESEARCH STUDY 22	546
Teacher-Student Interactions—Glenn Firestone	
and Nathan Brody	

PART FIVE: DEMOGRAPHY AND URBANIZATION	553

16 POPULATION   555

POPULATION OF THE UNITED STATES	559
Determinants of Population Size	560
Spatial Distribution	570
Composition	572
WORLD POPULATION	576
Population, Food, and Theory	576
Food Supply	577
Birth Control	579

RESEARCH STUDY 23 567
A Dip in Deaths Before Ceremonial Occasions
David P. Phillips and Kenneth A. Feldman

17
URBAN SOCIETY 585

ECOLOGY 587
ORIGIN AND EVOLUTION OF CITIES 590
The Preindustrial City 590
The Industrial-Urban Center 593
The Metropolitan City 593
URBAN TRENDS AND PATTERNS IN THE UNITED STATES 594
Suburbanization 594
Central Cities in Difficulty 599
Patterns of Urban Growth 601
Ecological Processes 605
Social Consequences of Urbanism 608
RESEARCH STUDY 24 611
Urbanism and Tolerance — Claude S. Fischer

GLOSSARY 617

REFERENCES 627

AUTHOR INDEX 665

SUBJECT INDEX 675

PHOTO CREDITS 683

SOCIOLOGY

1 INTRODUCTION

WHAT IS UNIQUE ABOUT SOCIOLOGY?
    Sociology as a Science
    The Subject Matter of Sociology

SOCIOLOGICAL THEORY
    Structure-Function Theory
    Conflict Theory
    Social Exchange Theory
    Symbolic Interactionist Theory
    Ethnomethodology

THE NATURE OF SOCIAL RESEARCH
    Selecting and Defining a Problem
    Techniques of Data Collection
    The Experiment
    Analysis
    Ethics in Research

PRACTICAL USES OF SOCIOLOGY
    The Pure Science Orientation
    The Applied Science Orientation
    The Critical Science Orientation
    Enlightenment and Engineering

4 Introduction

The following are entries from the journals of students in a number of introductory sociology classes at Ohio State University. The students recorded observations from their daily lives and then proceeded to analyze the observations from a sociological perspective:*

OBSERVATION As I was walking across campus today, I noticed a very attractive girl. It just so happened that she was also taking note of me. But at the same time that all of this was taking place, her boyfriend was noticing the looks we were exchanging. As my eyes caught her eyes saying "Hi, there!," I caught her boyfriend's eyes saying, "Keep off—she's mine!" I got the message, turned, and walked off.

PRINCIPLE Although no words were exchanged, communication occurred. By our facial expressions and the length of our glances, messages were exchanged: "Hi, there!" and "Keep off—she's mine!"

OBSERVATION On my floor in the dorm we started two bowling teams when the quarter began. We were all friends because we all enjoyed bowling and we were having a great time together until a week ago. We had to play each other in the tournament. We really had everything together and they started to fall apart. At any rate we beat them bad and believe me our floor has been extremely quiet since. We don't feel too warmly toward one another anymore.

PRINCIPLE The guys on the floor who bowl had been brought together by the common interest we share. We were sort of a big in-group. But when the big in-group was divided into two out-groups everything fell apart. When two groups are in competition, negative attitudes will be generated against the out-group.

OBSERVATION I went to see my doctor today as I had a sinus infection. While sitting in the waiting room, I noticed the magazines on the tables: *Time, Harper's, New Yorker, Forbes, Newsweek,* and *The Atlantic.* After seeing the doctor, I went to get my hair cut. At the barber shop I also noticed the magazines: *Pro-Quarterback, Outdoors, Pro-Basketball, Playboy, Penthouse,* and *Argosy.*

PRINCIPLE The doctor and the barber were both engaged in impression management. Each was seeking to project an image of himself. The doctor was portraying an intelligent individual with a well-rounded, educated background. It was as if he was saying to his patients, "I am a competent professional who can handle difficult matters." The barber was portraying a masculine individual with an interest in "manly" things. It was if he was saying to his customers, "I am a real man, an outdoor type."

---

* These edited excerpts, and others that appear throughout this text, are reproduced by permission of the students.

5 Introduction

OBSERVATION   I am in AFROTC and attended a military social gathering this evening. Although it was a function involving military personnel, we were not supposed to wear our uniforms. Somehow the cadets from our detachment didn't know this, so we all showed up in uniform. Even though we knew everyone else present was military we felt out of place.

PRINCIPLE   Deviancy is not an absolute standard but is dependent on the situation. You can carry on the identical behaviors in different situations and in the one be a conformist and in the other deviant. In fact, it doesn't even have to be a different group with different standards. It can be the same group with different standards operating in a different situation.

OBSERVATION   Last evening my roommates and I were talking about a guy and girl in our dorm who are going together. Both the guy and the girl are very nice looking although the girl is not very friendly. In our discussion we decided that the only reason the guy went out with her was because she was cute. Today while walking to class I saw another girl and boy kissing good-bye. The boy was extremely good looking while the girl was unattractive. I said to myself, "God, what does he see in her? Maybe she gives him what he wants!"

PRINCIPLE   We generally select partners who have a similar degree of physical attractiveness as we have ourselves. This is called the matching hypothesis of mate selection. In the "mating and dating game" we fear less rejection when we approach individuals who have a similar ranking as we do. They are more likely to respond to our advances. When, as in my second example, a couple violate this expectation that they will be roughly equal in attractiveness, we tend to assume that some other sort of "bookkeeping" arrangement is operating to balance out the ledger—the one partner compensating for low attractiveness by supplying wealth, status, sex, or some other "goodie."

OBSERVATION   Today our teaching assistant in chemistry gave us back our mid-term examinations. He put the grade curve on the board and told us the grade distribution. Out of 300 points, the highest anyone got was 286 points; the lowest score was 15 points. When I got back to the dorm I told Pete, my roommate, about the test and the high and low scores. Pete responded, "Some girls just can't do chemistry." But it so happens that a girl got the 286 points.

PRINCIPLE   This is a flagrant example of male prejudice toward women. Pete just assumed that women do poorly in chemistry. Our culture tends to define chemistry as a "masculine" subject. I wouldn't be surprised if some women do poorly in chemistry simply because many people define the situation for them as one in which they are expected to do poorly. Such definitions then become a self-fulfilling prophecy.

OBSERVATION A few months ago I bought a really nice sweater. I had been looking for a sweater like it for some time. But the first day I wore the sweater, disaster seemed to descend upon me. Someone dented my car's back fender while it was parked in the student parking lot. I bombed a test in chemistry. The back tire next to the dented fender went flat on my way to work. It poured rain on me while I was changing the tire. My boss chewed me out when I showed up late for work. I got a bad headache. When I got back to my apartment after work, my girlfriend was in a real bad mood. As a result of all this misfortune, I never wore the sweater again. I don't consider myself superstitious but I just don't take any chances.

PRINCIPLE I associate the sweater with "bad luck." I attribute magical properties to the wearing of it. I fear that if I wear the sweater, it may *cause* the same sort of circumstances to occur again.

OBSERVATION Our math classroom is on the third floor of a building that overlooks the top floor of a parking ramp. At best three or four cars are parked up there, although it contains enough space for at least 80 cars. The lower levels of the ramp are also fairly empty. The ramp is only for the use of the faculty. We students have to park some distance from campus and even then we have to get to school by 7:30 in the morning if we are to find a parking place.

PRINCIPLE Social stratification—ranking arrangements—meet us everywhere. The faculty enjoy many privileges. They have special offices; departmental chairpersons have more spacious offices; and deans and the university president have even more magnificent offices. The faculty have "faculty restrooms" which are distinct from those simply labeled "restroom." Each dean has his own private restroom. The faculty address us by our first names whereas we have to call them "Doctor" and "Professor." An instructor gets about a fourth of the classroom and can freely move about during class. We are cramped into four square foot spaces (desks) and lack freedom of movement.

OBSERVATION This afternoon in an intramural softball game I kept my hitting streak going by hitting a home run the first time I was up to bat. As I rounded the bases I heard people cheering. I overheard one man say, "Why don't you just let Mike bat all the time!" I really felt good. I have really never considered myself as an exceptional player but these people made me feel like one. And I've been playing better this season than I ever have in my life.

PRINCIPLE Our "selves" do not exist in a vacuum. They arise out of social interaction with other people. Our self-conceptions tend to be "reflected appraisals." We gain images of ourselves through the feedback that other people provide us. This in turn has consequences for our subsequent behavior. Believing myself to be a great hitter, I gained the confidence to become one.

OBSERVATION   Today at work the guys were really feeling good. We were joking around and letting off steam. A little later a guy came to work and we noticed that he was in a quiet, somber mood. When we asked him what was wrong he told us that his dad had died. Suddenly our behavior shifted from happy and fun mood into one of concern and sadness.

PRINCIPLE   We are social beings and hence we do not live in little worlds all by ourselves. We have to continually fit our actions to the actions of other people. Our roles are partly dictated by others' roles. When situations and role expectations change, we have to readjust our actions in a complementary fashion. This is what happened at work today.

OBSERVATION   One of the guys in my dorm suite is joining a fraternity. The rest of us think he must be crazy to put up with what he does. He has been beaten, humiliated, deprived of sleep, made to run ridiculous errands at ridiculous hours, and has messed up his school work since he does not have enough time to study. And believe it or not, he hasn't gone through "Hell Week" yet. When we asked him what he is getting out of it all, he only laughs and says his efforts will be worth it in the end.

PRINCIPLE   The fraternity is compelling my suitemate to undergo various group rituals. In doing so, they are promoting a "consciousness of kind"—an identity as a fraternity member. Such rituals emphasize the gulf between the in-group and the out-group. Also, by making my suitemate pay such a high human price for admission, they are telling him the high value placed on fraternity membership. In the course of this socializing process, he too is coming to acquire an even higher regard for fraternity life.

WHAT IS UNIQUE ABOUT SOCIOLOGY?

The topics covered in these journal entries span a wide range of human behavior. But they share one ingredient in common—they are written from a sociological point of view. **Sociology*** is distinguished by two characteristics: first, by its approach to phenomena—the approach of science; and, second, by its subject matter—human interaction. In brief, sociology is *the scientific study of human interaction*.

* Concepts set in color are defined in the glossary at the back of the book.

Introduction

SOCIOLOGY AS A SCIENCE

I have made a ceaseless effort not to ridicule, not to bewail, nor to scorn human actions, but to understand them.

Spinoza

It has been noted that a distinguishing mark of sociology is its approach to phenomena. One way to consider this matter is by examining an illustration—poverty and unemployment within the United States.

Some Nonsociological Views. There are those who argue that poverty and unemployment are symptoms of a social sickness and that something must be done about these conditions. Many recent Presidents have spoken out against both and have proposed various remedies. For example, President Lyndon B. Johnson (in his State of the Union address in January 1964) declared "unconditional war on poverty in America." However, not all Presidents have taken a position in opposition to poverty. Our twentieth President, James Garfield, observed: "The richest heritage a young man can be born to is poverty." And in the same era before the turn of the twentieth century, Andrew Carnegie, the "Steel king," noted, ". . . the greatest and best of our race have necessarily been nurtured in the bracing school of poverty—the only school capable of producing the supremely great, the genius." Hence, Carnegie concluded: "Abolish poverty and what would become of the race? Progress and development would cease."

Others, repelled by what they view as the moral bankruptcy, materialism, and decadence of the affluent classes, acclaim the have-nots as "the salt of the earth," a people uninhibited by "artificial values and constraints"—a virtuous people, upright, serene, independent, honest, kind, and happy. Related to this view, although less romantic, is the notion that the poor are more sinned against that sinning—that society itself through its inaction and debased values relegates the poor to "urban garbage heaps."

While some view the poor as "blessed," others see them as "cursed." According to this position, the poor "deserve what they get" because of their own individual deficiencies, "their tendency to 'squander' a week's pay," and their present-time orientation. Success is seen as a triumph for sheer determination and prudence, and the reward for ability. Whereas the "good life" is for "hard-working" people, so poverty is for the "lazy." One frequently hears this view: "You have a lot of people who don't want to work. You've got welfare. People will go on living on welfare. They like it that way. Why should they go to work if the government will support them?" Hence, as viewed through the eyes of this group, poverty is immoral, a reflection of idleness, dissipation, and irresponsibility.

The Pursuit of Objectivity. Although quite different, all these views share something in common—highly colored appraisals of poverty and unem-

9 Introduction

ployment that are coupled with judgments of "good–bad," "desirable–undesirable," and "moral–immoral." The proponents of such nonsociological views read their own biases into the world about them. As a consequence, they tend to see "facts" not as they are but as they wish or believe them to be. And here we note one distinguishing feature of sociology; it is a *science*. As such, sociology is characterized by the *rigorous, disciplined pursuit of objectivity*.

Of course sociologists, like everyone else, have their individual biases and moral convictions regarding such matters as poverty and unemployment. As Alvin W. Gouldner (1976) points out, objectivity is not neutrality. Neutrality implies that one does not takes sides between adversaries. But sociologists, like other scientists, often take sides on controversial matters (Hammond and Adelman, 1976). Objectivity, in contrast with neutrality, has to do with scientifically verifiable knowledge. Indeed, if we wish our side to triumph, we would be well advised to appraise a situation as realistically as we can. Only by such an objective approach can we devise effective tactics and strategies for achieving our goals.

The critical aspect distinguishing the sociological orientation from non-

Poverty. In studying human behavior, sociologists attempt to view facts as they are without injecting their own value preferences.

Patrick Reddy

sociological perspectives is this: sociologists rigorously cultivate a disciplined approach to the phenomena that they study so that they might determine facts as they are and not as they might wish them to be. This approach is the product of professional commitment and training. Much of sociological education beyond the bachelor's degree is oriented toward fostering this kind of commitment and developing those skills whereby valid, reliable knowledge can be realized. Moreover, there is the additional check —indeed, social pressure—provided by scientists' peers. Once a work is published in professional publications, other scientists, not necessarily sharing the writers' biases, come to scrutinize and criticize the work.

In studying poverty and unemployment, sociologists attempt to secure valid, reliable knowledge. Sociologists, for example, might wish to study popular conceptions of poverty, such notions as we considered earlier. This sort of study might reveal any number of things, for instance, the observation that poverty is a human-made category and not some sort of "inborn" or "natural" view of life conditions (Williamson, 1974; Williamson and Hyer, 1975). In this regard, Lewis, A. Coser, a sociologist, observes:

> . . . the poor are men [people] who have been so defined by society and have evoked particular reactions from it. From this perspective, the poor have not always been with us. In Oriental society, for example, deprivation was not socially visible and not within the focus of social awareness. The modern observer might have discerned there a great prevalence of want and misery, yet the members of the society themselves did not perceive poverty and were unaware of its prevalence. (1965, p. 141)

Sociologists might also wish to subject to scientific scrutiny the assertion that the poor lack the ability to defer gratification. Or they might desire to test the truth of the statement that the poor prefer welfare to work. However, consideration of these matters is deferred until Chapter 14.

Assumptions of Science. Underlying the scientific perspective of objectivity are three basic assumptions: (1) various phenomena within the universe are characterized by certain regularities or uniformities; (2) these regularities or uniformities operate independently of the characteristics of the observer; and (3) these regularities or uniformities can be discovered, at least in theory, through objective observation. In brief, science is predicated on the assumption that there is a "real world"—that something exists "out there," something that is divorced from individuals themselves, and that this something is empirically knowable (Mead, 1938). As Herbert Blumer (1977:288) notes: "The scientific community accepts the world out there, raises questions about the nature of certain parts of that world (which come to constitute the problem areas of science), and examines those parts to answer the questions."

Perhaps an illustration might be instructive. Chemists find that a pure sample of sodium chloride contains 60.7 percent of chlorine and 39.3 percent of sodium; all varieties of sodium chloride, regardless of their source, have identical proportions of the two elements present in them. The same condition holds for other compounds. Chemists refer to this repetitive pattern in the relationship between given elements as "The Law of Constant Composition." They assume that this generalization operates as a "law of nature," that it exists independently of the observer, and that objective observation—be it by an American Roman Catholic, a Chinese Communist, or a Kazak spiritualist—will yield this conclusion.

Similarly, sociologists assume that certain discoverable uniformities exist in people's behavior as members of society. Of course, human behavior has a great many variables influencing it—physical, psychological, social, cultural, and so forth. Nonetheless, sociologists maintain that human life hardly consists of just so many random and accidental events. Behavior falls into "patterns" of one sort or another. The public also operates on this principle. In our daily lives, for instance, we usually encounter little difficulty in assessing social status in terms of dress, hair style, speech, mannerisms, and the like. A surprising number of such regularities occur in human behavior, and lend themselves to reasonably reliable generalizations.

Conclusion. There are such things as **facts**—certain scientifically verifiable observations—and hence we can make reliable statements regarding what *is*. There are also **values**, conceptions regarding the desirability or undesirability of things (their beauty, merit, or worth)—in brief, notions of what *ought to be*. Science, be it chemistry or sociology, can only ascertain facts; it cannot tell us whether these facts are good or bad—whether it is ethically desirable or undesirable that every chemical compound contains unvarying proportions of its constituent elements or that American ghettos display particular social characteristics.

That science should concern itself only with "what is" is of course an ideal; in practice, things do not work out quite this way, for science involves *human* activity, carried on by individuals and by groups of individuals. It is this element that injects *subjectivity* into the picture. All human beings have values, and to the extent to which we are human, we cannot be completely objective.

Even at our best, we find values subtly invading our work. Indeed, the very fact of studying human behavior reveals concern with it, and the decision to focus on social rather than biological, psychological, or other factors betrays an implicit belief that the social factor is somehow "more significant." Similarly, values shape our selection of research problems (for example, the nature of ghetto life rather than the structure of business enterprise) and our preference for certain hypotheses or conceptual schemes as opposed to others. Recent research on perception and information processing even suggests that complete objectivity in observation may be impossible by virtue of selective perception (Lindsay and Norman, 1977). And, finally, our genes endow us with similar, though not identical, sensory capacities and nervous systems, a line of reasoning that leads us to conclude that the objectivity of science depends to a considerable degree on the ability of different observers to agree about their data and on their procedures for observation (Glass, 1965; Blumer, 1977).

In conclusion, there is not, there never has been, nor is it likely that there ever will be a value-free science. Science is not characterized by the complete absence of values but by a *rigorous, disciplined* attempt to look as objectively as is *humanly* possible on the phenomena that it studies. Hence, sociologists are enjoined to avoid such emotional involvement in their work that they cannot adopt a new approach or reject an old answer when their findings indicate that this is required. Moreover, sociologists are urged not to distort their findings in order to support a particular point of view. In brief, sociologists have an obligation not to turn their back on facts or distort them simply because they do not like them. This does not mean that sociologists are required to give up their moral convictions and biases. It only means that they must rigorously control these convictions and biases so that they may ascertain the facts.

THE SUBJECT MATTER OF SOCIOLOGY

> If you are interested in understanding your social environment . . . and making new discoveries and reaching new insights about that environment, there is a place in sociology for you.
> American Sociological Association, A Career in Sociology

We have observed that a distinguishing characteristic of sociology is that it is a science. But, some may protest, psychology, economics, political science, and anthropology make identical claims. Moreover, they too are concerned with human behavior. How do these other social sciences differ from sociology? This brings us to a consideration of sociology's subject matter.

Sociology focuses on **human interaction**—on the mutual and reciprocal influencing by two or more people of each other's feelings, attitudes, and actions. In other words, sociology does not so much focus on what occurs *within* people (primarily the province of psychology) as it does on what transpires *between* people. Hence, the focus of sociological inquiry is on people as social beings—their activities in relation to one another. Sociologists are interested in the way people structure their relationships—the manner in which their social ties with others are formed, sustained, and changed. They study families, cliques, religious sects, delinquent gangs, big organizations (such as factories and universities), communities, and societies.

In thinking about sociology's place in the social sciences, it is important

13   Introduction

Patrick Reddy

The study of social interaction. Sociologists are primarily interested in what transpires between people—in brief, in their activities as social beings in relation to one another.

that we avoid the tendency of viewing the various academic disciplines as somehow separated into "watertight" compartments (Faris, 1964). At best, the various academic disciplines like history, anthropology, psychology, economics, and political science are loosely defined—indeed, the border lines are so vaguely conceived that researchers following a particular interest often give little thought in practice as to whether they are "invading" another discipline's field of study. Far from being undesirable, such overlap often contributes to a freshness in approach and functions as a stimulus to the further advancement of the frontiers of knowledge.

SOCIOLOGICAL THEORY

Nothing is so practical as a good theory.
Kurt Lewin

Thus far, it has been noted that sociology entails the scientific study of human interaction. Obviously the topic of human interaction is virtually limitless. Its scope is so diffuse and massive that we find it difficult to comprehend—to think about, examine, and analyze. In brief, we need to weave some sort of net by which we can catch the world of observation—explain, predict, and influence it (Deutsch and Krauss, 1965). This is the purpose of theory.

Theory is a "way of binding together a multitude of facts so that one may comprehend them all at once" (Kelly, 1955: 18). Sociologist Jonathan H. Turner succinctly puts the matter in these terms:

> Theorizing can be viewed as the means by which the intellectual activity known as "science" realizes its three principal goals: (1) to classify and organize events in the world so that they can be placed into perspective; (2) to explain the causes of past events and predict when, where, and how future events will occur; and (3) to offer an intuitively pleasing sense of "understanding" why and how events should occur. (1974, p. 2)

In the chapters that follow, we shall encounter a variety of sociological theoretical orientations. Each provides us with a somewhat different perspective regarding human behavior. In some instances, a particular theory affords us a tool for getting at a matter that is difficult to grasp or understand by using an alternative theory. At times, aspects of one theory may clash with those of another theory. Since we shall be returning to such issues throughout the text, let us here simply summarize a number of the major perspectives. Their details will become clearer as we work with the theories in the chapters to come.

STRUCTURE-FUNCTION THEORY

Nineteenth century sociologists such as August Comte (1798–1857) and Herbert Spencer (1820–1903) were impressed by the similarities that they observed between biological organisms and social life. Spencer in particular was moved to proclaim that "society is *like* an organism" (Turner, 1974:16). Central to this perspective is the notion of a **system**—a complex of elements or components that are related to each other in a more or less stable fashion through a period of time.

The human body is seen as a system composed of a number of interrelated organs (the heart, lungs, kidneys, brain, and so on). Each organ performs a function or functions essential for the survival of the organism or the species to which it belongs. The organs represent the structures through which these requirements are typically met. The liver is one such structure, the largest gland of the body. It meets a number of indispensable requirements essential to the organism's survival. The liver splits fats and proteins into smaller substances so that the tissues can use them for energy; it forms products needed for blood coagulation, for transport of fat, and for immunity to infection; and it stores large quantities of fats, carbohydrates, and proteins and releases these foods as the tissues need them.

Institutions are viewed by some sociologists as analogous to organs. These social structures meet the vital requirements necessary for the survival and maintenance of society. Indeed, sociologists commonly classify institutions

15 Introduction

Courtesy of the American Sociological Association

Talcott Parsons. Over the past forty years Parsons has been the leading theorist of the structure-function approach within American sociology.

in terms of the chief function that they perform: the economic institution has as its focus the production and distribution of goods and services; the family institution, the reproduction, socialization, maintenance, and positional placement of children; the political institution, the protection of citizens from one another and from foreign enemies; the religious institution, the enhancement of social solidarity and consensus; and the educational institution, the transmission of the cultural heritage from one generation to the next.

Because sociologists of this school of thought focus their primary attention on structures and their functions, the perspective is termed **structure-function theory.** It enjoyed especial popularity during the 1940s, 1950s, and early 1960s and was identified with such sociologists as Talcott Parsons (1937; 1951; 1966; 1971), Kingsley Davis (1949), and Robert K. Merton (1968).

CONFLICT THEORY

Within social life there are some things defined as "good" that are scarce and divisible, so that the more there is for one party, the less there is for the other. Wealth, power, status, and the control of territory are examples of this. People typically seek to improve their outcome with regard to those things that they define as worthwhile and desirable. Where two groups of people both view themselves as having exclusive and legitimate claim to certain good things, so that each can realize what it defines as a rightful outcome only at the expense of the other, conflict usually results. **Conflict** entails a struggle over values or claims to wealth, power, status, or territory in which the opponents aim to neutralize, injure, or eliminate their rivals.

Probably the most famous exposition of a conflict approach is that set forth by Karl Marx and Friedrich Engels in the *Communist Manifesto* (1848). In language loud and clear they declared that the pivotal characteristic of social life is class struggle. According to Marx and Engels, a society's ruling class owes its position to its ownership and control of the means of production (the critical resources by which people derive their livelihood). By controlling the means of production, a ruling class undertakes to interpose itself between the rest of the population and the means by which this population meets its biological and social needs. In this manner a ruling class renders a population vulnerable and susceptible to its wishes and dictates. It dominates the whole moral and intellectual life of a people while making government, law, the military, science, religion, and education the vehicles for entrenching its rule and its position of privilege.

Although class conflict constitutes the central core of Marxian theory, many contemporary sociologists view conflict as taking place between a great many groups—race versus race, religion versus religion, consumers

16 Introduction

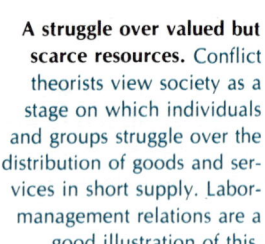

A struggle over valued but scarce resources. Conflict theorists view society as a stage on which individuals and groups struggle over the distribution of goods and services in short supply. Labor-management relations are a good illustration of this.

Patrick Reddy

versus producers, central city residents versus suburban residents, the Sunbelt states versus the Snowbelt states, taxpayers versus welfare recipients, and so on. These sociologists note that a recurring theme throughout much of human life is the question, "Whose will shall prevail, thine or mine?" Among conflict-oriented sociologists have been the late C. Wright Mills (1956), Tom B. Bottomore (1966; 1975), Ralf Dahrendorf (1959), Randall Collins (1975), and Richard P. Appelbaum (1978).

SOCIAL EXCHANGE THEORY

Most of our gratifications in life have their source in the actions of other human beings. Contentment in love, intellectual stimulation, companionship, economic sustenance, a sense of worth, protection from predators—these and many other goals in human life—can only be attained by inducing others to behave in certain ways toward us. This assumption is the foundation of **social exchange theory**—people are viewed as ordering their relationships with others in terms of a sort of mental bookkeeping that entails a ledger of rewards, costs, and profits.

According to social exchange theory, people enter into and sustain patterns of interaction with certain other people because they find such interaction rewarding, whatever the reasons. But in the process of seeking rewards, people inevitably incur costs. Costs refer to negative considerations (obligations, fatigue, boredom, anxiety, concern, and so on) or to positive elements that are forgone by continuing the relationship. The profit derived from a social exchange represents the difference between rewards and costs. Some sociologists (Heath, 1976) view social exchange as a "rational choice theory" since individuals are seen as continuing a relationship only so long as they define it as being more rewarding than it is costly.

Peter Blau (1967), a social exchange theorist, argues that it is inevitable that people generally end up with the friends, lovers, and marriage partners that they "deserve." He notes that if individuals want to reap the benefits of associating with others, they must offer their partners enough to make it worth their while to remain in the relationship. The more people have to offer, the more demand there will be for their company. Accordingly, others will themselves have to offer more before they can hope to win such people's friendship. In this fashion the principle of supply and demand insures that people will get only partners as desirable as they deserve. Other sociologists who are commonly identified as social exchange theorists are James S. Coleman (1973), George C. Homans (1974), and Peter P. Ekeh (1974).

Courtesy of the American Sociological Association

Peter Blau. Blau has been a leading American proponent of the social exchange theory.

SYMBOLIC INTERACTIONIST THEORY

A fundamental premise of sociology is that humans are social beings; we cannot be human all by ourselves. Various "social insects" (ants, bees, and termites) likewise aggregate in organized groups. But in contrast with human beings, the behavior of these insects appears to be integrated primarily on a physiological and instinctive basis. If human beings are largely lacking in such inborn mechanisms, what is the foundation of human groups and societies? Some sociologists, **symbolic interactionists,** point to communication, or more particularly symbols, as the key to understanding social life. A **symbol** is any act or object that has socially come to be accepted as standing for something else.

Symbolic interactionists follow in the tradition of George Herbert Mead (1863–1931). Mead argued that human beings evolved the capacity to interact with others through the use of shared symbols. By means of shared symbols, human beings impart "meaning" to their activities; they come to define situations and interpret behavior. People form perspectives through a social process in which they define things for one another. In turn they act toward each other and modify their actions in terms of such socially derived meanings (Blumer, 1969; 1977; Meltzer, Petras, and Reynolds, 1975).

Mead (1932; 1934; 1938) pointed out that symbols, particularly language, not only enable human beings to carry on communication with one another (*inter*individual communication). They are also vehicles for thinking (*intra*individual communication). We carry on an internal conversation with ourselves. We talk and reply to ourselves in much the same way that we carry on a conversation with others. We ask ourselves, for instance, "If I want to produce this given response in this person, what will it take to do it? What would it take to make me act in this way?" We address ourselves and respond to the address. In this fashion we fit our acts to the acts of others, mapping, testing, suspending, and revising our behavior in response to their

Imagining how we appear to others. Symbolic interactionists indicate that we mentally exchange roles with other people so as to establish what we can expect of them and what they can expect of us. In this manner we devise our actions so as to achieve a mutual integration of our activities. Symbols are the vehicles by which we engage in inter-individual and intra-individual communication.

Patrick Reddy

behavior. Among sociologists identified with the symbolic interactionist school have been the late Manford H. Kuhn (1960), Herbert Blumer (1962; 1969; 1971; 1977), Ralph H. Turner (1962; 1968), Howard S. Becker (1963), and Norman K. Denzin (1970).

ETHNOMETHODOLOGY

As we go about our everyday activities, our social world gives the appearance of being orderly and patterned. We attend sociology lecture on Monday, Wednesday, and Friday at the same hour, we drive our cars on the right side of the road, we set aside Friday and Saturday evenings, Christmas, and New Year's Eve for merriment, we receive our paychecks on some regular basis such as the last day of each month, we smoothly carry out exchange transactions with innumerable store clerks who we never previously met, and so on. We tend to take such everyday "happenings" for granted; they are background understandings, the "stuff" out of which we fashion our social lives.

Some sociologists, those identified with **ethnomethodology,** ask, "How is a particular social activity done?" They examine human behavior that takes place on the "taken-for-granted" level, illuminating the commonplace. Ethnomethodologists Don H. Zimmerman and D. Lawrence Wieder note:

> We ask such questions as: How are members going about the task of investigating the scenes of their actions so that they see and report patterning and structure in these scenes? How are events being analyzed so that they appear as connected? By what procedures are descriptions being done so that they portray order? How is the factual character of such accounts established? and How is the sense or appearance of a world in common and common understanding concerning its shared features accomplished? (1970, p. 290)

Courtesy of the American Sociological Association

Charles Horton Cooley. Cooley (1864–1929) was a pioneer social psychologist who formulated many of the concepts associated with the symbolic interactionist theory.

Ethnomethodologists study how people go about creating and sustaining for one another the *presumption* that the social world has a real character (see Research Study 10 in Chapter 5 and Research Study 13 in Chapter 7). In other words, they are interested in the complex ways in which individuals consciously and unconsciously go about fashioning, maintaining, and changing their "sense" of an external social reality and order (Turner, 1974; Zimmerman, 1978). They seek to strip the taken-for-granted background expectancies of life of their cloak of invisibility. Ethnomethodology is closely identified with the work of Harold Garfinkel (1964;1967). Other ethnomethodologists include Harvey Sacks (1972), Aaron V. Cicourel (1964; 1968; 1974), David Sudnow (1967; 1972), and Hugh Mehan and Houston Wood (1975).

THE NATURE OF SOCIAL RESEARCH

Art and science have their meeting point in method.
Edward G. Bulwer-Lytton

How do sociologists go about the scientific study of human interaction? Let us begin by noting that social research is not necessarily a simple matter of asking a few questions or making a few observations. Perhaps an illustration or two might be instructive. Some years ago a brewery making two kinds of beer conducted a survey to find out people's beer preferences as a guide to its merchandisers. It asked people known to favor its general brand name: "Do you drink the light or the regular?" To its astonishment, the company discovered people reporting they preferred light over the regular by better than three to one. The truth of the matter was that for years the company, in order to meet consumer demands, had brewed nine times as much regular beer as light beer. It decided that, in asking people this question, it in effect had asked: "Do you drink the kind of beer preferred by people of refinement and discriminating taste, or do you just drink the regular stuff?" Hence, a seemingly straightforward and simple question may in fact be quite "loaded" and produce biased results.

Let us consider another illustration, the political orientation of Americans. At first appearance this seems to be a relatively simple matter. A good many of us might say, "Well, let's just go out and ask a representative sample of Americans a question or two about it." This is precisely what four polling organizations did. But as Table 1.1 reveals, the findings of the organizations differed. By asking the same questions in somewhat different ways the pollsters secured different results (Lipset, 1976).

It is apparent that social research is not the simple matter it may first appear to be. For example, people want very much to end pollution of the environment. However, when a particular extra tax figure is mentioned, a good many people conclude that such programs are not worth the cost. See Figure

TABLE 1.1
Political Orientations of Americans*

Gallup Organization
Question: If an arrangement of this kind, that is, two new political parties, were carried out, and you had to make a choice, which party would you personally prefer—the conservative party or the liberal party?
Results: Conservative, 40 percent; liberal, 30 percent; undecided, 30 percent.

Louis Harris & Associates
Question: How would you describe your own political philosophy, as conservative, middle-of-the-road, liberal, or radical?
Results: Conservative, 30 percent; middle-of-the-road, 43 percent; liberal, 15 percent; radical, 3 percent; undecided, 9 percent.

National Opinion Research Center (NORC) of the University of Chicago
Question: We hear a lot of talk these days about liberals and conservatives. I'm going to show you a seven-point scale on which the political views that people might hold are arranged from extremely liberal to extremely conservative. Where would you place yourself on this scale?
Results: Conservative alternatives, 28 percent; liberal alternatives, 28 percent; the mid-point position, 37 percent; don't know, 6 percent.

Survey Research Center (SRC) of the University of Michigan
Question: We hear a lot of talk these days about liberals and conservatives. I'm going to show you a seven-point scale on which the political views that people might hold are arranged from extremely liberal to extremely conservative. Where would you place yoruself on this scale or haven't you thought much about it? (Identical to the NORC question except for the last option.)
Results: Conservative alternatives, 25 percent; liberal alternatives 21 percent; the mid-point position, 26 percent; haven't thought much about it, 21 percent.

* Polls conducted between November 1974 and March 1975.

Source: Adapted from Seymour Martin Lipset (1976) The waving polls. *The Public Interest,* 43 Spring): 70–89.

1.1. One reason why subtle changes in the wording of a question produces different results is that many people are not well-informed or do not have a deeply held opinion on a given issue; they are likely to respond to a question to which they have not given much thought. In other cases, an issue is too complex to be summed up by the responses to one or two questions. All these comments add up to the following point: Social research that is worth its salt is a highly sophisticated and skilled undertaking. It would seem advisable, therefore, for us to give additional thought to the nature of social research.

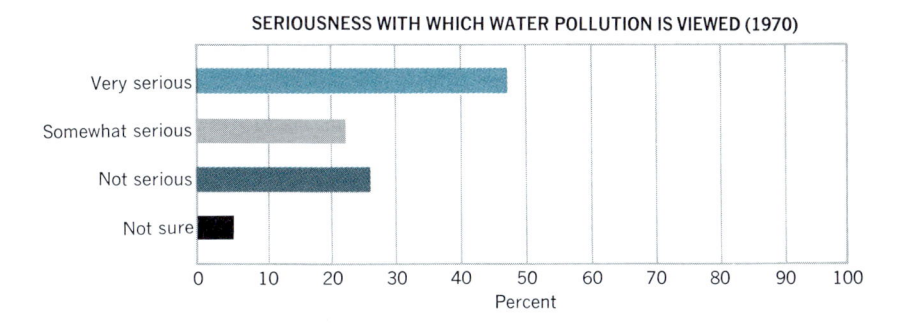

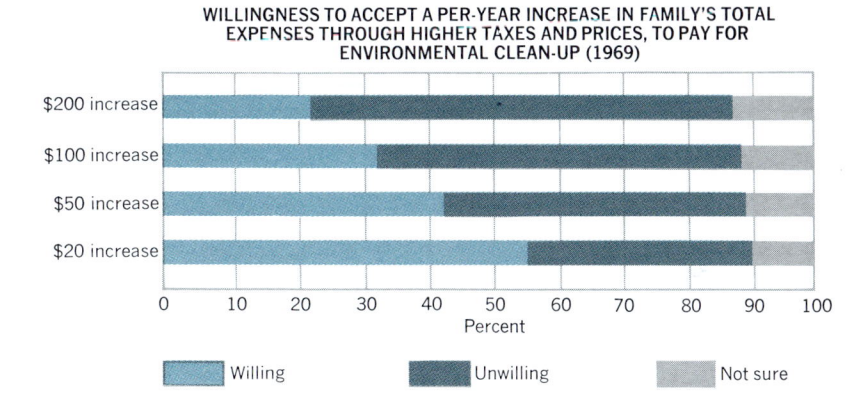

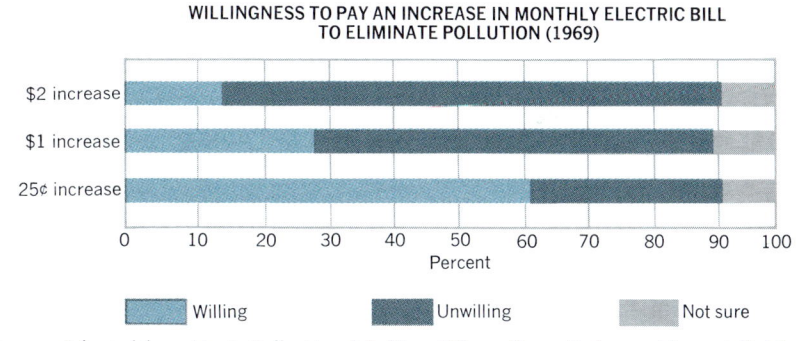

SERIOUSNESS WITH WHICH WATER POLLUTION IS VIEWED (1970)

WILLINGNESS TO ACCEPT A PER-YEAR INCREASE IN FAMILY'S TOTAL EXPENSES THROUGH HIGHER TAXES AND PRICES, TO PAY FOR ENVIRONMENTAL CLEAN-UP (1969)

WILLINGNESS TO PAY AN INCREASE IN MONTHLY ELECTRIC BILL TO ELIMINATE POLLUTION (1969)

Figure 1.1 Discrepancy between desire to end pollution and willingness to foot the bill for it.

Source: Adapted from Harris Polls: Hazel Erskine, "The polls: pollution and its cost. *Public Opinion Quarterly*, 38 (1972): 124, 133, and 134.

SELECTING AND DEFINING A PROBLEM

Hypotheses are the scaffolds, which are erected in front of a building and removed when the building is completed. They are indispensable to the worker; but he must not mistake the scaffolding for the building.

Johann W. von Goethe

The range of topics for social research is as broad as the range of human behavior itself. Our first task, then, is to locate a problem that we feel

22   Introduction

demands solution. As part of this effort, we often find it necessary to formulate **hypotheses.** A hypothesis is a proposition that can be tested to determine its validity. It may prove to be correct or incorrect, but in any event it leads to an actual test. Without hypotheses, our research tends to become unfocused — a random wandering about in the name of science.* Sound hypotheses aid us in establishing the direction in which to proceed, in delimiting and singling out pertinent facts, and determining which facts may be included and which omitted.

Included in this and the chapters that follow are a number of boxed inserts containing Research Studies. Each Study summarizes a significant piece of sociological research. Some of these Studies set forth specific hypotheses. Chapter 6, for instance, contains a study of Muzafer Sherif in which he investigated a number of hypotheses including the following: If two groups compete with each other, they will evolve unfavorable stereotypes of each other. Hypotheses, then, are tentative guesses or hunches that we employ as guides to investigation.

Not all the Research Studies, however, contain a set of hypotheses. Where considerable research has been done in an area or where theory is well developed, the formulation of hypotheses often poses little difficulty. Unhappily, these conditions do not always prevail. At times, there are few well-trodden paths for us to follow. Instead of launching a study with well-defined hypotheses, we may have to settle, at least initially, for an *exploratory* study. Under these circumstances, we seek to develop a problem for more precise investigation, to formulate hypotheses, or to establish priorities for further research. We may also wish to undertake another type of study in which we seek to assess the characteristics of situations, a *descriptive* study.

In any event, whether we undertake a study with or without hypotheses, we should know what we intend to accomplish before we actually get underway. F. S. C. Northrop compares the beginning of a study to a ship's leaving a port for some distant destination. He (1947:1) notes that "a very slight erroneous deviation in taking one's bearings at the beginning may result in entirely missing one's mark at the end, regardless of the sturdiness of one's craft or the excellence of one's subsequent seamanship."

TECHNIQUES OF DATA COLLECTION

Having selected our research problem, our next task is to formulate a plan whereby we can gain suitable information. Let us consider, therefore, a number of common techniques of data collection.

Observation. Observation probably represents at once the most primitive and the most modern of research techniques. It may entail, for instance, the rather casual, uncontrolled observation of researchers who disguise themselves, so to speak, in order that they may be accepted as members of a group (called *participant observation*.) Nels Anderson (1923), for example, often

---

* Such random wondering, however, may be useful if our primary purpose is to suggest hypotheses for testing.

23 Introduction

traveled and lived with hobos without revealing the fact that he was a sociologist, and Howard S. Becker (1951), also a sociologist, became accepted as a young piano player by jazz musicians. Perhaps the best-known sociological study employing participant observation is William Foote Whyte's *Street Corner Society* (1943), a study of a slum community that has become a sociological classic. A portion of the study is summarized in Research Study 1. Observation may also entail the use of a laboratory, a setting often employed in the study of small groups. The laboratory usually consists of a large, well-lighted room for the group under study and an adjoining room for observers who listen and watch from behind one-way mirrors.

Observation in a laboratory setting. These photos show the small group laboratory at Ohio State University. Two rooms are separated by a one-way mirror that allows observers in the control room to view subjects in the experimental room without themselves being observed. In this fashion, the subjects' spontaneous behavior is less likely to be impaired. One photo shows two observers in the control room. The window to the left of the equipment looks into the experimental room. Viewed from the experimental room, shown in the other photo, the control room window is simply a mirror. The televisionlike equipment is an added feature of this facility. In smaller rooms located nearby in the complex, subjects can individually view in isolation on television screens the activity taking place in the experimental room. This allows researchers to compare the perceptions or reactions that subjects have to various behavior without the subjects themselves influencing one another. The equipment also allows researchers to videotape behavior taking place in the experimental room for more detailed later examination and study.

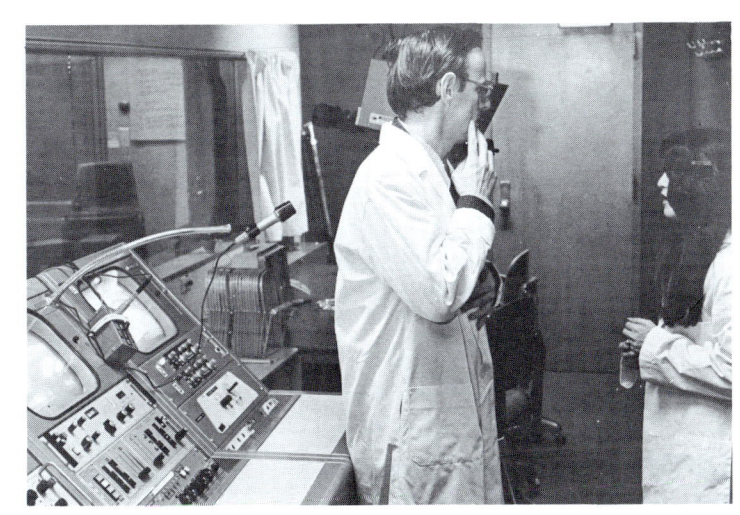

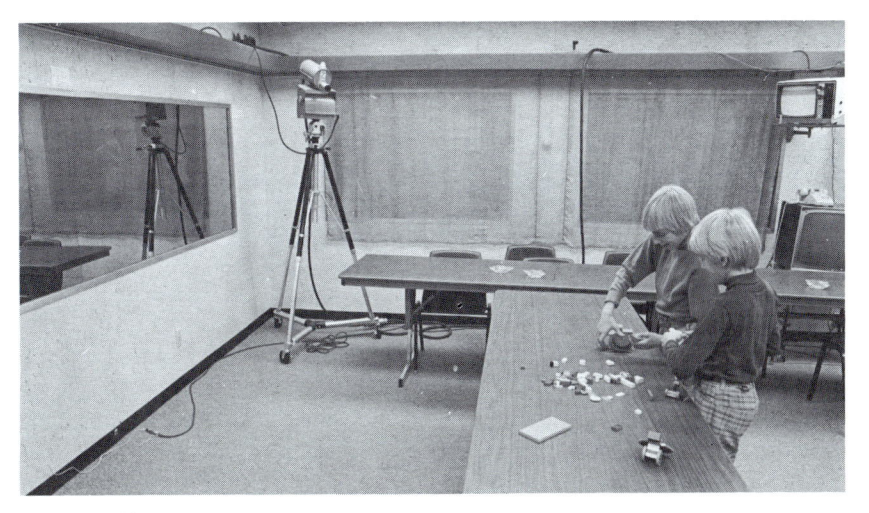

Patrick Reddy

One advantage of observation is that it is independent of people's ability or willingness to report on given matters. Many individuals lack sufficient self-insight to tell us about certain aspects of their behavior; or, because their behavior is illicit, taboo, or deviant, they may be reluctant to do so. The following account of an interview with a mother that dealt with her child-rearing practices provides a good illustration of this point:

> During the interview she held her small son on her lap. The child began to play with his genitals. The mother, without looking directly at the child, moved his hand away and held it securely for a while . . . later in the interview the mother was asked what she ordinarily did when the child played with himself. She replied that he never did this —he is a very "good" boy. She was evidently unconscious of what had transpired in the very presence of the interviewer. (Maccoby and Maccoby, 1954, p. 484)

Observation, however, also has certain limitations (Selltiz, Wrightaman, and Cook, 1976): (1) the spontaneous occurrence of an event is often unpredictable, and hence a trained observer cannot always be present; (2) there is the practical limitation of applying observational techniques to phenomena involving a considerable span of time (for example, a life history); and (3) there are occurrences that people may be able and willing to talk about that are inaccessible to direct observation (for example, sex behavior, religious behavior, dreams).

RESEARCH STUDY 1

STREET CORNER SOCIETY*

William Foote Whyte

Problem. William Foote Whyte came from an upper-middle-class background. When he graduated from Swarthmore College in 1936, he received a fellowship from Harvard University. This grant provided him with three years of financial support for any line of research he wished to undertake. Since he was interested in social reform, he decided to study a slum district in Boston. He chose "Cornerville," an Italian slum, since it best fitted his stereotypes of what a slum district should look like. He admits "I made my choice on very unscientific grounds" (1955:283).

Method. After a number of false starts, a social worker in the Norton Street Settlement House arranged for Whyte to meet Doc, the twenty-nine-year-old head of the Nortons, one of the local youth gangs. Doc agreed to "sponsor" Whyte in the Italian community—to allow Whyte to observe and participate in activities and relationships as "Doc's friend." Whyte "hung out with" the young men of the gang, bowling, playing baseball, shooting pool, playing cards, and chatting about gambling, horse races, sex, and other matters. He also lived in the neighborhood for three-and-one-half

---
* Adapted from William Foote Whyte (1955) *Street Corner Society*. Enlarged edition. Chicago: University of Chicago Press.

years. Eighteen of these months he lived with an Italian family and learned the Italian language.

Whyte writes:

As I began hanging about Cornerville, I found that I needed an explanation for myself and for my study. As long as I was with Doc and vouched for by him, no one asked me who I was or what I was doing. When I circulated in other groups or even among the Nortons without him, it was obvious that they were curious about me....

I soon found that people were developing their own explanation about me: I was writing a book about Cornerville. This might seem entirely too vague an explanation, and yet it sufficed. I found that my acceptance in the district depended on the personal relationships I developed far more than upon any explanations I might give.... If I was all right, then my project was all right; if I was no good, then no amount of explanation could convince them that the book was a good idea. (1955, p. 300)

Findings. In the course of his observations, Whyte gained a good many insights regarding youth gangs, community politics, and racketeering. Some of his most important findings had to do with the social impact that the Norton gang had on its member's self-conceptions and self-images. During the winter and spring months, bowling was the principal social activity of the Nortons. On Saturday evenings, the men would divide into teams and play one another. They would also engage in individual matches.

Whyte was initially perplexed by the fact that an individual's athletic ability did not appear to be the primary factor influencing his bowling performance. For instance, on sheer athletic ability, Frank should have been an excellent bowler. Indeed, he had played semiprofessional baseball with a number of teams. Oddly enough, Frank also made a poor showing when playing in community baseball games.

Alec provided another example. He was an outstanding bowler when he played for the "fun of it" on weekday evenings. But when the Norton gang would assemble on Saturday evenings, his game "fell apart." Doc and Danny, on the other hand, were only average bowlers yet they would consistently defeat the others in bowling contests.

Conclusions. Based on his observations, Whyte concluded that a man's bowling performance was related to the status he held within the Norton gang. Doc and Danny enjoyed the highest status and also had the highest scores. Frank and Alec ranked quite low and also had the lowest scores. The Nortons defined it as inappropriate that low status members should defeat the top-ranked members.

Whyte points out that there are many "mental hazards" associated with bowling. There are critical moments when a player needs the steadiest of nerves if he is not to "tighten up" and lose control. Hence, confidence plays a large part in shaping a bowler's performance. When a low-ranked Norton was bowling well, his group members defined his successes for him as a matter of "luck" and heckled him. It was otherwise with Doc and Danny.

On the basis of such evidence, Whyte concluded that there is a relationship between an individual's performance and group structure. He found other evidence that tended to conform this proposition. The mental health and psychological well-being of the Norton members seemed to be affected by their group relationships. Thus, when Doc suffered a number of setbacks that jeopardized his role as the group's leader, he began experiencing "dizzy spells."

Interviews. Another way we may secure information is through the interview—"a meeting of persons face to face, especially for the purpose of formal conference on some point" (*Shorter Oxford English Dictionary*). Hence, an interview is a conference with a purpose, be it to select a candidate for a vacancy, to diagnose a patient's illness, or to gain sociological information. If we wish to know how persons feel or what they experience, what their emotions and motives are like, and their reasons for acting as they do, we may ask them. Or if we desire information about their unobserved behavior, again we may ask them. We may or may not take their report at face value; we may interpret it in terms of some psychological or sociological theory. But in any event, the starting point is the subjects' own report about themselves. Moreover, the interview gives us access to an event that took place in the recent or remote past but which otherwise would remain undocumented, for instance, the history of a preliterate tribe, a political coup, or a race riot.

Like observation, however, the interview has its limitations. Because individuals are involved in the data that they are reporting, they may consciously or unconsciously give us biased reports. Individuals, for example, may withhold or distort information because, if they were to tell us the truth, they would feel threatened or face a loss in self-esteem (Clark and Tifft, 1966). Further, some people are unable to provide us with certain types of information by virtue of a lack of self-insight, repression, and so on; this, as we noted earlier, is an advantage of observation.

Questionnaires. An interview may also take the form of a questionnaire — a useful tool for collecting data from large, diverse, and widely scattered groups of people. The questionnaire places heavy reliance on people's written report for information regarding their feelings, thoughts, and actions. Generally, individuals receive the questionnaire in the mail and fill it out themselves. The questionnaire offers a good many advantages. For one thing, it is less expensive than an interview (since interviewers usually receive financial remuneration). Moreover, it can be administered simultaneously to a great many people (in contrast, since trained interviewers are generally scarce, interviews may take place over a period of time during which a population's attitudes may change).

AN ADVANTAGE OF OBSERVATION

OBSERVATION Today seemed to be one of those days when you just don't seem to know what to do with yourself. So I was wandering through the halls of the dorm and I stopped by the room of one of my friends. She was looking for her cigarettes. She told me, "I really don't need them. I can do without 'em." But she kept getting more frustrated looking for her cigarettes. Finally she started cussing up and down and bummed one off a girl across the hall. Basically she is a quiet, easy-going person, and once she was smoking away on a cigarette she calmed down.

PRINCIPLE My observations of her behavior made her statement about "needing cigarettes" questionable. Through observing her behavior I probably got a more accurate picture of her "need" than if I had gone about asking her if she "needed to smoke and whether she could do without cigarettes."

The questionnaire, however, suffers from many of the same shortcomings as the interview. And it is estimated that, for purposes of filling out even the simplest questionnaire, at least 10 percent of the adult population of the United States are illiterate (13 percent of American adults cannot pass a basic reading test). The greatest problem, however, is that from 20 to 70 percent of the people who receive a questionnaire in the mail fail to complete it; this in turns makes the sample unrepresentative (for example, lower-class groups are less likely to complete a questionnaire than upper-class groups; hence, returns may be biased in the direction of upper-class behavior).

Uses of Available Data. Significant sociological contributions to knowledge are not limited to those realized through the gathering of original data in field studies. A *new* utilization of data already collected may have considerable worth and merit. Population data supplied by governmental agencies, for example, provide rich sources of research materials. The monumental study of suicide by Emile Durkheim (1858–1917), a pioneer French sociologist and a profound student of social organization, was based on data gained from governmental records. Durkheim (1951) investigated suicide rates among various groups of Europeans and found that some groups had higher rates than others—for example, Protestants had higher rates than Catholics; unmarried, higher rates than married; soldiers, higher rates than civilians—and that there were higher rates of suicide in times of peace than in times of war and revolution, and in times of economic prosperity and recession than in times of economic stability. Based on such findings, Durkheim concluded that different suicide rates (as distinct from the individual case, which is a problem for psychology) are the consequence of variations in social organization, particularly of differences in the degree to which individuals are integrated in group life. Hence, where individuals are caught up in a web of meaningful social bonds, they are less inclined toward suicide.

THE EXPERIMENT

Experimental observations are only experience carefully planned in advance.
Sir Ronald J. Fisher, The Design of Experiments

We have considered a number of common techniques for collecting data. The ideal model for scientific research in which various techniques come to be applied is the controlled experiment. Obviously, the basic method of scientific demonstration is to design our research so that the data will logically require either the acceptance or rejection of a hypothesis. This requires that we control all relevant factors in order to eliminate other possible relationships. The *controlled experiment* best meets this requirement (Carlsmith, Ellsworth, and Aronson, 1976; Selltiz, Wrightsman, and Cook, 1976).

In a controlled experiment, we measure two groups that are identical in all relevant respects. We introduce a change in one group—the *experi-*

mental group—but not in the other group—the *control* group. Thus, the two groups are identical, except for our having introduced some change in the experimental group. We then compare the two groups, the difference between the two groups being attributed to the change introduced within the experimental group.

Circumstances, however, do not always permit us to follow this model, and hence in practice we frequently find it necessary to make variations of one sort or another in it. The *ex post facto* (after the fact) experiment provides a good illustration of this. We may find it impossible, for instance, to gain a precise, accurate picture of a group prior to such an event as an earthquake, a race riot, or a prolonged drought. Nonetheless, we may want to discover what impact the event had on people. Under these circumstances, we may create an *ex post facto* experiment in which we compare two or more groups, one of which was exposed to the event in question and the other which was not. Such a procedure obviously presents a good many problems—for instance, finding another group that is identical with the group in question except for having experienced the event. Usually, we have to satisfy ourselves with finding as close a "match" as is possible. Clearly, this procedure is not entirely satisfactory, as it presents a wide-open gate through which many uncontrolled variables can march. Through the years social scientists have evolved still other techniques for deriving empirical generalizations, particularly statistical methods (in which, for instance, the problem of control can be handled by means of partial correlations) and comparative methods (including cross-cultural research). But these matters go far beyond the scope of an introductory sociology textbook.

Perhaps our understanding of the controlled experiment can be deepened by considering an actual sociological study. Research Study 2 summarizes a study by Russell Middleton dealing with the effectiveness of motion pictures as instruments for combating prejudice. Middleton's study provides a good illustration of research that expands the frontiers of sociological knowledge while simultaneously providing important information for reaching a socially desired goal (a more democratic society). After reading this account, ask yourself: "Had Middleton not employed a control group, had he merely relied upon the experimental group, to what extent would his inferences have been distorted?"

RESEARCH STUDY 2

ETHNIC PREJUDICE AND SUSCEPTIBILITY TO PERSUASION*

Russell Middleton

Problem. As motion pictures and television have come to occupy a growing place in the recreational life of this country, it would seem that the possibilities for the mass influencing of attitudes would be vastly increased. In keeping with this view, some have suggested that motion pictures that urge tolerance toward minority groups and foreign nationalities can play a major part in reducing the expression of ethnic prejudice among those individuals exposed to them. But is this indeed the case? Some studies reveal, for instance, that people often evade propaganda that is at odds with their existing attitudes, and that at times propaganda "boomerangs"—it has an effect directly opposite to that which the propagandist intended. Hence, it was to this matter of the effectiveness of antiprejudice propaganda that Russell Middleton, a sociologist, directed his attention.

Method. For his study, Middleton selected the film *Gentleman's Agreement,* a movie that carries a strong message against anti-Semitic prejudice and that sets forth an appeal for brotherhood, equality, and democracy. The movie had received wide praise from film critics—indeed, it won the 1947 Academy Award. *Gentleman's Agreement* also had the additional virtue of having been first released in 1947 when most of Middleton's subjects—students at a southern state-supported university—were still small children. Accordingly, only about 5 percent of his subjects had to be eliminated from the study because they had previously seen the movie.

From the university students, Middleton selected an experimental group (a group to which he showed the movie) and a control group (a group to which he did not show the movie). Both groups completed an attitude questionnaire regarding Jews: the experimental group before and again after the movie; the control group before and again after the intervention of a comparable period of time. Middleton introduced the control group into the study to check for any attitude changes that could have resulted from other factors, for instance, the mere fact of having taken an attitude "test" a second time. In other words, Middleton wanted to make certain that any changes he noted

in the attitudes of the experimental group were the product of the film and not some intervening variable or variables.

In order to encourage the students to be as frank as possible in completing the questionnaire, Middleton tried to protect their anonymity. To do this, he had the students sign the questionnaires with their mothers' maiden names. This made it possible for Middleton to match the before with the after questionnaire for each individual without identifying the person.

Findings. The results of the study, presented in Figure 1.2, reflect the wisdom of Middleton's having introduced the control group, since both the control and experimental groups displayed some attitude changes. Nonetheless, the evidence strongly suggests that the film played a major part in reducing the expression of anti-Semitic prejudice. Of those in the experimental group, 69.3 percent had lower scores on anti-Semitism on the second questionnaire than on the first; this compared with 42.2 percent for those in the control group. Moreover, subjects in the experimental group were five times more likely to display a reduction of eleven or more points in anti-Semitism than those in the control group. Reductions of four to ten points were also found to be more extensive among those in the experimental group. Yet the movie was hardly a panacea for anti-Semitism: some 50 percent of the individuals in the experimental group did not experience an appreciation diminution in expressed anti-Semitism; indeed, some actually displayed an increase.

To determine more about the possible boomerang consequences of the film, Middleton compared the experimental and control groups with regard to the proportion showing an increase in anti-Semitism scores on the second questionnaire. Since twice as many of those in the control as those in the experimental group had greater scores, Middleton concluded that the movie by itself probably had no significant boomerang effect.

Conclusions. Middleton interprets his findings as revealing that a movie such as *Gentleman's Agree-*

---

* Adapted from Russell Middleton, "Ethnic Prejudice and Susceptibility to Persuasion," *American Sociological Review,* 25 (1960), 679–86.

ment can have considerable impact on the expression of anti-Semitic prejudice. He does caution us, however, on two matters. First, since the second questionnaire was administered a few days after the showing of the film, we do not know how *last-ing* an effect the movie had. Second, the study tells us little about how deep seated the changes were, that is, whether the motion picture merely exerted pressure toward a *surface* conformity to its anti-prejudice theme.

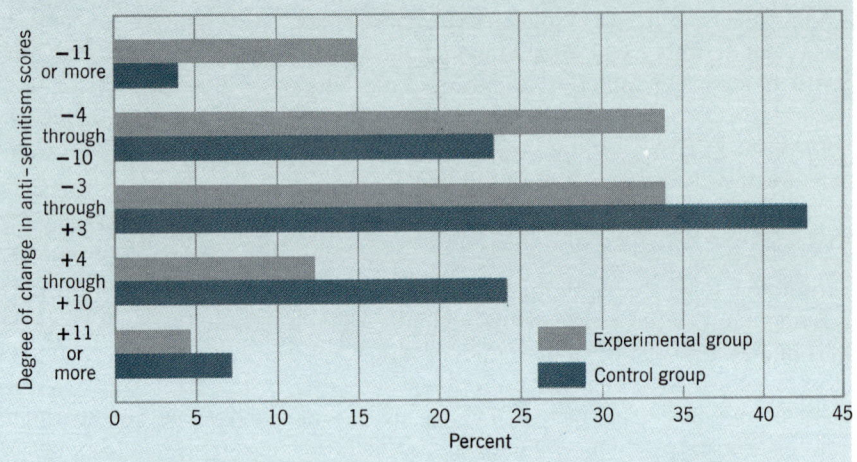

Figure 1.2. Degree of change in expressed anti-Semitism following the showing of the movie *Gentleman's Agreement*.

Source: Adapted from Russell Middleton, "Ethnic Prejudice and Susceptibility to Persuasion," *American Sociological Review,* 25 (1960), 682, Table 2.

ANALYSIS

Once we have secured our data, our final task in a research undertaking is to analyze it so as to find the answers to the questions posed by our research project. Analysis involves us in a search for meaningful links between the facts that have emerged in the course of our research. Middleton, for instance, had to determine the relationship between the viewing of *Gentleman's Agreement* and student attitudes toward Jews as measured by his anti-Semitism scale. Where our hypotheses are simple and our research plan is quite precise, these answers are often readily apparent. The more complex our hypotheses and our research plan, the more complicated generally will be our analysis.

Facts, even statistics, do not in and of themselves necessarily supply us with the answers to our questions. Questions are usually easy to ask but much less easy to answer. We may ask, for instance, is the distribution of income in this country becoming more or less unequal:

> . . . one reads that the top 20 per cent of families, which receive a little over 40 per cent of total income, now pay 50 per cent of total taxes, and the top five per cent, which receive 16 per cent of total income, pay 25 per cent of total taxes. This statistic is accurate and conveys the

impression that our present tax system distributes the tax burden rather fairly. One also reads that the top 20 per cent pay in taxes about the same proportion (33 per cent) of their income as the lowest 20 per cent. This statistic, too, is accurate in its own way and, while not contradicting the first, conveys a quite opposite impression. One can do quite marvellous things with statistics. . . . (Kristol, 1974, p. 4)

Analysis, then, is hardly a simple or easy task. It is a human undertaking fraught with all the limitations of humanness, including the subtle selection of facts to fit pre-existing biases (Hraba and Richards, 1975; Useem, 1976). Different people may "see" different linkages between facts. Sophisticated research, however, seeks to minimize this problem. Sociologists enjoy a variety of statistical tools that are helpful for analyzing facts, but a treatment of these is usually deferred to advanced courses in sociology.

ETHICS IN RESEARCH

Hurt not others in ways that you yourself would find hurtful.

Udana-Varga (Buddhism)

Over the past decade, considerable controversy has been generated regarding the ethics of particular research studies (Rivlin and Timpane, 1975). The Central Intelligence Agency, in its 25-year quest for control of the human mind, tested LSD and other psychochemicals on unsuspecting subjects, resulting in the death of at least one individual (Szulc, 1977). The U.S. Public Health Service sponsored research in which a control group of southern Blacks* went 40 years without treatment for syphilis. The State Health Department filed 52 charges against the State University of New York in 1977 alleging, among other things, that researchers delved illegally into people's sexual behavior and fantasies (the university subsequently admitted to 35 improper experiments). And at Stanford University, psychologist Philip Zimbardo and his associates (Zimbardo, Haney, and Banks, 1973) set up a mock prison in which the "guards" (college students) subjected the "prisoners" (also college students) to such sadistic abuse that four of the ten "prisoners" developed acute anxiety, crying spells, and severe depression and a fifth developed a psychosomatic rash over his entire body.

Stuart W. Cook, the chairperson of the American Psychological Association's Committee on Ethical Standards, cites the following as questionable practices encountered in social science research:

---

* Controversy exists as to whether or not to capitalize the first letter of "Black" and "White." I have followed the approach of capitalizing both. The terms refer to either a "people" or an "ethnic group"; capitalization recognizes a group's "peoplehood" or "ethnic status" and accords dignity to it. A similar rationale exists for capitalizing such terms as Chicano, Jew, Italian, and Puerto Rican.

1. Involving people in research without their knowledge or consent
2. Coercing people to participate
3. Withholding from the participant the true nature of the research
4. Deceiving the research participant
5. Leading the research participants to commit acts which diminish their self-respect
6. Violating the right to self-determination: research on behavior control and character change
7. Exposing the research participant to physical or mental stress
8. Invading the privacy of the research participant
9. Withholding benefits from participants in control groups
10. Failing to treat research participants fairly and to show them consideration and respect (1976, p. 202)

The major scientific associations have formulated codes of ethics for the treatment of research participants (American Anthropological Association, 1973; American Political Science Association, 1968; American Psychological Association, 1973; and American Sociological Association, 1971). For example, the American Sociological Association states that the search for social truths must operate within constraints:

> Its limits arise when inquiry infringes on the rights of individuals to be treated as persons, to be considered . . . as ends and not as means. Just as sociologists must not distort or manipulate truth to serve untruthful ends, so too they must not manipulate persons to serve their quest for truth. The study of society, being the study of human beings, imposes the responsibility of respecting the integrity, promoting the dignity, and maintaining the autonomy of these persons. . . .
>
> Every person is entitled to the right of privacy and dignity of treatment. The sociologist must respect these rights. . . .
>
> All research should avoid causing personal harm to subjects used in research. (1971)

Clearly, research must not be seen as license to violate human rights.

PRACTICAL USES OF SOCIOLOGY

> To him who devotes his life to science, nothing can give more happiness than increasing the number of his discoveries, but his cup of joy is full when the results of his studies immediately find practical application.
>
> *Louis Pasteur*

We have considered a number of ways by which sociologists go about acquiring valid, reliable knowledge concerning human interaction. But, we may ask, what practical use is such knowledge; what relevance has sociology for the problems that confront the world? This is admittedly an old and vexing question.

A good many American sociologists were personally interested in social reform and saw sociology as a potentially powerful instrument for relieving human suffering and guiding humans in the search for a better future. Hinkle and Hinkle (1954:4) point to the prevalence of rural and religious backgrounds and the deep concern with ethical matters among leading sociologists in the first decades of this century — indeed, a surprising number launched their careers as Protestant ministers. In succeeding decades, despite changes in the philosophical and social climate, sociology has secured many of its recruits from among the highly idealistic, those individuals who see hope for the solution of our problems in scientific study of society (see Figure 1.3). Today many students take sociology courses in search of intellectual tools to fashion a society with a new authenticity and a new freedom.

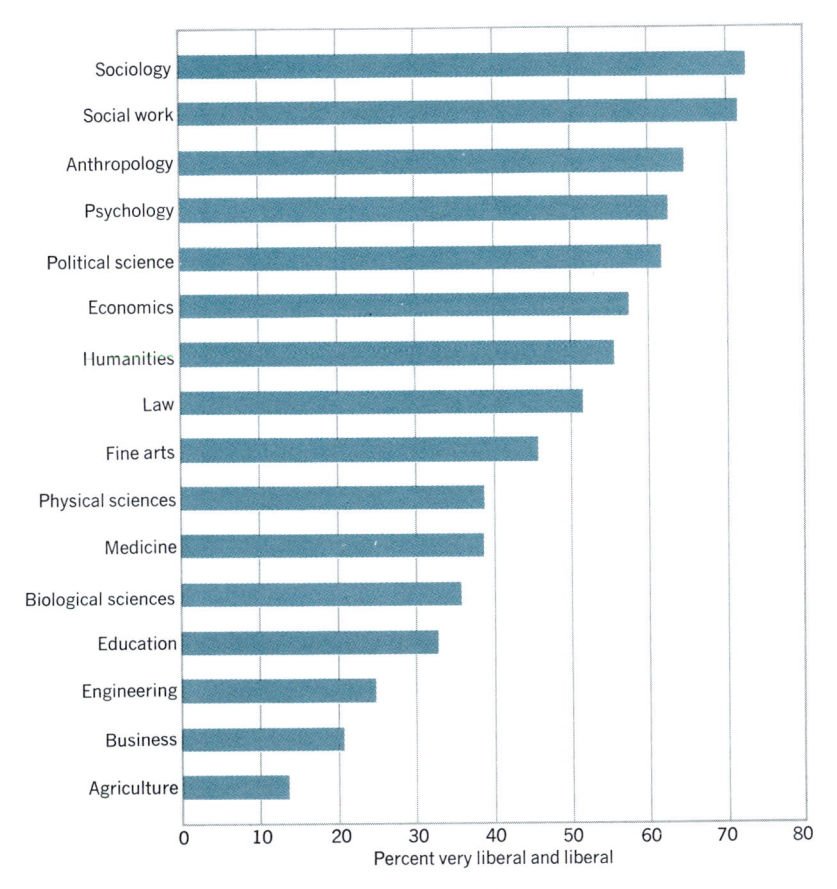

Figure 1.3. Faculty positions on liberalism — conservatism scale by field. These findings are based on a massive survey of college faculty conducted during the spring of 1969 with the financial support of the Carnegie Commission and the United States Office of Education. The scale was constructed from questions in the survey.

Source: Adapted from Seymour Martin Lipset and Everett Carll Ladd, Jr., "The Politics of American Sociologists," *American Journal of Sociology*, 78 (1972), 71, Table 2.

Although most sociologists share the hope that their work will lead to a better understanding of human behavior, they disagree about sociology's role in bringing about a better society (Street and Weinstein, 1975). Some sociologists take the view that sociology is a pure science; others that it is an applied science; and still others that it is a vehicle for social criticism. Let us examine each of these viewpoints in turn.

THE PURE SCIENCE ORIENTATION

It can never be the task of an empirical science [such as sociology] to provide binding norms and ideals from which directions for immediate practical activity can be derived.

Max Weber, The Methodology of the Social Sciences

The view that sociology is a pure science is closely identified with the position of Max Weber (1864–1920), a German sociologist whom most sociologists rank at or near the top of any list of illustrious sociologists. According to Weber, the validity of values is a matter of faith, not of knowledge. Sociologists must study values but not commit themselves to any values in their role as scientists: "I am ready to prove from the works of our historians that whenever the man of science introduces his personal value judgment, a full understanding of the facts *ceases*" (Weber, 1958: 146). Hence, Weber held that sociology must be *value-free* and that sociologists must owe allegiance to no flag.

It is not too surprising that many American sociologists should have found Weber's position appealing. During its formative years, sociology struggled to gain respectability and acceptance within the scientific community. It is easy to forget that in the early decades of this century even William Graham Sumner, whose Social Darwinism would place him today at the far right in the range of social theory, clung precariously to his endowed chair at Yale, continually under suspicion of irreligiousness by virtue of his studies of the customs of other societies. Only in the last decade or so has a suspicion that there is something subversive about sociology largely died out. It is possible now to say that one is a sociologist and be free of identification as a "socialist."

Partly as a response to this early suspicion of sociology, many sociologists argued that their discipline should remain aloof from involvement with social problems and concern itself strictly with the enlargement if sociological knowledge. This was the dominant position of the profession during the 1940s, 1950s, and early 1960s. The established leaders of sociology advocated a neutral, amoral sociology—one in which sociologists were bound to the tenet: "Thou shall not commit a value judgment." Robert Bierstedt, a prominent sociologist of the period, expressed the view as follows:

> Sociology is a pure science, not an applied science. The immediate goal of sociology is the acquisition of knowledge about human society,

not the utilization of that knowledge. Physicists do not build bridges, physiologists do not treat people afflicted with pneumonia, and chemists do not fill prescriptions at the corner drugstore. Similarly, sociologists do not determine questions of public policy, do not tell legislators what laws should be passed or repealed, and do not dispense relief to the ill, and lame, the blind, or the poor. . . . (1963, pp. 12–13)

Brewton Berry, another leading sociologist, outlined a somewhat similar position for his field of race relations. Responding to critics who accused sociologists of "fiddling about leisurely" studying race problems in the face of urgent calls for remedial social engineering, Berry wrote:

We fully appreciate the seriousness and urgency of the situation, but we believe that knowledge and understanding are prerequisites for wise and effective action. We are sympathetic, for instance, with the medical research scientists who work away in their laboratories while an epidemic rages in the community. Why, some will say, do they not do something immediately useful? Why not put into practical use such knowledge and skill as they have, imperfect though it be? Why waste their efforts on research when the times demand action? It is our opinion that, in the long run, the research scientists will relieve more suffering by their investigations than by abandoning their study and devoting themselves to therapy. (1965, p. 18).

THE APPLIED SCIENCE ORIENTATION

Any process of inquiry unguided by intellectual passions would inevitably spread out into a desert of trivialities.
Michael Polanyi, Personal Knowledge: Towards a Post-Critical Philosophy, 1964

During the 1960s and 1970s there emerged a group of "new-breed" sociologists who challenged the position advanced by such sociologists as Weber, Bierstedt, and Berry (Gouldner, 1962; Becker, 1967; Colfax, 1970; Lee, 1973, 1976). For these sociologists the notion of a value-free and unbiased sociology is a "myth." They argue that sociologists are as much social beings as the people they study and that they are not free of the social demands of colleagues, research organizations, government granting agencies, political systems, university administrators, students, and friends. Viewed from this perspective, it is impossible to do research that is uncontaminated by personal and political sympathies. Knowledge is not neutral. Even relatively "neutral" research has social consequences and overtones of bias. Howard S. Becker and Irving Louis Horowitz observe:

The disclosure that social scientists have undertaken research designed to further the interests of the powerful at the expense of those of the powerless (e.g., riot control at home and "civic action" abroad) showed how even apparently innocent research might serve special political interests. Prison research has for the most part been oriented to problems of jailers rather than those of prisoners; industrial research, to the problems of managers rather than those of workers; military research, to the problems of generals rather than those of privates. Greater sensitivity to the undemocratic character [of society] . . . has revealed how research frequently represents the interests of adults and teachers instead of those of children and students; men instead of women; of the white middle class instead of the lower class, blacks, chicanos, and other minorities; of the conventional straight world instead of freaks; of boozers instead of potheads. (1972, p. 48)

Critics of the ethical neutral stance of Weber, Bierstedt, and Berry contend that neutrality actually masks a very definite commitment: "The choice that has generally been made by sociologists is to put their skills at the service of the establishment, that is to say, of groups who wield a great deal of economic and political power in the society" (Biblarz, 1969:4). Indeed, "to do

Pure versus applied science. Some sociologists believe that their discipline should be "value-free." Others hold that sociology should link itself with the larger hopes, aspirations, and purposes of humanity and improve social conditions and extend human freedom.

Patrick Reddy

nothing in today's world is as political in its effect as to do something; to assent is as political as to dissent" (Berreman, 1971: 19). Further, such sociologists charge that the apostles of sociological "neutrality" are remiss in their public and civic responsibilities, that they come to champion moral insensitivity—a crass disregard for such things as the suffering of the poor and minority groups, the destructiveness of war, and the high social costs of crime and delinquency. Hence, these sociologists believe that scientists should direct their research activities to the improvement of human life.

The writings of C. Wright Mills (1916–1962) have had considerable influence on the thinking of many sociologists. In *The Sociological Imagination* (1959) Mills argued that sociologists should not consider their sole mission to be the development of abstract knowledge. They equally have the task of shedding light on the human condition and linking the troubles of people with the larger realities of the social order. If people are to free themselves from the "traps" they encounter in their daily lives, Mills believed that they need to make the connection between their "private troubles" and "public issues." The fundamental message of *The Sociological Imagination* is that sociologists must look at the structure of society and find points of intervention whereby human conditions might be improved and human freedom extended.

THE CRITICAL SCIENCE ORIENTATION

> The radical sociologist must serve as a constant social critic. . . . A radical sociology must elaborate a counter definition of social reality. It must explain how badly the present society functions, how people's private frustrations stem from the social structure, how unnecessary and oppressive the present institutional arrangements are, and how much better an alternative social order would work. It must further, provide the practical knowledge, techniques, and skills to the counter institutional movement that is trying to create a decent social order.
>
> Albert Szymanski, Toward a Radical Sociology, 1970

The critical science orientation differs from the applied science orientation primarily in the degree to which it is committed to fundamental social change. Applied science proponents tend to be reformists—they aim to achieve goals and effect values that are already acknowledged to be inherent in a political democracy, for instance, expanding rights and job opportunities for women and Blacks. Critical science advocates, in contrast, tend to see society as so grievously flawed that only basic changes in the American class structure and government and the establishment of new political, economic, and ethical goals will suffice.

Further, as Paul Starr observes:

> Merely to call attention to some facts, however true, is to challenge moral or political views that systematically ignore or distort them. So social science, conducted even in the purest spirit, easily becomes a

kind of social criticism whenever it deals with subjects that people care deeply about. (1974, p. 403)

In brief, "to tell it as it is" threatens the interests of some groups. But sociologists who share the critical science perspective see this as an essential aspect of their scientific role.

ENLIGHTENMENT AND ENGINEERING

What are we to make of these divergent conceptions of sociology, the one championing neutrality, the other partisanship? Can we arrive at any meaningful conclusion on this matter? The author of this text believes that we can. Many sociologists reject both the view that sociology must be *nothing but* self-contained knowledge—entirely insulated from the world of social action—and the view that sociology must be *nothing but* a guide to action. They feel quite sympathetic with the following position set forth by Alfred North Whitehead, a distinguished philosopher:

> Science is a river with two sources, the practical source and the theoretical source. The practical source is the desire to direct our actions to achieve predetermined ends. . . . The theoretical source is the desire to understand. I most emphatically state that I do not consider one source as in any sense nobler than the other, or intrinsically more interesting. I cannot see why it is nobler to strive to understand than to busy oneself with the right ordering of one's actions. Both have their bad sides; there are evil ends directing actions, and there are ignoble curiosities of the understanding. (1951, p. 107)

Subscription to this viewpoint does not mean that some sociologists, by virtue of temperament or interest, may not concentrate their energies in the one realm or the other. It only means that many of them do not see a hard and fast boundary separating pure from applied or critical science, enlightenment from social engineering (Olsen, 1971).

Some of sociology's most fruitful work has come from "applied" research, such as the enrichment of reference group theory (see Chapter 6) resulting from the American Soldier studies dealing with army morale and related matters (Stouffer, 1949a; 1949b). And Goffman's study (1962) of mental hospitals added to our understanding of "total institutions" (for example, TB sanitariums, mental hospitals, jails, convents, and army barracks), while simultaneously revealing aspects of social organization in mental hospitals that could be altered to provide more help and better care for their patients. Further, applied research provides a test for sociological theory (Lazarsfeld and Reitz, 1975), such as the work of LaMar T. Empey and Jerome Rabow (1961) in applying sociological formulations to the treatment of delinquents in Provo, Utah.

SUMMARY

1. Sociology is distinguished by two characteristics: first, by its approach to phenomena—the approach of science; and second, by its subject matter—human interaction. In brief, sociology is the scientific study of human interaction. As a science it is characterized by the rigorous, disciplined pursuit of objectivity. In terms of its subject matter, sociology is concerned with the process by which two or more people mutually and reciprocally influence each other's feelings, attitudes, and actions.

2. Theory is "a way of binding together a multitude of facts so that one may comprehend them all at once." It is the net we weave so that we can catch the world of observation—explain, predict, and influence it.

3. Structure-function theory views institutions as analogous to organs. These social structures meet the vital requirements (functions) necessary for the survival and maintenance of the larger social system.

4. Conflict theory views the struggle over scarce, divisible good things as the central feature of social life. A recurring theme throughout much of human life is the question, "Whose will shall prevail, thine or mine?"

5. Social exchange theory conceives of people as ordering their relationships with one another in terms of a sort of mental bookkeeping that entails a ledger of rewards, costs, and profits. People enter into and sustain patterns of interaction with certain other people because they find such interaction rewarding, whatever the reasons.

6. Symbolic interactionist theory, following in the tradition of George Herbert Mead, argues that human beings evolved the capacity to interact with others through the use of shared symbols. By means of shared symbols, human beings impart "meaning" to their activities; they come to define situations and interpret behavior.

7. Ethnomethodology asks, "How is a particular social activity done?" It is primarily concerned with human behavior taking place on the "taken-for-granted" level.

8. The first task in social research is to locate a problem that we feel demands solution. As part of this effort, we often find it necessary to formulate hypotheses. A hypothesis is a proposition that can be tested to determine its validity.

9. Observation, interviews, questionnaires, and the use of available data are a number of common techniques that sociologists employ in the study of human interaction. The ideal model in which these techniques come to be applied is the controlled experiment.

10. Once we have secured our data, our final task in a research undertaking is to analyze the data so as to find the answers to the questions posed by our research project. Analysis involves us in a search for meaningful links between the facts that have emerged in the course of our research.

11. The major scientific associations have formulated codes of ethics for the treatment of research participants. Every person is entitled to the right of privacy and dignity of treatment. All research should avoid causing personal harm to the subjects.

12. Although most sociologists share the hope that their work will lead to a better understanding of human behavior, they disagree about sociology's role in bringing about a better society. Some sociologists take the view that sociology is a pure science; others that it is an applied science; and still others that it is a vehicle for social criticism. On the other hand, many sociologists do not see a hard and fast boundary separating pure from applied or critical science.

PART ONE

THE SOCIAL WORLD

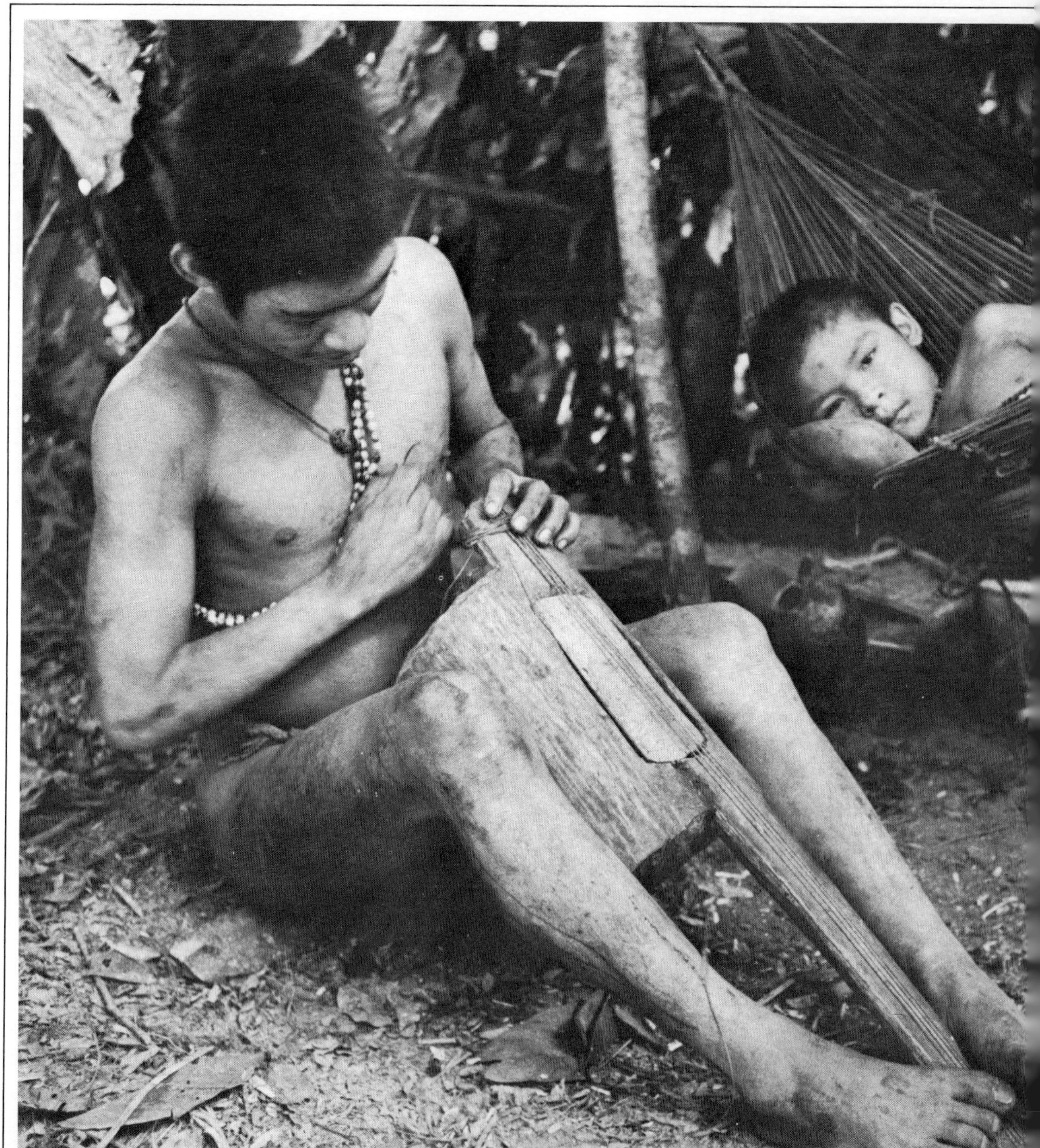

2
CULTURE: AN OVERVIEW

THE NATURE OF CULTURE
    What Is Culture?
    The Definition of the Situation

NORMS
    Folkways and Mores
    Law
    Negotiated Order

VALUES

SYMBOLS AND LANGUAGE
    The Importance of Symbols
    Language

SUBCULTURE AND COUNTERCULTURE
    Subculture
    Counterculture

OBSERVATION I returned to my room today to find my roommate hiding his booze and joints [marihuana]. He then proceeded to pick up all the *Playboys, Penthouses,* and other assorted magazines and hide them under his mattress. After that he took down two of his naked girlie posters and hid them. About 7:30, Jack's Dad and Mom knocked on the door and came in to visit for a while. They had come up to town in the afternoon, and called Jack telling him they were coming over.

PRINCIPLE Jack lives a life at college quite different from that he lives at home. When his parents called Jack changed our room and hid those things that were inconsistent with his life at home and with the roles that he wanted his parents to think he played while at school. Jack was afraid that the cultural rules of his parents would not allow for all the things he did at school that were quite permissible within the dorm. In truth, of course, Jack's way of life here at school is countercultural when viewed against the standards of his parents. But I can't help feeling that Jack and his parents play a little game. His parents didn't come barging into our room unexpectedly but tipped off Jack that they were coming; in this way they were saved from discovering how Jack actually lived. And Jack for his part took the cue and hid the potentially offensive stuff.

Over the past three decades the United States has spent hundreds of billions of dollars on foreign aid programs. Despite its efforts, the United States has failed to win either the affection or esteem of many of the peoples it has assisted. Edward T. Hall (1973), an anthropologist, has looked into this matter. He notes that many of the difficulties Americans have experienced are not untypical of the problems that arise when peoples of different countries have dealings with one another.

Hall cites a number of examples to highlight his point:

> Despite a host of favorable auspices an American mission in Greece was having great difficulty working out an agreement with Greek officials. Efforts to negotiate met with resistance and suspicion on the part of the Greeks. The Americans were unable to conclude the agreements needed to start new projects. Upon later examination of this exasperating situation two unsuspected reasons were found for the stalemate: First, Americans pride themselves on being outspoken and forthright. These qualities are regarded as a liability by the Greeks. They are taken to indicate a lack of finesse which the Greeks deplore. The American directness immediately prejudiced the Greeks. Second, when the Americans arranged meetings with the Greeks they tried to limit the length of the meetings and to reach agreements on general principles first, delegating the drafting of details to subcommittees. The Greeks regarded this practice as a device to pull the wool over their eyes. The Greek practice is to work out details in front of all concerned and con-

45 Culture: An Overview

tinue meetings for as long as is necessary. The result of this misunderstanding was a series of unproductive meetings with each side deploring the other's behavior. (1973, p. xv)

In another case, an American agricultural mission encountered problems in teaching modern agricultural methods to Egyptian villagers. The Americans often asked the farmers how much they expected their fields to yield at harvest-time. The farmers responded by becoming agitated and angry. The Americans did not realize that to the Arabs only God knows the future and anyone who attempts to look into the future is regarded as somewhat insane. In essence, by asking the question that they did, the Americans were insulting the Arabs by implying that the Americans thought them to be demented.

THE NATURE OF CULTURE

[Culture is] that complex whole which includes knowledge, belief, art, morals, law, custom, and any other capabilities and habits acquired by man as a member of society.

Edward B. Tylor, Primitive Culture, 1871

How are we to understand the contrasting behavior of peoples of different societies? The answer, in part, rests with *culture*.

WHAT IS CULTURE?

Culture is the socially standardized ways of thinking, feeling, and acting that the human acquires as a member of society. It provides us with a set of common understandings—a kind of map—for life's activities. These cultural guideposts present us with a set of ready-made definitions of the situation which each of us only slightly retailors in our own individual way (Kluckhohn, 1960). Culture is a sort of configuration of do's and don'ts, a recurring pattern of mental Stop and Go signs and preferences that are implicit or expressed (Benedict, 1946): "Notice this," "Ignore that," "Imitate this action," "Avoid that action," and so on. Clyde Kluckhohn (1960: 21), a distinguished anthropologist, notes that "a good deal of human behavior can be understood and indeed predicted, if we know a people's design for living [their culture]."

We can see the pervasive influence of culture in this interesting illustration of Kluckhohn's:

Some years ago I met in New York City a young man who did not speak a word of English and was obviously bewildered by American ways. By "blood" he was as American as you and I, for his parents had gone from Indiana to China as missionaries. Orphaned in infancy, he was reared by a Chinese family in a remote village. All who met him found him more Chinese than American. The facts of his blue eyes and light hair were less impressive than a Chinese style of gait, Chinese arm and hand movements, Chinese facial expression, and Chinese modes of thought. The biological heritage was American, but the cultural training had been Chinese. He returned to China. (1960, pp. 21–22)

For the most part, human behavior is not haphazard or random. It is characterized by organization, regularity, and continuity. In other words, a good deal of our behavior is socially standardized. Perhaps we can gain a better understanding of this matter by considering two illustrations, one dealing with perception, the other with biological processes.

Culture and Perception. We never really "see" the physical world about us. Rather, the world we experience is a product of the interaction between our anatomy, the physical aspects of the universe, and what we have learned

Cultural differences in the language of space. Arab interaction involves a considerable degree of physical contact. Arab men touch one another and visually maintain eye contact. Most American men find physical contact among males distasteful and feel one's masculinity is challenged by prolonged "staring."

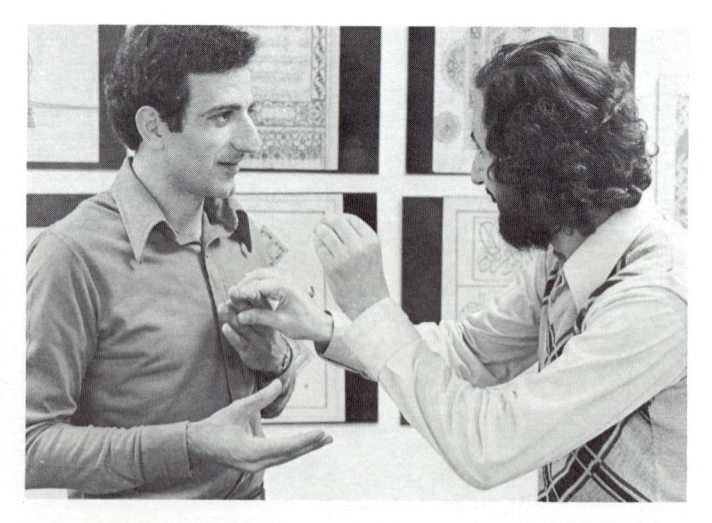

Patrick Reddy

from our past experience (Blumer, 1977; Lindsay and Norman, 1977). As a consequence, our perception is never a photographic image of the physical world. It is not surprising, therefore, that people differ in the world that they experience. Indeed, it can be argued that *we experience the world not as it is, but as we are.*

Although many factors enter into our perception of the world, one of the most important of these is culture. Anthropologist A. Irving Hallowell (1951) gives an interesting example of the part culture plays in influencing our perceptions. He discussed with a group of his students the differing names that various peoples have given to a group of stars in the constellation Ursa Major (Big Dipper, Great Bear, otter, plow, and so on) and the influence that the assignment of such names has had on the people's perception of the stars. When he finished, feeling he had made the point, one student spoke up asserting: "But it *does* look like a dipper." As Hallowell responded, it probably *does* look like a bear (an otter or whatever) to those who use that label.

Social influences affect perception in a very marked way. Perception is *selective;* it involves a good deal of omitting. At almost every moment of our waking life, we encounter countless stimuli that we might notice but in fact never do. Only by hitting on a few salient features and ignoring the others are we able to "make sense" out of most situations. In brief, we "tune in" some stimuli and "tune out" others. Hence, cultural definitions, by influencing individuals' perceptions of people, objects, and events, serve to lock individuals of different groups and societies into somewhat different worlds.

An interesting study illustrating how cultural definitions can affect perceptions was made by Gregory Razran (1950). One hundred and fifty men were shown pictures of thirty young women, all strangers to them. They were asked to rank each photograph on a five-point scale that would indicate their general liking for the girl, her beauty, her character, her intelligence, her ambition, and her "entertainingness." Two months later, the same group was again shown the identical photographs but with surnames added. For some of the photographs, Jewish names were given, such as Finkelstein and Cohen; to others, Irish surnames such as O'Shaughnessy and McGillicuddy; to others, Italian surnames such as Valenti and Scadano; and to others, old American surnames such as Davis and Clark.

The labeling of the photographs with the surnames had a marked effect on the manner in which they were perceived. The addition of Jewish and Italian names resulted in a substantial drop in general liking and a smaller drop in the judgment of beauty and character. The falling of likeability of the "Jewish girls" was twice as great as for "Italians" and five times as great as for "Irish." On the other hand, it also resulted in a general rise in the ratings in ambition and intelligence for the girls with Jewish surnames. Clearly, cultural definitions had a marked effect on the perception of the photographs and on the judgment of the characteristics attributed to the girls. Not only were the men's perceptions selective, they also "read into" the photographs aspects which were not present but which jibed with their cultural definitions.

Culture and Biological Processes. Culture channels, molds, and modifies a good deal of our biological functioning. Some patterns of every culture crystallize about the inevitables of our existence as biological organisms. If we are to survive, society must make provision for the satisfaction of our basic needs, including hunger, thirst, sex, fatigue, elimination, and internal temperature control. We experience, for instance, generalized hunger as localized sensations of emptiness and dull and acute stomach pain that is accompanied by periodic contractions of the stomach muscles. But our precise reaction to these internal stimuli cannot be predicted by physiological knowledge alone. Whether we will experience hunger twice, three times, or even six times a day depends in large measure on our culture. What people eat is of course limited by availability of food, but it is also influenced by culture. Milk and its products are viewed as luxury foods among the Baganda of East Africa, while the peoples of West Africa regard them as inedible and probably poisonous. Many American Indian tribes consumed fish, but the Navahos and Apaches of the Southwest considered them nauseating and unfit for human consumption. And the beliefs of most Americans that snakes

The San of the Kalahari Desert in southern Africa. The San are a hunting and gathering people whose social bonds derive primarily from kinship ties. Although living in an environment that affluent Americans would define as harsh, the San manage to satisfy their subsistence needs with only a few hours work each day allowing them ample time for leisure activities. However, their distinctive cultural arrangements are imperiled by the progressive encroachments of outside political and economic interests and groups.

Stern/Black Star

Culture: An Overview

and insects are not suitable for food are quite similar to the Muslin–Jewish belief that pork is unfit for consumption. Culture, then, serves to pattern the manner by which people will satisfy their hunger drive.

The importance of culture in human biological functioning has been documented by studies dealing with group responses to pain. Considerable evidence indicates that the perception and tolerance of pain are not purely physiological responses (Wolff and Langley, 1968; Zimbardo and Ruch, 1975). Margaret Mead (1950), for example, records no morning sickness among pregnant Arapesh women of New Guinea. Her data suggests that this may be related to this people's almost complete denial of pregnancy until shortly before birth. Similarly, Irving Kenneth Zola (1966) found that the Irish typically handle their illnesses by denial and the Italians by dramatization. Such findings are consistent with those of Mark Zborowski (1969), who studied the responses of three ethnic groups to pain. He found that Italians and Jews tended to express their feelings and emotions quite freely, whereas "Old Americans" tended to hide them. Although the Italians and Jews reacted similarly toward pain, they nonetheless differed in their attitudes regarding it; hence, visibly similar behavioral patterns may serve quite different purposes among various groups. This work of Zborowski is summarized in Research Study 3.

RESEARCH STUDY 3

CULTURAL COMPONENTS IN RESPONSES TO PAIN*

Mark Zborowski

Problem. Pain is basically a physiological phenomenon. Yet like so many other physiological phenomena, cultural factors play a considerable part in influencing an individual's attitudes toward and reactions to pain. Any number of observers have noted this fact—indeed, a belief prevails among American medical personnel that Italian and Jewish patients have a tendency to "exaggerate" their pain. Is this belief well founded? It is to this matter that Zborowski addresses himself in the present study.

Method. Within the setting of a Veterans Administration Hospital, Zborowski examined the modes of expression and the meaning of pain among Jewish, Irish, Italian, and "Old American" (at least "third generation") patients. All were hospitalized war veterans, the majority of whom suffered from neurological diseases (mainly herniated discs and spinal lesions). Zborowski collected his data by interviewing patients of the selected groups, observing their behavior when they were in pain, and discussing their cases with medical personnel. In

Continued on next page.

* Adapted from Mark Zborowski, *People in Pain*. San Francisco: Jossey-Bass, 1969.

addition, Zborowski interviewed "healthy" members of the respective ethnic groups so as to determine their attitudes toward pain.

Findings. Zborowski found that Jews and Italians tended to react similarly toward pain. Both groups possessed cultural traditions that permitted them freely to express their feelings and emotions through words, sounds, and gestures. Hence, Italian and Jewish patients tended to talk and complain about their pain, and to express it by groaning, moaning, and crying. Moreover, they generally revealed little shame concerning their displays of suffering; they willingly admitted that they complained a great deal, called for help, and expected others to give them sympathy.

Although the two groups *reacted* quite similarly to pain, they nonetheless differed in their *attitudes* toward it. Italian patients seemed primarily concerned with the immediacy of the pain experience and found the actual pain sensation quite disturbing. Patients of Jewish origin, in contrast, focused mainly on the symptomatic meaning and broader significance of pain (its consequences for their health, welfare, and eventually for the welfare of their families). This underlying difference reflected itself in the two groups' attitudes toward pain-relieving drugs. When in pain, Italian patients often called for pain relief and welcomed the analgesic effects produced by the drugs. On finding relief, the Italian tended to forget his sufferings and to manifest his normal disposition. The Jewish patient, however, was often reluctant to accept analgesic drugs; he tended to be apprehensive about the habit-forming aspects of the drug and to feel that the drug only masked his pain and did not cure him of the disease. Moreover, when relieved of pain by analgesic drugs, many Jewish patients continued to be depressed and worried.

"Old American" patients tended to be somewhat stoic in their reaction to pain, repeatedly stating in interviews that there was no point in complaining, groaning, and moaning because "it won't help anybody." They tended to "report" on their pain—to assume the detached role of an unemotional observer who gave an efficient description of his state for a correct diagnosis and treatment. Although readily admitting that they cried when their pain became unbearable, they tended to do it when alone—indeed, withdrawal from society seemed to be a frequent "Old American" response to strong pain. As in the case of the Jewish patients, "Old Americans" often experienced a future-oriented anxiety, worrying lest the pain signal serious illness. But whereas the Jewish attitude tended to be one of pessimism or skepticism, the "Old American" attitude was one of optimism. To many "Old Americans," the body is a machine that has to be well taken care of, be periodically checked for dysfunctioning, and—when out of order—be taken to an expert who "fixes" it. Hence, their anxieties were often relieved when "something was being done." Security and confidence seemed to increase in direct proportion to the number of tests, X rays, examinations, injections, and the like that were administered.

Irish patients tended to be rather helpless in explaining their illness and were prone to seek the cause within themselves. This attitude found reflection in their passive and uncomplaining role as patients, which differentiated them from the cooperative but often griping patients of "Old American" background. Throughout the study, Irish patients expressed worry and pessimism about the outcome of their illness and its effect upon their body and masculinity.

Although the researcher found certain overall regularities among members of the ethnic groups, there were, of course, individual differences and variations. Interestingly enough, a Jewish or Italian patient born in the United States of American-born parents tended to *behave* like an "Old American" but often expressed *attitudes* similar to those expressed by Jewish or Italian immigrants. In brief, such a patient tended to be stoic in his overt reaction to pain; but if he were of Jewish origin, he was likely to express attitudes of anxiety regarding pain; and, if he were of Italian origin, he was likely to express attitudes that indicated little concern with the broader significance of the pain.

Conclusions. Zborowski's work suggests that cultural patterns play an important part in influencing how an individual thinks about and reacts to pain. Moreover, it reveals that simply because two groups display similar reactions to pain (for instance, Jews and Italians), they do not necessarily share similar attitudes toward it. Hence, visibly similar reactive patterns may have different functions and serve different purposes in various cultures.

THE DEFINITION OF THE SITUATION

The meaning of things lies not in the things themselves but in our attitude towards them.
Antoine de Saint-Exupéry, The Wisdom of the Sands, *1948*

Social life requires that we *fit* our developing lines of action to the actions of other people (Blumer, 1969; 1977). Whatever we do—exchange a greeting, carry on a conversation, rob a bank, drive our car along a city street, make love, or complete an examination—we must take other people and their behavior into account. Accordingly, we need to *interpret* people's behavior and they in turn must interpret our behavior. This involves us in a continual process whereby we arrive at agreed on meanings. Only by sharing a similar perspective with others can we weave an integrated web of ongoing interaction. In brief, social interaction requires that we have certain common understandings or *shared* definitions of the situation. Culture is the cognitive (mental) map that outlines for us in rather broad terms what we can expect of others and what they can expect of us (Vander Zanden, 1977).

The definition of the situation is an important concept within sociology (McHugh, 1968; Perinbanayagam, 1974). The sociologist W. I. Thomas (1937: 42) provided its classic formulation: "Preliminary to any self-determined act of behavior there is always a stage of examination and deliberation which we may call the definition of the situation." Thomas noted that in life we act in an "as if" fashion. We mentally define each path of contemplated behavior in terms of what we anticipate will result if we follow one path and not another.

A study by Robert H. Lauer (1974) highlights the importance of people's definitions of situations. He measured the effects that objective and perceived rates of change had on individuals' level of anxiety. Students at a midwestern university completed a questionnaire dealing with the changes that had occurred in their lives during the previous year: family relationships, occupation, financial affairs, health, education, religion, and the like. Their responses provided an objective measure of changes in their life circumstances.

The students were also asked to indicate the extent to which they agree with three statements (512):

> The world we live in is changing so fast it leaves me breathless at times.
>
> There is so much information accumulating that I can't keep up with everything I need to know.
>
> Generally, it seems to me that the passage of time is more like a rushing river than a slowly trickling stream.

The students' responses to these statements provided a measure of their perceived rate of change, that is, their definition of the situation.

Finally, the students completed a test measuring their level of anxiety (for instance, they were asked to respond "true" or "false" to such statements as "I work under a great deal of tension"; "I am happy most of the time"; and "I frequently find myself worrying about something"). Lauer found that the way the students *defined* the situation was more crucial in influencing their level of anxiety than was the actual situation as measured by objective criteria.

As revealed by Lauer's study, people's definitions of situations have profound consequences for them—in this case, influencing their level of anxiety in response to stressful life circumstances. But of even greater significance, as people come to share definitions of situations—evolve a culture—they fashion the social means by which they can come to terms with and cope with their environment. These shared definitions of situations represent people's social legacy as contrasted with their biological heredity.

DEFINITIONS OF SITUATIONS

OBSERVATION Tonight I wanted to study for my sociology midterm, so I went down the hall to study in one of our dorm's lounges. As I entered the room, I shut the door slowly to prevent it from slamming and tip-toed very quietly to a stuffed chair. During the entire time I was in the room, no one talked—not even a whisper—and the only sound I heard was an occasional turning of a page. I thought that it was amazing since there is no formal sign, rule, agreement, or anything that proclaims that everyone must be quiet. Nevertheless, everyone is. On weekends the room is employed for parties; students simply understand that the room is to be used for merriment and noisemaking.

PRINCIPLE It is interesting to note how we go about defining situations. During weekdays the lounge has informally come to be defined as a "study room," one in which people are not to talk loudly (or talk at all). Yet the identical room becomes socially defined as a "recreation room" on weekends in which noisy actions are not only acceptable but expected. In the course of living together, the dorm students have evolved common understandings by which they fit their actions together and manage their lives.

Culture: An Overview

Human beings, then, are heir to a social tradition — culture. They are lacking in biological programming which preordains most of their behavior. For instance, the round pebbles scattered about on the ground do not in and of themselves suggest stone knives. Many processes had to be learned and many thousands of years had to pass before human beings learned to make knives out of stone. Even the simplest tool is the fruit of long experience and trials and errors. Children do not have to go through the entire inventive process again. They can learn how to make and use material from their elders in accordance with the definitions evolved by ancestral generations. In this sense culture is cumulative. It permits each new generation to spring from the achievement shoulders of the preceding one.

NORMS

It has been noted that culture provides us with a set of guideposts — ready-made definitions of situations — by which we align our individual actions to create social or joint actions. These guideposts are **norms**. Norms are rules that specify appropriate and inappropriate behavior. They tell us what we *should, ought,* and *must* do as well as what we *should not, ought not,* and *must not* do. Norms are expectations — conceptions of ideal behaviors — that are shared by the members of a society-at-large or by the members of particular groups within a society.

Norms, however, not only afford us a *means* for guiding our actions so that we might fit them to the actions of others. We also tend to attribute to norms an independent quality, making them objects in their own right. In this respect, norms consist of recognized and preferred ways of thinking, feeling, and acting. Hence, norms are also *ends*. They are standards for behavior.

In sum, norms have a dual character. First, they are a means, social tools by which we align our actions to create joint actions. Second, they are an end (or goal), social standards to which we are expected to align our conduct (Stokes and Hewitt, 1976).

FOLKWAYS AND MORES

Certain laws have not been written, but they are more fixed than all the written laws.
Seneca the Elder, Controversiae, *1st Century A.D.*

We would find it difficult to discuss norms very long without making some distinctions between them. In approaching this matter, we do not face any shortage of classificatory schemes. However, one approach in particular has found its way into the sociological literature and has had a far-reaching impact on the field. In 1906, a Yale professor and one of our country's early sociologists, William Graham Sumner, published an influential book about norms entitled *Folkways*. This work introduced the concepts *folkways* and *mores* into sociological terminology.

Through the years the concepts have taken on somewhat different connotations than they had in Sumner's usage. Generally, sociologists distinguish between folkways and mores on the basis of two criteria: (1) the degree of importance people attach to a given rule, and (2) the severity of sanctions (punishments) meted out to the wrongdoer. **Folkways** refer to norms that are looked on by the members of society (or a group within the society) as *not* being extremely important and that may be violated without severe punishment. **Mores** (*mos* is the singular of mores), on the other hand, are norms that are looked on by the members of a society (or a group within the society) as being extremely important and the violation of which results in severe punishment. As often happens when two criteria are simultaneously used in classifying a phenomenon, the two distinctions may not be completely correlated with one another; that is, a given behavior may be defined as quite important yet only nominal punishment may be meted out to the violator and vice versa.

What are some of the folkways of American culture? Women should not wear hair rollers to work or school. One should bathe frequently and keep one's teeth clean. People should keep their lawns cut. People should offer their neighbor a ride in their car if both are going in the same direction. One should not drink whiskey in a chapel. One should be on time for appointments.

FOLKWAYS

OBSERVATION Today I was in the men's restroom using a urinal. I was going about my business and while standing there I noticed that I was looking straight ahead at the blank wall in front of me. When I realized this I looked to both sides and noticed several other guys also staring straight ahead. Everyone is afraid to look to the right or left for fear of being deemed a little "strange" or "queer." But it is interesting if you observe carefully, that upon lining up at the urinal, guys usually take a quick glance out of the corner of their eyes, checking out the people next to them.

PRINCIPLE This is a good illustration of a folkway. You aren't supposed to size up other guys or else people will think you are a homosexual. Yet most guys violate the norm when lining up at the urinal, but so quickly that they aren't caught.

The sanctions associated with folkways are relatively mild and are generally applied informally. Gossip, ridicule, and ostracism constitute the retribution extracted for their violation. But as Kingsley Davis (1949: 59) notes, the sanctions are cumulative; if we persistently violate the same norm, the retribution grows accordingly. And if we violate a large number of different folkways, the punishment for the violation of each is likely to be greater than if we violated one alone. Ordinarily, people do not attach moral significance to the folkways. People who do not take baths and do not brush their teeth may be viewed as crude but not as sinful; people who do not keep their appointments are considered thoughtless, not evil.

As contrasted with folkways, mores are seen as extremely important to societal well-being, and severe punishment awaits violators. When negatively stated—as "thou shall not's"—mores are referred to as **taboos**. What are some of the mores and taboos of American culture? One must be loyal to America (a mos); one must not commit treason (a taboo). One must have only one spouse; one must not practice bigamy. One must respect human life; one must not murder (unless the individual is identified as having been placed beyond the realm of the taboo, for instance, "enemy" soldiers or "burglars").

Usually the retribution for violating the mores is severe. Violators may be put to death, imprisoned, outcast, mutilated, tortured, and the like. People attach moral significance to the mores. Americans generally view people who commit treason, bigamy, and murder as sinful, evil, and wicked.

It is very difficult to draw a hard and fast line between mores and folkways. In fact, it is misleading to make a dichotomy between them. Rather, folkways and mores may be viewed as poles on a continuum along which norms fall:

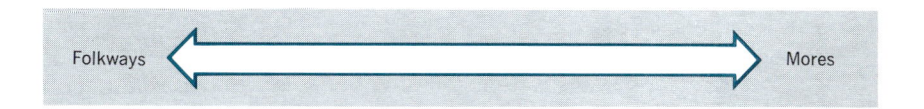

Folkways ⟷ Mores

Thus, the distinction between folkways and mores is a matter of degree rather than necessarily of kind—a question of degree of importance and degree of severity in punishment. Accordingly, some norms fall somewhere in the middle of the continuum, for example, the norm that Whites should not marry Blacks and vice versa (in some sections of South, however, it remains a strong taboo).

LAW

A law is not a law without coercion behind it.

James A. Garfield, 20th President of the United States

The distinguishing characteristic of **law** is the legitimate use of physical coercion by a legitimate party. The law has teeth, and teeth that can bite. To be effective, however, force need not be implemented; it need merely remain in the wings, ready at any moment to make its appearance (Goode, 1972). E. A. Hoebel (1958: 470–471), an anthropologist, notes: "The essentials of legal coercion are general acceptance of the application of physical power, in threat or in fact by a privileged party, for a legitimate cause, in a legitimate way, and at a legitimate time." Hence, the persons who administer laws may make use of physical force with a low probability of retaliation by a third party (Collins, 1975; Turk, 1976). The distinction between mores and folkways on the one hand and laws on the other is primarily a question of *who* institutes the sanctions. The folkways and mores are spontaneously and collectively enforced by the members of the society. Law, in contrast, involves enforcement by an individual or organization whose function is so defined.

NEGOTIATED ORDER

Man should be studied as he is — active, curious, imaginative, complex, intricately dependent upon his milieu.

William E. Roweton, Revitalizing Educational Psychology, 1976

Some sociologists conceive of society as a people's enactment of their culture in accordance with norms (Parsons, 1966). Viewed from this perspective, culture is made the major explanation of individual behavior. The human organism is seen as blindly enacting a programmed routine. Society becomes a community of well-programmed social robots. Such a view, however, is much too simplistic (Wrong, 1961; Stokes and Hewitt, 1976).

Other sociologists, especially those identified with the symbolic interactionist and ethnomethodological orientations, emphasize that social life is fluid and continually changing (Strauss et al., 1963; 1964; Mehan and Wood, 1975; 1976; Martin, 1976; Day and Day, 1977). Social order is not seen as something that automatically happens. Rather, people construct social order — a sense of social reality — as they repeat, reaffirm, and recreate their social acts. Hence, social order is **negotiated order.**

Anselm Strauss and his associates (1963) describe the process of negotiated order in these terms:

Culture: An Overview

Order is something at which members of any society, any organization, must work. For the shared agreements, the binding contracts—which constitute the grounds for an expectable, nonsurprising, taken-for-granted, even ruled orderliness—are not binding and shared for all time. Contracts, understandings, agreements, rules—all have appended to them a temporal clause. That clause may or may not be explicitly discussed by the contracting parties, and the terminal date of agreement may or may not be made specific; but none can be binding forever—even if the parties believe it so, unforeseen consequences of acting on the agreements would force eventual confrontation. Review is called for, whether the outcome of review be rejection or revision, or what not. In short, the bases of concerted action (social order) must be reconstituted continually, or as remarked above, "worked out." (1963, p. 148)

Negotiated order. Social order does not automatically happen. People construct order by arriving at shared understandings. Consider how pedestrians fashion order on a crowded sidewalk. If two sets of robots were to move toward one another, each set maintaining its line of march, few would make it past the point where they met. Notice how the woman in the photo communicates through eye contact with the man her intention of crossing in front of him. Both parties have to take the other's action into account in devising their own action.

Don McCarthy

Research Study 4 summarizes a study by Strauss and his associates (1964) dealing with the negotiation of order in hospitals.

Despite the insights afforded by their research, Strauss and his associates provide only a limited view of hospital life. Their treatment of negotiated order tends to overlook how the world outside of the hospital impinges on what goes on inside of it. With the rapid urbanization of the United States, vast technological innovations in medicine, and the establishment of new mechanisms for financing health services (primarily Blue Cross and Blue Shield and Medicare and Medicaid), an entire "medical-industrial complex" has arisen, for instance, large hospitals, nursing homes, comprehensive health care clinics, medical schools, and large pharmaceutical firms. This emerging health care system is highly organized and centralized, with major interlocks and inroads to state and federal governments. Hence, the arena for examining negotiated order needs to be expanded to encompass the conflict of interests and sentiments that take place among groups outside a hospital and which have consequences for a hospital's internal operation (Day and Day, 1977).

RESEARCH STUDY 4

NEGOTIATED ORDER IN PSYCHIATRIC HOSPITALS*

Anselm Strauss, Leonard Schatzman, Rue Bucher, Danuta Ehrlich, and Melvin Sabshin

Problem. To the outsider, hospitals appear to be tightly structured organizations operating in strict accordance with well-defined, bureaucratic rules and regulations. Anselm Strauss and his colleagues — a team of three sociologists, a social psychologist, and a psychiatrist — were interested in studying what actually happens in hospitals, especially psychiatric hospitals.

Method. Two hospitals were studied: the Chicago State Psychiatric Hospital (a large and relatively old Illinois facility) and the 80-bed psychiatric wing of Michael Reese Hospital (a prestigious and well-staffed private hospital in Chicago). The researchers employed three methods for gathering data: anthropologist-style field work involving contact with people under "natural living condi-

* Adapted from Anselm Strauss, Leonard Schatzman, Rue Bucher, Danuta Ehrlich, and Melvin Sabshin, *Psychiatric Ideologies and Institutions*. New York: The Free Press of Glencoe, 1964.

tions"; informal interviewing; and questionnaires administered to selected professional groups within the hospitals.

Findings. On the surface, the hospitals presented a picture in which physicians were primarily concerned with organizing treatment for their patients; nurses and aides with achieving manageable wards and providing therapeutic activities and services; and patients with managing their sick selves and adjusting to institutionalized lives. The one overriding goal to which all parties seemingly subscribed was "to get patients better."

In practice, however, this general mandate proved of little direct help in understanding the social interaction within the two hospitals. Among the various administrative, professional, and lay groups (and even within these groups), there existed different conceptions regarding the nature, causes, and treatment of mental illness. This in turn led to conflicting definitions of situations (diagnoses and prognoses) and to divergent therapeutic regimes and practices. Conflicts of interest continually emerged that resulted in individuals and groups jockeying for position. For example, should a patient fail to show progress, the nurses might grow restless with a physician's approach and institute their own supplementary, even contradictory, program. Or the staff might attempt to transfer an unruly patient from one ward to another behind the physician's back.

For the most part—and contrary to popular stereotypes—the researchers did not find a formal, rigid set of operating rules. As with most large-scale organizations, hardly anyone knew all the rules, much less in exactly what situations they applied, to whom, in what degree, and for how long. A considerable turnover in staff and patients contributed to this confusion. Further, rules, once formulated, would fall into disuse, only to undergo periodic administrative resurrection should someone find it advantageous to do so. Almost all the "house rules" were more like general understandings than commands. Such "rules" could be stretched, argued, reinterpreted, ignored, or applied at convenient moments. And finally, despite the best laid plans developed rationally by people, unforeseen things happened that called for new working arrangements.

Within the great unruled areas of hospital life, individuals entered into agreements of one kind or another. Such agreements could be of long or short duration. They could be spelled out in detail or left vague. Hospital personnel were well aware of the need for making various types of agreements, activities that they labeled "politicking," "persuading," "bargaining," and "negotiating." Such agreements were the foundation for "negotiated consensus." This consensus had a limited time period and periodically had to be reviewed, revised, and recreated.

Conclusion. Strauss and his colleagues conclude:

A skeptic, thinking in terms of relatively permanent or slowly changing structure, might remark that the hospital remains the same from week to week, that only the working arrangements change.... Practically, we maintain, no one knows what the hospital "is" on any given day unless he has a comprehensive grasp of the combination of rules, policies, agreements, understandings, pacts, contracts, and other working arrangements that currently obtain. In a pragmatic sense, that combination "is" the hospital at the moment, its social order. Any changes that impinge upon this order—whether ordinary changes, like introduction of a new staff member or a betrayed contract or unusual changes, like the introduction of new technology or new theory—will necessitate renegotiation or reappraisal, with consequent changes in the organizational order. There will be a new order, not merely the re-establishment of an old order or reinstitution of a previous equilibrium. It is necessary continually to reconstitute the bases of concerted action, of social order. (p. 312)

VALUES

> Man's chief purpose... is the creation and preservation of values: that is what gives meaning to our civilization, and the participation in this is what gives significance, ultimately, to the individual human life.
>
> Lewis Mumford, *Faith for Living, 1940*

In our daily living, we continually evaluate objects, ideas, acts, feelings, events, and people. We are concerned with what is good, beautiful, moral, and worthwhile—in brief, with **values**. Values are the criteria or conceptions individuals use in evaluating things as to their relative desirability or merit.

Lest we confuse values with norms, let us stress that values represent commonly shared conceptions of the desirable, while norms constitute *rules* for behavior. Further, while norms contain penalties, values do not. Perhaps this matter may be clarified if we think about when and how children begin to develop values in contrast to norms: children may obey a parental rule lest they be punished, but they themselves may not as yet come to judge the behavior in its own right as desirable. This awareness often occurs later in time (Piaget, 1932; Kohlberg, 1976; Lickona, 1976).

In order to gain a clearer conception of values, it might be helpful if we indicate some of the major value configurations within the *dominant* American culture.

1. *Materialism.* Americans are prone to evaluate things in material and monetary terms. Many of us are inclined to appraise the success of a father in terms of his income and his ability to provide financially for his family. We often judge our pastors and ministers in terms of their ability to raise money, pay off the debt, and attract more and more parishioners. We expectantly await the yearly announcement of the contract terms of leading baseball and football players who have had "big" years. Our candidates seeking re-election to public office spend much of their time attempting to convince people of their fine record in financial and material achievement and improvements (Fichter, 1971). Even in the supposedly uncommercial halls of learning the awed whisper is heard, "Why, he is a $50,000-a-year professor!" As Kluckhohn notes, "Only Americans think that the relative standing of students in a course can be measured on a continuous scale from zero to 100" (1960, 186). We tend to emphasize the quantitative—the biggest, the largest, the highest, and so on. We tend to get quite excited about things as opposed to ideas, people, and aesthetic creations.

2. *Success.* Another value, closely allied with that of materialism, is the stress Americans place on personal achievement. Perhaps more than any other, Abe Lincoln stands forth as the American culture hero. The rail-splitter

who became President embodies the cardinal American virtues. Lincoln was industrious, resolute, thrifty, hardworking, shrewd, intelligent, ambitious, and eminently successful in climbing the ladder of opportunity from the lowermost rung of laborer to lawyer and President (Merton, 1968).

Part of the American faith is that "there is always another chance" and that "if at first you don't succeed, try, try, again." If we ourselves cannot succeed, then we have the prospect for vicarious achievement through our children. We see failure as a confession of weakness and we rationalize, "It's his own fault that he did not get ahead." The American exaltation of success is reflected in countless staple phrases such as "bettering yourself," "getting ahead," and "how are you getting on?"

3. *Work and Activity.* Foreign observers are struck with the hustle and bustle of American life. Work and activity are exalted in their own right; they are not merely means by which success may be realized; in and of themselves they are valued as worthwhile. Kluckhohn notes (1960: 178–79), "No conversational bromides are more characteristically American than 'Let's get going'; 'Do something'; 'Something can be done about it.'" Americans tend to be optimistic believers that "work counts"; middle-class Americans in particular are firm subscribers to the "cult of busyness." Many Americans are not happy unless they are *doing* something.

In large measure, it was the rejection of the "hard work-success" ethic by some youths in the late 1960s (hippies and others) that contributed to their rejection by older Americans. Many of these youths cultivated a "hang-loose" orientation characterized by a rejection of "Establishment" values (Langman, 1971). In part, the older generation's condemnation of marihuana has stemmed from its identification of the drug with young people's defiance of traditional patterns (an equating of marihuana with sensory freedom and a present-time ethos). Significantly, many adults—forgetting their own bouts with the law in the days of Prohibition and overlooking the serious contemporary health problem posed by alcoholism—have viewed alcohol as the socially approved drug of choice for "well-adjusted, responsible, hardworking people" when engaging in social interaction and relaxation. In contrast, they tend to define the use of marihuana as involving neurotic, irresponsible behavior.

4. *Progress.* A belief in the perfectibility of society, humankind, and the world has been a kind of driving force in American history. "Throughout their history Americans have insisted that the best was yet to be. . . . The American knew that nothing was impossible in his brave new world. . . . Progress was not, to him, a mere philosophical ideal but a commonplace of experience" (Commager, 1947). Within the American vocabulary such words as "backward," "outmoded," "old-fashioned," and "stagnant" have taken on a connotation of "undesirable." Americans tend to equate "the new" with "the best."

The Tasaday of the Philippines. The Tasaday are a "stone age" people recently "discovered" by the outside world. They are gentle people for whom aggression, competition, and acquisitiveness are highly devalued behaviors. Their values stand in sharp contrast to those that prevail within the dominant segments of American life.

John Launois/Black Star

5. *Rationality.* A great many Americans place faith in the rational approach to life. We continuously search out more "reasonable," "time-saving," and "effort-saving" ways of doing things. We esteem science as a tool for controlling nature and for solving our problems. We often search for intellectual and scientific supports for our behavior.

6. *Democracy.* "Democracy" has become almost synonymous with "the American way of life." We have fought our wars in its name. We extol the Declaration of Independence with its insistence that "all men are created equal" and "governments [derive] their just power from the consent of the governed." Through the years we have expanded the scope of the democratic creed to include even more groups, a fact reflected in the progressive extension of voting rights. In 1787, when the Constitution was framed, less than one-quarter of adult Americans were allowed to vote. Eleven of the colonies restricted voting rights to property owners and taxpayers. Following the Civil War, the 14th and 15th Amendments undertook to guarantee that no citizens should have their right to vote denied on account of "race, color, or previous condition of servitude," a right that 100 years later is only coming to be realized. In 1913, voters were given the right to elect United States Senators, a privilege retained by state legislatures until the ratification of the 17th Amendment. In 1920, culminating a seventy-year cam-

paign, the 19th Amendment extended voting rights to women. And today the vote has been extended to 18-year-olds.

We have singled out for analysis six value configurations within the United States. We have by no means meant our consideration to be inclusive or exhaustive; at best it is suggestive. Nor should we fail to note that a considerable gap often exists between what people define as desirable and their actual behavior.

SYMBOLS AND LANGUAGE

> It is a very inconvenient habit of kittens (Alice had once made the remark) that, whatever you say to them, they *always* purr. "If they would only purr for 'yes,' and mew for 'no,' or any rule of that sort," she had said, "so that one could keep up a conversation. But how *can* you talk with a person if they always say the same thing?"
>
> Lewis Carroll, Through the Looking Glass, 1871

Human beings live their lives in a symbolic environment. They respond directly to symbols and mentally organize their relationships to other people and to the external world by means of symbols (Lindesmith, Strauss, and Denzin, 1978). A **symbol** is any act or object that has socially come to be accepted as standing for something else. It provides a code or "shorthand" for representing and dealing with various aspects of the world about us (Hewitt, 1976).

COMMUNICATION IS NOT LIMITED TO WORDS

OBSERVATION I went to a dance tonight with three other girls. We sat down and glanced around the room at the other people. We kind of sized up the guys. If a guy looked cute I would let my eyes meet with his eyes. I looked at him a longer time than I would if I was not interested in him. This way I would let him know that I was interested. If the guy was also interested, he looked at me a few seconds longer than usual; in this way he indicated to me that he was taking notice of me too. We then looked around the room only waiting for the chance for our eyes to meet again. Naturally, it happened but this time he also would give me a little smile. I smiled back and in a few minutes he generally would come over and ask me to dance.

PRINCIPLE Communication takes place in ways other than with words. We communicate with others by gesture and body language. At the dance we signaled to each other our availability. In this way we saved ourselves the embarrassment of rejection. We clue the other person in to the fact that we would welcome dancing with them.

Symbols are human-made and take a good many forms. Probably the most familiar examples are the spoken and written words that we use in our interaction with others. But language is not the only means by which we communicate with other persons. At times, we communicate with objects that have become more or less socially recognized as stand-ins for other things. In many societies, flags, masks, clothing, hair styles, body adornments, tattooing, and related devices function to communicate social status, the significance of an occasion, and a variety of other messages. Similarly, in the American upper-middle-class suburb, the home serves as a sort of stage on which visitors play the role of audience while the family displays its possessions. These possessions communicate the degree to which the family has realized the goal of success as measured in material terms.

We also communicate with other persons by various gestures—that is, through the movement and positioning of the body. Within American life, the subtle raising of the eyebrow, the shaking of hands, kissing, waving good-bye, meeting someone else's eyes or looking away, shifting positions in a chair, and various forms of "body language" tell us significant things about the feelings and attitudes of others (Fast, 1970; Duncan, 1972; Argyle, 1975). Although we assume such actions are random and incidental, they too tend to be culturally patterned. Americans, for instance, tend to end a statement with a droop of the head or hand, a lowering of the eyelids; they wind up a question with a lift of the hand, a tilting of the chin, or a widening of the eyes; and with a future-tense verb they frequently gesture with a forward movement. But regardless of the form they take, symbols are the instruments or vehicles that make social interaction possible.

THE IMPORTANCE OF SYMBOLS

Most of us are familiar with the story of Helen Keller, a woman who was deprived of her sight and hearing in infancy. Although she could not see or hear, she could feel and smell, and in these ways she was able to effect some degree of contact with other people. In her autobiography (1908) she tells of her early experiences with her teacher, Ann Mansfield Sullivan, with whom she first had contact when she was seven. The morning after her arrival, Ann Sullivan gave Helen a doll. The teacher allowed her to play with the doll a little while, and then she slowly spelled in her hand the word "d-o-l-l":

> I was at once interested in this finger play and tried to imitate it. When I finally succeeded in making the letters correctly I was flushed with childish pleasure and pride. Running downstairs to my mother I held up my hand and made the letters for doll. I did not know that I was spelling a word or even that words existed; I was simply making my fingers go in monkey-like imitation. In the days that followed I learned

to spell in this uncomprehending way a great many words, among them *pin, hat, cup,* and a few verbs like *sit, stand,* and *walk.* But my teacher had been with me several weeks before I understood that everything has a name. (1908, pp. 22–23)

In her writings, Helen Keller describes the changes that language brought in her life. The acquisition of words brought about an intellectual and emotional revolution. *She became aware of herself and other people.* At one point she writes: "When I found the meaning of 'I' and 'me' and found that I was something, I began to think. . . . Then, consciousness first existed for me" (1938: 117). Her memory of her first seven years was vague, and she hesitates to apply the term "idea" or "thought" to her mental processes during that time. Helen Keller's case testifies to the critical part symbols (particularly language) play in human life. Without symbols, we could not communicate with other persons; indeed, we would find ourselves solitary beings, for we would not be able to establish meaningful contact with others. People who are both deaf and blind are literally "people without symbols" unless through special training they acquire symbolic means for communication.

Practically all human interaction depends on symbolic communication. As we noted earlier in this chapter, we must share common definitions of situations if we are to align our actions with those of other people. Symbols permit the transfer of information and mental states from one person to another:

If a person shouts "Fire!" in a public building . . . he is attaching symbolic designation to the situation. As he shouts, others become aware of the situation in a way that shows they previously were not aware of it. The mental states of these other people have become similar to that of the person who shouts "Fire!" Moreover, the individual who warns the others reacts to his own warning in much the same way they do—that is, he hears his own voice and takes an attitude toward the situation that resembles the attitudes of the others—perhaps a desire to get out of the burning building. (Hewitt, 1976, pp. 29–30)

Symbols also enable us to advance our mastery of the world about us; without symbolic interaction, we could achieve only the simplest inventions and the most elementary thought processes. When we reflect on what we have learned from direct experience and compare it with what we have acquired by communication with others, we begin to appreciate how startlingly limited is our own experience. Our knowledge is almost entirely dependent on an accumulation of information transmitted from one generation to another. In brief, humankind's ability to develop culture and to transmit culture stems primarily from its ability to manipulate symbols—to engage in *symbolic interaction* (Rose, 1962).

LANGUAGE

Speech is civilization itself.
Thomas Mann

Speech may well constitute our most distinctive characteristic as human beings. Leslie White, a cultural anthropologist, observes that

> without articulate speech we would have no *human* social organization. Families we might have, but this form of organization is not peculiar to man; it is not *per se, human*. But we would have no prohibitions of incest, no rules prescribing exogamy [outgroup marriage] and endogamy [in-group marriage], polygamy or monogamy.... Without speech we would have no political, economic, ecclesiastic, or military organization; no codes of ethics; no laws; no science, theology, or literature.... Indeed, without articulate speech we would be all but toolless.... In short, without symbolic communication in some form, we would have no culture. "In the Word was the beginning" of culture — and its perpetuation also. (1949, pp. 33–34)

Language is a group product, a socially structured system of sound patterns (words and sentences) with standardized meanings (Vander Zanden, 1977). Words provide us with labels—"handles"—which we apply to various aspects of our environment. As such, language is an organizing device by which we partition the world into manageable units and domains of relevance. It permits us to group our perceptions into categories. Further, through the mechanism of sentences (meaningful linkages among words) we are capable of mentally joining our perceptions together in a great variety of ways.

Language facilitates the conceptualizing process so essential to life. It allows us to group together various elements within our environment on the basis of our needs and wants. We can filter and channel stimuli into meaningful groupings: dog, Senator, beer, mother, green, divorce, clock, telephone, singing, and so on. In so doing, we can simplify and generalize—"place" aspects of the world into categories and address our problems quickly and readily.

Language also helps us to experience life in terms of recurring patterns of order, constancy, and regularity. By pigeonholing stimuli in terms of word categories, we find it possible to relate current perceptions and experiences to past sets of sensations. We can view an object as the same object despite changes in stimulus display (despite the fact that it varies from moment to moment and from perspective to perspective). Further, we can treat two things that differ in some ways as equivalent, as the same kind of object (for example, Fords, Chevrolets, and Dodges as automobiles). By allowing us to group perceptions and experiences within categories, language enables us to minimize confusion and avoid being overwhelmed by an incoherent flood of stimuli (Vander Zanden, 1977).

SUBCULTURE AND COUNTERCULTURE

Considerable variation often exists *between* the cultures of different societies. Variation also may occur *within* the culture of the same society. Sociologists have used the concepts *subculture* and *counterculture* to refer to such variability within a society (Yinger, 1960; 1977; Spates, 1976). Let us examine each of these concepts in turn.

SUBCULTURE

A group may possess certain distinctive ways of thinking, feeling, and acting that in a number of respects set its members apart from the larger society. We refer to these distinctive ways of thinking, feeling, and acting as **subculture.** Although participating in a large society and sharing in most of its culture, individuals may simultaneously engage into a set of behaviors peculiar to their own group.

In the past two decades considerable attention has come to be focused on the "subculture of poverty" — commonly shortened to simply "culture of

SUBCULTURES

OBSERVATION I work in a fast service food chain. The employees use a distinctive vocabulary that most customers do not understand: "TC" (toasted cheese), "DC" (double-cheeseburger), and "O" (onion). We also use "ham" for "hamburger" and "cheese" for "cheeseburger." A customer listening might easily conclude that we serve ham and cheese sandwiches (which we don't). Further, "TMO (turn me on) on 4A" means that there is an attractive customer at register 4A.

Likewise, in the dorm the guys have a unique vocabulary: "munchies" (hunger or food), "studley" (when someone is all dressed up), "turk" (stupid), "crank it up" (turn up the stereo), "nun" (a girl who never puts out), "porker" (a large girl), "got burnt" (flunked a test), and "chief" (friend).

PRINCIPLE A group may possess a set of distinctive ways of thinking, feeling, and acting that, in a number of respects, sets its members apart from the larger society — a subculture. We find subcultures among various occupational and dorm groups, a fact reflected in their professional terminology or jargon.

The Social World

poverty." According to this view, initially formulated by anthropologist Oscar Lewis (1959; 1961; 1966; 1968), poor people from societies with vastly different cultures are markedly similar to each other in certain attitudes, values, and patterns of behavior. Lewis observes that the poor in class-stratified capitalist societies (including the United States, Mexico, and Puerto Rico) lack effective participation and integration within the larger society. They are victimized by a lack of economic resources, segregation, discrimination, and pervasive fear. Clustered in the ghettos of New York, Mexico City, and San Juan, the poor experience strong feelings of marginality, helplessness, dependence, and inferiority. Such circumstances, Lewis argues, breed weak ego structures, a lack of impulse control, a strong present-time orientation (with relatively little ability to defer gratification and to plan for the future), and a sense of resignation and fatalism. These lifeways — this culture of poverty — is both an adaptation and a reaction of the poor to their disadvantaged position within society. But perhaps of greatest importance, according to Lewis, once it is established the culture of poverty becomes *self-perpetuating*. Its distinct social ethos of defeatism, dependence, and a present-time orientation comes to be transmitted to successive generations through socialization; in this fashion it becomes embedded as a cultural way of life among poor people.

A youth subculture. Western societies prolong the period between childhood and adulthood while simultaneously segregating young people in schools for a large part of their time. This segregation reaches extreme expression in college communities. These factors have given rise to a kind of youth subculture.

Patrick Reddy

A good many social scientists reject Lewis's portrayal of poverty (Valentine, 1968; Leacock, 1971; Gouldner, 1977; Womack, 1977; Critchfield, 1978). Elliot Liebow (1967), for instance, who studied a Black streetcorner men's group in Washington, D.C., depicted the economically poor Black male, not as a carrier of an independent culture of poverty, but as very much immersed in American life. The Black man shares the same goals as other American men—Liebow argues that he too wants a stable marriage and job—but differs in his ability to realize these goals; the Black man is the victim of a racist social order. Liebow suggests that the similarities between Black father and son do *not* result from "cultural transmission" (as Lewis argues), but from the fact that the son goes out and *independently* experiences the same victimization as his father. The process only *appears* to be self-sustaining.

The debate that surrounds the culture of poverty theory is hardly a trivial matter. It has major policy implications (and it also highlights the point made in Chapter 1 that knowledge is not neutral). If the alleged cultural patterns of the poor are of greater significance in their lives than the condition of being economically poor, then it is more important for the power holders of society to do away with these lifeways than to do away with poverty. Hence, many influential Americans believe that there is a negative culture of poverty and that it must be uprooted if we are to solve the problem of poverty. This attitude has been implicit in social welfare programs that concentrate on services rather than money, that train the unemployed in how to *act* as employees (proper grooming, speech, and manners) rather than train them in meaningful skills, and that attempt to create "a stable family structure" among poor Black Americans (as if that of the White middle class is so stable!). Much American policy has concentrated on eradicating the culture of poverty rather than poverty itself. Political radicals, in contrast, call for the fundamental restructuring of current capitalist society.

COUNTERCULTURE

Counterculture, in contrast with subculture, points to the fact that a group smaller than a society may not only be distinctive but its members may share ways of thinking, feeling, and acting that in some respects are *opposed to and clash with* those of the larger society. Not uncommonly, people find themselves caught in frustrating and conflict-laden situations. They may respond with new standards and guideposts for behavior (as found in extremist political groups and delinquent gangs) that are at odds with those of the larger society.

The Hare Krishna movement has a good many countercultural overtones (Judah, 1974). It is one of the largest and most visible groups operating in the United States with roots in Indian (Hindu) thought. The movement was founded in the United States about 1965 by a then relatively unknown,

Hare Krishna. As viewed by the American public, the Hare Krishna movement is counter-cultural. The distinctive dress and shaved heads that render the membership exceedingly visible are defined as "weird" although not "dangerous."

Patrick Reddy

seventy-year-old Hindu swami, A. C. Bhaktivedanta (he died in 1977). A rigid code of behavior is imposed on members. Gambling, frivolous sports and games, narcotics, alcoholic beverages, tobacco, and illicit sex is forbidden (sexual relations are permitted only between individuals married by a qualified devotee in Krishna Consciousness). The daily life of individual members entails considerable ritualism, ceremony, and chanting. The movement's stated goal is the salvation of the world through its conversion to Krishna Consciousness, a state of being thought to produce a mystical experience of love, freedom from anxiety, and peaceful bliss.

Some of its members have had a prior hippie life-style involving the use of psychedelic drugs. As members of the movement, they abandon drug-induced ecstacies and instead pursue a continuous Krishna "high." Some live in spiritual communes, others in movement-run monasteries, and still others live "in the world" following otherwise secular careers with their "minds in Krishna." By virtue of their distinctive dress, shaved heads, chant-ins, ware-hawking, unique beliefs, and proselytizing in airports and other places, the American public defines the movement as countercultural.

SUMMARY

1. Culture is the socially standardized ways of thinking, feeling, and acting that a person acquires as a member of society. It provides us with a set of common understandings—a kind of map—for life's activities. These cultural guideposts present us with a set of ready-made definitions of the situation that each of us only slightly retailors in our own individual way.

2. The world we experience is a product of the interaction between our anatomy, the physical aspects of the universe, and what we have learned from our past experience. Our perception is never a photographic image of the physical world. Many factors enter into our perception of the world, one of the most important of which is culture. As a consequence, peoples of different cultures experience somewhat different worlds.

3. Culture channels, molds, and modifies a good deal of our biological functioning. Some patterns of every culture crystallize about the inevitables of our existence as biological organisms. Our precise reaction to internal biological stimuli cannot be predicted by physiological knowledge alone.

4. Social life requires that we fit our developing lines of action to the actions of other people. This requires that we have certain common understandings or shared definitions of the situation. Culture provides us with the shared definitions whereby we can mentally chart our behavior.

5. Norms are ready-made definitions of situations by which we align our individual actions to create social or joint actions. They are rules that specify appropriate and inappropriate behavior.

6. Norms have a dual character. They are a means, social tools by which we align our actions with those of other people. They are also an end, social standards to which we are expected to align our conduct.

7. Sociologists distinguish between folkways and mores on the basis of two criteria: (1) the degree of importance people attach to a given rule, and (2) the severity of punishments meted out to the wrongdoer. Folkways refer to norms that are looked on as not being extremely important and that may be violated without severe punishment. Mores are norms that are regarded as being extremely important and the violation of which results in severe punishment.

8. The distinguishing characteristic of law is the legitimate use of physical coercion by a legitimate party. The distinction between mores and folkways on the one hand and laws on the other is primarily a question of who institutes the sanctions. The folkways and mores are spontaneously and collectively enforced by the members of a society. Law, in contrast, involves enforcement by an individual or organization whose function is so defined.

9. Symbolic interactionists conceive of social order as negotiated order. People construct a sense of social reality as they repeat, reaffirm, and re-create their social acts. They enter into agreements with one another and arrive at a negotiated consensus.

10. Values are the criteria or conceptions that individuals use in evaluating things as to their relative desirability or merit. Among the major value configurations of the dominant American culture are materialism, success, work and activity, progress, rationality, and democracy.

11. Individuals live their lives in a symbolic environment. A symbol is any act or object that has socially come to be accepted as standing for something else. It provides a code or shorthand for representing and dealing with various aspects of the world about us.

12. Language is a group product, a socially structured system of sound patterns (words and sentences) with standardized meanings. Language facilitates the conceptualizing process so essential to life. It allows us to group together various elements within our environment on the basis of our needs and wants.

13. A group may possess a set of distinctive

ways of thinking, feeling, and acting that in a number of respects sets its members apart from the larger society. We refer to this set of distinctive ways of thinking, feeling, and acting as subculture.

14. Counterculture, in contrast with subculture, points to the fact that a group smaller than a society may not only be distinctive but its members may share ways of thinking, feeling, and acting that in some respects are opposed to and clash with those of the larger society.

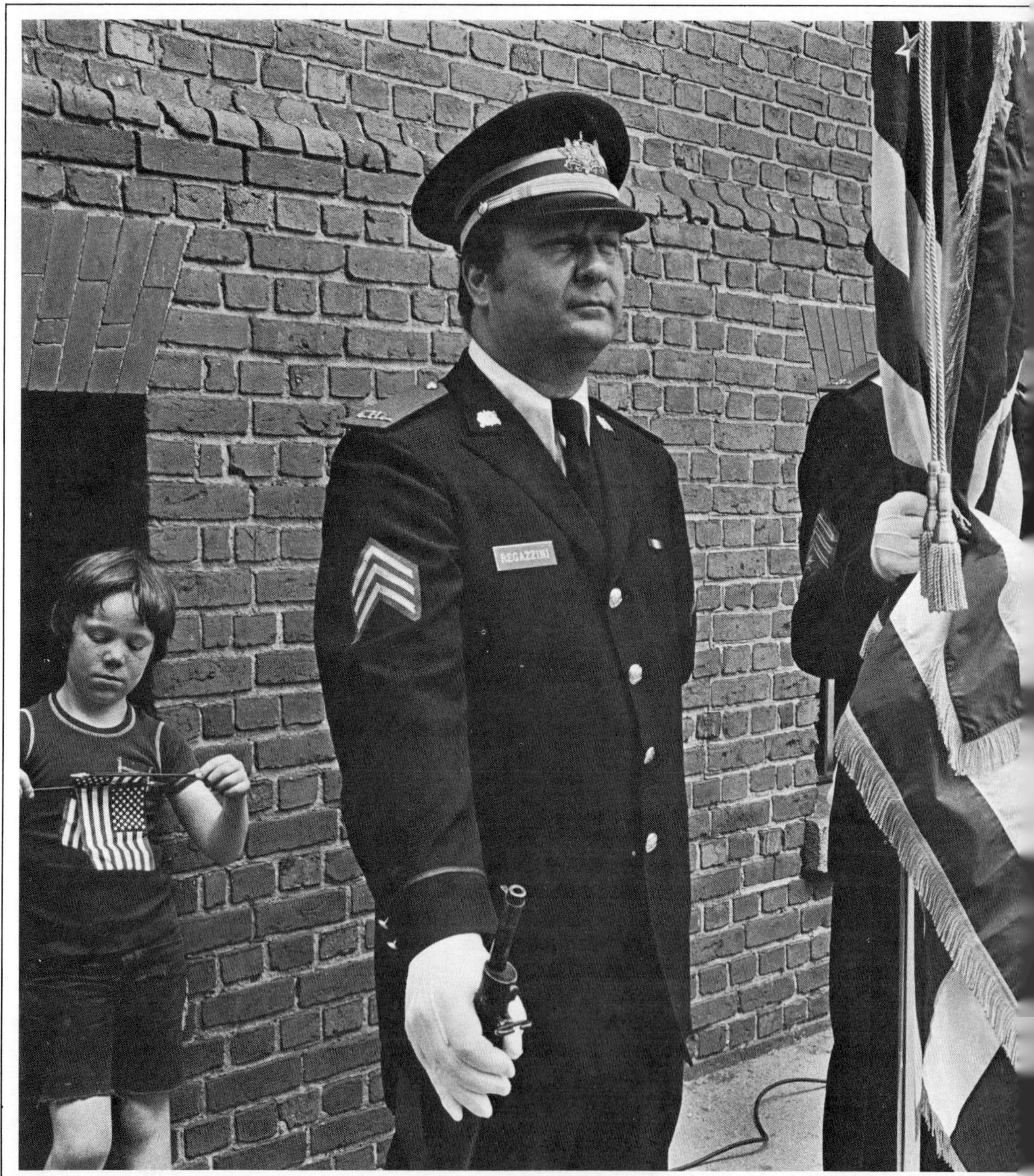
REGAZZINI

3
SOCIALIZATION

NATURE AND NURTURE
 The Relationship Between Heredity and Environment
 Sociobiology
 The Inadequacy of Human Environment Alone
 The Inadequacy of Human Heredity Alone
 The Dynamic Interplay of Heredity and Environment

THE SELF
 The "Looking-Glass Self"
 Self-Appraisals
 Mead's Theory of the Development of the Self
 Socialization Across the Life Span

OBSERVATION I spent this weekend at the home of my roommate. She has a five-year-old sister, Lisa. On Saturday afternoon Lisa was playing with Jennie, a five-year-old friend from down the block. The girls were playing house. Lisa was the mother and Jennie played two roles, that of Susie, a little girl, and Paul, the husband. Lisa acted as the mother several times to "Susie," telling her to be careful not to run out into the street and to be "a good little girl." On other occasions she acted as the wife of "Paul." She kissed "him," prepared "his" dinner, and cleaned the house.

PRINCIPLE It was evident that the children were "trying on" the roles of other people. Lisa was putting herself in the position of her mother and "acting out" the requirements associated with the roles of mother and wife. In so doing, Lisa was "taking on" these behaviors, incorporating them within her personality. Also, by taking the role of the mother toward "Susie," she was sharpening and clarifying the role expectations of being a little girl (her real life role relative to her own mother). In their games, children rehearse behaviors that characterize the roles they will assume in the course of their lives. This illustrates Mead's theory regarding the socialization process. It was somewhat upsetting to me though, since it seemed to me that Lisa was becoming socialized within a sexist tradition, one in which a woman is expected to be only a housewife and mother.

We are not born human. It is only slowly and laboriously in the course of social interaction with others that we attain the distinctive qualities of "human nature" (Park and Burgess, 1921:79). As infants we are born into a social environment; we can remain alive only in this environment; and from birth on we take our place within such an environment (Rheingold, 1969:781). Hence, humanness is a social product.

We become human through **socialization**—a process of social interaction by which we acquire those ways of thinking, feeling, and acting essential for effective participation within society. Culture—its norms, values, and symbols—is what is learned in socialization. Socialization is the process whereby society recreates itself in the young.

Since children are uninitiated in the ways of culture, the birth of new generations subjects society to a recurrent "barbarian invasion." Most infants are fairly malleable in the sense that within broad limits they are capable of becoming adults of quite different sorts. Through socialization, children become inducted into their society's cultural ways; as a related consequence, they may become more or less unfit for participation in many other societies. This point is made in a striking fashion by Edmund Carpenter, an anthropologist, who lived for a period among the Aivilik, an Eskimo people:

> For months after I first arrived among the Aivilik, I felt empty, clumsy. I never knew what to do, even where to sit or stand. I was awkward in a busy world, as helpless as a child, yet a grown man. I felt like a mental defective. (1965:55)

Only as Carpenter learned the cultural patterns of the Aivilik and became accepted by them did he feel comfortable in the new setting.

NATURE AND NURTURE

Broadly considered, socialization is the process by which the infant is molded into a social being, by which a mere biological organism becomes transformed into a person. Without socialization, society could not perpetuate itself beyond a single generation, and culture could not exist. Moreover, without socialization, we could not become human since the ever repeated renewal of culture within each of us would not occur. Both the individual and society are mutually dependent "on this unique process of psychic amalgamation whereby the sentiments and ideas of the culture are somehow joined to the capacities and needs of the organism" (Davis, 1949:195). Let us begin our discussion of "this unique process of psychic amalgamation" by considering heredity and environment.

THE RELATIONSHIP BETWEEN HEREDITY AND ENVIRONMENT

The way a question is asked limits and disposes the ways in which any answer to it — right or wrong — may be given.

Susanne K. Langer, Philosophy in a New Key

The relationship between heredity and environment has long intrigued humans. Indeed, the nature-nurture controversy can be traced back to the classical Greek era of Plato and Aristotle (Vander Zanden, 1978). Through the years the nature-nurture controversy has been phrased in quite different ways. Various schools of thought have asked different questions and, not surprisingly, have come up with different answers.

Scientists initially asked *which* factor, heredity or environment, is most important in fashioning a given trait such as a mental disorder or an individual's level of intelligence. Later they sought to determine *how much* of the differences among people are due to differences in heredity and *how much* to differences in environment (Jensen, 1973a; 1973b). And more recently a number of scientists have phrased the question in terms of *how* specific hereditary and environmental factors *interact* to produce particular characteristics (Lerner, 1976, 1978; Vander Zanden, 1978).

Scientists no longer ask the question, "Which is more important, heredity or environment?" Counterposing heredity and environment in this manner results in a hopeless dichotomy. Carried to its logical conclusion the formulation defines biologically programmed behavior as that which occurs in the absence of environment and learned behavior as that which does not

Identical twins. Identical twins develop from a single fertilized egg which by some accident gets split into two parts early in embyonic development. Genetically, each twin is essentially a carbon copy of the other. Researchers investigating the relative contributions that heredity and environment make in fashioning a given trait have placed considerable reliance on studies of identical twins. A major problem with this research is that the twins commonly share an astonishingly similar environment, even to the point of being dressed alike.

Patrick Reddy

require an organism. The "how much" question likewise poses difficulties. It assumes that heredity and environment are related to each other in such a way that the contribution of one is *added* to the contribution of the other so as to determine a given behavior.

Both the "which" and "how much" questions overlook the *interaction* that takes place between heredity and environment (Anastasi, 1958; Overton, 1973; Vander Zanden, 1978). An analogy might prove helpful to our understanding of this matter. Consider the following questions: "Which is more important to ordinary table salt, sodium or chlorine?" and "How much of the properties of table salt are due to sodium and how much to chlorine?" Chemists point out that neither question makes sense. Without either sodium or chlorine we would not have salt. Further, salt is not a mixture of sodium and chlorine that can be mechanically separated (for instance, with a sieve) so as to assess the relative contribution of each.

Sodium is a soft solid; it reacts violently with water and hence would produce dangerous results if placed in the mouth. Chlorine has properties equally characteristic; it is a greenish-yellow gas highly irritating and choking to the throat and lungs when inhaled. When the two elements are brought together, a rapid reaction takes place; the sodium and chlorine combine to form a white crystalline solid, sodium chloride or common table salt. The new substance is entirely —*qualitatively*— different from either sodium or chlorine. When tasted, nothing unpleasant happens; in fact, it is a necessary food. We can recognize that sodium and chlorine exist separately as such, but with respect to salt they never exist separately—they are always in a process of continuous molecular interaction. This interaction is critical and gives salt its distinct character.

A somewhat similar situation exists with heredity and environment. Individuals are the joint products of their heredity and their environment. **Heredity** refers to that which is inherent and inborn; it involves the genetic transmission of traits from parents to offspring. **Environment** refers to the sum total of the external factors that affect the organism. Counterposing heredity and environment results in a false and meaningless dichotomy. None of the reactions that a human displays could occur without a particular environment or in the absence of a given genetic heritage. Heredity is what the new life starts with; environment is what makes its continuance possible. Although genes and environment exist separately, with respect to the individual they never exist separately but always in a process of continuous *interaction* (see Figure 3.1).

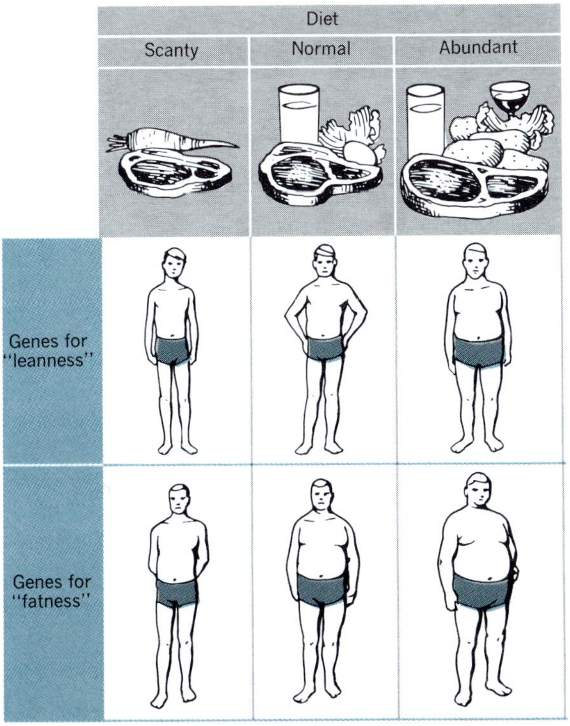

Figure 3.1 Gene-environment interaction. A person who has a gene for "fatness" may actually weigh less than a person with a gene for "leanness," if the former lives on a scanty diet and the latter on an overabundant one.

Source: Reprinted by permission of Yale University Press from *Mankind Evolving* by Theodosius Dobzhansky. Copyright © 1962 by Yale University.

Recent experiments reveal the importance of the joint contribution that nature and nurture make to behavior. Neurobiologists, for instance, sew one eye of a kitten shut shortly after its birth. A number of months later they reopen the eye and find that the cat cannot see with it. The absence of visual stimulation affects the way stimuli are processed by the cat's brain. Only a small fraction of the nerve cells in that portion of the brain concerned with vision respond with electrical signals when the neurobiologists shine light on the deprived eye. In contrast, nearly all the cells respond when they shine light on the normal eye. Such research demonstrates that early experience interacts with genetic endowment to produce sight (Kolata, 1975; Daw, Berman, and Ariel, 1978).

SOCIOBIOLOGY

Man was formed for society.
>Sir William Blackstone, Commentaries on the Laws of England, 1765

An updated version of the nature-nurture debate has emerged over **sociobiology** (Wilson, 1975; Dawkins, 1976; Ellis, 1977; Barash, 1977). Sociobiology is the study of the biological basis for all social behavior. Much of the controversy was triggered by the publication in 1975 of *Sociobiology: A New Synthesis*. Its author is Edward O. Wilson, a widely recognized zoologist at Harvard University. Wilson built his reputation as a leading authority on social insects. In this book he expands his interest to encompass the entire animal kingdom.

Wilson suggests that a hereditary basis may underlie many kinds of social behavior including "cannibalism" and "infanticide" among bees, "castes" and "slavery" in ant colonies, "harem formation" in mammalian societies, and "homosexuality" among human beings. His basic tenet derives from Darwinian evolutionary theory: in the course of evolution organisms develop their anatomy and body chemistry so as to increase the chances for their species' survival. Wilson expands this formulation to include a genetic programming for certain forms of social behavior.

The way in which Wilson develops his argument is illustrated by his approach to *altruism*. Altruism is defined as self-sacrificing behavior that helps to insure the survival of other members of one's own species. Wilson notes that honeybee workers will sting an intruder at the hive, driving the invader off but in the process insuring their own death (the fishhook-like sting rips off along with much of an insect's inner viscera). Termites will explode themselves to protect their colony from predators. Similarly, several small birds (robins, thrushes, and titmice) give warning signals to others of their kind should a hawk appear (thereby drawing the predator's attention to themselves). And during wars, human beings are known to throw themselves on top of grenades to shield comrades or aid the rescue of others at the price of certain death to themselves.

Altruistic behavior has long proven a puzzle for evolutionary theorists. Why should altruism evolve if it entails surrendering one's own life? Seemingly, individuals displaying self-sacrificing behavior would die out while selfish ones would survive and prosper. Wilson provides this answer. In the course of evolution, natural selection has been broadened to include the process he terms "kin selection." Kin selection means that the survival of a group is favored by counteracting the effects of individual selection. Because all the members of the family or group *share* the gene for self-sacrificing behavior, the larger social unit will survive even though a few individual members may not. These survivors in turn multiply and transmit altruistic genes to later generations.

Wilson's *Sociobiology* has received a mixed reception among sociologists. Pierre L. van den Berghe (1976:731) asserts that the book is "nothing short of a towering theoretical achievement of exceptional elegance and parsimony." And Gerhard Lenski observes:

> As sociologists, we have too often ignored the fact that social organization is not a uniquely human phenomenon. . . . Human societies rest on a biological foundation—whether we like it or not. When we ignore this fact in our analyses . . . we jeopardize at the outset every effort in basic theory construction. Recognition of this fact does not commit us to . . . biological determinism. It only obliges us to take seriously once again a set of forces that most sociologists have chosen largely to ignore for half a century or more. (1976, p. 530)

Other sociologists, like Barbara Chasin, take a much more critical stance:

> Biological frames of reference such as Wilson's have been used consistently to establish an ideological justification for the status-quo. There is not very much that is new in Wilson's basic outlook. It is merely the latest restatement of the scientifically erroneous and politically reactionary conception that the world we live in is caused by our genes, not our social institutions. (1977, p. 525)

Viewed from this perspective, Wilson's theory provides a genetic justification for socioeconomic, racial, and sexual inequality (Allen et al., 1975).

Still other sociologists argue that simply because certain forms of behavior are biologically prewired within social insects does not mean that a like explanation holds for human social behavior (Sahlins, 1976). All of this clearly suggests that additional research is required. Wilson's work, however, has highlighted the fact that sociologists need to be better informed about biology and biological research (Tiryakian, 1976).

THE INADEQUACY OF HUMAN ENVIRONMENT ALONE

An ape is an ape even though it wears golden ornaments.
Latin proverb

Our discussion has emphasized the critical contributions that biological and social factors *both* make in the shaping of human beings. Humanness is dependent on an adequate heredity *and* environment. By itself, for instance, environment cannot overcome the limitations imposed by heredity. Winthrop and Louise Kellogg (1933), two psychologists, performed a most interesting and instructive experiment dealing with this matter. They brought into their home a female baby chimpanzee seven-and-a-half months old, Gua, and reared the ape in company with their own ten-month-old son, Donald. It would have been preferable had they reared the ape and child together from birth. Nevertheless, their findings are insightful. So far as possible, the Kelloggs treated the two infants in the same way: both were exposed to the same daily regimen that included training in postural and body habits, in walking and feeding, play, and all the other habits that American parents transmit to their children. The child and the ape played and ate together, and were given the same food and clothing. Initially, Gua learned as readily as the child. In some respects, by virtue of her more rapid physical maturation, she learned more quickly, as, for example, in games requiring strength, agility, and muscular coordination. Hence, at seven-and-a-half months, Gua easily climbed into a high chair, a skill that took Donald eighteen-and-a-half months to master.

But Gua and Donald responded much alike to a number of sensory—perceptual responses—for example, both reacted vigorously to tickling. Further, the noises initially made by the two infants were quite similar—both employed essentially similar sounds to indicate hunger, thirst, physical discomfort, and a desire for toys, utensils, and other objects. And both infants soon learned to follow correctly all sorts of vocal commands. Indeed, the ape was at first more correctly responsive to human commands than was Donald. On the command "Show me a bow-wow," Gua would point correctly to a picture of a dog; to the question "Do you want an orange?" she would make certain barklike sounds to indicate "Yes."

But when Donald began to acquire language, the chimp was soon outdistanced. With the acquisition of language, Donald undertook to interact with others in a way that seemingly was forever barred to the chimp. Despite the Kelloggs' patient efforts at teaching, Gua never acquired a single human word.

A somewhat similar experiment was undertaken by Keith and Cathy Hayes, two other psychologists who took a baby chimpanzee, Viki, into their home shortly after her birth and treated her like a human child for three years (Hayes, 1951). On the whole, Viki's development closely paralleled that of a normal human child. Just as a human child copies its parents' activities, so Viki dusted; washed dishes; sharpened pencils; sawed, hammered, and sandpapered furniture; painted woodwork; and pressed photographs in books. But Viki's inability to master language proved to be a crucial handicap. By manipulating Viki's lips as she vocalized, the experimenters were able to make her say "mama." Moreover, at two-and-a-half-years of age, Viki could pronounce in whispering fashion "papa" and "cup," but she sometimes confused the words. To most lay and professional observers, Viki's behavior seemed like that of a human except for language skills. In many respects, she functioned like a "language deficient" child. The research of the Kelloggs and the Hayeses demonstrated that a normal human environment is not sufficient to enable chimpanzees to learn a human language.

Over the past two decades, a number of psychologists have picked up where the Kelloggs and the Hayeses left off and have succeeded in teaching a dozen or so apes to employ symbols. Allen and Beatrice Gardner (1974) have had considerable success in teaching Washoe, a female chimp, to use the sign language of the deaf. Ann (1976) and David Premack (1976) have taught another chimp, Sarah, to send and receive messages through words consisting of plastic shapes that can be stuck to a magnetized board (for instance, "banana" is represented by a pink plastic square, "give" by a green bow tie, and so on). And researchers at the Yerkes Primate Research Center in Atlanta (Rumbaugh, 1977) have taught Lana to "converse" with humans by means of a computerized keyboard (the console contains 75 buttons and if Lana pushes the buttons in the following sequence, "Please, machine, give milk," an automated dispenser with a straw will fill with milk). Through such procedures Washoe has learned over 180 words, Sarah, 120 words, and Lana, 71 words.

This research suggests that there is a continuum of communicative skills ranging across various levels of sophistication. Although the abilities evidenced by the chimps are related to human skills, they are not equivalent to human linguistic capabilities. Regardless of the ultimate linguistic potential of chimps, they are far more adept at learning visual-manual communications than the auditory-vocal processes central to human language. Perhaps of even greater significance, the methods by which chimps must be trained are quite different from the spontaneous, self-organizing acquisition processes characteristic of children (Limber, 1977). Thus, even though chimps have learned to swear, transmit signs to one another, invent names, translate from spoken to sign language, and use words to joke, show emotion, and lie, their efforts are not truly equivalent to the symbolic manipulation of human beings.

THE INADEQUACY OF HUMAN HEREDITY ALONE

Man is the only one that knows nothing, that can learn nothing without being taught. He can neither speak nor walk nor eat, and in short he can do nothing at the prompting of nature only, but weep.

Pliny the Elder, Natural History, *1st century*

Research with chimps demonstrates the limitations of even an enriched environment in the absence of an adequate heredity. But what about heredity? Will heredity prevail regardless of environment? An understanding of the importance of environment—more particularly, social interaction—for the development of the human personality can be gained from a description of two separate cases involving extreme isolation from human associations (Davis, 1947). The two cases—Anna and Isabelle—are alike in some respects. Both were illegitimate children who had been kept in seclusion. When discovered, each was about six years of age and appeared to be feebleminded. Moreover, neither could speak. Let us examine each case in turn.

Anna's first five-and-a-half months after birth were complicated by frequent changes of domicile. Various efforts at adoption failed, and eventually Anna was returned to the home of her mother and grandfather. The mother maintained Anna physically over a period of years in an attic-like room, but neglected her to an extreme degree. When "discovered" by authorities and removed from these conditions, Anna could not talk, walk, or do anything that showed intelligence, and appeared extremely emaciated and undernourished. Although possessing normal reflexes, she was in most other respects an apathetic, vegetative creature. Anna was placed in the county home and later in a school for retarded children where she died of hemorrhagic jaundice at ten years of age.

In the four years following her discovery, Anna made progress toward becoming "human." She became capable of feeding herself, washing her hands, brushing her teeth, dressing herself (except for fastening her clothes), and keeping her clothing clean. Most remarkable of all, she finally acquired some speech; she talked mostly with phrases but would repeat words and attempt to carry on a conversation. By virtue of Anna's early death, firm conclusions regarding the case are not possible. Further, it is necessary to entertain the hypothesis that she was mentally deficient. Nevertheless, her later development suggests that she was able to acquire various skills and capabilities that she never could have realized in her original condition of isolation.

The case of Isabelle is different from that of Anna in at least two respects. First, Isabelle's mother, although deaf, spent much of her time with the girl in a dark room shut off from the rest of the family. Second, Isabelle was given prolonged, systematic, and expert training in speech and other skills by members of the staff of The Ohio State University. When "discovered," Isabelle acted in many ways like an infant. She appeared to be utterly unaware of any type of relationship—for instance, when presented with a ball

Humanness evolves out of social interaction. These children are experiencing the human interaction essential for the emergence of a social being. As the cases of Anna and Isabelle demonstrated, heredity by itself produces little more than a vegetable.

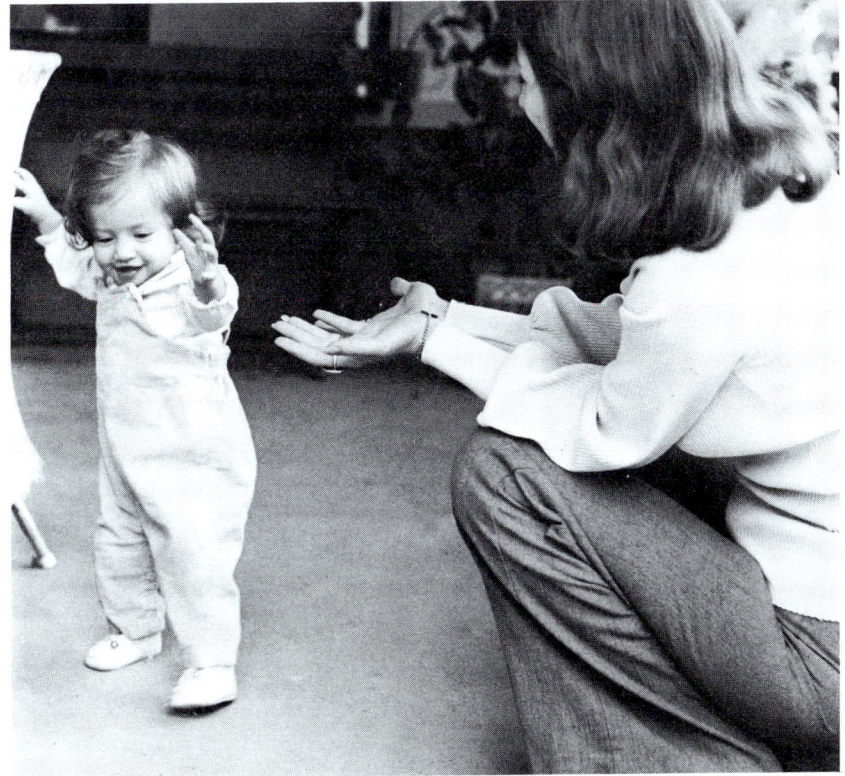

Patrick Reddy

for the first time, she held it in the palm of her hand, then reached out and stroked the investigator's face with it, a behavior comparable to that of a child of six months. Instead of speech, she made only a strange croaking sound. She displayed much fear and hostility toward strangers. Specialists concluded she was feebleminded: "The general impression was that she was wholly uneducable and that any attempt to teach her to speak, after so long a period of silence, would meet with failure" (Davis, 1947:436).

Despite this pessimistic prognosis, the individuals in charge of Isabelle launched a systematic and skillful program of training. After one week of intensive effort, she made her first attempt at vocalization. After the first hurdles were mounted, a curious thing happened. Isabelle went through the usual stages of learning characteristic of children from one through six years of age, not only in proper succession, but far more rapidly than normal. Within two-and-a-half months after her first vocalization, she was putting sentences together. Nine months later, she could identify words and sentences in books, write well, add to ten, and retell a story after hearing it. Within two-and-a-half years, she reached the normal educational level for children of her age. At fourteen, she had passed the sixth grade; appeared to be a bright, cheerful, energetic child; and participated in school activities as normally as other children. Isabelle is reported to have married and raised her own normal family. Jarmila Koluchová (1972; 1976), a Czechoslovakian psychologist, reports somewhat similar outcomes for two identical twin boys, who after experiencing severe deprivation in early childhood, achieved normal intellectual and social development when placed by authorities in a favorable home and school environment.

We have recounted that both Anna and Isabelle displayed an exceedingly low intellectual level at six years of age, so much so that both appeared to be congenitally feebleminded. Yet both reached a considerably higher level later on. But whereas Isabelle reached a normal mentality within two-and-a-half years, Anna was still markedly inadequate at the end of four years. We cannot rule out the possibility that Anna was feebleminded. Yet an alternative hypothesis is also possible. The specialists in charge of Isabelle launched an intensive training program oriented toward giving her mastery of speech. Anna never had such training; indeed, for the first nine months after her "discovery," Anna was placed in an institution where she was virtually isolated and where her care often fell to adult inmates, many of whom were mentally defective. Isabelle's early mastery of language may well have been a critical factor accounting for the subsequent differential development of the two girls. At any rate, both cases point to the importance of social interaction for the development of the human personality. Moreover, the cases suggest the inadequacy of our biological equipment in the absence of social interaction for producing a human personality. The cases of Anna and Isabelle on the one hand, and of Gua and Viki on the other, amply testify that both an adequate heredity and environment are essential for producing a human personality.

THE DYNAMIC INTERPLAY BETWEEN HEREDITY AND ENVIRONMENT

At times, we are prone to oversimplify the relationship between heredity and environment. We often think of heredity as determining the nature of the internal trigger that the stimulus from the environment may release to produce a given effect. And indeed, in some behavior, this appears to be true. Certain responses are found closely linked with given stimuli. These responses include the reflex patterns of behavior, and are fairly stable from individual to individual and from society to society. Illustrations include changes in the palmar grasping reflex (touching the palm of an infant's hand results in a grasping action), which wanes by seven months of age, or the blinking reflex of the eye in the presence of sudden, strong light. Still other triggers are so constituted that they resist most of the range of pressures that are possible in an ordinary environment—for instance, they may fail to respond to the stimulus of red or green, and result in color blindness.

Yet the matter is frequently not this simple. Environment may affect the trigger mechanism itself. Hence, the "right" kind of prenatal environment is essential or the individual may have no eyes at all or eyes that are blind—for instance, if the mother contracted German measles (rubella) or syphilis during her pregnancy. And as we noted in the previous chapter, our environment sensitizes us to certain stimuli and desensitizes us to others.

From early childhood, life demands of the individual more, rather than less, complex kinds of behavior. Such behavior is less and less dependent on *maturation*—changes in the organism that are associated with physical and chemical processes and that occur without conscious effort or training. With the passage of time, human behavior becomes more and more dependent on learning. And this is critical: *in learning, the human organism modifies itself by responding.*

Learning is not merely a process of maturation or unfolding. A microscopic examination of the tulip bulb reveals a blossom in miniature that, under proper environmental conditions, is merely elevated, enlarged, and colored until it assumes the familiar form of the spring flower. Much human behavior is not of this sort. In this regard, Dr. José M. R. Delgado, a renowned brain researcher, observes:

> We must first start with the realization that the mind, to all intents and purposes, does not exist at birth; in some brain areas as many as 80 to 90 per cent of the neurons don't form until afterwards. Personal identity is not something we are born with. It is a combination of genetic bias, the sensory information we receive, our educational and cultural inheritance. In other words, *the mind is not revealed as the child matures; it is constructed.* (Quoted by Scarf, 1970, p. 170. Italics added.)

Genetic determination is like the blueprint of a house, Delgado contends:

But the house itself is not there; you can't sleep in a blueprint. The kind of building you eventually have will depend on the choice of which bricks, which wood, which glass are used—just as the virgin brain will be shaped by what is given to it from the environment. (Scarf, 1970, p. 170)

Jean Piaget (1952a, 1952b, 1954, 1967), an internationally recognized developmental psychologist, arrives at somewhat similar conclusions. Piaget's primary interest has been the study of children's cognitive development—the sequential stages that children undergo in acquiring the ability to think (see Research Study 5). He depicts children as acting on and modifying the world in which they live, and in turn being shaped and transformed by the consequences of their own actions. This dynamic interplay between an individual and the environment is in Piaget's view the foundation of all intelligence and knowledge (Vander Zanden, 1978).

According to Piaget, human development consists of adaptation. Children construct a series of mental models (*schemas*) for coping with their world. They typically stretch a model as far as possible to accommodate new observations. However, life periodically confronts them with the inescapable conclusion that many of their observations do not fit their current model. Children are then compelled to restructure their world view in accordance with new experience. Hence, children are required to invent increasingly better models concerning their environment as they mature (Vander Zanden, 1978).

Cognitive development. According to Jean Piaget, children act on their environment and gain feedback from it. They modify their conceptions of the world on the basis of this feedback so as to make their mental models better fit reality. Thus, cognitive development entails a continual process of adaptation.

Patrick Reddy

Socialization

A good illustration is afforded by Piaget's research dealing with the conceptions that children have regarding dreams. In response to questioning, one four-year-old indicated that she dreamed about a giant and explained, "Yes, I was scared, my tummy was shaking and I cried and told my mommy about the giant." Asked, "Was it a real giant or was it just pretend? Did the giant just seem to be there, or was it really there?" she answered, "It was really there but it left when I woke up. I saw its footprint on the floor" (Kohlberg and Gilligan, 1971:1057).

In Piaget's view this child's response should not be dismissed as the product of a wild imagination. From a four-year-old's perspective, dreams are real. As she grows older, she will have new experiences that will cause her to question this conception of dreams. She may note, for example, her failure to find a "footprint" on the floor. This will cause her to change her model regarding dreams so as to realize a better fit with reality. She will conclude that dreams are not in fact real events.

The process of revising models continues through additional steps. In time the child will realize that dreams are not seen by other people. Still later, she will recognize that dreams are internal happenings although she will credit them with a material existence. Finally, at about six to eight years of age, she will become aware that dreams are nonmaterial events (thoughts) that take place within the mind. In sum, as noted by Delgado and Piaget, the human organism literally changes itself through responding (through interaction with the environment). As we interact, we generate consciousness; we create ourselves. More specifically, we develop a "self."

RESEARCH STUDY 5

COGNITIVE DEVELOPMENT

Jean Piaget

Intelligence thus begins neither with knowledge of the self nor of things as such but with knowledge of their interaction and it is by orienting itself simultaneously towards the two poles of that interaction that intelligence organizes the world by organizing itself.

Jean Piaget

Problem. No one in recent years has had a greater impact on educational and psychological thought than Jean Piaget (1896–   ) a Swiss developmental psychologist. Although Piaget began publishing in the 1920s, he did not become a major figure on the American scene until the 1960s. His chief concern has been with the study of how children's thinking changes over time and becomes the thinking of adults.

Method. Piaget's principal method has been to make careful daily observations of his own three children's development. Although he has performed some experiments, Piaget has employed only a few subjects and has often omitted the control group technique typical of a rigorous experimental procedure.

Findings. Piaget conceives of development as separated into stages. The stage concept implies that the course of human development is divided into step-wise levels. Each phase is characterized by clear-cut differences in behavior. Piaget identifies four stages in the development of cognition (intelligence).

The first stage is the *sensorimotor period,* which lasts from birth to about two years of age. The major task of this stage revolves around infants' coordination of their motor activities (grasping, crawling, walking, and so on) with their sensory inputs (visual, auditory, and tactual cues), for instance, looking at an object and then reaching out and successfully grasping it. A second achievement of the period occurs at about eight months of age as children acquire the notion of *object permanence*—the awareness that things continue to exist when one is not perceiving them (very young infants believe that an object ceases to exist when they no longer see it.) According to Piaget, the major limitation of the sensorimotor period is that children are unable to portray the world mentally to themselves by means of symbolic representations. Hence, they are limited to the immediate here-and-now.

The second stage is the *preoperational period,* which spans the ages from two to seven. The chief achievement of this period is the developing capacity of children to employ symbols, especially language. Symbolic functioning enables children to deal with things in another time and place since they can mentally represent to themselves past and future aspects of the external world.

The third stage is the *period of concrete operations,* the elementary school years. Children gain the ability to solve *conservation* problems. They come to recognize that the quantity or amount of something remains the same regardless of changes in its shape or position. By way of illustration, consider the task depicted in Figure 3.2. A child is presented with two identical rows of six checkers. The checkers are aligned so that each checker in the top row is directly below a checker in the bottom row. The child is then asked if the two rows have the same number of checkers, if the top row

Figure 3.2. Conservation experiments. Children are first shown two rows of checkers arranged in the manner of *A* above. They are asked if both rows contain the same number of checkers. Then in full view of the children the experimenter spreads out the checkers in the bottom row as in *B* below. Children are again asked if both rows contain the same number of checkers.

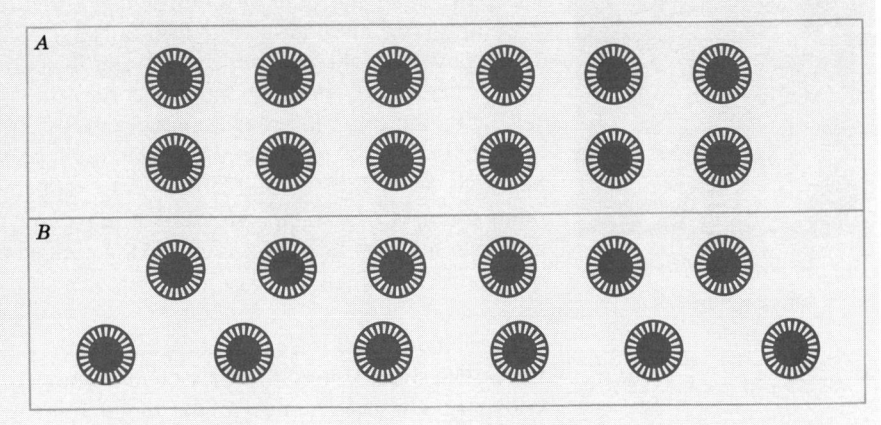

has more, or if the bottom row has more. Four-year-old children and eight-year-old children both respond that the rows have the same number of checkers. If the experimenter then spreads out the checkers in the bottom row, and again asks children the same question, four-year-olds now reply that the bottom row has more checkers "because it is longer" (or in some cases, that the top row has more checkers "because they are all bunched up"). In contrast, eight-year-olds recognize that both rows still contain the same number of checkers (the children are said to "conserve number").

The final stage in Piaget's system is the *period of formal operations,* which occurs during adolescence. Individuals become capable of engaging in logical and abstract thought and thus can handle contrary-to-fact hypotheses (if coal is white, then snow is _____). They achieve a true understanding of causation and engage in the type of thought characteristic of scientific reasoning.

Conclusion. As explained in greater length in the chapter, Piaget views human development as an ongoing process of adaptation. Children arrive at progressively better models of the world as they interact with their environment. In the course of this interaction, they increasingly refine the conceptions by which they interpret and in turn cope with the world about them. Hence, as children "grow up," the form of their thought changes. At each stage in cognitive development, their thought is qualitatively unique. It is not simply a miniature version of adult thought.

THE SELF

> Man can be defined as the animal that can say "I," that can be aware of himself as a separate entity.
>
> *Erich Fromm*

Patrick Reddy

The self. The self involves thoses ideas and definitions we have about ourselves. Such concepts arise out of social interaction.

Most of what is learned in socialization is a series of complex interpersonal relationships (Brim, 1966). In orienting ourselves to other people, we must anticipate their responses to our actions and appraise the adequacy of our behavior. Accordingly, the heart of socialization is the emergence and gradual development of the **self**. The self is the conception that individuals acquire of themselves through social interaction with others (the qualities that individuals attribute to themselves). It involves the system of concepts we employ in attempting to define ourselves (Gergen, 1971). In everyday speech, we note the existence of the self in such phrases as "proud of oneself," "talking to oneself," "losing control of oneself," "ashamed of oneself," "hating oneself," and "loving oneself." In so doing, we express certain attitudes and feelings about our own personality. Our own person becomes both subject and object. We reflect on ourselves. Within our mind's eye, so to speak, we take a place on the outside and view our thoughts, feelings, and actions within the context of a socially acquired frame of reference. Hence, an essential characteristic of the self is its reflexive character.

The self does not refer to a corporeal body. It is a psychic, not a physical, entity. We should avoid the error of attempting to find "it" somewhere in the body. The self lacks a physical existence in the sense that it is not located in the head, brain, heart, eyes, chest, or genitals. Further, it is a mistake to think of the self as a definitely bounded unity with a kind of absolute autonomy of its own. It is not something that comes into full-fledged being at a given moment, such as at the time of birth or conception, and which continues to exist after death. The self lacks spiritual or mystical properties. It is not something that exists prior to and apart from a social environment. Rather, the self is a social product and can exist only in a social context (Lindesmith, Strauss, and Denzin, 1978).

THE "LOOKING-GLASS SELF"

We have observed that an essential characteristic of the self is its reflexive character. Within our imagination, we take a position outside of our own personality, so to speak, and from this assumed position we observe our thoughts, feelings, and actions as if we were someone else. Now of course we never really leave our own personality in any objective sense. Rather, we merely exercise our imagination in such a manner that we take a place on the outside for the purpose of self-observation. Further, we are not entirely objective in our self-appraisal; our self-perceptions are often erroneous and distorted. Frequently, it would be simply too painful, discomforting, and threatening to see ourselves as others see us. Hence, we merely think that we see ourselves objectively.

An essential problem of selfhood is this: How can we get outside of ourselves in such a way as to become an object to ourselves? Or, to put the question another way, how can we be both object and subject to ourselves? Charles Horton Cooley (1864–1929), a pioneer social psychologist, provides an answer to this question. We can do it only through others. By temporarily assuming the position of other people, we may look at ourselves, as it were, through their eyes. Cooley (1902, 1909) conceived of this process when he coined the phrase, the **looking-glass self**. He suggests that there is an ever recurring process going on in the mind of each of us, a process characterized by three separable phases.

Phase 1: Perception. We imagine how we appear to other people. In this phase, we imagine how other people perceive us. If we have a large pimple on our nose, we imagine that this is what others see when they view us.

Phase 2: Interpretation or Definition. In this phase, we imagine how others judge us. Returning to our illustration, we are aware of how people typically interpret a pimple on one's nose. We may assume that they view it as a blemish that detracts from one's appearance, and a relatively "humorous" blemish at that. Actually, however, others may simply overlook our pimple.

THE SELFHOOD PROCESS

OBSERVATION It became clear to me today that if I continue spending money at the rate I have been doing, I won't have enough to see me through the rest of the quarter. I have been thinking of ways that I can cut down on unnecessary expenses. Lately I've been seeing a girl as often as I can, which unfortunately isn't often enough. Whenever we go out, it usually involves the spending of money. I realize that somehow I'm going to have to tell her that I'm very short on cash and that I can't afford to go to many places for the rest of the quarter. But I'm bothered about how to tell her. I have to make certain that it doesn't sound like the brush-off—that "no money" doesn't sound like "I don't want to see you anymore." So I began thinking to myself, "How can I tell her in such a way that she will understand?" I've been going over various ways of phrasing it and also anticipating what she will say.

PRINCIPLE This illustrates the selfhood process. I've been carrying on an inner conversation with myself. I mentally exchange roles: I am alternatively my girlfriend and then "me." I imagine how my girlfriend will interpret what I say and do. I "try out" various ways of approaching her on this matter, essentially saying to myself, "How would I respond if someone said such-and-such to me?"

In a word, we imagine how others evaluate our behavior, in this case, the pimple. But our interpretation need not be correct; it may be erroneous.

Phase 3: Response. We experience some sort of feelings on what we regard to be others' judgment of us. On the basis of the first two processes, we may experience fear, sympathy, pity, hate, anger, love, contempt, embarrassment, envy, or some other emotional response. In the case of our illustration, we may experience embarrassment over our pimple, or perhaps anger that others can be so "unfair" since a pimple is a happening over which we normally lack control.

Although the process associated with the looking-glass self is ever recurring, we usually are not explicitly or consciously aware of its taking place; that is, it occurs more or less "in the back of our minds." Yet under some circumstances, we may be quite aware of the process, especially when we are concerned with "what kind of impression we are making." While making a speech in class we may feel extremely "self-conscious." We may wonder, "What are they thinking of me?" Or approaching the professor after class to ask a question, we may relentlessly scrutinize the professor for telltale clues that we believe will reveal whether the professor considers us to be "smart" or "stupid."

Although the concept "looking-glass self" is most appropriate, it can be misunderstood. It does not imply that our self-conception changes radically every time we confront a new person. Accordingly, some sociologists (Turner, 1968) distinguish between self-images and self-conceptions. A **self-image** is a mental conception or picture that we have of ourselves which is relatively temporary; it is subject to change as we move from one situation to another. Our **self-conception** is a more overriding view of ourself, a sense of self through time—"the real me," or "I myself as I really am" (Turner, 1968:94). The deposits of self-images usually build up over time, resulting in relatively definite and stable self-conceptions. As a consequence, the succession of self-images serves to *edit* rather than supplant our self-conceptions.

SELF-APPRAISALS

Treat people as if they were what they ought to be and you help them to become what they are capable of being.

Johann W. von Goethe

Basic to the writings of Charles Horton Cooley and George Herbert Mead, both distinguished pioneers in the field of social psychology, is the notion that *individuals' self-conceptions emerge from social interaction with other people and, in turn, that individuals' self-conceptions influence their actual behavior* (Mead, 1932, 1934, 1938). It is not simply that children can *discover* themselves only in the actions of others toward them:

> More than that, the self is *formed* out of the actions of others, which become part of the individual as a result of his having identified with these others and responded to himself in their terms. Retrospectively, one can ask "Who am I?" *But in practice, the answer has come before the question.* The answer has come from all the definitions of one's roles, values, and goals that others begin to furnish at the moment of birth. "You are a boy; you are my son; you are French"; "You are a good boy and fully a part of this group" (with rewards confirming the words); or "You are a bad boy" (with significant others driving the point home by the sanctions they administer). (Yinger, 1965, p. 149)

And what we think of ourselves and how we feel about ourselves affects our actions (see Research Study 6).

The responses others make toward us influence how we come to see ourselves; they provide us with feedback regarding the "kinds" of persons we are (Coombs, 1969). The late Harry Stack Sullivan (1947; 1953), a distinguished psychiatrist, suggested that our self-appraisals have their origins in our interpersonal relationships, especially those within the family. Our self-appraisals tend to be "reflected appraisals." If children are accepted, approved, respected, and liked for what they are, they will very likely acquire an attitude of self-acceptance and self-respect (Coopersmith, 1967; Sears, 1970; Gecas, 1971, 1972). But if the significant people in their lives—especially their family members—belittle, blame, and reject them, they are likely to develop unfavorable attitudes toward themselves. As they are judged by others, they will tend to judge themselves. For the most part, social psychological research has supported the postulate that we influence one another's self-conceptions (Videbeck, 1960; Quarantelli and Cooper, 1966; Gergen, 1965, 1972; Guardo, 1969; Bloom, 1977).

Although our self-appraisals derive from the reflected appraisals that significant others provide us, they are not the only source for our self-conceptions. David R. Franks and Joseph Marolla (1976) point out that we also achieve feedback regarding our power and competence based on the impact we have on the world about us. Through interaction with others and through the effects we produce in our material environment, we gain a sense of our adequacy, energy, skill, industry, and so on.

Robert W. White makes somewhat the same point:

> [Self-esteem] has often been dealt with as if it were wholly a question of how one is treated by other people. . . . I do not want to underestimate the importance of the love and the esteem we receive from others, but I believe that even in infancy the whole matter must be viewed as an interaction. . . . It is important, therefore, to make allowance for the child's action upon his environment, of the extent to which this action is apt to be successful, and consequently of the confidence he builds up that he can influence his surroundings in desired ways. We can suppose that a placid child who has always received

generous narcissistic supplies, without doing much to earn them, will enjoy an agreeable level of self-esteem, provided he never enters a harsher environment. Self-esteem will be much more substantial, however, in the more active child who feels confident that he can elicit esteem from others by competent performances. . . . It is to this second person that we would attribute large ego strength. The first would strike us as too much at the mercy of his surroundings. (1965, p. 201)

In sum, we are not simply passive beings acted on by others; we are *active* agents in the shaping of our own beings (Wrong, 1961; Turner, 1962; Vander Zanden, 1978).

RESEARCH STUDY 6

"BORN LOSERS"*

Jeanne Marecek and David R. Mettee

Problem. Research suggests that self-conceptions have a considerable influence on people's behavior. "Born losers" are good illustrations of this principle. Such individuals appear to suffer failure after failure and misfortune after misfortune. Even when they are on the verge of a "surefire thing," something always seems to go amiss and success eludes them. Psychologists suggest that these individuals set situations up in such a manner that they insure failure for themselves. They define themselves as "failures" and then undertake to be "true to self" by failing. Only in this way can they maintain a consistent conception of themselves (Aronson and Carlsmith, 1962).

Hypotheses. Jeanne Marecek and David R. Met-

* Adapted from Jeanne Marecek and David R. Mettee (1972). "Avoidance of continued success as a function of self-esteem, level of esteem certainty, and responsibility for success." *Journal of Personality and Social Psychology,* 22:98–107.

tee, two social psychologists, studied the rejection-of-success phenomenon. They formulated two hypotheses. First, persons with chronic low self-esteem will reject or minimize a success for which they believe themselves responsible. Second, persons with chronic low self-esteem will accept a success that is due to a windfall or a "lucky break."

Method. Seventy-two college women completed a questionnaire consisting of 81 self-esteem items from the California Psychological Inventory (a personality test). After answering each true-false question, the subjects were asked to indicate their level of certainty about their response by circling one of three possibilities: "C," certain; "SD," some doubt; and "U," uncertain. The questionnaires were then scored. Women in the upper third of the self-esteem distribution were designated "high self-esteem"; those in the bottom third, "low self-esteem."

All the high and low self-esteem subjects were individually given a task in which they earned points by matching geometric figures on a display board with those contained in the deck of cards. After ten of the twenty matching trials (the halfway point), the women were casually informed that their scores were quite good—"very few people get that high on average." But half of the subjects in each of the two esteem groups were told that their success was entirely a matter of luck. The other half were informed that their achievement was the result of their skill. The women then completed the trials.

Findings. Following the halfway point, Marecek and Mettee found that (1) all high self-esteem groups showed significant improvement; (2) low self-esteem women who had been uncertain regarding their self-appraisal improved as much as did the high self-esteem subjects; (3) low self-esteem subjects who had been certain of their low self-appraisal and who had been informed that their first-half success was the product of *luck* improved *more* than did any other group; and (4) low self-esteem women who had been certain of their low self-appraisal and who had been told that their success was due to their own *skill* did *not* show any improvement.

Conclusions. The results demonstrate that low self-esteem does not necessarily preclude success. Only those individuals who are certain of their low self-esteem avoid success and then only if they believe that success is self-determined. When individuals with deeply rooted, chronic low self-esteem define success as fate-determined (due to luck), they show dramatic improvement in their task performance; they enthusiastically embrace a successful outcome. But when they perceive success as the product of their own efforts and talents, they shun success so as to maintain a consistent self-conception. They do not strive to achieve. They find themselves locked by their self-perceptions into patterns of self-imposed failure.

MEAD'S THEORY OF THE DEVELOPMENT OF THE SELF

From the moment of birth we are immersed in action, and can only fitfully guide it by taking thought.

Alfred North Whitehead, Science and the Modern World

We owe much to George Herbert Mead (1932; 1934; 1938) for our understanding of the self. According to Mead, the key to children's development of the self is to be found in their acquisition of *language*. Through the use of language, we arouse the same tendencies in ourselves as we do in others; we put ourselves in the place of others. Before we can initiate any action in other people, we mentally say to ourselves: "If I want to produce this given response in this person, what will it take to do it? What would it take to make me act in this way?" Mead uses the illustration of an instructor who asks a student to bring a chair to the classroom. The student probably would fulfill the request, but if not, the instructor would very likely do so. In the act of asking the student to secure a chair, the instructor first must conjure up the act within his or her own imagination.

The use of language enables us to carry on, as it were, an internal conversation. We hear ourselves; we respond to ourselves. We talk and reply to ourselves in much the same fashion that we carry on a conversation with other people. We can be objects to ourselves. Hence, we judge how other people will respond to the words we ourselves utter. In this manner, we can appraise within our imagination the judgment others have of our attitudes, feelings, and actions. Obviously, this ability is critical for the process of the looking-glass self.

Ralph Turner (1968a), a sociologist following in the symbolic interactionist tradition, clarifies and extends Mead's formulation. As periodically noted in this book, social interaction involves us in a process whereby we fit our developing actions to those of other people. In speaking or acting, we have some interpretation in mind for our behavior. Whether we provide a vocal utterance, a flirtatious glance, a wave of the hand, a shrug of the shoulder, or a clenched fist, we hope to signal something to another person.

When speaking or acting, we typically adopt a state of *preparedness* for certain kinds of responses from the other person. If we offer a clerk a ten-dollar bill for a purchase, comment to a friend on the weather, or embrace our lover, we expect that the other person will respond with an action that will appropriately fit our own. As the other person responds, we enter a stage of *testing and revision*. We mentally interpret the other's behavior, noting whether or not it falls within the range of behaviors that we anticipated. In so doing, we engage in a process of inner communication with ourselves.

As we appraise the other's behavior and assign meaning to it, we plan our subsequent course of action. For example, if the person responded in an unexpected way, we might terminate the interaction, attempt to "go back" and reassert our original intention, disregard the other's response, or abandon our initial gesture and follow the other person's lead. Social interaction involves us in a process of self-communication.

Mead believed that the ability of children to understand and later employ language is central to the socialization process (a position supported by the cases of Anna and Isabelle). This ability apparently begins developing at an early age, certainly by the time children reach their second birthday (Denzin, 1972; Vander Zanden, 1978). According to Mead, children typically pass through three stages in evolving a conception of themselves as objects, a recognition essential for the internal communication that underlies the selfhood process: the "play stage," the "game stage," and the "generalized other stage."

In *play*, children take the role of *one* person at a time and seek to act out the behavior associated with this role, for instance, their mother, their father, their sister, and similar "models." Such a model is termed a **significant other**. Two-year-old children may examine a doll's pants, pretend to find them wet, reprimand the doll, and take it to the bathroom. In so doing, children view the situation from the point of view of a particular person, in this case probably their mother, and then proceed to act as this person would act. But in imitating the attitudes of their mothers, children take over their mothers' attitudes toward themselves. They alternately play the role of children and mothers. They put themselves in the position of their mothers, and then respond as children to the words they utter when they were playing mother.

In the first stage, that of play, children take the role of only one other person at any given time. In the second stage, that of the *game*, children take many roles. In an organized game, such as baseball, children need to take within their imagination the role of everyone else in the game. All nine other positions (including that of the rival team's batter) are tightly interwoven with their own position. If the rival batter bunts the ball down the third base line, the child as the first baseman must know what the pitcher, third baseman, shortstop, and others will do. They must have the responses of each position involved in their own position. They must know what everyone else is going to do in order to carry out their own play. The game constitutes a social situation that requires all the participants to know what the others expect. Children must come to see themselves not only from the viewpoint of one other person (such as mother, police officer, or cowboy as in the case of play) but from the viewpoint of all the individuals occupying a variety of positions within the game. In games, the response of every player to every other player is organized in terms of definite rules. In grasping the

THE DEVELOPMENT OF THE SELF

OBSERVATION When I turned on the television set this evening to watch the news, my two-year-old daughter, Jackie, turned to her doll and said, "Now, Baby, please be quiet. I want to watch the news." During the program Jackie made several comments to her doll that echoed things I frequently tell her: "Now, Baby, I want to hear this!" "Honey, please be quiet until this is over!"

PRINCIPLE George Herbert Mead suggests that socialization occurs as the child acts out through games and play the behavior of others. In imitating my attitudes and actions, Jackie was taking over—adopting—my attitudes and actions. She was placing herself in my position and undertaking to act as I act toward her. In so doing, she was incorporating my attitudes and actions within herself, making them her attitudes and actions.

rules of the game, children acquire within themselves an organized system of positions; they can participate in the mutual responses that constitute the actual game.

In Mead's third stage, individuals come to relate themselves to the community of which they are members. Groups and societies possess an organized character in which people enact their culture. The society or social group that gives to individuals their unity of self is called **the generalized other.** The attitude of the generalized other is the attitude of the entire group or society. It involves individuals' organized conceptions of the expectations of others who interact with them. Although we acquire our conception of these expectations from particular people (our mother, teacher, or scout leader), these expectations are generalized to embrace all people within similar contexts.

The inner conversations that we carry on with ourselves take place from the perspective of the generalized other. To think about our behavior is to interact with ourselves from the standpoint of an abstract community of persons. Thus, as conceived by Mead, the generalized other is the means by which we are linked to society. By virtue of the generalized other, our behavior comes to be influenced by the expectations of our social group. We incorporate (internalize) the organized attitudes of our community within ourselves so that social control becomes self-control.

101 Socialization

The importance of games in socialization. According to George Herbert Mead, children learn in the course of their games the part that rules and social expectations play in social interaction.

Patrick Reddy

SOCIALIZATION ACROSS THE LIFE SPAN

Learning is but an adjunct to ourself,
and where we are, our learning likewise is.
William Shakespeare, Love's Labour's Lost, Act IV

Traditionally we have tended to think of socialization as occurring almost exclusively during childhood. Yet socialization is a never-ending process; it continues throughout life. Initiates are socialized within the patterns of a labor union, upward mobile individuals within a new social class, new patients within a hospital ward, "senior citizens" within a Golden Age village, dental students within their profession, religious converts within a new religion, and new employees within a factory or business establishment. Indeed, many people spend much of their lives in organizations whose explicit mandate is to change them. We expect individuals to acquire basic skills in school, to get advanced training in universities, to recover from "faulty behavior patterns" in mental hospitals, to be "resocialized" through corrective programs in prisons, or to learn special work skills in trade schools. Clearly it would be a mistake to conclude that socialization processes are restricted to a particular period in life or to the intimate environs of the family.

Until recently, the selfhood processes so critical to socialization were thought by many developmental psychologists to occur only after children reached six or seven years of age. They tended to depict children under six years old as passive and egocentric, incapable of thinking about others (Chandler and Greenspan, 1972). Only within the past several years have developmental psychologists come to recognize that children younger than six exhibit people-oriented and sharing behaviors (Flavell, 1974; Pufall, 1975; Marvin, Greenberg, and Mossler, 1976). Harriet L. Rheingold, Dale F. Hay, and Meredith J. West (1976) have observed infants of 10 months calling their parents' attention to objects by pointing to them. And infants of 11 months have been seen to hold up a toy and to give it to an adult.

Rheingold and her associates conclude:

> In showing an object to another person, the children demonstrate not only that they know that other people can see what they see but also that others will look at what they point to or hold up. We can surmise that they also know that what they see may be remarkable in some way and therefore worthy of another's attention. . . . We propose that sharing behaviors, from the first holding up of objects for others to see, the first offering of an object to another . . . qualify as developmental milestones. That children so young share contradicts the egocentricity so often ascribed to them and reveals them instead as already able contributors to social life. (p. 1157)

A sense of self does not develop suddenly in an all-or-none manner (Bertenthal and Fischer, 1978). Michael Lewis (1977; Lewis and Brooks, 1975), a developmental psychologist, observed 96 infants with rouge on their noses in front of a mirror. The infants' mothers applied the rouge under the guise of wiping their noses. None of the children under twelve months of age responded to the paint. However, twenty-five percent of those 15 to 18 months of age and seventy-five percent of those 21 to 24 months of age touched their noses. This reaction suggested that the youngsters recognized themselves.

Various developmental psychologists report empathic awareness among children as young as fifteen months of age (Borke, 1972). Martin L. Hoffman cites the following case:

> Michael, aged 15 months, and his friend Paul were fighting over a toy and Paul started to cry. Michael appeared disturbed and let go, but Paul still cried. Michael paused, then brought his teddy bear to Paul but to no avail. Michael paused again, and then finally succeeded in stopping Paul's crying by fetching Paul's security blanket from an adjoining room. Several aspects of this incident deserve comment. First, it is clear that Michael initially assumed that his own teddy bear, which often comforts him, would also comfort Paul. Second, Paul's continued crying served as negative feedback that led Michael to consider alternatives. Third [since Michael's parents were certain that he had never seen Paul being comforted with the blanket], he was somehow able to reason by analogy that Paul would be comforted by something he loved in the same way that Michael loved his own teddy bear. (1975, p. 612)

Children's language capacities begin to develop rapidly at about two years of age, making possible an increasing awareness of other people's viewpoints (Vander Zanden, 1978). Helen Borke (1973) reports that by three years of age both American and Chinese (Taiwan) children are capable of distinguishing between happy and unhappy reactions in other people and can recognize social situations associated with these responses. Observers note that nursery school children (youngsters between three and five years of age) spend the greatest part of their time in school interacting with others, primarily talking. Moreover, most of their speech is mutually responsive and adapted to the utterances or nonverbal behavior of their partners (Garvey and Hogan, 1973). And Michael P. Maratsos (1973) found in his research that nursery school children are far more explicit when communicating with a blindfolded person than with an individual who can see. These and other findings testify to the continual and progressive development of selfhood capabilities in children (Bigner, 1974; Turnure, 1975; Urberg and Docherty, 1976).

The elementary school years bring about a rapid growth in children's knowledge of the social world and of the requirements for social interaction (Kerckhoff, 1972; Vander Zanden, 1978). Research by W. J. Livesley and D. B. Bromley involving schoolage English children reveals that "the eighth year is a critical period in the developmental psychology of person perception" (1973:147). Children under eight tend to describe people largely in terms of external, readily observable attributes such as their personality traits, families, possessions, and physical characteristics. At about eight years of age, they exhibit a rapid development in their vocabularies for evaluating people, and become more specific and precise in their appraisals. Moreover, they show a greater ability for recognizing people's subtle qualities and for analyzing and interpreting their behavior.

With increasing age, children's self-conceptions also undergo change. Elementary school children describe themselves in terms of concrete, objective categories such as their home addresses, physical appearance, possessions, and play activities. A nine-year-old fourth-grade boy describes himself in these terms:

> My name is Bruce C. I have brown eyes. I have brown hair. I have brown eyebrows. I'm nine years old. I LOVE! Sports. I have seven people in my family. I have great! eye site. I have lots! of friends. I live on 1923 Pinecrest Dr. I'm going on 10 in September. I'm a boy. I have a uncle that is almost 7 feet tall. My school is Pinecrest. My teacher is Mrs. V. I play Hockey! I'm almost the smartest boy in the class. I LOVE! food. I love fresh air. I LOVE School. (Montemayor and Eisen, 1977, p. 317)

In contrast, adolescents use more abstract and subjective descriptions such as personal beliefs and motivational and interpersonal characteristics. A seventeen-year-old senior high school girl describes herself in these terms:

> I am a human being. I am a girl. I am an individual. I don't know who I am. I am a Pisces. I am a moody person. I am an indecisive person. I am an ambitious person. I am a very curious person. I am not an individual. I am a loner. I am an American (God help me). I am a Democrat. I am a liberal person. I am a radical. I am a conservative. I am a pseudoliberal. I am an atheist. I am not a classifiable person (i.e., I don't want to be). (1977, p. 318)

Orville G. Brim, Jr. (1966), a sociologist, also points out that the content of socialization differs at different stages of the life cycle. We learn different things at different times and places in our lives. He notes a number of ways in which socialization during adulthood differs from that of childhood. First,

105 Socialization

Socialization across the lifespan. Socialization is a never-ending process that encompasses one's entire life.

Patrick Reddy

society tends to be primarily concerned with children's values and motives, whereas with adults it focuses largely on their actual behavior. Second, whereas childhood socialization is primarily directed toward elementary skills (toilet-training, language competence, and so on), adult socialization requires a synthesis of elements from already-learned responses. Third, adult socialization tends to emphasize realism as opposed to the idealism associated with childhood socialization (for instance, children are taught not to lie but later they learn that they are expected to tell "white lies"). Fourth, later socialization places greater emphasis than does early socialization on the mediating of conflicting demands that derive from contradictory role expectations (see Chapter 4). In these and other ways the content of socialization changes as individuals move through the life cycle.

SUMMARY

1. Socialization is a process of social interaction in which we acquire the socially expected ways of thinking, feeling, and acting essential for effective participation within society. Culture, its norms, values, and symbols, is what is learned in socialization.

2. The relationship between heredity and environment has long intrigued humans. Rather than counterposing heredity and environment, many scientists are now interested in specifying how hereditary and environmental factors interact to produce particular characteristics.

3. An updated version of the nature-nurture controversy has emerged over sociobiology. Sociobiology is the study of the biological basis for all social behavior. This approach has received a mixed reception among sociologists.

4. Humanness is dependent on an adequate heredity and environment. By itself, environment cannot overcome the limitations imposed by heredity, a fact demonstrated by studies with chimps. Research reveals that a normal human environment is not sufficient to enable chimps to learn a human language.

5. The cases of Anna and Isabelle point to the importance of social interaction for the development of the human personality. These cases reveal the inadequacy of our biological equipment in the absence of social interaction.

6. In learning, the human organism modifies itself by responding. As children act on and modify the world in which they live, they in turn are shaped and transformed by the consequences of their own actions.

7. Most of what is learned in socialization is a series of complex interpersonal relationships. In orienting ourselves to other people, we must anticipate their responses to our actions and appraise the adequacy of our behavior. Accordingly, the heart of socialization is the emergence and gradual development of the self. The self is the conception that individuals acquire of themselves through social interaction with others.

8. An essential problem of selfhood is this: How can we get outside of ourselves in such a way as to become an object to ourselves? In other words, how can we be both object and subject to ourselves? Charles Horton Cooley provides an answer through his formulation of the "looking-glass self."

9. Our self-conceptions emerge from social interaction with other people. In turn, our self-conceptions influence our actual behavior. As a consequence, our self-appraisals tend to be "reflected appraisals." Further, what we think of ourselves and how we feel about ourselves affects our actions.

10. According to George Herbert Mead the key to children's development of the self is to be found in their acquisition of language. The use of language enables human beings to carry on an inner conversation with themselves. In Mead's view, children typically pass through three stages in evolving a conception of themselves as objects: the "play stage," the "game stage," and the "generalized other stage."

11. Socialization is a never-ending process; it continues throughout life. However, the content of socialization changes as individuals move through the life cycle.

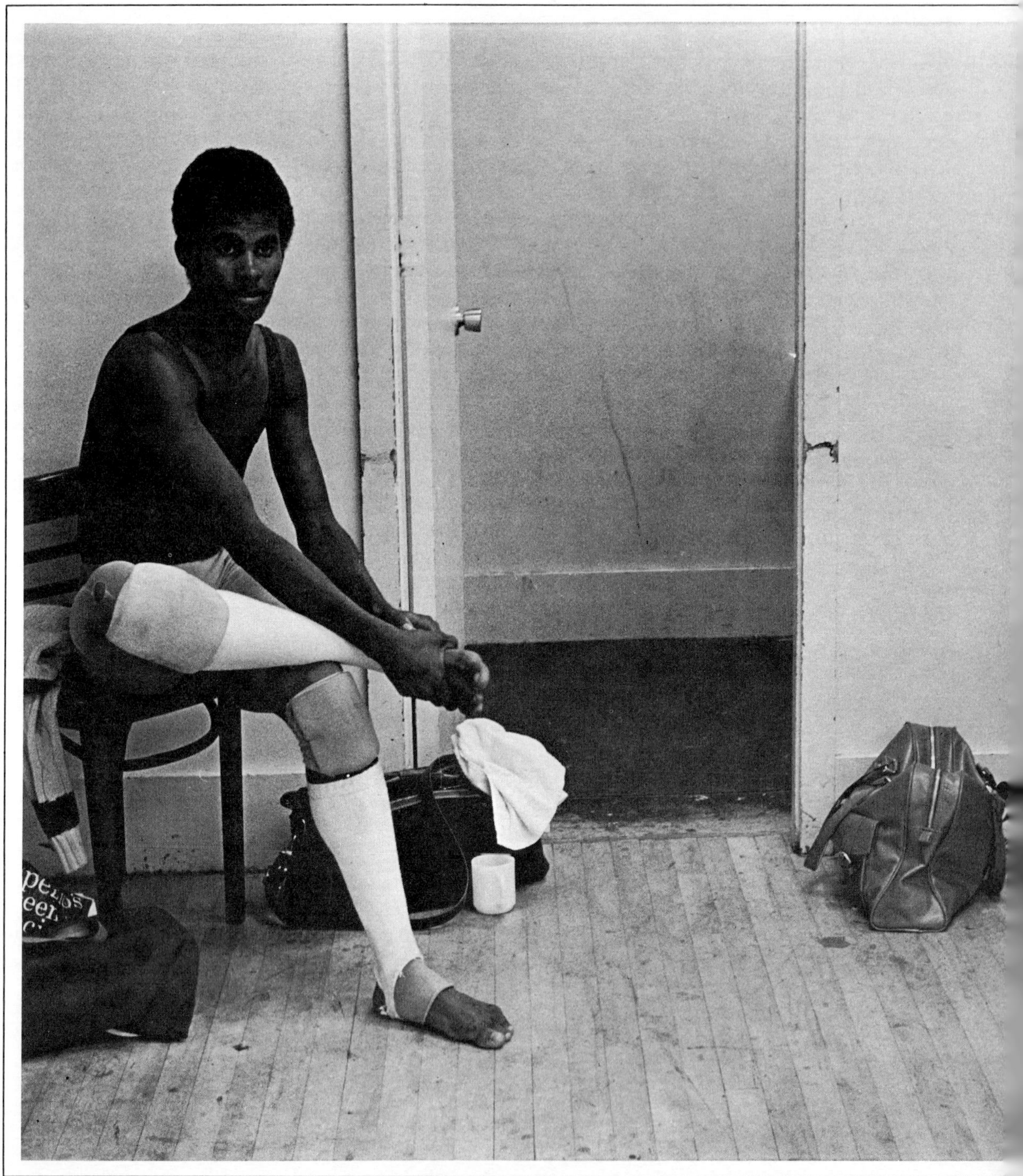

4
ROLES: THE FASHIONING OF EVERYDAY LIFE

BASIC CONCEPTS
  Roles
  The Role-Set
  Social Structure
  Role-Taking and Role-Making
  Impression Management

ROLES AND IDENTITY
  "Who Am I?"
  Valid Identity

ROLE STRAIN
  Role Conflict
  Mechanisms for Dealing with Role Conflict
  Role Ambiguity

OBSERVATION   This is Saturday's installment but it is being written on Sunday for reasons that will soon be obvious. Last night my roommate and I decided to hit the bars. Actually we made only one bar. At the bar several varieties of interesting behaviors were being exhibited, all socially approved because of the location and time it occurred: guys trying to "make it" with chicks, dressed to the max, hanging it all on that first impression, putting their best into their rap (impression management); rowdies in the back playing Foos Ball, swearing and spitting and letting off steam; and the bummed-out crowd getting smashed to insensibility, dripping across their tables and melting to the floor. An interesting lot really.

Eventually, the night wore down and the glitter in the air settled out and stopped glowing, and I was left in my apartment with my roommate, two girls, and an upset stomach. The behavior of the others began to change in a most singular manner, the sicker and sicker I got. They were expressing worry and concern over my condition—they couldn't do anything else as I was so damn sick.

PRINCIPLE   Roles are complementary and comprise a role-set. As I became sick, the roles the other people were playing (good time charlies) re-adjusted themselves complementary to the role I was being forced to take—"a sick person." It no longer was a swinging fun scene. Whether or not their sympathies were in earnest, their behavior pointed to the socially appropriate behavior patterns called for toward a sick individual.

William Shakespeare in *As You Like It* wrote:

All the world's a stage,
And all the men and women merely players:
They have their exits and their entrances;
And one man in his time plays many parts . . .

It is perhaps difficult to believe that this oft-quoted passage from Shakespeare has any relevance for the modern study of human interaction. Nonetheless, aside from the poetry, there are noteworthy parallels between Shakespeare's characterization of social life and that of contemporary sociologists. When actors portray characters in a play, their performance is influenced by the script, the performance of fellow actors, the director's instructions, and the reactions of the audience. In some respects, culture is similar to a play's script; it provides a framework by which we broadly map out our behavior—by which we play our "roles." But our behavior does not take place in a vacuum. We continuously assess and reassess our own behavior in relation to that of other people; we take both our own actions and those of others into account as we prepare to "stage" our future actions. Moreover, in real life, the "director" is often present as a supervisor, parent, or teacher, while the "audience" consists of those who observe our behavior (Biddle and Thomas, 1966).

As with most analogies, this one has its weaknesses. In real life parents, clerks, engineers, and others do not "read their lines" or carry out the requirements of their roles in a robotized or mechanical manner. Nor are people in everyday life commonly aware of "enacting" culture as such. Ralph Linton, an anthropologist, writes:

> It has been said that the last thing which a dweller in the deep sea would be likely to discover would be water. He would become conscious of its existence only if some accident brought him to the surface and introduced him to air. Man, throughout most of his history, has been only vaguely conscious of the existence of culture and has owed even this consciousness to contrasts between the customs of his own society and those of some other with which he happened to be brought into contact. (1945, p. 125)

In other words, we tend to take our culture for granted; our "enactment" of culture becomes more or less second nature to us.

BASIC CONCEPTS

Sociologists employ terms like "role," "role-set," and "social structure" as an intellectual shorthand. Concepts are tools that facilitate scholarly thinking and communication. A professional language allows scientists to talk with one another compactly and dispassionately. Words, especially everyday words referring to daily behavior, vibrate with overtones. They are filled with a variety of connotations and double and triple meanings. Hence, a professional language, provided it is not overused or unnecessarily used, is a definite asset to scientific work.

ROLES

When we enter the presence of other people, we mentally attempt to "place" or "locate" them within the broader scheme of social life: elderly woman, meter reader, thief, police officer, clerk, athlete, wife, grandparent, friend, drug addict, and so on. In so doing we scrutinize people for a variety of cues, certain telltale "signs" or "marks," that tell us about the categories to which they belong—for instance, do they wear wedding rings indicating that they are married; do they wear suits and ties or are they dressed in "work clothes" indicating something about their occupation and social class; do they get about with crutches indicating information about their state of health; and so on. In this manner, we come to define the situation; we activate within our minds a map, so to speak, that guides us in identify-

Patrick Reddy

Roles. When we enter a new setting, we undertake to define the situation. We attempt to identify people's roles so as to mentally establish the actions we can expect of them and the actions they can expect of us. When we enter a restaurant we have never previously patronized, we can quickly begin fitting our developing lines of action together by assuming that the "same" set of behaviors will transpire as we previously encountered in other restaurants.

ing the mutual set of expectations that will operate within the relationship (what we can expect of them and what they can expect of us). In brief, we attempt to identify their **roles**.

John Lofland observes:

> Roles are *claimed* labels, from behind which people present themselves to others and partially in terms of which they conceive, gauge, and judge their past, current and projected action. And roles are *imputed* labels toward which, and partially in terms of which, people likewise conceive, gauge, and judge others' past, present and projected action. (1967, pp. 9–10)

Hence, roles specify *who does what, when, and where* (Vander Zanden, 1977).

Roles allow us to collapse or telescope a large number of behaviors into manageable bundles (Goffman, 1959). We can collect all the particulars of an unfolding social situation and simplify them by grouping them together within a broad category or class. Moreover, roles permit us to assume that some degree of "sameness" holds from one social setting to another. We can take it for granted that stable meanings characterize social interaction, a perspective that reduces surprise and reassures us that the world as it appears today will appear in essentially the same manner tomorrow (Cicourel, 1970). Alfred Schutz notes:

I hold on to the familiar image I have of you. I take it for granted that you are as I have known you before. Until further notice I hold invariant that segment of my stock of knowledge which concerns you and which I have built up in face-to-face situations, that is, until I receive information to the contrary. (1964, p. 39)

A word of caution is in order regarding the use of the concept "role" in this book. Although the concept "role" assumes a critical part in sociological thought and research, sociologists differ in the use which they make of it. This fact is often disconcerting to students in introductory sociology courses and, indeed, to professional sociologists.

Some sociologists distinguish between a "role" and a "position" (or a "status"). For these sociologists, the emphasis of position falls on what people *ideally should* do; it has as its focus the behavior that is socially expected of a category of people in relation to certain other categories of people (for instance, the behavior "expected" of mothers in relation to their children, clergy in relation to parishioners, and Whites in relation to Blacks). The concept of "role" is then employed to refer to how individuals *actually perform* in a given position, as distinct from how they are supposed to perform. This distinction between position and role highlights for us the gap that often exists between what people *should* do and what they *actually* do. Viewed from this perspective, one *occupies* a position (or status) and *plays* a role. Thus, although we occupy a great multitude of positions, at any time we are likely to play only one, or at best a few, roles.

THE ROLE OF A SICK PERSON

OBSERVATION Yesterday Dave, Lenore, Ed, and I went to give blood over at the blood center. Lenore wasn't too hot on the idea and said the thought of giving blood made her sick. But since we all were going, she came along. At the blood center she must have passed out about six times. We got her home and after about seven hours she was still passing out. So we brought her to the emergency room of University Hospital to see why she kept passing out and they just told her to stay in bed. We wheeled her all the way home in a wheelchair and Dave and Ed even carried her up the stairs and to bed. Well, she kept passing out during the night. We called the emergency room this morning to ask if we should bring her over again. They put a doctor on the phone and he told us that she had to be faking it; he said no person could possibly still be that weak 24 hours after just giving a pint of blood.

PRINCIPLE Lenore was playing the role of a sickly girl since she was getting so much attention. All these guys came to visit her and gave her so much attention and especially Ed (he stayed with her the whole night to make sure she was okay). And she got to miss a midterm she didn't think she was going to do too well on.

Although sociologists may differ in their use of the concept "role," we should not conclude that they are necessarily talking about wholly different things. More often, they are simply using different terms to refer to the same phenomenon. Nor should we conclude that one definition is "right" and another "wrong." There is nothing sacred in a definition, although, admittedly, a profusion of definitions results in regrettable problems in communication. Concepts and their definitions are human-made; they are simply tools that are more or less useful for some specific scientific or other scholarly purpose. If we are to avoid confusion in reading sociological literature, however, it is necessary that we ascertain just how an author is defining "role" and the related concepts of "position" and "status."

THE ROLE-SET

Man is a knot, a web, a mesh into which relationships are tied.
Antoine de Saint-Exupéry, Flight to Arras, *1942*

Roles do not exist by themselves in isolation from one another; each role has its complementary or associated role or roles (Merton, 1957; Turner, 1962; 1968a; 1968b; Turner and Shosid, 1976). The role of mother, for instance, has no meaning apart from the role of the child; the role of professor, no meaning apart from that of student; the role of minister no meaning apart from that of parishioner. Usually a role is linked with a number of interdependent, complementary roles—termed a **role-set**. The role of nurse is a

Figure 4.1. A simplified representation of the role-set associated with the role of nurse. Within that social structure we term "the hospital," the role of "nurse" is linked to an array of other roles. The role is reciprocal to these other roles.

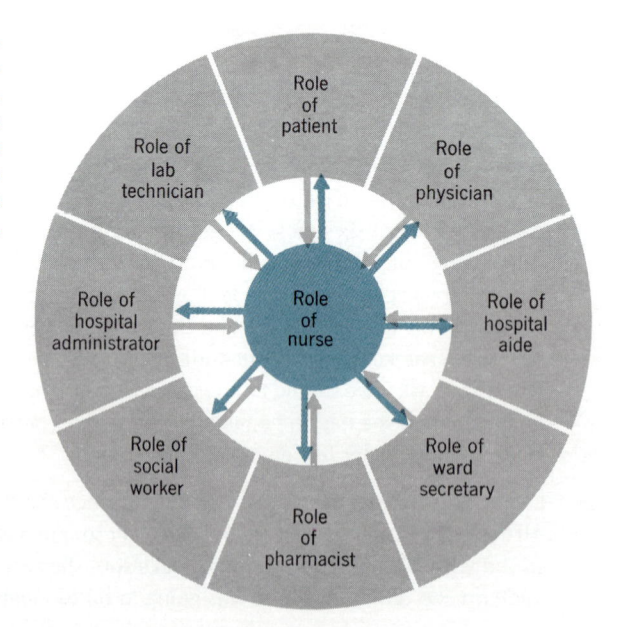

Role-set. The role of nurse is tied to an array of other roles including those of patient and hospital aide. Individuals are linked together within social structures by the fact that their roles are reciprocal: the rights of one end of the relationship are the duties of the other end, and vice versa.

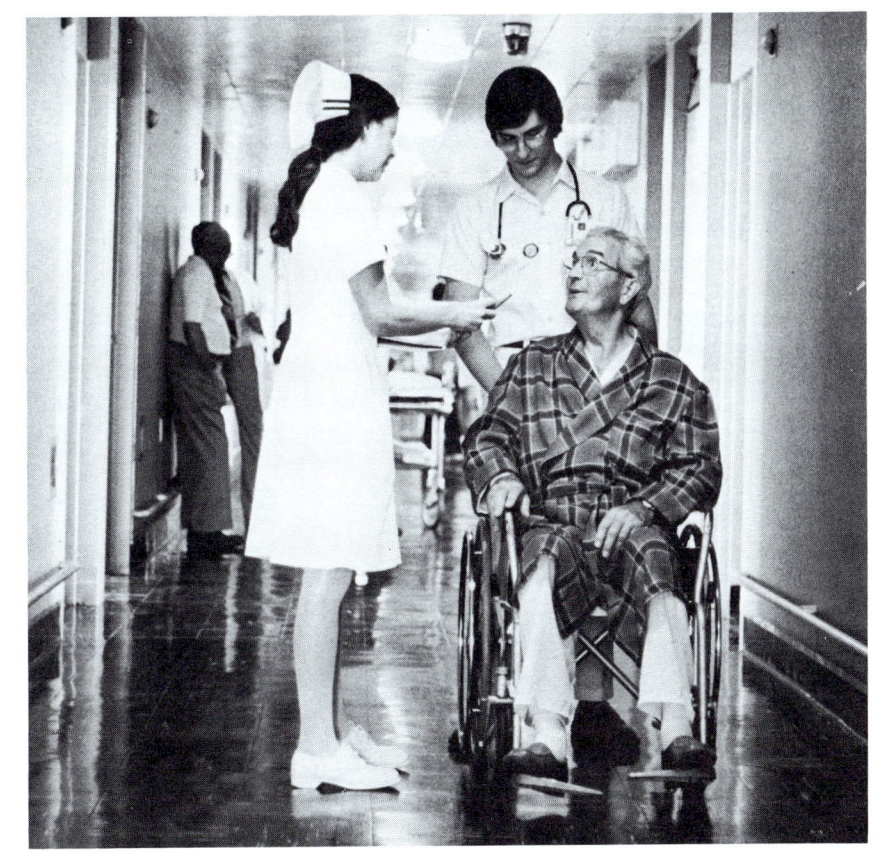

Patrick Reddy

case in point. It is tied to an array of other roles, including that of patient, physician, hospital aide, nursing supervisor, lab technician, ward secretary, and so on (see Figure 4.1).

Roles impinge on us as sets of norms that define our **rights**—the actions that we can legitimately insist that others perform—and **duties**—the actions which others can legitimately insist that we perform (Goffman, 1961:92). The rights that attach to a role are the duties attached to its reciprocal role or roles, and vice versa. Hence, nurses are required to do certain things for patients—they are expected to ascertain any unusual symptoms, to administer medications on schedule, to provide for the patient's physical care, and to allay the patient's anxieties. These are the duties of the role "nurse"; they are the reciprocal rights of the role "patient." In contrast, the rights of the nurse are the duties of the patient—nurses have the right to expect that patients will follow their instructions, that they will permit nurses to administer medications, and that they will inform nurses of their symptoms.

Roles are shorthand conceptions involving rights and duties. We are locked by life into the same social arena through networks of reciprocal roles. In sum, we are linked to one another through role relationships; the rights of one end are the duties of the other (Vander Zanden, 1977).

The concept of role-set finds expression in the process of the self that we considered in Chapter 3. We mentally take the stance of another individual and imaginatively portray what he or she expects of us in a given role (for instance, as a nurse or teacher). In so doing, we appraise our duties, or, in sociological terminology, we "take the role of the other." Simultaneously, we imagine the other person's duties toward us (for example, as a patient or student). By mentally exchanging roles in this fashion we can grasp the requirements for social interaction—what kinds of behaviors we can expect from them and them from us. The selfhood process provides the mechanism by which we can formulate our lines of action so as to realize joint action.

SOCIAL STRUCTURE

In the course of our daily lives we sense that human activities have a considerable element of organization to them. We more or less know what various individuals are likely to do (Goffman, 1974). Sociologists employ the concept of **social structure** to refer to the fact that many aspects of human interaction are characterized by a high degree of stability. A social structure is a configuration in which different categories of people are bound together within a network of relationships.

One way of viewing social structure is to conceive of it as a web of interconnected role-sets. Hence, the role-sets of physicians, patients, administrators, nurses, aides, and lab technicians, as they interlock with one another and become activated within networks of relationships, constitute that social structure that we term "hospital." Similarly, in much the same fashion, the role-sets of teachers, pupils, principals, school board members, and superintendents comprise the educational institution.

The concept of social structure recognizes the fact that our social world does not consist of just so many isolated individuals; rather, it consists of individuals who are classed as being of like kind (for instance, mothers, clergy, or Blacks) and who in turn are systematically linked in a web of relationships with certain other kinds of individuals (for instance, children, parishioners, or Whites). In relating ourselves to others, we define situations by attributing meaning to our own actions and to the actions of others. Individuals who share a common culture—similar cognitive (mental) maps—discriminate situations and actions in virtually the same manner. This eases the process by which they fit their lines of action together to achieve joint action (Blumer, 1969; Denzin, 1970). Consequently, as we experience much of social life, interaction does not occur in a random, unordered manner, but rather in terms of certain more or less patterned relationships.

ROLE-TAKING AND ROLE-MAKING

Life is not a having and getting, but a being and a becoming.

Matthew Arnold

The notion of social structure draws our attention to the relatively stable aspects of human interactions, namely, those sets of tried-and-proven recipes by which we construct our daily existence (Garfinkel, 1967). Some social scientists, especially those of the structure-function tradition (see Chapter 1), stress the recurrent and organized aspects of social life. They depict individuals as culturally programmed actors who "enact" the requirements spelled out by their societies' norms (Linton, 1936; Parsons, 1937, 1951, 1966). However, sociologists of the symbolic interactionist and ethnomethodological traditions (see Chapter 1) are critical of the structure-function formulation (Turner, 1962; Blumer, 1969; Cicourel, 1970). They label it a " 'black box' type of causal explanation" in which rights and duties enter at one end of the box only to mysteriously come out the other end as observed behaviors (Offenbacher, 1967).

Ralph H. Turner (1962, 1968a), a symbolic interactionist, points out that the notion that individuals play their roles in conformity with prevailing norms contains a much too simple and static picture of human life. Interac-

DEVISING OUR BEHAVIOR

OBSERVATION The university has a rule against smoking in classrooms but many professors do not enforce it. While in class today I got an irresistible urge to smoke. The classroom is a large auditorium and I was off near a corner. I was fairly certain that the professor would not spot me smoking, but my fellow students were another matter.

I undertook to "feel out" whether the students around me would let me get away with smoking. First, I took out the cigarette and tapped it on my desk a few times. Next I took out a match box and played with the cover. Then I took the cigarette and put it in my mouth, all the time twirling it around with my fingers.

"No objections? Well hell, light it up," I thought to myself. I sat there blowing smoke into the air but all the time keeping alert for any signs of disapproval. A girl two seats over gave out a cough and started waving smoke away from her face. I put the cigarette out.

PRINCIPLE Just what is and isn't allowed in life is not always clear. And if it is clear, there is no guarantee that people will enforce a particular norm. This was the case in class today. We devise our behavior with other people's responses in mind. We test the impact of our actions on others, mentally making inferences about their feelings toward us. I implemented step-by-step a course of action, all the time appraising the reactions of my classmates. I got as far as lighting up and taking a few drags, when a girl two seats over started kicking off cues that she disapproved of my smoking. So I in turn put out my cigarette.

tion has a tentative quality to it. It involves the selfhood process in which we continually test and revise our behavior in accordance with the meanings we mentally assign to people's actions. We seek to determine the intention and direction of acts, examining and interpreting them so as to uncover their implications for our own plans. Hence, the activities of others enter as a positive factor in the shaping of our own conduct. We abandon, alter, intensify, or replace given lines of activity in order to align and fit our actions to those of others (Blumer, 1966;1969). This process by which we *devise* our performance based on our interpretation of people's behavior is termed **role-taking** (Turner, 1962;1968a).

Interaction is built up point by point as we continually take one another's actions into account. Thus, our behavior is provisional and subject to change in accordance with our perception and interpretation of other's activities. Even though repetitive and well-established, each instance of a social act nonetheless requires its being formed *anew* (Blumer, 1969).

More often than not, however, we experience many situations in everyday life as problematic. We are confronted with uncertainty and obstacles of one sort or another. This leads us to innovation and improvisation; we create, shape, and modify roles in the course of social interaction. Hence role-taking also involves an element of **role-making**. In so doing we *produce* culture (Turner, 1962; Garfinkel, 1967; Stokes and Hewitt, 1976).

One example is the school superintendent (Gross, Mason, and McEachern, 1958). In many American communities, the superintendent functions as the manager of one of the largest local organizations—the school system. Such duties encompass not only the financial management of the enterprise; the superintendent is also its chief personnel officer. These responsibilities often pose conflicting expectations for the superintendent.

Take the matter of hiring and promoting teachers. Professional organizations, P.T.A. groups, teachers, school board members, local patriotic organizations, taxpayers, and politicians may make diametrically opposite demands on the superintendent in carrying out this duty. A local politician or school board member whose word carries great weight at city hall or with the city finance committee may ask the superintendent to recommend a friend or relative for a principalship vacancy. Big taxpayers may expect a voice in the selection of school executives. Patriotic groups may wish to scrutinize the "loyalty" of candidates. Professional organizations, P.T.A. groups, and teachers expect the superintendent to make decisions on the basis of merit alone. Likewise, contradictory pressures come to bear on the superintendent in teacher salary and budget recommendations: some groups and individuals call for new tax levies; others insist that salaries and budgets are already high enough.

In dealing with these conflicting pressures, the superintendent must adjudicate, balance, adjust, and juggle the contradictory requirements. Typically the superintendent gives in to this interest group here and that interest group there, all the while maneuvering and negotiating—advancing at this point, holding the line at some other point, and backtracking at still some other point. In the process, the contours of the role are hammered out, trimmed, and shaped; through *action* the role is fashioned.

In a similar manner, women and Blacks have brought about major changes in the requirements of their roles over the past decade or so. By acting in the manner of first-class citizens, they compelled arrangements of institutional sexism and racism to bend (Vander Zanden, 1977). Thus, as we pointed out in Chapter 2, social order is not a fixed given in human affairs. It is an order negotiated through the endless process by which humans fashion shared meanings and arrive at a working consensus.

Role-taking as role-making. Even when we are engaged in the playing of rather standardized roles, we add our own unique qualities to it. We continually improvise behavior and interpret the expectations of a role. Consequently, role-taking involves us in role-making.

Patrick Reddy

IMPRESSION MANAGEMENT

The world is governed more by appearances than by realities, so that it is fully as necessary to seem to know something as to know it.

Daniel Webster

We have noted that in social interaction we scrutinize people for words and deeds that will permit us to locate them within one or more social structures. In arriving at a definition of the situation, we undertake to assess people's roles in order to determine what we can expect of them and what they can expect of us. The counterpart of this process of assessment is what Erving Goffman (1959, 1967) terms **impression management**. Impression management is a process by which we undertake to define the situation for others by generating words, gestures, and actions that will lead them to act in accordance with our wishes.

Generally, we have a stake in the interaction that takes place between ourselves and others—we stand to gain or lose from it. Hence we are motivated to create a particular image of ourselves in the minds of other people. Only by influencing their ideas of us can we effect an advantageous outcome for ourselves. Through structuring others' definitions, we elicit—"ask for"—certain reciprocal behaviors from them. Because they take into account what we publicize about ourselves, we use the arts of concealment and strategic revelation to create various impressions (Goffman, 1959, 1974; Perinbanayagam, 1974).

Central to the process by which we undertake to manage the impressions which others form of us is **front**—the communications that serve to define the situation for an audience (Goffman, 1959; Ball, 1966; Stone, 1970; Perinbanayagam, 1974). One aspect of front is the *setting*—the scenery and props we use in staging our performance, for instance, the furniture, décor, physical layout, and other background items characterizing the offices of

IMPRESSION MANAGEMENT

OBSERVATION When I can, I hang around with a girl who is very popular and exceptionally attractive. We go out with one another now and then, although our relationship is not by any means intimate. Although we have very little in common, I believe that in the back of my mind I date her because I feel that my status is greater when I am seen with her. I believe that others say to themselves, "What a man he must be to attract a chick like that."

PRINCIPLE I am engaged in impression management, attempting to fabricate a positive image of myself in the minds of my peers (in truth, also in my own mind). I feel that being seen with this girl will elevate my status. However, I basically don't believe that I am exploiting her, since she looks to me to help her with math and chemistry when she runs into difficulty. I guess we both "use" one another.

Roles: The Fashioning of Everyday Life

Impression management. Because we have a stake in the outcomes of social interaction, we undertake to create a particular image of ourselves in the minds of others. By publicizing and transmitting certain meanings, we attempt to define the situation for others. In so doing, we generate those cues that will lead others to act as we might wish.

Patrick Reddy

business executives, college presidents, lawyers, and physicians. Another aspect is *personal front*—the expressive equipment that is intimately associated with the performers themselves, for example, clothing, grooming, posture, speech, bodily gestures, facial expressions, and titles ("Doctor," "Professor," "Mr. President," and so on).

Although front may be elaborately staged, it commonly occurs in very simple terms within everyday life (Fast, 1970). A smile is an example. A smile is not only a sign of humor or pleasure but also an apology, a symbol of defense, or even an excuse. I present you with a weak smile as I sit down next to you in a crowded cafeteria to say, "I don't mean to intrude but this is the only vacant place." Or if I am thrown against you in the bus, my smile says, "Sorry, I'm not trying to be nasty."

Impression management may also be undertaken by *teams* of individuals—casts of players. A family often seeks to project a collective image of itself to the neighbors, and each family member is expected to support a consistent "line" of self presentation to the world of outsiders. Similarly, workers often cooperate in concealing from their supervisors certain secret modes of gratification, job shortcuts, errors and mistakes, and unauthorized work breaks. Under these circumstances a bond of reciprocal dependence links teammates together. Each is forced to rely on the other, for any member of the team has the power to "give the show away" or to disrupt it by inappropriate behavior (Goffman, 1959).

One way we handle impression management is through the manipulation of *regions*—places that are bounded to some degree by barriers of perception. Goffman (1959) distinguishes between front regions (frontstage)—where the performance is presented—and back regions (backstage) where a performance is prepared. Very often individuals in the back region knowingly engage in actions that contradict their frontstage performances. Signs reading "Authorized Personnel Only" may highlight the separation between regions. Restaurants, for instance, seal off the dirty work of food preparation—garbage, grease, spoiled food, and unwashed glasses and dishes—from the enticing front-stage atmosphere. And backstage, waiters and waitresses can drop the pose of geniality that they maintain in the presence of the customers.

Goffman's treatment of the presentation of self in everyday life underscores the subtle and frequently hidden variations in our behavior that occur as we move from one social situation to another. However, the picture we gain of human beings is not particularly commendable and human life emerges as one gigantic "con game." As Kenneth J. Gergen (1968) points out, Goffman's treatment is insufficient. It provides a discerning view of the chameleonlike behavior of people but gives little consideration to behavior we feel to be "authentic." In many contexts, as with friends, lovers, and family members, we experience relationships as genuine, sincere, and honest; we perceive these meaningful others not as means to some ulterior end but as ends in their own right.

ROLES AND IDENTITY

> Everyone is always and everywhere, more or less consciously, playing a role. . . . It is in these roles that we know each other; it is in these roles that we know ourselves.
>
> *Robert Ezra Park,* Race and Culture, *1950*

To *be* a particular kind of person is not merely to possess the proper attributes. It is also necessary that we sustain the behaviors our fellow group members attach to this kind of person (Goffman, 1959). Our sense of being a particular kind of person influences our selection of various roles. Simultaneously, our sense of being a particular kind of person is shaped by our roles. Hence, the relation between the kind of person we are and our roles is a reciprocal one.

123 Roles: The Fashioning of Everyday Life

"WHO AM I?"

The person is composed of the roles he enacts.
  Hans H. Gerth and C. Wright Mills, Character and Social Structure, 1953

Viewed in its simplest fashion **identity** is our answer to the question "Who am I?" The answer arises out of role-taking. Our roles, by placing us in relation to others in role-sets and more broadly in a social structure, establish *where* and *what* we are in social terms. And establishing where and what we are, we derive a sense of *who* we are. Hence, in the course of role-taking we come to know each other and, perhaps more importantly for us, we come to know ourselves.

Identity. Our identity provides us with answers to the question "Who am I?"

Patrick Reddy

Our sense of identity arises out of social interaction:

> Identities are socially bestowed. They must also be socially sustained, and fairly steadily so. One cannot be human all by oneself and, apparently, one cannot hold on to any particular identity all by oneself. The self-image of the officer as an officer can be maintained only in a social context in which others are willing to recognize him in this identity. If this recognition is suddenly withdrawn, it usually does not take very long before the self-image collapses. (Berger, 1963, p. 100)

Thus, role-taking determines our personality—not in the sense of being the only determinant but of being an inescapable one.

VALID IDENTITY

Men can starve from a lack of self-realization as much as they can from a lack of bread.
Richard Wright, Native Son, *1940*

Our need for a valid identity is basic; we all need to "be somebody" (see Research Study 7). Our society offers us great variety in the kinds of person we can become. But the particular somebody we become is of less importance than that we come to recognize ourselves as authentic beings (Rainwater, 1970). Our sense of a valid identity arises out of social interaction. It is established when others *place* us as a social object by assigning us the same identity that we announce for ourselves. It is the coincidence of placements and announcements that is the basis of a valid identity.

The maintenance of a valid identity constitutes a lifelong task, beginning in infancy and continuing until death. We seek to build valid identities that will meet our needs. In so doing we use the resources that our culture makes available to us. We try on identities that emerge from the cultural material available to us and test them by making appropriate announcements. If these announcements meet with success, we generally maintain the identity until it is no longer validated by others or is no longer congruent with our inner promptings (Rainwater, 1970).

But for the most part life is not a simple matter. Valid identities are not always easy to come by or to maintain. One of the deepest anxieties we can experience is that resulting from a loss of identity. Indeed, we are anchored to reality and purpose by a firm sense of who we are. Amnesia presents an extreme illustration of this fact:

> There are few human conditions more frightening than amnesia, where the individual, cut off from such a sense [of identity], drifts aimlessly, his actions without meaning or purpose to himself. When an amnesia victim goes to some authority in his plight, it is to get help in finding out *who* he is. And it is always striking to see how zealously other people set to work to hook him back onto the identity from which he

Roles: The Fashioning of Everyday Life

Identities as a social product. We construct our identities—conceptions of who we are and a sense of our social value—through what others tell us about ourselves in the course of everyday life. In this sense reality does not exist; rather we *fashion* reality through the dynamic flow of life experience, and, more importantly, through the meanings we assign to such experience. Accordingly, valid identities are not established once and for all, but are a continual lifetime process.

Patrick Reddy

has come loose. Whatever his problems may be, there seems to be no way to get at them until he recommits himself to a particular identity in a world of other identities, and until he becomes a specific person again. (Goodenough, 1963, p. 176)

One important source of identity problems is role strain. Anything that interferes with our placement in the social structure—that makes uncertain the expectations operating upon us—has consequences for our identity. This is so since roles establish what and where we are in social terms. They provide us with answers to the question "Who am I?" Role strain serves to place us in situations where the answers supplied to us are in conflict or where they are nebulous and ill-defined. Let us consider this matter of role strain more closely.

RESEARCH STUDY 7

FACE-SAVING AT THE SINGLES DANCE*
Bernard Berk

Problem. Erving Goffman (1967) points out that maintaining "face" is essential to sustained social interaction. *Face* refers to an individual's sense of worth and respect. People commonly experience a loss of face as psychologically disconcerting and painful. Accordingly, they undertake face-saving actions that are designed to minimize feelings of embarrassment, rejection, and stigma. Bernard Berk was interested in identifying various techniques that people employ in everyday life to ward off potentially damaging evaluations by others.

Method. Within the United States singles dances bear somewhat the stigma of "lonely hearts clubs." Attendance at such dances is often taken to mean that the individual is a "social reject," "misfit," or "loser." The impersonal nature of singles dances has led them to be labeled "body exchanges," "meat markets," "cattle auctions," and other derogatory nicknames. Berk, a sociologist, attended over seventy singles dances in Los Angeles, San Francisco, Boston, and New York as a participant (he "went to the dances to meet women"). In due course he became interested in the sociological aspects of singles dances and secured the help of four research assistants and thirty students in collecting observations and interviewing subjects.

Findings. Patrons must cope with the stigma of attending a singles dance and with the potential rejection associated with seeking a partner. In so doing, they typically employ a variety of face-saving strategies:

- They may *enhance their presentations* by emphasizing positive attributes and downgrading negative aspects—coming with a same-sex friend, arriving late, and leaving early in order to project an image of respectability and popularity.
- They may *limit their involvement* by creating displays of detachment from the event or others—physically locating themselves in an inaccessible place or totally engrossing themselves in a conversation with a same-sex friend.
- They may *one-down others*—label the other patrons "creeps," "dogs," "stuck-up bitches," and so on.
- They may *deny* the stigmatic aspects of the situation, deliberately choosing to highlight the socially positive features of the dance.
- They may *withdraw*, leaving the situation entirely.
- They may attempt to *change the self*, modifying their stigmatizing characteristics (seeking therapeutic help, taking dancing lessons, and so on).
- They may *accept* popular definitions of themselves, succumbing to shame and incorporating the stigma within their social identity.

Conclusion. Berk does not claim that his list of coping mechanisms is exhaustive. However, the techniques are suggestive of those which people employ to minimize threats to their self-esteem. The study highlights the importance of "facework" in social interaction.

---

* Adapted from Bernard Berk, "Face-Saving at the Singles Dance," *Social Problems,* 24 (1977):530–544.

ROLE STRAIN

> To live is to adapt.
> *Johann W. von Goethe*

Role strain refers to circumstances in which people experience difficulties in meeting the demands and expectations associated with a role. It covers a variety of situations that individuals find to be stressful. For our purposes, we shall consider two sources of role strain: role conflict and role ambiguity.

ROLE CONFLICT

Individuals may be exposed to incompatible expectations—role conflict. In other words, people find themselves confronted with incompatible demands that they cannot completely or realistically fulfill. The crux of the matter lies in the fact that a social relationship involves at least two people, each of whom has a set of expectations concerning the behavior of the other. Conflict arises either because role partners have contradictory expectations or because those of one partner are unwelcome to the other. We shall single out here the following sources of role conflict for more detailed treatment:

1. Individuals may be confronted with the expectations of roles that they find incompatible or uncongenial with certain of their personality characteristics.
2. Individuals may be confronted with conflicting expectations stemming from their simultaneous assumption of two or more roles.
3. Individuals may be confronted with conflicting expectations deriving from their relationships with people who are identified with other roles in their role-set.
4. Individuals may be confronted with conflicting expectations associated with contradictory definitions of the appropriate responses demanded by a role.
5. Individuals may be confronted with conflicting expectations stemming from a lack of interrole consensus.

Let us consider each of these sources of role conflict in turn.

Roles Uncongenial with Particular Personalities. Individuals may be confronted with the demands and dictates of roles that they find incompatible or uncongenial with certain of their personality characteristics:

Self-Definitions   VERSUS   Others' Expectations
and Needs

This is most apparent in the case of *ascribed* positions—that is, positions assigned to individuals independent of their unique qualities or abilities.

ROLES AND PERSONALITY

OBSERVATION It really hit home to me today how we may very literally be "different" individuals depending on the role we take at the time. I was in the supermarket and I observed a woman pushing her cart down the aisle. She was one of our cafeteria workers in the dorm dining hall. Now I have seen this woman daily for the past two school years and she is a terrible grouch. She is downright ornery and nasty to the students and she doesn't act any better toward her fellow workers.

Well, as I walked down the aisle and also noticed her on several other occasions in the supermarket, she was the most affectionate person I have ever seen when dealing with the two children who were with her. She was so sympathetic and understanding of the kids that I found it hard to believe. She came across in this setting as a kindly, warm person.

PRINCIPLE At any given time the roles we take have a profound impact on the kind of person we are. We may find that a particular role is uncongenial; we may resent the role and take it out on others who assume complementary roles in the role-set, for instance, students and co-workers. Other roles, for example, mother, we may find more acceptable to us — we may like playing it with consequences for our personality. In this sense, we display different dimensions of our personality depending on the role highlighted for us at the time.

Societies commonly use at least four reference points for the ascription of positions: (1) sex (gender); (2) age; (3) family (for instance, mother-child, brother-sister, uncle-nephew) relationships; and (4) birth into a socially established group (for example, class, caste, or religious group). At times, the cultural patterns associated with these roles may call for rather specific personality characteristics.

Race and ethnic membership (ascribed positions) still function to some degree within the United States as a source for the ascription of rather distinct personality types. Blacks are culturally defined as musical and athletic, Jews as shrewd and mercenary, Irish as quick-tempered and witty, and so forth. Members of given racial or ethnic groups often find, in relating to members of other groups, that a rather subtle but explicit expectation exists that they be the men and women of the stereotype. Yet by virtue of temperament and other needs, many individuals are either unwilling or incapable of responding in the designated fashion; they may find the obligations associated with a particular racial or ethnic stereotype uncongenial and unacceptable.

Conflicting Roles. Individuals may be confronted with contradictory expectations by virtue of their simultaneous assumption of two or more conflicting positions:

Roles: The Fashioning of Everyday Life

| Expectations Associated with Role A | VERSUS | Expectations Associated with Role B |

Accordingly, quite different and even antagonistic behavior may be demanded of them. William S. Gilbert comments humorously on such dilemmas (a commentary that no longer seems quite so humorous in view of the real-life revelations associated with the Nixon Administration) in the following dialogue between Ko-Ko and Pooh-Bah in *The Mikado*:

KO-KO   Pooh-Bah, it seems that the festivities in connection with my approaching marriage must last a week. I should like to do it handsomely, and I want to consult you as to the amount I ought to spend upon them.

POOH-BAH   Certainly. In which of my capacities? As First Lord of the Treasury, Lord Chamberlain, Attorney-General, Chancellor of the Exchequer, Privy Purse, or Private Secretary?

KO-KO   Suppose we say as Private Secretary.

POOH-BAH   Speaking as your Private Secretary, I should say that, as the city will have to pay for it, don't stint yourself, do it well.

KO-KO   Exactly—as the city will have to pay for it. That is your advice.

POOH-BAH   As Private Secretary. Of course you will understand that, as Chancellor of the Exchequer, I am bound to see that due economy is observed.

KO-KO   Oh! But you said just now "Don't stint yourself, do it well."

POOH-BAH   As Private Secretary.

KO-KO   And now you say that due economy must be observed.

POOH-BAH   As Chancellor of the Exchequer.

KO-KO   I see. Come over here, where the Chancellor can't hear us. (They cross the stage.) Now, as my Solicitor, how do you advise me to deal with this difficulty?

POOH-BAH   Oh, as your Solicitor, I should have no hesitation in saying "Chance it—"

KO-KO   Thank you. (Shaking his hand.) I will.

POOH-BAH   If it were not that, as Lord Chief Justice, I am bound to see that the law isn't violated.

KO-KO   I see. Come over here where the Chief Justice can't hear us. (They cross the stage.) Now, then, as First Lord of the Treasury?

POOH-BAH   Of course, as First Lord of the Treasury, I could propose a special vote that would cover all expenses, if it were not that, as Leader of the Opposition, it would be my duty to resist it, tooth and nail. Or, as Paymaster-General, I could so cook the accounts that, as Lord High Auditor, I should never discover the fraud. But then, as Archbishop of Titipu, it would be my duty to denounce my dishonesty and give myself into my own custody as First Commissioner of Police.

KO-KO   That's extremely awkward. (Cerf and Klopfer, 1963:354–355)

Ko-Ko's final statement sums up the matter: many people find themselves in awkward situations by virtue of having to play simultaneously two or more conflicting roles.

College students often report that they experience role conflict when their parents pay them a visit. They feel "on stage" before two audiences holding somewhat contradictory expectations. They think their parents view them in some respects as dependent "children" while their peers see them as "adults." Moreover, the life-styles of the two groups frequently clash.

Incompatible expectations likewise confront many public officials. Political party loyalty may conflict in letter as well as spirit with the impartial behavior expected of a judge or administrator. Military chaplains provide another illustration. As officers in the armed forces they are expected to remain socially distant from the enlisted personnel and promote military aims. As priests, ministers, or rabbis, they are expected to be accessible to the rank-and-file and pursue the path of their religious vocation (Burchard, 1954; Abercombie, 1977). All these situations share in common two conditions: (1) the same person simultaneously assumes two positions; (2) the two positions confront the individual with conflicting expectations.

Role conflict. Is the police officer to be a stern, tough enforcer of the law or a sympathetic, understanding friend to the community?

Don McCarthy

131 Roles: The Fashioning of Everyday Life

ROLE CONFLICT

OBSERVATION For the past three years I have worked on the loading dock of a large retail appliance store. Well, five months ago I received a promotion and was made the supervisor. I used to load trucks with all the guys that now work under me, and at times I feel very uneasy when I have to get after the guys to work faster and harder. I understand how aggravating it is for a boss to constantly hound you for more work. All of these guys are my friends, but in my new role I am required to get them to do things that I always hated to do myself. I have to play the role of both supervisor and friend, and it isn't the best situation to be in, believe me!

PRINCIPLE I am confronted with conflicting expectations because I am assuming two contradictory roles simultaneously—supervisor and friend. The boss expects me to get the most work I can out of the guys; the guys expect me to be understanding and take it easy on them.

Role-Set Conflicts. Earlier in the chapter we noted that many roles have a number of reciprocal or complementary roles associated with them—a role-set. By virtue of a role-set, many individuals find themselves in several different kinds of relationships. Each of these relationships may call for quite different behavior; indeed, at times the expectations may be in conflict:

| Expectations Associated with Reciprocal Role A | VERSUS | Expectations Associated with Reciprocal Role B |

The school superintendent, for instance, must deal with parents, teachers, school board members, politicians, officials of patriotic organizations, and so on. Generally speaking, the more diversified the related roles, the greater will be the role strain—that is, the greater the difficulty experienced in job performance (Snoek, 1966). The superintendent's role fits well up on the scale of diversification.

Conflict Among Expectations. A role typically calls for several responses in relation to another role. But the responses dictated may be at variance with one another:

| Expectation A of a Role | VERSUS | Expectation B of a Role |

In the doctor–patient relationship, for instance, three facets characterize the doctor's role: (1) The doctor is expected to be a scientist-warrior on the frontiers of knowledge. In terms of this facet of the relationship, the doctor is expected to see the patient from a detached point of view much in the same fashion as the doctor would view a guinea pig—as a subject for scientific research, experimentation, and testing. (2) The doctor is expected to be a gentle technician—savior of the sick. Here humanitarian and self-sacrificing principles are expected to govern the doctor's behavior; the doctor's task is one of curing the ill. (3) Finally, the doctor is expected to be a small-business retailer of knowledge, which the doctor has obtained at considerable cost. While aggressive bill collecting is consistent with the small-business retailer aspects of the doctor's role, it is inconsistent with the image of the gentle healer or the altruistic scientist (Lee, 1944).

Supervisors are similarly confronted with conflicting demands in their interaction with the people under them. They are often uncertain as to what constitutes a "real" leader. They wonder: "Should I be a good Joe and mix with my people, or should I maintain my position as a supervisor?" They are asked to be both a commanding parental figure and a reassuring, comforting big brother or sister. There seems to be no accepted, well-defined answer to the dilemma posed by these contradictory expectations.

Conflict Stemming from a Lack of Interrole Consensus. Individuals do not always see eye-to-eye on what they expect of each other:

Individual A's Definition of the Expectations (the Duties and Rights) Associated with A's own Role	VERSUS	Individual B's Definition of the Expectations (the Duties and Rights) Associated with A's Role

People may disagree on their respective rights and duties. Such disagreements may derive from a variety of sources. Individuals may lack consensus on what expectations are included in a given role; newly hired secretaries, for example, may feel that they are entitled to a fifteen-minute coffee break each morning and afternoon, whereas their boss may disapprove of coffee breaks. Individuals may disagree on the range of permitted or prohibited behavior; a boss, for instance, may disagree with a newly hired secretary in believing that, although a ten-minute coffee break is permissible, a fifteen-minute coffee break is not. Individuals may disagree on the situation in which given expectations may apply; a boss and a newly hired secretary, for example, may disagree in believing that the secretary should take coffee breaks only during slack seasons when the work load is light. In any event, where consensus is lacking, concerted action by individuals is impaired, and they are likely to be anxious and uncertain regarding their privileges and obligations.

MECHANISMS FOR DEALING WITH ROLE CONFLICT

Individuals confronted with unwelcome or incompatible expectations—with role conflict—find themselves in stressful circumstances. They are pulled in differing directions by opposing forces. How do people deal with such circumstances? In truth, the mechanisms for handling role conflict run into the hundreds, and a consideration of them here would lead us far afield. Hence, our discussion is at best merely suggestive.

One approach for dealing with conflicting expectations is **compartmentalization**. Individuals subdivide their lives, so to speak, and within a given context act in accordance with the dictates of one role while ignoring the other. In a word, individuals temporarily abdicate one of the conflicting roles; they wall themselves off from it. Many college students, for example, may abdicate the role of a dependent "child" before their peers and that of an independent "adult" before their parents. Compartmentalization becomes a feasible approach to the extent to which two roles are ordinarily taken on different stages, such as one at school and another at home.

Role conflict may be handled through a **hierarchy of obligations**. See Figure 4.2. Individuals interacting with one another usually recognize that certain obligations take precedence over others. For example, in the case of death in one's family, obligations to comfort the bereaved and to make funeral arrangements take precedence over occupational obligations. Indeed, excuses frequently reflect this type of conflict resolution: "I would like to but I can't because . . . ," followed by assertion of a higher priority.

Individuals can also handle their role conflict through banding together for *mutual support and concerted action*. Whatever they may believe to the contrary, the occupants of a position are not alone. The very fact that they are placed in a position means that there are others who share a similar fate. By virtue of this fact, individuals need not deal with conflicting expectations in a wholly private manner. By banding together, they can often constitute a force sufficient to lessen or negate the power of those in some counterpositions. Thousands of librarians, for example, sparsely distributed among the towns and villages of America and not infrequently subject to censorial pressures, receive strong support against censorship from the American Library Association.

Still another mode of individual resolution takes the form of *reducing dependence on the group or role partner supporting one of the expectations*. Individuals achieve this by leaving the group, by redefining its value to them, or by making it irrelevant to the conflict situation. The first method is illustrated by priests who resign from the clergy (see Research Study 8). The second is illustrated by a woman who, caught in a conflict between her position as a wife and her position as a career woman, responds by redefining her marriage as of lesser importance. The third method is illustrated by chaplains in the armed forces who make their officer rank irrelevant in their relations with the enlisted personnel (Secord and Backman, 1964).

Role conflict need not be handled in a rational manner. For example, Elton F. Jackson (1962) found that many people respond to the stresses posed by role conflict with psychophysiological symptoms. Those with role inconsistencies were more likely than others to be troubled with spells of dizziness, upset stomachs, nervousness, insomnia, nightmares, and similar symptoms.

Figure 4.2. Some mechanisms for handling role conflict.

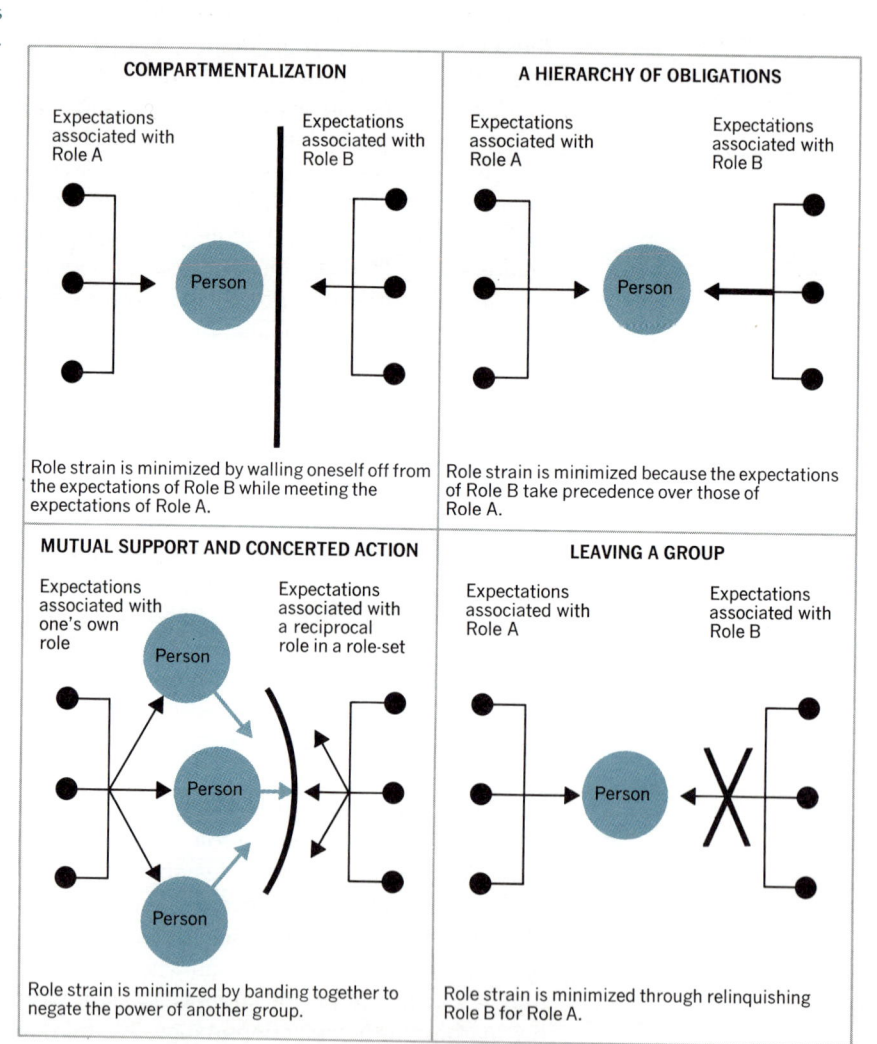

COMPARTMENTALIZATION
Role strain is minimized by walling oneself off from the expectations of Role B while meeting the expectations of Role A.

A HIERARCHY OF OBLIGATIONS
Role strain is minimized because the expectations of Role B take precedence over those of Role A.

MUTUAL SUPPORT AND CONCERTED ACTION
Role strain is minimized by banding together to negate the power of another group.

LEAVING A GROUP
Role strain is minimized through relinquishing Role B for Role A.

RESEARCH STUDY 8

BECOMING AN EX-PRIEST*
Frances A. DellaCava

Problem. Within daily life people move in and out of a good many roles. Some roles, however, tend to be core roles about which other roles are organized. Such roles entail a high level of commitment. The role of a Roman Catholic priest is an example of a high commitment role. Despite this fact, many individuals have left the priesthood. Based on data from the National Opinion Research Center (NORC), Richard A. Schoenherr and Andrew M. Greeley (1974) estimate that in the six years between 1966 and 1972 over one-eighth of the Roman Catholic clergy within the United States resigned. In this study Frances A. DellaCava undertook to identify the process by which individuals leave the priesthood.

Method. DellaCava gathered data for the study by open-ended, depth interviews with 35 ex-priests. Seven were contacted through the National Association for Pastoral Renewal and three from individual sources. The remaining 25 men were suggested by the initial sample of 10 former priests (a snowballing technique for securing respondents). The ex-priests were questioned concerning the expectations that they had had for the priesthood, their satisfactions in the role, their role conflicts, and the process by which they had become disenchanted with the priesthood.

Findings. Induction into the priesthood is carried out in physical isolation from the secular world so as to maximize the effectiveness of the Church's socialization. After becoming a priest, a man's life is restricted to those activities that are defined as extensions of the priestly role. Nevertheless, a priest is not immune from the influence of the larger world. Public opinion data reveal that a majority of American priests differ with the official papal position regarding birth control and celibacy.

All the ex-priest's in DellaCava's sample reported problems with the authority structure of the Roman Catholic Church, disenchantment with the nature of their work and with their fellow priests, and disagreement with some of the Church's positions on theological and social issues. All but three cited celibacy as a major problem for them. Indeed it was celibacy that in most cases was the key issue in the decision to resign.

The process of leaving the priesthood usually began with a shift in social relationships. The man typically found himself more "involved" with women as he widened his contact with the lay world (for instance, in college communities or urban poverty programs). These liaisons at first were defined in nonsexual terms. However, the relationships afforded new self-images and self-definitions. In turn, the priests tended to seek out other priests like themselves who provided support for their nontraditional theological views and their emerging life-styles. In so doing, their ties to the established religious community were weakened. These new relationships with supportive priests functioned as a waystation between the clerical and secular worlds. Such groups facilitated the erosion of the men's identities as priests and created new identities for them outside the priesthood.

Continued on next page.

---

* Adapted from Frances A. DellaCava, "Becoming an Ex-Priest: The Process of Leaving a High Commitment Status," *Sociological Inquiry*, 45 (1975):41–49.

Generally the priests experienced a growing awareness of acute inconsistency within their lives. Many of their relationships, especially those with women, were not consistent with traditional expectations regarding the priestly role. At first they tended to deny to themselves that their relationships with women were unorthodox; rather they attempted to interpret them as part of a legitimate concern for and a love of other persons. When professions of love, affection, and sexual intercourse occurred, they were categorized as "lapses."

As "friendship" with a woman continued and interaction with fellow priests was limited almost exclusively to the "deviant group," the priest ceased to deny the relationship and instead came to acknowledge and accept it. Some of the priests rationalized the break with their vows of celibacy as an extension and culmination of spiritual love. Others came to "believe" that it was only a matter of time before the Pope would permit the clergy to marry and therefore concluded that there was no point in their waiting until the rule was officially changed. By reinterpreting their new relationships as either conformity to the ideal norms of the priesthood (celibacy being defined as at odds with the true expression of Christian love) or as the forerunners of a formal change in priestly obligations, the inconsistency between past commitments and present standards was resolved. In the process the men relinquished their identities as priests and established new identities based on their new activities and relationships.

Conclusion. DellaCava concludes:
The conditions under which conflict over celibacy becomes translated into resignation from the priesthood are: (1) establishment of new primary relationships which provide support for the move out; and, (2) construction of mechanisms of legitimation which make the new decision acceptable within the context of the prior option for celibacy and priesthood. Both of these conditions are vital to the successful resocialization which is a prerequisite to leaving the priesthood. (p. 49)

ROLE AMBIGUITY

We have considered how role conflict may contribute to role strain (difficulties in meeting the expectations associated with a role). Individuals may experience role strain for still another reason: their roles may lack clarity. The guideposts by which they find direction and social anchorage may be ambiguous and nebulous. Finding themselves in a more or less amorphous setting, they may become confused as to what is expected of them. For our purposes here, we shall consider three types of role ambiguity: (1) lack of clarity deriving from the newness of a role, (2) lack of clarity stemming from rapid social and cultural change that alters the established expectations associated with a role, and (3) lack of clarity deriving from discontinuities encountered in passage from one role to another. Let us examine each of these sources of role ambiguity in turn.

Emergent Roles. Newly emerging and developing roles generally lack clear-cut expectations whereby individuals can guide their behavior. Walter I. Wardwell, in a study of a relatively new occupation—that of chiropractor—notes how a lack of clarity contributes to strain:

... lack of clarity in the definition of the role hampers adjustment, producing strain. ... There is vast ignorance on the part of patients and potential patients as to what chiropractors do, and, more important, chiropractors themselves disagree on the question of what chiropractic treatment should be. The "straights" limit themselves to spinal manipulation alone, sometimes "adjusting"-only upper cervical vertebrae, while the "mixers" also use heat, light, air, water, exercise, diet regulation, and electric modalities in their treatment. State laws differ as widely in the scope of practice they permit. In most states chiropractors are limited to spinal manipulation and simple hygienic measures, while in others they may perform minor surgery, practice obstetrics, and sign death certificates.

Today there are an estimated 20,000 chiropractors in active practice (as against 278,500 medical doctors). More than five million people visit chiropractors each year. The American Medical Association has long opposed chiropractic, labeling it "an unscientific cult whose practitioners lack the training and background to diagnose and treat human disease." The medical establishment stereotypes chiropractic as appealing to the value systems of the rural and poorer populations, " 'legitimizing' the sick status of patients with whom physicians can find nothing wrong." At the same time, the chiropractor is seen as relieving the physician of "troublesome, time-consuming" patients. Despite this opposition and hostility from the medical profession, chiropractic is becoming firmly entrenched as an alternative form of health care. Chiropractors are licensed in all fifty states, and their services can be reimbursed through Medicare and, in most states, Medicaid and Workmen's Compensation Boards (Brody, 1975).

Role Ambiguity Associated with Rapid Change. Individuals may experience role strain when immersed within a rapidly changing social and cultural setting. They may find that established norms and values have altered beyond the point of the instability that they have come to expect through past experience. Such an undermining of individuals' stable expectations may be of varying duration and intensity. At the extreme, it may progress to the point where people literally "do not know what to expect," posing severe identity problems for them.

Post-World War II race relations within the United States provide an illustration of this. Large numbers of Blacks were drawn from small towns and rural communities and propelled into an urban, industrial world. As the Black population migrated to urban centers, the traditional structure of race relations, characterized by Black subordination and adapted to a feudal, rural environment, became no longer appropriate. Old guideposts governing relations between the races became irrelevant and old identities were undermined.

Accompanying these changes were new definitions of Black rights. Of landmark importance was the action of the Supreme Court in its 1954 school ruling in which it overturned the old "separate but equal" doctrine formulated in 1896 in *Plessy v. Ferguson* (a decision that had relegated Blacks to second-class citizenship and gave legal sanction to a segregated racial order) and redefined Blacks as first-class citizens. Presidential statements and Congressional enactment of new civil rights laws reinforced the effect of the Supreme Court's decision. These developments were closely associated with another important stimulus to new Black self-definitions, the emergence of the new nations of Africa. The late Rev. Martin Luther King, Jr. observed:

> . . . today he [the Black] looks beyond the borders of his own land and sees the decolonization and liberation of Africa and Asia; he sees colored peoples, yellow, black and brown, ruling over their own new nations. He sees colored statesmen voting on vital issues at the United Nations. . . . (1965, p. 26)

Changes of such magnitude produced considerable ambiguity as to just what the definition of the Black position in American life would and should be. The slogan "Black Power," with its connotations of racial pride, self-respect, and unity, represented an effort to evolve new guideposts and definitions together with new social identities.

Rapid social change, then, has an unsettling impact on role definitions and expectations. People find that old social anchorages no longer support them and old standards no longer guide them. New social perceptions and life styles emerge. Under such circumstances people often experience alienation, a condition in which they no longer feel attached to or a part of the existing social and political structure. They search for new guideposts and identities and become susceptible to sources that offer new standards and definitions to them. Such developments, as we have seen, have fed a variety of social movements within America's Black ghettos.

Discontinuities Encountered in Role Passage. Role strain may arise where a discontinuity or gap exists in the expectations associated with the transition from one role to another (Glaser and Strauss, 1971; Vizedom, 1976). Adolescents in American society present a classic illustration of this. Probably no society makes the transition from childhood to adulthood more difficult than we do in the United States (Kerckhoff, 1972; Dragastin and Elder, 1975; Sebald, 1977). We have developed very few patterns that dramatize the "coming of age" of adolescents. We have provided them with few guideposts by which to find direction. At adolescence, we expect boys and girls to stop being children, yet we do not expect them to be men or women. Any definitions that they have of their changing age roles are quite inconsistent. They are told they are no longer children but are treated like depen-

139 Roles: The Fashioning of Everyday Life

Discontinuities in role passage. Few patterns exist within the United States to provide the adolescent with consistent, sharply defined role expectations. It is not entirely clear when childhood ends and adulthood begins.

Patrick Reddy

dents, supported by their parents, and mistrusted for the tragedies that befall some adolescents—auto accidents, juvenile delinquency, unwanted premarital pregnancies, and drug addiction. In a word, there are many situations in which they scarcely know whether they are expected to act like adults or children. It is little wonder that some American youth experience identity problems.

Many societies make the trial of the adolescent much easier (Muensterberger, 1961; Schiamberg, 1969; Brown, 1969). Preliterate peoples often provide initiation ceremonies—puberty rites—that make the transition from one age to another both definite and relatively easy. The adolescents' people may subject them to various thoroughly distasteful, painful, and actually humiliating experiences during the ceremony, but then they are recognized as being grown up. They may be buried for a short while in an anthill or be forced to run up a hill without spilling the water from the containers they carry on their heads. But the tasks are clearly defined, and they know that if they pass the tests, they will be recognized as adults.

Research confirms that many individuals in the United States undergo changes in their self-images and self-conceptions during adolescence (Erikson, 1963, 1968; Monge, 1973; Waterman, Geary, and Waterman, 1974). Roberta G. Simmons, Florence Rosenberg, and Morris Rosenberg (1973) studied a sample of 1,197 Baltimore-area pupils in grades three through twelve. They found that 12- to 14-year-olds display a higher level of self-consciousness, greater instability of self-image, and lower levels of self-esteem than do younger children. Self-consciousness declines somewhat in later adolescence while the self-image becomes somewhat more stable. Nonetheless, even in late adolescence, the pupils showed greater self-consciousness and instability in self-image than did the eight- to eleven-year-olds. See Figures 4.3 and 4.4.

Figure 4.3. Increase in self-consciousness by age. The median score of eight-year-olds is subtracted from the median score of each subsequent age group. The points above "0" show a higher level of disturbance after age eight; points below "0" show a lower level.

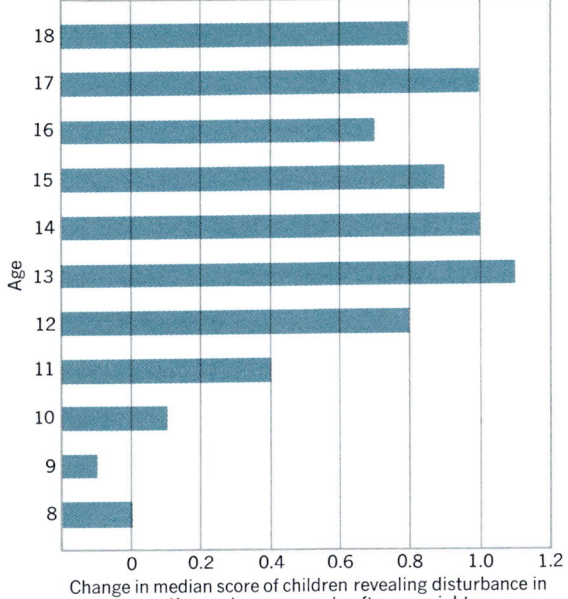

Source: Adapted from Roberta G. Simmons, Florence Rosenberg, and Morris Rosenberg, "Disturbances in the Self-Image at Adolescence," *American Sociological Review,* 38 (1973), 559.

Figure 4.4. Increase in unfavorable content of the self-image by age. The median score of eight-year-olds is subtracted from the median score of each subsequent age group.

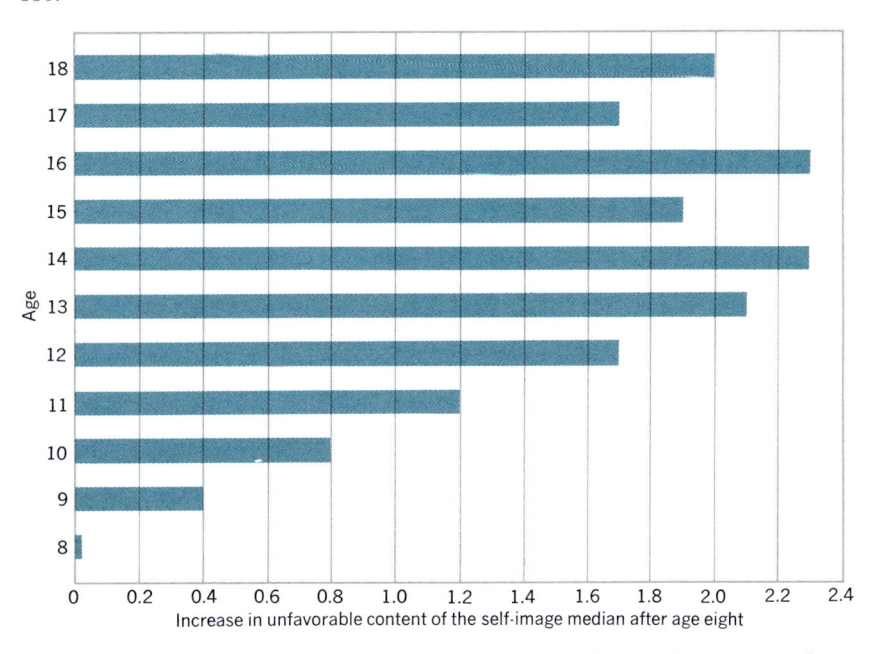

Source: Adapted from Roberta G. Simmons, Florence Rosenberg, and Morris Rosenberg, "Disturbance in the Self-Image at Adolescence," *American Sociological Review,* 38 (1973), 560.

SUMMARY

1. Social interaction requires that we define a situation. In defining a situation, we undertake to identify the roles of other people. Roles specify who does what, when, and where. They allow us to know what we can expect of others and what they can expect of us. Roles permit us to collapse or telescope a large number of behaviors into manageable bundles.

2. Roles do not exist by themselves in isolation from one another. A role is linked with a number of interdependent, complementary roles termed a role-set. Roles impinge on us as sets of norms that define our rights—the actions that we can legitimately insist that others perform—and duties—the actions that others can legitimately insist we perform. The rights that attach to a role are the duties attached to its reciprocal role or roles, and vice versa. We are locked by life into the same social arena through networks of reciprocal roles—the rights of one end of a relationship being the duties of the other.

3. Sociologists employ the concept of social structure to refer to the fact that many aspects of human interaction are characterized by a high degree of stability. A social structure is a configuration in which different categories of people are bound together within a network of relationships. One way of viewing social structure is to conceive of it as a web of interconnected role-sets.

4. Interaction has a tentative quality to it. It involves the selfhood process in which we continually test and revise our behavior in accordance with the meanings we mentally assign to people's actions. We abandon, alter, intensify, or replace given lines of activity in order to align and fit our actions to those of others. This process by which we devise our performance based on our interpretation of people's behavior is termed role-making.

5. We often experience social situations as problematic. We are confronted with uncertainty and obstacles. This leads us to innovation and improvisation; we create, shape, and modify roles in the course of social interaction. Hence role-taking involves an element of role-making.

6. Impression management is a process by which we undertake to define the situation for others by generating words, gestures, and actions that will lead them to act in accordance with our wishes. Central to the process by which we undertake to manage the impressions others form of us is front—the communications that serve to define the situation for an audience. Impression management may also be undertaken by teams of individuals. One way we handle impression management is through the manipulation of regions—places that are bounded to some degree by barriers of perception.

7. Viewed in its simplest fashion identity is our answer to the question "Who am I?" The answer arises out of role-taking. In the course of role-taking we come to know each other and, perhaps more importantly for us, we come to know ourselves.

8. Our need for a valid identity is basic; we all need to "be somebody." Our sense of being an authentic person arises out of social interaction. It is

established when others assign us the same identity that we announce for ourselves.

9. Role strain refers to circumstances in which people experience difficulties in meeting the demands and expectations associated with a role. One source of role strain is role conflict—individuals are exposed to incompatible expectations. Conflict arises either because role partners have contradictory expectations or because those of one partner are unwelcome to the other.

10. One approach for dealing with conflicting expectations is compartmentalization—individuals subdivide their lives and within a given context act in accordance with the dictates of one role while ignoring the other. Role conflict may also be handled through a hierarchy of obligations—individuals usually recognize that certain obligations take precedence over others. These are but two of the numerous mechanisms for dealing with role conflict.

11. In addition to role conflict, individuals may experience role strain by virtue of the fact that their roles lack clarity. Finding themselves in a more or less amorphous setting, they may become confused as to what is expected of them.

PART TWO

GROUP BEHAVIOR

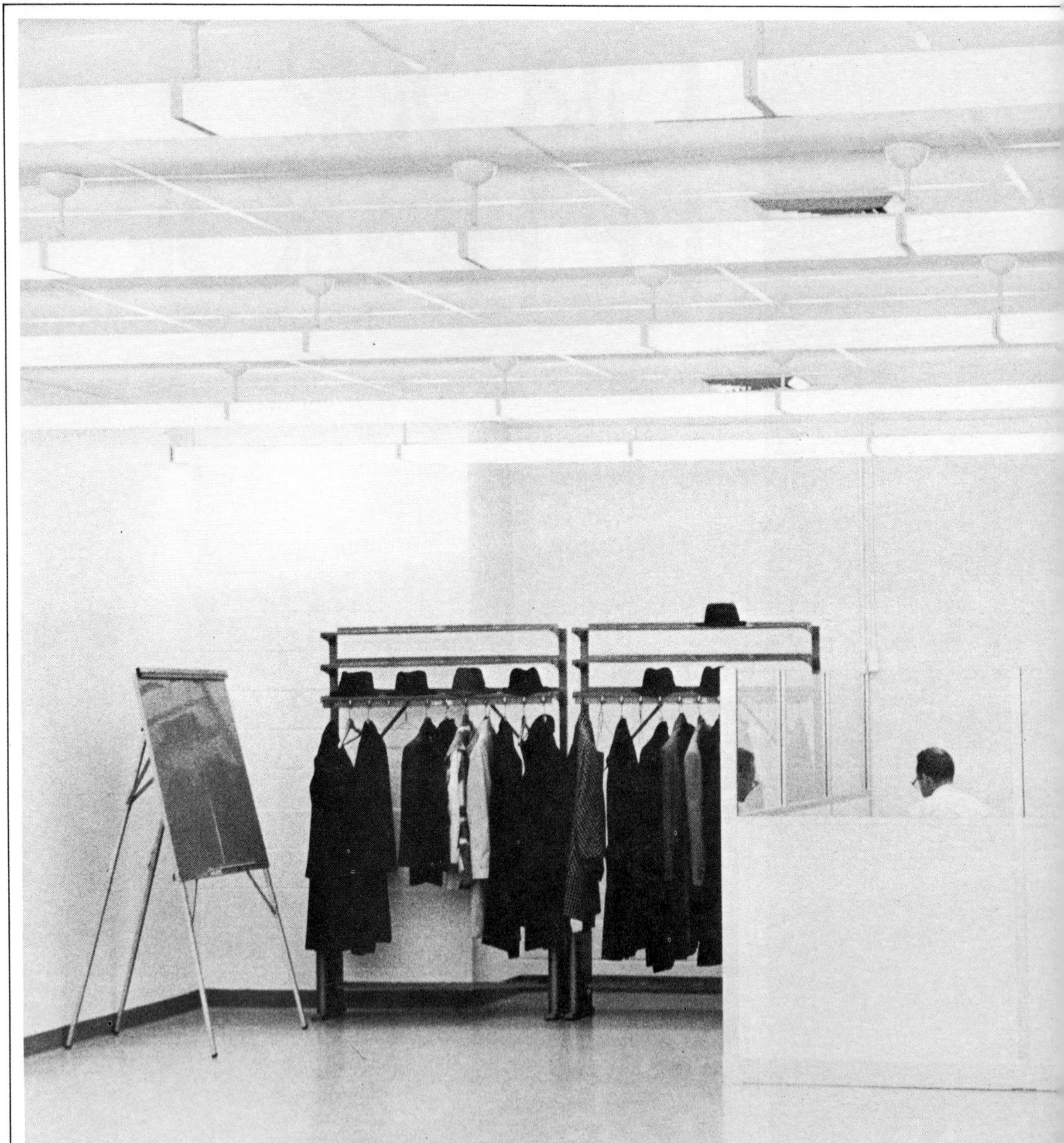

5
GROUPS AND FORMAL ORGANIZATIONS

THE NATURE OF GROUPS

STATISTICAL CATEGORIES

SOCIAL CATEGORIES

SOCIAL GROUPS
  Primary and Secondary Groups
  In-Groups and Out-Groups
  Reference Groups

FORMAL ORGANIZATIONS
  The Nature of Bureaucracy
  Weber's Conception of Bureaucracy
  Social Consequences of Bureaucracy
  Alternative Formulations Regarding Formal Organizations
  Informal Organization

OBSERVATION I went home over the weekend. While doing an errand downtown, I ran into Hank, my old high school buddy. For the past nine months, Hank has been working as a bank teller in a downtown bank. I noticed an astonishing change in the way Hank dresses and acts. Over the past couple of summers we worked together for a construction company resurfacing highways. We always used to "shoot the bull" and go out and get "blasted" together—really tore up the town. I can't remember him ever being out of greasy jeans and T-shirts. Now that Hank has a job at the bank, he wears double knit slacks and button-down shirts. While talking with him today I thought I was with a completely different guy. He wasn't the same old "shoot the bull" Hank. He acted very businesslike, reserved, and dignified which made me feel quite uncomfortable. I asked him to come up to the university to visit me so we could "party down." He said that he doubted if he would have the time and that it probably wouldn't look too good if the bank president found out about it. Hank has come to acquire the patterned behaviors expected by his banking associates.

PRINCIPLE To understand a person's behavior, we need to know which group is providing him with his frame of reference. The group that provides these standards is a reference group. Hank's behavior has changed because he has shifted reference groups. When attending high school and working for the construction company, he had a rowdy "hell-of-a-fellow" reference group. When he became a bank teller, he detached himself from his previous reference group and attached himself to a business reference group. This explains the very marked change in Hank's behavior.

Our humanness is rooted in group life. The cases of Anna and Isabelle which were discussed in Chapter 3 provided stark evidence in support of this fact. Isolated from human interaction for their first six years, they were little more than biological vegetables when "discovered" by authorities and removed from their secluded conditions. Anna and Isabelle subsequently acquired "human personalities" only as they were immersed in social environments and exposed to group experiences.

Additional evidence for the importance of the human group for us is found in settings in which individuals are deprived of meaningful group interaction. Huey P. Newton, a Black Panther leader imprisoned for twenty-two months, much of it in solitary confinement, observes:

> During the first few days out of jail, I wondered when reality would come again—in relation to myself, to the world around me, to all that was happening to me. I had literally forgotten how to live outside.
> I had to develop all over again my old reflex actions to avoid being startled or puzzled by certain phenomena. . . . [L]ife around me at first seemed jerky and out of synchronization. All the sounds, movements, and colors coming on simultaneously—television, telephone, radio, people talking, coming and going, doorbells and phones ringing—were dizzying at first. Ordinary life seemed hectic and chaotic, and quite

overwhelming. I even had to figure out what to eat and what time I was going to bed. In prison, all this had been decided for me. (1973, pp. 290–291)

Newton's observations find confirmation in the experiences of American POW's in the Korean War. The most significant feature of the Chinese prisoner camp program was the systematic destruction of the prisoners' formal and informal group structure. American officers were isolated from their men and replaced by Chinese leaders. The Chinese banned all nonindoctrination meetings and broke up non-Communist group activity by reassigning POW leaders or key members to other camps. Distrust was systematically fomented by playing the prisoners off against each other. From informers or spies, the Chinese received detailed information about a prisoner's activities and then subjected the prisoner to intense interrogation about them. Such detailed surveillance of the men's activities made them feel that their ranks were so infiltrated by the enemy that it was not safe to trust anyone. Division was further promoted by bestowing special favors upon collaborators and by demoralizing the Americans with germ-warfare confessions and peace appeals made by some of their number. Such tactics reduced the person to a social isolate — to the naked impotence of an unsupported individual — and so prepared the way for varying degrees of collaboration (Schein, 1957). In other words, the POW was stripped of meaningful group membership: the POW group no longer functioned as a viable instrument for supporting opposition to the enemy, for meeting various social and psychological needs, and for maintaining American patriotic allegiance. As such, the POW became vulnerable to Chinese pressures for collaboration.

THE NATURE OF GROUPS

We would find it difficult to discuss groups very long without finding that we use the term "group" to refer to many different collections of people — dog owners, women, Italian-Americans, schizophrenics, jewelers, grandparents, students, Billy Graham enthusiasts, bald-headed men, clique members, widows, Democrats, smokers, members of the middle class, Texans, and so on. Within some of these "groups," there may be other groups — students, for example, are divided into first-graders, college sophomores, graduate students, and so on; males and females; married and nonmarried students; Democrats, Republicans, Socialists, and Independents; Catholics, Jews, Moslems, Lutherans, atheists, and the like; majors in sociology, chemistry, physical education, and a variety of other fields; members of the student senate, the football team, the YMCA, the mountain climbers club, fraternities, and a good many other organizations. In fact, there are more groups in any society than there are individuals in it.

This multitude of groups is so diversified that we find it difficult, if not impossible, to characterize them except in very general terms. In the broadest sense, each of our illustrations above constitutes a **group**—a collection of people with certain common attributes. Since this concept of a group is so broad, sociologists have attempted to distinguish between types of groups.

Chemists have arranged the substances that they study into a number of classes—elements—that form the building blocks of compounds. Biologists have arranged plants and animals into classes, called species, and in turn species are divided into varieties. Sociologists, however, have not yet succeeded in realizing a fully satisfactory classification of groups. Classifications do not, as such, exist in the nature of phenomena. For analytical purposes, we impose categories on phenomena. Hence, the same phenomenon may be classified in any number of ways, although not all the possibilities are equally logical or useful.

In classifying groups, we find particularly useful the scheme originally suggested by Robert Bierstedt (1948), which we have modified here to suit our needs. We may single out three properties or criteria for the purpose of distinguishing among groups: (1) *consciousness of kind*—the tendency of people to recognize others like themselves; (2) *social relations between individuals*—the mutual and reciprocal influencing by two or more people of each other's feelings, attitudes, and actions; and (3) *goal-oriented associations*—social units deliberately constructed to seek specific ends. Employing these three criteria, we may distinguish among four types of groups as exhibited in Figure 5.1: statistical categories, social categories, social groups, and formal organizations.

TYPES OF GROUPS

OBSERVATION I belong to a Women's Liberation rap group which meets every Tuesday evening. We started as a statistical category in that we all are women (53 percent of the country's population). We became a social category when along the way we had our consciousness raised and became aware of the oppression we experienced in common. When we came to perceive ourselves as members of an oppressed group, we started interacting on this basis and constituted a social group. When we organized for the purpose of advancing the interests of women we became a formal organization.

PRINCIPLE As a statistical category, we were a demographic entry in the Census records. As a social category, a consciousness of kind had come to exist. As a social group, we entered into relationships wherein we reciprocally influenced one another's feelings, attitudes, and actions. As a formal organization, we deliberately formalized our relationship to realize a goal.

Figure 5.1. Types of groups.

	Consciousness of kind	Social relations between individuals	Goal-oriented associations
Statistical categories	−	−	−
Social categories	+	−	−
Social groups	+	+	−
Formal organizations	+	+	+

Before proceeding with a consideration of each of these four types of groups, we should note that this is not an inclusive classification. Some groups are not included in the scheme—for example, those that involve social relations but lack a consciousness of kind, and those made up not of individuals but of other groups. Further, we should recognize that none of these groups is necessarily stable and hence, in the course of time, may become transformed into one of the other types. Bald-headed men, a statistical category, would become a social category if they developed a consciousness of kind, a social group if they entered into social relations on the basis of being bald-headed, and a formal organization if they established an association, as in the case of the St. Cloud, Minnesota, Bald-Headed Men's Club. Finally, this classification is not a temporal or evolutionary continuum; a statistical category may become a formal organization immediately without first becoming a social category and then a social group, and the reverse could also take place with the dissolution of an association. With these reservations in mind, let us consider each of these groups at greater length.

STATISTICAL CATEGORIES

Statistical categories are formed, not by the members themselves, but by sociologists, statisticians, demographers, and others. The individuals making up statistical categories are characterized by neither consciousness of kind, social interaction, or formal organization. Nevertheless, they constitute a group in the broad sense of the term in that they represent a collection of people with certain common attributes. The labor force, preschool children, persons who have had tuberculosis, redheads, schizophrenics, and right-handed persons are illustrative of statistical categories.

It would be easy to dismiss statistical categories as just a matter of "counting noses" and therefore of little consequence. Yet such knowledge may have considerable practical utility. If we know how many babies were born last year and the mortality rates for children from infancy to six years, we have fairly accurate knowledge on how many pupils will be entering elementary school in a few years hence. Insurance companies employ similar data for fixing the rates on their policies. Government officials also find information on statistical categories useful—for instance, a concentration of a population in the younger and the older age groups has consequences for social security and medicare programs.

SOCIAL CATEGORIES

Social categories differ from statistical categories in one important respect—a consciousness of kind. The individuals making up social categories recognize the fact of their membership, and this recognition affects their behavior. Members of social categories are aware of something that they share in common with others like themselves—that is, "I am one of them." Usually, some visible and conspicuous feature serves to identify the members of social categories and to differentiate them from others—for example, such "signs" as skin color, sex, grammar, accent, mannerisms, dress, gestures, food habits, family names, or response to patriotic symbols. Males, females, Blacks, Chinese, Texans, members of occupational groups, and members of similar social class, to cite a few illustrations, are social categories.

The consciousness associated with membership in a social category does not involve continual awareness, and may often be quite unconscious in the Freudian sense—for instance, one is hardly aware in all contexts of being a male, a Black, a Texan, or a professor. Nor does membership in a social category require that the members enter into social relations with one another simply on the basis of sharing certain features in common. Hence, one woman encountering another woman does not necessarily initiate interaction with her simply because she recognizes a consciousness of kind; the same holds true for Blacks, Chinese, Texans, members of occupational groups, and members of similar social classifications. Moreover, social categories lack formal organization. One need not join the League of Women Voters to be a woman or the National Association for the Advancement of Colored People (NAACP) to be a Black. In some—but not all—cases, membership in a social category provides a basis for entering into social interaction and even for establishing formal organizations—for instance, the League of Women Voters and the NAACP. But the important thing is this: a social category merely involves a consciousness of kind and does not *necessarily* lead to social interaction or formal organization among people.

SOCIAL GROUPS

> He who is unable to live in society, or who has no need because he is sufficient for himself, must be either a beast or a god.
>
> — Aristotle, *Politics, 1*

Social groups are similar to social categories in that their members are aware that they share something in common—a consciousness of kind. They differ from social categories in one important respect—social relations between individuals. The members of a social group are in *interaction* with one another—that is, there is a mutual and reciprocal influencing by two or more people of each other's feelings, attitudes, and actions. Acquaintances, friends, relatives, clique members, work associates, teammates, neighbors, and business clients are illustrations of social groups. Sociologists find it useful to distinguish between various types of social groups, including primary and secondary groups, in-groups and out-groups, and reference groups. Let us examine each of these in turn.

PRIMARY AND SECONDARY GROUPS

> No man is an island, entire of itself; every man is a piece of the continent.
>
> — John Donne, *Devotions, 1624*

In the sociological classification of social groups, one of the broadest and most fundamental distinctions is that between small, intimate *primary* groups and large, impersonal *secondary* groups. The concept of primary groups was introduced to American sociology in 1909 by Charles Horton Cooley, a pioneer social psychologist whom we discussed in Chapter 3. We may think of **primary groups** as involving two or more people who enjoy an intimate, cohesive relationship with one another.

Primary group relationships are facilitated by (1) face-to-face contact, (2) smallness of the group, and (3) frequent and intense contact (Davis, 1949). For intimacy to arise, it is usually necessary that people be in physical proximity. Seeing and talking with each other makes possible the subtle exchange of ideas, feelings, and opinions. Group size is also important. It is simply impossible to be in sensory contact with many people at the same time. Small groups enable individuals to come to know one another personally. Finally, the duration of the relationship is critical. Other things being equal, the longer people are together, the more numerous and deeper the contacts between them. Social ties deepen with time as people gradually develop interlocking habits.

Social Functions of Primary Groups. We enter into primary group relationships with the members of our immediate family, our companions and friends, and our daily associates. These groups are primary in the sense of

154 Group Behavior

being fundamental to each of us and to society. They are fundamental, first, because within them, particularly within our family, we are initiated into the patterns of our culture. Primary groups are the breeding ground wherein we acquire our norms, values, and symbols. In a word, they are the agencies that equip us for social living. Hence, the primary group is an essential bridge between the individual and the larger society, serving to transmit, to mediate, to interpret, and, in the end, to sustain society's cultural patterns.

Primary groups. Primary groups are characterized by spontaneity and good fellowship.

Patrick Reddy

Primary groups are fundamental, second, because they constitute the chief focus for realizing social satisfactions. Within them, we find our most worthwhile social experiences and meet our various needs—for example, companionship, ego worth, love, security, and a general sense of well-being. We commonly become most aware of just how important they are to us when we abruptly change primary groups, as for instance, when we leave home to attend college, get married, or take a job. We experience "homesickness"—that is, nostalgia for a primary group from which our immediate ties have suddenly been severed. Hence, the primary group meets a variety of psychological needs.

Primary groups are fundamental, third, because by virtue of their emotional tone and their binding social ties, they function as basic instruments of social control. As members of primary groups, we enjoy unparalleled opportunities for making our attitudes known; for checking, modifying, or correcting one another's views; and for bringing dissenters into line. In contrast, we experience the impact of larger and more impersonal groups only occasionally and sporadically. This power of primary groups is further augmented by their extraordinary capacity for rewarding conformity and punishing deviation since we are so dependent upon them for realizing meaningful social experiences and for meeting various psychological needs. Primary groups also define "social reality" for us; they not only "structure" the ways in which we perceive the world but they shape our self-perceptions through the "feedback" they give us concerning the appropriateness of our behavior (McClosky and Dahlgren, 1959). Hence, primary groups function not only as "carriers" of cultural norms but as "enforcers" of them.

Degree of Primariness. Groups differ from one another in the *degree* to which they exhibit qualities of primariness. A **secondary group** is the polar opposite of a primary group. We may view the primary group as constituting one pole of a continuum, and the secondary group as constituting the other

A PRIMARY GROUP

OBSERVATION I have two aces (very, very close friends). We do a lot of things together. We met the very first day that we came to college, and we call ourselves "partners" and "cats." We eat together, party together, and ridicule each other. The ridicule is accepted because we are good friends. It is not unlikely for two of us to team up on the other odd one. When the deal comes down, I will do anything for them and they will do anything for me.

PRINCIPLE This is an example of a primary group—people who enjoy an intimate, cohesive relationship with one another. Primary group relationships are facilitated by face-to-face contact, smallness of the group, and frequent and intense contact. Social ties deepen with time as people gradually develop interlocking habits.

pole. Specific groups are distributed along this continuum between the poles according to their degree of primariness. In some languages, such as French and German, different forms of address symbolize the distinction between primary and secondary group relations. *Vous* and *Sie,* meaning "you" in French and German respectively, are polite forms of address and are used in impersonal relationships—for example, in dealing with a store clerk, a bus driver, or an elevator operator. *Tu* and *du,* also meaning "you," are used in more personal, intimate relationships—for example, in relation to friends and family members.

Secondary group relationships are illustrated by everyday touch-and-go contacts in which people need have little or no knowledge of the other. Within secondary group relationships, people tend to interact more formally than in primary group relationships; they are more careful and calculating, more inclined to "watch themselves." Little sentiment is generally attached to secondary group relationships. We view them as means of getting things done, and not as ends in their own right. Whereas in primary group relationships we center our attention on people themselves, in the secondary group relationship we see people as an instrument (object) for realizing our goals. We can buy cigarettes from anybody. We focus our attention on getting them, not on people who sell them. In fact, the less sellers intrude themselves, the better; vending machines will do just as well.

Importance of Primary Groups. Studies of combat units highlight in vivid fashion the importance of primary groups. Much evidence points to the fact that the stronger the primary group ties of the troops fighting together, the better their combat record. In their perceptive study of the German army in World War II, Edward A. Shils and Morris Janowitz argue that it was the ability of the Wehrmacht to reproduce in the infantry company the intimacy and bonds previously furnished by the soldiers' civilian primary groups that largely explained its success. Although it has often been asserted that the extraordinary tenacity of the German army was a product of the strong National Socialist (Nazi) political convictions of the German soldiers, Shils and Janowitz found little support for this hypothesis. Except for a minority of hard-core Nazis, the values involved in political and social systems or ethical schemes had little impact on determination to fight. "Nazism," said a captured German, "begins ten miles behind the front lines." Indeed, considerable ignorance and apathy prevailed among German troops regarding the course of the fighting. Shils and Janowitz observe:

> For the ordinary German soldier the decisive fact was that he was a member of a squad or section which maintained its structural integrity and which coincided roughly with the *social* unit which satisfied some of his major primary needs. He was likely to go on fighting, provided he had the necessary weapons, as long as the group possessed leadership with which he could identify himself, and as long as

he gave affection to and received affection from the other members of his squad and platoon. In other words, as long as he felt himself to be a member of his primary group and therefore bound by the expectations and demands of its other members, his soldierly achievement was likely to be good. (p. 284)

Ideological considerations likewise played but a small part among the American G.I.'s fighting in Vietnam (Moskos, 1967, 1969). Although generally giving a good account of themselves in combat, American soldiers were extremely unlikely to voice patriotic rhetoric or overt political sentiments. Indeed, anti-ideology itself constituted an integral part of the soldiers' belief system. They tended to dismiss or meet patriotic slogans and exhortations with "What a crock," "Be serious man," or "Who's kidding who?" For the most part, they saw no relationship between their presence in Vietnam and the national policies that brought them there. One soldier put it this way: "Maybe we're supposed to be here and maybe not. But you don't have time to think about things like that. You worry about getting zapped and dry socks tomorrow. The other stuff is a joke." Yet despite their pronounced embarassment in the face of patriotic rhetoric, they displayed a kind of elemental nationalism in the belief that the United States is the best country in the world.

Relationships in the city. Although considerable impersonality characterizes the city and secondary group relationships abound, primary group ties nonetheless flourish.

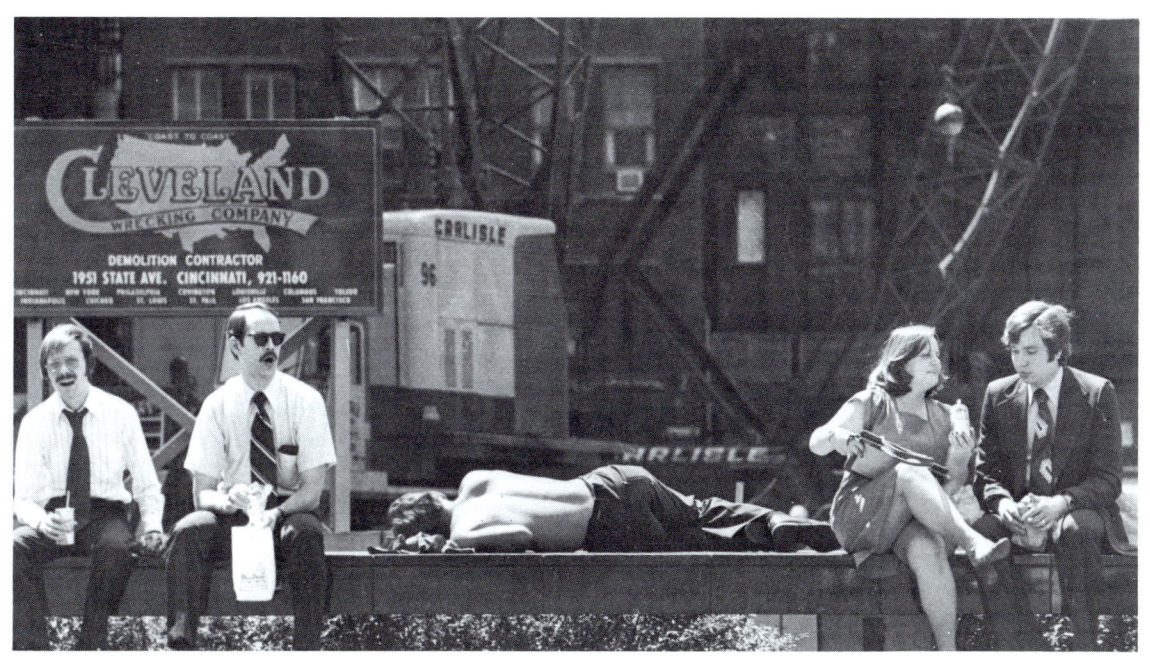

Patrick Reddy

Overall, then, the issues of national policy that brought them to Vietnam were for the most part irrelevant to American combat soldiers. Rather, they were concerned with the physical conditions under which they had to manage and with maximizing their survival chances. They had to cope with the routine physical stresses of combat existence, such things as the weight of the pack, the tasteless food, thirst, diarrhea, mosquitoes, leeches, rain, heat, mud, and loss of sleep. And not only was there the imminent danger of the loss of their own lives or limbs, but there was also the sight of wounded and dying comrades.

Under these harsh circumstances of ground warfare, the individual G.I. necessarily had to develop and take part in primary group relationships. The bonds that developed were in very large part the outgrowth of the very private war each individual was fighting for his own survival. It was on the primary group that the G.I. was dependent for his moral, physical, and technical support and for meeting has basic needs. As such, his fighting effectiveness was in large part the product of the strength of his squad's primary group ties.

IN-GROUPS AND OUT-GROUPS

An important distinction commonly made between social groups is that between *in-groups* and *out-groups*. An **in-group** is a social unit of which individuals are a part or with which they identify. An **out-group**, on the other hand, is a social unit of which individuals are *not* a part or with which they do *not* identify. Very simply, an in-group is a "we-group" and an out-group is a "they-group." The in-group includes ourselves and anybody whom we happen to include when we use the pronoun "we." The out-group includes those whom we exclude when we use the pronoun "they." In-groups may include both primary and secondary group relationships; for instance, we may view such primary groups as our family and work group and such secondary groups as our nation and professional association as in-groups. A sense of solidarity, loyalty, and cooperation prevails within in-group relationships. In contrast, we feel a sense of indifference, disgust, competition, and at times outright conflict with the members of out-groups.

Our understanding of the process whereby in-group antagonism is generated toward out-groups has been appreciably advanced by the experimental work undertaken by Muzafer Sherif and his associates. Using a summer camp as their setting and eleven- and twelve-year-old boys as their subjects, Sherif and his associates found that intergroup competition for valued but scarce resources was an important source contributing to the emergence of out-group antagonism. The research, summarized in Research Study 9, also demonstrated that the possibilities for achieving harmony between in-groups and out-groups are greatly enhanced when the groups come together to pursue superordinate goals (ends both groups desire but which they cannot realize singly).

RESEARCH STUDY 9

EXPERIMENT IN GROUP CONFLICT*

Muzafer Sherif

Problem. Conflict between groups—whether between boys' gangs, social classes, racial and ethnic groups, or nations—has no simple cause, nor is humanity yet in sight of a cure. Nonetheless, it is possible to identify certain general factors that typically give rise to conflict between in-groups and out-groups and certain other factors that, occasionally at least, serve to reduce hostility.

Hypotheses. Among the hypotheses tested by Muzafer Sherif and his associates as part of a larger study in group conflict were the following:

1. If two groups compete with each other, they will evolve unfavorable stereotypes of each other.
2. If two groups are hostile toward each other, merely bringing them into contact with one another will not markedly reduce intergroup conflict and tensions.
3. If two groups who have been hostile toward each other want something badly enough, and if they can get it only by working together, they will join efforts to reach their goal.
4. If two groups who feel hostile toward each other join their efforts to reach some common goal, their stereotypes toward each other will become more favorable.

Method and Findings. Sherif and his associates set up an experiment in which they employed a summer camp as the setting. For their subjects, they chose boys eleven or twelve years old, all of whom were healthy, socially well-adjusted, somewhat above average in intelligence, and from stable, White, Protestant, middle-class homes—in brief, boys with a homogeneous background. This procedure was designed to rule out from the beginning explanations of hostility or friendly intergroup attitudes in terms of differences in socioeconomic, ethnic, religious, or family backgrounds. The experiment proceeded through several stages as follows:

1. During the first six days of the boys' stay in camp, Sherif and his associates aimed to develop two separate groups, each having high cohesiveness and each unaware of the other's existence. Although the two campsites were not far apart, they were out of sight and earshot of each other; each group had its own facilities for swimming, boating, making campfires, and the like. Group cohesiveness was fostered through the promotion of common and interdependent activities characterized by goals integral to actual situations—cookouts, preparing campfires, improving swimming facilities, treasure hunts, and so on. Before the end of the first stage, each group had adopted a name ("Eagles" and "Rattlers"), had developed a recognized status hierarchy among its members, had formulated individual role assignments, and had evolved various norms (for example, concerning "toughness" and cursing).

2. The second six days, Stage 2, consisted of experimental efforts to create friction between the Rattlers and the Eagles. The experimenters brought the two groups into competitive contact with one another through a tournament of games (baseball, touch football, a tug-of-war, a treasure hunt, etc.) in which cumulative scores were kept for each

Continued on next page.

---

* Adapted from: Muzafer Sherif, O. J. Harvey, B. Jack White, William R. Hood, and Carolyn W. Sherif, *Intergroup Conflict and Cooperation: The Robbers Cave Experiment.* Norman, Okla.: University of Oklahoma Book Exchange, 1961.

group (not for individuals). The tournament started in a spirit of good sportsmanship, but as it progressed, good feelings evaporated. The members of each group began to call their rivals "stinkers," "sneaks," and "cheaters." Friction became commonplace. The Eagles, after a defeat in a tournament game, burned a banner left behind by the Rattlers; the next morning, the Rattlers seized the Eagles' flag when they arrived on the athletic field. Other incidents of name-calling, scuffling, and raiding developed. The antagonism of the members of each group for the members of the other group was confirmed through sociometric indices and a questionnaire that the boys completed dealing with their out-group and in-group stereotypes. These data, together with the researchers' observations, were taken as providing confirmation for the first hypothesis.

3. The third six-day period was designed as an integration phase. At this juncture, Sherif and his associates undertook to test the second hypothesis that pleasant social contacts between members of conflicting groups would not reduce friction between them. The hostile Rattlers and Eagles were brought together for social events: going to the movies, shooting off firecrackers, eating in the same dining hall, and so on. But far from reducing conflict, these situations only provided new opportunities for the rival groups to berate and attack each other—for instance, in the dining hall, they would hurl paper, food, and vile names at each other. This evidence was taken as providing confirmation of the second hypothesis.

Sherif and his associates then turned to a test of the last two hypotheses and experimentally created a series of urgent and natural situations that challenged the boys. In this way, superordinate goal activities were introduced. One of these followed the shutting off of the common water supply by the experimenters, a development explained by the experimenters as the work of "vandals." A plan was formulated whereby the damage was repaired through a good deal of work on everyone's part. As the boys began to complain of thirst, Eagles and Rattlers found themselves working side by side. A similar opportunity offered itself when the boys requested another movie. The experimenters told them that the camp could not afford to rent another one. The two groups then got together, chose the film by a vote, jointly financed the venture, and enjoyed the showing together. In due course, intergroup frictions were virtually eliminated, new friendships developed between individuals across group lines, and the groups actively sought opportunities to mingle, entertain, and "treat" each other. This shift from hostility to friendliness was reflected in the changes that occurred in sociometric indices and in each group's stereotypes of the other between the end of Stage 2 (after intense competition) and the end of Stage 3 (after the institution of superordinate goals). Figure 5.2 presents the results of a questionnaire designed to measure stereotypes that was administered to the boys at the end of Stage 2 and again at the end of Stage 3.

Conclusions. Efforts to reduce friction and prejudice between groups have usually followed rather different methods. Much attention has been given to one approach in particular: "Bring people of differing and hostile groups together and unfavorable group stereotypes will disappear." According to this thinking, "Contact brings friendliness." Yet things do not always work out quite this way. As Sherif's experiment reveals, social contacts may only serve as occasions for intensifying conflict. On the other hand, possibilities for achieving harmony are greatly enhanced when groups are brought together to work toward common ends. Then favorable information about a disliked group may be seen in a new light, and leaders may be in a position to take bolder steps toward cooperation.

Figure 5.2. Stereotypes that each group of boys held of the other group at the end of Stage 2 and the end of Stage 3.

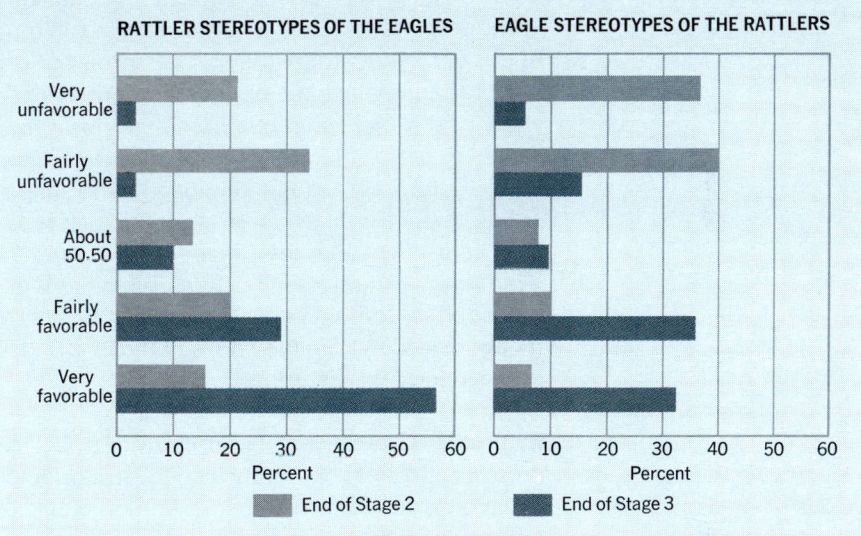

Source: Adapted from materials in Muzafer Sherif et al., *Intergroup Conflict and Cooperation: The Robbers Cave Experiment* (Norman, Okla.: University of Oklahoma Book Exchange, 1961).

REFERENCE GROUPS

If a man does not keep pace with his companions, perhaps it is because he hears a different drummer.

David Thoreau, *Walden*

Complex societies, such as our American society, are organized about an almost infinite variety of functioning groups, and all of us find ourselves members of a surprising number of them. In appraising individuals' behavior, it is essential to know which group furnishes the frame of reference for their behavior within a situation—in brief, which group is their **reference group**. A reference group is a social unit that provides the standards and perspective regulating an individual's behavior within a given context. A reference group may be an actual membership group or a group to which we aspire in membership (we then achieve the relationship through psychological identification). Nonmembership identifications are of considerable importance in understanding treason, renegadism, immigrant assimilation, upward class mobility, and social marginality. Under these circumstances people take as their reference group individuals other than those in their membership group (Hyman and Singer, 1968).

In the army, for example, it appears that low-ranking personnel who identify with officers (a nonmembership reference group) are more likely to receive promotions than those individuals who identify with the rank-and-file (their membership group). Other consequences, however, also flow from such identification. Because the norms of the nonofficer in-group and the norms of the out-group (the official norms of the army embodied within the officer stratum) are often at odds, conformity to the norms of an out-group is equivalent to nonconformity to the norms of the in-group. For enlisted personnel to adopt the standards of the officer group, a group to which they aspire but do not belong, this orientation may serve the twin functions of aiding their rise into that group (anticipatory socialization) and of easing their adjustment after they have become part of it. But for those individuals who make such an identification and fail to win promotion, the orientation has adverse consequences—allegiance to the norms of the officer group means defection from the norms of the in-group, with all its attendant penalties (Merton and Kitt, 1966).

Reference Groups and Groupthink. Strong in-group identifications and pressures toward conformity lead to **groupthink**, a decision-making process in which group consensus is so paramount that an individual's critical facilities become ineffective. Something of this sort led the Kennedy Administration into the ill-fated Bay of Pigs invasion of Cuba. The Kennedy policymakers had either not bothered to assemble the relevant facts or had simply overlooked the size and strength of the Castro army. Later, when the poorly conceived venture was crushed by Castro's forces (solidifying the Cuban-Soviet alliance and leading the Russians to attempt the installation of atomic missiles in Cuba), President Kennedy remarked, "How could we be so stupid?"

Irving L. Janis (1971), a social psychologist, has examined the groupthink process operating in the Kennedy inner circle—the President, his brother Robert, Dean Rusk, McGeorge Bundy, Arthur Schlesinger, Jr., Douglas Dillon, and Robert McNamara. The decision-makers were blinded by oversimplified and shared stereotypes of the Castro regime (the Communists were weak, stupid, and incompetent). Further, they saw themselves as moral crusaders acting on behalf of Western democracy. No one wished to break the illusion of unanimity. Arthur Schlesinger, Jr., later wrote:

Groups and Formal Organizations

> In the months after the Bay of Pigs I bitterly reproached myself for having kept so silent during those crucial discussions in the cabinet room. . . . I can only explain my failure to do more than raise a few timid questions by reporting that one's impulse to blow the whistle on this nonsense was simply undone by the circumstances of the discussion. . . . Our meetings were taking place in a curious atmosphere of assumed consensus. Had one senior adviser opposed the adventure, I believe that Kennedy would have canceled it. Not one spoke against it. (1965, pp. 255 and 259)

And finally, Robert Kennedy assumed the role of a "mind-guard," stifling dissent and fostering the warm glow of group unanimity.

Reference Groups and Attitude Change. Strong reference group attachments may lead to groupthink. In some circumstances, such identifications may also contribute to attitude change. This is highlighted by a study undertaken by Leonard Pearlin (1954). He investigated the attitudes toward Blacks of White coeds at a segregated southern woman's college (at the time the laws of North Carolina required school segregation). The majority of the students experienced at the college a climate of opinion that was much more favorable toward Blacks than that to which they had been exposed prior to coming to college. Hence, many of the students came into contact with norms and attitudes that were inconsistent or in conflict with those they had previously experienced.

Reference groups. Individuals employ the standards of their reference group to define their behavior and evaluate themselves.

Patrick Reddy

The data from the Pearlin study indicate that the least prejudiced White students were those who had experienced a weakening of ties to pre-college Southern White membership groups, while the more prejudiced were those who had retained firm affiliations with such groups. Likewise, the least prejudiced students were those who most strongly referred themselves to college groups, while the more prejudiced were those who referred themselves less strongly to campus groups. Thus, the shift toward favorable attitudes toward Blacks was in part the product of a *double-edged* process. On the one hand, there occurred a weakening of ties to pre-college groups. This weakening of ties was accompanied by a decrease in the effectiveness of the pre-college groups in regulating the individual's attitudes in an unfavorable direction toward Blacks. On the other hand, it was not sufficient that one simply "drift away" from previously established social relationships. Of equal importance in the modification of attitudes was the establishment of strong identification with those groups possessing attitudes favorable toward Blacks. By virtue of identifying with new reference groups, the women shifted their attitudes in accordance with those harbored by the new groups.

The process of acquiring more favorable attitudes toward Blacks involves both *disattachment* and *attachment:* disattachment from previous reference groups unfavorable to Blacks and attachment to new reference groups favorable to Blacks. Attitude changes cannot be reckoned solely in terms of exposure to new attitudes. Not all students underwent a modification of their attitudes toward Blacks, although they had been exposed to the new ideas. Whether individuals undergo a modification of their attitudes depends to a considerable extent on the nature of their relationship to groups holding the opposing sentiments. Generally, where a shift in attitudes occurs, there will be found a detachment from those groups from which one initially derived and found support for one's attitudes. Correspondingly, the shift in attitudes will be in the direction of the sentiments of those groups with which one develops the firmest attachments and identifications.

FORMAL ORGANIZATIONS

We are born in organizations, educated by organizations, and most of us spend much of our lives working for organizations. We spend much of our leisure time paying, playing, and praying in organizations. Most of us will die in organizations, and when the time comes to bury us, the largest organization of all—the state—must grant official permission.

Amitai Etzioni, Modern Organizations, *1964*

Formal organizations are similar to both social categories and social groups in that their members are aware that they share something in common—a consciousness of kind. And like social groups, but unlike social categories, they are characterized by interaction between their members.

Formal organizations differ, however, from both social categories and social groups in one important respect—they are goal-oriented associations. Formal organization arises when individuals deliberately construct a social unit to seek specific objectives (Blau and Schoenherr, 1971).

Our American society is characterized by a great many formal organizations—General Motors, the Elm Street Garden Club, the University of Wisconsin, the American Bar Association, the Republican party, the United States Postal Service, the Missouri Synod of the Lutheran Church. In fact, we have so many organizations that a whole set of other organizations has appeared to supervise them—the Securities and Exchange Commission, the National Labor Relations Board, the National Collegiate Athletic Association (NCAA).

Within the past few decades, the United States has increasingly become a society of big, semiautonomous, and tightly knit formal organizations. Indeed, some sociologists like Herman Turk (1970:1) conceive of modern societies and cities as networks of "organizations which appear, disappear, change, merge, and form . . . relations with one another." There is not only "big government"—federal as well as state and municipal (within which civil services and the armed forces represent large, tightly organized power centers of their own)—there is also the big farmers' federation, the big hospital, the big university, the big labor union, and many others. Business was the first sphere in American society in which the large organization appeared, explaining in part why we tend to associate "bigness" with "business." Many of the decisive interactions in American society today—and increasingly on the governmental level—are interactions between highly organized, large, powerful, and professionalized organizations, each with its own specific concerns.

THE NATURE OF BUREAUCRACY

A large-scale, complex organization such as an American university requires an elaborate division of labor. An army of specialists facilitates the activities of administrators, professors, and students: librarians, maintenance personnel, physicians, counselors, police officers, secretaries, plant engineers, cooks, nutritionists, accountants, and many others. Specialization promotes efficiency. If individuals are given one task to perform, they generally can become more skilled and efficient at it than if they have to perform a great many different tasks. Yet elaborate specialization demands some overall coordination and integration of the activities within a larger whole. The structure directing, coordinating, and controlling the efforts of many individuals performing different tasks is *bureaucracy*.

Bureaucracy is simply a hierarchical arrangement between the parts of an organization in which the pyramiding order is based on division of function and authority (Miller and Form, 1964). This sociological view of bureaucracy contrasts sharply with the widespread use of the term to refer to government inefficiency. The government bureaucrat is commonly stereotyped as an officious, rule-conscious, responsibility-dodging clerk entangled in red tape and preoccupied with busy-work. Yet as one business executive said after serving in government, "We in business have bureaucracy just like the government. Only we call it 'system.' "

Bureaucracy has existed in a good many times and places, including ancient Egypt and China. Many sociologists believe that bureaucracies are an inevitable accompaniment of organizational growth and specialization (Blau and Schoenherr, 1971; Blau, 1973; Hummon, Doreian, and Teuter, 1975; and Mileti, Gillespie, and Haas, 1977). As an organization increases in number of people, more subdivisions evolve to accommodate them. In turn, specialization and subdivision require some social mechanism for integrating and coordinating the various activities—hence bureaucracy. Organizational complexity works toward a similar end. As technology, marketing arrangements, and long-term economic planning become more complicated and intricate, an expansion of the administrative sphere is required.

WEBER'S CONCEPTION OF BUREAUCRACY

Max Weber (1864–1920), an influential German sociologist, dealt with bureaucracy as an **ideal type**. An ideal type is not a model or description of any existing structure. Rather it is an analytical construct created by the sociologist. The term "ideal" has nothing to do with evaluations of any sort. An ideal type is derived by abstracting the most characteristic aspects that are present in a real phenomenon, in this case, bureaucracy. Ideal types enable sociologists to generalize and to "oversimplify" the data by disregarding what are held to be minor differences in order to emphasize what are thought to be major similarities. Hence, the descriptions associated with ideal types do not portray total "reality." Ideal types are tools. In the case of bureaucracy, the ideal type enables sociologists to abstract certain characteristics often associated with organizational structure—for example, common elements within the United States government, General Motors, Ohio State University, the AFL–CIO, the Roman Catholic Church, and the Democratic party. Yet we need to remember that each concrete case provides its own unique exceptions.

Weber (1946) noted the following characteristics of bureaucracies.

Division of Labor. The regular activities of the organization are broken down into a clear-cut division of labor. This makes it possible to hire only specialized experts in each position and to make every one of them responsible for the effective performance of given duties.

Hierarchy of Authority. The hierarchy typically takes on the shape of a pyramid in which officials are held accountable to their superior for their subordinates' decisions and actions as well as their own. At each level of the hierarchy, officials enjoy the right of issuing directives to their subordinates, and they have the duty to obey them. The scope of their authority, however, is clearly circumscribed and limited to those directives relevant to the organization's official operation.

Rules Governing Behavior of Positional Incumbents. The organization's operation is governed by a consistent system of abstract rules and regulations. These rules and regulations define the responsibilities of the incumbents of the various positions and the relationships between them. They assure the coordination of the different tasks and uniformity in the performance of the various activities, regardless of the number of persons involved. These common rules function as a source for the predictability of behavior. They provide for continuity in operations regardless of changes in personnel.

Impersonality of Personal Contact. Officials are expected to assume an impersonal orientation in their dealings with clients and subordinates. The exclusion of personal considerations from official business is a prerequisite for impartiality and efficiency. Personal detachment assures that rational standards will govern the organization's operation. It fosters equitable treatment of all persons and promotes democratic administration. Hence, the very factors that make government bureaucrats unpopular with their clients — an aloof attitude and a lack of genuine interest in their problems — function to benefit the client and the subordinate.

Technically Competent Participants. In principle, bureaucratic offices are filled by persons who possess the technical competence necessary to perform the required duties; political, family, or other connections do not give individuals claim to preferred posts. The advantage of this is clear — trained individuals are more likely to do their jobs well than those whose positions rest upon political favors, family ties, or personal friendship. Usually, individuals' qualifications are tested by examination (for instance, civil service examinations) or by certificates that demonstrate their competence (for example, college degrees).

Careers. Employment in the organization constitutes a career. Officials are appointed to their positions, not elected; they are dependent on their superior in the organization rather than on a body of constituents. In principle, promotion is based on seniority and achievement, or both. After a probationary period, officials gain the security of tenure and are protected against arbitrary dismissal. Such security renders the individual less susceptible to outside pressures.

SOCIAL CONSEQUENCES OF BUREAUCRACY

It's all papers and forms, the entire Civil Service is like a fortress made of papers, forms, and red tape.

Alexander Ostrovsky, The Diary of a Scoundrel, *1868*

In formulating the characteristics of bureaucracy, Weber implicitly supplied us with an analysis of its *functions*. A division of labor contributes to efficiency. A hierarchy of authority promotes control over an array of positions and contributes to the effective coordination of effort. Rules and regulations provide for continuity in operations regardless of personnel changes and serve as a source for the predictability of behavior. Impersonality fosters the equitable treatment of all people and promotes democratic administration. Technical competence insures that qualified individuals are placed in responsible positions. And job security makes the individual less susceptible to outside pressures.

There are, however, limits to what can be accomplished by large hierarchical organizations, although the opposite view is more often in vogue. James Q. Wilson, a political scientist, observes:

> If enough people don't like something, it becomes a problem; if the intellectuals agree with them, it becomes a crisis; any crisis must be solved; if it must be solved, then it can be solved—and creating a new organization is the way to do it. If the organization fails to solve the problem (and when the problem is a fundamental one, it will almost surely fail), then the reason is "politics," or "mismanagement," or "incompetent people," or "meddling," or "socialization," or "inertia." (1967, p. 6)

Yet, as Wilson notes, some problems cannot be solved and some government functions cannot be done well.

Moreover, bureaucracies not only contribute to the survival and effective operation of social systems but they may also be *dysfunctional;* that is, they may impair the adaptation or adjustment of social systems. Indeed, the popular conception of bureaucracy as an overgrown, impersonal, and inefficient organization—saturated with "red tape" and "bungling"—suggests that perhaps there may be more to the story than Weber noted (see Table 5.1). "Paperwork" is one such problem. Studies by the Commission on Federal Paperwork reveal that the federal government employs about 5,000 forms for public use and another one million forms for internal use by its various agencies. It is estimated that if the time all federal employees spend on paperwork is counted as one lump sum, it equals the worktime of nearly one million full-time employees.

As we have noted, bureaucrats are also encouraged to stick to the rules. Concern for promotion and a desire to be highly regarded by superiors often engenders among bureaucrats an outlook that overemphasizes rules, proce-

TABLE 5.1
Reshaping Bureaucracy: An Old Problem

Andrew Jackson (1837):
> I am accused of usurping power, when my whole life has been one continual battle against the tendency of bureaucracy or aristocracy—the concentration of power in the hands of the few.

Woodrow Wilson (1914):
> Very few governments are organized, I venture to say, as wise and experienced businessmen would organize them if they had a clean sheet of paper to write on.

Herbert Hoover (1928):
> Bureaucracy is ever desirous of spreading its influence and its power.

Harry Truman (1955):
> There was too much duplication of functions, too much "passing the buck," and too much confusion and waste. . . . Reorganization should be an unending process.

Lyndon Johnson (1965):
> I am busy currently reviewing the structure of the executive branch of this Government. I hope to reshape it and reorganize it to meet more effectively the tasks of the twentieth century.

Richard Nixon (1971):
> It is important that we move boldly to consolidate the major activities of the Government.

Jimmy Carter (1976):
> We must give top priority to a drastic and thorough revision and reorganization of the federal bureaucracy.

dures, and paperwork. Presumably, rules are formulated to facilitate the achievement of the organization's goals—the rules are a *means* to an end. Yet an exaggerated concern with routines and regulations leads to a situation where the rules become *ends* in themselves.

Bureaucracies may exhibit another dysfunction, the so-called **Peter Principle** formulated by Lawrence J. Peter. Simply stated, the Peter Principle says: "In a hierarchy every employee tends to rise to his level of incompetence" (Peter and Hull, 1969: 25). Put another way, individuals get promoted so long as they are competent; but eventually many people reach positions that exceed their talents and abilities. Once this has occurred, they usually no longer receive promotions although they are maintained by the bureaucratic arrangement in the positions in which they are incompetent. Indeed, given sufficient time and the existence of a hierarchy having many ranks, Peter's Corollary follows: "In time, every post tends to be occupied by an employee who is incompetent to carry out its duties" (p. 27). Still the essential work gets done: "Work is accomplished by those employees who have not yet reached their level of incompetence" (p. 27). Although the Peter Principle may overstate the matter, it nonetheless points to a problem with bureaucratic structures.

Robert Michels (1911/1966) claims that bureaucratic organizations have a further dysfunction, indeed a fundamental flaw: they inevitably lead to the concentration of power in the hands of a few who in turn use their positions to advance their own fortunes and self-interests. He terms this the **iron law of oligarchy**. Michels cites many reasons for this tendency—leaders become adept at organizational manipulation; they erect barriers to challenges by opponents; they acquire control over an organization's finances, communication networks, and disciplinary agencies; they can buy off or absorb (coopt) potential rivals; and they are seldom challenged by the rank-and-file who for the most part remain indifferent and apathetic. He believes that the developmental course of various European socialist parties and labor unions confirms his thesis that leaders seldom reflect the democratic aspirations espoused by their organizations. Although the model has been found applicable to many labor unions, professional associations, private clubs, and legislative bodies (Selznick, 1952; Lipset, Trow, and Coleman, 1956; Tannenbaum, 1965; Schlesinger, 1965), sociologists point out that the formulation is vastly overstated as an "iron law" (Gouldner, 1955; Olsen, 1968; Collins, 1975).

Bureaucracies, then, have both functional and dysfunctional consequences. But we should not lose sight of the fact that they are able to accomplish things that could not be realized without them. The complexity of modern life necessitates large-scale, formal organization.

ALTERNATIVE FORMULATIONS REGARDING FORMAL ORGANIZATIONS

It is always a windfall for truth when well-established facts collide with a well-constructed theory.

Jean Rostand, Substance of Man

Weber's formulations have dominated sociology for nearly a half century. The focus has fallen on social structures as abstract entities and has tended to ignore the actions of individual participants. Peter M. Blau and Richard A. Schoenherr (1971), both distinguished sociologists, set forth this approach in these terms:

> Formal organizations, as well as other social structures, exhibit regularities that can be analyzed in their own right, independent of any knowledge about the individual behavior of their members.... it is time that we "push men finally out" to place proper emphasis on the study of social structure in sociology. (pp. viii and 357)

Primary groups as the foundation of formal organization. Many large-scale formal organizations, such as the Girl Scouts of America, find their roots in the close, personal bonds prevailing within local community groups.

Patrick Reddy

Such sociologists have studied organizations without paying much attention to the processes by which given structural features are produced and reproduced in the course of day-by-day interaction.

Recent developments within sociology have expanded the perspectives from which formal organizations are studied. Criticisms of the traditional position of Weber and Blau and Schoenherr have surfaced as research and theory have begun to grapple with a series of new issues (Silverman, 1971; Turner, 1977). Although the critiques have emanated from such diverse sources as symbolic interactionism, ethnomethodology, conflict sociology, Marxism, and social exchange theory, their tendency has been to undermine the conventional approach at the same point—the *production* of organizational reality through the actions of particular people and particular groups of people (Benson, 1977).

Symbolic interactionists direct their attention to the processes through which organizational arrangements and patterns are negotiated, reproduced, and altered. In Chapter 2 we examined a study by Anselm Strauss and his associates (1964) that described the process by which patients, physicians, nurses, and others "work out" concerted action and fashion those understandings and agreements that constitute "the hospital." Peter K. Manning (1977) has studied two police narcotic units and likewise finds that many of the conventionally understood features of organizations—goals, rules, and procedures—often have a fictional character to them. In the course of the everyday operation of these police agencies, the official guidelines are so loose that they permit wide variations in responses. Through negotiated interaction, the narcotics officers arrive at mutual understandings regarding specific cases. Ethnomethodologists like Don H. Zimmerman take a related approach and seek to establish how individuals within an organization employ, manipulate, and suspend rules in constructing their workaday worlds and a sense of social order (see Research Study 10).

Conflict sociologists and Marxists see organizations as social arrangements structured by power relationships. Power is viewed as the essential core from which other organizational aspects proceed. An organization's goals, technologies, division of labor, and reward systems are shaped by the power of established interests inside and outside the organization's boundaries. Organizations, then, are not "neutral" social arrangements but structures that operate on behalf of particular groups (Benson, 1977; Goldman and Van Houten, 1977; Heydebrand, 1977).

Social exchange theorists are interested in the manner in which organizations transact rewarding and costly actions in order to realize their respective objectives. Viewed from this perspective, organizations are not self-contained entities but rather units involved in a network of relationships with other units (Kroeger, 1975; Cook, 1977). All these alternative approaches to formal organization open to examination a series of problems ignored and shunted aside by conventional sociological formulations.

RESEARCH STUDY 10

THE PRACTICALITIES OF RULE USE*

Don H. Zimmerman

Problem. Sociologists have typically regarded bureaucratic rules as being substantially more explicit and coherent than the norms we usually encounter in everyday settings. Bureaucratic personnel are seen as implementing officially stated policies and procedures designed to achieve rationally defined goals. But what happens in practice? Are bureaucratic rules habitually followed? What part do such rules play in the day-by-day operations of large-scale organizations? Don H. Zimmerman, an ethnomethodologist, addresses these questions in this study.

Method. Zimmerman spent six months studying the work of receptionists in a public welfare agency. He examined how the receptionists used rules for assigning applicants to caseworkers. Zimmerman was known to the agency's staff as a sociologist working on his doctoral dissertation. He took field notes, made tape-recordings of work-related conversations, and periodically conducted unstructured interviews with the personnel to gain insight into various practices and events.

Findings. It was the responsibility of the receptionists to process applicants for public assistance and apportion them among caseworkers who handled their claims. Applicants were assigned a social worker based on the rule "first come, first served." From the point of view of the receptionists, the caseworkers, and Zimmerman, the rule appeared to produce a moving, coordinated, sequenced, and orderly flow of applicants through the system. However, receptionists were also concerned with affording the *appearance* of a systematic, smooth flow of individuals. This required

them periodically to deviate from the "first come, first served" rule. They based such violations on explicit as well as tacit understandings regarding the practical requirements of their work—that is, in light of certain taken-for-granted assumptions about "what everyone who works here knows."

By way of illustration, on one occasion a caseworker was taking an unusually long time interviewing her first client of the day. As the morning passed, the third applicant assigned to the caseworker became concerned with the delay and told the receptionist that she was afraid she would miss a "12:30 doctor's appointment." Accordingly, the receptionist switched the applicant to another worker. In so doing, the receptionist "suspended" the rule—a turn was skipped and changes were made in the intake book. The receptionist rationalized her deviance as resolving a "snag" and "keeping the people moving."

Another example involved the case of an applicant who specifically requested a particular social worker. Here too the rule was suspended as a "one time only" exception and in order to avoid "making an issue of it." Still another example of the rule's suspension involved the assignment of "difficult" or "troublesome" applicants to a particular caseworker known to be adept at handling "special problems."

Conclusion. Zimmerman points out that in the course of the ongoing, everyday activities of an organization, people continually develop what a rule means. They invoke rationalizations that *satisfy* themselves and others as to what is or is not "reasonable" compliance with a rule in given situations. Individuals, then, do not mechanically enact rules as programmed robots. Rather rules serve as a common-sense method of accounting for their behavior. Rules also afford a sense that life's activities proceed in an orderly manner; people can feel that their courses of action are rational, coherent, and precedented.

---

* Adapted from Don H. Zimmerman, "The Practicalities of Rule Use," in Jack D. Douglas, Ed., *Understanding Everyday Life*, Chicago: Aldine Publishing Company, 1971.

INFORMAL ORGANIZATION

Work relationships are much more than the lifeless abstractions contained within a chart listing an organization's officers and departments. It is only rarely that the ideal situation portrayed by the formal organization corresponds with the actual situation. Formal organizations breed **informal organizations**—networks of personal and social relations that arise within a formal organization but which are not defined or prescribed by it. Elaborate patterns of "kidding," swearing, gambling, unauthorized work breaks, "goldbricking," and the like derive from informal social relationships. Within the larger formal structure, primary groups often emerge.

The roots of informal organization are embedded within formal organization and are nurtured by the very formality of its arrangements. Official rules must be general enough to have sufficient scope to cover the great variety of situations that arise. Hence, the application of the general rules to a given case poses problems of judgment. Informal practices emerge that provide solutions. Further, to escape from the "red tape" that typically develops within bureaucracies, participants customarily reach informal working agreements with one another. Although such agreements are not explicitly formulated, they serve to facilitate the organization's efficient operation. Moreover, the impersonality that characterizes formal relationships is disquieting and unsatisfying to many individuals. They long for congenial relations with others in which they may find warmth, rapport, and friendship. Hence, formal organization breeds informal organization. Informal organizations serve to supplement, modify, and even oppose the formal organization.

A variety of studies have noted how an informal or unofficial organization

Informal organization. Lunchtime cliques are primary groups that arise within formal organizations and pattern personal and social relationships.

Patrick Reddy

of work activities develops within the framework of formal organizations (Roy, 1952;1953;1954; Harper and Emmert, 1963). One study in particular has stood out through the years as somewhat of a "classic" and has exerted considerable influence on sociological investigations: the research carried out from 1927 through 1932 by F. J. Roethlisberger and William J. Dickson (1939) at the Western Electric Hawthorne Works in Chicago. Western Electric is a subsidiary of the American Telephone and Telegraph Company and among other things manufactures telephones for the Bell System.

Although many of the findings of the Roethlisberger and Dickson study have since been called into question (Carey, 1967), one aspect nonetheless has had enduring merit, namely, its "discovery" of the operation of informal organization within the framework of larger, formal organizational structures. As part of the Hawthorne research, an intensive study was made of one small group of fourteen men who assembled switches for use in telephone switchboards, a job requiring some individual work and some group cooperation. Observation soon revealed that there were uniformities in the behavior of the group that did not follow the formal organization's blueprint. Informal relations developed among the men and gave rise to organized patterns of conduct — in brief, informal organization. Talking, singing, and horseplay were common. As a rule, the men were very businesslike and worked rapidly during the morning hours. In the late afternoon, however, they would work more slowly and talk more. Job trading was quite common. Moreover, the men divided themselves into two cliques, although there were a few isolates who were not members of either group (see Figure 5.3). Among the members of the same clique, there developed friendship ties, horseplay, betting, an exchange of candy bars, and lunchtime conversation.

Figure 5.3. The internal organization of the group: Bank wiring observation room.

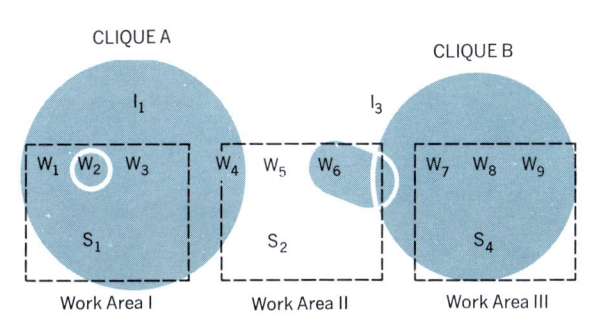

Clique A included: W_1, W_3, W_4, S_1, and I_1.
Marginal to Clique A: W_2.
Clique B included: W_7, W_8, W_9, and S_4.
Marginal to Clique B: W_6.
Outside either clique: W_5, S_2, and I_3.

Source: From *Management and the Worker* by F. J. Roethlisberger and William J. Dickson. Copyright 1939 by the Harvard University Press. Reprinted by permission of the publisher.

Group Behavior

INFORMAL ORGANIZATION

OBSERVATION I have a job in the warehouse of a large lumber company. The guys have developed a lot of neat little gimmicks to goof off at work. Let me describe one of them. We have one supervisor but access to two restrooms. This means that the supervisor cannot cover both restrooms simultaneously. If the "super" cannot find someone, we tell him that the guy has gone to the restroom. In reality, however, the guy is hiding out, relaxing somewhere behind a pile of lumber. The "super" usually hollers, "What's taking him so G____d____ long?" Mad as hell, he goes to get the guy, looking first in one restroom and then in the other. When the "super" heads for the first restroom, we give a little whistle. The guy hears the whistle and hustles back to work. When the "super" returns complaining that he can't find the guy, one of us says, "Oh, he's already back. He's over there loading lumber. He was in the other restroom."

PRINCIPLE We have created at work an informal organization within the formal organization. This informal organization operates to beat the system. It allows us to goof off without getting caught.

The men shared a set of norms that were not officially defined by the formal organization:

1. You should not turn out too much work. If you do, you are a "rate-buster."
2. You should not turn out too little work. If you do, you are a "chiseler."
3. You should not tell a supervisor anything that will react to the detriment of an associate. If you do, you are a "squealer."
4. You should not attempt to maintain social distance or act officious. If you are an inspector, for example, you should not act like one. (p. 522)

Management had established a normal day's output at 6600 wiring connections, while the men defined a reasonable day's work as only 6000 connections. Hence, the norms of the informal organization ran counter to the rules and expectations of management. Current studies of "time theft" — on-the-job socializing, day-dreaming, reading novels and magazines, and so on — suggest that the average worker in the United States "steals" three hours and forty-five minutes from his or her employer each week (*New York Times*, November 25, 1977:5).

The informal organization of the men in the Hawthorne plant performed a twofold function: (1) to protect the group from internal indiscretions; and (2) to protect it from outside interference, including that of management. The men enforced these norms through sarcasm, ridicule, and "binging" (punching the fellow worker on the arm). Clique membership similarly operated as an instrument of social control. Individuals whose behavior was viewed as reprehensible were excluded from cliques; they were, in a sense, socially ostracized.

SUMMARY

1. A group is a collection of people with certain common attributes. We may single out three properties or criteria for the purpose of distinguishing among groups: (1) consciousness of kind — the tendency of people to recognize others like themselves; (2) social relations between individuals — the mutual and reciprocal influencing by two or more people of each other's feelings, attitudes, and actions; and (3) goal-oriented associations — social units deliberately constructed to seek specific ends.

2. Statistical categories are formed, not by the members themselves, but by sociologists, statisticians, demographers, and others. The individuals making up statistical categories are characterized by neither consciousness of kind, social interaction, or formal organization.

3. Social categories differ from statistical categories in one important respect — a consciousness of kind. The individuals making up social categories recognize the fact of their membership, and this recognition affects their behavior.

4. Social groups are similar to social categories in that their members are aware that they share something in common — a consciousness of kind. They differ from social categories in one important respect — social relations between individuals. The members of a social group are in interaction with one another.

5. Primary groups involve two or more people who enjoy an intimate, cohesive relationship with one another. Such groups are primary in the sense of being fundamental to each of us and to society. They are fundamental, first, because within them, particularly within our family, we are initiated into the patterns of culture. Primary groups are fundamental, second, because they constitute the chief focus for realizing social satisfactions. And third, primary groups are fundamental because by virtue of their emotional tone and their binding social ties, they function as basic instruments of social control.

6. An in-group is a social unit of which individuals are a part or with which they identify. An out-group, on the other hand, is a social unit of which individuals are not a part or with which they do not identify. Very simply, an in-group is a "we-group" and an out-group is a "they-group."

7. A reference group is a social unit that provides the standards and perspective regulating an individual's behavior within a given context. A reference group may be an actual membership group or a group to which we aspire in membership. Strong in-group identifications and pressures toward conformity lead to groupthink — a decision-making process in which group consensus is so paramount that an individual's critical facilities become ineffective.

8. Formal organizations arise when individuals deliberately construct a social unit to seek specific objectives. The structure directing, coordinating, and controlling the efforts of many individuals performing different tasks is bureaucracy. Bureaucracy is simply a hierarchical arrangement between the parts of an organization in which the pyramiding order is based on division of function and authority.

9. Max Weber dealt with bureaucracy as an ideal type. He noted the following characteristics of bureaucracies: division of labor, hierarchy of authority, rules governing behavior of positional incumbents, impersonality of personal contact, technically competent participants, and careers.

10. In formulating the characteristics of bureaucracy, Weber implicitly supplied us with an analysis of its functions. It may also exhibit dysfunctions — characteristics that impair the survival and effective operation of a social system. One example is the Peter Principle — individuals get promoted so long as they are competent; but eventually many people reach positions that exceed their talents and abilities. Robert Michels claims that bureaucratic organizations have a further dysfunction — they inevitably lead to the concentration of

power in the hands of a few who in turn use their positions to advance their own fortunes and self-interests. He terms this the "iron law of oligarchy."

11. Recent developments within sociology have expanded the perspectives from which formal organizations are studied. Criticisms of the traditional position of Weber and others have surfaced as research and theory have begun to grapple with a series of new issues. Although the critiques have emanated from such diverse sources as symbolic interactionism, ethnomethodology, conflict sociology, Marxism, and social exchange theory, their tendency has been to undermine the conventional approach at the same point — the production of organizational reality through the actions of particular people and particular groups of people.

12. Formal organizations breed informal organizations that arise within a formal organization but which are not defined or prescribed by it. The roots of informal organization are embedded within formal organization and are nurtured by the very formality of its arrangements.

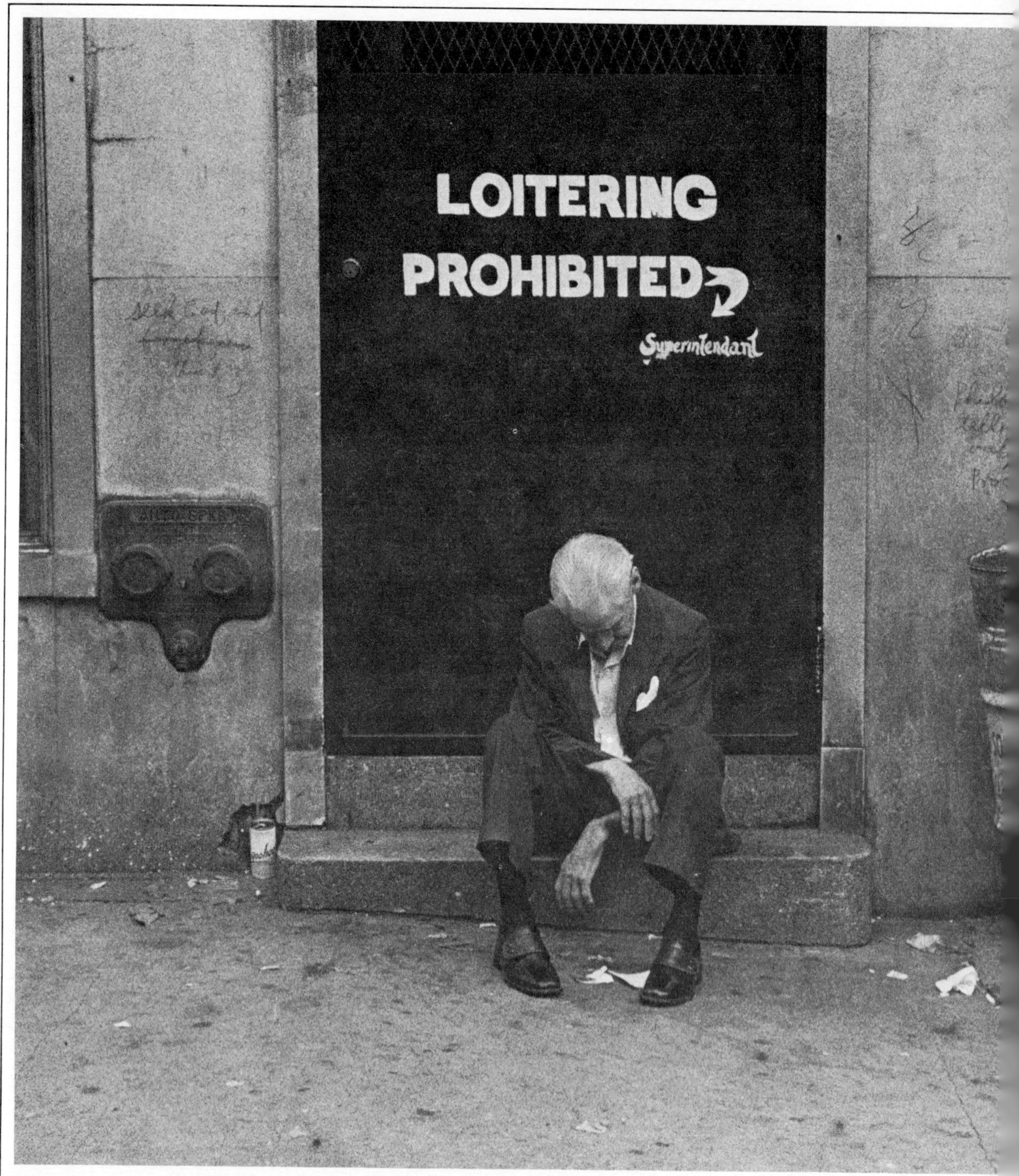
LOITERING
PROHIBITED
Superintendant

6
CONFORMITY AND DEVIANCE

CONFORMITY
  Factors Producing Conformity
  Group Forces and Conformity in Judgment

DEVIANCE
  Social Definitions of Deviance: Drug Use
  Deviance and Social Life
  The Prevalence of Deviance
  Rehabilitation Versus Deterrence

THEORIES OF DEVIANCE
  Anomie and Deviance
  Conflict and Deviance
  Differential Association and Deviance
  Labeling and Deviance

OBSERVATION As I was passing the Library I heard the strangest noise. It sounded like someone on roller skates. I turned around and sure enough I saw a guy skating from one class to the next. My roommate who was walking with me said, "What a jerk!" A lot of the kids were looking at him kind of funny, like he was some sort of weirdo and made nasty cracks about him.

PRINCIPLE Skating, though not conventional, made a lot of sense. It was kind of ingenious. It was faster than walking and certainly no more ridiculous than riding a bike. But when judged by other students, his form of transportation was seen as abnormal and out of the ordinary. Thus he looked like an outcast and stuck out like a sore thumb.

James S. Slotkin (1950:70–71) relates an interesting case that points to the part culture plays in providing us with socially "approved" standards for our behavior. At a psychiatric hospital, during a hot summer spell, a diagnostic mental examination was given to a patient who had been brought to the hospital a few days before. His responses appeared quite normal until the following dialogue took place:

Q. How did you happen to come here?
A. I don't know. I was just minding my own business.
Q. Who brought you here?
A. The police.
Q. What had you been doing?
A. Nothing. Just minding my own business.
Q. What were you doing at the time?
A. Just walking along the street.
Q. What street?
A. [He gave the name of one of the busiest streets in the city.]
Q. What had you done just before that?
A. It was hot, so I took my clothes off.
Q. All your clothes?
A. No. Not my shoes and stockings.
Q. Why not those too?
A. The sidewalk was too hot.

In itself, the man's behavior was more rational than that of any other man on the street at that time who sweltered in a suit. Yet we judge behavior by its conformity to norms rather than by its intrinsic reasonableness. On the basis of this and other data, the man was diagnosed a schizophrenic and confined to a mental institution. In capsule form, this man and society's reaction to him constitute the topic of the chapter: conformity and deviance.

CONFORMITY

> People are always talking about originality, but what do they mean? As soon as we are born, the world begins to work upon us, and this goes on to the end.
>
> Johann W. von Goethe,
> quoted in Johann P. Eckermann's Conversations with Goethe,
> May 12, 1825

If humans are to live with one another—if they are to carry on daily interaction—there must be rules, and people must be able to assume that, by and large, these rules will be observed:

> Whatever people want—food, clothing, shelter, sex, fame, contract bridge—they must get it by working with and through other people. They must take up positions in organized and complex social enterprises: families, clubs, schools, armies, political associations, ball teams. Each of these may be thought of as a way of fitting together the diverse actions of many people so that the work of the world gets done. But if the actions of many people are to be fitted together, there must be understandings about who is supposed to do what and under which circumstances. Some understandings may be "better" than others in the sense that, if they are followed, they will get the job done better. But the first prerequisite to organized human activity is that there be *some* understandings, however arbitrary they may be. (Cohen, 1966, p. 3).

But why, we may ask, do people conform to group rules? What factors serve to produce obedience to norms?

FACTORS PRODUCING CONFORMITY

> Most of the things we do, we do for no better reason than that our fathers have done them or our neighbors do them, and the same is true of a larger part than what we suspect of what we think.
>
> Oliver Wendell Holmes, Jr., speech, Boston, January 8, 1897

Sociologists identify three principal factors that contribute to conformity: (1) we internalize many norms; (2) we often are unaware of alternative modes of behavior; and (3) we may realize that to violate norms may result in our incurring punishment, while conformity produces rewards. Let us examine each of these factors more closely.

First, as members of a society, we continuously undergo socialization, a process by which norms are transmitted to us. Many of these norms we *internalize*—we incorporate them within our personality; we accept them without thought or questioning; they become second nature to us. Hence, conformity need not be a product of a concern that we shall be punished or

184 Group Behavior

Conformity. Even those American youth who pride themselves on their individualism seem, on most occasions, to follow cultural patterns not of their own making. They dress, for instance, in the outfit prevalent among their "crowd."

Patrick Reddy

go unrewarded. In accepting the group, we develop self-conceptions that in effect regulate our conduct in accordance with the norms of the group. The matter of conformity or nonconformity does not come to mind; by doing what group members do, we achieve pride, self-identity, a sense of security — products of group belonging. It is our group, *our* norm. In such cases, social control is *self-control*.

Second, it usually does not occur to us that alternative standards exist. Norms constitute guideposts; they represent the social "tools" that enable us to relate ourselves to others and to meet our daily needs. In considerable measure, we see and experience the world about us in accordance with the culture patterns of our society. We are culture bound. Nonconformist patterns simply do not come to mind; they are not alternatives known to our society.

Third, our conformity may be the product of our realization that to do otherwise is to incur punishment, while conformity produces rewards. The rule breaker is met with dislike, hostility, gossip, and ostracism; the conformist with praise, popularity, prestige, and other socially defined "good things." We soon learn that there are real disadvantages to nonconformity, advantages to conformity. Thus, Herbert Porter of the Committee to Re-Elect the President (the 1972 Nixon campaign organization), during the Senate Watergate hearings in 1973, said that he had not spoken up against his bosses' wrongdoings "probably because of the fear of group pressure that would ensue, of not being a team player." He went on to explain that loyalty to the President and his team had taken precedence over loyalty to principles or to country.

Punishments and rewards need not be formal and tangible as this commentary on soldiers in military units testifies:

> The individual recruit is powerless. He finds solace in the company of his fellows, who are new and bewildered like himself, but who now, with all escapes blocked by fear of formal punishment, further each other's adjustment to the inevitable by applying sanctions of their own to those who "can't take it." *The fear of being thought less than a man by one's buddies can be as powerful a control as the fear of the guardhouse.* (Stouffer, 1949a, p. 412)

On the other hand, the soldier's ability "to take it" becomes a source of respect and admiration — he becomes a "regular guy."

GROUP FORCES AND CONFORMITY IN JUDGMENT

Success, recognition, and conformity are the bywords of the modern world where everyone seems to crave the anesthetizing security of being identified with the majority.

Martin Luther King, Jr., Strength in Love, 1963

Over the past forty years, Muzafer Sherif has been an innovative and imaginative social psychologist. One of his major studies involved the process whereby people evolve norms in group settings, come to internalize these norms, and then use these same norms as guidelines for their behavior. Sherif employed in his experiment an optical illusion — the "autokinetic phenomenon." If a small, fixed point of light is briefly exposed in a completely dark room, it appears to move, although it is in fact stationary. Individuals differ in their estimates of how far the point "moves." Sherif found that, when individuals were tested alone, each developed a characteristic range for the reported movements. The central tendency within this range served as their reference point. In repeated sessions, individuals tended to maintain the range and reference point that they had originally established. He then brought together in *groups* individuals who in solitary sessions had established very *different* ranges and reference points. Within group settings, they were again exposed to the light and asked to report aloud on their appraisal of the light's "movement." Their judgments tended to converge; the subjects responded with approximately the same range and central tendency as the others in the group. When brought back again for *individual* sessions, the group-derived norms persisted; the subjects did not return to their previously established norms.

Sherif discovered still another fact:

> . . . every individual was not necessarily aware of the fact that he was being influenced by others, or that he and other individuals were converging toward a common norm. In fact, the majority of the sub-

EVOLUTION OF NORMS

OBSERVATION Today is the second day of final exam week. I think every girl on my floor of the sorority house is smoking cigarettes, including myself. Yet until a week ago, most of us were nonsmokers. I abhor smoking, especially since the smoke makes me sick. Since all of us have been uptight during the past week, we have been smoking cigarettes to "calm our nerves." This is the explanation I give for smoking; it is the same explanation given by my sorority sisters. But now that I reflect about it, I find that I am no more at ease than if I were not smoking. Besides I would not have this sick feeling.

PRINCIPLE This is a good example of the emergence of a new norm in a group setting. My sorority sisters have evolved a norm specifying how to deal with tension and relax: smoke cigarettes. We accept our group's definitions. "It is our group, our norm." Yet as in the Asch experiments, we lack the confidence to contradict our group even when, as in my case, the evidence runs contrary to the group's definitions.

Figure 6.1. A sample comparison. Asch gave the subjects in the experimental groups the following instructions: "This is a task which involves the discrimination of lengths of lines. You see the pair of white cards in front. On the left is a single line; on the right are three lines differing in length; they are numbered 1, 2, and 3 in order. One of the three lines at the right is equal to the standard line at the left— you will decide in each case which is the equal line. You will state your judgment in terms of the corresponding number. There will be twelve such comparisons. As the number of lines is few and the group small, I shall call upon each of you in turn to announce your judgment, which I shall record here on a prepared form. Please be as accurate as possible. Suppose we start at the right and proceed to the left."

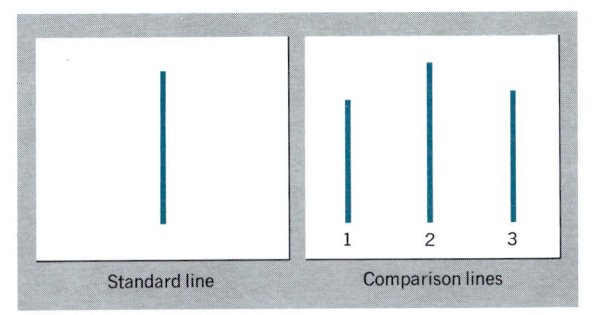

Source: Solomon E. Asch, *Social Psychology.* © 1952, p. 452. Reprinted by permission of Prentice-Hall, Inc., Englewood Cliffs, N. J.

jects reported not only that their judgments were made before the others spoke but also *that they were not influenced by the others.* (Sherif and Sherif, 1969, p. 210)

The influence of the group in channeling and directing our judgments is even more dramatically demonstrated in an ingenious experiment by Solomon E. Asch (1952, 1965). Unlike Sherif, Asch did not present his subjects with a vague situation. Instead, students were asked to match in length lines from two sets of white cards. In one set, each card displayed a single black line (the standard); in the other set, each card contained three lines, one the same length as the standard, the other two perceptibly longer or shorter. (See Figure 6.1.) When answers were written anonymously, control group students matched the lines with almost complete accuracy. However, when "naïve" subjects (the experimental groups) were asked to match the lines publicly after other "instructed" subjects (Asch's confederates) had intentionally given *incorrect* answers, a goodly number of the naïve subjects also gave *incorrect* answers. (Approximately one-third of all the subjects' judgments contained errors identical with or in the direction of the rigged errors of the majority.)

Why, Asch asked, did individuals yield to group pressures even though the group was wrong? On the basis of his interviews, he concluded that three different kinds of reactions contributed to the subjects' yielding to majority opinion:

1. *Distortion of perception.* A few subjects were not aware that their estimates had been distorted or displaced by the majority. These subjects came to perceive the rigged majority estimates as correct.
2. *Distortion of judgment.* Most of the yielding subjects concluded that their own perceptions were inaccurate while those of the majority were correct. Lacking confidence in their own perceptions, these individuals reported not what they saw but what they felt must be right.
3. *Distortion of action.* These subjects frankly admitted during the interviews that they did not report what they saw. They revealed that they yielded simply

Group Behavior

because they did not want to appear different or defective in the eyes of other group members.

The Asch experiment provides vivid testimonial to the part group norms play in regulating human behavior.

DEVIANCE

The more laws, the more offenders.
Thomas Fuller, M.D., *Gnomologia, 1732*

Norms are not a point or a line, but a *zone* (Williams, 1970:413). Usually, a "permissive" zone of variation is allowed around even the most specific and strongly supported norms. Hence, in actual practice, a norm provides for a band of behavior that is viewed as permissible even though it departs from the strict letter of the rule: a norm allows for *variant* behavior, new or at least different behavior that falls within the borders of the institutionally acceptable (Merton, 1959). The extent of this zone differs among norms and for the same norm under differing conditions. For example, when people come to feel that the group or society is threatened—as under conditions of war or after a great catastrophe—this band of permissiveness tends to contract, as exemplified by declaration of martial law.

Apparently, in all societies, the behavior of some people at times goes beyond that which is institutionally allowed. Norms of course tell us only what

DEGREES OF DEVIANCE

OBSERVATION I drive to the university each morning from a nearby town with two other guys. As we were coming in on the freeway, we observed a car get pulled over by a cop for what was obviously speeding. We all laughed at the "turkey with the escort." Then Dave observed that I regularly go five miles over the speed limit. I told Dave not to worry, "the cops give you an extra five miles an hour." But he got serious and said that I was speeding and breaking the law. This got me mad and I told him that there was a big difference between going 60 miles an hour and going 80 miles an hour. Dave replied, "Right, but you both are breaking the law. The law sets the speed limit at 55 miles an hour." I got even angrier and told Dave that "the turkey was breaking the law a lot more than me." He said, "That's stupid. The law is the law." Jack spoke up and said, "Dave, Jim's right. Notice that the cop didn't pull Jim over when he passed us to get that other turkey."

PRINCIPLE I've been thinking about what went on in the car this morning. In society we tend to tolerate a certain degree of deviance with respect to certain norms. However, we eventually reach a point where we begin recognizing that the deviance is excessive and then take measures against the deviant.

people should and should not do; they do not necessarily tell us what people *actually* do. Thus, we need to consider **deviance** —behavior that is viewed by a considerable number of people as reprehensible and beyond the tolerance limit. Deviance is *not* a property *inherent* in certain forms of behavior; it is a property *conferred* on these forms by social definitions, that is, by people rendering judgments regarding the desirability or undesirability of given behaviors (Becker, 1963; Horowitz and Liebowitz, 1968; Lemert, 1972;1976). Hence, in a very real sense, groups create deviance by making rules, the infraction of which they then define as deviance. And since societies differ in their rules, they differ in the acts that they view as being deviant. Table 6.1, for instance, presents data from 110 societies that indicate the range of variability existing with respect to twenty-two aspects of sexual behavior.

TABLE 6.1
Number and Percentage of Societies Punishing Specific Types of Sexual Behavior

Number of Societies Measured	Percentage Punishing Given Behavior	Type of Behavior and Person Punished
54	100	Incest
82	100	Abduction of a married woman
84	99	Rape of a married woman
55	95	Rape of an unmarried woman
43	95	Sexual relations during the postpartum period
15	93	Bestiality by an adult
73	92	Sexual relations during menstruation
88	89	Adultery (the paramour punished)
93	87	Adultery (the wife punished)
22	86	Sexual relations during the lactation period
57	86	Infidelity of the fiancée
52	85	Seduction of another man's fiancée
74	85	Illegitimate impregnation (the woman punished)
62	84	Illegitimate impregnation (the man punished)
30	77	Seduction of a prenubile girl (the man punished)
44	68	Male homosexuality
49	67	Sexual relations during pregnancy
16	44	Masturbation
97	44	Premarital relations (the woman punished)
93	41	Premarital relations (the man punished)
12	33	Female homosexuality
67	10	Sexual relations with own betrothed

Source: Adapted from Julia S. Brown, "A Comparative Study of Deviations from Sexual Mores," *American Sociological Review,* 17 (1952), 138. Reprinted by permission of the American Sociological Association and the author.

SOCIAL DEFINITIONS OF DEVIANCE: DRUG USE

As sociologist John A. Clausen observes, "drug use illustrates, perhaps better than any other form of deviance, the extent to which the existence of a social problem depends on definitions made within a society at a given time" (1976:143). Human beings have a long history of using chemical comforters (drugs to change their mood, feeling, or perception). Alcohol and marihuana are among the oldest of all socially used drugs. For example, in a pharmacy book written about 2737 B.C. by the Chinese Emperor Shen Nung, marihuana was recommended for "female weakness, gout, rheumatism, malaria, beriberi, constipation, and absent-mindedness." But which chemical substances are defined as legitimate, which effects as valuable, and which risks as tolerable are questions various groups and societies have decided in different ways (Orcutt, 1975; Zentner, 1977).

Within the United States, the Federal Drug Commission, the Bureau of Narcotics, and other government agencies take formal positions on whether a given drug is "good" or "bad," and if "bad," how bad. Indeed, some drugs enjoy official approval in everyday American life. For example, the use of caffeine, a mild stimulant, has been institutionalized through the American breakfast, coffee break, and coffee shop. And the possession of alcohol, a central nervous system depressant that has produced physical dependence in an estimated six million Americans and psychological dependence in perhaps five times that number, is free of penalty. Further, its use is encouraged to such a degree in recreational and business settings that nonusers are regarded by many as being somewhat peculiar. And until relatively recently, much the same held true for the use of nicotine (smoking).

In sharp contrast with coffee, alcohol, and tobacco, the mere possession of marihuana, a mild "hallucinogen," is still an offense punishable by fine or imprisonment in some parts of the United States. Yet marihuana does not produce physical dependence when used in moderate amounts and its psychological dependence is judged by many scientific authorities to be less than that of alcohol and tobacco (Fort and Cory, 1975; Conger, 1977).

In the United States marihuana arrests soared from 18,000 in 1965 to 188,682 in 1972 and to a peak of 445,600 in 1974 (according to FBI crime statistics). In 1975, arrests fell to 416,100 and have continued to fall since then as some states have eased their penalties and some local police agencies have relaxed their enforcement of anti-marihuana laws (Schellhardt, 1977). Of interest, a 1977 Gallup survey found that 24 percent of American adults said that they had used marihuana at least once (a figure double what it was in 1973 and six times what it was in 1969).

In sum, decisions as to which drugs are legitimate depend on the norms and values that characterize a society or powerful groups within it. "These judgments lie in the eye of the beholder, not in the drug" (Nowlis, 1971:13).

NORMS NEED NOT BE RATIONAL

OBSERVATION It was a lovely fall day today so I decided to study outside on a blanket near the dorm. Other students were lying about sunbathing. As I was halfheartedly studying, an attractive girl came by, spread out her blanket near me, and then proceeded to take off her clothes like she would to take a shower or make love (oh wow!). Underneath her jeans and T-shirt she had on a bikini. As I was taking this all in, it occurred to me that her bikini was much more revealing than if she had taken her clothes off and exhibited a bra and panties. Yet had she done the latter, she would have been deemed a deviant and been subject to arrest by campus police for indecent exposure.

PRINCIPLE Neither our norms nor our definitions of deviance are necessarily rational. Here a woman exposed more of her body in a bikini than would have been the case with a bra and panties. Nonetheless, her behavior was in keeping with the other sunbathers and was defined as acceptable. Clearly, norms are evolved by humans and exhibit all the vagaries of the human experience, at times reaching ridiculous levels. But then . . . Oh, yes! We got to chatting and we're going out together this evening!

DEVIANCE AND SOCIAL LIFE

Most of us define deviance as "bad"—behavior that constitutes a "social problem." This is not surprising since deviance may undermine the smooth flow of social interaction and impair social organization (Cohen, 1966; Wilson, 1975). Much of social life is constructed through the coordinated actions of numerous people. If some people fail to perform their actions at the proper time in accordance with prevailing expectations, social organization may be impaired (for instance, the family that finds itself deserted by a parent, the army whose commanding officer defects in the middle of a critical military operation, or the company whose supplier fails to honor a contract in delivering certain essential building materials).

Deviance may also undermine people's willingness to play their roles and contribute to ongoing social activity. Where some get rewards, even disproportionate rewards, without playing by the rules—for example, "idlers," "fakers," "chiselers," "sneaks," and "deadbeats"—others may develop bitterness and resentment. Morale, self-discipline, and loyalty may suffer. Further, *trust*—confidence that others will, by and large, play by the rules—is impaired (Denzin, 1970:279). In involving themselves in a collective enterprise, people commit some resources, forego some alternatives, and make some investment in the future. They do so based on the assumption that others will do the same. When others fail to undertake the appropriate and reciprocal behaviors, people feel themselves betrayed—their own efforts seem pointless, wasted, and foolish. Consequently, their determination to play by the rules may be undermined (Cohen, 1966).

While sociologists recognize that deviance may impair social organization, they also point out that in still other respects deviance actually facilitates effective social functioning. There are a number of ways in which this may come about. First, organizations commonly evolve rules that are designed to expedite various tasks. Yet, at times, such rules—"red tape"—actually interfere with the smooth operation of the organization; they defeat rather than serve the purposes of the organization. For instance, a university's rules may stipulate that graduate teaching assistants may be hired by a department's chairperson only after the college budget has been approved. Often, however, if the chairperson were to follow this procedure, other universities would already have "signed up" the better graduate students. So the chairperson may go ahead and make commitments in violation of the regulations. In this case, the deviance occurs on behalf of the organization.

Second, norms rarely are expressed as a firm rule or official code (see Chapter 2). Deviance may thus serve to clarify norms. Each time a group censures some acts of deviance, it highlights and sharpens the contours of a rule. Indeed, one of the interesting features of control institutions is the amount of publicity they generally attract. In earlier days, the correction of deviant offenders took place in the public market in full view of a crowd. In our day, we are confronted by a heavy flow of newspaper, radio, and television reports that serve much the same function:

> Why are these reports considered "newsworthy" and why do they rate the extraordinary attention they receive? Perhaps they satisfy a number of psychological perversities among the mass audience, as many commentators have suggested, but at the same time they constitute our main source of information about the normative outlines of society. They are lessons through which we teach one another what the norms mean and how far they extend. In a figurative sense, at least, morality and immorality meet at the public scaffold, and it is during this meeting that the community declares where the line between them should be drawn. . . . [The trespasser] informs us, as it were, what evil looks like, what shapes the devil can assume. In doing so, he shows us the difference between kinds of experience which belong within the group and kinds of experience which belong outside it. (Erikson, 1962, p. 310)

Moreover, in the process of opposing the deviant, the group may strengthen itself. A common enemy serves to arouse common sentiments and to revive and maintain solidarity (Coser, 1962; Lauderdale, 1976).

Third, deviance often provides a signal or warning that invites attention to defects in an organization. As such it may afford an impetus to social change (Coser, 1962). And, fourth, deviance provides a means by which nondeviant members of a group may indirectly violate or evade norms when it is to their advantage to do so. For instance, a "ratter"—a police officer—who "carries tales" to a supervisor—may be used by members of the police force as a "pipeline to the Chief" (Reed, Burnette, and Troiden, 1977). Deviance has many diverse consequences for the larger human enterprise.

THE PREVALENCE OF DEVIANCE

I hate this "crime doesn't pay" stuff. Crime in the U.S. is perhaps one of the biggest businesses in the world today.
>Paul Kirk, quoted in the Wall Street Journal, February 26, 1960

Statistics on deviance are among the most unsatisfactory of all social statistics (Booth, Johnson, and Choldin, 1977). Hence, in truth, we cannot at present gauge the prevalence of deviance within the United States with any great accuracy. Official crime records (the FBI's annual "Uniform Crime Reports") suffer from any number of limitations. For one thing, a large proportion of the crimes that are committed go undetected; others are detected but not reported; and still others are reported but not officially recorded (for instance, local officials occasionally manipulate their reports for political purposes).

A study undertaken several years ago by the National Opinion Research Center for the President's Crime Commission highlights the unreliability of official crime statistics. The Center conducted a household survey to discover how many families had been the victims of certain major crimes, and to compare this "victimization rate" with the "crime rate" reported by citizens to local police departments and through them to the FBI. These data revealed that about half again as many robberies, twice as many serious assaults and thefts, three times as many burglaries, and four times as many rapes occur as FBI reports indicate (the rates for murder and auto theft, on the other hand, appeared to be quite accurate). Matters were even worse in the central cities, where the true crime rates for certain offenses were as much as ten times greater than the reported rate. Similarly, a 1974 study undertaken by the Law Enforcement Assistance Administration (LEAA) found considerable variation between FBI reports and estimates based on interviews with 25,000 citizens in eight cities (see Table 6.2).

TABLE 6.2
Difference in the Volume of Crime Reported by the FBI and Estimated by LEAA*

	FBI	LEAA
Rape	3,090	6,600
Aggravated assault	24,095	37,600
Robbery	34,274	78,100
Burglary	119,984	325,600
Grand larceny	60,714	140,700
Petty larceny	101,085	259,500
Auto theft	65,966	65,700

* Comparison based on reports for eight cities in the United States.
Source: News release, Law Enforcement Assistance Administration, April 1974.

Official crime reports. Most crime in the United States goes unreported and hence does not come to the attention of law-enforcement agencies.

Patrick Reddy

Still other studies have noted that rates for some crimes, particularly **white collar crime**, are not routinely compiled (Sutherland, 1949; Wheeler, 1976; Geis and Meier, 1977). White collar crimes are committed by persons of affluence, often in the course of their business activities: corporate crime, fraud, embezzlement, corruption, bribery, tax fraud or evasion, stock manipulation, misrepresentation in advertising, restraint of trade, infringements of patents, and so on. By way of illustration, consider the following revelations:

- General Motors, unknown to consumers, places a Chevrolet engine in an Oldsmobile chassis.
- Bert Lance, Budget Director during the early months of the Carter Administration, routinely permitted himself large interest-free overdrafts in the Georgia banks which he headed. The Federal Reserve Board forbids loans as large as the Lance overdrafts to national-bank officers, and an overdraft is commonly defined as a loan. Lance also allegedly misemployed corporate funds by using his bank's plane for personal and political trips.
- Experts who specialize in fraud cases estimate that at least $15 billion is secretly pocketed each year by American business officials through commercial bribery and kickbacks (Jensen, 1976).
- A 1977 federal grand-jury named Tongsun Park, a South Korean business executive, and twenty-four present and former members of Congress as recipients of cash gifts or campaign contributions from Park. The indictment charged that Park arranged trips to South Korea by members of Congress believed "to be influential in matters affecting" South Korea. On such trips, the indictment said, "officials of the Republic of Korea would attempt to influence" the lawmakers "to take official actions in favor of" Korea.
- Arson-for-profit is rapidly becoming a big business in the United States. Owners of hotels, warehouses, factories, and housing in slum neighborhoods on occasion heavily insure their property and then arrange to have it burned down. Losses from arson have been nearly doubling each year since 1974, resulting in insurance claims running into billions of dollars (Clarity, 1977).

The most highly publicized revelations of white collar crime during the 1970s revolved about the Nixon Administration. Members of the House Judiciary Committee, in their articles of impeachment, found

> clear and convincing evidence that the President caused action—not only by his own subordinates but by agencies of the United States, including the Department of Justice, the Federal Bureau of Investigation, and the Central Intelligence Agency—to cover up the Watergate break-in. This concealment required perjury, destruction of evidence, obstruction of justice—all of which are crimes.

Moreover:

> Richard M. Nixon, in violation of his constitutional duty to take care that the laws be faithfully executed and his oath of office as President, seriously abused powers that only a President possesses. He engaged in conduct that violated the constitutional rights of citizens, that interfered with investigations by federal authorities and congressional committees, and that contravened the laws governing agencies of the executive branch of the federal government. This conduct, undertaken for his own personal political advantage and not in furtherance of any valid national policy objective, is seriously incompatible with our system of constitutional government.

President Nixon, of course, was compelled to resign the Presidency. But even prior to his indictment, President Ford pardoned him for all crimes he committed while President.

Official crime statistics also tend to overlook organized crime within the United States. Crime is big business and is managed and carried out in much the manner of any other business. The worlds of legitimate and illegitimate activity come together in many spheres of life. Carl B. Klockars details one such sphere in his study of a professional fence summarized in Research Study 11.

RESEARCH STUDY 11

THE PROFESSIONAL FENCE*

Carl B. Klockars

Problem. Sociologists have provided a good deal of research on crime and delinquency. However, most of this work has entailed survey research studies involving prison populations, the analysis of official crime statistics, and reports on youth gangs. The emphasis has fallen on traditional forms of crime. In contrast, relatively little is known about professional crime and the linkages that exist between the legal and illegal communities. It is to these latter matters that Carl B. Klockars addresses himself.

Method. After much effort and a number of false starts, Klockars located a professional fence, "Vin-

* Adapted from Carl B. Klockars, *The Professional Fence*. New York: The Free Press, 1974.

cent Swaggi" (a pseudonym), who agreed to cooperate with him and provide him with information. The study is a life-history of Swaggi. Klockars provides lengthy quotations from Swaggi and intersperses his own observations and interpretations.

Findings. A professional fence is an individual who runs a business in which stolen goods are sold to the public. Swaggi acts as a go-between for thieves and customers. He runs a general merchandise store that consists of both legitimate and illegitimate goods, a vast range of items including dental tools, plumbing fixtures, clothing, jewels, toys, typewriters, and office equipment. Much of his operation consists of creating the illusion that he sells merchandise at low prices because it is stolen. His customers include police officers, clergy, ordinary retailers, small-time wholesalers, ghetto housewives, and secretaries — all individuals hunting for a "real steal."

Much of Swaggi's merchandise consists of legitimate goods that other retailers and wholesalers have been unable to "move" and which Swaggi purchases cheaply from them. It is his legitimate business that provides a "cover" for his illegitimate activities. His stolen merchandise comes from professional thieves, hijackers, shoplifters, and ordinary truck drivers who "drop off" overload items.

Swaggi faces the continuous problem of avoiding arrest for the possession of stolen property. He employs a good many devices and procedures so as to alter and conceal the identity of stolen merchandise. He creates the appearance of legitimacy or obliterates the appearance of illegitimacy by changing or destroying identification numbers, removing identifiable characteristics (removing gems from their settings and refashioning minks), falsely claiming that particular receipts cover stolen goods, forging receipts, maintaining receipts with vague descriptions of merchandise, and mixing stolen stock with legitimate stock:

In his illegitimate trade he models his operations after the normal procedures and practices of the business world. In his legitimate trade he buys and sells with an eye toward covering his illegitimate activities. This managed similarity is designed to frustrate the . . . law and render it incapable of discriminating between the fence's legal and illegal activities (p. 101)

Swaggi has served only eighteen months of prison time in his nearly thirty years as a fence. He points out that the typical two-year maximum jail term for receiving stolen property is seldom served. Moreover, even the maximum penalty is far less severe than that commonly meted out to the armed robber, narcotics pusher, or burglar.

In a legal sense Swaggi is a criminal. But Swaggi does not conceive of himself as such. He asserts, "If I don't buy it, somebody else will. So what's the difference? I might as well make money with him instead of somebody else" (p. 139). He denies that he causes harm to anyone and insists that many people benefit from his activities. As is frequently the case with human beings, Swaggi shows an amazing ability to redefine what others view as immoral and rationalize it as moral. In the process he has fashioned an identity for himself as a morally righteous person.

Conclusion. We often conceive of the world as divided between "good people" and "bad people," each living their lives in relative isolation from each other (except in those circumstances when "bad people" prey on "good people"). In contrast, Klockar's study reveals the ties and relationships that exist within a society between individuals in the legitimate and illegitimate spheres.

REHABILITATION VERSUS DETERRENCE

There is a widespread public complaint that the present system of criminal justice does not deter criminal conduct.... The simple and obvious remedy is to give the courts the manpower and the tools, including prosecutors and defense counsel, to try criminal cases within sixty days after indictment and then let us see what happens. I predict that this would sharply reduce the crime rate.

Chief Justice Warren E. Burger, address August 10, 1970

Over the past decade, considerable controversy has emerged in both public and scholarly circles over the relative merits of rehabilitation and punishment as approaches for dealing with deviants. Prior to 1800 the notion was prevalent that the punishment of deviants is required if the injured community is to feel morally satisfied. Toward the latter part of the eighteenth and the early part of the nineteenth centuries, the idea that prisons might "rehabilitate" criminals became more prevalent. The word "penitentiary" was coined to describe a place where a criminal might repent and resolve to follow a more socially acceptable course of behavior. Through the years the American prison system has in part been organized on the premise that prisons can and should rehabilitate their inmates. Although prisons often failed in this mission, penologists nonetheless maintained that either effective means of rehabilitation remained to be found or that the means were known but were not being properly implemented (Tullock, 1974).

Beginning in the 1960s, a number of criminologists began questioning these assumptions. During the 1970s, the chorus of critics rapidly expanded. These critics suggest that there is a basic flaw in existing strategies, namely that education and psychotherapy even at their best cannot overcome or reduce the powerful tendency for offenders to continue their criminal ways. And they cite statistics on the high rate of recidivism (relapse into criminal behavior) to back up their argument. The critics of rehabilitation deny that crime resembles "disease," something foreign and abnormal to people that presumably can be "cured." Rather, they argue that some degree of crime is normal within a society and that a very large proportion of offenders are likewise normal and merely responding to the facts and conditions of social life (Martinson, 1974).

Probably the most prominent critic of rehabilitative procedures is James Q. Wilson (1975), a Harvard University political scientist who has enjoyed close ties over the past decade with the Nixon, Ford, and Carter Administrations. Wilson blames academic criminologists for assuming that the search for the *causes* of crime will lead to effective *policies* for controlling crime. For example, it may be true that youth growing up in a household where parents exercise ineffective control over their children are more disposed to becoming delinquents than other children. But no one knows how to give every child competent and loving parents. Wilson argues that the appeal of "rehabilitative" strategies has rested on the idea that such strategies get

Conformity and Deviance

down to "basics." But he notes that it is impossible to give a delinquent a new childhood. And prison programs that teach convicts how to be auto mechanics, read, or understand their inner impulses merely increase their life alternatives. However, such programs do not guarantee that the inmates will prefer auto mechanics to theft.

Wilson believes that changing people is difficult. Instead he calls for *deterrence*—for the swift and certain punishment of law violators. He views humans as essentially rational beings, self-interested individuals who rationally pursue what is best for themselves. For many Americans, especially ghetto youth who find jobs inaccessible and the juvenile justice system overloaded, underfunded, and ineffective, crime pays. Wilson believes, therefore, that a "good" and "swift" sentencing system is needed that "minimizes the chance of an offender's repeating his crime."

In Wilson's opinion, a policy of deterrence also has other merits. He cites official criminal statistics to show that roughly six percent of all prisoners are chronic offenders who account for over half of all the recorded delinquencies and two-thirds of all the violent crimes committed by the entire prison population. By keeping such individuals in prison and off the streets, the crime rate would presumably be reduced. Further, certain and swift punishment would allegedly prevent the population-at-large from believing that they can "get away with it" should they engage in criminal conduct.

Rehabilitation versus deterrence. The controversy over the relative merits of rehabilitation and punishment as approaches for dealing with deviance is one that has recurred across the centuries.

Patrick Reddy

As sociologist Jack P. Gibbs points out, deterrence is more a doctrine than a theory, "a vague congery of ideas with no unifying factor other than their being the legacies of two major figures in moral philosophy, Cesare Beccaria and Jeremy Bentham" (1975:5). Criminologists employ the concept of deterrence to describe the prevention of deviant behavior through the use of, or by the threat of, legal penalties. On the whole, recent sociological studies suggest that the *certainty* of apprehension and punishment does tend to lower crime rates (Chiricos and Waldo, 1970; Waldo and Chiricos, 1972; Tittle and Rowe, 1973, 1974; Kraut, 1976). Few studies, however, have found an association between the *severity* of punishment and crime (Bowers and Salem, 1972; Tittle and Logan, 1973; Gibbs, 1975).

Although most sociologists recognize that the prospect of punishment has *some* deterrent effect under *some* circumstances, they tend to be more concerned with specifying the *conditions* under which sanctions influence behavior (Tittle and Logan, 1973; Anderson, Chiricos, and Waldo, 1977). By way of illustration, the norms and sanctions of a group to which we owe strong allegiance may operate as an even stronger force than the threat of societal punishment in bringing about conformity (Silberman, 1976; Meier and Johnson, 1977; Anderson, Chiricos, and Waldo, 1977). By the same token, such informal standards and pressures may counteract the deterrent effects of legal sanctions (Tittle and Rowe, 1974).

The applicability of the deterrence doctrine to white collar crime remains to be determined, a matter of no small consequence since estimates place the cost of white collar crime to the nation as at least 200 times that of burglary. Of interest, Wilson has little to say about white collar crime. Similarly, some criminologists believe that the effectiveness of deterrence may be primarily limited to burglary and other property crimes but has much less influence on crimes of passion, such as murder.

Some Americans advocate capital punishment as one form of deterrence (Van Den Haag, 1976). Critics of capital punishment point out, however, that the victims of legalized killing by the state are usually the poor, Blacks, Chicanos, and the pleaders for unpopular causes (Shapiro, 1976). Finally, most authorities recognize that capital punishment is hardly a cure-all remedy for crime. As Samuel Johnson observed during the eighteenth century, the surest place to find most of the pickpockets of London at one time plying their trade was in the crowd assembled to witness one of their number being hanged.

THEORIES OF DEVIANCE

Sociologists are concerned with the question of why deviance exists. Theories of deviance have taken a number of different forms (Sagarin, 1975; Frazier, 1976). Some focus on the nature of society (the anomie and conflict theories), others on the characteristics and socialization of deviants (differential association theory), and still others on the nature of people's reaction against certain behaviors and individuals (labeling theory).

ANOMIE AND DEVIANCE

Today traditional morality is shaken and no other has been brought forward to replace it. The old duties have lost their power without our being able to see clearly and with assurance where our new duties lie.

Emile Durkheim, Sociology and Philosophy, 1906

Emile Durkheim, an influential French sociologist and profound student of social organization, introduced the concept of **anomie** to sociology in his 1897 study of suicide rates. Through the years sociologists have come to view anomie as a condition within a society or group in which there exists a weakened respect for some of the norms. Although literally the term means "without rules," anomie is not the same thing as the absence of norms. Rather, individuals are in part oriented to the norms but in an ambivalent manner; they lean either to conformity, but with misgivings, or toward deviance, but with misgivings.

The Disparity Between Cultural Goals and Approved Means. There are a great many factors that can contribute to anomie. Robert K. Merton (1968), a leading American sociologist, identified one source: a disparity between the *goals* held out to the members of a society and the institutionalized *means* by which these goals may be achieved. Merton distinguishes between those norms that set goals and those norms that indicate the approved ways by which the goals can be realized. The goals constitute people's aspirations; they are the things "worth striving for." A society also defines the allowable procedures for moving toward these objectives. But the regulatory norms need not be identical with technical or efficiency norms. Many procedures would be quite efficient in realizing the goals but are ruled out—the exercise of force, fraud, and so on.

Merton focuses his attention on American society. He suggests that, to a degree not true of most other societies, Americans are expected to reach out for the goal of worldly success. Within the United States, Merton argues, striving for success is encouraged to such an extent that it virtually becomes

Robert K. Merton. Merton holds that anomie is the source of much deviant behavior.

Courtesy of the American Sociological Association

a culturally obligatory pattern (witness the sanguine forecasts and hopes inked in on the margins of senior yearbooks). Accumulated wealth has come to symbolize success; money is prized for itself. Money, however, is highly abstract and impersonal. Whether acquired fraudulently or institutionally, it can be used to purchase the same goods and services.

Moreover, in the American Dream there is no final stopping point:

> The measure of "monetary success" is conveniently indefinite and relative. At each income level, as H. F. Clark found, Americans want just about twenty-five per cent more (but of course this "just a bit more" continues to operate once it is obtained). In this flux of shifting standards, there is no stable resting point, or rather, it is the point which manages always to be "just ahead." An observer of a community in which annual salaries in six figures are not uncommon, reports the anguished words of one victim of the American Dream: "In this town, I'm snubbed socially because I only get a thousand a week. That hurts." (1968, p. 190)

Yet many Americans do not enjoy access to the socially approved means for realizing success. Lower-class and minority group members in particular often find themselves handicapped by little formal education and few economic resources. And Americans tend to attach a stigma to manual labor. For those individuals who internalize the goal of pecuniary success—and not all individuals do—strong strains exist toward unorthodox practices and nonconformity. One answer to the dilemma becomes that of obtaining the prestige-laden ends by any means whatsoever—illicit means (crime, vice, and the like). Within this context, Al Capone and contemporary Mafia overlords represent a triumph over morally prescribed "failure." But a high frequency of deviant behavior is not simply generated by a "lack of opportunity" or by an exaggerated pecuniary emphasis. A society with a comparatively rigid class or caste structure may lack opportunity and simultaneously extol wealth—as for instance in the medieval feudal system. It is, however, only when a society extols certain *common* symbols of success for the *entire* population while structurally restricting access to approved means for acquiring these symbols for *a considerable part of the same population* that antisocial behavior ensues on a large scale.

Types of Responses to Anomie. Merton identifies five types of individual adaptation to the pressures posed by anomie (the gap between culturally defined goals and the socially structured means for realizing the goals). He sets forth these adaptations in the scheme shown in Figure 6.2.

Conformity. Conformity to both cultural goals and institutional means represents the most common adaptation. Indeed, as we shall see in Chapter 9, widespread commitment to cultural goals and institutional norms represents an important source of societal integration.

Figure 6.2. A typology of modes of individual adaptation to anomie.

Modes of adaptation	Cultural goals	Institutionalized means
I Conformity	+	+
II Innovation	+	−
III Ritualism	−	+
IV Retreatism	−	−
V Rebellion	±	±

+ = Acceptance
− = Rejection
± = Rejection of prevailing values and substitution of new values

Source: Reprinted with permission of The Free Press, from *Social Theory and Social Structure*, rev. ed., by Robert K. Merton. Copyright 1949, 1957 by the Free Press.

Innovation. In this form of deviant behavior, people hold fast to the culturally emphasized goals while abandoning culturally approved ways of seeking them. Merton argues that America's extreme emphasis on success actually invites individuals to use forbidden but nevertheless effective means for realizing accumulated wealth. Illustrations of this type of deviancy include organized vice (prostitution and gambling), rackets, and crime (including "white-collar" crime).

Ritualism. Ritualism involves the abandoning or scaling down of the lofty cultural goals of great pecuniary success to the point where one's aspirations can be satisfied. Although individuals reject the cultural obligation of attempting "to get ahead" — or in any event lower their horizons — they continue to abide compulsively by the approved means. An example of this kind of adaptation is the zealously conformist bureaucrat who makes a fetish of red tape:

> ... men, having internalized moral norms to a degree that does not allow them to be violated, find sanctuary in routine. They reluctantly abandon their aspirations while clinging, perhaps on that account all the more tightly, to the routines of their roles [positions]. These are the ritualists of our society, uncounted though probably legion: the organization automatons, the routineers, the religious compulsives. (1964, pp. 218–219)

Retreatism. Retreatism involves the rejection of *both* cultural goals and approved means *but without the substitution of new norms* — for example, outcasts, vagrants, vagabonds, drug addicts, and chronic alcoholics. Such individuals "are in society but not of it."

Rebellion. Rebellion entails the rejection of *both* cultural goals and approved means and the substitution of *new* norms — for example, radical social movements. This form of adaptation arises when the institutional system is regarded as a barrier to the satisfaction of legitimate goals. Under such circumstances, the allegiance of persons may be withdrawn from the existing social structure and transferred to new groups with new ideologies.

Critique of Merton's Theory of Anomie. Merton's writings on anomie have enjoyed a prominent place within American sociology. They have not, however, gone without criticism. Let us briefly outline a number of them.

Some critics (Cohen, 1965) claim that Merton views deviants as atomistic and individualistic beings—persons more or less in a box by themselves who work out a solution to their stressful circumstances without regard for what other people are doing. Thus, critics charge, Merton fails to take *social interaction* into sufficient account (the bearing other people's experience and influence have in channeling a person's response to anomie).

Other critics charge that Merton's theory suffers from "the assumption of discontinuity"; that is, Merton treats the deviant act as though it were an abrupt change of state, a leap from a state of strain or anomie to a state of deviance. In contrast to Merton's formulation, Cohen notes:

> Human action, deviant or otherwise, is something that typically develops and grows in a tentative, groping, advancing, backtracking, sound-out process. People taste and feel their way along. They begin an act and do not complete it. They start doing one thing and end up by doing another. They extricate themselves from progressive involvement or become further involved to the point of commitment. These processes of progressive involvement and disinvolvement are important enough to deserve explicit recognition and treatment in their own right. (1965, pp. 8–9)

Further, not all deviant behavior is a response to conditions of anomie. Simpson and Simpson observe:

> Not all deviance . . . stems from gaps between goals and means. Some subcultural deviance—for example, the extramarital sex activity in some lower-class circles—can be viewed simply as a failure to accept the same norms as are prevalent in most of the population. The deviants may not regard themselves as such, but their behavior has the effect of deviance since it is so considered by the middle-class people who control the courts and other agencies which can impose sanctions [penalties]. (1964, pp. 410–411)

Finally, sociologists William Simon and John H. Gagnon (1976) point out that Merton's formulation focuses primarily on means and not sufficiently on goals. It is essentially an anomie rooted in conditions of chronic economic recession and depression. But, Simon and Gagnon assert, there is also an "anomie of affluence":

In contrast to a social order that makes promises and fails to keep them, we must now consider a social order that for many segments of the society makes promises and then proceeds to keep them. But a society that keeps these promises with such ease and abundance can trivialize them to the point where achievement no longer affords what has been called "consummatory gratification." ... Attainment of goals ceases to provide ... confirmation [of competence, moral worth, and/or good fortune] precisely when the objects or experiences that have symbolized achievement become part of the easily accessible and therefore unspectacular, everyday quality of life." (p. 361)

CONFLICT AND DEVIANCE

These written laws are just like spiders' webs; the small and feeble may be caught and entangled in them, but the rich and mighty force through and despise them.
Anacharsis to Solon (ancient Greece)

In the past decade, conflict has proven to be a popular explanation for deviance (Quinney, 1974, 1975; Platt, 1975; Spitzer, 1975; Galliher and McCartney, 1977). Marxists in particular have offered an image of society in which a ruling class exploits and otherwise robs the masses yet avoids punishment for its crimes. Others, victimized by exploitation, are driven to commit acts in their struggle to survive that leads the ruling class to brand them as criminals (Sagarin, 1975). William Chambliss indicates, "The criminal law is ... first and foremost a reflection of the interests and ideologies of the governing class" (1974:37). Similarly, Richard Quinney asserts:

Law is the tool of the ruling class. Criminal law, in particular, is a device made and used by the ruling class to preserve the existing order. In the United States, the state—and its legal system—exist to secure and perpetuate the capitalist interests of the ruling class. (1974, p. 8)

Sociologists Raymond J. Michalowski and Edward W. Bohlander (1976) point to a number of ways in which American criminal justice serves the "capitalist ruling class." First, crime is defined primarily in terms of offenses against property (burglary, robbery, auto theft, vandalism, and the like) while corporate crime is deemphasized. Second, the penalty prescribed for crimes against property is imprisonment while the most common form of penalty for business-related offenses is a monetary fine:

In the State of Ohio, for example, all of the acts listed under "offenses against property" are punishable by incarceration, while only forty percent of the offenses listed under the "pure food and drug law" can result in a deprivation of liberty. Furthermore, while nearly all of the property crimes are determined to be felony offenses punishable by prison sentences, ranging from one year to life, there is not a single violation of the pure food and drug law classified as a felony, and the maximum period of incarceration for any of these violations is 100 days. (p. 102)

Third, Michalowski and Bohlander assert that affluent groups have the least likelihood of being prosecuted, and if prosecuted, they enjoy the maximum advantage in defending themselves against the charges. And fourth, local police agencies define their task as one of enforcing common-law crimes while "violations against consumers or the commonwealth, such as air and water pollution, are generally handled, if at all, by small regulatory agencies with little power and only minimal funding relative to the task at hand" (1976:103).

However, not all conflict sociologists are Marxists. Some sociologists simply take the view that people frequently find themselves involved in a struggle over scarce resources and social values. In brief, individuals feel themselves separated by incompatible objectives. Many goods and services are in scarce supply so that the more there is for some, the less there is for others. Further, people often differ in what forms of behavior they define as being moral or immoral and commendable or deplorable. When individuals find themselves at odds, the problem becomes: Whose interests shall be served and whose values shall prevail? Such issues become a question of power, and as such may become caught up in the political process.

It would appear that within the United States at the present time some behaviors traditionally defined as deviant are indeed becoming politicized. In the past, America attempted a "nonpolitical" or "welfare" approach to deviance. It handed over such "problems" as drug addiction, homosexuality, alcoholism, mental illness, and poverty to professionals—social workers, psychologists, and psychiatrists. However, this traditional approach is under attack: drug addicts and homosexuals are pioneering their own organizations in response to harassment, women with unwanted pregnancies are demanding and receiving legal abortions, welfare recipients are mobilizing their resources in opposition to traditional welfare approaches, Black Power advocates are demanding indigenous control over schools in Black ghettos, and prisoners are organizing against prison abuse, harassment, and exploitation (Horowitz and Liebowitz, 1968:280–296).

In a very real sense, deviance may be seen as a conflict between at least two factions: those members of society who enjoy power and who make and enforce rules, and those members who are subordinate and whose behavior violates such rules. Viewed from this perspective, social problems are defined by a society's elitist groups as those arenas where dangerously intense and unfavorable polarization is occurring, power is being effectively challenged, dominant institutions are faltering, manipulation is failing, and subtle coercion is insufficient. Simultaneously, social problems are defined

Conformity and Deviance

by the victims, by those who feel themselves exploited and abused by existing arrangements, in quite different terms. Viewed by elitist groups, it is the breakdown of exploitation that produces the social problem; viewed by the victims it is the dominant institutions that constitute the problem (Sagarin, 1973).

Conflict approaches to deviance call our attention to many aspects of social inequality that emerge in the enactment and administration of laws. However, many of its formulations need to be refined (Horwitz, 1977). For example, it is not always clear as to which specific individuals or groups are covered by such terms as "ruling elites," "governing classes," "powerful interests," and the like (Hagan and Leon, 1977). Further, conflict hypotheses need to be tested. For instance, William J. Chambliss and R. B. Seidman assert, "When sanctions are imposed, the most severe sanctions will be imposed on persons in the lowest social class" (1971:475). Yet Theodore G. Chiricos and Gordon P. Waldo (1975) examined the prison sentences received by 10,488 inmates for seventeen offenses within three southeastern states and found no support for this conflict proposition. Clearly, additional research is called for on this and related matters.

Conflicting values: The abortion controversy. People frequently differ regarding what they consider to be moral and immoral behavior. Under these circumstances, whose values shall prevail? Who shall translate their values into the operating standards of society? Who shall define who is or is not deviant? Conflict theorists suggest that the answers to these questions reside in which party to a conflict commands the greater power.

Patrick Reddy

DIFFERENTIAL ASSOCIATION AND DEVIANCE

Some sociologists have focused on how deviant patterns are culturally transmitted. Edwin H. Sutherland's theory of differential association best represents this approach. Sutherland states his theory in these terms:

> Criminal behavior is learned in interaction with other persons in a process of communication. . . . The principal part of the learning of criminal behavior occurs within intimate personal groups. . . . When criminal behavior is learned, the learning includes (a) techniques of committing the crime, which are sometimes very complicated, sometimes very simple; (b) the specific direction of motives, drives, rationalizations, and attitudes. . . . The specific direction of motives and drives is learned from definitions of the legal codes as favorable or unfavorable. . . . A person becomes delinquent because of an excess of definitions favorable to violation of law over definitions unfavorable to violation of law. This is the principle of differential association. (Sutherland and Cressey, 1970, p. 75)

In a very real sense, then, socially disapproved behaviors arise through the same process of socialization as socially approved ones.

Sutherland emphasizes the part that social interaction plays in producing deviance. He emphasizes that an individual becomes a deviant through being exposed to deviant patterns and isolated from antideviant patterns. A person "inevitably assimilates the surrounding culture," and hence criminals are criminals because of "differential association"; that is, through association with criminals, the individual acquires criminal patterns of behavior, whereas the noncriminal—through association with noncriminals—acquires noncriminal patterns. Not everyone, however, in contact with criminality adopts or follows the criminal pattern: only those who have an *overabundance* of such associations in comparison with anticriminal associations (Cressey, 1960).

As with other theories of deviance, Sutherland's approach has come under close scrutiny. Some charge that the theory does not apply to some types of crime, namely, those in which neither the techniques nor the appropriate definitions and attitudes are acquired from other deviants: for example, criminal violators of financial trust; naïve check forgers; "accidental" criminals; occasional, incidental, and situational offenders; nonprofessional shoplifters and non-career-type criminals; and persons who commit crimes of passion. Still others assert that Sutherland does not adequately take into account the "acceptance" and "receptivity" patterns of various individuals. One form of this criticism suggests that criminals and noncriminals are sometimes reared in the "same environment"—criminal behavior patterns are presented to two persons, but only one of them becomes a criminal. In other words, Sutherland does not take into account the fact that two individuals may be confronted with the same patterns of behavior but perceive them quite differently, producing quite different consequences.

LABELING AND DEVIANCE

. . . the character of every act depends upon the circumstances in which it is done.
Justice Oliver Wendell Holmes, Jr., opinion in
Schenck v. U.S. (1919)

By 1970 labeling theory had become the dominant sociological perspective on deviance (Cole, 1975). But as the 1970s progressed, opposition to labeling theory became almost as fashionable as labeling had been a decade earlier (Goode, 1975; Sagarin, 1975; Gove, 1976). Labeling sociologists—such individuals as Howard S. Becker (1963), Kai Erikson (1962, 1964), and Edwin M. Lemert (1972, 1976)—take the view that no act by itself is inherently criminal or noncriminal. Rather, in the course of their interaction, people react to one another's behavior. Central to this process is the evolution and formulation of definitions, meanings that embody images, evaluations, and designations—in brief, *labels*. People then take into account these labels as they fashion their further actions. In many cases, they evolve an identity derived from the content of a particular label and as a result enter on a career of deviance. This perspective derives from the symbolic interactionist tradition.

Labeling theorists observe that whether people's acts will be seen as deviant depends in part on what they do (whether they have violated some norm) *and in part on what other people do about it.* In brief, deviancy depends on which rules society chooses to enforce, in which situations, and with respect to which people. Thus, Blacks may get censored for what Whites may do; women censored for what men may do; certain individuals censored for what their friends are also doing; and some may be labeled as deviants even though they have not violated a norm but simply because they are so accused (for example, they "dress" or "walk" like a homosexual or a "pervert"). Of critical importance is the social audience and whether it *labels* an individual a deviant.

Labeling people as deviants has consequences for them. It tends to set up conditions conducive to subsequent deviancy. Kai Erikson observes:

> The community's decision to bring deviant sanctions against the individual . . . is a sharp rite of transition at once moving him out of his normal position in society and transferring him into a distinctive deviant role. The ceremonies which accomplish this change of status, ordinarily, have three related phases. They provide a formal confrontation between the deviant suspect and representatives of his community (as in the criminal trial or psychiatric case conference); they announce

DEVIANCE IS A MATTER OF SOCIAL DEFINITION

OBSERVATION I am still getting over my New Year's Eve hangover (written on January 2). It is interesting how our society taboos intoxication and yet makes it mandatory to get smashed on New Year's Eve. Actually I don't care that much for drinking but if I don't get smashed on New Year's Eve I'd be deviant—"uptight," "straight." The same thing happens at Mardi Gras. You are supposed to live it up and do all sorts of crazy things that you can't do on other occasions. April Fool's Day is another case. You can do all kinds of tomfoolery that would make you a kook on other days.

PRINCIPLE It is weird the way society falls all over you if you violate some norms—even sends you to the Workhouse if you're drunk. Then it turns around and makes you a deviant if you don't do these very same things. On given days society institutionalizes behavior that on other days it would label deviant.

> some judgment about the nature of his deviancy (a verdict or diagnosis for example), and they perform an act of social placement, assigning him to a special role (like that of a prisoner or patient) which redefines his position in society. (1964, p. 16)

According to this view, society forces individuals through a degradation ceremony—it socializes them in the cultural patterns of the new role (a drug user, homosexual, mental patient, prisoner) and assigns them an inferior status—all of which fosters a deviant self-image (Farrell and Nelson, 1976). Individuals so labeled may react by entering "career" deviance.

An important aspect of these ceremonies is that they are often almost irreversible. The status of deviant—a mental patient, a forger, a rapist, a drug addict, a homosexual—is a master status that overrides all other statuses in influencing how others will act toward the individual. Such individuals become *stigmatized*. In so doing they are virtually forced into a deviant group with people sharing a common fate as a way of coping with frustrating and conflict-laden situations: a deviant counterculture (Becker, 1963).

Critics suggest that two major premises of labeling theory are substantially incorrect (Gove, 1975,1976; Wellford, 1975). First, the theory holds that society's reaction to deviants does not initially derive from the "deviants'" behavior but from the fact that they occupy positions on the margins of society (individuals who lack power and resources such as youth, lower-class people, and minority group members). Critics dispute this formulation (Bernstein, Kelly, and Doyle, 1977) and insist that it is the behavior or condition of the people themselves that is primarily responsible for their being labeled as deviants. An example is mental illness (Mechanic, 1972; Townsend, 1975; Loman and Larkin, 1976). Walter R. Gove argues that the theory's explanation of how and why people enter the mentally ill role is incorrect, for it appears that the substantial majority of people who are hospitalized are suffering from a serious disturbance deriving from *internal* psychological or metabolic malfunctioning. As he appraises the evidence, labeling theorists overstate the degree to which societal reaction contributes to mental hospitalization. See Research Study 12.

A second premise of labeling theory that critics find questionable is the assertion that a deviant status becomes more or less permanent. The theory presumes that once individuals are stigmatized as deviants, it becomes exceedingly difficult for them to return to a normal status. Yet as noted earlier in the chapter, a punitive societal reaction often acts as a deterrent that prevents individuals from engaging in further deviant acts. This is true for those heroin addicts who eventually kick their habit (McAuliffe, 1975). Nor is labeling necessarily a one-way street in which individuals passively accept their stigmatized labels—some successfully fight back (Rogers and Buffalo, 1974). And research by Anthony R. Harris (1976) reveals that their definition as "criminals" does not lead many inmates, especially Black prisoners, to a "spoiled identity," a loss of ego "integrity," or "self-derogation."

RESEARCH STUDY 12

SOCIETAL REACTION AS AN EXPLANATION OF MENTAL ILLNESS: AN EVALUATION*

Walter R. Gove.

Problem. In the past decade or so "labeling theory" has emerged as one of the most pervasive and influential sociological approaches for interpreting deviance. Walter R. Gove sets himself the task of assessing the validity of the approach as it applies to mental illness.

Hypotheses. Labeling theory views mental illness as a socially constructed role deriving from conditions external to the individual (as opposed to those theories that see mental illness arising from internal emotional conflicts or metabolic/biochemical imbalances). As formulated by Thomas Scheff (1966; 1968), the theory holds:

1. Nearly everyone at sometime commits acts that correspond to the public's image of mental illness;

2. Should by chance such acts become public knowledge, the individual may, depending on the circumstances (unspecified by Scheff), be referred to some official agency;

3. Once "referral" occurs, the individual is routinely processed as mentally ill and hospitalized in a mental institution.

In sum, the theory hypothesizes that an individual becomes publicly labeled as a deviant ("mentally ill") and then is forced by the societal reaction into a deviant role—such individuals are victimized.

Next, the labeling theory hypothesizes that once placed within a mental hospital, the individual is socialized within the new role: the hospital is a debilitating institution where patients come to accept (enact) the role of "insane" and develop attitudes and skills appropriate to a regimented institutional

Continued on next page.

---

* Adapted from Walter R. Gove, "Societal Reaction as an Explanation of Mental Illness: An Evaluation," *American Sociological Review*, 35 (1970), 873–884.

life (while simultaneously losing those attitudes and skills relevant for living in the "real world"). Further, individuals are "stigmatized" as mentally ill ("insane"), reinforcing their self-image as deviants (facilitating socialization in the mentally ill role) and setting them apart from "normal people" ("nut," "kook," "crazy Jane") — in brief, they become estranged from the larger society (Goffman, 1961).

Method. In contrast with previous Research Studies considered in the text, Gove did not gather original data. Rather, he surveyed a vast amount of literature and data — material collected by others — and made *new* utilization of it. His contribution was bringing together "old" material in a "new," creative, imaginative fashion.

Findings. Labeling theory holds that the deviant (the "mentally ill" person) is someone who is victimized. Gove found, however, that little systematic evidence supports this notion. He cites a pioneering study by Marion Yarrow, Charlotte Schwartz, Harriet Murphy, and Leila Deasy (1955) that investigated how wives come to define their husbands as mentally ill. The research revealed that the wives made every effort to *avoid* seeing their husband's behavior as anything but normal; when this failed, they attempted to minimize the importance of the deviant behavior and to balance it off against more normal behavior. Only when the wife could no longer cope with the husband's bizarre or depressed behavior did she take action to have him hospitalized. Evidence from other studies likewise suggests that people are typically hospitalized because they have severe psychiatric disorders that are extremely difficult for themselves and/or others to handle (for example, they are suicidal or disoriented).

Gove's survey of the literature also leads him to challenge Scheff's notion that individuals, brought to the attention of officials or agencies as mentally ill, are routinely routed to mental hospitals. Hospital acceptance of voluntary mental patients is hardly routine: Gove notes two studies which show that a private mental hospital accepted for admission 58 percent of the applicants and two public mental hospitals 39 and 41 percent respectively. And a number of studies suggest that even in circumstances involving court hearings, as many as 22 percent of the cases result in the individual being released (not committed).

Gove next turns his attention to the labeling theory's view of hospitalization as an agent socializing individuals to the mentally ill role and contributing to the stigmatizing. He notes that the majority of psychiatric patients are hospitalized for only a relatively brief time (in the contemporary era of tranquilizers and open-door policies) — in brief, patients typically do not spend enough time in the hospital to become truly institutionalized. Further, while admittedly having debilitating consequences for some individuals, hospitals also have positive, health-generating results; for instance, with the assistance of mental health workers, many individuals are able to reach a new "working consensus" in family affairs. And finally, Gove challenges the notion of stigma. He observes that two-thirds of mental patients are not rehospitalized (Angrist, Lefton, Dinitz, and Pasamanick, 1968); thus most patients do not continuously occupy the mentally ill role nor experience its accompanying stigma. Moreover, studies (Freeman and Simmons, 1961) reveal that fewer than half of ex-mental patients feel stigmatized (in one study only 24 percent felt stigmatized by relatives).

Conclusion. Gove concludes that it is a person's disturbed behavior that generally leads to the mentally ill role. Labeling theory, he believes, is unable to explain the development of mental illness — that is, it fails to explain why people initially commit deviant acts. Gove insists that a person's behavior determines the expectations of others to a much greater degree than the reverse (labeling theory proponents take the opposite approach). He does not deny, however, that societal reactions to mentally ill people are important, but concludes that labeling theorists vastly overestimate the importance of such reactions.

SUMMARY

1. Sociologists identify three principal factors that contribute to conformity: (1) we internalize many norms; (2) we often are unaware of alternative modes of behavior; and (3) we may realize that to violate norms may result in our incurring punishment, while conformity produces rewards.

2. As revealed by the research of Muzafer Sherif, people evolve norms in group settings, come to internalize these norms, and then use these same norms as guidelines for their behavior. Research by Solomon E. Asch shows that some individuals yield to group pressures even when the group is wrong.

3. Deviance is behavior that is viewed by a considerable number of people as reprehensible and beyond the tolerance limit. Deviance is not a property inherent in certain forms of behavior; it is a property conferred on these forms by social definitions. Drug use within the United States illustrates the extent to which the existence of a social problem depends on such definitions.

4. Deviance may undermine the smooth flow of social interaction and impair social organization. Sociologists point out, however, that in some respects deviance actually facilitates effective social functioning.

5. Statistics on deviance are among the most unsatisfactory of all social statistics. A large proportion of the crimes that are committed go undetected; others are detected but not reported; and still others are reported but not officially recorded. Further, the rates for some crimes, particularly white collar crime, are not routinely compiled.

6. Over the past decade, considerable controversy has emerged in both public and scholarly circles over the relative merits of rehabilitation and punishment as approaches for dealing with deviance. Although most sociologists recognize that the prospect of punishment has some deterrent effect under some circumstances, they tend to be more concerned with specifying the conditions under which sanctions influence behavior.

7. Theories of deviance have taken a number of different forms. Robert K. Merton suggests that one source of deviance is anomie that arises from a disparity between the goals held out to the members of a society and the institutionalized means by which these goals may be achieved.

8. Conflict sociologists suggest that people find themselves involved in a struggle over scarce resources and social values. When individuals find themselves at odds, the problem becomes one of determining whose interests will be served and whose values will prevail; in brief, who will and will not be branded as criminals. Such issues become a question of power, and as such become caught up in the political process.

9. Some sociologists have focused on how deviant patterns are culturally transmitted, a theory of differential association. Socially disapproved behaviors are viewed as arising through the same process of socialization as socially approved ones.

10. Labeling sociologists take the view that no act by itself is inherently criminal or noncriminal. Rather, in the course of their interaction, people react to one another's behavior. Central to this process is the evolution and formulation of labels. People then take these labels into account as they fashion their further actions. In many cases, they evolve an identity derived from the content of a particular label and as a result enter a career of deviance.

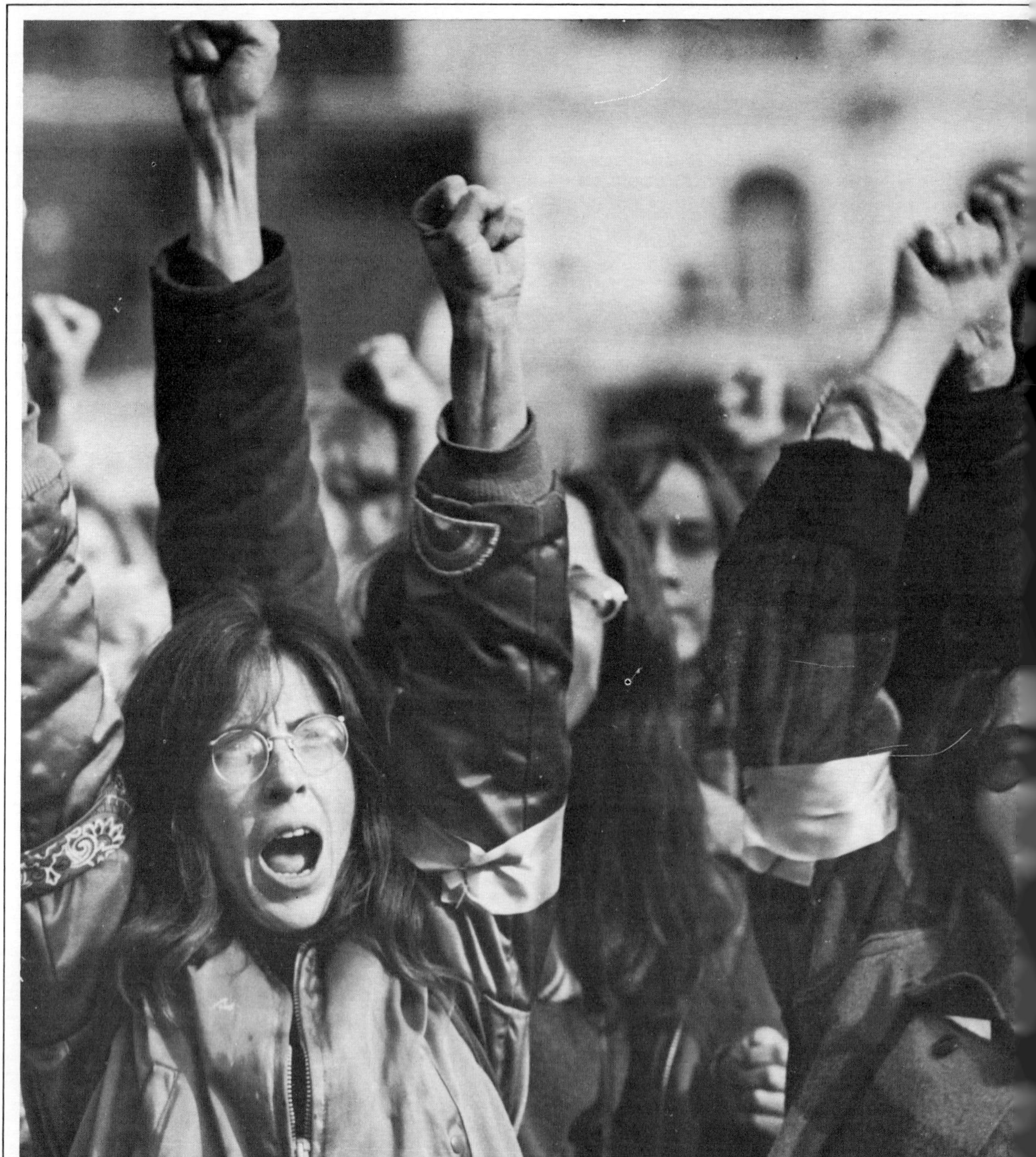

7
Collective Behavior and Social Movements

DETERMINANTS OF COLLECTIVE BEHAVIOR
Structural Conduciveness
Structural Strain
The Growth of a Generalized Belief
Precipitating Factors
The Mobilization of Participants for Action
The Operation of Social Control

CROWD BEHAVIOR
Contagion Theories
The Convergence Theory
The Emergent Norm Theory
Crowd Selection of Targets

THE MASS
Mass Communication
The Significance and Effects of Mass Communication

THE PUBLIC
Public Opinion
Public Conceptions of Social Problems

SOCIAL MOVEMENTS
The Nature of Social Movements
Elements of Social Movements

OBSERVATION I work in a large department store. Today the store had its annual "one dollar sale" on linens. When I got to work my supervisor sent me to the linens department to help out just for today as they expected considerable business. The store opened as usual at 9:30 and a massive tidal wave of women descended on the linens department. At the time I was wheeling a cart of sheets past the cash register heading for the place where I was to stack them in a pile. At least twenty women suddenly bolted for the cart, shoving me out of the way. They were by no means a gentle bunch as they elbowed one another and clawed at the sheets. To be honest, they scared the hell out of me. It was a real mob scene. I just backed off and let them do as they pleased.

PRINCIPLE The crowd behavior this morning seems to me to be best explained by the convergence theory. The one dollar sale had selected out from the population-at-large a number of bargain-hungry people. Each had assembled outside the store early, determined to get some merchandise before the store sold out. Thus these individuals had converged on the store sharing similar predispositions and ready for "action."

The 1960s and 1970s were turbulent years on American college campuses. During this period the student movement passed through three phases. The first phase, that of civil rights, was launched on the spur of the moment by what at first appeared to be a relatively inconspicuous development. On February 1, 1960, four Black freshmen from North Carolina Agricultural and Technical College entered a Greensboro variety store and bought some merchandise. About four-thirty in the afternoon they sat down at a lunch counter reserved for Whites, but had not been served by the time the store closed an hour later. The movement did not take on an organized form until the next day, when some seventy-five A & T students "sat-in" at the same lunch counter. The sit-in movement spread throughout the South, involving Black youth from at least thirty-nine colleges and White youth from another nine. By May 1, 1960, 1194 Blacks had been arrested for their part in the demonstrations. In the next four years White college students from the North went South during the summer months to participate with Blacks in civil rights and voter registration drives.

Berkeley's Free Speech Movement ushered in the second phase of the student movement during the fall of 1964, the campus-oriented "student power" campaign:

> Improbable as it may have seemed to outsiders, events at the Berkeley campus of the University of California during the last three months of 1964 constituted a small-scale but genuine revolution. Through continuous violation of university regulations, sit-ins, almost daily mass demonstrations, and finally a strike by students and teaching assistants, the authority of both the administration and the faculty had become virtually nonexistent at Berkeley by December. (Lipset and Seabury, 1965, p. 340)

Collective Behavior and Social Movements

The immediate cause of "The Berkeley Student Revolt" was the university's barring of social- and political-action groups from a 26-foot-long strip of walkway at the entrance to the campus, an area that traditionally had functioned as a site for informal debate. A student protest movement was quickly organized, the Free Speech Movement (FSM), which in due course extracted major concessions from university officials. But perhaps of even greater significance, "Berkeley" focused the attention of college students throughout the nation on the issue of "student power"—the right of students to participate in decision-making processes affecting education and college life.

The third phase of the student movement was associated with the antiwar campaign of the late 1960s and early 1970s. Its most dramatic developments followed in the wake of President Nixon's order on May 1, 1970, sending U.S. troops into Cambodia, thus expanding the Vietnam War. On hundreds of campuses students engaged in protest activities. At Kent State University

College demonstrations. In the late 1960s and early 1970s, many American college campuses were the scene of student demonstrations against the Vietnam War and other issues.

Courtesy of the Columbus, Ohio, Citizen-Journal

in Ohio, small bands of college youth broke store windows and threw stones at the police in the Kent business district a few blocks from the campus. Later, a thousand students gathered at the ROTC building and some of their number set it on fire. In response to these developments, Ohio Governor James Rhodes ordered units of the national guard to the campus with instructions to protect property and lives and to break up any assembly on the campus whether it was peaceful or violent.

About noon on May 4, a crowd of students assembled at the edge of the Kent State Commons, a central area on the campus. Warning was given to the crowd to disperse and shortly thereafter the guard began the use of tear gas to scatter the students. A number of students hurled a few of the tear gas canisters back at the guard. The guard then marched in formation to the top of Taylor Hall hill. When they reached the top, firing began which resulted in the death of four students and the wounding of nine others (Lewis, 1972). Eventually the end of the draft and the withdrawal of American troops from Indochina restored peace to college communities within the United States.

In contrast with the student movements, accompanied as they were by the development of organized group action, the majority of the residents of Seattle, Washington, underwent an episode of relatively *unstructured* mass hysteria in April, 1954. The immediate source was a belief that some unusual agent was causing widespread damage to automobile windshields:

> Most commonly, the damage reported to windshields consisted of pitting marks that grew into bubbles in the glass of about the size of a thumbnail. On the evening of the 15th, the Mayor of Seattle declared the damage was no longer a police matter and made an emergency appeal to the Governor and to President Eisenhower for help. Many persons covered their windshields with floormats or newspaper; others simply kept their automobiles garaged. Conjecture as to cause ranged from meteoric dust to sandflea eggs hatching in the glass, but centered on possible radioactive fallout from the Eniwetok H-bomb tests conducted earlier that year. In support of this view many drivers claimed that they found tiny, metallic-looking particles about the size of a pinhead on their car windows. (Medalia and Larsen, 1958, p. 180)

The Seattle episode arose in part out of public response to highly suggestive reports received from the mass media — *Life* magazine, for instance, talked in its report about windshields being damaged by "ghostly little pellets." Chemical research later revealed that there was no evidence of pitting that could not be accounted for by ordinary road damage. People simply had looked *at* their windshields for the first time instead of *through* them.

Explanations involving mass hysteria have also been advanced to account for episodes of UFO sightings. The first flying saucer "flap" had its beginning on June 24, 1947, when Kenneth Arnold, flying his private plane near Mt.

Rainier, saw nine "disclike objects." A wire service man called them "saucers" and a flurry of additional sightings followed. More recently the movies *Star Wars* and *Close Encounters of the Third Kind* have renewed public interest in flying objects piloted by creatures from outer space. Periodic scientific reports, including that undertaken in the 1960s on behalf of the Air Force by the distinguished physicist, Edward U. Condon, have argued that there are no UFOs. On the whole such reports have attributed "sightings" to comets, meteors, orbiting satellites, weather balloons, conventional aircraft, planets, and atmospheric illusions that people define as UFOs—in brief, if people think there are UFOs, they go out and look for them. But since there has always been a small residue of cases that have remained unexplained, some segments of the population continue to be unconvinced.

DETERMINANTS OF COLLECTIVE BEHAVIOR

The above cases are illustrations of **collective behavior**. By collective behavior, sociologists mean ways of thinking, feeling, and acting that develop among a large number of people and which are relatively spontaneous and unstructured. Collective behavior involves groups that are not guided in a straightforward fashion by prevailing cultural patterns. Such collectivities lack defined procedures for selecting and identifying members and leaders. Although the collectivity is oriented toward an object of attention and arrives at some shared objective, these are not formally defined in advance nor do defined procedures exist whereby decisions are reached (Turner and Killian, 1972).

Collective behavior differs from other forms of group behavior in that it is not organized in terms of established cultural norms and lines of social interaction (Blumer, 1964). But the distinction is not categorical or absolute (Turner, 1964). In clarifying this matter, it is useful to consider the following continuum:

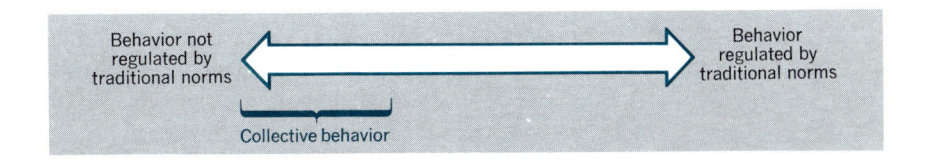

| Behavior not regulated by traditional norms | ⟷ | Behavior regulated by traditional norms |

Collective behavior

At one pole (the left pole), we find forms of human behavior in which cultural patterns play little or no part, for example, panic behavior. As we move along the continuum toward the pole of highly structured social action, we find collective behavior imperceptibly grading into other forms of behavior, for example, social movements, which, as in the case of the Berkeley Free Speech Movement, take on many of the characteristics of an association.

Much of the significance that collective behavior has for human life derives from the very fact that it is not rigidly guided by custom and tradition. As such, collective behavior is an important source of new norms and modes of action. Many of today's most respected religious denominations, including the Methodists and the Quakers, originated in religious movements and excited revivalistic crowd behavior. Yesterday's fads, such as ties, wrist watches, collars attached to shirts, and oxfords, are today's customs. And eighteenth-century innovations stemming from The Revolution of 1775 have become the framework of nineteenth- and twentieth-century American constitutional order. Through collective behavior, new cultural patterns and modes of social interaction may emerge.

Any number of sociologists and social psychologists have attempted to identify the determinants of collective behavior. One theory, that of Neil Smelser (1963), has attracted particular interest and provides a good model for the causation of collective behavior. In his *Theory of Collective Behavior,* Smelser suggests six determinants of collective behavior: structural conduciveness, structural strain, growth and spread of a generalized belief, precipitating factors, mobilization of participants for action, and operation of social control. Each of these six conditions is said to be a *necessary* condition for the production of collective behavior, while all six are said to be sufficient. Although critics have found fault with Smelser's approach (Snyder and Tilly, 1972; Marx and Wood, 1975; Milgram, 1977; McCarthy and Zald, 1977), it does provide a useful way of organizing material.

STRUCTURAL CONDUCIVENESS

Structural conduciveness refers to social conditions that *permit* collective behavior of a particular sort to take place. Hence, for a financial panic to occur, such as in the stock market crash of 1929, a money market is required where assets can be exchanged freely and rapidly. In contrast, in societies where property can be transferred only to the firstborn son on the father's death, financial panic is ruled out since the holders of property lack sufficient maneuverability to dispose of their assets upon short notice (Smelser, 1963; Mann, Nagel, and Dowling, 1976). Similarly, a race riot—a battle between two racial groups—requires that two racial populations be in close physical proximity to each other. At most, however, conduciveness is merely permissive of a given type of collective behavior. A money market, for example, even though its structure is conducive to panic, may operate for long periods without a financial crisis, and two racial groups may live in close proximity for long periods without violent encounters.

STRUCTURAL STRAIN

By itself, conduciveness does not cause collective behavior. It permits it to occur only if the other conditions are also present. People become vulnerable to collective behavior when they feel that something is wrong in their social environment. The experience of frustration and stress often leads to such cumulation of tension that people become susceptible to courses of action not normally indicated by their culture. Indeed, the more severe the strain, the more likely it is that an episode of collective behavior will occur (Smelser, 1963; Kerckhoff and Back, 1968).

The 1960 student sit-ins, for instance, reflected Black discontent and restlessness over the slow pace of desegregation that followed in the wake of the Supreme Court's 1954 school desegregation ruling. Segregationists had demonstrated amazing maneuverability, resourcefulness, and resilience in maintaining the old system. An occasional barrier had come down here and there but desegregation at best was "token." And with the exception of a relatively minor act in 1957, Congress had refused to enact any civil rights legislation since the Reconstruction Period (a major civil rights act was passed four years later in 1964).

Prior to the Seattle windshield-pitting episode, local newspapers had carried intermittent reports of the Pacific H-bomb tests and the resultant fallout, hinting darkly at doom and disaster as reflected in the following headlines:

PANIC BEHAVIOR

OBSERVATION In our dorm we had a fire drill at 2:30 this morning. Being awakened in the middle of the night is bad enough but to a fire alarm is really scary. My roommates started screaming and running to the window to look outside and see if anything was happening. Someone down the hall started yelling "Fire" and ran for the stairs. Naturally everyone dropped the idea of it being only a false alarm (which it really was) and thought the dorm really was on fire. We all jammed up at the stairway door and could not get through. We were all pushing and shoving. It was just horrible. It seemed forever before we managed to get outside.

PRINCIPLE This illustrates panic behavior, and shows the part Smelser's determinants of collective behavior played in it. Structural conduciveness existed in that a lot of us were clustered in the same wing of the dorm and hence could be affected by each other's reactions. In this case, preexisting structural strain was not in evidence, but the fire alarm (which signaled "fire" to us) produced intense anxiety; our anxiety was compounded by our being disoriented on being jolted from sleep. A generalized belief came into existence regarding imminent danger posed by fire. The precipitating event was really not one thing but two events: first, the sounding of the fire alarm; second, the cry, "Fire." We were mobilized to action, in this case flight, when one girl bolted for the stairway door. This set off a chain of fleeing girls.

"3 H-Bomb Victims Face Death: Doctor Reports on Fishermen"
"Witness Says: Hydrogen Test Out of Control"
"Atomic Scare Ties Up Japan Fishing Fleet"

In short, the windshield-pitting epidemic was preceded by a period in which diffuse anxieties were allowed to accumulate (Medalia and Larsen, 1958). Similarly, in the late 1970s millions of Americans, disenchanted with politics and science, were longing for apocalypse, for a mystical development that would instantly solve the world's problems and inaugurate a new age of love and tranquility. For those who could not believe in the Second Coming of Christ or other Messianic hopes, there were the UFOs (Gardner, 1978).

THE GROWTH OF A GENERALIZED BELIEF

Before collective behavior can occur, the situation of strain must be interpreted by potential participants in a meaningful manner. Individuals must feel that they have the "answers" to their stressful circumstances (Smelser, 1963). Social movements commonly provide "answers" in the form of an **ideology**. Communism, for instance, views our social ills as rooted in inequitable economic relationships and spells out our salvation in terms of a socialistic order. In the case of the Berkeley movement, the "multiversity" became defined as the root cause of student tension. A Free Speech Movement leaflet expressed the belief in these terms:

> The university has become grotesquely distorted into a "multiversity"; a public utility serving the purely technical needs of society. . . .
>
> Research and training replace scholarship and learning. In this system even during the first two years, the student is pressured to specialize or endure huge, impersonal lecture courses. He loses contact with his professors as they turn more to research and publishing, and away from teaching. . . .
>
> As a human being trying to enrich himself, the student has no place in the multiversity. Instead he becomes a mercenary, paid off in grades, status, and degrees, all of which can eventually be cashed in for hard currency on the job market. His education is not valued for its enlightenment and the freedom it should enable him to enjoy, but for the amount of money it will enable him to make. Credits for courses are subtly transformed into credit cards as the multiversity inculcates the values of the acquisitive society. (Distributed on campus January 4, 1965)

Mass hysteria is characterized by a somewhat different kind of belief than that characterizing social movement, but nonetheless a belief—a hysterical belief, an idea that empowers an ambiguous element in the environment with a generalized capacity to threaten or destroy. It was this type of belief regarding radioactive fallout that underlaid the Seattle windshield-pitting episode.

PRECIPITATING FACTORS

Conduciveness, strain, and a generalized belief — even when combined — do not by themselves produce an episode of collective behavior. Generally, some sort of event is required to "touch off" or "trigger" mass action. A precipitating event creates, sharpens, or exaggerates conditions of conduciveness and strain; it also provides adherents of a belief with explicit evidence of the workings of evil forces or greater promise of success. Revolutions, for instance, are commonly precipitated in this manner: General Gage's 1775 march from Boston to Concord and Lexington; the seizure of the royal prison fortress by an angry French crowd in 1789; and the March 11, 1917, Tsarist decrees against Petrograd strikers. In the case of "The Berkeley Student Revolt," the precipitating event was the university's banning of political activities on the 26-foot strip of brick walkway at the campus entrance. And it was the May 1, 1970, Cambodian incursion that triggered the developments surrounding Kent State and other universities.

Similarly, in the case of panic, such determinants as conduciveness, strain, and a generalized belief merely establish a *predisposition* to flight. It is usually a specific event, however, that sets the flight in motion. A precipitating factor serves to "confirm" the generalized suspicions and uneasiness of anxious people; it provides an occasion for structuring an ambiguous situation through rumors, "explanations," and predictions. This structuring by a dramatic event — an explosion, a governmental collapse, a bank failure, a political assassination — is essential in the determination of panic.

THE MOBILIZATION OF PARTICIPANTS FOR ACTION

Once the above determinants have been established, the only necessary condition that remains is to bring the affected group into action. This point marks the outbreak of hostilities, the beginning of agitation for reform or revolution, or the onset of panic. One example is the spontaneous student sit-in that took place in a Greensboro variety store in 1960. In mobilizing people for action, leaders often play a critical part. In the Berkeley Free Speech Movement, for instance, Mario Savio, a twenty-two-year-old philosophy major, played a leading role. On December 2, 1964, Savio encouraged a rally of 1000 students to "sit-in" the administration building with these rousing words (as a result of the sit-in, 814 students were arrested, a development that in turn triggered a student strike):

> There is a time when the operation of the machine becomes so odious, makes you so sick at heart, that you can't take part; you can't even tacitly take part, and you've got to put your bodies upon the gears and upon the wheels, upon the levers, upon all the apparatus and you've got to make it stop.

In the case of the Seattle windshield-pitting episode, the mayor made a public announcement carried by the mass media that the damage was no longer a police matter and sent an emergency appeal to the Governor and to President Eisenhower for help. Through contagion, the mass hysteria created fear that fed on itself.

THE OPERATION OF SOCIAL CONTROL

The operation of social control is not like the other determinants. Social control is really a counterdeterminant that prevents, interrupts, deflects, or inhibits the accumulation of the others. Social control may be designed to *prevent* the occurrence of an episode of collective behavior through minimizing conduciveness and strain (for instance, war on poverty programs and new civil rights legislation) or to mobilize deterrents *after* an episode has begun to materialize (for instance, repressive police measures and curfews). Social control influences how far, how fast, and in what direction an episode of protest will develop, the success with which a movement mobilizes its constituency, the course of organizational development a movement takes, and the kinds of tactics a movement is able to employ (Humphreys, 1972; Oberschall, 1973; Wilson, 1977).

Agents of social control are not always successful in their efforts to block mounting episodes of collective behavior. Indeed, at times their actions may have backlash consequences. The efforts of Southern segregationists to repress the student civil rights movement only served to deepen and solidify the participants' self-conceptions of themselves as militants (Fendrich, 1977). The shooting of student demonstrators at Kent State had the effect of moving the great majority of those exposed to the shootings to the political "left" and intensified anti-government and anti-war sentiment (Adamek and Lewis, 1973). Thus, the actions of control agents may strengthen a movement by justifying the investment that individuals have already made and promote radicalism by feeding an "us against them" polarization (Wilson, 1977). The impact of control activities, however, is complex. Close police surveillance, constant harassment, the threat of arrest, and police infiltration of spies may also generate distrust among movement members and make it difficult for them to coordinate their work (Wilson, 1977).

CROWD BEHAVIOR

One of the most familiar and at times spectacular forms of collective behavior is the **crowd**. A crowd is a temporary, relatively unorganized gathering of people who are in close physical proximity. As Herbert Blumer (1946) points out, a wide range of behavior is encompassed by the concept. Accordingly he distinguishes among various kinds of crowd behavior and identifies four basic types. The first, a *casual crowd,* is a collection of people who have little in common with one another except that they may be viewing a common event such as looking through a department store window. The second, a *conventional crowd,* is a number of people who have assembled for some specific purpose and who act in accordance with prevailing norms such as individuals in attendance at a baseball game or concert. The third, an *expressive crowd,* is an aggregation of people who have gotten together for self-stimulation and personal gratification such as occurs at a religious revival or a rock festival. And fourth, an *acting crowd,* is an excited, volatile collection of people who are engaged in rioting, looting, or other forms of aggressive behavior in which established norms carry little weight.

Like the lay public, sociologists have been intrigued by crowd behavior. This has resulted in three principal theories regarding crowds: (1) contagion, (2) convergence, and (3) emergent norm.

CONTAGION THEORIES

Every man has a mob self and an individual self, in varying proportions.
D. H. Lawrence, This Quarter, 1929

Contagion theories have stressed the part that rapidly communicated and uncritically accepted feelings, attitudes, and actions play within crowd settings. Such theories have focused their attention on the apparent unanimity that prevails within crowds. To casual observers, crowd members seem to act in an identical manner, dominated by a common impulse. So strong is this appearance of unanimity that laypeople find it easy to speak of the crowd in the singular, as if it were a real being—"the crowd roars," "the angry mob surges forward," and so on. This view of the crowd has enjoyed considerable popularity and has functioned as a focal point for much sociological thinking regarding crowd behavior (Bagehot, 1875; Le Bon, 1896; Blumer, 1946; Lang and Lang, 1961).

In different degrees, theorists of the contagion bent have accepted Gustav Le Bon's "law of the mental unity of crowds":

> Under certain given circumstances . . . an agglomeration of men presents new characteristics very different from those of the individuals composing it. The sentiments and ideas of all the persons in the gather-

CONTAGION THEORY OF CROWD BEHAVIOR

OBSERVATION Friday evening a bunch of guys from my fraternity hit a local bar for some heavy drinking. We began by ordering a bucket of beer and pushing two picnic-sized tables together so each of us would have some elbow room. As usual we started out slowly, taking our time drinking and more or less enjoying the atmosphere. However, one bucket of beer doesn't last too long with ten guys, so about an hour later we ordered another bucket. By midnight we had gone through four buckets and were all pretty drunk. About this time we were good and warmed up, and started chugging (gulping) glasses of beer. The chuggings became a contest in which we made quarter side bets. After "downing" a few beers, most of us dropped out because our guts couldn't take the punishment. Two guys were left, chugging each other for a dollar. Mike was a big guy weighing over 240 pounds while Zeke was a little guy of about 170 pounds. It wasn't long before our little group became the center of interest for the people in the bar. Everyone was rooting for Zeke, probably because he was a little guy and thus the underdog. All the people were egging Mike and Zeke on, yelling "chug-a-lug." Although both Mike and Zeke were about smashed, they decided to chug two glasses at once for ten dollars. The excitement in the bar reached a real peak. You would have thought it was the Beer Chugging World Championship on Wide World of Sports. Even a number of bartenders came over to witness the happenings. After the first glass Mike had to race for the men's room where he "lost his guts." Everyone cheered Zeke and patted Zeke on the back.

PRINCIPLE The behavior of the crowd is best explained by the contagion theory. Through imitation, suggestibility, and circular reaction, intense feelings were communicated between the bar's patrons and an excited mood progressively built up. People came to react in a similar manner, all dominated by the same impulse. The patrons were caught up in an atmosphere in which they were cheering Zeke on, hoping for the "impossible" feat of a small guy beating a big guy.

ing take one and the same direction, and their conscious personality vanishes. (pp. 23–24)

Thus, Le Bon's fundamental idea is that people undergo a radical transformation in a crowd. They can become cruel, savage, and irrational, Jekyls turned into Hydes. In the crowd individuals become capable of violent actions that would horrify them if they carried them out when alone.

This "mob mind" view of crowds stresses the apparent lack of differentiation in the behavior of crowd participants. Crowds are seen as dominated by a uniform mood and imagery that is developed through social contagion. Mechanisms that are often cited as contributing to contagion are *imitation*—the tendency for one to do the same thing that others are doing; *suggestibility*—a state in which the individual is particularly susceptible to images, directions, and propositions emanating from others; and *circular reaction*—

Collective Behavior and Social Movements

a process whereby the emotions of others elicit the same emotions in oneself, in turn intensifying the emotions of others (for example, A sees B getting excited and then also becomes excited, intensifying the excitement of B, and in turn A becomes all the more excited, and so on).

THE CONVERGENCE THEORY

Although contagion theorists stress the temporary *transformation* of individuals under crowd influence, there has always been an undercurrent of suspicion that participants are merely revealing their "true selves"—that the crowd merely serves as a pretext to translate hidden and often destructive impulses into overt action. When this suspicion is singled out as the key assumption about crowd behavior, a theory emerges that stresses the *convergence* of a number of individuals who share the *same predispositions*. Theorists of this school commonly identify a special class or category of people as "crowd-prone." At the very least, they argue that the emergent action in the crowd is a function of what people bring to the scene as well as what occurs in the crowd situation (Berk, 1974; Johnson and Feinberg, 1977).

Convergence. In some cases, a crowd assembles by selecting out from the larger population those individuals sharing common characteristics or interests. In the photo below, people are assemblying to view an automobile demolished earlier in the day in a serious accident which resulted in fatalities.

Patrick Reddy

Hadley Cantril (1941), in his study of the Leeville, Texas, lynching, notes that the active members came chiefly from the lowest economic bracket, and several had previous police records. As a class, poorest Whites were the most likely to compete for employment with Blacks and were most likely to find their own status threatened by the presence of successful Blacks. The lack of commitment to lawful procedure among criminal elements and the aggravated state of relations between poor Whites and Blacks allegedly provided a reservoir of people who were ready for a lynching with a minimum of provocation. This view finds its reflection in the popular stereotype of the crowd as an undifferentiated "rabble" composed of poorly educated, low-status, highly suggestible individuals; it assumes that behind the civilized facade of humanity lurks a savage animal ready to emerge if given the opportunity.

A more subtle application of the convergence approach attempts to find in collective outbursts categories of people who are not fully committed to the dominant norms. William Safire (1977), a columnist for the *New York Times*, takes this view of the billion dollar looting and pillaging that took place during the two-day electric power breakdown in New York City in July, 1977. He argues that the Black and Hispanic ghetto looters were motivated by "the spreading non-ethic that looting is O.K. if you can get away with it." According to this theory, the participants had not accepted White middle-class values and considered it fair game to acquire goods during moments of social crisis.

THE EMERGENT NORM THEORY

The mob gets out of hand, runs wild, worse than raging fire, while the man who stands apart is called a coward.

Euripides, Hecuba, 425 B.C.

A third theory marks its departure by challenging the very image of the crowd contained in contagion and convergence theories. The emergent norm school stresses the *differences* in motives, attitudes, and actions that characterize crowd members. It underlines the *lack* of unanimity in many crowd situations: the presence of impulsives; suggestibles; opportunistic yielders; passive supporters; rebellious, deviant, and uninhibited individuals; and so on. It points out that most members of so-called aggressive crowds are not engaged in hostile activity but are merely interested and curious bystanders. The theory denies that people find themselves spontaneously infected with the emotions of others in such a fashion that they want to behave as others do (Turner, 1964; Turner and Killian, 1972; Couch, 1968; Wanderer, 1968).

Proponents of this view note, for instance, that the participants in the 1965 Los Angeles Watts rioting were not confined to an "underclass" of the Black community but rather were drawn from all classes—in brief, evidence of a class link was lacking. Based on their study of the Watts riot, Raymond J. Murphy and James M. Watson conclude:

> . . . we have presented indirect but compelling evidence that the *motivations of persons* supporting the riot *vary* with their relative positions in the structure of the community. Those who are better off seem to evidence considerable anti-white sentiment which is significantly related to their participation in violence. Those less fortunate rebel against discrimination and appear to be motivated mainly by economic discontent. Mistreatment or exploitation by whites (merchants and police) seems to be a source of riot support for all levels in the ghetto. Such evidence of *differential motivation* points to the hypothesis that the more fortunate members of the community compare themselves with the white majority and feel frustrated at their inability to gain benefits in keeping with their status aspirations. (p. 114. Italics added)

CROWD BEHAVIOR

OBSERVATION Usually I don't care for sports. My Dad took my brother and me to a baseball game at Three Rivers Stadium to see the Pirates play. I didn't think I would enjoy the game; I really don't understand it. But the effect that the crowd in the stadium had on me was unbelievable. The crowd had nothing more in common than their love for the Pirates, yet this was a strong enough bond to knit them together as one unit. Their tremendous enthusiasm, yelling, shouting, and applauding caught me up and soon I found myself excited, yelling, and shouting with everyone else.

PRINCIPLE In some respects all three theories of crowd behavior would be relevant to this situation. The contagion theory indicates that a uniform mood arises through imitation, suggestibility, and circular reaction; emotional display breeds still more emotional display and engulfs people in its momentum. The convergence theory suggests that individuals sharing a common predisposition find their latent impulses activated in a crowd setting. In this case Pirate fans and a type of person "turned on" by the excitement of a game—people with preexisting sentiments in common—were selected out from the population-at-large and constituted a reservoir of crowd-prone individuals. The emergent norm theory argues that in a crowd setting unlike people experience pressure to conform to a norm developed in a particular setting. It could be debated whether some sort of "new" norm evolved in Three Rivers Stadium as many of the fans had been socialized at previous games in behavior "appropriate" for Pirate fans. Nonetheless, the crowd did suppress moods unfavorable to the Pirates and rewarded behavior rallying the Pirates to victory.

Taking their cue from Sherif's experiments with the autokinetic phenomenon and Asch's work with distortions of judgment in group settings (see Chapter 6), sociologists of this school explain crowd behavior as the consequence of a social norm. The crowd is seen as evolving a norm (for example, one ought to loot, burn, or harass police) that it then proceeds to enforce: it rewards behavior consistent with the norm, inhibits behavior contrary to it, justifies proselyting, and institutes restraining action against those who dissent. Since behavior in a crowd is different either in degree or kind from that in noncrowd situations, the norm must be specific to the situation — hence, an *emergent* norm.

Emergent norm theorists argue that people within crowd settings experience a normative pressure against nonconformity; the crowd is seen as suppressing incongruous moods through generating fear of crowd retaliation. In this manner, crowd members and observers come to see the dramatic happenings of crowd action not in detail but as a whole, and overlook the fact of differential crowd expression — in brief, a collective illusion of unanimity is produced. For instance, a buoyant, chattering person, wandering into a funeral service, quickly becomes quiet. It is not that the individual automatically becomes infected with the mood of the mourners. Rather, silence results from the individual's awareness of the appropriate norm for behavior within a funeral context (Milgram, 1977).

CROWD SELECTION OF TARGETS

An essential part of the formation of a hostile crowd is the emergence of a shared, negative image of some social object that provides the focal point for unified action. In crowds, no less than in other settings, social definitions play a critical part. Faced with an ambiguous or unstructured situation, people reach some degree of consensus regarding appropriate behavior through an interactive process of milling (Johnson and Feinberg, 1977). These shared definitions come to be represented in common symbols that provide the rallying point for crowd attention. Two general conditions help to focus collective attention on some social object. First, it is *physically accessible* — the crowd views it as being nearby. Second, it is *psychologically accessible* — the crowd comes to define the object in such a manner that unrestrained hostility may be directed against it.

The rioting that characterized our nation's cities between 1964 and 1971 provides a good illustration of this. Feeling themselves cheated and betrayed by an affluent America and coming to define many of their problems in racial terms, some ghetto Blacks came to attack the symbols of the "White Establishment" — the police and property. As one police official at the time observed:

> ... the police officer, wherever he may be, is the visible symbol of *status quo*—the "power structure," the "establishment," the authority of government, by whatever name you wish to brand it. In other words, the policeman is a physical object against which persons believing themselves to be oppressed can vent their frustrations. (*U.S. News & World Report,* August 10, 1964, p. 33)

Similarly, property became a symbol of White power and racism:

> The inmates of the ghetto have no realistic stake in respecting property because in a basic sense they do not possess it. They are possessed by it. Property is, rather, an instrument for perpetuation of their own exploitation. Stores in the ghetto—which they rarely own—overcharge for inferior goods. They may obtain the symbols of America's vaunted high standard of living—radios, TV's, washing machines, refrigerators—but usually only through usurious carrying costs, one more symbol of the pattern of material exploitation. They do not respect property because property is almost invariably used to degrade them. (Clark, 1965, p. 10)

While more privileged America may look upon the police and property as essential for its survival, in the ghettos survival often depends on disrespect for both, at least as many Blacks come to experience and define them. Hence, in this sense, the police and property were readily accessible crowd targets, both in terms of physical accessibility and psychological availability.

THE MASS

Crowds are a form of collective behavior that may arise when people are in close physical proximity. Some forms of collective behavior also emerge among individuals who are separated and hence not in social interaction with one another. However, despite the absence of contact, their lines of action converge on a common object, for instance, people who watch the same television program, engage in a land rush, follow a murder trial in the press, sing the same song, switch to the same deodorant, and are excited by the same national event. This form of collective behavior is termed the **mass**—a relatively large number of separate individuals, each of whom responds independently to the same stimulus in the same fashion.

Mass behavior, even though consisting of a great many individual lines of action, may take on momentous significance. If these lines converge, the influence of the mass may be enormous, as shown in the far-reaching effects on institutions that result from shifts in mass interest or taste—a loss in the appeal of a political party such as that associated in recent years with the erosion of Republican strength or changing reading habits that have resulted in the demise of such mass circulation magazines as *Look* and *The Saturday Evening Post.*

Mass behavior often finds expression in fashions and fads. A **fashion** is a behavior that endures for a short time and enjoys widespread acceptance within a society. Fashion finds expression in such things as styles of clothing, grooming, auto design, and home architecture (Robinson, 1976). The dress that was in vogue five years ago often seems out of place today. Crew cut haircuts so popular in the 1950s are currently a source of ridicule. The automobile of three years ago that appeared so exquisitely beautiful and appropriate looks outdated and even somewhat odd now.

A **fad** is a behavior that endures for a short time and enjoys acceptance among a limited segment of a society. Fads differ from fashions by virtue of their more restricted appeal (and often shorter duration). Adolescents appear to be especially prone toward fad behavior within the United States. Fads find reflection in amusements, new games, popular tunes, dance steps, health practices, movie and television idols, and slang (Peterson and Berger, 1975). They generally play only incidental roles in the lives of the individuals who adopt them. Some fads, however, come to preoccupy individuals and become virtually all-consuming passions. Such fads are referred to as **crazes** Financial speculations frequently assume craze dimensions. In the famous Holland Tulip Mania of the 1630s the value of tulip bulbs came to exceed their weight in gold; the bulbs were not planted but were bought and sold among speculators. In the Florida Land Boom of the 1920s, lands were sold and resold at skyrocketing prices without buyers even seeing them. Clearly communication is central to mass behavior, a matter to which we now turn our attention.

MASS COMMUNICATION

It [television] is a medium of entertainment which permits millions of people to listen to the same joke at the same time, and yet remain lonesome.

T. S. Eliot, New York Post, *September 22, 1963*

Communication is the process by which individuals transmit information, ideas, and attitudes to one another. As such, it entails an effort to establish "commonness" so that the sender and the receiver become "tuned" together for a given message. As part of this process, a source "encodes" a message—individuals take an idea or feeling that they wish to share and put it into a form that can be transmitted, namely, a signal. Once coded and sent via a signal, the message becomes independent of its sender. For the act of communication to be completed, it is then necessary that a receiver (the destination) "decode" the signal in order to comprehend the message. Figure

Figure 7.1. The communication process.

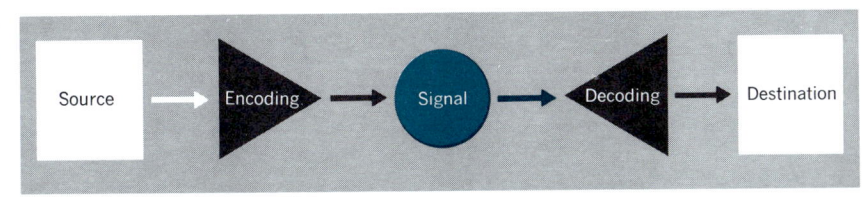

[Diagram: Source → Encoding → Signal → Decoding → Destination]

7.1 provides a diagram of this process. Difficulty, of course, can occur at any stage in the process, resulting in communication distortion or failure. Hence, when we have sent an important letter, we not uncommonly worry about communication breakdown—will it reach the person, will the person understand it as we intended, will the person respond in the manner we hope, and so on?

In **mass communication**, the message stems from a *single, organized source* (a formal organization—a newspaper, a broadcasting or television station, or a publishing house); is directed toward *a large, scattered, and heterogeneous audience;* and is received through *a mechanical device* (such as print or a TV screen). These characteristics make for an *impersonal* relationship between communicator and audience. Generally, we include television, radio, films, newspapers, magazines, books, and billboards in this category.

In mass communication, information flows largely in one direction. In contrast, in interpersonal communication, more sensory channels are generally involved (people can see, hear, and even touch and smell each other); as a consequence, direct information and auxiliary cues (a nod, a yawn, a wink) move rapidly back and forth between people, each of whom functions both as a sender and as a receiver. We refer to this as *feedback*—a process whereby others respond to our acts of communication. The feedback we acquire from our own messages and from others' becomes the corrective basis for achieving a greater degree of communication. In mass communication, of course, feedback is not entirely absent; it occurs in the form of audience ratings, opinion polls, and marketing research. Despite this difference, however, the basic elements in mass and interpersonal communication closely parallel each other. In both instances, individuals encode and transmit messages, select and decode messages, and elicit responses (Larsen, 1964).

THE SIGNIFICANCE AND EFFECTS OF MASS COMMUNICATION

Conditions of modern life have lent increasing importance to mass communication. Before the advent of modern mass media, most people lived their entire lives in local community settings in which they were dependent for in-

Television-viewing: Favorite American pastime. According to the A. C. Nielson Company, a firm specializing in the assessement of program popularity, the television set is on an average of 53 hours a week in homes with preschool children. This compares with 43 hours a week in average American households.

Patrick Reddy

formation on personal, face-to-face contact with their fellows. In the early days of our nation, it often took months for many people to learn of significant national and world developments. In the War of 1812, for instance, the British and the Americans engaged in the bitter Battle of New Orleans two weeks *after* a treaty of peace had been signed at Ghent, and it took an additional three weeks before word of Andrew Jackson's victory reached Washington. For information regarding the latest concoction for remedying one's aches and pains, rural Americans (then constituting nearly 90 percent of the population) were dependent on the itinerant peddler. Today, by virtue of the "communications explosion" (more than 96 percent of American households have TV sets), a *particular* news announcement, speech, or advertisement is heard by thousands or millions of people at a given moment. Further, millions of people are *repeatedly* exposed to mass communication, drawing them into a vast social world beyond the confines of their immediate day-to-day lives. Hence, the development of the mass media may be one of the most important social facts of the twentieth century (Groombridge, 1975; Bunce, 1976).

There are two popular views with respect to the effect that mass communication has on people's attitudes and behavior. The first depicts the media as a giant hypodermic needle. In the hands of a few skilled operators—crafty politicians, "Madison Avenue people," and other sell-artists—the needle discharges into the passive body of the mass endless propaganda that renders it susceptible to the manipulators' wares—whether products, ideas, attitudes, candidates, goals, or states of mind (Wheeler, 1976). Still another view—"the marketplace of ideas" model—invokes an image of the mass as an enlightened body, carefully and rationally sifting and winnowing its attitudes and behavior (be it selecting a candidate or choosing a dentrifice) from those provided by the mass media. Both views are alike in assigning considerable weight and importance to mass communications in the shaping and changing of people's attitudes and behavior.

The matter, however, is not quite as simple as the proponents of either school of thought would have us believe. Indeed, research suggests that mass communication *ordinarily* does not serve as a necessary and sufficient cause of attitudinal and behavioral change among people (Schramm, Lyle, and Parker, 1961; Hartnagel, Teevan, and McIntyre, 1975). A number of studies, some performed in the laboratory and some in the social world, indicate that persuasive mass communication functions far more often as an agent for attitude reinforcement than as an agent of conversion. Indeed, *most* efforts at mass communication most significantly influence behavior by confirming the beliefs that people already hold (Klapper, 1960).

Any number of factors appear responsible for the tendency of mass communication to reinforce rather than to change attitudes and behavior. Among these are *selecting processes of exposure and perception* (Hyman and Sheatsley, 1973; Kretch and Crutchfield, 1973). People tend to expose themselves to mass communications that are congenial or favorable to their existing opinions and interests; further, they tend to avoid unsympathetic material (Lazarsfeld, Berelson, and Gaudet, 1948; Berelson, Lazarsfeld, and McPhee, 1954; Patterson and McClure, 1976). Republicans, by and large, listen only to Republican speakers; Democrats expose themselves primarily to Democratic speeches. Similarly, Leon Festinger (1957) found that among the heaviest readers of particular automobile advertisements are the recent purchasers of that make, and Dorwin Cartwright (1949) found that people already active in a cause are more likely than others to see material intended to recruit additional volunteers.

Selective perception also operates. People tend to misperceive and misinterpret persuasive communications in accordance with their own existing opinions. Hence, anti-Semites tend to misread the tolerance propaganda put out by Jewish groups; political partisans misinterpret the position of their candidate to bring it more clearly into line with their own position on issues; partisans on both sides tend to judge neutral speeches as favoring their own viewpoints; and partisans are more likely than others to accept as "fact" news reports supporting their own position (Berelson and Steiner, 1964; Vander Zanden, 1972).

THE PUBLIC

Within contemporary societies new issues are continually arising, capturing the attention of a great many people. Individuals and groups view their interests as being served or impaired by the course of human developments. Social change is seldom neutral, usually conferring advantage on some and disadvantage on others. This gives rise to publics, a **public** is a collection of people who share a common interest on an issue about which there is considerable controversy. Some of the interaction that occurs among publics involves direct face-to-face discussion, as in arguments with friends and family members, but most of the interaction is carried on through indirect media of mass communication. Publics mostly arise in societies characterized by structures that permit argument and discussion as methods of arriving at the provisional settlement of controversial issues. In such societies, there is not just one public but many publics, one for every controversy that arises and attracts the attention of a sizable number of people. Within the United States, for instance, when Congress is in session, there is a public for every controversial bill that receives any appreciable attention. Clearly, publics overlap in membership, yet each public is a separate and distinct unit. Publics are distinguished from a mass by the element of discussion and the exchange of ideas among their members.

The boundaries of publics are quite fluid. A public may change without alteration of existing alignments through the addition of new members or the withdrawal of old members. It expands as more people become sufficiently interested to enter into discussion on an issue, and it contracts as people lose interest.

PUBLIC OPINION

A universal feeling, whether well or ill founded, cannot be safely disregarded.
Abraham Lincoln, speech, Peoria, Ill., October 16, 1854

Public opinion is the attitude of a public. It emerges out of the give-and-take among people divided on an issue. The existence of active concern and discussion on an issue transforms individual private opinions into some kind of public opinion. When the points of view on an issue coalesce so that the members of the public agree, the matter passes from the realm of public opinion and enters that of consensus. At times, however, the controversy may continue until the issue drops from attention or results in overt conflict.

Public opinion begins to form through a good many exploratory ventures in collective behavior. Only with the passage of time do more formal, rational commitments to action occur. Nelson N. Foote and Clyde W. Hart (1953) have suggested that we view the processes occurring within the public in terms of an idealized series of phases. In the first or *problem phase*, a segment of the population comes to define a situation as problematic and troublesome. People begin to explore alternative solutions to the problem in a tentative, groping way. Hence, a public emerges as a situation comes to be defined as a problem through social interaction. In the second or *proposal phase*, a dominating sense of urgency leads to the advancement of many plans of action, resulting in controversy, argument, and discussion. During these two phases, much of the sentiment is only partially verbalized; it consists in large part of vague feelings and gestures that are hardly recognized consciously by the participants themselves. During the third or *policy phase*, explicit discussion occurs concerning the plans of action that emerged during the preceding phase; this discussion culminates in group decision and a commitment toward a given line of action. The way is now prepared for the final or *program phase* in which group decision is converted into action; formal organization now exists for the implementation of the program. Foote and Hart suggest that a transitional phase may also occur that links the completed cycle to the beginning of a new cycle. This they call the *appraisal phase*, one in which new problems come to be defined because of the discrepancy between what was sought and what was realized.

Although opinion in all publics does not necessarily move through these five phases, the model is useful in focusing our attention on a number of critical factors. Indeed, it is probably more instructive if we view the phases as *aspects;* many of the "phases" occur simultaneously and continuously in some publics and not in the cyclical fashion formulated by Foote and Hart. Many publics revolve about enduring problems in which sentiment constantly shifts, decisions are continually being made, and programs are continuously being implemented, for example, public opinion regarding civil rights, poverty, disarmament, and the like.

PUBLIC CONCEPTIONS OF SOCIAL PROBLEMS

Earlier in the chapter we noted the part that structural conduciveness and strain play in the emergence of collective behavior. Societal conditions influence people's experiences and hence may render them susceptible to courses of action not normally prescribed by their society's norms (Useem, 1975). But as Herbert Blumer (1971) shows, a social problem does not exist for society *unless* its members define it as existing. Social malfunctioning and injurious conditions may be present but go unrecognized. Although environmental pollution and harmful food additives have existed for decades, only recently have they been identified as "problems." Likewise, Peter Conrad (1975) traces the recent discovery of "hyperkinesis" as a label for certain deviant behaviors in children and their treatment with Ritalin and other psychoactive drugs. And Stephen J. Pfohl (1977) documents the recent definition of child abuse as a problem. Indeed, people may even attribute problem status to a nonexistent condition as did the colonists of Salem, Massachusetts, who believed in witches and actively sought them out.

To a large extent, social problems are what people say and think they are. They are social in nature because they are a product of group definitions. As such, our attention is directed toward those constellations of power, influence, and authority that process, funnel, and filter the problems a society sets itself (Ross and Staines, 1971; Reasons, 1974; Tallman, 1976). In large contemporary societies, such as the United States, this involves those processes by which publics place given issues on the "national agenda" and label them social problems. Research Study 13 provides a good illustration of this, the oil spill off Santa Barbara, California, in 1969.

Collective Behavior and Social Movements

Blumer states the matter in these terms:

> Societal recognition gives birth to a social problem. But if the social problem is to move along on its course and not die aborning, it must acquire social legitimacy. It may seem strange to speak of social problems having to be legitimated. Yet after gaining initial recognition, a social problem must acquire social endorsement if it is to be taken seriously and move forward in its career. It must acquire a necessary degree of respectability which entitles it to consideration in the recognized arenas of public discussion. In our society such arenas are the press, other media of communication, the church, the school, civic organizations, legislative chambers, and the assembly places of officialdom. If a social problem does not carry the credential of respectability necessary for entrance into these arenas, it is doomed. (1971, pp. 302–303)

Should a problem manage to secure legitimacy, it enters a new stage in its career (Blumer, 1971; Spector and Kitsuse, 1973). In legislative committees and chambers an official plan of action is hammered out, all of which entails compromises, concessions, tradeoffs, assessments as to what is workable, responses to vested interests, and so on. The net result is usually an outcome that is a far cry from what the early sponsors of the program envisaged. When the ensuing legislation is implemented by administrators in bureaucratic agencies, it is further interpreted, modified, twisted, and reshaped.

Simultaneously, groups who are in danger of losing certain privileges seek to restrict the implementation of the program and bend its operation in self-serving directions. Those who anticipate benefits from the legislation strive to blunt the counterattacks of their opponents while searching for new opportunities of their own. Frequently governmental agencies take over the issue, making it their own and neutralizing the original protest groups. This reshaping of a social problem as it passes through various phases in the collective process may render it unrecognizable to its earliest sponsors. Such has been the retold story of countless reform efforts—antitrust legislation, pure food and drug laws, highway and aviation programs, civil rights legislation, social security and medicare programs, and President Johnson's war on poverty measures. In sum, movement begets countermovement, and between the two a swirling, dynamic interaction occurs.

RESEARCH STUDY 13

ACCIDENTAL NEWS: THE GREAT OIL SPILL*

Harvey Molotch and Marilyn Lester

Problem. In this study Harvey Molotch and Marilyn Lester explore how newsmaking occurs in the United States. They employ a case study, the oil spill off Santa Barbara, California, in January 1969, which resulted from the uncontrolled eruption of oil from Union Oil's Platform A. Most studies of news coverage take the perspective that newsmaking consists of bringing to the public attention the important happenings of the day through reporting on an objective reality "out there." Molotch and Lester break with this tradition. They follow an ethnomethodological approach and ask how news events are "created" out of the infinite number of occurrences that take place on any given day. These researchers see their task not as one of investigating distortions of objective reality but as one of identifying the processes by which some selected occurrences manage to be translated into public events for a mass constituency.

Method. The research strategy employed in the study involved the contrasting of two available worlds of news. One was created locally by the community's only daily newspaper, the *Santa Barbara News Press*. The other was created by newspapers elsewhere in the United States. In the first two years after the spill (which still had not been completely contained six years later), the Santa Barbara paper carried 860 separate news stories on the subject involving a total of 598 occurrences. A random sample of 195 of these occurrences were selected for further study. Nineteen additional newspapers were chosen for examination in terms of their geographical location, circulation, and national prestige. Two are papers with nationwide circulation (the *Wall Street Journal* and the *Christian Science Monitor*); two are prestigious dailies (the *New York Times* and the *Washington Post*); others are less prestigious but large circulation dailies (for instance, the *Boston Globe* and the *Chicago Tribune*); and still others relatively smaller, local papers (for example, the *Bakersfield Californian* and the *Hartford Times*). The microfilm of each newspaper was inspected for stories on the 195 occurrences.

---

* Adapted from Harvey Molotch and Marilyn Lester (1975) "Accidental news: The great oil spill as a local occurrence and national event." *American Journal of Sociology,* 81:235–260.

Findings. On the average the non-Santa Barbara papers covered 7.7 percent of the sampled occurrences. See Figure 7.2. Of particular interest is the content of the nonlocal news stories. A sharp conflict of interest existed between conservationists and local officials on the one hand and the oil companies and federal government on the other. The former groups opposed the efforts of the latter groups to continue and expand the offshore oil drilling program in the Santa Barbara Channel. Accordingly, the conservationists and local officials attempted to promote statements to the effect that drilling was unsafe, that the oil leak was never completely brought under control, and that considerable ecological damgage was occurring. The oil companies and federal government were engaged in promoting statements and reports minimizing the oil damage.

Molotch and Lester found that nationwide coverage of activities favorable to the oil companies was much more extensive than that given to conservationists (93.2 percent versus 6.8 percent), especially in comparison with the alternative coverage possibility provided by the *Santa Barbara News Press* (54.5 percent versus 45.5 percent). Accordingly, the oil companies and federal government were much more successful in turning available occurrences into public events that reflected their needs than were the conservationists and the local interests.

Conclusion. Individuals and groups often have differing and competing uses for occurrences and hence have differing conceptions of what constitutes a newsworthy event. One dimension of power is the ability to have one's account become the perceived reality of others—in brief, the capacity to create and sustain the realities of publics. Molotch and Lester indicate:

Our view is that federal executives and large corporations, among other groups, have routine access to the event-creating processes. Their greater newsworthiness, their place in the "hierarchy of creditability," is built into the organization of news and of news agencies. In the media's daily task of "doing events," it is assumed to be a fact. It is not, then, that the oil companies did inherently more newsworthy things; in fact, from our own perspective it appears that they could do rather routine things and get covered, whereas an increasing number of nonroutine (and occasionally bizarre [sit-ins, sail-ins, and fish-ins]) occurrences of the conservationists received proportionately less coverage. (p. 257)   Continued on next page.

Figure 7.2. Percentage of occurrence coverage by newspaper over a two-year period.

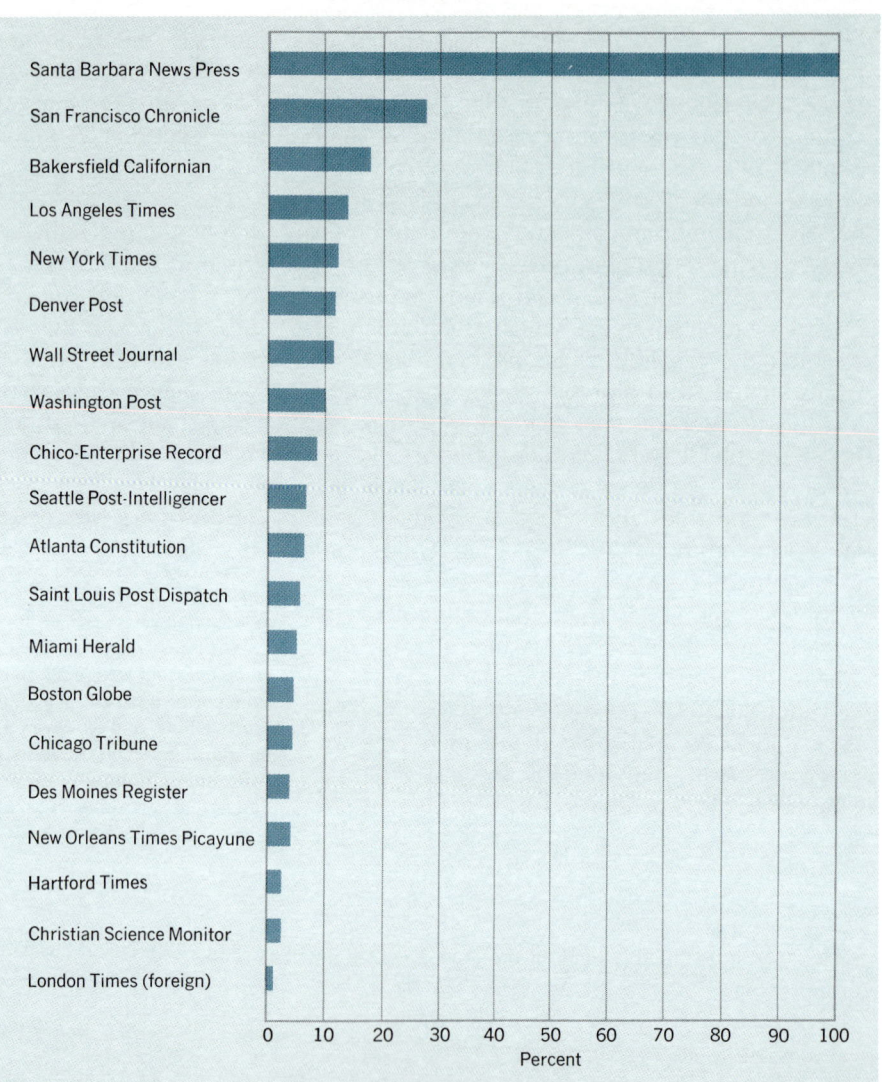

Newspaper	Percent
Santa Barbara News Press	~100
San Francisco Chronicle	~28
Bakersfield Californian	~18
Los Angeles Times	~14
New York Times	~12
Denver Post	~12
Wall Street Journal	~11
Washington Post	~10
Chico-Enterprise Record	~8
Seattle Post-Intelligencer	~7
Atlanta Constitution	~6
Saint Louis Post Dispatch	~6
Miami Herald	~5
Boston Globe	~5
Chicago Tribune	~5
Des Moines Register	~4
New Orleans Times Picayune	~4
Hartford Times	~3
Christian Science Monitor	~3
London Times (foreign)	~1

Source: Adapted from Harvey Molotch and Marilyn Lester (1975) "Accidental news: The great oil spill as local occurrence and national event." *American Journal of Sociology,* 81:p. 241, Table 1.

Issue-specific social movements. Some social movements arise over a specific issue and then die when members win their cause or lose interest. However, others, on accomplishing their goal and facing extinction, find a new and viable function. The March of Dimes, for example, organized to combat polio, gained a new lease on life by shifting its focus to birth defects after the development of the polio vaccines.

Patrick Reddy

SOCIAL MOVEMENTS

> Those who profess to favor freedom yet deprecate agitation, are men who want crops without plowing up the ground; they want rain without thunder and lightning. They want the ocean without the awful roar of its many waters. . . . Power concedes nothing without demand. It never did and it never will. . . . Men may not get all they pay for in this world, but they must certainly pay for all they get.
>
> *Frederick Douglass, Black abolitionist, 1857*

As we observed earlier in the chapter, the boundaries of collective behavior tend to be vague, shading into the study of the dynamics of both individual behavior and organized group behavior. Perhaps the most ephemeral and least structured collectivity is panic behavior. On the other hand, in marked contrast with panic behavior, social movements are collectivities that have duration through time and give evidence of group structuring. Indeed, the longer a social movement's life and the larger and more powerful it becomes, the more it is likely that rules and traditions become codified, and some degree of stability and continuity is effected — in brief, it increasingly takes on the characteristics of a formal organization (Turner and Killian, 1972).

THE NATURE OF SOCIAL MOVEMENTS

A **social movement** is a more or less persistent and organized effort on the part of a relatively large number of people to bring about or resist change (Vander Zanden, 1959). Central to the concept of social movement is the notion that people intervene in the process of social and cultural change; people are viewed as actors, not simply as passive responders to the flow of culture or to the troubling features of their environment. Further, people undertake joint action; social movements are not the discrete activities of a good many scattered individuals but involve people acting together with a sense of engaging in a common enterprise. In brief, social movements are vehicles by which people collectively seek to influence the course of human events. It is little wonder, then, that social movements are the stuff of which history books are written—accounts of great leaders, the rise and fall of political movements, and the social dislocations and changes effected by revolutions. The Crusades; the Reformation; the American, French, and Russian revolutions; the antislavery movement; the labor movement; Christianity; and fascism—these, like many other social movements, have profoundly affected the societies that they touched (Killian, 1964).

ELEMENTS OF SOCIAL MOVEMENTS

In describing and analyzing social movements, sociologists not uncommonly focus their attention on such elements as goals, ideology, organization, tactics, and appeal. Let us consider each of these matters in turn.

Goals. Goals refer to the objectives toward which the movement's activities are directed. Some movements pursue objectives that entail changing society either through challenging fundamental values or by seeking modifications within the framework of the existing value scheme. The former, *revolutionary* movements, advocate the *replacement* of the existing value scheme; the latter, *reform* movements, urge a change that will *implement* the existing value scheme more adequately. The civil rights movement of the early 1960s had a reform emphasis—it aimed to effect values that were already acknowledged to be inherent in political democracy. In contrast, movements of Black nationalism have had a revolutionary emphasis—their aim has been to institute basic change in our republican form of government, to rearrange the American class structure, and to inaugurate a system of "Black political autonomy."

Movements not only arise to institute change but also to block change or to eliminate a previously instituted change—*resistance* movements. The John Birch Society is a good illustration of this, a movement organized in 1958 to resist many of the social reforms instituted in the past half-century (in 1973, it had 225 full-time employees and a bustling million-dollar publishing empire). Its founder was Robert Welch, Jr., a retired businessman who, in the movement's ideological bible, *Blue Book of the John Birch Society,* depicts democracy as government by "mobocracy" and brands the late President Eisenhower as a "dedicated, articulate agent of the Communist conspiracy" (Nobile, 1973). In general, the movement sees the existence of a large-scale, massive conspiracy to despoil the American way of life. Activities of members are motivated largely by the conviction that most of the leaders of our major economic, religious, educational, and political institutions are willing or unwitting Communist agents. Hence, the movement falls into the standard pattern of recent American resistance movements in opposing social reforms by calling them Communistic. The Ku Klux Klan is another example of a resistance organization (Vander Zanden, 1965; Schaffer, 1971).

There are still other movements — *expressive* movements — that are not so much oriented toward institutional change as toward a renovating and renewing of people from *within* — often with the promise of some future redemption. Pentecostal and "holiness" sects provide good illustrations of this. Although arising principally among the underprivileged, they do not concern themselves with broad social betterment — with saving the world — but with saving individuals out of a world that is getting worse and worse. They believe that the second coming of the Messiah is near at hand and that there is no hope for the unsaved except through conversion and regeneration.

Ideology. Crane Brinton (1958), in his classic study, *The Anatomy of Revolution,* observes, "No ideas, no revolution." He might equally well have noted, "No ideas, no social movement." In brief, a set of ideas — an *ideology* — is an indispensable element within a social movement. An ideology provides people with conceptions of the movement's purpose, its rationale for existence, its indictment of existing arrangements, and its design for action. As such, it functions as a kind of social glue that joins people together in a fellowship of belief; it is an instrument of unification — of solidarity. But an ideology does even more. It not only binds otherwise discrete individuals together, it unites them with a *cause.* In so doing, it prepares people for self-sacrifice on behalf of the movement. Nationalistic movements are a good illustration of this. An ideology of nationalism has fired contemporary peoples in Asia and Africa with a vivid and at times all-consuming sense of their existence as nations — or at least a desire to create nations where none existed before. Nationalism has supplied great portions of humanity with a deeply seated sense of unconditional identification with a nation, even to the extent of being prepared to lay down their lives for it, however deeply they may differ among themselves on other matters.

As we noted earlier in this chapter, people become vulnerable to collective behavior when they feel that something is wrong in their environment. Ideologies commonly identify the source of such ills and supply people with answers to them. As part of this effort, the ideologies of movements provide people with definitions of good and evil and their personification in heroes and villains. Such contrast conceptions help to set the we-group apart from the they-group. The enemy is dehumanized and becomes a legitimate target of hate or rejection—imperialists, moral degenerates, Christ-killers, reds, and so on. Indeed, the strength of a movement is often related to the vividness and tangibility of its devil. When Hitler was asked whether he thought the Jew must be destroyed, he answered: "No. . . . We should have then to invent him. It is essential to have a tangible enemy, not merely an abstract one" (quoted by Hoffer, 1951:89–90).

An ideology also helps to wall off a movement's adherents from contaminating influences from the larger society; that is, it seeks to interpose a fact-proof screen between the faithful and the realities of the world. It does this by claiming that ultimate and absolute truth is already embodied in its program, and that there is no truth or certitude outside of it. Hence, of the Bible, Martin Luther could exclaim: "So tenaciously should we cling to the word revealed by the Gospel, that were I to see all the Angels of Heaven coming down to me to tell me something different, not only would I not be tempted to doubt a single syllable, but I would shut my eyes and stop my ears, for they would not deserve to be either seen or heard" (quoted by Frank-Brentano, 1939:246). And the official history of the Communist party of the Soviet Union states: "The power of Marxist-Leninist theory lies in the fact that it enables the Party to find the right orientation in any situation, to understand the inner connection of current events, to foresee their course, and to perceive not only how and in what direction they are developing in the present but how and in what direction they are bound to develop in the future" (quoted by Fisher, 1947:236). Such beliefs insulate members from the real world and embolden them in their efforts on behalf of the movement.

Organization. As individuals interact with one another in pursuit of a movement's goals, they come to evolve an organization composed of differentiated and interrelated positions. Distinctions between followers and functionaries emerge—between ordinary members whose participation is sporadic and whose roles are unspecialized and members who are more or less continuously active and whose roles are likely to be more specifically defined.

Specialization may also develop among functionaries, giving rise to leader, bureaucrat, and intellectual types. The *leader*—often the founder or the successor to the founder—is generally both prophet and agitator; the leader is the individual most prominently identified with the movement in the eyes of both members and outside observers. Often, such individuals are endowed with a variety of charismatic qualities; that is, they are seen as heroic and magnetic figures, endowed with special grace, power or insight — for instance, Lenin, Luther, Malcolm X, Hitler, and Robespierre. The *bureaucrat* tends to be an administrator; the bureaucrat's task is one of coordinating the movement and supervising its apparatus. Whereas the leader tends toward idealism, the bureaucrat tends toward pragmatism; the bureaucrat views the movement's values in less absolute terms and more readily tolerates compromises with these values in order to help the movement gain its objectives. Students of the Nazi movement point to the importance in Hitler's rise to power of such "sophisticated realists" as Von Papen, Von Ribbentrop, and Hjalmar Schacht, who stood in sharp contrast to the fanatical "Old Fighters" (Killian, 1964:442). Whereas the leader simplifies and symbolizes the movement's values and the administrator promotes them, the *intellectual* elaborates and justifies them. The intellectual gives the appearance of being reasonable, logical, and well informed; the intellectual adds a flavor of respectibility to the movement and, hence, appeals to those thoughtful persons who might otherwise not be reached by more obvious propaganda. Although these three kinds of functionaries are described as discrete types, there may be considerable overlap among them. Stalin, for instance, functioned as a charismatic figure, an administrator, and party ideologist.

Tactics. Tactics refer to the manner in which a social movement goes about achieving its goal or goals. Expressive movements tend to place their greatest reliance on education, personal "example," and individual proselytizing, although on occasion they have sought to reinforce their conversion efforts with threats and force. The tactics of reform, revolutionary, and resistance movements are usually designed to move large masses of people. The means may vary among movements: some rely primarily on negotiation, lobbying, and carefully applied pressure; some use various degrees of "nonviolent" force, such as mass boycotts, strikes, fasts, sit-ins, and processions; and still others make use of violence, terror, and intimidation.

Appeal. Of abiding interest to students of social movements has been the matter of what kinds of people (in terms of broad personal or social characteristics) are attracted to given movements and what the sources of this attraction are. Perhaps no movement has been subjected to greater scrutiny in this regard than that of communism. According to Marxist theory, it is the most exploited and the oppressed who should most readily respond to Communist appeals. But has this prophecy held true? One of the most thorough studies undertaken to answer this question is that of Gabriel A. Almond (1954) and his associates at the Center of International Studies of Princeton University. The study consisted of a sample of former Communists from

France, Italy, England, and the United States, with about an equal number from each country. Although there were many former party members who grew up in extreme want, this was hardly typical. In terms of their parents' income status, only 10 percent grew up in poverty, while 7 percent were reared in high-status, 52 percent in middle-status, and 30 percent in low-status families. Similarly, data on the occupations of the sample at the time of their joining the party hardly revealed a picture of privation, want, or oppression: 22 percent were professionals; 23 percent, students; 1 percent, small entrepreneurs; 6 percent, white-collar workers; 4 percent, supervisors and lower managerial personnel; 24 percent, skilled workers; 1 percent, farm labor; and 13 percent, unskilled workers. Further, in terms of education, some 40 percent had attended college.

According to Almond, Communist parties have somewhat differing appeals in different national settings. In England and the United States, the Communist parties are small, deviational movements, with considerable appeal to the emotionally maladjusted: (1) people who join the party because it provides them with an opportunity to express destructive and negative impulses in an intellectually and morally satisfying way (hatred and rage, otherwise unacceptable impulses, become redefined as acceptable when directed against "the enemies of the masses"); (2) people who are lonely and isolated and who join the party to gain a sense of communion and community by merging themselves with an all-encompassing political movement; and (3) people who feel inadequate, weak, and unworthy and who join the party to derive a sense of identity, dignity, and esteem through total commitment to a holy, sacred cause. In contrast, in France and Italy, Almond argues, Communist parties fulfill political needs—needs for protest against an inequitable distribution of wealth, power, and status and against stalemated societies that offer no promise of future improvement. In such societies, Communist parties draw on historically endemic feelings of estrangement and hopelessness among working-class and peasant groups.

SOCIAL INEQUALITY

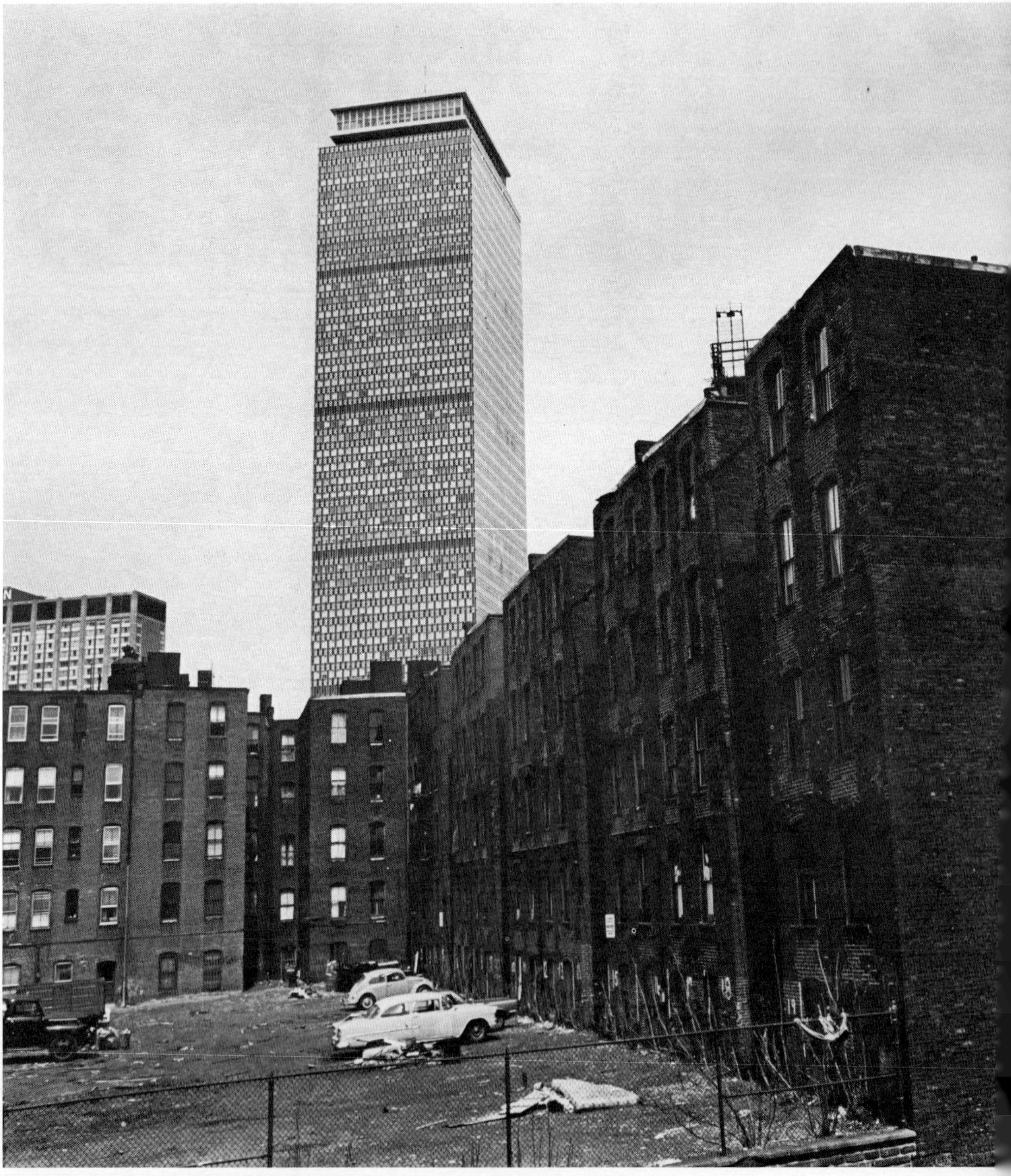

8
SOCIAL STRATIFICATION

INEQUALITY
   Power Hierarchies
   Privilege Hierarchies
   Status Hierarchies

SOURCES OF SOCIAL STRATIFICATION
   Functionalist Theories
   Conflict Theories

APPROACHES FOR STUDYING STRATIFICATION
   The Objective Approach
   The Subjective Approach
   The Reputational Approach

THE SIGNIFICANCE OF SOCIAL CLASSES
   Health
   Child-Rearing Practices
   Marital and Family Relations
   Religious Life
   Political Behavior

SOCIAL MOBILITY
   Caste and Class Systems
   Social Mobility in the United States
   The Status Attainment Process

OBSERVATION Today I visited the bank where I work summers. I noticed that I addressed the tellers and secretaries by their first names. These people are employees of similar rank to myself. Bank officers I address as "Mr." plus their last name. Bank officers of similar rank, however, address one another by first name. They do the same with people under them. When I stop to think about it, I address people of older generations as "Mr." or "Mrs." People of my same or a younger generation I address by their first name. My professors I address as "Doctor" plus their last name. I do the same with my physician.

PRINCIPLE The rules regarding how we address a person reflect social ranking. People of the same or a lower status we address by their first name. People of a higher status we address by using a title plus their last name. Employing a title in addressing a person displays deference. It further establishes "social distance" between us; it makes quite explicit our status differences.

We do not live in a neutral world. Instead, we continually evaluate and appraise one another. We render judgments on people's relative worth, desirability, and value, rating and ranking them in terms of a social ladder or hierarchy. Hence, in social life we constantly differentiate among people as superior or inferior, higher or lower. This differential ranking—this grading of people into horizontal layers or strata—is referred to as **social stratification**. The layers we term **classes**. Classes are human-constructed categories by which we classify people and order our actions with respect to them.

Broadly considered, it is questionable whether any society, even the simplest, lacks some form of stratification. In this sense, social inequality is universal. This fact finds expression in the unequal distribution among the members of any society of certain scarce, divisible "good things." Although we in the United States pride ourselves on our earthy "plain folks" tradition, we nonetheless have our wealthy and our poor and most of us take great care to cultivate socially appropriate symbols. In the Soviet Union, leading Communist officials ride in black cars along well-policed Moscow avenues to lavish residences and country villas; other Muscovites make their way home from factories to huddle in cramped apartments (Shipler, 1977). In China, with the ebbing of the Cultural Revolution, some people are paid a good deal more than others; some ride in chauffeur-driven limousines while others pedal bicycles or walk; and some Chinese wear well-tailored gray "Mao suits" while the masses make do with baggy blue (Bartley, 1976; Cony and Kann, 1977). Throughout the world we find the high and the low, and, in some societies, a big in-between.

INEQUALITY

In forging and fashioning our actions, we require knowledge of the ranking of other individuals or groups in comparison with ourselves. We especially need to know where they stand relative to us with regard to three hierarchies: (1) power, (2) privilege, and (3) status (Weber, 1946). Each of these three hierarchies has consequences for our everyday fortunes and fate. **Power** determines which of us is able to translate our preferences into the reality of social life; it provides answers to the question of whose interests will be served and whose values will reign. **Privilege** entails our physical and psychological comfort as these are associated with the control and possession of goods and services. **Status** involves our sense of worth and respect, particularly the extent to which we feel ourselves admired and thought well of. Distinguishing between power, privilege, and status helps us to clarify the matter of social inequality. Each constitutes a somewhat different experience area and provides a somewhat different kind of social ranking arrangement.

POWER HIERARCHIES

The genie was able to do marvelous things; but Aladdin held the lamp, and he who holds the lamp tells the genie what to do.

M. E. Sharpe; Tangling with Technology, 1971

Power hierarchies find expression in behaviors of dominance and submission. There are those who rule, lead, and influence and those who are ruled, follow, and yield. Wherever we look, from families to juvenile gangs to nation-states, we find that some disproportionately realize their will in the course of everyday life. This is true even of one-to-one and love relationships, a fact elevated to recent consciousness by the Women's Liberation Movement (West and Zimmerman, 1977). Hence, as sociologist Amos Hawley (1963:422) observes: "Every social act is an exercise of power, every social relationship is a power equation, and every social group or system is an organization of power."

Power affects people's ability to make the world work on their behalf. It allows some to impose limits on the ability of others to effect their will, to screen these others off from access to skills, knowledge, and other critical resources. Those who are able to impose their definitions of the situation on the arena of social interaction and structure the working arrangements of life in their favor can make advantage self-perpetuating. To gain mastery of skills, knowledge, and critical resources is to gain mastery of people. It is to interpose oneself (or one's group) between people and the means whereby people meet their biological, psychological, and social needs.

Karl Marx and Friedrich Engels (1848/1955) viewed the ownership of property as the key ingredient for realizing and maintaining social power. In Marxist thinking, the dividing line between possessors and nonpossessors of property has marked the critical break in the class structure of each historical period. Thus, from the writings of Marx and Engels we gain a tidy two-class view of history, one of oppressor and oppressed: the stage of slavery — slaveowners and slaves; the stage of feudalism — landed aristocracy and serfs; and the stage of capitalism — bourgeoisie (capitalists) and proletariat (workers). Each period witnessed the emergence of a different sort of property that became the foundation of a new social order: humans (slavery); land (feudalism); industrial tools (capitalism). Since private property was seen as the root of oppression, Marx and Engels (1848/1955:24) concluded: "the theory of the Communists may be summed up in the single sentence: Abolition of private property."

Much of the appeal of Marxist analysis lies in its seemingly straightforward simplicity. It appears to strip away the superficial verbage and qualifications of which academics are so fond and "to tell it like it is": bourgeoisie and proletariat stand in confrontation, one against the other. Yet it is this very simplicity that is deceiving; it hides or distorts other dynamic processes involving property. Debtor and creditor have stood against each other throughout history; indeed, a dominant feature of American nineteenth century politics was the cheap money cry of agrarians (the Greenback and Free Silver movements). Consumers and sellers have similarly confronted one another, a fact highlighted in the present period and in the consumer revolts of Blacks of the 1960s (the ghetto riots). Further, genuine and deep-rooted conflict — competition over markets and labor supplies — have internally divided capitalists. Simultaneously, divisions among racial and ethnic groups, skilled and unskilled workers, and union organizations have impaired labor solidarity.

Ownership of property (the means of production) constitutes only one source of power. The possession of the *means of administration* constitutes still another. Present-day Communist nations provide a good illustration of this. Milovan Djilas (1957), a Yugoslavian Marxist and once Marshal Tito's chief lieutenant, has strongly condemned the rise of what he calls "the new class." He views the Communist new class as "made up of those who have special privileges and economic preference because of the administrative monopoly they hold" (39). The party bureaucracy constitutes the new elite: "It is the bureaucracy which formally uses, administers, and controls both nationalized and socialized property as well as the entire life of society. The role of the bureaucracy in society, i.e., monopolistic administration and control of national income and national goods, consigns it to a special privileged position" (44). Djilas further defines the matter in these terms: "Power is an end in itself and the essence of contemporary Communism" (169). All of this suggests that it is not necessarily ownership of the means of production that determines class, since ownership is only one kind of power (Dahrendorf, 1959).

It is also worth noting that nowadays one can go a long way in the United States without property. A good deal of power derives from office rather than ownership. Seniority, tenure, and professional certificates come to be "securities" upheld by law even though they are not entirely transferable to one's heirs (Hacker, 1975:9). Neither Harry Truman, Dwight Eisenhower, Richard Nixon, nor Gerald Ford launched their careers from a base of financial, industrial, or landed property, and yet each reached the pinnacle of power within the United States. The same holds true for the vast majority of American corporation executives, top government officials, and high military leaders. For instance, neither the heads of General Motors or Exxon make the list of American millionaires yet each holds one of the most powerful posts in America. Not only do they, and others like them, hold comparatively little in the way of property, their influence lasts only so long as they hold down their particular office; their hold on power is tenuous and they are easily replaceable.

PRIVILEGE HIERARCHIES

There are but two families in the world—Have-much and Have-little.

Cervantes, Don Quixote, *1615*

Max Weber (1947) highlighted for us the importance of privilege hierarchies. As viewed by Weber, a privilege rank (he used the term "class") is made up of people who share roughly similar incomes and hence have kindred **life-chances**. By life-chances, he meant the typical probability that an individual or group will possess a given level of (1) goods and services, (2) external conditions of life, and (3) subjective satisfaction or frustration. Life-chances include everything from the chance to stay alive during the first year after birth to the chance to remain healthy, and if sick to get well again quickly, the chance to avoid becoming a juvenile delinquent, the chance to complete a given level of schooling, and the chance to enjoy the fine arts (Gerth and Mills, 1953). Thus life-chances refers to something more than vital statistics (health and mortality expectations at given ages). Broadly considered, it refers to one's level of living or socioeconomic level.

For the great majority of people, the most meaningful dimension of their level of living is their direct personal or family income. Income is distributed quite unevenly within the United States. The richest fifth of American families receives more than all the income received by the bottom three-fifths; further, whereas the poorest fifth receive less than six percent of the total national money income, the top fifth take over forty percent. See Table 8.1. These figures are of particular interest since, as we will point out later in the chapter, sociologists find that there is little in life that is not associated with income.

260 Social Inequality

Social stratification. Social inequality pervades American life.

Patrick Reddy

TABLE 8.1
Percent Family Income Received by Each Fifth and Top 5 Percent

Income received by	1950	1965	1974
Lowest fifth	4.5%	5.2%	5.4%
Second fifth	11.9	12.2	12.0
Middle fifth	17.4	17.8	17.6
Fourth fifth	23.6	23.9	24.1
Highest fifth	42.7	40.9	41.0
Highest 5 percent	17.3	15.5	15.3

Source: Pocket Data Book, USA 1976. Washington, D.C.: Government Printing Office, p. 224, table 320.

Privilege reflects itself not only in access to goods and services. It also finds expression in various subjective satisfactions and frustrations. Work provides a good example of this. Those ranking high in the privilege hierarchy generally have a wider range of work choices and options; their work tends to be "interesting" and deemed "socially significant"; and a close connection exists between work and leisure (solidifying contacts and contracts through golf, tennis, and night-clubbing, and through memberships in exclusive country and social clubs). It is otherwise for the disprivileged who find that work is either unavailable, intermittently available, or menial, tedious, and stultifying.

STATUS HIERARCHIES

What we call prestige ... propounds [many] problems. ... Often a miser is unable to amass it; a punctual man cannot keep it in order; and a spendthrift is unable to spend it. The most accurate book-keepers are incapable of showing the items of prestige in their yearly balance-sheets. Yet people are always alluding to it; it is feared and jealously guarded; sacrifices are made for it; it enables successes to be won, and serves as a cloak for weakness.

Lewis Leopold, Prestige, *1913*

Status is an intangible, not a tangible quality. It is an expansive feeling of being somehow special and valuable. As such, status is something which we carry about in our heads; it has no independent, objective existence. This is not to deny that we frequently seek to make status tangible through titles, special seats of honor, honorary degrees, deference rituals, demeanor, emblems, and conspicuous displays of leisure and consumption. But even so, these constitute merely *symbols* of status; we have to impute meaning and significance to such displays.

Status, then, involves us in a continual process of evaluation. We carry on an internal process of self-indication in which we map our actions in relation to others based on judgments of our comparative superiority and inferiority; we fashion our acts so as to reveal the "proper" degree of reverence or irreverence, honor or dishonor, respect or disrespect. We mutually affect one another's self-constructed subjective worlds by what we symbolically tell each other through our actions.

Much of interaction consists of subtle negotiation over the displays of deference, reverence, awe, and honor that we are respectively to receive and extend. Even a seemingly simple conversation often entails an implicit bargain that we will be attentive to what others say if they in turn will be appropriately attentive to what we say—an exchange of "ego massages." At times the exchange may appear on the surface to be rather one-sided; we may remain a passive listener but receive a sense of importance by being in the company of a person who we deem to be prestigious—a sort of status contagion.

Within the United States we employ a good many standards in evaluating and placing people in terms of their status rankings: physical attractiveness; occupation; source and size of income; length and type of education; residential neighborhood; type and size of home; ranks of associates; manners; leisure-time activities; family; racial, ethnic, and religious memberships; skills and talents; and many more. Various of these elements coalesce in what sociologists term **style of life** (Weber, 1946, 1947). Although sheer magnitude of consumption constitutes an important element in an individual's style of life, of equal importance is the *manner* of consumption. The lifeways of the highest ranked are distinguished from those "below" them by the "appropriateness," "deportment," and "dignity" they reveal in using given goods and services. Consumption can be either "vulgar" or "tasteful," "highbrow" or "lowbrow."

THE IMPORTANCE OF STATUS SYMBOLS

OBSERVATION About 10:30 every night a man who calls himself "Sandwich Man" comes around the dorm and sells us hot submarines that he makes himself. The guys do a lot of joking around and tease one another that if they don't get with it and study they'll end up selling subs. Some of us happened to watch Sandwich Man leave tonight and darned if he didn't hop into a late model Cadillac. This really set us back on our heels.

PRINCIPLE Americans place a good deal of emphasis on status (which we tend to measure largely in monetary terms). A hot sub salesman ranks low in the American stratification system. The guys reflected this fact in their jokes. But when we found out Sandwich Man drove a Cadillac we considered him much more successful than we did before. We saw him as enjoying a higher status since he had a symbol (a nice car) of high status.

Status not only finds expression in various styles of life but also in **deference**—the ritual or ceremonial dramatizing of an individual's or group's priority. Deference often takes the form of **presentation rituals**. Individuals or groups attest to their regard, awe, or respect for superiors through symbolic acts. The tradition of abasement before a monarch or sacred idol provides a good illustration of this. Bowing and scraping are all variations of superiority and inferiority by height; they contain the body language message, "You are higher than I am, so you are dominant" (Fast, 1970:51).

Deference may also be displayed through **avoidance rituals**. Since close association would violate the aura of respect, awe, and dignity associated with high status (it would become "soiled" through contact), those of lesser rank may be required to maintain distance from the bearers of honor and prestige. The Brahmins (aristocratic priests) of the Hindu caste order afford a good illustration of this; members of lower castes and especially the "Untouchables" were believed ritually to pollute or contaminate Brahmins by entering their territorial space. Still another illustration is provided by the use of titles. Since people and their names are commonly equated, others may be required to avoid mention of the name and instead employ a title: "Your Majesty," "Your Excellency," "Sir," "Mr. President," "Doctor," and so on (Goffman, 1967).

SOURCES OF SOCIAL STRATIFICATION

Humanity left to its own does not necessarily re-establish capitalism, but it does re-establish inequality. The forces tending toward the creation of new classes are powerful.
Mao Tse-Tung, 1965 interview

It has been noted that, broadly considered, all societies have some form of social stratification. Why this should be so is an intriguing question. In the course of human history two strikingly divergent answers have emerged. The first—the conservative thesis—has supported the status quo, arguing that an unequal distribution of social rewards functions as a necessary social instrument for getting the essential tasks of society performed. In contrast, the second view—the radical thesis—has been highly critical of the status quo, seeing social inequality as a dog-eat-dog and exploitative arrangement arising out of a struggle for valued goods and services in short supply. Modern theories of inequality fall broadly into one or the other tradition. Those stemming from the conservative tradition are commonly labeled "functionalist" theories; those with roots in the radical tradition are usually referred to as "conflict" theories (Lenski, 1966; Kemper, 1976).

FUNCTIONALIST THEORIES

> For the sake of the prosperity of the worlds, He [the Lord] caused [the various castes] to proceed from his mouth, his arms, his thighs, and his feet. . . . But in order to protect this universe, He, the most resplendent one, assigned separate [duties and] occupations to those who sprang from his mouth, arms, thighs, and feet.
>
> *Hindu priests*, The Laws of Manu, *about 200* B.C.

Probably the clearest formulation of the contemporary functionalist position appears in a paper by Kingsley Davis and Wilbert E. Moore (1945). Although more than thirty years have passed since its original publication, the issues raised by the paper are still being debated by sociologists. Davis and Moore argue that social stratification is a *necessity*. This necessity arises out of the requirement faced by society of placing people in all the positions comprising the social structure and then of motivating them to perform the duties associated with these positions. Put still another way, if a society is to maintain itself, certain tasks or work must be done. Accordingly, society needs to motivate people at two different levels: (1) it must instill in the proper individuals the desire to fill certain positions and (2) once in these positions it must instill in the occupants the desire to act out the associated roles. Society must concern itself with human motivation since the duties associated with the various positions are not all equally pleasant to the human organism, are not all equally important to societal survival, and are not all equally in need of the same ability or talent.

From the above considerations, Davis and Moore insist that a society must have, first, some kind of rewards that it can use as inducements for its members, and, second, some way of distributing these rewards differentially according to positions. Inequality constitutes the motivational incentive for meeting the twin problems of filling certain positions and of getting the occupants to act out the associated roles. These differential rewards are, so to speak, "built into" positions making for social stratification.

Davis and Moore go on to argue that in all societies those positions that are most highly rewarded are generally those (1) which are functionally most important (demand), and (2) which are occupied by the most talented or qualified incumbents (supply). They note, however (in keeping with the classical economic model of supply and demand), that societies do not overreward positions that are easy to fill, even if they are important. The position of farmer, for instance, is vital to the physical maintenance of most contemporary populations. Yet recent technological and scientific advances in American agriculture have produced a surplus of individuals capable of filling the position. Hence the position of farmer is not generally rewarded highly. In contrast, a position may be defined as of the utmost importance yet the supply of talented or qualified individuals may be small in relation to the demand. Under such circumstances society needs to give sufficient reward to the position in order to guarantee that the position will be competently and plentifully filled. For example, American society defines good health as an important value and hence the physician is viewed as an extremely important person. Yet a medical education is so burdensome (the studying and hours are commonly defined as so onerous) and expensive that virtually none would undertake it if the position of physician did not carry a reward commensurate with the sacrifice.

Critics quickly challenged the Davis–Moore formulations (Tumin, 1953; Huaco, 1963, 1966; Grandjean, 1975; Broom and Cushing, 1977). Some have observed that the positions of highest societal responsibility—government, science, technology, and education—are financially not highly rewarded in the American system. The heads of America's largest corporations earn considerably more than the President of the United States and cabinet members. Further, some baseball, football, and basketball stars receive incomes in seven figures. The same is true of some stock market speculators and racketeers. Can one logically argue that such individuals have a higher "function" in American society than top government officials?

Other critics contend that people are *born* into family positions of privilege and disprivilege (Anderson, 1971). Where people end up, even in "open" class societies, is strongly influenced by birth. Thus almost twenty percent of American medical doctors are children of medical doctors (Schumacher, 1961). And research (Sherlock and Morris, 1972) reveals that sixty-six percent of dental students have fathers who are professionals, managers, and proprietors (although only two percent of the fathers are dentists). Rather than some sort of Meritocracy—where each person begins the competitive race from the same line—the starting blocks are so widely staggered that the runners in the rear have only a remote chance of catching up with those ahead, while those starting ahead must virtually quit to even begin to lose ground (Anderson, 1971). T. B. Bottomore (1966), a British sociologist, observes, "Indeed, it would be a more accurate description of the social class system to say that it operates, largely through the inheritance of property, to *ensure* that each individual *maintains* a certain social position, determined by his birth and *irrespective of his particular abilities*" (p. 11. Italics added).

CONFLICT THEORIES

Any city, however small, is in fact divided into two, one the city of the poor, the other of the rich; these are at war with one another.

Plato, The Republic, 370 B.C.

Conflict theorists, as their name implies, view social inequality as arising out of the struggle for valued goods and services in short supply. They focus on the interests that divide people within society, leading to domination and exploitation within human relationships. They see society as a stage on which struggles occur for power, privilege, and status, and in which advan-

Figure 8.1. Percentage distribution of total employment (counting jobs rather than workers) for selected years and projected for 1980 and 1985. Karl Marx and other early socialists had prophesied that capitalist society would inevitably polarize into manual workers and big capitalists, with the virtual eclipse of the middle class. Just the opposite has happened. White-collar workers (generally occupants of middle-class positions) now exceed manual workers, exclusive of those in the service category.

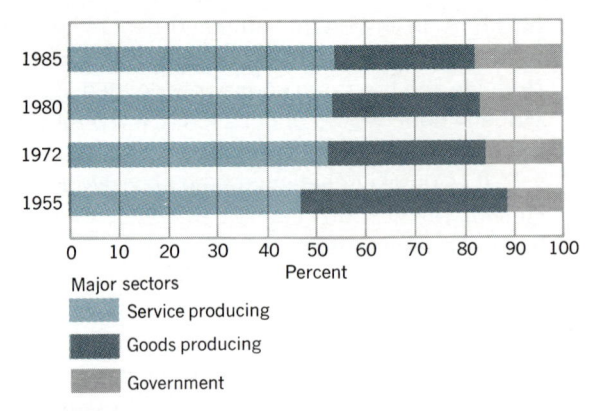

Major sectors:
- Service producing
- Goods producing
- Government

Source: Ronald E. Kutscher, "The United States Economy in 1985," *Monthly Labor Review,* 96 (1973), 40.

taged groups seek to maintain their advantage through the coercive oppression of the disadvantaged (Mills, 1956; Dahrendorf, 1959; Lenski, 1966).

Probably the most famous exposition of a conflict approach is that set forth by Karl Marx and Friedrich Engels in the *Communist Manifesto* (1848). They declared that the pivotal characteristic of social organization is class struggle (at least until a later hypothetical stage of communism would be reached). According to Marx and Engels, capitalist society was being transformed into "two great hostile camps, into two great classes directly facing each other—bourgeoisie and proletariat" (see Figure 8.1). The struggle between these classes determined the social relations between people; it shaped the entire social fabric. In particular, the bourgeoisie (the ruling capitalist class), which owed its position to the ownership and control of the means of production, also controlled, though in subtle ways, the whole moral and intellectual life of the people; law, government, religion, art, literature, science, and philosophy (all of which were viewed as constituting a "superstructure" deriving from class interests of the ruling group) were directly in the service of the capitalist class. In due course, however, Marx and Engels argued that the proletariat would see its "true interests" (they would become "class conscious") and overthrow the capitalist social order.

History, however, has dealt harshly with the Marxian predictions. Class consciousness and organization—the ingredients deemed so essential for revolution—have largely failed to develop in the large industrial nations. Herbert Marcuse observes: "The prevalence of a nonrevolutionary—nay, antirevolutionary—consciousness among the majority of the working class is conspicuous" (1972:72).

And contrary to Marxian expectations, the world's most highly developed capitalist nations have proved to be the most resistant to Communism—the United States, Great Britain, and Germany. Indeed, wherever the working class has been strong, capitalism has been strong. Where revolutions have occurred, the conquests were effected not by urban proletarians, but by varying combinations of intellectuals, the military, and peasantry. Communism has won its most enthusiastic and potent converts in the essentially agricultural and quasi-feudalistic nations of Latin America, Africa, and Southeast Asia (Hodges, 1964).

APPROACHES FOR STUDYING STRATIFICATION

Before examining the effects of social stratification, it would be well to clarify what is meant by the notion of "social class." Most of us make reference in our everyday conversations to the "upper class," "middle class," and "lower class." In many instances these terms carry the fairly strong implication that these social classes are rather distinct groups, each possessing unique cultural patterns (Berkowitz, 1975). Two views prevail in sociology concerning the accuracy of this conception of stratification, especially as applied to the American scene.

The first view of American stratification emphasizes the existence of distinct and bounded social classes. Some have defined these classes as status groups (Warner, 1949), others as strata with conflicting interests (Marx and Engels, 1848/1955; Bottomore, 1966; Anderson, 1971), and still others in terms of a blue collar–white collar division (Blau and Duncan, 1967; Vanneman and Pampel, 1977). A variation of the class-as-group conception is the idea of a "culture of poverty" which we considered in Chapter 2.

The second view portrays American society as essentially classless, a society in which class lines are blurred by the continuous and uninterrupted nature of power, privilege, and status hierarchies. Proponents of this view point to the absence of large gaps in occupational prestige rankings (Reiss, 1961; Hodge, Siegel, and Rossi, 1966; and Siegel, 1971), political attitudes (Glenn and Alston, 1968), and income levels (see Table 8.2 and Figure 8.2). Seen from this perspective, the various "social classes" are culturally quite similar and represent gradations in rank rather than hard-and-fast social groups (Rodman, 1968; Nisbet, 1970).

These differing conceptions derive in large measure from different methods for studying stratification: (1) the objective approach, (2) the subjective approach, and (3) the reputational approach. Although a good deal of overlap exists among these approaches, still there are appreciable differences in the results provided by each. Further, each method affords certain advantages and disadvantages in the study of social stratification. Which is "best" depends on what is being studied and what is to be predicted with it. Let us examine each of these approaches more carefully.

TABLE 8.2

How Incomes Differ by Job: Median Family Income, 1976

Occupation of Family Head	
Self-employed professionals, technicians	$28,565
Managers, administrators	$22,747
Salaried professionals, technicians	$21,423
Sales workers	$18,898
Craftsmen	$17,419
Clerical workers	$15,377
Operatives	$14,835
Nonfarm laborers	$13,455
Service workers	$12,550
Farm operators	$10,580
Farm laborers	$ 8,754
Private household workers	$ 4,937

Source: Press release, U.S. Census Bureau, October 4, 1977.

Figure 8.2. Family income levels in current and constant (1975) dollars, 1955–1975.

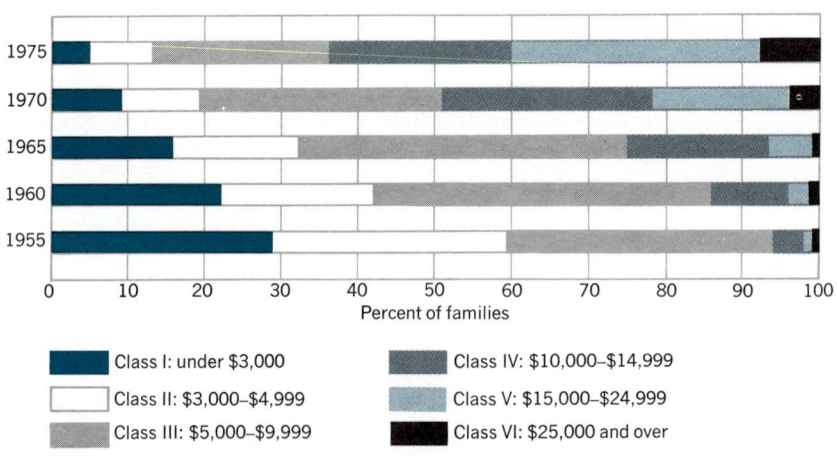

- Class I: under $3,000
- Class II: $3,000–$4,999
- Class III: $5,000–$9,999
- Class IV: $10,000–$14,999
- Class V: $15,000–$24,999
- Class VI: $25,000 and over

Source: U. S. Bureau of the Census.

THE OBJECTIVE APPROACH

The label **objective approach** can be misleading. It is not meant to imply that the approach is more "scientific" or "unbiased" than either of the others. It is simply employed to indicate that class membership is a function of some rather easily measured statistical variable. The most common variables used are income, occupation, or education (or some combination of these characteristics). The objective approach views class as a *statistical category*. Such categories are formed, not by the members themselves, but by sociologists or statisticians.

Sociologists employing the objective approach may decide to make income their criterion and divide an income range into a number of categories, for instance six, rendering six social classes as depicted in Figure 8.2. This approach enjoys the advantage of providing a rather clear-cut statistical measure for investigating various correlates of class, such things as child-rearing practices; incidence of mortality, mental illness, and divorce; and political attitudes. The objective approach is probably the most commonly used for measuring social class since it is the simplest and cheapest — statistical data from a variety of sources (for example, the Bureau of the Census) tend to be readily available.

Although the objective approach enjoys undoubted advantages, it also suffers from a number of disadvantages. Probably the most serious of these is noted by the late W. Lloyd Warner, an eminent sociologist, who with his associates investigated the stratification systems of communities in various parts of our nation:

> An analysis of comparative wealth and occupational status in relation to all the other factors in the total social participation of the individuals we studied demonstrated that, while occupation and wealth could and did contribute greatly to the rank-status of an individual, they were but two of many factors which decided a man's ranking in the whole community. For example, a banker was never at the bottom of the society, and none in fact fell below the middle class, but he was not always at the top. Great wealth did not guarantee the highest social position. Something more was necessary. (Warner and Lunt, 1941:82)

THE SUBJECTIVE APPROACH

The **subjective approach** (sometimes also referred to as a "self-classification" or "self-placement" approach) to social stratification views class as a *social category* (Tucker, 1968; Schreiber and Nygreen, 1970; Kluegel, Singleton, and Starnes, 1977). Social categories differ from statistical categories in that they are characterized by a consciousness of kind. Richard Centers, a social psychologist, exemplifies this type of subjective orientation to class:

Classes are psycho-social groupings, something that is essentially subjective in character, dependent upon class consciousness (i.e., a feeling of group membership), and class lines of cleavage may or may not conform to what seem to social scientists to be logical lines of cleavage in the objective . . . sense.

Class . . . can well be regarded as a *psychological* phenomenon in the fullest sense of the term. That is, a man's class is a part of his ego, *a feeling on his part of belonging to something;* an *identification* with something larger than himself. (1949, p. 27. Italics in original.)

Researchers employing the subjective approach generally directly ask respondents this type of question: "If you were asked to use one of these names for your social class standing, which would you say you belong to: the middle class, lower class, upper-middle class, working class, or upper class?" The answers secured from a national sample of adults in 1964 were as follows (Hodge and Treiman, 1968):

Upper class	2.2%
Upper-middle class	16.6
Middle class	44.0
Working class	34.3
Lower class	2.3
Don't believe in classes	.6
Total	100.0%

The subjective approach to class has a number of advantages. It can be applied to large units such as a nation (see, for instance, Table 8.3), whereas, as we shall shortly see, the reputational approach is limited to small communities where people are acquainted with each other. Further, the subjective approach is a useful tool for predicting political behavior since what people *think* they are influences how they vote. But the approach also suffers from a number of disadvantages. The class with which individuals identify may represent their aspirations rather than their current associations. Moreover, when placing themselves in the national class structure, people make very few distinctions among classes, while in their daily lives they often make subtle and fine distinctions in ranking themselves and other persons.

THE REPUTATIONAL APPROACH

In contrast with the subjective approach, where individuals are asked to rank *themselves,* the **reputational approach** asks people how they classify *others.* This approach views class as a *social group,* one characterized by a consciousness of kind and social interaction. It rests on knowledge of who associates with whom. Probably the most influential series of studies employing the reputational approach were those undertaken in the 1930s by W.

TABLE 8.3
How Americans Rate the Prestige of Selected Occupations*

Physician	78
University professor	78
Lawyer	71
Dentist	70
Head of a large business firm	70
Accountant	68
Business executive	67
High school teacher	64
Lives off income from property	57
Registered nurse	54
Secretary	53
Real estate agent	49
Skilled construction worker	46
Office clerk	43
Factory machine operator	38
Sales clerk	34
Plumber	34
Truck driver	33
Assembly-line worker	30
Gas station attendant	25
Janitor	21
Migrant worker	18
Lives from public assistance	16

* Based on a scale from 0 to 100

Source: Adapted from Donald J. Treiman (1977) "Job prestige scores." *Human Behavior,* 6 (November):25, and *Occupational Prestige in Comparative Perspective* (New York: Academic Press, 1977).

Lloyd Warner and his associates (Warner, 1949,1959; Warner and Lunt, 1941,1942; Warner and Srole, 1945; Warner, Havighurst, and Loeb, 1944; Warner and Low, 1947; Davis, Gardner, and Gardner, 1941; Hollingshead, 1949).

Warner and his colleagues studied the class structure of three communities: "Yankee City" (Newburyport, Massachusetts), a New England town of about 17,000 population; "Old City" (Natchez, Mississippi), a southern town of about 10,000 population; and "Jonesville" (Morris, Illinois), a Midwestern town of about 6000 population. Warner's reputational approach is reflected in his conception of class, which he defined as "two or more orders of people *who are believed to be,* and are accordingly ranked by all the members of the community, in socially superior and inferior positions" (Warner and Lunt, 1941:82. Italics added).

Figure 8.3. The social perspectives of the social classes in "Old City." The phrases in bold type portray the images that a given social class has of itself.

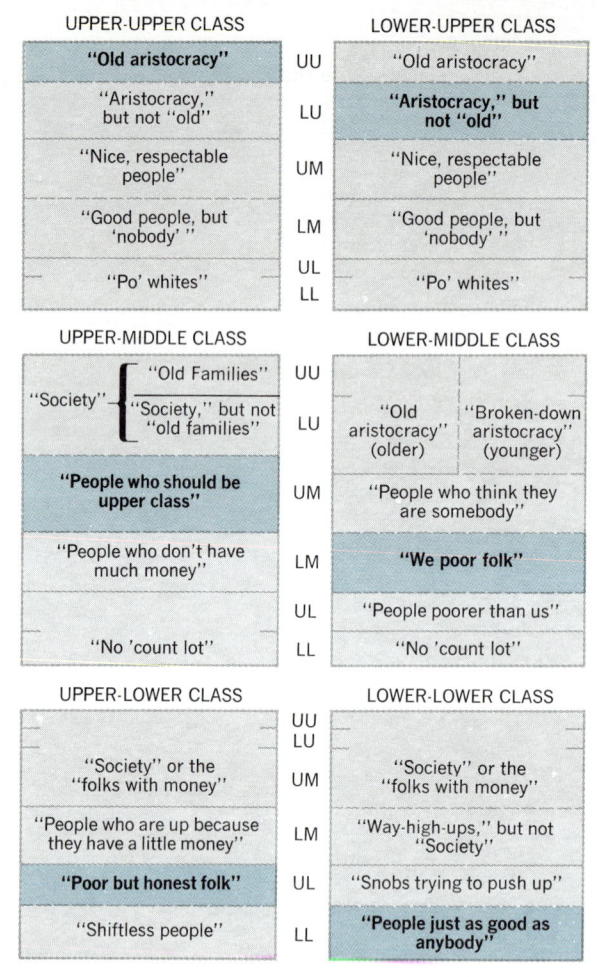

UPPER-UPPER CLASS		LOWER-UPPER CLASS
"Old aristocracy"	UU	"Old aristocracy"
"Aristocracy," but not "old"	LU	**"Aristocracy," but not "old"**
"Nice, respectable people"	UM	"Nice, respectable people"
"Good people, but 'nobody'"	LM	"Good people, but 'nobody'"
"Po' whites"	UL / LL	"Po' whites"

UPPER-MIDDLE CLASS		LOWER-MIDDLE CLASS
"Society" { "Old Families" / "Society," but not "old families"	UU / LU	"Old aristocracy" (older) / "Broken-down aristocracy" (younger)
"People who should be upper class"	UM	"People who think they are somebody"
"People who don't have much money"	LM	**"We poor folk"**
	UL	"People poorer than us"
"No 'count lot"	LL	"No 'count lot"

UPPER-LOWER CLASS		LOWER-LOWER CLASS
	UU / LU	
"Society" or the "folks with money"	UM	"Society" or the "folks with money"
"People who are up because they have a little money"	LM	"Way-high-ups," but not "Society"
"Poor but honest folk"	UL	"Snobs trying to push up"
"Shiftless people"	LL	**"People just as good as anybody"**

Source: Reprinted from *Deep South* by Allison Davis, Burleigh B. Gardner, and Mary R. Gardner, by permission of The University of Chicago Press. Copyright © 1941 by The University of Chicago.

In appraising the class composition of a community, Warner and his associates interviewed people from many walks of life. It soon became clear to the interviewers that people used different terms for designating individuals who were their equals and individuals who were above or below them in rank, for instance, "old aristocracy," "the folks with the money," "way-high-ups," "nice, respectable people," "good people but nobody," "po' whites," and "people just as good as anybody." Based on statements of this sort, Warner and his associates would piece together a community's class structure. Figure 8.3 depicts the class structure of "Old City." Figure 8.4 portrays the stratification pyramids of "Jonesville" and "Yankee City."

Figure 8.4. Stratification pyramids in "Jonesville" and "Yankee City." In Jonesville, a Midwestern community, W. Lloyd Warner identified five classes: one upper class, two middle classes, and two lower classes. In Yankee City, a considerably older Eastern community, he distinguished six classes, the upper class being divided by an "old family"-"new family" chasm. Birth was crucial for membership in the "old family" ("upper-upper") class. Its members could trace their lineage and wealth through many generations. In terms of wealth, the "new family" ("lower-upper") class could meet the *means* test, but its members failed to meet the *lineage* test so essential for upper-upper class membership.

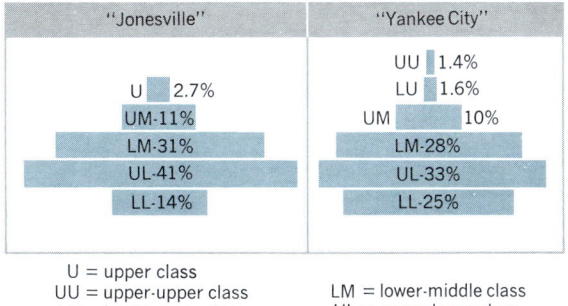

"Jonesville"	"Yankee City"
U 2.7%	UU 1.4%
UM-11%	LU 1.6%
LM-31%	UM 10%
UL-41%	LM-28%
LL-14%	UL-33%
	LL-25%

U = upper class
UU = upper-upper class
LU = lower-upper class
UM = upper-middle class
LM = lower-middle class
UL = upper-lower class
LL = lower-lower class

Source: Adapted from W. Lloyd Warner, *Democracy in Jonesville*. (New York: Harper & Row, 1949), 24–25.

The reputational approach to social stratification is particularly useful in predicting patterns of social interaction and membership in community organizations. But as a research tool, it suffers from certain liabilities. The most serious problem associated with this method is the difficulty of applying it to large metropolises where by virtue of the prevalence of secondary group contacts reputational assessment is impossible. Further, the same range of characteristics that produces a given class in a small community cannot be assumed to produce the same class in a large city; the upper class of small American cities is largely composed of people who are middle class when we look at class from the perspective of the metropolis. Nonetheless, even if we do not accept Warner's picture of American stratification in detail, he and his associates have provided us with valuable data on the operation of status mechanisms, especially those to be found within small communities.

The Warner studies were undertaken prior to World War II. Recently Richard Coleman and Lee Rainwater have updated our understanding of the class structure of urban America (Dellinger, 1977). They integrated the subjective and reputational approaches in a study of 900 residents of Kansas City and Boston. Subjects were queried concerning contemporary living levels within the United States. These urbanites ranked each other and themselves in the following fashion:

People Who Have Really Made It. Included in this elite class of wealthy individuals are the old rich (the Rockefellers), the celebrity rich (Paul Newman), the anonymous rich (a millionaire shopping center developer), and the run-of-the-mill rich (a well-heeled physician).

People Who Are Doing Very Well. Corporate executives and professional people make up this class. They reside in large, comfortable homes, belong to semiexclusive country clubs, occasionally vacation in Europe, and send their children to private colleges or large state universities.

People Who Have Realized the Middle-Class Dream. Although enjoying the "good life" as defined in material terms, the members of this class lack the luxuries of those in the higher classes. They are typically suburbanites who live in a three-bedroom home with a family-TV room.

People Who Have a Comfortable Life. Members of this class enjoy a "comfortable" life in the less fashionable suburbs.

People Who Are Just Getting By. The husband is likely to be employed as a blue-collar worker and the wife as a waitress or store clerk. The couple may own or rent a small home but find that "getting by" places a strain on their joint income.

People Who Are Having a Real Difficult Time. Both the husband and wife work and are proud that they are not on welfare. Their income is low and they spend much of their leisure time viewing television.

People Who Are Poor. Many of these families are on welfare.

Coleman finds that considerable changes have occurred among the upper classes over the past twenty years. Family background and wealth count for less than they previously did. In contrast, "social personality" and "gregariousness" have come to assume considerable importance:

> Although people think money is the most important thing, the lifestyle that they manage and the image they can project of their total being and what kind of person they are—the values they reflect—are truly the most important things. (Quoted by Dellinger, 1977, p. 29)

THE SIGNIFICANCE OF SOCIAL CLASSES

> In class society everyone lives as a member of a particular class, and every kind of thinking, without exception, is stamped with the brand of a class.
>
> Mao Tse-Tung, Quotations, 1966

Members of different social classes typically enjoy differing life chances and behave differently in a wide variety of respects. Such differences are fundamental and pervasive. Although class membership is seldom the exclusive factor affecting behavior, it is a factor that seldom is entirely absent.

HEALTH

Any number of studies have shown a relationship between social class and health. For instance, the higher the social class of the parents, the less likelihood there is that an infant will die during its first year (Brooks, 1975). An association also exists between occupation and cause of death, even beyond that which is explained by differentials in job hazards (for example, the high incidence of deaths resulting from respiratory diseases among miners). Thus, professionals, managers, and proprietors are considerably less likely to die from tuberculosis, stomach and duodenal ulcers, intestinal obstructions, or syphilis than service workers or laborers (Tuckman, Youngman, and Kreizman, 1965). Similarly, the higher the class, the lower the prevalence, morbidity, and morality associated with hypertensive heart disease (Howard and Holman, 1970).

Two factors appear to interact in producing the relationship between social class and health. First, higher class members have traditionally enjoyed better sanitation, preventive measures, and medical treatment (Antonovsky, 1972). Second, people who develop chronic illness are more likely to "drift" downward in social status or find their upward mobility impeded because their disability prevents them from gaining and maintaining many jobs (Harkey, Miles, and Rushing, 1976).

A variety of studies have also investigated the relationship between social class and mental health. One of the most sophisticated of these, based on a representative sample in midtown New York, found a decided relationship between the two (Srole et al., 1962; Myers and Bean, 1968):

Mental Health Categories	Highest Stratum	Lowest Stratum
Well	30.0%	4.6%
Mild symptom formation	37.5	25.0
Moderate symptom formation	20.0	23.1
Impaired	12.5	47.3

Other research comes to a somewhat similar conclusion, namely that lower social classes have higher rates of mental illness (Turner and Wagenfeld, 1967; Rushing, 1969; Eaton, 1974; Redlich and Kellert, 1978).

CHILD-REARING PRACTICES

Studies reveal a relationship between social class and child-rearing practices (Kohn, 1969; Walters and Stinnett, 1971; Gecas and Nye, 1974; Scheck and Emerick, 1976; Wright and Wright, 1976). Middle-class parents regard it as of primary importance that children be able to decide for themselves how to act and that they have the personal resources to act on their decisions. To working-class parents, however, it is most important that children act reputably and that they not break "proper" rules. Further, middle-class parents tend to be more supportive and controlling of their children, and more likely to discipline their children by utilizing reason and appeals to guilt than are lower-class parents. However, there appears to be little difference among the classes in the use or incidence of physical punishment (Erlanger, 1974).

Swinehart, based on interviews with mothers of third-grade children in a St. Louis sample, found appreciable class differences in the parents' child-rearing objectives; as class rank increased, the mothers' emphasis on meeting their children's social and emotional needs increased, while the emphasis placed on meeting the children's physical needs decreased (see Table 8.4).

TABLE 8.4
Maternal Objectives in Child-Rearing, Based on a St. Louis Sample of Mothers of Third-Grade Children

Emphasis	Lower-Lower	Upper-Lower	Lower-Middle	Middle-Middle	Upper-Middle	Upper
Meeting children's social and emotional needs	11%	21%	18%	27%	32%	43%
Guiding children's behavior, "building character"	14	32	48	43	32	25
Meeting children's physical needs	43	21	14	5	7	4
Other responses	32	25	20	25	28	28

Source: Adapted from James W. Swinehart, "Socio-Economic Level, Status Aspiration, and Maternal Role," *American Sociological Review,* 28 (1963), 395, Table 1.

MARITAL AND FAMILY RELATIONS

Through the years, sociologists have accumulated an impressive body of data demonstrating the relationship between social class and family patterns. Whom we date and in turn marry, the age at which we marry, the respective authority of the husband and wife in the marriage, our chances for making marriage succeed—these and other matters are associated with our social class. Hollingshead (1949), in his study of Elmtown youth, found that dating at the high school level appears to be decisively biased by class affiliation; in fact, 61 percent of the daters belonged to identical social-class levels, and 96 percent limited dating partners to their own or an adjacent level. And Hodges' investigation (1964) of more than 3000 San Francisco area families revealed that nearly one-half of the marriages involved spouses who were from identical (parental) social-class levels, and 95 percent were from identical or adjacent levels.

Class differences are related to still other aspects of marriage. Hence, the higher the *composite* social status of the husband, the more likely is his wife to find satisfaction with the companionship features of the relationship, the more likely is his wife to be enthusiastic about her husband's ability to express love and affection, and the more likely is his wife to indicate overall satisfaction with her marriage. Of the elements making up the husband's composite social status, his education appears to be the most critical variable in his wife's overall satisfaction with the marriage (the higher a husband's education, the more likely is his wife to report she is satisfied with the way the marriage functions). In terms of occupation and income, however, satisfaction appears to fall off in the upper brackets (most drastically in the higher income groups), so that the greatest overall satisfaction is reported by wives in the middle occupational and income groups (Blood and Wolfe, 1960).

Social class is also associated with marital stability (Goode, 1956; Bernard, 1966; Urdy, 1966,1967). For both Whites and Nonwhites, there is an inverse relationship between status and marital disruption when status is measured either by education (a minor exception is women with graduate training) or by male occupational status. On the basis of his examination of special census data, J. Richard Urdy reports:

> Generally speaking, there is lowest marital stability in the lowest-status occupations, with highest instability in men in personal service and domestic service. Occupational status has the same relationship to marital stability in non-white and white males, except that non-white rates are more than double the white rates. The relationship between occupational status and marital stability for men is direct and unequivocal. (1966, p. 208)

RELIGIOUS LIFE

Christian churches commonly stress the view that before God all people are equal without regard for their social or racial differences. Nonetheless, American churches are predominantly class-typed institutions (Gockel, 1969; Goldstein, 1969). The upper, middle, and lower classes typically favor certain churches and avoid others, a fact reflected in Table 8.5. In most American communities, the people of the upper classes belong to those Protestant denominations that feature services of quiet dignity and restrained emotion, such as the Episcopal or Congregational groups. The "common people" are more often seen at the Methodist and Baptist churches, or in Catholic churches (reflecting their origins as part of the "new" immigration from southern and eastern Europe). Revivalistic and fundamentalist sects hold the greatest appeal for members of the lower classes.

Some social scientists suggest that these religious patterns reflect attitudes of conformity and support for the established order among the upper classes. In contrast, the lower classes attempt to compensate for their economic misfortunes and failures through a commitment to salvation in the Hereafter (Pope, 1942; Warner, 1949; Yinger, 1957). It is important to point out, however, that the frequency of religious participation bears little relationship to socioeconomic status (Mueller and Johnson, 1975).

TABLE 8.5
Average Family Income, Occupational Socioeconomic Status, and Education Within Selected Religious Groups*

Group	Family Income	Occupational Socioeconomic Status Score	Education (Years)
Jewish	$9,839	53.4	13.3
Episcopalian	9,173	50.0	13.5
Congregationalist	9,067	44.7	12.9
Presbyterian	8,013	43.2	12.5
Morman	7,188	41.0	12.0
Methodist	7,185	37.3	11.6
Catholic	7,132	35.9	11.1
Lutheran	7,120	35.6	11.1
Baptist	5,612	30.5	10.1

* Based on a 1962 census sample of 12,000 U.S. households. Unhappily, a more recent study of this size has not been undertaken.

Source: Adapted from Galen L. Gockel, "Income and Religious Affiliation: A Regression Analysis," *American Journal of Sociology,* 74 (1969), 637, Table 1.

POLITICAL BEHAVIOR

Numerous studies show that social class affects people's political behavior (Erbe, 1964; Hansen, 1975; Kim, Petrocik, and Enokson, 1975). Regardless of the specific measure used by the investigator—income, education, occupation, home ownership, rent, or some combination of these—the results are most uniform: the higher the social class, the more likely is an individual to register, to vote, to be interested in politics, to discuss politics, to belong to politically relevant organizations, and to attempt to influence the political views of others.

Political attitudes are also affected by social class. A variety of surveys reveal that class differences are greatest in regard to issues that obviously and directly affect the interests of people at upper-, middle-, and lower-class levels differently. On the whole, lower-income groups are more in favor of government control of business, extending government welfare activities, and sacrificing institutional property rights and unlimited opportunities for individual achievement in the interests of increasing security. Further, evidence suggests that the lower classes have more extreme nationalistic attitudes, greater religious traditionalism, and generally a more restricted outlook on the world (presumably associated with limited education). Although it is tempting to catch up the main differences in a simple generalization that upper classes are more conservative and lower classes more radical, the relationship is not quite this simple (Glenn, 1975). Hence, as social class ascends, tolerance on civil liberties' issues increases (based on responses to questions about the right of free speech for Communists, critics of religion, advocates of nationalization of industry, and so on). A similar picture emerges on many civil rights' issues, for instance, the higher the status, the more favorable the image of Blacks and the greater the readiness for school desegregation (Noel and Pinkney, 1964; Vander Zanden, 1972; Ransford, 1972).

SOCIAL MOBILITY

Thus far in this chapter we have emphasized the more stable aspects of social stratification. We now turn our attention to **social mobility**—the movement of individuals or groups from one social level (stratum) to another. There are at least two basic reasons why social mobility occurs within a society (Lipset and Bendix, 1959). First, societies change, and whether change is slow or rapid, it leads sooner or later to a change in the demands a society makes on individuals. Those who have inherited high positions may lack the competence demanded of them in the new circumstances. Further, the exclusion from high rank of capable members of the lower strata may cause tensions that eventuate in their attacking the traditional stratification structure and either modifying it or extracting concessions from the privileged groups. Second, just as changes occur in the demand for various kinds of talent, so there are constant shifts in the supply. No elite controls the natural distribution of talent or other abilities, though it may monopolize the opportunities for education and training. Hence, sooner or later recourse must be had to recruitment of individuals from the lower ranks. The first of these factors has to do with societal demand; the second, with the supply of competent personnel.

CASTE AND CLASS SYSTEMS

When social mobility is conspicuously absent within a society—where inherited inequality prevails—we speak of a **caste system**; in contrast, when mobility proceeds independently of social origin—where equality of opportunity prevails so that people's status is determined by their own abilities rather than by circumstances of their birth—we speak of a **class system**. In either event, we have stratification; but in the former, individuals are placed in the same stratum as their parents, whereas in the latter, individuals are ranked independently of their parents. A somewhat similar distinction is conveyed by the concepts of **ascribed status** and **achieved status**. In the case

280 Social Inequality

CLASSISM

OBSERVATION I work as a teller in a branch bank located in a working class neighborhood. Today, Friday, was payday for workers in area factories. As usual the bank closed promptly at five o'clock. Some of the workers had gotten off of work and hurried over to the bank to cash their paychecks only to find that the bank had closed moments before. The bank manager locked the door and would not allow any of the working class patrons in. About five minutes after five a man of about thirty-five appeared at the door. He was dressed in a suit that must have cost at least $350 and he carried a briefcase. His manner and bearing suggested that he was a businessman. He knocked at the door and when the manager appeared he told the manager that he wanted to open a savings account. The manager looked the man over and glanced out at the man's late model car parked by the curb. The manager let him in and instructed me to handle the man's business.

PRINCIPLE This illustrates the unequal allocation of privileges within our society. The manager sized up the man as someone of relative affluence and accorded him special consideration. In contrast, the working class guys were turned away.

of ascribed status individuals are assigned roles without regard to their unique talents or characteristics. In contrast, achieved status involves the allocation of roles to individuals on the basis of their unique abilities or qualities (Linton, 1936; Davis, 1949; Kemper, 1974).

When we mention "caste," we commonly think of Hindu India. Generally, the Hindu castes (especially of the period about 1900 A.D.). are cited as the most typical example of the caste type of stratification. The crucial feature of the Hindu system is that membership in a given stratum is generally ascribed and unalterable. Members of the lower castes are considered inherently inferior and enjoy the least desirable positions, regardless of their behavior. Rigid rules of avoidance operate within the caste system since certain types of contacts are defined as spiritually polluting. Choice of marriage partners is strictly endogamous—marriage must take place within the caste. Members of the highest castes maintain their superior ranking by exercising powerful sanctions, and they rationalize their superior status with elaborate philosophical, religious, psychological, or genetic explanations (Davis, 1949; Berreman, 1960).

The United States constitutes one of the best examples of a class-type society. The American dream pictures a society in which all of us can improve our social ranking. The American folk hero is Abe Lincoln, the "poor boy who made good," the "rail-splitter" who progressed from a "log cabin to the White House." The United States is founded not on the idea of a classless society but on notions of a class system where equality of opportunity prevails. Yet despite the ideal of equal opportunity, our society places some reliance on status ascription. This is most apparent in the assignment of roles on the basis of race, sex, and age.

A high caste wedding in India. The choice of partners under the Hindu system must take place among individuals of the same caste. Here the bride and bridegroom sit next to Brahmin priests.

United Nations/J. Isaac

SOCIAL MOBILITY IN THE UNITED STATES

A large number of sociological studies have been made of the patterns and amount of social mobility within the United States. This evidence suggests that considerable social mobility occurs. Studies of *intra*generational mobility—the occupational career patterns of individuals in terms of their mobility between jobs and occupations during their lifetime—reveal that a very large proportion of Americans have worked in different communities, in different occupations, and in different jobs. Job mobility occurs as people seek to maximize their status and income (Sørensen, 1975). However, there are limits to the variety of most people's mobility experience—most notably, it is primarily confined to mobility on either side of the dividing line between manual work and the nonmanual occupations; little permanent occupational mobility takes place across this basic line.

*Inter*generational mobility studies involve a comparison of the social status of parents and their children at some point in their respective careers (for instance, as assessed by their occupations at approximately the same age). Such research reveals that a large minority, perhaps even a majority consisting of up to two-thirds of the American population, moves up or down at least a little in the class hierarchy in every generation.

Political radicals have argued that an advanced stage of industrialization, such as that achieved in the United States, is likely to produce an increasing "rigidification" of social classes. Studies show, however, that social mobility has not slackened off; if anything, American society is less rigid today in terms of social advancement than it was in the past (Jackson and Crockett, 1964; Tully, Jackson, and Curtis, 1970; Lipset, 1972; Hauser, Dickinson, Travis, and Koffel, 1975). A survey of the backgrounds of "big business" executives reveals that only 10.5 percent of the current generation are sons of wealthy families; as recently as 1950 the figure stood at 36.1 percent, and at the turn of the century, 45.6 percent. Moreover, in the post-World War II period the proportion of those from economically "poor" backgrounds nearly doubled in the ranks of the top echelons of American business (from 12.1 percent in 1950 to 23.3 percent in 1964); simultaneously there was an appreciable decline in the percentage from wealthy families (from 36.1 percent in 1950 to 10.5 percent in 1964). Factors contributing to these developments include the replacement of the family-owned enterprise by the public corporation; the bureaucratization of American corporate life; the recruitment of management personnel from the ranks of college graduates; and the awarding of high positions on the basis of competitive promotion (Lipset, 1972).

It is worth noting that there is little difference among various industrialized nations in the rates of occupational mobility between the blue-collar and white-collar classes (Cutright, 1968; Lipset, 1972; Hazelrigg and Garnier, 1976). The basic processes affecting rates of social mobility appear to be structural—linked to the pace of economic development rather than to political or economic systems—and are thus comparable in socialist and capitalist nations. A comparison of social mobility in highly industrialized Czechoslovakia, a Communist country, and the United States shows that the openness of both systems is surprisingly great (Machonin, 1970).

SOCIAL STATUS MAY OPERATE THROUGH "GUILT BY ASSOCIATION"

OBSERVATION When I was walking over to the Library, I saw a girl talking with a guy who would not be considered good-looking or a good date. In all honesty, my girlfriends and I would consider the guy a creep. Out of curiosity I stood some distance away and watched the girl laugh and talk with the guy, seemingly enjoying herself immensely. The guy was doing the same. All of a sudden the girl caught sight of three girls who seemed to be her friends and who waved to her as they approached. Immediately the original girl turned and walked away from the guy. I could sense his hurt and bewilderment.

PRINCIPLE Social status often operates through "guilt by association." If you are friendly or associate with someone of lower status, it reflects unfavorably upon you, and deflates your status. On the other hand, if you associate with people "above you" in rank, it reflects favorably upon you, and inflates your status. It is as if people assume that "Birds of a feather flock together."

THE STATUS ATTAINMENT PROCESS

In recent years the focus of sociological interest has shifted from concern with the extent of social mobility to the factors underlying status transmission and attainment. By shifting the question from how far individuals move across class levels to the factors that lead to this movement, sociologists are able to establish the causal relationships involved in the mobility process (Wilson and Portes, 1975). The initial impetus to this research has been the model of the socioeconomic life cycle developed by Peter M. Blau and Otis Dudley Duncan (1967,1972; Duncan, Featherman, and Duncan, 1972).

The Blau-Duncan model entails a sequence of stages in the life cycle: first, birth into a family with an already established status ranking; second, a period of formal schooling; and third, adult life as the bearer of a particular occupational status. This model permits us to trace the influence of a person's socioeconomic origin on eventual occupational status through several intervening variables, especially education. More specifically, the "basic model" of the achievement process involves six factors: three pertaining to social background (father's education, father's occupational status, and number of siblings), one intervening variable (years of formal education), and two measures of the individual's later status (occupational ranking and income).

In order to capture the specific contributions of each stage, Blau and Duncan employed a mathematical technique termed **path analysis**:

> We think of the individual's life cycle as a sequence in time that can be described, however, partially and crudely, by a set of classificatory or quantitative measurements taken at successive stages. . . . Given this scheme, the questions we are continually raising in one form or another are: how and to what degree do the circumstances of birth condition [determine] subsequent status? And how does status attained . . . at one stage of the life cycle affect the prospects for a subsequent stage? (1972, p. 163)

Blau and Duncan employed data collected by the Census Bureau in 1962 from a sample of the American adult male population. They concluded that parental status typically has little *direct* effect on a son's occupational attainment. Rather, the primary effect of parental status is *indirect* through influencing a man's education (one of the virtues of path analysis is its ability to sort out direct from indirect effects). The length of formal education was the factor that most affected both early and later occupational attainment.

A second factor that had an appreciable impact (although less than that of education) was the level in the occupational status hierarchy at which an individual started his career. The lower a man began, the higher he had to rise, and the less likely he was to reach the top status positions. George L. Maddox and James Wiley note:

Head start. Some children are advantaged in the race for desirable positions by early childhood experiences that foster the skills necessary for academic success.

Patrick Reddy

> Serial dependence is produced by making the entry into roles conditional on performance in temporally prior roles. Failure, deviance, mediocre or exceptional achievement—each affects the probabilities of entry into subsequent roles, especially if these events are formally recorded. Every society has some way of "remembering" socially relevant aspects of an individual's biography, and that information is used to structure his current opportunities. In modern societies, individual role histories are efficiently assembled by records-keeping departments of impersonal bureaucracies. (1976, p. 25)

Current evidence suggests that the processes of educational and occupational attainment may be somewhat different for working men and women (Tyree and Treas, 1974; Treiman and Terrell, 1975; McClendon, 1976). It is known, for instance, that whether or not the mother worked outside the home and the occupation she held affects her daughter's occupational destination (Rosenfeld, 1978). Racial differences in the status attainment process are also known to exist (Hout and Morgan, 1975; Stolzenberg, 1975).

During the same period in which Blau and Duncan were at work, William H. Sewell and his associates at the University of Wisconsin were engaged in closely related research. The Wisconsin group undertook to specify various social psychological factors that serve as intervening or mediating links between an individual's family of origin and his or her later placement in the status hierarchy (Sewell, Haller, and Ohlendorf, 1970; Gasson, Haller, and Sewell, 1972; Hauser, 1973; Sewell and Hauser, 1975;1976). Sewell does not view his work as an alternative to the more general Blau-Duncan model but as an endeavor to supplement and complement it. Overall, both groups of researchers conclude that an individual's initial occupational placement and status are primarily a function of the amount of schooling completed. Research Study 14 provides a summary of the Wisconsin research.

RESEARCH STUDY 14

THE STATUS ATTAINMENT PROCESS*
William H. Sewell and Robert M. Hauser

Problem. The United States is characterized by a class society, one that allows for the movement of individuals up and down in the status hierarchy. Given this arrangement, why is it that some Americans are more successful than others in educational attainment, occupational status, and income? Over the past fifteen years, William H. Sewell and his associates at the University of Wisconsin have provided some of the best known studies in American sociology dealing with this matter.

Method. In the spring of 1957, all the high school seniors in Wisconsin completed questionnaires providing information on their post-high school educational and vocational plans, the educational, occupational, and economic backgrounds of their parents, their perceptions of the influence that parents, teachers, and friends had on their plans, and a number of related matters. The students' IQ scores were also available based on tests taken during their junior year. In 1964, seven years later, a follow-up study was carried out with a representative portion of the original sample (one-third of all the students). A questionnaire, mailed to parents, provided information on the post-high school achievement of the students. Between 1964 and 1967 Sewell and his associates also obtained information about the parents' and students' earnings from state income tax and federal Social Security records. Elaborate precautions were taken to preserve the confidentiality of the information.

Findings. The major link between the socioeconomic origins of individuals and the socioeconomic achievements they evidence early in their careers is post-high school education. Indeed, the path to higher occupational status is primarily through college education. Once educational attainment is statistically taken into account, the additional effects of parental status on occupational attainment are found to be insignificant.

Educational aspirations and attainment are influenced by a variety of factors. Mother's and father's education, father's occupation, and parental income taken together account for fifteen percent

---

* Adapted from William H. Sewell and Robert M. Hauser, "Causes and Consequences of Higher Education: Models of the Status Attainment Process." In William H. Sewell and Robert M. Hauser, Eds. *Schooling and Achievement in American Society.* New York: Academic Press, 1976.

of the total variance found among the individuals in terms of the years of post-high school education completed. When academic ability (IQ performance) is added to the model, the explained variance in educational attainment almost doubles, rising from 15 to 28 percent.

Sewell and his associates then examine a set of "social psychological" factors including high school grades, parental and teacher encouragement of higher education, friends' post-high school plans, the individual's college plans, and the individual's occupational aspirations. By totaling the effects of parental status characteristics, mental ability, and the social psychological variables, the Wisconsin researchers are able to explain 54 percent of the variance in educational attainment. This model also accounts for 43 percent of the variance in occupational attainment and seven percent of the variance in 1967 earnings (this figure is low presumably because of the very early stage in career development being considered).

The Wisconsin research suggests that social psychological factors intervene between parental status and an individual's later status attainment. Occupational attainment, then, is seen as the outcome of two related processes: those by which educational and occupational aspirations are formed and those by which the aspirations become translated into a position in the status hierarchy. Educational expectation, encouragement, and performance influence educational attainment which in turn, together with occupational expectation, causes occupational attainment.

Conclusion. Sewell and Hauser conclude:

To return to our model, we feel that it has been highly successful in . . . [explaining] the attainment process in the educational, occupational, and economic spheres—and this is what we as sociologists are concerned with. Our . . . model has clearly demonstrated the importance of socioeconomic origins for educational, occupational, and earnings attainments. It has illuminated the rather complex process by which the effects of socioeconomic background on educational, occupational, and economic attainments are mediated by various social psychological experiences. (1976, p. 26)

SUMMARY

1. In social life we constantly differentiate among people as superior or inferior, higher or lower. This differential ranking or grading of people into horizontal layers is referred to as social stratification. Broadly considered, it is questionable whether any society, even the simplest, lacks some form of stratification.

2. In forging and fashioning our actions, we need to know where other individuals or groups stand relative to us with regard to three hierarchies: (1) power, (2) privilege, and (3) status. Power determines which of us is able to translate our preference into the reality of social life. Privilege entails our physical and psychological comfort as these are associated with the control and possession of goods and services. Status involves our sense of worth and respect, particularly the extent to which we feel ourselves admired and thought well of.

3. Power hierarchies find expression in behaviors of dominance and submission. Ownership of property constitutes one source of power. The possession of the means of administration constitutes still another.

4. A privilege rank is made up of people who share roughly similar life-chances. Life-chances refers to the typical probability that an individual or group will possess a given level of (1) goods and services, (2) external conditions of life, and (3) subjective satisfaction or frustration.

5. Status is an intangible, not a tangible quality. However, we frequently seek to make it tangible through titles, special seats of honor, honorary degrees, demeanor, emblems, and conspicuous displays of leisure and consumption. Status also finds expression in different styles of life and deference rituals.

6. In the course of human history two strikingly divergent explanations have been advanced for social stratification. The first—the conservative thesis—has supported the status quo, arguing that an unequal distribution of social rewards functions as a necessary social instrument for getting the essential tasks of society performed. In contrast, the second view—the radical thesis—has been highly critical of the status quo, seeing social inequality as a dog-eat-dog and exploitative arrangement arising out of a struggle for valued goods and services in short supply. Probably the clearest formulation of the conservative or functionalist thesis is the position outlined by Kingsley Davis and Wilbert E. Moore. The most famous exposition of the

radical or conflict approach is that set forth by Karl Marx and Friedrich Engels.

7. Sociologists have used three methods for studying social stratification. The first method is the objective approach—class membership is viewed as a function of some rather easily measured statistical variable such as income, occupation, or education. The second method is the subjective approach—class membership is seen as constituting a social category characterized by a consciousness of kind. The third method is the reputational approach—class membership is viewed as resting on people's knowledge of who associates with whom.

8. Members of different social classes typically enjoy differing life chances and behave differently in a wide variety of respects. Such differences are fundamental and pervasive, finding expression in health, child-rearing practices, marital and family relations, religious life, and political behavior.

9. Social mobility involves the movement of individuals or groups from one social level (stratum) to another. When mobility is conspicuously absent within a society—where inherited inequality prevails—we speak of a caste system. When mobility proceeds independently of social origin—where equality of opportunity prevails so that people's status is determined by their own abilities rather than by circumstances of their birth—we speak of a class system.

10. Studies of intragenerational mobility—the occupational career patterns of individuals in terms of their mobility between jobs and occupations during their lifetime—reveal that a very large proportion of Americans have worked in different communities, in different occupations, and in different jobs. Studies of intergenerational mobility—a comparison of the social status rankings of parents and their offspring—reveal that a large minority, perhaps even a majority consisting of up to two-thirds of the American population, moves up or down at least a little in the class hierarchy in every generation.

11. Research dealing with the status attainment process reveals that it is the level of schooling that has the principal influence on an individual's subsequent occupational attainment. Parental status serves to influence a child's aspirations. These aspirations then contribute to the individual's education attainment which in turn influences the individual's first occupational placement and, through it, later occupational attainment.

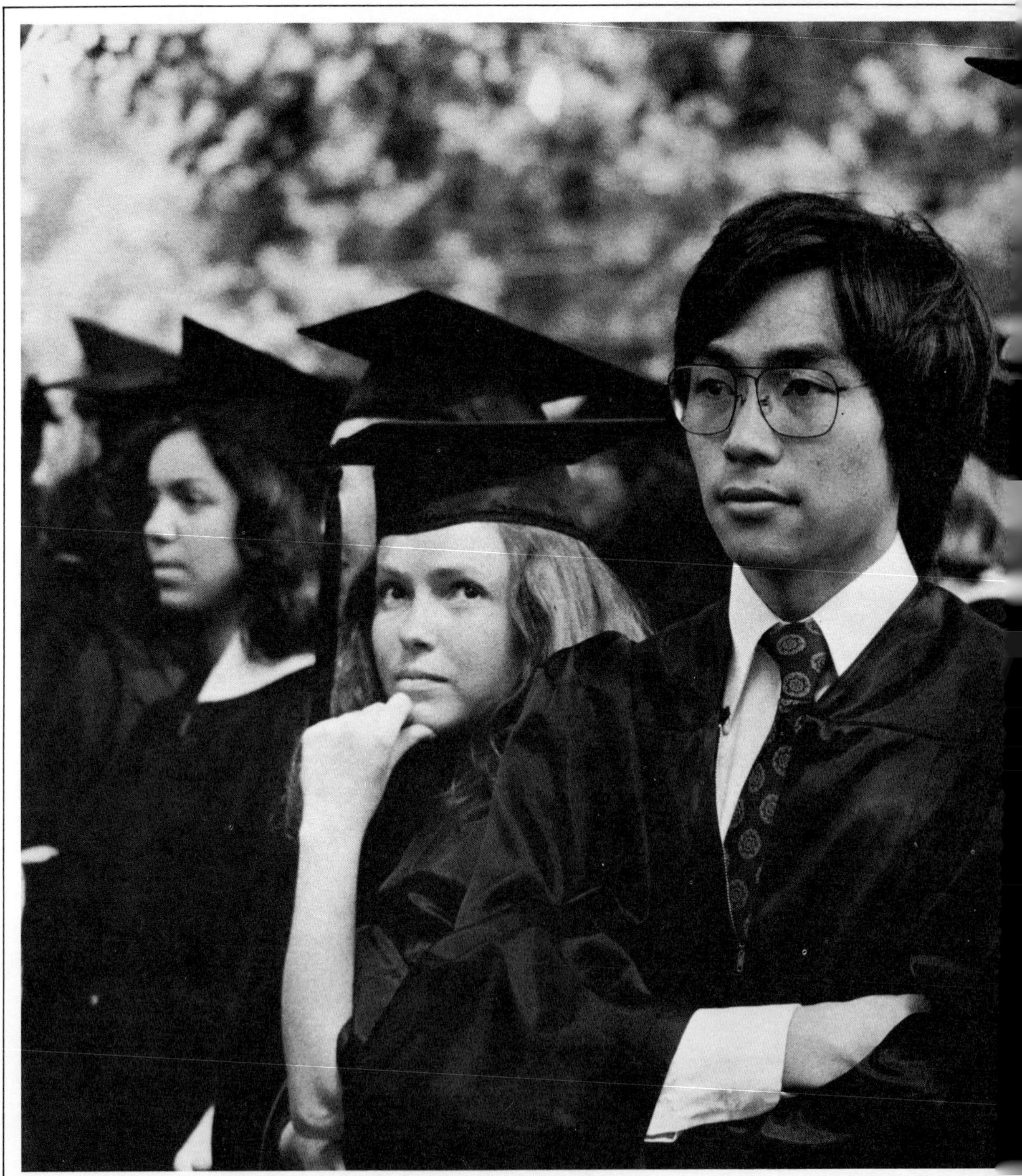

9
RACE AND ETHNIC RELATIONS

RACIAL AND ETHNIC INEQUALITY
    Dominant and Minority Group Relations
    Ethnocentrism
    Prejudice and Discrimination
    Institutional Racism

SOURCES OF RACISM
    Diversity and Categorization
    Competition
    Unequal Power

SOCIAL UNITY AND DISUNITY
    Consensus
    Functional Reciprocity
    Coercion
    Assimilation, Segregation, and Pluralism

MINORITY RESPONSES TO DOMINATION
    A Typology of Responses
    The Black Protest

OBSERVATION I consider myself to be quite liberal when it comes to race relations and to be nonprejudiced toward Blacks. Today, however, something occurred which really stunned me and got me thinking. For a number of years I've been working as a clerk in the sporting goods department of a national retail chain. Once in a while my sister drops by to see me. After she left today, a Black coworker who I consider to be one of my buddies told me he thought that my sister was real sharp and he asked me to fix him up with a date. That really set off the adrenalin in me. My skin flushed and I was dumbfounded—frightened and angry. I no longer saw him as my friend but as a "jive n___" trying to put the make on my sister. He asked me if I disapproved of interracial dating. Rather then respond to him I sought out a customer to wait on and avoided the whole issue.

PRINCIPLE It is easy to consider oneself nonprejudiced until the racial issue hits close to home. Much racial prejudice within the United States is rooted in sexual fears. Racist Whites believe that Blacks are oversexed and incapable of entering into a total and meaningful male-female relationship that is not colored by sexual exploitation. I cannot conceive of my sister voluntarily entering into a sexual relationship with a Black man. To me he would have raped her. I have concluded that I must be a racist.

Contact between racial and ethnic groups is probably a phenomenon as old as humanity itself. Excavations involving skeletal fossils of protohumans and early humans reveal that groups with differing characteristics coexisted and in some cases interbred (Howells, 1973; Harris, 1975). Archeological evidence also affords indisputable evidence that long before the dawn of history, people were continually on the move, invading the territory of others and borrowing ideas from their enemies and from strangers (indeed, archeologists gain a glimpse into early history by tracing peoples' migrations through their differing types of artifacts, designs on pottery, dwellings, forms of art, and so on). Similarly, ancient folklore recounts such migrations—the Bible, for example, tells of the early Hebrews in Ur of the Chaldees, of their years of slavery in Egypt, of their wanderings over the Sinai Peninsula, of their eventual entrance into the Promised Land, and of their wars with the tribes already settled there. And the mixed genetic nature of all modern "races" bears ample testimony to earlier migration, contact, and interbreeding.

RACIAL AND ETHNIC INEQUALITY

> The problem of the Twentieth Century is the problem of the color-line.
> W.E.B. DuBois, The Souls of Black Folk, 1903

People in various parts of the world differ in certain hereditary characteristics such as skin color, hair texture, various facial features, stature, and head shape. We term populations differing in the incidence of such hereditary traits **races**. Likewise, people the world over exhibit extraordinary cultural diversity in language, religion, economic arrangements, government, food habits, clothing styles, and family patterns. We term populations differing in their cultural practices **ethnic groups**. Throughout history people have attributed social significance to racial and ethnic differences and made them the basis for social inequality.

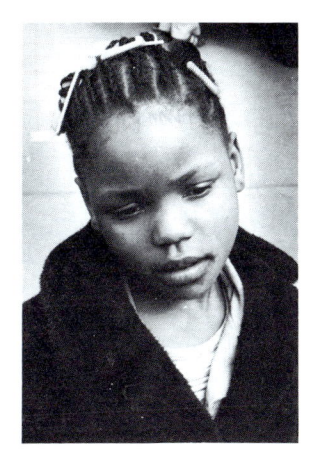

Patrick Reddy

Children and racism. Children are often the most severe victims of a racist society.

DOMINANT AND MINORITY GROUP RELATIONS

Racial and ethnic inequality finds expression in group relations that are characterized by dominance and subordination. Sociologists term the advantaged group the **dominant group** and the disadvantaged group the **minority group**. Five features commonly distinguish the relationships between the two groups (Wagley and Harris, 1964; Vander Zanden, 1972).

First, the minority suffers various disabilities at the hands of the dominant group including discrimination, segregation, exploitation, and persecution. It is not only that the dominant group enjoys advantage relative to the minority group—the minority group is commonly one *source* of the dominant group's advantage. The subjugation of one group confers privilege on the other group. The term *minority*, however, does not necessarily have any numerical connotation. Despite its literal meaning, a minority is *not* a statistical category. Under some circumstances, as under many colonial conditions, the minority group may be the numerical majority. This is true of Blacks in South Africa. And until recently, a limited number of Europeans dominated "minority peoples" in Asia, Africa, and Indonesia.

Second, the disabilities experienced by minorities are related to certain characteristics that its members share, either physical or cultural or both, which the dominant group holds in low regard and even contempt. This disapproval ranges from suspicion and ridicule to virulent hatred. Most commonly such notions are embedded in doctrines of racial superiority and inferiority.

Third, both minority and dominant groups are self-conscious social units; they are characterized by a *consciousness of kind*. Individuals are very much aware of their membership in one or the other group and this recognition affects their behavior. The traits the members of each group share in common feed strong in-group feelings that are increased by intergroup conflict. Such intense social and psychological affinity—deep-rooted loyalty and allegiance to "my people"—leads to the type of protracted struggle that has characterized the Israelis and Palestinians, Irish Catholics and Irish Protestants, and South African Whites and Blacks.

Fourth, membership in a dominant or minority group is most commonly ascribed and not a matter of individual choice. Frequently, people think of themselves as being alike by virtue of their common ancestry, either real or presumed. If an offspring is of mixed ancestry, the child is usually defined as a member of the minority group. For instance, within the United States an individual who is physically indistinguishable from the dominant White group but who has a known Black grandparent is defined as a Black. In Nazi Germany it was of no avail that a "Jew" looked like German non-Jews, had been converted to Christianity, and had taken a Christian spouse—the person was still, according to the Nazis, a "Jew."

And fifth, dominant and minority members tend to marry within their own group. In-group marriage is sometimes enforced by the dominant group, sometimes by the minority, and frequently by both. Indeed, many sociologists believe that the most sensitive barometer of the relations between two groups is their tolerance of intergroup marriage.

Sociologists employ a variety of concepts in analyzing the relationships between dominant and minority groups. Among the most common of these are ethnocentrism, prejudice, discrimination, and institutional racism. Let us turn to a consideration of each of these terms.

ETHNOCENTRISM

That pernicious sentiment, "Our country, right or wrong."

James Russell Lowell (1819–1891)

It is not uncommon for the members of a society to believe that they, and they alone, belong to the "best people" (Brewer and Campbell, 1976). Indeed, as Ruth Benedict (1940), an anthropologist, points out, "The formula 'I belong to the Elect' has a far longer history than has modern racism." Among even the most technologically "primitive" peoples, this formula frequently emerges as an integral part of their whole life experience. They see themselves grandiosely as "*the* human beings." The designation applies exclusively to their own group. Tungus, Lapp, Zuñi, Déné, Kiowa, and the rest are names by which peoples know themselves, and these terms are equated with "humanity." Outside their own closed group, human beings in the true sense do not exist. Other people are seen within this highly provincial outlook:

> They were not people with whom my own tribe had common cause. God did not create them of the same clay, or they did not spring out of the same water jar, or they did not come up through the same hole in the ground. But my own little group was under the special providence of God; he gave it the middle place in the "world" and foretold that if ever it was wiped out, the world would perish. To my tribe alone he gave the ceremonies which preserve the world. (1940, p. 156)

This tendency for a people to put their own group in a central position of priority and worth is known as **ethnocentrism**. William Graham Sumner described this point of view as one in which one's own group is the center of everything, and all others are scaled and rated with reference to it" (1906:13).

It was ethnocentrism that led China's Emperor Chien Lung to dispatch the following disdainful message to Great Britain's George III in reply to the latter's request that trade ties be established between the two nations.

> Our Celestial Empire possesses all things in prolific abundance and lacks no produce within its own borders. There is, therefore, no need to import the manufactures of outside barbarians in exchange for our own produce. But as the tea, silk, and porcelain, which the Celestial Empire produces, are absolute necessities to European nations and to yourselves, we have permitted, as a signal mark of favor, that foreign business houses [at Canton] be supplied, and your country thus participate in our beneficence. . . . As your Ambassador can see for himself, we possess all things. I set no value on objects strange or ingenious, and I have no use for your country's manufacturers. . . . I do not forget the lonely remoteness of your island, cut off from the world by intervening wastes of sea, and I overlook your excusable ignorance of the usages of our Celestial Empire. I have consequently commanded my Minister to enlighten your Ambassador on the subject. (Quoted in *New York Times*, February 28, 1926, p. 15)

Ethnocentrism often makes in-group virtues into out-group vices. Robert K. Merton notes how the very same behavior may undergo a complete change of evaluation in its transition from the in-group to the out-group:

> Did Lincoln work far into the night? This testified that he was industrious, resolute, perseverant, and eager to realize his capacities to the full. Do the outgroup Jews or Japanese keep these same hours? This only bears witness to their sweatshop mentality, their ruthless undercutting

of American standards, their unfair competitive practices. Is the in-group hero frugal, thrifty, and sparing? Then the out-group villain is stingy, miserly and penny-pinching. All honor is due the in-group Abe for his having been smart, shrewd, and intelligent and, by the same token, all contempt is owing the out-group Abes for their being sharp, cunning, crafty, and too clever by far. (1968, p. 482)

Ethnocentrism is a common and pervasive social phenomenon. It is found in virtually all groups—families, gangs, cliques, universities, fraternities.

PREJUDICE AND DISCRIMINATION

Sometimes, it's [racial prejudice] like a hair across your cheek. You can't see it, you can't find it with your fingers, but you keep brushing at it because the feel of it is irritating.

Marian Anderson, September 1960

Ethnocentrism entails strong *positive* feelings toward an in-group. It is often, although not inevitably, accompanied by **prejudice**—*negative* conceptions, feelings, and action orientations regarding the members of a particular group (generally an out-group). Prejudice is an *attitude,* and as such it involves a *state of mind.* It is to be distinguished from **discrimination**, which entails *overt action* in which members of a group are accorded unfavorable treatment on the basis of their religious, cultural, or racial membership. Prejudice, then, merely constitutes a predisposition to act, a predilection for certain kinds of action, but *not* the actual response itself. In contrast, discrimination involves the actual response or series of responses that an individual makes.

Discrimination occurs without prejudice and prejudice without discrimination. Overall, however, some correspondence exists between prejudice and discrimination such that the more prejudiced are also more likely to

DISCRIMINATION

OBSERVATION My parents live in a virtually all-White suburb. Through the years my best buddy has been Mike, a guy who lives two houses over. This evening I was over at Mike's house playing pool in the recreation room. Mike's dad came into the room and asked if I knew anyone respectable that I could recommend for a job in one of his drugstores. I told him I would ask around and then I said, "Why don't you put an ad in the newspaper?" He answered: "I can't do that because a Black might answer the ad. I can't hire 'em. You can't trust them."

PRINCIPLE I suspect that it is not uncommon for White business managers to try to get around civil rights laws by this method. Since he hires by a grapevine approach, he can limit applicants to an informal White job network.

practice discrimination. Yet there are numerous occasions in real life when there is far from a one-to-one relation between them. In the 1930's, for instance, Richard T. LaPiere (1934), a sociologist, traveled throughout the United States with a Chinese couple. In the course of the trip, LaPiere and the Chinese couple asked for service in hundreds of hotels, auto camps, tourist homes, and restaurants. They were refused service only once. Six months later, LePiere wrote each of the establishments and asked if Chinese guests were welcome. Over 90 percent replied that they would *not* accommodate Chinese, clearly in contradiction to their earlier actions. Here is a clear case of verbal prejudice combined with no actual face-to-face discrimination.

The *situation* in which individuals find themselves does much to determine which attitudes will be activated within an intergroup context. For instance, Lewis M. Killian (1952,1953) found in his Chicago study of Appalachian Whites that as patrons of a "hillbilly" tavern the men would have beaten up a Black rather than permit him to be served. But in the nonsegregated restaurant next door, of which they were also regular patrons, the men ate lunch on a desegregated basis. And many of them not only worked in plants with Blacks, but shared the same restrooms and dressing rooms. Thus in different situations, different expectations operate to guide people's actions. Further, Blacks differ from one another in such characteristics as age, education, occupation, sex, and marital status, all factors influencing White perceptions and definitions (Liska, 1974). As a result of the complexity of most social situations, there is no simple way in which the actions of one individual toward another can be accurately predicted solely from knowledge of the one person's attitude toward the other (Warner and DeFleur, 1969; Wicker, 1969,1971; Ajzen and Fishbein, 1973).

Since situational factors play such a large part in intergroup relationships, there are those authorities who believe that the fight against segregation and discrimination is more important than the fight against prejudiced attitudes and feelings. They point out that laws can be effective weapons against people's overt acts although they do not necessarily change people's minds. By analogy, laws against murder and theft do not aim to eradicate people's inclination to kill or steal; rather, they serve as a deterrent designed to prevent these impulses from becoming translated into behavior. Similar parallels exist between prejudice and discrimination. Robert M. MacIver summarizes the position in these terms:

> No law should require men to change their attitudes. . . . In a democracy we do not punish a man because he is opposed to income taxes, or to free school education, or to vaccination, or to minimum wages, but the laws of a democracy insist that he obey the laws that make provisions for these things. (1954, p. viii)

Social Inequality

Barometer of racial attitudes. Some sociologists suggest that the most sensitive barometer of racial attitudes in a society is the incidence of interracial dating and marriage.

Patrick Reddy

It is also worth noting that under some circumstances laws may affect prejudice by adding moral and symbolic weight to the principle embodied within the civil rights legislation. Law contributes to the moral atmosphere that prevails within a society, and may have an educational impact on its members. Physicians' attitudes toward medicare provide a good illustration of this. Seldom has a law been more bitterly opposed by any group than was medicare by the medical profession. Nonetheless, the proportion of physicians favoring the program jumped from 38 percent before the law was passed to 70 percent ten months after it was passed (but not implemented), and then to 81 percent six months after it was implemented (Colombotos, 1969).

INSTITUTIONAL RACISM

> What white Americans have never fully understood—but what the Negro can never forget—is that white society is deeply implicated in the ghetto. White institutions created it, white institutions maintain it, and white society condones it.
>
> *Report of the National Advisory Commission on Civil Disorders, 1968*

The concepts of prejudice and discrimination tend to focus on the *individual*. The emphasis falls on relations between prejudiced *individuals* and victimized *individuals*. While useful, the concepts fail to call our attention to the ways in which people of one racial group are systematically oppressed or exploited by the institutions of a society controlled by another racial group, a phenomenon that Stokely Carmichael and Charles V. Hamilton (1967) label **institutional racism**. Carmichael and Hamilton highlight the distinction between individual racism and institutional racism in these terms:

> When white terrorists bomb a black church and kill five black children, that is an act of individual racism, widely deplored by most segments of the society. But when in the same city—Birmingham, Alabama—five hundred black babies die each year because of the lack of proper food, shelter and medical facilities, and thousands more are destroyed and maimed physically, emotionally and intellectually because of conditions of poverty and discrimination in the black community, that is a function of institutional racism. When a black family moves into a home in a white neighborhood and is stoned, burned or routed out, they are victims of an overt act of individual racism which many people will condemn—at least in words. But it is institutional racism that keeps black people locked in dilapidated slum tenements, subject to the daily prey of exploitative slumlords, merchants, loan sharks and discriminatory real estate agents. (1967, p. 4)

Individual racism, then, consists of overt acts of discrimination or violence committed by individuals; institutional racism, in contrast, is less overt, far more subtle, and less identifiable in terms of specific individuals committing the acts.

The United States has long been portrayed as a land of opportunity, one in which individuals find their social placement on the basis of individual merit. According to the American democratic creed, individuals should be evaluated on the basis of their competence and talents rather than their racial, ethnic, religious, or family memberships. In practice, however, American institutions have functioned to impose more burdens and give fewer benefits on an on-going basis to the members of one racial group than to another. More specifically, decisions have been made, issues defined, beliefs and values enshrined, commitments entered into, and resources allocated in such a fashion that Blacks, Chicanos (Mexican-Americans), and Native Americans have been systematically deprived and even exploited.

One mechanism of institutional racism is **gatekeeping**, the decision-making process by which members of a society are admitted to positions of power, privilege, and status. The people who tend the gates are often career individuals with experience and credentials in the fields they monitor. They are found in schools and universities, employment agencies, and business and governmental hiring offices. But even more importantly, such individuals have traditionally been White (Erickson, 1975).

Gatekeepers evaluate the qualifications of others to determine whether these others will or will not be permitted to do what they wish. Qualifications, however, are a relative matter. Which group's standards will be employed in evaluating whether individuals are talented and competent—"upstanding," "bright," "responsible," and "desirable"? Will the standards of excellence be those of Whites? Blacks? the Polish? Chicanos? And of equal importance, which individuals will be the judges who determine which people meet the standards of excellence? Will the judges be Whites? Blacks? the Polish? Chicanos?

Historically, the White power structure has tended the critical gates of society. It has determined who would be permitted to pass through the portals it controlled to good jobs, good schools, good housing, and good health facilities. And on the whole it has admitted those who fitted its own image—who adhered to its value system as reflected in family patterns, the owner-

Institutional racism. Centuries of institutional racism have relegated many Blacks to marginal business enterprises and jobs.

Patrick Reddy

ship and use of property, and personal behavior. To the degree to which other groups have had unique subcultures (for instance, as reflected in Black ghetto life or Chicano life in the Rio Grande Valley), their members have been filtered out of the "system"—or, put still another way, the socially defined good things (wealth, power, and status) have been funneled toward privileged Whites (like the chips flowing to those having a stacked deck of cards).

The consequences of institutional racism pervade American life. Black men, for example, receive lower wages than White males working in the same occupation (Stolzenberg, 1975). Further, despite Black gains in the 1960s, the income, educational, and occupational gap between Blacks and Whites still remain substantial (Villemez and Rowe, 1975; Featherman and Hauser, 1976). See Figure 9.1. Although anti-discrimination laws have been

Figure 9.1. Widening income gap between Blacks and Whites.

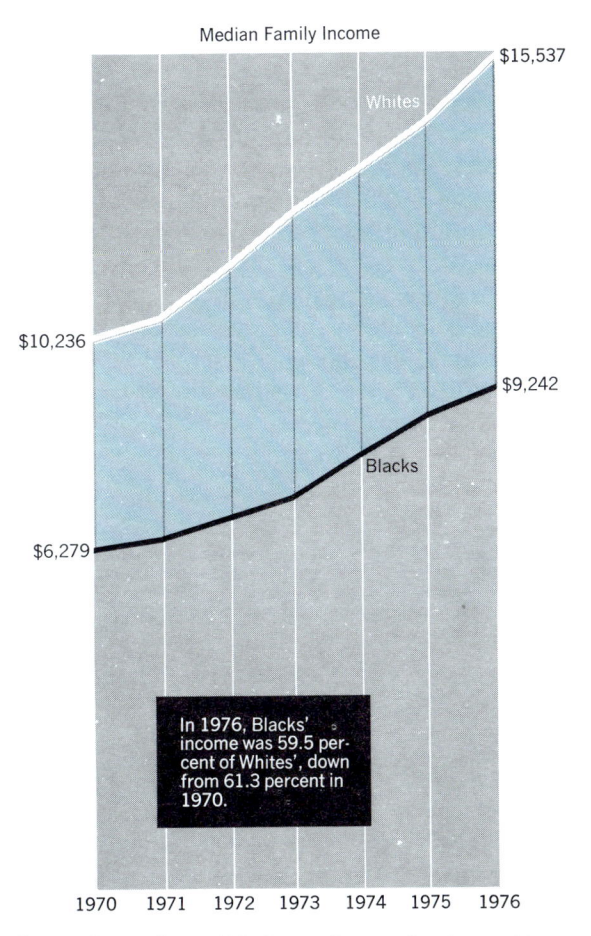

Median Family Income

Whites: $10,236 (1970) → $15,537 (1976)
Blacks: $6,279 (1970) → $9,242 (1976)

In 1976, Blacks' income was 59.5 percent of Whites', down from 61.3 percent in 1970.

1970 1971 1972 1973 1974 1975 1976

Source: Press release, U.S. Census Bureau, October 4, 1977.

TABLE 9.1

Statistics for Native Americans (Indians)

Population	About 1 million
Tribes	493
Number of reservations	267
Income per capita (1975)	
Native Americans	$1573
All U.S.	$5869
Unemployment (1977)	
Native Americans	40%
All U.S.	7%
Life expectancy at birth (1969–1971)	
Native Americans	65.1 years
All U.S.	70.9 years

Source: U.S. Departments of Commerce, Labor, and Interior.

passed to immunize Blacks against hiring bias, it is estimated from Census data that in 1969 it cost Blacks $1647 just to be Black (Johnson and Sell, 1976). Some economists say that institutional racism results in a dual labor market (Averitti, 1968; Gordon, Edwards, and Reich, 1975). Nonwhites are primarily concentrated in a secondary labor market offering low wages, insecure, dead-end employment, and few avenues of escape into the more advantageous primary market of well-paid, secure jobs. During periods of economic contraction, minorities are the first to be removed from the payrolls, providing an economic "buffer" or "shock absorber" for dominant group Whites. Nor should it be overlooked that some Whites, especially White employers and managers, realize tangible benefits from Black subordination (Dowdall, 1974). Table 9.1 provides data relevant to Native Americans (Indians).

SOURCES OF RACISM

> If we were to wake up some morning and find that everyone was the same race, creed and color, we would find some other causes for prejudice by noon.
>
> U.S. Senator George Aiken, Vermont

How does a racist social order arise? The evidence suggests that the processes involved are complex but that three ingredients are commonly present. First, people differentiate among populations, placing individuals in distinct social categories based on some visible and conspicuous feature or features. Second, competition takes place between groups for certain socially valued things, serving to generate prejudice. Third, the groups are unequal in power so that the more powerful group is able to actualize its claim to an unequal and larger share of the socially valued things. Let us consider each of these ingredients in turn.

DIVERSITY AND CATEGORIZATION

Categories are necessary to social life. They enable us to group things into "classes" or "pigeonholes," and to respond to them in terms of this placement rather than in terms of their uniqueness. In this fashion we reduce the complexity of our world through subsuming the diverse under the general. Because of any number of historical circumstances, people come to evolve given categories for classifying other persons (for instance, they are slaves, newcomers, foreigners, or heathens). Certain characteristics with high social *visibility* (for example, somatic traits, food habits, religious rites, language, and occupation) serve as identifying symbols of the category.

Hence, for racism to arise, it is essential that there be some visible and conspicuous feature or features present by which categories of people can be distinguished. In terms of our interests here, people must be able to identify one another in terms of ethnic (cultural) or racial membership. The distinguishing traits may be of a physical, cultural, or combined physical-cultural character. In the absence of such traits, the boundaries between the in-group and the out-group could not be maintained. Within the United States, for instance, Chinese, Indians, Filipinos, Puerto Ricans, and Blacks are distinguished from the dominant Whites by certain hereditary physical traits that they share in common with the other members of their respective

WHITE RACISM

OBSERVATION Today I was in the drug store when two Black guys walked in. It scared me because I thought to myself they may be stick-up men. I stayed clear of them in the store. I waited until they had completed their purchases and had left the store before I approached the cashier. When I left the store I saw they were ahead of me. I took my time walking behind them so as to put distance between us. Black guys just give me a creepy feeling. I guess I'm afraid they'll rape or hurt me.

PRINCIPLE This is an illustration of racism. On the rational level I know that I shouldn't feel the way I do. Yet really I can't help myself. Black guys just make me uptight. It is a gut-level thing. I can tell myself all I want that I have nothing to fear but it doesn't do any good. This shows how rooted prejudice can become in our personalities; it derives from the racist nature of our society.

groups. Cultural traits similarly may provide identifying clues; names (Cohen, Valenti, McGillicuddy), language, mannerisms, dress, gestures, food habits, religious practices and emblems (a Star of David).

By virtue of racial and ethnic categories, we "size up" people in terms of a limited array of characteristics. Such categories foster *object* relations as opposed to *person-centered* relations. We view a person as an exemplar of a group rather than as a unique human being. The individual comes to be identified first of all as a White, a Black, an Italian, or a Chicano—an *It* rather than a *Thou* (Gergen, 1967). Thus categories serve to order our experiences while simultaneously influencing *what* we experience.

COMPETITION

Within any social system, people act in relation to certain things that can be shared by everyone. These things are not scarce in the sense that one individual's sharing in them reduces or interferes with others' enjoyment. Religious salvation and national prestige provide illustrations of this. Christians can all share in salvation without detracting from the salvation of others. National prestige is similarly "participated in" rather than "divided up." On the other hand, there are some things that are scarce and divisible, such things as wealth, status, and leisure. In each case, the more there is for one person, the less there is for others (Williams, 1947; Labovitz and Hagedorn, 1975).

People typically seek to improve their outcome with regard to those things that they define as good, worthwhile, and desirable. Where the outcomes of two distinct groups are perceived to be mutually exclusive and legitimate, so that each can realize what it defines as a rightful outcome only at the expense of the other, competition will ensue. Goal attainment by one group is inversely related to goal attainment by the other. In other words, if two groups both believe they have a just claim upon the same scarce, divisible "good" things, their relationship will be characterized by competition—indeed, even conflict. In contrast, where a group does not define itself as having a rightful claim to certain valued things—for instance, where it accepts its low status as in the case of some caste orders—competition need not occur.

Where the relations between two groups are perceived as competitive, negative attitudes (prejudice) will be generated toward the out-group. Any number of experiments are suggestive in demonstrating the relationship between competition and prejudice. The reader will recall the research undertaken by Muzafer Sherif (summarized in Research Study 9 in Chapter 5) in which he experimentally brought two groups of boys into competitive contact with one another through games and tournaments. In short order, members of both groups developed negative stereotypes and feelings toward those in the other group.

It is also worth nothing that evidence from a study by R. J. Hamblin (1962) suggests that the mere *anticipation* of *future* competition with another group may be sufficient to generate out-group prejudice.

Similarly, Edna Bonacich (1972, 1975, 1976) details how competition generates ethnic antagonism within a **split labor market** — one in which there exists a large difference in the price of labor at the same occupational level. Conflict develops out of the divergent interests of three key groups: business, higher-paid labor, and cheaper labor. The business class aims at having as cheap and docile a labor supply as possible so that it might compete effectively with other businesses and maximize profit. Historically it seeks cheaper sources of labor through importing overseas groups (the importation of slaves from Africa to the United States until the 1860s and, in the post-Civil-War period, of immigrants from Ireland, Italy, and Southeast Europe) or using indigenous conquered peoples (native Indian populations throughout Latin America).

The higher-paid group feels threatened by the prospect of cheaper labor, fearing its own circumstances will be imperiled. If the cheaper labor is of a differing racial or ethnic group, class antagonism typically takes the form of racism; the rhetoric concentrates on ethnicity and race although at root it may largely express class conflict. Where the more expensive labor is strong enough, it resists displacement through *exclusion* or *caste systems*.

Exclusion movements attempt to prevent the physical presence of cheaper labor by barring immigration, driving immigrants out, or both. The anti-Chinese movement in California during the 1870s is an example (Miller, 1974). When the Republican and Democratic parties failed to heed White labor's wishes, the Workingman's party arose and swept the state with the cry, "The Chinese must go." The Chinese were severely persecuted, subject to violence, riots, bloodshed, pillage, and incendiarism. Within San Francisco it was not uncommon to see Chinese pelted with stones or mud, beaten or kicked, harassed on the streets, and tormented by having their queues cut.

In the case of caste systems, the higher-paid labor resorts to exclusiveness rather than exclusion. Caste is essentially an aristocracy of labor in which the higher-paid group controls certain jobs and gets paid at a higher wage-scale. The labor aristocracy evolves an elaborate battery of segregationist laws, customs, and beliefs that serves to entrench its advantaged position. It seeks to deny the cheaper labor access to education by which it may gain upward mobility and to political institutions by which it may alter its fortunes. Exclusion and caste, then, represent two different reactions to a split labor market; in either case, they constitute a victory for higher-paid labor in its competitive encounter with cheaper labor.

It is important to point out, however, that racism need *not* be an *inevitable* accompaniment of intergroup contact. Anthropologist Ethel John Lindgren (1938) reports that two groups in western Manchuria — the Tungus (a nomadic group) and a group of farming Cossacks — lived in essentially peaceful and harmonious relations despite the presence in both groups of ethnocentric notions. There was, it seems, a mutual economic interdependence, an intercultural complementing, an absence of competition between the two peoples for land and resources, and shared antipathies toward the Chinese. The case lends support to the thesis advanced in this book that the attitudes that the members of a group evolve toward an out-group tend to be consistent with their perceptions of the relationships they have with the out-group. Research Study 15 summarizes the Lindgren study.

RESEARCH STUDY 15

AN EXAMPLE OF CULTURE CONTACT WITHOUT CONFLICT*

Ethel John Lindgren

Problem. We often assume that conflict is an inevitable accompaniment of contact between different groups. But is it? It is to this matter that Ethel John Lindgren directed her attention.

Method. In the course of her anthropological field work in northwestern Manchuria in the 1930s, Lindgren lived among the Tungus and the Cossacks. From this vantage point, she had an opportunity to observe the nature of the relationships that existed between these two racially and culturally unlike peoples.

Findings. Lindgren found that the Tungus and the Cossacks had lived together, trading and associating with each other, for generations, yet had nonetheless managed to avoid conflict. Racially, the Reindeer Tungus are a Mongoloid people with physical characteristics quite similar to those of the Chinese. In contrast, the Russian Cossacks are a burly Caucasoid people. Culturally, the two peoples are also quite distinct. The Tungus are an illiterate, nomadic people who dwell in tents and depend on their domesticated reindeer, hunting, and trade with the Cossacks for subsistence. The Cossacks are a literate, sedentary people who dwell in village homes and rely for their subsistence on agriculture, stock-raising, some squirrel hunting, and trading with the Tungus. Religiously, the Tungus are nominal Christians, yet their ancient religious beliefs persist; they place considerable reliance on their shamans who are skilled in curing the sick, predicting the future, and communicating with spirits. For their part, the Cossacks are zealous Christians, although they are not without their superstitions and folk beliefs.

Despite these major differences, Lindgren notes:

I heard no Tungus or Cossack express fear, contempt, or hatred in relation to the other group as a whole or any individual composing it. A few traits of the opposite group are habitually criticized, and a few praised on the basis of a comparison with the corresponding traits of the speaker's culture. (p. 607)

---

* Adapted from Ethel John Lindgren, "An Example of Culture Contact without Conflict: Reindeer Tungus and Cossacks of Northwestern Manchuria," *American Anthropologist*, 40 (1938), 605–621.

The Tungus, for example, criticize the Russians because thefts occur in their communities, a crime unknown among the Tungus, while the Cossacks themselves praise the Tungus for their honesty, implying its superiority to their own. The Cossacks, for their part, criticize the Tungus for their random violence under the influence of alcohol, behavior the Tungus themselves deplore. Despite such criticisms, Lindgren observes: "Expressions of dislike and distrust with regard to individuals in the other group are of exactly the same type as those applied within the group itself, and admiration seems to predominate over criticism" (p. 607). Further, Lindgren was unable to discover any tradition or record that the relations between the two groups had ever been other than amicable, although she inquired of the elderly for such evidence.

The Tungus and Cossacks come in contact with one another on a variety of occasions during the year; hence, ample opportunities are provided for clashes between them. The markets provide one major source for contact. Two or three times each winter, when the Tungus are busy hunting squirrels, the Cossack traders travel with horse-drawn sledges up the frozen rivers and meet the Tungus at a forest rendezvous, where a market is held. Two or three times each summer, when the Cossacks are busy farming, the Tungus come with their reindeer to the Cossack settlements. The markets last from two to five days. The Tungus trade furs to the Cossacks in exchange for needles, thread, axes, iron pots, copper kettles, gun powder, lead, flour, and shirts, coats, and jackets. The trade is conducted between individuals who call each other "andak" or "friend." A Tungus often boasts about the wealth and superior products of his Cossack andak, who in turn boasts of his Tungus hunter's achievements.

The Tungus and Cossacks also encounter one another in the woods while hunting. Neither the Tungus nor the Cossacks divide the hunting grounds in any way within their own groups, nor do they come to a collective agreement with the other group on the subject. Nevertheless, the first to arrive in a valley, Tungus or Cossack, is left undisturbed. If members of either group discover fresh marks of the other, they will eagerly seek out the others' camp for the sake of company, and probably a little trade. Longer visits also occasionally occur.

Conclusions. How are we to explain the apparent lack of conflict between the Tungus and Cossacks? Lindgren suggests a number of plausible reasons:

1. The two groups have always been small in number and about equal in size. In 1908, both groups numbered about 800, and at the time of Lindgren's visit, there were some 160 Tungus (their number having been depleted by smallpox) and 150 Cossacks.
2. The two groups were not in competition for land or resources. The Tungus nomadized within an area of over 7000 square miles, giving a low population density of about .02 per square mile.
3. Outside foreign pressures tended to draw the Tungus and the Cossacks together. About 1908, the Chinese undertook to impose a tax on fur trade, a development that both the Tungus and Cossacks resented, and which strengthened the bonds between them.
4. Culturally, the two groups complemented one another. Both benefited economically from the trade between them. Religiously, the groups were quite compatible: the Tungus were nominally Christians, while the Cossacks took delight in praising the insight of the Tungus shamans and in describing shaman prophecies that had come true. Friction arising from intermarriage did not occur since the groups seldom intermarried, primarily because of the fact that the opposite sexes of the two groups had little opportunity to get together. Nevertheless, Tungus children adopted by Cossacks habitually made Cossack matches.

Conditions during and since World War II have not permitted Western social scientists to study the Tungus and the Cossacks again to determine if changes have occurred in their amicable relationships. It is conceivable that population changes, a depletion of game, and interferences with the fur trade may have promoted discord and strife.

UNEQUAL POWER

There are two ways of exerting one's strength: one is pushing down, the other is pulling up.
Booker T. Washington

Competition — the pursuit of incompatible goals — means that to the extent that one group obtains its goals the opposing group must fail to obtain its goals. Competition, however, rarely takes place between equals. Power becomes a factor: the ability to control the behavior of others in order to realize one's own goals even without their consent. Power, then, determines whether one group will be able to actualize its claim to an unequal and larger share of the socially defined "good" things — in brief, whether one group will be able to subordinate the other, in effect establishing a racist order.

External Colonialism. European "expansion," beginning in the fifteenth and sixteenth centuries and resting heavily upon power and force deriving from superior weaponry, brought with it a variety of outcomes. Where the native population consisted of small, sparsely settled, nomadic groups (as, for example, in Brazil, the United States, and the Western Cape in South Africa), the characteristic pattern of contact was frontier expansion of the Whites punctuated by sporadic skirmishes, raids, and guerilla warfare. Usually the outcome was virtual genocide of the natives or encapsulation of their scattered remnants on reservations. Where, in contrast, the European conquerers encountered large, densely settled, politically centralized, agricultural, and even urban nation-states (as in Mexico), the outcome was quite different:

> Military conquest was not accompanied by extermination but by subjugation. The dominant group established its control either by "beheading" the indigenous societies and substituting itself as the new aristocracy, or by using the ruling class of the defeated peoples and ruling through it. In both situations the native masses became politically subordinate and economically exploited through some form of serfdom, forced or "contract" labor, debt peonage, or share-cropping tenancy. (Van den Berghe, 1967, p. 125)

Assimilation Versus Internal Colonial Models. There are two sociological positions regarding the experience of Blacks and Chicanos within the United States. The one argues that Blacks and Chicanos are like European immigrants and will in due course become assimilated; the other claims that they are like Third World colonized groups (Murguia, 1975). Indeed, those who argue the merits of either position in the dispute tend to talk past one another as if speaking different languages.

Political conservatives say that Blacks and Chicanos are simply the last migrant groups to reach American cities, and as with European arrivals of earlier periods, it will take several generations for them to achieve equality (Kristol, 1969; Sowell, 1975). They emphasize the advantages of private enterprise and oppose special programs to aid Blacks and Chicanos. On the whole conservatives have led the fight against special admissions programs to colleges and professional schools, efforts to achieve greater desegregation through busing, and curriculum changes that would stress racial and ethnic identity. And they point out that colonized peoples have traditionally been numerical majorities whereas in the United States Blacks and Chicanos are numerical minorities.

In contrast, many political liberals and radicals take the position that the experience of Blacks and Chicanos relative to Whites is comparable to "internal colonies" in relation to a "mother country" (Blackwell, 1976). For instance, Kenneth Clark, a Black psychologist, argues that the position of Blacks in the United States constitutes internal colonialism:

> Ghettos are the consequence of the imposition of external power and the institutionalization of powerlessness. In this respect, they are in fact social, political, educational, and above all — economic colonies. Those confined within the ghetto walls are subject peoples. They are victims of the greed, cruelty, insensitivity, guilt and fear of their masters. (1964, pp. 10–11)

Raymond S. Franklin and Solomon Resnik take Clark's argument a step further:

> The meager savings and profits which are generated in the ghetto are sucked into the white "foreign" sectors through foreign-owned financial institutions and foreign-owned income-earning assets. . . . [The] general exchange between the black underdeveloped ghetto society and its white foreign controller is between the ghetto's export of low-paid labor surpluses for higher-priced imported goods and technical services. The consequences of this particular pattern of trade tend to be periodic balance-of-payments crises in the form of ghetto deficit. The deficits are met in two ways: (1) by foreign aid in the form of welfare payments by the "imperial" controllers used to keep the "natives" compliant, and (2) by the relative cheapening of the ghetto's main exportable commodity — surplus labor, a large portion of which is frozen within the boundaries of the ghetto. (1973, p. 86)

Viewed from this perspective, riots, theft, and other crimes against "White foreigners" operating in and adjacent to ghetto territory are forceable transfers of wealth (a redistribution of property).

Robert Blauner suggests that what makes the Black ghettos an expression of colonized status (and distinguishes them from White ethnic communities of an earlier period) are three special features:

First, the ethnic ghettos [made up of Poles, Italians, Jews] arose more from voluntary choice, both in the sense of the choice to immigrate to America and the decision to live among one's fellow ethnics. Second, the immigrant ghettos tended to be a one and two generation phenomenon; they were actually way-stations in the process of acculturation and assimilation. . . . But more relevant is the third point. European ethnic groups . . . generally only experienced a brief period, often less than a generation, during which their residential buildings, commercial stores, and other enterprises were owned by outsiders. The Chinese and Japanese faced handicaps of color prejudice that were almost as strong as the Blacks faced, but very soon gained control of their internal communities, because their ethnic culture and social organization had not been destroyed by slavery and internal colonization. (1969, p. 397)

Thus proponents of the internal colonialism model argue that Black problems within America are unique and old answers are irrelevant to the improvement of the Black situation.

SOCIAL UNITY AND DISUNITY

Our consideration of racism brings us to this question: How do societies manage to hold together in the face of racial and ethnic hostilities that at times reach intense proportions? Of course, not all societies do succeed in maintaining social unity—Pakistan and Bangladesh, for instance, split apart in 1971, as did the United States (at least temporarily) in 1860. Yet despite deep-seated intergroup antagonisms, a great many contemporary societies achieve some measure of social unity.

It is useful in considering social integration if we view groups and societies as concretions of *opposing* tendencies (Simmel, 1955; Schermerhorn, 1967). Social life is characterized by change, by an interplay of forces advancing, retreating, converging, or diverging in patterns of greater or lesser stability. Those forces that hold a social unit within the whole (an individual within a group or a group within society) we designate as *centripetal;* forces that spin-off or separate a social unit from the whole we designate as *centrifugal.* Centripetal and centrifugal tendencies are simultaneously present in every society, and each, if unchecked, will exhibit cumulative growth toward its own extreme. Hence, centripetal tendencies move toward integration—a state of being whole or entire; in contrast, centrifugal tendencies move toward segmentation—a state of being separate or divided. Consensus, functional reciprocity, and coercion are factors associated with the degree of integration prevailing within a society.

CONSENSUS

More than one hundred years ago, Auguste Comte (1798–1857), a leading nineteenth-century social philospher who is often acclaimed the "founder of sociology," contended that the chief unifying force in society is **consensus**. By this term, Comte (1871) referred to the customs and interests shared in common by a people—that is, things in which people were *alike*. His observation has much validity. Where individuals share common norms, values, beliefs, and symbols, they are knit together by an all-encompassing, seamless web of culture. They view and experience much the same social world. Indeed, their oneness derives from this very fact—they are so *alike*. Their life activities are guided by mutually shared expectations; and hence, in large measure, they are culturally carbon-copy replicas of one another. Few, if any, societies, however, are characterized by virtually complete consensus. Indeed, most contemporary societies integrate widely different subcultures that possess quite different—even clashing—behavior patterns. Thus, although consensus is a major dimension of human life, so also is dissension and conflict (van den Berghe, 1963).

Consensus may also derive from a felt allegiance to a common social unit. Such ties produce a feeling of oneness that gives those who are charged with it a sense that they are kith and kin. Such allegiance may arise from the sharing of broad tribal, racial, religious, linguistic, regional, or national bonds. The slogan "Black Power," with its connotations of group pride, solidarity, and collective self-awareness, provides a good illustration of this. By calling on people to feel, think, and act Black, it fostered a sense of community and forged new bonds within Black ghettos.

Although a corporate sentiment of oneness promotes social solidarity, we should not overlook the fact that it simultaneously generates the very opposite—social segmentation:

> This feeling is a double-edged feeling. It is at once a feeling of "consciousness of kind" which, on the one hand, binds together those who have it so strongly that it overrides all differences arising out of economic conflicts or social gradations and on the other, severs them from those who are not of their kind. It is a longing not to belong to any other group. (Ambedkar, 1955, p. 11)

Thus, those factors that promote social distance from out-groups are likely to be the very factors promoting in-group allegiance; the very forces operating with centripetal thrust in one context (promoting a given group's integration) frequently operate with centrifugal thrust in another context (promoting a larger group's or society's segmentation). Hence, the slogan "Black Power," while fostering Black unity, was interpreted by some Blacks as a rallying cry to separate themselves from White America.

FUNCTIONAL RECIPROCITY

The true security is to be found in social solidarity rather than in isolated individual effort.
Fëdor Mikhailovich Dostoevsky

We need to appraise still another force that often contributes to social integration, namely **functional reciprocity** — the mutual and supplementing interchanges that take place between *unlike* parts of a system. Herbert Spencer (1971), a leading nineteenth-century social philosopher, referred to this phenomenon of differentiation and interdependence as "the division of labor"; Emile Durkheim (1933), an eminent French sociologist, termed it "organic solidarity." Regardless of what they call it, sociologists generally recognize the fact that the individuals or groups making up a society may share few cultural patterns or social allegiances in common, yet the whole nonetheless "hangs together." Interdependence forces social groups to cooperate with each other, regardless of the presence or absence of consensus, in order that each may achieve a variety of goals that it cannot achieve alone. Individuals and groups of diverse values and interests have to take each other's desires into account since each needs the other to maximize its own outcomes.

An Illustration: Social Integration in South Africa. Contemporary South Africa presents a good example of a society in which functional reciprocity plays an important part in social integration. White Afrikaners and Black Africans have almost nothing in common for which they would willingly die together, and in both groups strong tendencies exist toward achieving functional autonomy. Yet, through three centuries of contact, innumerable social relationships have come to link the people of the two racial groups. A complex interweaving of activities, especially in the economic sphere, has operated as a strong force for interracial accommodation despite legal and social barriers.

One of the most salient characteristics of South Africa is its racial and cultural pluralism (van den Berghe, 1965; Kaufman, 1976; Northrup, 1976; Leger, 1977). Of its population of 25.8 million, 18 percent are White; 70 percent, African; 9 percent, Coloured (a mixed hybrid population); and 3 percent, Asiatic. Moreover, the country is a meeting point of three broad cultural currents: the European, the African, and the Indian. Internally, each of these cultural groups is further subdivided: the European by English-speaking Whites (1.9 million) and White Afrikaners (2.9 million — people descended from early Dutch, French, and German settlers and speaking Afrikaans, a Dutch derivative); the African by tribal, religious, and linguistic traditions; and the Indians by religious (Islam and Hindu) and linguistic (Hindi, Tamil, Telugu, Urdu, and Gujarati) traditions.

Dominant-group Whites (particularly the Afrikaners) have vigorously pursued a policy of "apartheid" (an Afrikaans word meaning "apartness")

Figure 9.2. Native reserves in South Africa.

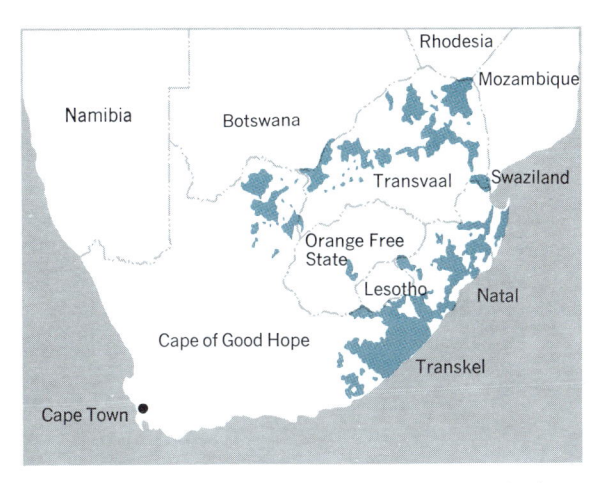

Source: Adapted from Pierre L. van den Berghe, *South Africa: A Study in Conflict* (Middleton, Conn.: Wesleyan University Press, 1965), facing p. 118.

toward the Africans. This policy has been characterized by (1) the maintenance of paternalistic White domination, (2) extensive racial segregation and discrimination, and (3) the political and economic subjugation of nonEuropeans. The blueprint of the South African government calls for maximization of segregation, although government policy is prepared to accept a lesser degree of physical separation when it is found to be expedient. As part of this program, South Africa maintains a round-the-clock territorial separation of a large portion of its African population in "Native Reserves" (see Figure 9.2). The government has been trying to organize nine "homelands" for the Blacks in these fragmented rural reservations according to "tribal" ancestry and without regard to the wishes of the Blacks. Each of these "homelands" is supposed to evolve into an independent nation, a program that many Blacks see as a subterfuge for continued White domination.

In considering South Africa, we are confronted with this question: How does South Africa hold together; that is, how does South Africa achieve integration, as partial and precarious as it may nevertheless be? Social unity clearly is not provided by value consensus—indeed, value conflict and dissension characterize South Africa. European notions of individual land ownership clash with African notions of communal tenure; Europeans view cattle as consumption goods (to be used for milk, meat, and hides) in contrast to the African view of cattle primarily as capital goods (to be held for prestige purposes); Europeans consider time as a valuable and rigorously measurable commodity, a view alien to traditional African values; and European conceptions of marriage, sex, and family sharply diverge from African values (e.g., African premarital sexual standards are more permissive, leading Europeans to stereotype Africans as "lascivious" and "oversexed").

In contrast to those societies depending primarily on value consensus for realizing social integration, South Africa finds a measure of social unity through functional reciprocity:

> . . . there emerged in Zululand [a territory within South Africa] a social system containing Blacks and Whites which had a cohesion of its own, arising from the common participation of Zulu and Whites in economic and other activities in which they became more and more dependent on one another. Force established White rule and the threat of force maintained it. But the Zulu want of money, and their desires for White goods and education, created a system of social relationships in which Whites and Zulu co-operated to earn their separate livings. Even White force was used to protect individual Zulu against breaches of law by other Zulu, and by Whites. The system contained many sources of dispute and friction, but these arose largely out of new forms of co-operation between the colour-groups. (Gluckman, 1955, p. 150)

The participation of Whites and Blacks in a common system of production is a critical integrative factor in South Africa. Indeed, the dependence of the African masses on the "White" economy has been one of the chief inhibiting factors to mass protest actions.

Ultimately, however, South Africa is held together because the Whites wield superior force. Whites conquered the country by force of arms, or the threat of arms, and by superior technology. Force established White dominance, and force keeps it going. Recent years have witnessed the institution of even more repressive measures. "Pass laws" rigorously restrict the movement of Africans. All Blacks over sixteen years of age must carry passbooks and present them on demand to the police (in the year ending June 30, 1974, some 511,163 Blacks were arrested for curfew and related pass law violations). The pocket-sized documents (containing name, photograph, and fingerprints) list where the carrier is authorized to live and work. In theory all South African Blacks "belong" to their homelands. In practice nearly nine million live in the "White areas" (constituting 87 percent of the land and generating 99 percent of the gross national product) and three million migrants move back and forth between areas.

South African civil liberties have been progressively whittled away, organizations have been proscribed, and long treason trials and midnight raids have been instituted. Men and women are deported, banished, banned, and imprisoned without trial. Hence, an extensive system of mass routine terror has become a critical ingredient in White domination and in South African social integration. Accordingly, let us now turn to a consideration of still a third mechanism for realizing social integration, coercion.

COERCION

> There is plenty of law at the end of a nightstick.
> *Grover Whalen*

Those social forces contributing to consensus and functional reciprocity may be insufficient in strength to counterbalance the opposing forces making for dissension and functional autonomy. Under such circumstances, a social system may separate into two or more independent units. Nations may split apart (for example, India and Pakistan in 1947); political parties may fragmentize (for example, the American Whig party in the 1850s); families may divide (for example, through divorce); religious groups may splinter (for example, Judaism into Orthodox, Conservative, and Reform branches); friends and lovers may part; and so on.

Separation (segmentation) may often be thwarted through **coercion**—the imposition of external regulation and control on persons or groups through threats or use of force. The ability to take life—to effect physical violence—can constitute an important instrument of social control. In effect, force constitutes the final court of appeals in human affairs; there is no appeal from force except the exercise of superior force. To be effective, however, force need not be implemented; it need merely remain in the wings, so to speak, ready at any moment to make its appearance.

Many sociologists, in recognition of this fact, distinguish between force and power. *Force* refers to the *application* of sanctions; it is the implementation of coercive remedies. *Power,* in contrast, entails the *capacity* or *ability* to introduce force within a social situation; it is the *potential* for instituting force but *not* the actual implementation of force itself.

Some writers stress the view that force constitutes the foundation for all societies, save those with the least social differentiation:

> Only with the development of the state did human societies become equipped with a form of social organization which could bind masses of culturally and physically heterogeneous "strangers" in a single social entity. Whereas primitive peoples derive their cohesion largely from a common culture and from kinship and other kinds of personal ties, state societies are held together largely by the existence of a central political authority which claims a monopoly of coercive power over all persons within a given territory. Theoretically, with a sufficiently strong development of the apparatus of government, a state society can extend law and order over limitless subgroups of strangers who neither speak the same language, worship the same gods, nor strive for the same values. (Wagley and Harris, 1958, p. 242)

Contemporary South Africa constitutes a good illustration of a social order that at least in part is held together through recourse to coercive remedies.

ASSIMILATION, SEGREGATION, AND PLURALISM

In considering social integration and segmentation, sociologists find it useful to distinguish between "assimilation," "segregation," and "pluralism." We may visualize these concepts in terms of the following continuum:

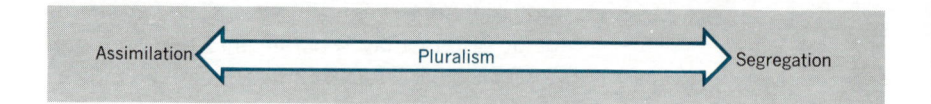

Assimilation ←—— Pluralism ——→ Segregation

Assimilation entails a process whereby groups with diverse ways of thinking, feeling, and acting become fused together within a social unity and a common culture. As such, assimilation is an "integrating" process. The fusion of groups may be largely realized through a unilateral approximation of one group to the culture of the other, for instance, the relinquishing by European immigrant groups within the United States of their native cultures and the assuming of Anglicized cultural patterns. Assimilation may also be achieved by a bilateral, reciprocal fusion in which a genuine third culture appears through the merging of two or more cultures, for example, the Mestizo (Indian and Spanish) culture of Latin America and the English (Norman and Saxon) culture.

Segregation entails a process (or state) whereby people are separated or set apart. It is a "segmenting" process. Segregation may be territorial; groups may undertake to disengage from interaction by means of spatially distinct areas of habitation. This may be accomplished voluntarily by a group that seeks to insulate itself from others (for example, the Amish of Pennsylvania

"EXCEPTION TO THE RULE"

OBSERVATION My roomate and I are from quite different backgrounds. She grew up on a farm. I was brought up in a middle class, Jewish home. We get along beautifully but once in a while I have to laugh at something she says. Today we were eating lunch together, and she commented, "You know, Becky, you're really a great person. You're not like other Jews." I asked her how many other Jews she knew well and she said not too many. But she said those she knew fitted the stereotype. They were pushy, obnoxious, and loud. She said she was really concerned when she found out I was Jewish. I guess I must be inconsistent with her image of a Jew.

PRINCIPLE I think this example is kind of sad. Instead of changing her image of a Jew, my roomate will simply consider me as an "exception to the rule." Contact between groups may fail to challenge stereotypes, because instead of altering or eliminating the stereotype, the individual exempts the "non-fitting" person. The person is "not really" a Jew.

Self-segregation: The Old Order Amish. The Amish originated in Alsace and the upper Rhineland area of Germany and Switzerland during the Reformation conflicts of the sixteenth century. Oppressed by religious persecution, they migrated to Pennsylvania in the early 1700s. They are a kin-oriented, rural-dwelling, religion-centered people who focus on two major goals: (1) "the Christian way of life" as defined by the sect's interpretation of the Bible, and (2) successful farming as defined by agricultural abundance rather than financial success. The Amish are highly successful as farmers, and their farms are acknowledged to be among the best in the world. Although very conservative generally, the Amish are not conservative in their farming techniques. They have adopted the new methods of rotating crops, applying fertilizer, and introducing new commercial agricultural products. While prohibiting the use of the tractor, they do employ some modern farm equipment, including cultivators, sprayers, binders, and balers. The Amish, far from being ashamed of their nonconformity to many American standards, pride themselves on being a "peculiar people" who do not conform to the standards of the world. Nonconformity is held to be obligatory in those areas in which "worldly" standards are in conflict with those of the Bible.

Pennsylvania Dutch Tourist Bureau

and the Basques of Idaho); it may also be accomplished involuntarily where a dominant group imposes separation on a minority (for example, the Indian reservation policy employed for years within the United States). Segregation may also find expression in discrimination, where members of a group are accorded unfavorable treatment on the basis of their religious, ethnic, or racial membership.

Pluralism entails a process whereby people with differing cultural backgrounds live together harmoniously and peacefully, permitting the expression of their distinctive ways of life within a range consonant with the national welfare. Switzerland provides an example of this. Historically, the Swiss nation originated from the desire of a group of heterogeneous communities to preserve their local independence through a system of mutual defense alliances. Today, a majority of the Swiss speak a variety of German known as *Schwyzertütsch;* about 21 percent speak French; another 5 percent, Italian; and slightly more than 1 percent speak an ancient language known as Romansh. Contrary to widespread misconception abroad, most Swiss know only one language well and are not bilingual or multilingual. Within this setting, Switzerland officially recognizes all four languages, although only German, French, and Italian have been declared "official languages" into which all federal documents are translated. In addition to language differences, the various cantons also display notable differences in costume, dialect, and patterns of life. And although a majority of the people are Protestant, there is a sizable Catholic population. Religious and ethnic prejudices are by no means nonexistent, yet the Swiss have learned to live harmoniously with their differences.

MINORITY RESPONSES TO DOMINATION

No man is good enough to be another man's master.
George Bernard Shaw, Major Barbara, 1905

Over the past twenty-five years race relations in the United States have undergone some phenomenal changes. Contributing to these developments have been the civil rights movement of the 1960s, the Black Power movement, and protest movements of Chicanos and Native Americans. This brings us to a consideration of how minority group members think and feel about their disadvantaged status. How do they react to segregation, discrimination, and racism? It is to these matters that we now turn our attention.

A TYPOLOGY OF RESPONSES

We can identify four common themes in minority reactions to domination (Noel, 1969):

1. *Acceptance.* Members of a minority group may come to acquiesce in their disadvantaged and disprivileged status; for example, resignation and "Uncle Tomism."
2. *Aggression.* Members of a minority may respond by striking out against a status that is disadvantaged and subordinate; for example, attacks against dominant-group members and their property, "irresponsible" and "awkward" work, and protest activities and movements.
3. *Avoidance.* Members of a minority group may respond by attempting to shun — to escape from — situations in which they are likely to encounter prejudice and discrimination; for example, avoidance of contact with dominant-group members, migration, and separatism (Zionism and Black Nationalism).
4. *Assimilation.* Members of a minority group may seek to become socially and culturally fused with the dominant group; for example, passing and acculturation.

For our purposes, we may view avoidance and assimilation as opposites, each representing a pole of a continuum:

Assimilation ⟷ Avoidance

Each pole constitutes an "outer limit" or standard between which transitional or intermediate reactions can be located. When minority-group members are confronted with a potential intergroup situation, they must tend either to avoid contact with the dominant group or merge themselves with it. Of course, there are different degrees of avoidance and assimilation, and hence a specific reaction falls somewhere along the continuum, depending on the extent to which it reflects an avoiding or assimilating tendency.

We may also view acceptance and aggression as opposites:

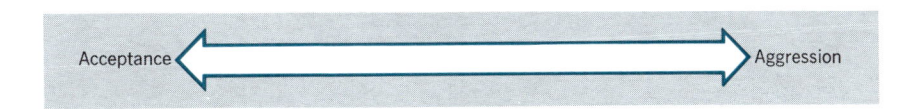

Acceptance ⟷ Aggression

When minority-group members are confronted with contact with dominant-group members, they must either tend to acquiesce in their disadvantaged and subordinate status or strike out against it.

These two continua pose choices confronting minority-group members in an intergroup situation. First, they must either allow contact to take place or they must avoid (or, at least, minimize) it. Second, once in the intergroup situation, they must either acquiesce in their subordinate and disadvantaged status or strike out against it.

Minorities generally do not follow one exclusive pattern of reaction. Intergroup relations are much too complex for any one pattern to prevail at all times. Rather, at times one pattern of response may come into play; at still other times, another; and often some combination of responses operates. Hence, based on our two continua, we may identify four mixed reaction patterns: acceptance-avoidance, acceptance-assimilation, aggression–avoidance, and aggression-assimilation:

```
Assimilation                          Avoidance
      ↑  ⟵⟶                         ⟵⟶  ↑
      │        ╲                 ╱        │
      │          ╲             ╱          │
      │            ╲         ╱            │
      │              ╲     ╱              │
      │                ╳                  │
      │              ╱     ╲              │
      │            ╱         ╲            │
      │          ╱             ╲          │
      │        ╱                 ╲        │
      ↓  ⟵⟶                         ⟵⟶  ↓
Acceptance                            Aggression
```

The civil rights movement led by the late Rev. Martin Luther King, Jr., during the early 1960s is illustrative of an aggression–assimilation type response; Black separatist movements are illustrative of an aggression–avoidance type response, as are the Irish Republican Army and the Palestinian Liberation Organization.

THE BLACK PROTEST

One ever feels this two-ness — an American, a Negro; two souls, two thoughts, two unreconciled strivings; two warring ideals in one dark body, whose dogged strength alone keeps it from being torn asunder.

W. E. B. DuBois, The Souls of Black Folk, 1903

A good many Blacks have always resented the disadvantaged and disprivileged status assigned them in American life. However, at least until recently, Blacks on the whole lacked the power to do much about it. In large measure, acceptance constituted the principal Black reaction to dominance. Yet, even so, periodic ripples of Black protest did occur. During slavery, over two hundred slave plots and revolts were recorded (Burns, 1963). The Civil War and Reconstruction brought new strivings, but these were crushed with the overthrow of Reconstructionist governments and more particularly by the evolution of the Jim Crow (segregated) system in the 1890s (Woodward, 1966).

The twentieth century brought the formation of a number of civil rights organizations, the most important being the National Association for the Advancement of Colored People (NAACP). The NAACP evolved a highly developed, selectively applied, legalistic approach, one that led in 1954 to the Supreme Court's overthrow of the legal foundations of segregation (in the 1954 case of *Brown v. Board of Education,* the Supreme Court unanimously ruled that the "separate but equal" doctrine, which had been used to bar Black children from White public schools, was unconstitutional). This NAACP approach was essentially one of "tokenism" — a small gain here and a small gain there involving a given institution, university, park, or other public facility, gains often realized by middle-class Blacks *for* middle-class Blacks and having little implication for the great mass of American Blacks. Moreover, the Black masses were not drawn into the struggle, since one or a few plaintiffs were sufficient to enable NAACP lawyers to launch their legal attack. The Black protest of the 1960s and 1970s broke, at least in part, with this tradition. Protest shifted from an emphasis on primarily legal and educational means to direct *mass* action (demonstrations, boycotts, sit-ins, and urban civil "disorders").

Sociologists have noted that a major factor in the evolution of the "new" Black protest has been the emergence among the Black masses of a growing sense of **relative deprivation** — a gap between what people actually have and what they have come to expect and feel to be their just due. The prosperity of the 1950s and 1960s gave many Blacks a taste of "the good life," a taste of the affluent society. A good many Blacks had gained enough to hope realistically for more. Thus, grievances about squalid housing; a narrow range of job possibilities; frequent unemployment; low pay; exploitation by landlords, shopkeepers, and employers; and police brutality were felt as severely frustrating. The movement emerged not so much as a protest fed by despair as one fed by *rising* expectations. National surveys revealed that a majority of Blacks felt that they had been doing better than five years previously and expected to do even better in the next five years (Vander Zanden, 1972).

The decade of the 1960s opened with the sit-ins and freedom rides and continued through Birmingham, the March on Washington, and Selma with the battle cry, "Freedom Now." Yet by 1964 and 1965, episodes of rioting began unfolding in the nation's Black ghettos; the rhetoric of protest became increasingly demanding, blanket charges of pervasive White racism were more common, and some Blacks began actively to discourage Whites from participating in protest demonstrations and civil rights organizations. Probably nothing better symbolized the changing mood and style of Black protest than the change in the dominant symbol from "Freedom" to "Black Power." Although interpreted in a great many ways, the slogan of "Black Power" had the underlying theme of Black pride, Black unity, and economic and political power for the Black community.

A sense of relative deprivation, then, fed the rise of the civil rights movement; it also played a part in the later emergence of the Black Power Movement and the ghetto riots. During the 1960s, civil rights leaders and top government officials (including Presidents Kennedy and Johnson) promised a lot—a new day for Black Americans to be realized through civil rights legislation and the war on poverty (a Great Society)—but delivered little; Blacks were led to believe that they would be much better off, but little dramatic improvement occurred. Probably the closest one can come to social dynamite is to promise people freedom and a Great Society and then deliver handouts. Many Blacks found themselves much in the position of the underprivileged urchin who has his nose pressed against the window, longing for the goodies inside; in the past, segregation and discrimination barred him from entering the door—now he could enter the store, but he lacked the economic resources for securing the goodies. Hence the new expectations went unfulfilled, or in any event were fulfilled too slowly. All this intensified feelings of relative deprivation, and the ghetto riots and the Black Power Movement followed.

The Black Protest subsided by the early 1970s. This occurred for a number of related reasons (Killian, 1975). First, the existence of new laws and administrative policies, many of them a response to the Black Protest, made it possible for Blacks to pursue their goals through existing institutional channels. Second, the ranks of the more visible and aggressive Black leaders were decimated by imprisonment, emigration, and assassination thereby weakening the more militant organizations. Third, on the local level the White power structure was able to coopt and bring many young Black militants into government and White political organizations. Fourth, the Black movement was plagued by confusion as to whether it should pursue an assimilationist (civil rights) or a separatist (Black nationalist) program, a dilemma posed by the fact that the Black population has been too large to integrate quickly within American life while simultaneously being too small and scattered to go it alone as an independent nation.

Although the Black Protest has subsided, the Black cultural revival (with a strong emphasis on Black standards of beauty and Black pride and unity) has become so pervasive that all segments of the Black population have been awakened by it. During the 1970s many Blacks turned to the task of electing Black office-seekers and organizing local self-help programs (Conyers and Wallace, 1976; Nelson and Meranto, 1977). They have concentrated on the nuts-and-bolts of winning elections—registering voters, setting up telephone banks with voter names, getting supporters to the polls, and establishing pool-watching operations to guard against vote-stealing. And they have concentrated on such community-level activities as securing mortgages for Black homeowners, establishing and running businesses, and getting jobs for the poor and training them to keep them. However, despite the relative calm of the 1970s, many authorities agree that the potential for another shift toward violence still exists (Killian, 1975; Scott, 1976; Nelson and Meranto, 1977).

Black Power movements. The slogan "Black Power," spawned in 1966, has fostered a sense of deep racial pride and unity among Blacks, particularly among Black youth.

Patrick Reddy

SUMMARY

1. People in various parts of the world differ in certain hereditary characteristics such as skin color, hair texture, various facial features, stature, and head shape. We term populations differing in the incidence of such hereditary traits races. Likewise, people the world over exhibit extraordinary cultural diversity in language, religion, economic arrangements, government, food habits, clothing styles, and family patterns. We term populations differing in their cultural practices ethnic groups.

2. Ethnocentrism often accompanies intergroup contact. It involves the tendency to put one's own group in a central position of priority and worth and evaluate other groups with reference to it.

3. Ethnocentrism entails strong positive feelings toward an in-group. It is often accompanied by prejudice—negative conceptions, feelings, and action orientations regarding the members of a particular group. Prejudice is an attitude, and as such it involves a state of mind. It is to be distinguished from discrimination, which entails overt action in which members of a group are accorded unfavorable treatment on the basis of their religious, cultural, or racial membership. The situation in which individuals find themselves does much to determine which attitudes will be activated within an intergroup contact.

4. The concepts of prejudice and discrimination tend to focus on the individual. The emphasis falls on relations between prejudiced individuals and victimized individuals. While useful, the concepts fail to call our attention to the ways in which people of one racial group are systematically oppressed or exploited by the institutions of a society controlled by another racial group, a phenomenon called institutional racism. One mechanism of institutional racism is gatekeeping, the decision-making process by which members of a society are admitted to positions of power, privilege, and status.

5. Evidence suggests that the processes by which a racist social order arises are complex but that three ingredients are commonly present. First, people differentiate among populations, placing individuals in distinct social categories based on some visible and conspicuous feature or features. Second, competition takes place between groups for certain socially valued things, serving to generate prejudice. Third, the groups are unequal in power so that the more powerful group is able to actualize its claim to an unequal and larger share of the socially valued things.

6. There are two sociological positions regarding the experience of Blacks and Chicanos within the United States. The one argues that Blacks and Chicanos are like European immigrants and will in due course become assimilated; the other claims that they are like Third World colonized groups (giving rise to internal colonialism).

7. It is useful if we view groups and societies as concretions of opposing tendencies. Social life is characterized by change, by an interplay of forces advancing, retreating, converging, or diverging in patterns of greater or lesser stability. Consensus, functional reciprocity, and coercion are factors associated with the degree of integration prevailing within a society.

8. Auguste Comte contended that the chief unifying force in society is consensus. By this term he referred to the customs and interests shared in common by a people, those things in which they are alike. Where individuals share common norms, values, beliefs, and symbols, they are knit together by an all-encompassing, seamless web of culture.

9. Sociologists recognize the fact that the individuals or groups making up a society may share few cultural patterns or social allegiances in common, yet the whole nonetheless "hangs together." One factor responsible for such cohesion is functional reciprocity—the mutual and supplementing interchanges that take place between unlike parts of a system. Interdependence forces social groups to cooperate with each other in order that each may achieve a variety of goals that it cannot achieve alone.

10. Those social forces contributing to consensus and functional reciprocity may be insufficient in strength to counterbalance the opposing forces making for dissension and functional autonomy. Under these circumstances separation may often be thwarted through coercion—the imposition of external regulation and control on persons or groups through threats or use of force.

11. In considering social integration and segmentation, sociologists find it useful to distinguish between assimilation, segregation, and pluralism. Assimilation entails a process whereby groups with diverse ways of thinking, feeling, and acting become fused together within a social unit and a common culture. Segregation involves a process (or state) whereby people are separated or set apart. Pluralism entails a process whereby people with differing cultural backgrounds live together harmoniously and peacefully, permitting the expression of their distinctive ways of life within a range consonant with the national welfare.

12. Minority group members commonly respond in a great many different ways to their disadvantaged and disprivileged position. For analytical and classificatory purposes, we distinguished between four responses: assimilation, avoidance, acceptance, and aggression. Confronting an intergroup situation, a minority group member must either allow contact to take place or must avoid (or, at least, minimize) it. Once in the intergroup situation, the individual must either acquiesce in the minority status or strike out against it.

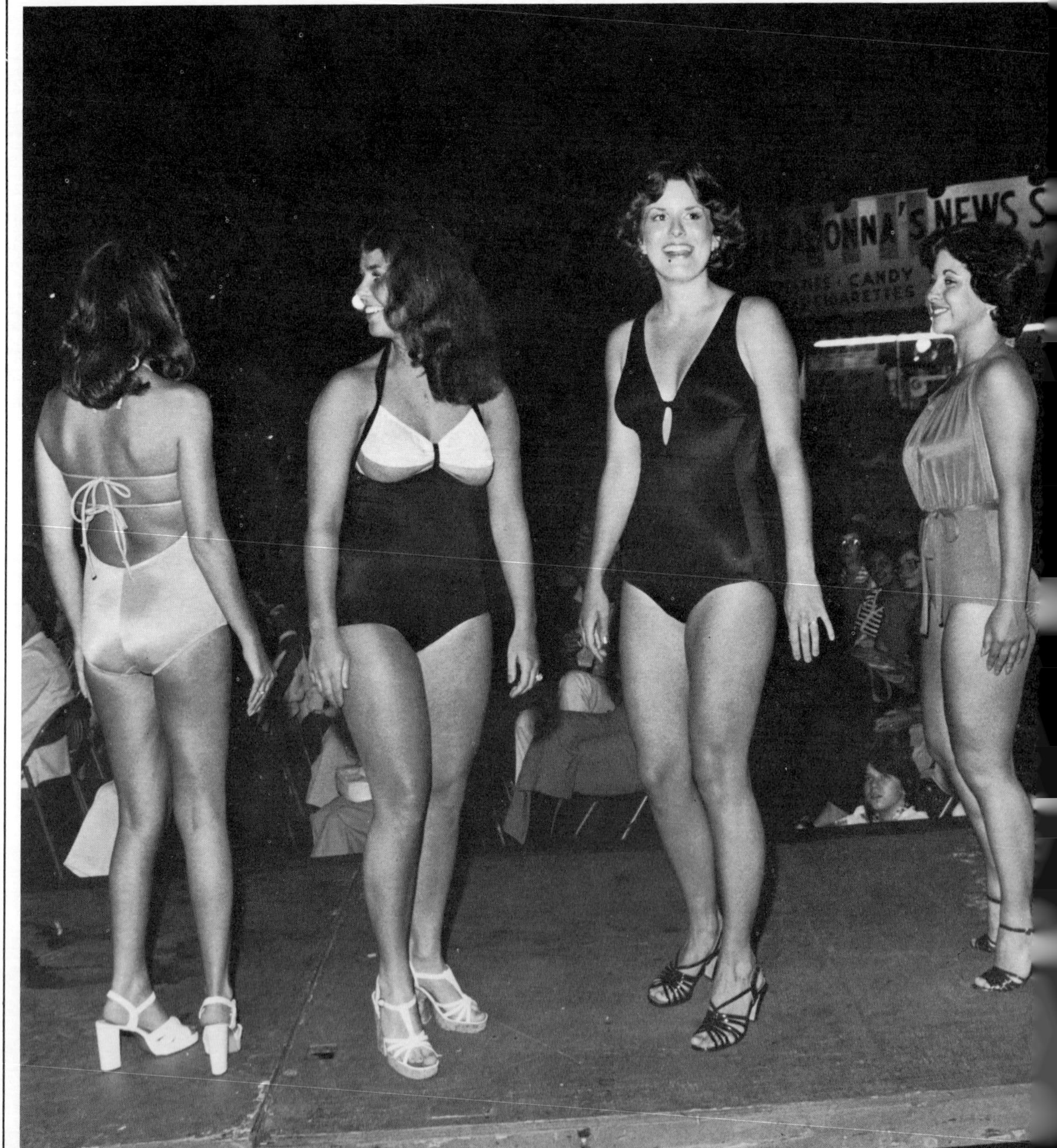
NEWS
CANDY

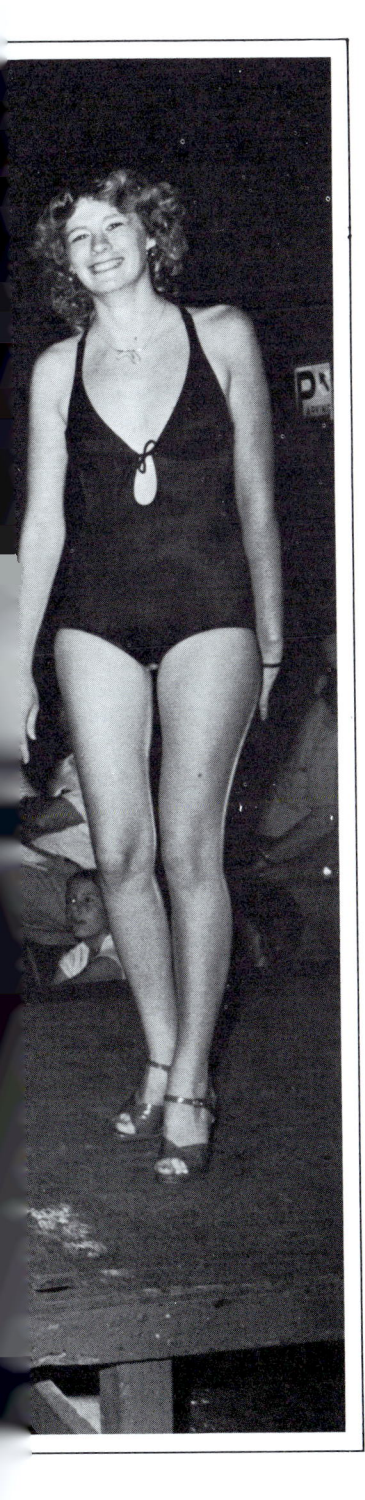

10
GENDER ROLES AND INEQUALITY

GENDER ROLES
  Gender Roles and Culture
  Gender Roles and Biology
  Acquiring Gender Behaviors and Identities
  Gender and Achievement Motivations and Expectations

SEX STRATIFICATION
  Homemaking and Childcare
  The Wage Economy
  Sexual Inequality, Exploitation, and Abuse

GENDER ROLES AND CHANGE
  The Women's Movement
  Androgynous Roles

OBSERVATION My parents were divorced when I was about two years old and my mother always worked. I can remember that even at a very young age I had to cook the dinner so it would be ready when mom got home. And I regularly did the washing, putting the clothes in the wash machine and then into the dryer. Well today I was cooking lasagna for dinner and folding my jeans that I had just washed when one of my classmates came over to pick up a book. He said, "What are you, a faggot? That's women's work to cook and do the wash." It made me real mad because my girlfriend and I divide up the apartment tasks without regard to sex-typed expectations.

PRINCIPLE My classmate thought that I was in some way defective as a man because I happen to cook and do washing. I don't look at it that way. The work has to get done and whether I or my girlfriend does it really is not the issue. We have an androgynous relationship when it comes to household responsibilities.

At birth we are classed as a male or a female based on anatomical cues. Like race, our gender is ascribed to us, a role that few of us can dispute or change. Physical characteristics become the foundation for a complex web of social expectations and obligations. Such sex-coded requirements bear on our political and legal condition, our work and economic condition, our recreational and play condition, our cosmetic and style condition (including grooming, adornment, and dress), and our protocol and etiquette condition (Money, 1977). **Gender** is a set of ideas—certain social conceptions by which a society allocates by sex various roles (for instance, homemaker or wage earner) and defines certain attributes (for instance, "hardheaded" or "softbrained"). It is a device of "sex-linkage." When artificial lines are drawn around the activity of each sex in this manner, physical differences become exaggerated by symbolic and social ones (Strathern, 1976). It is little wonder that being male or female is a core identity that leaves its signature on everything we do.

GENDER ROLES

What are little boys made of? What are little boys made of? Frogs and snails and puppy dogs' tails, that's what little boys are made of. What are little girls made of? What are little girls made of? Sugar and spice and all that is nice, and that's what little girls are made of.
J. O. Halliwell, Nursery Rhymes of England, 1844

Apparently all societies have seized on the biological dichotomy between men and women for the assignment of **gender roles**. These are sets of expectations that provide the guidelines for the behavior of men and women. They

Gender roles. Many Americans, especially youth, are challenging traditional sex-linked behavior patterns. Although they may make sport of these patterns, one cannot help wondering if male chauvinism may not be more deeply ingrained than many young people would like to admit.

Patrick Reddy

specify which sex does what, when, and where. Hence, we are all born into societies with well-established cultural patterns for men and women. The members of a society generally take great pains to fit and shape us in accordance with their social definitions of what constitutes appropriate masculine and feminine behavior.

GENDER ROLES AND CULTURE

The differences between the two sexes is one of the important conditions upon which we have built the many varieties of human culture that give human beings dignity and stature. In every known society, mankind has elaborated the biological division of labour into forms often very remotely related to the original biological differences that provided the original clues. . . . Sometimes one quality has been assigned to one sex, sometimes to the other. . . . Some people think of women as too weak to work out of doors, others regard women as the appropriate bearers of heavy burdens, "because their heads are stronger than men's." . . . In some cultures women are regarded as sieves through whom the best-guarded secrets will sift; in others it is the men who are the gossips.

Margaret Mead, Male and Female, 1949

Many Americans have reached a point where they no longer trust traditional notions of what is masculine and what is feminine. Not too many years ago it was widely assumed that any differences found between men and women in attitudes, feelings, and behavior must rest on a biological foundation and hence be immutable. But what previously appeared to be plausible explanations of sex differences are now seen as myths used to justify sexism and discrimination (Rosenblatt and Cunningham, 1976).

Although social scientists acknowledge the biological basis for the distinction between the sexes, they have viewed with skepticism claims that biological differences between the sexes are the principal source of behavioral differences. The wide variety found in the behavior patterns of men and women from one society to another, and the changes observed from one time to another in sex-linked behavior patterns within the same society, point to a social foundation for a great many such differences. In many societies women are the ones primarily responsible for homemaking and child-rearing. In the Marquesas Islands, however, cooking, housekeeping, and babytending are defined as male roles. Interestingly enough, the people of Marquesas rationalize their behavior as stemming from the fact that women are not maternally inclined. Among the Tasmanians, the most dangerous type of hunting—swimming out to remote rocks in the sea to stalk and club sea otters—was the task of women. Similarly, women formed the bodyguard of Dahomeyan kings because they were deemed to be especially fierce fighters.

Knowledge of these cultural variations challenges our beliefs regarding what is "natural." In the Western world, for instance, women have long been excluded from many jobs because the men who controlled these jobs defined women as by nature "stupid," "delicate," and "fickle." However, among the Arapesh of New Guinea, women regularly carry heavier loads than men "because their heads are so much harder and stronger."

Societies likewise differ in their conceptions of male and female personality. The anthropologist Margaret Mead (1935) found within a 100-mile radius of New Guinea three peoples with widely differing notions of what constitutes appropriate masculine and feminine behavior:

The Arapesh. The Arapesh make very few distinctions between male and female personalities, although like all societies they practice a certain division of labor between the sexes. From our American viewpoint, both Arapesh men and women are maternal in parental aspects and feminine in sexual aspects. Both sexes are cooperative, nurturant, unaggressive, mild, and responsive to the needs and demands of others. Sex did not seem to be a powerful driving force for either men or women.

The Mundugumor. As with the Arapesh, the Mundugumor view "masculine nature" and "feminine nature" as essentially the same. But in marked contrast to the Arapesh, both Mundugumor men and women are ruthless, aggressive, positively sexed individuals, with the maternal cherishing aspects of personality at a minimum. Both men and women approximate a personality type which within the United States would be found in an undisciplined and very violent male. Hostility, hatred, and suspicion are the dominant characteristics of these people (who also practice cannibalism).

The Tchambuli. Contrasted with the Arapesh and the Mundugumor, and like Americans, masculinity and femininity are highly differentiated among the lake-dwelling Tchambuli. But here we find a genuine reversal of the culturally approved sex-temperaments of our own society, with the woman the dominant, impersonal, managing partner and the man the less responsible and emotionally dependent figure. Toward one another, men are suspicious and sensitive; toward women, timid and uncertain. Male security lies largely in what women give them. Women are hearty, casual, easygoing, and friendly among themselves; among men they are self-reliant and inclined to take the initiative, viewing men as the "weaker" sex.

Hence what is socially defined as approved behavior for men and women in one culture may be defined as inappropriate in another culture.

Despite the enormous cross-cultural variability in gender roles, there nonetheless is a certain degree of consistency in the sexual division of labor. Some activities are more likely to be undertaken by one sex than the other (see Table 10.1). This is true of childcare, a task that rather uniformly falls on women (Murdock and Provost, 1973; Rosaldo, 1974; Chodorow, 1974). Women, of course, are the only ones biologically capable of birth and nursing functions. But this fact does not necessarily dictate that a mother be her child's sole caretaker. In many societies older siblings and the elderly (including men) have childcare duties (Rosenblatt and Cunningham, 1976). Such childcare arrangements, for instance, allow many women of West Africa to engage in extensive trade (Mintz, 1971). Nevertheless, the heavier burden of childcare even for children beyond the nursing age tends to be allocated to young and middle-aged women.

It is estimated that in many societies throughout the world women supply thirty to forty percent of the calorie intake of a people (Rosenblatt and Cun-

TABLE 10.1

The Division of Labor in Cross-Cultural Perspective (224 Societies)

	Number of Societies in Which Activity Is Performed By:				
Activity	Men Always	Men Usually	Either Sex	Women Usually	Women Always
Hunting	166	13	0	0	0
Trapping small animals	128	13	4	1	2
Herding	38	8	4	0	5
Fishing	98	34	19	3	4
Clearing agricultural land	73	22	17	5	13
Dairy operations	17	4	3	1	13
Preparing and planting soil	31	23	33	20	37
Erecting and dismantling shelter	14	2	5	6	22
Tending and harvesting crops	10	15	35	39	44
Bearing burdens	12	6	35	20	57
Gathering fruits, berries, nuts	12	3	15	13	63
Preserving meat and fish	8	2	10	14	74
Cooking	5	1	9	28	158
Metalworking	78	0	0	0	0
Boat building	91	4	4	0	1
Basket weaving	25	3	10	6	82
Carrying water	7	0	5	7	119
Grinding grain	2	4	5	13	114

Source: Adapted from George P. Murdock (1935) Comparative data on the division of labor by sex. Social Forces, 15:551–553.

ningham, 1976). In food gathering and early agricultural societies lacking the plough, women often contribute more than the men (Murdock and Provost, 1973; Sanday, 1973; Aronoff and Crano, 1975). Indeed, women in sub-Saharan Africa provide as much as eighty percent of the labor necessary for food production (Germain, 1975). In contrast, as reflected in Table 10.1, men tend to be concentrated in activities involving hunting and plough agriculture.

Many anthropologists have attempted to explain this traditional division of labor as an adaptive device evolved during primitive times. Men's greater muscular strength led them to assume the hunting role and to translate their power advantage into sexual dominance (D'Andrade, 1966). In contrast, women (by virtue of their childbearing and nursing functions) found their mobility restricted and tended to stay near to their homes. Accordingly, men assumed public (away from home) roles while women assumed domestic (close to home) roles (Rosaldo, 1974). Some argue that this adaptive arrangement became genetically programmed within the human organism in the course of evolution. Others insist that the traditional division of labor embedded itself within the cultural tradition, becoming self-perpetuating as it was transmitted from one generation to the next through socialization.

Needless to say, such theoretical formulations are highly speculative. Not all social scientists find them entirely convincing. Simply because women nurse infants does not "naturally" lead them to be "homebodies" and cooks. Hunting is an intermittent activity and a mother's occasional absence a few times a week for several hours need not interfere with her lactating activity. And since band and village communities were organized about kinspeople, plenty of baby sitters were available. Further, since men did not have eight-to-five jobs, it is not clear why they could not have tended the children (Harris, 1977). Finally, even should the theory prove correct, physical strength no longer commands the importance it once did within our contemporary technological age. Hence the traditional division of labor is no longer necessitated by the dictates of group survival.

GENDER ROLES AND BIOLOGY

The first thing that strikes the careless observer is that women are unlike men. They are "the opposite sex"—(Though why "opposite" I do not know; what is the "neighboring sex"?). But the fundamental thing is that women are more like men than anything else in the world.

Dorothy Sayers, Unpopular Opinions, *1946*

How important is biology in producing those behavioral differences we observe between men and women? There are those who assert that sexual differences are firmly rooted in physiology (Broverman et al., 1968; Gray, 1971; Hutt, 1972a; 1972b). And there are also those who look to environmental explanations and claim that biology plays little or no part. But as we noted when considering the nature-nurture controversy in Chapter 3, the question is not one of whether heredity or environment is more important but how these factors interact to produce given behaviors. Further, by phrasing the issue in terms of sexual *differences* we tend to overlook the fact that such differences are relatively minor compared to the overall *similarities* shared by men and women (Archer, 1976).

Until relatively recently it was assumed that two quite separate roads exist, one leading from XX chromosomes at conception to womanhood and the other from XY chromosomes to manhood. The research of John Money (Money and Ehrhardt, 1973; Money and Tucker, 1975), a medical psychologist at Johns Hopkins Medical Center, suggests that there are not two roads but one road with a number of forks where each of us turns in either a male or female direction. According to Money, we become male or female by stages.

For the first several weeks following conception the XX and XY embryos proceed along the same sexually neutral course. About the sixth week the XX or XY chromosomal combination "instructs" the two undifferentiated gonads to become ovaries or testes. These organs then have the function of secreting the appropriate sex hormones. Hormones are chemical messengers that are secreted into the bloodstream. In males the major sex hormone is testosterone (one of a group of hormones called androgens) while in females the two principal sex hormones are progesterone and estrogen. Each sex has a certain amount of the other sex's hormones although such hormones are found in lower levels.

The body appears to differentiate as a female except where the secretions of the embryonic testes push the organism in a male direction. Nature's first choice is to make an Eve rather than an Adam. Unless the "something more" takes place in the correct proportions at the proper junctures in development, the fetus will take a female turn. When the developmental process goes amiss at one or more critical points, individuals develop with the reproductive organs of both sexes. Individuals whose reproductive structures are sufficiently ambiguous that they cannot be defined as exclusively male or female are termed **hermaphrodites**.

For some years Money and his associates (Money and Ehrhardt, 1973) have been studying female children who were exposed to excess levels of male hormones (androgen) before birth (their mothers had been administered hormonal supplements to prevent miscarriage). Of a group of twenty-five such girls, twenty claimed to be "tomboys." Compared with a control group of girls whose mothers had experienced normal pregnancies, the androgen-exposed group are reported to have indulged in more energetic play, chosen masculine clothes, and preferred boys' to girls' toys. Although all the control-group girls indicated that they wanted to be mothers when they grew up, one-third of the androgen-exposed girls said they would prefer not to have children.

Money believes that the human embryo has a bisexual potential. Certain behaviors become programmed in the fetus by the relative proportions of the sex hormones received at critical developmental junctures. It is as if some inner behavioral dial is set at "male" or "female" (Scarf, 1976). Hence, in Money's view, certain of the embryo's neural circuits become "imprinted" and subsequently function at puberty to activate either "male" or "female" behaviors.

Money's critics claim that he does not make sufficient allowance for cultural influences. Possibly the androgen-exposed girls were reared differently by their parents who sought to compensate for their daughters' virilization (in some cases the administration of the prenatal hormones had resulted in an enlarged clitoris and partially fused labia). Certainly having a daughter or being a female with a malelike phallus affects a person's self-conceptions and the attitudes and behaviors of others (Rogers, 1976; Quadagno, Briscoe, and Quadagno, 1977). It is conceivable that these girls were unsure of their role as potential mothers. However, except for their possible concern regarding their reproductive ability, the androgen-exposed girls were not different from the controls in dreaming about heterosexual romance and dating boys (nor did they report homosexual fantasies). Further, it is questionable whether "tomboyish" behavior can be considered rare or abnormal in girls. Samples of both college and noncollege adult women reveal that from 51 to 87 percent retrospectively report that they were tomboys during childhood (Hyde, Rosenberg, and Behrman, 1974, 1977).

In fairness to Money, however, it should be noted that he concludes from his research on hermaphrodites that the most powerful factors in the shaping of gender identity are environmental:

> The chances are that society had nothing to do with the turnings you took in the prenatal sex development road, but the minute you were born, society took over. When the drama of your birth reached its climax, you were promptly greeted with the glad ritual cry, "It's a boy?" or "It's a girl!" depending on whether or not those in attendance observed a penis in your crotch. . . . The label "boy" or "girl," however, has tremendous force as a self-fulfilling prophecy, for it throws the full weight of society to one side or the other as the newborn heads for the gender fork [in the road], and the most decisive sex turning point of all. . . . [At birth you were limited to] something that was ready to become your gender identity. You were wired but not programmed for gender in the same sense that you were wired but not programmed for language. (Money and Tucker, 1975, pp. 86–89)

Hence, according to Money (1977), biological factors do not themselves produce differences in male or female behavior but affect the threshold for the elicitation of such behavior.

Much attention has been devoted in popular and scientific literature to claims that men are "naturally" more aggressive than women. This was one of the few sex-linked differences that Eleanor E. Maccoby and Carol N. Jacklin (1974) were able to document in their detailed assessment of the current state of scientific knowledge on male-female differences. They conclude that males are biologically primed to respond aggressively. In contrast, Lesley Rogers has reviewed much the same evidence and reaches the opposite conclusion: "On available evidence the differing concentrations of androgens in males and females cannot explain human sex differences in sexual and aggressive behavior" (1976:177). Clearly our knowledge on these matters is as yet not solid enough to derive any hard-and-fast conclusions.

It has of course been demonstrated in many species (including chickens, mice, rats, hamsters, and monkeys) that aggressive behavior is influenced by the level of male hormones (Rogers, 1976; Quadagno, Briscoe, and Quadagno, 1977). For instance, administering testosterone to male chickens increases their attack behavior (Andrew, 1966). However, the increase in aggression occurs only when the bird is matched against a total stranger.

When it is tested with its own social group, previously established peck-order habits override the hormonal effect (Guhl, 1964). Similarly, administration of testosterone restores aggressive behavior in castrated male mice (Bronson and Desjardins, 1971). But even here learning factors can mask the action of the male hormones. Past experience of winning or losing fights with other mice has a greater influence on an animal's behavior than do testosterone levels (Bevan, Daves, and Levy, 1960). In sum, we need to understand how biological and social factors interact to produce given male and female behaviors.

ACQUIRING GENDER BEHAVIORS AND IDENTITIES

It is the bliss of childhood that we are being warped most when we know it the least.
William Gaddis, The Recognitions

From birth to death our social environment tells us that men and women are different, or in any event should be different. Much of social life dictates that we act in conformity with cultural definitions that specify the behavioral expectations and obligations associated with male and female roles. However, within the past fifteen years considerable interest has arisen in maximizing children's potentials and in guaranteeing individual rights. This has raised concern that some sex-typed behaviors and attitudes serve to limit children and adults of both sexes, locking them into a highly gender-stereotyped world. An understanding of the development of gender behaviors and identities is an important first step toward revising and, if possible, minimizing environmental constraints and expanding human horizons (Garrett and Cunningham, 1974). **Gender identities** are the conceptions that individuals have of themselves as being male and female. Let us consider three major theories dealing with the process by which children acquire sex-typed behaviors and identities.

Psychoanalytic Theory. The *psychoanalytic* formulations of Sigmund Freud (1856–1939) have had a profound impact on public and scientific thinking regarding sexual behavior and identities. In Freud's view, "anatomy is destiny": a fundamental relationship exists between genital differences and the psychological characteristics of men and women. Freud said that all humans pass through a fixed set of chronologically ordered stages during the critical first six years of their lives.

During the oral stage, lasting from birth to about eighteen months, infants experience the world primarily in terms of their mouths, deriving pleasure from sucking and biting. From about eighteen months to three years, children enter the anal stage in which pleasure is focused on retaining and expelling feces and urine. Boys and girls experience the oral and anal stages in essentially the same manner. It is during the phallic stage—lasting from the third to seventh year—that the developmental courses of males and females diverge, with each sex following a separate path.

During the phallic stage, boys find their penises a source of great interest and pleasure. They also feel sexual love for their mothers and hostile rivalry with their fathers, termed by Freud the *Oedipal complex* (named for the Greek myth of Oedipus, who killed his father and married his mother). However, boys recognize that their fathers are more powerful than they are. Because boys have sexual designs on their mothers and wish to do away with their fathers, they imagine that their fathers bear considerable ill will toward them. And they fear that their fathers will punish them by cutting off their penises, giving rise to castration anxiety. Through complicated psychological maneuvers which Freud never specified, boys resolve the Oedipal situation by repressing their erotic desires for their mothers and identifying with the potential aggressors, their fathers. By virtue of this identification, they acquire masculine self-conceptions and later erotically seek out females.

For girls, the process of Oedipal conflict (often termed the *Electra complex*) is quite different. At about the time boys experience castration anxiety, girls confront the stark and painful realization that they have no penis:

> [Girls] notice the penis of a brother or playmate, strikingly visible and of large proportions, at once recognize it as the superior counterpart of their own small and inconspicuous organ, and from that time forward fall a victim to envy for the penis. (Freud, 1948, p. 190)

Girls hold their mothers responsible for their lack of a penis. They renounce their mothers and feel sexual love for their fathers. But girls soon recognize that they cannot replace their mothers in their fathers' affections and come to identify with their mothers. In so doing they incorporate within themselves feminine behaviors and attitudes and later seek suitable men to love. Nonetheless, Freud believed that women never satisfactorily resolve their feelings of sexual inferiority. Thus he sought to explain the prevalence of women in weaving occupations as an unconsciously motivated attempt to attach hairs in order mystically to veil the absence of a penis.

No one can seriously challenge the considerable impact that Freud has had on twentieth-century thought. However, his work is difficult to evaluate since it makes few predictions that can be tested by accepted scientific procedures. Since unconscious motivation is by definition not accessible to the conscious mind, it is difficult to observe or study. To the extent to which his ideas have been scientifically testable, they have in most instances been found wanting (Fisher and Greenberg, 1977). His analysis of women has been especially criticized, particularly his biased assertion that the clitoris and vagina are inferior organs to the penis. Nonetheless, Freud's contribution has been historically important in highlighting the notion that our sexual identities and behaviors have their roots in previous social experience (Hyde and Rosenberg, 1976).

Cultural Transmission Theory. We are engulfed in a social environment that constantly provides us with sex-typed conceptions and stereotypes. This observation forms the basis for the *cultural transmission theory of gender acquisition*. It asserts that individuals are essentially neutral at birth and that biological differences are insufficient to account for later male and female differences in gender identities. Viewed from this perspective, individuals acquire those ways of thinking, feeling, and acting characteristic of males or females through their social experiences, most particularly socialization (see Chapter 3).

Language provides a good illustration of the cultural transmission process. As we noted earlier in the text, language is the chief symbolic vehicle making social interaction possible. Language contains many explicit messages regarding cultural definitions of male and female roles. In the English language, for example, women are included under the rubic *man*. Further, there are *chairmen, congressmen, policemen, postmen, businessmen, foremen, craftsmen, laymen, servicemen, statesmen, spokesmen, newsboys,* and *cleaning women* (Walum, 1977).

Shortly after birth infants are given "boys' " or "girls' " names, linguistic markers of male or female status. Males are provided with short, brisk, and hard-hitting names (Bret, Lance, Mark, Bruce, Craig). Even when the name is multisyllabic (Michael, Joshua, William, Richard, Thomas), the nickname tends to imply hardness and energy (Mike, Josh, Bill, Dick, Tom). In contrast, women's names tend to be longer, more melodic, and softer (Deborah, Victoria, Jessica, Catherine, Virginia) and easily succumb to the diminutive *ie*-ending (Debbie, Vickie, Jessie, Cathy, Ginnie).

Children are also symbolically cued as to their gender roles in a good many other ways. Surveys reveal that parents furnish boys' and girls' rooms differently (Rheingold and Cook, 1975). The rooms of boys are more often decorated with animal motifs; those of girls, with floral motifs, lace, fringe, and ruffles. The toys found in the rooms also differ. Boys are provided with more vehicles, military toys, sports equipment, toy animals, and mechanical toys; girls, more dolls, doll houses, and domestic toys. Clearly, different sets of principles guide parental behavior regarding male and female children.

Adults also relate differently with male and female children (Cantor and Gelfand, 1977). Josephine V. Brown and her associates (1975) found in a sample of urban Black mothers that the mothers rubbed, patted, touched, kissed, rocked, and talked more to male than to female newborns. Research also suggests that adults tend to act more positive toward opposite-sexed than toward same-sexed children (Gurwitz and Dodge, 1975).

Psychologists suggest that three principal mechanisms operate in the socialization process: reinforcement, imitation, and observational learning. *Reinforcement* occurs in the course of conditioning. Learning takes place as behavior is strengthened by its consequences. In their daily lives children are actively rewarded and praised for what adults and their peers view as

Sexist toys. Children are bombarded with sexist messages telling them the "proper" gender roles for men and women. Note the occupations assigned to each sex on this child's playboard. Women are "dancers," "nurses," and "homemakers," while men are "firemen," "astronauts," "cowboys," "policemen," and "workers."

Patrick Reddy

sex-appropriate behavior (Mischel, 1970). When organisms exhibit behavior that yields various gratifications for them, the behavior is reinforced by this consequence and therefore is more likely to recur.

Imitation means that individuals do what they see other people doing. In Chapter 3 we considered the importance of play for children by affording them opportunities for the rehearsal of adult roles, a process termed *anticipatory socialization* (Merton, 1968). Through role-taking dramas in which they imaginatively "try on" the behaviors of parents, spouses, doctors, teachers, and others, children prepare themselves for the later real-life enactment of adult roles (Mead, 1934; Caplan and Caplan, 1973). Hence the fact that children spend much of their leisure-time involved in sex-typed activities assumes considerable significance. Boys tend to engage in adventurous group games with rather elaborate rules (cops and robbers, cowboys and Indians, war games, and contact team sports). Girls tend to participate in more turn-taking games (jumprope and hopscotch) and scenarios that reconstruct home activities. In many ways children's play patterns contribute to the preservation of traditional gender-role divisions by equipping boys with social skills needed for occupational careers while equipping girls with the social skills better suited to family careers (Lever, 1976).

Observational learning refers to the fact that children do not actually have to perform a behavior in order to learn it. Through observation, children acquire a good deal of information (Bandura, 1965; 1967; 1971; 1973). Frequently they do not use this information until a situation arises in adolescence or adulthood that calls for knowledge of particular gender-appropriate behaviors (Hyde and Rosenberg, 1976). Television is one source for observational learning. According to the A. C. Nielsen Company, a firm that specializes in assessing the popularity of television programs, the television set stays on an average of fifty-three hours a week in homes with preschoolers (this compares with forty-three hours a week in the average American household). From television programs children gain a great deal of information regarding love, sex, marriage, and occupational roles and relationships, much of it saturated with traditional stereotypes. For instance, commercials commonly depict the male figure as an expert on the advertised product. Even in the case of laundry products (with which many women are presumably quite familiar), the male is frequently portrayed as the most knowledgeable person.

Labeling Theory. The cultural transmission theory draws our attention to the important part that society plays in shaping the sex-typed behaviors of its members. However, the image we derive from the theory is one of passive individuals who become programmed for given behaviors through the operation of forces external to them. *Labeling theory* (also termed cognitive developmental theory) provides a corrective to this perspective by highlighting for us the fact that children *actively* seek to acquire gender roles.

According to Lawrence Kohlberg, a developmental psychologist, children come to label themselves as "boys" or "girls" when they are between eighteen months and three years of age (Kohlberg, 1966, 1969; Kohlberg and Ullian, 1973). Once they so categorize themselves, children undertake to acquire and master those behaviors that fit their gender concepts, a process termed *self-socialization*. Kohlberg distinguishes his labeling approach from the cultural transmission theory in these terms. According to the cultural transmission model, the following sequence occurs: "I want rewards; I am rewarded for doing boy things; therefore I want to be a boy." In contrast,

341 Gender Roles and Inequality

Kohlberg depicts the following sequence: "I am a boy; therefore I want to do boy things; therefore the opportunity to do boy things (and to gain approval for doing them) is rewarding" (1966:89).

Initially children's conceptions of maleness and femaleness are oversimplified, exaggerated, and cartoonlike stereotypes. Hair styles, clothes, stature, and occupation appear to be the overriding consideration for young children. Thus children fail to pick up real-life variations as in the case of a four-year-old girl who adamantly insisted that only boys can be physicians although her own mother was a doctor. Of interest, genital anatomy plays a relatively minor part in children's thinking about sex differences during their early years. Allan Katcher (1966) found that when four- and five-year-olds are asked to assemble dolls so that the genitals match other parts of a doll's body and clothing, most children are unable to complete the task.

At first children's understanding of gender is rather tentative (Slaby and Frey, 1975; Thompson, 1975). It is not until they are between four and six years of age that they acquire the notion of *gender-constancy*—the idea that one's gender is a permanent part of the self. Before these ages children fail to recognize that a person cannot shift from a woman to a man and vice versa.

Since self-categorization occurs so early in life, John Money and his associates find that if hermaphrodites are to be switched in gender roles, it must take place before they are three years old. By this time children have labeled themselves as male or female, and any later change in their gender role is associated with inadequate sex-typing and poor psychological adjustment (Money and Ehrhardt, 1972).

GENDER AND ACHIEVEMENT MOTIVATIONS AND EXPECTANCIES

At the present time when women are beginning to take part in the affairs of the world, it is still a world that belongs to men—they have no doubt of it at all and women have scarcely any.
Simone De Beauvoir, The Second Sex, *1949*

An underlying theme in popular and scientific literature is that men and women differ in certain achievement-related characteristics (Maccoby and Jacklin, 1974; Lenney, 1977). Although considerable emphasis has fallen on societal (external) barriers to women's achievement, there are those who insist that psychological (internal) barriers also operate toward a similar end. Some social scientists argue that women have lower initial expectations for success than do men (Parsons, Ruble, Hodges, and Small, 1976). Others like Lois W. Hoffman (1972) and Talcott Parsons and Robert F. Bales (1955) say that women have more "affiliative" or "expressive" needs (nurturant, affectionate, integrative, and sympathetic qualities) than achievement needs. And still others like Matina S. Horner (1968, 1972) suggest that women have a "fear of success." Common to such formulations is the notion that women possess personality traits that impair their achieving success. Women are portrayed as being victimized by their socialization in many of the same ways that they were reputed by Freud to be victimized by their biology.

Horner's theory of achievement motivation has commanded particular interest. She claims that women's motive to avoid success is a stable characteristic of the personality that is acquired early in life in accordance with gender-role standards. As a consequence women feel uncomfortable when they are successful in competitive situations since they believe that such behavior is inconsistent with standards of femininity. Further, women anticipate social rejection if they are successful in competitive tasks. In sum, whereas men are viewed as failures if they are not successful, women are judged to be failures if they are successful.

Horner based her conclusions on research she carried out with a sample of undergraduate students at the University of Michigan. In the study (1968), she asked ninety women to tell a story based on the following beginning: "After first-term finals, Anne finds herself at the top of her medical school class." Over sixty-five percent of the women were disconcerted, troubled, or confused by the cue. They associated negative consequences with unusual excellence in women including loss of femininity and social rejection.

Eighty-eight college men also participated in the study, responding to the following cue: "After first-term finals, John finds himself at the top of his medical school class." Less than ten percent of the men wrote fear of success stories. Subsequently the male and female students were given a variety of tasks to perform under competitive and noncompetitive conditions. Horner found that women who expressed a fear of success performed more poorly in competitive than in noncompetitive situations. In contrast, most of the men and those women who had not shown fear of success performed better under competitive conditions.

It is now widely recognized that Horner's research was flawed in a good many respects (Tresemer, 1974; Levine and Crumrine, 1975). For instance, she did not adequately define "success" and there is little consensus on scoring students' essays in terms of what exactly constitutes fear-of-success imagery. Nonetheless, many social scientists would concur with John Condry and Sharon Dyer in their appraisal of the impact of Horner's study:

> Unquestionably we owe a great debt of gratitude to Matina Horner. It was her thoughtful analysis of the issues that has generated most of the ... [current] research, and although not all of the authors agree with her conclusions, few would deny the importance of the topic or the intellectual force of her writings. In some respects she may have been wrong, but in the words of Francis Bacon, "truth emerges more readily from error than from confusion." ... We have focused our attention on error, if error it be, but we should not lose sight of the fact that without Horner's work and theory we might still be floundering in a disarray of conflicted notions and ambiguous theories. (1976, p. 79)

343 Gender Roles and Inequality

Many social scientists now accept the view that such qualities as competitiveness, assertiveness, and competence are not sex-linked either on the basis of genetics or early socialization (Darley, 1976). Some of what is termed "fear of success" simply reflects realistic expectations about the negative consequences of deviance from norms of what constitutes sex-appropriate behavior. Much of the difficulty women experience with achievement and competition derives from the situation and the meaning that a situation has for them (Condry and Dyer, 1976; Lenney, 1977), a fact highlighted by Research Study 16. Women do not have a general disposition to avoid success but rather they, like men, will avoid success when success conflicts with norms relating to gender role, and will seek success when norms permit or require it (Darley, 1976). Thus many women have not been troubled about pursuing success in homemaking roles. Further, patterns of occupational choice and achievement are also affected by perceptions of the available alternatives (Meeker and Weitzel-O'Neill, 1977). In many cases women are not convinced that the opportunity structure is open to them (Berman and Haug, 1975).

Considerable research reveals that definitions of the situation play a considerable part in individuals' level of self-confidence (Lenney, 1977). For instance, when J. G. Simon and N. T. Feather (1972) asked their students in introductory psychology to indicate how confident they were of passing the *first* exam of the course, women were less confident than men. But when they asked the same question of the students immediately prior to the *final* examination, there were no differences between the sexes in reported confidence (Simon and Feather, 1973). Once having received grades and other feedback regarding their abilities, women were as confident as men were.

RESEARCH STUDY 16

SKEWED SEX RATIOS AND TOKEN WOMEN*

Rosabeth Moss Kanter

Problem. Conclusions regarding "women's behavior" often fail to distinguish between the effect of the gender role and the effect of the situation. For instance, what Horner attributes to "fear of success" (a trait acquired by women through socialization processes) may be due to "fear of visibility" in male-dominated corporation settings. Sociologist Rosabeth Moss Kanter sought to shed light on these matters by studying male-female interactions in a large-scale organization in which

Continued on next page.

women comprise a relatively small proportion of the work group.

Method. Kanter undertook a field study of one of America's largest industrial corporations. She studied in detail a division in which women were being admitted to the sales force for the first time. In local and regional sales offices a lone woman commonly found herself with ten or twelve male coworkers (in a few cases two women were together).

Findings. The women in the sales force were highly visible and captured a larger share of a group's awareness than did their male associates. Their relationships and behavior were continually considered "newsworthy," leading any number of the women to complain of "overobservation." Further, their acts tended to take on added symbolic significance as signs of "how women do in sales." But whereas the women had no difficulty having their presence noted, they found that their technical abilities were likely to be eclipsed by their physical appearance. Hence, in order to make their work skills and competence known, they felt they had to work twice as hard as the men. However, at the same time, they experienced pressure to maintain a low profile and blend unnoticeably into the predominant male culture lest they be viewed as "too aggressive" and "too much a hustler."

The women's presence had the effect of heightening the consciousness of males as males and increasing their camaraderie in various work and social settings. The token women seemed to elicit exaggerated displays of aggression and potency from the men: episodes of sexual teasing and innuendo and prowess-oriented "war-stories." Further, in sales meetings the men often made the women feel as "outsiders" and "intruders," for instance, by posing a question as to whether the men would be allowed to swear or go drinking and then invariably going ahead with the act. Women were also kept on the periphery of colleague interaction while simultaneously being placed in situations where they had to pass "loyalty tests" (the price of being "one of the boys" was a willingness on occasion to turn against "the girls").

Token women found that stereotyped assumptions and mistaken attributions tended to force them into playing limited and caricatured roles in the system. Hence the women frequently felt themselves treated in more wifelike and datelike ways than a man would be treated by another man. Kanter observed four role traps for lone women in male groups: "mother" (a sympathetic, good listener); "seductress" (the sex object); "pet" (group mascot); and "iron-maiden" (militant and unapproachable). Women often found it easier to feign acceptance of the stereotyped roles than to fight them. Thus, accurate conclusions about work attitudes and behavior cannot be reached by studying women in token positions since an element of compensation or distortion is often involved.

Conclusion. Kanter concludes that "token" women operate under a number of handicaps in work settings:

> Their possible social isolation may exclude them from situations in which important learning about a task is taking place and may also prevent them from being in a position to look good in the organization. Performance pressures make it more dangerous for tokens to fumble and thus give them less room for error. Responding to their position, they often either underachieve or overachieve, and they are likely to accept distorting roles which permit them to disclose only limited parts of themselves. (p. 987)

In sum, despite the controversy over affirmative action quotes, numbers do appear to be important in shaping outcomes for minorities in new work situations.

SEX STRATIFICATION

> The first class antagonism which appears in history coincides with the development of the antagonism between man and woman in monogamian marriage, and the first class oppression with that of the female sex by the male.
> *Friedrich Engels,* The Origin of the Family, Private Property, and the State

In all known societies there appears to be some degree of male dominance (Friedl, 1975). Greater power, status, and social benefits are commonly bestowed on men than women. The term **sexism** is applied to institutional arrangements that maintain a gender order of inequality and justify it by an ideology of male biological superiority and female biological inferiority. Sexism infects the entire social fabric. The sociologist Jessie Bernard describes the pervasiveness of sexism in these terms:

> [Sexism is] the unconscious, taken-for-granted, assumed, unquestioned, unexamined, unchallenged acceptance of the belief that the world as it looks to men is the only world, that the way of dealing with it which men have created is the only way, that the values which men have evolved are the only ones, that the way sex looks to men is the only way it can look to anyone, that what men think about what women are like is the only way to think about what women are like. (Quoted by Gornick and Moran, 1971, p. xxv)

By virtue of sexism, the question of who shall get what, when, and how is usually answered in terms that favor males (Collins, 1975). It is men who occupy the top political offices, who get the best jobs, who enjoy positions of eminence in their communities, who escape from many menial household tasks, who control the scheduling of sexual intercourse, and who achieve most of the organisms (although many women are capable of multiple organisms during a single act of intercourse, a relatively rare occurrence among men).

Sex stratification is maintained in a variety of ways. First, there is occupational discrimination and segregation by sex resulting in "male" occupations (politics, law, accounting, engineering, medicine, and dentistry) and "female" occupations (nursing, elementary school teaching, and secretarial work). Second, American law, based on the Napoleonic code, has defined marital relationships in terms that have seriously disadvantaged wives. Third, social pressures, gossip, ridicule, and ostracism have operated on the informal level to relegate women to domestic roles. Fourth, belief and value systems have defined the prevailing sexual division of labor as "natural," "inborn," "moral," and "sacred." Fifth, the state, the family, the school, the church, mass media, popular entertainment, and language have channeled men and women into separate life spheres. And sixth, co-optation and tokenism have been employed to bring a limited number of unusually talented women into the system and to legitimize the claim that the meritorious are rewarded (Holter, 1973; Krauss, 1974).

HOMEMAKING AND CHILDCARE

Women should remain at home, sit still, keep house, and bear and bring up children.
Martin Luther, Table-Talk, 1569

Sexual inequality is sustained by assigning the economic-provider role to men and the child-rearing role to women. The dichotomy between the public and domestic spheres has been a compelling one. Public labor has been rewarded with power, money, and prestige whereas labor in the domestic realm is generally isolated and undervalued.

The American family system has bound women to their reproductive function. In many respects motherhood has been made central to our society's definition of the adult female—the mandate that a woman have children and rear them well (Hardin, 1974; Russo, 1976). Norms specify that the woman who bears a child must be the person who is primarily responsible for its rearing. According to this cultural ideal, each woman raises one man's children in an individual household that is viewed as private property and private space (Gordon, 1970). Until recently this value led to the virtual absence of institutions providing childcare services outside the home (Zellman, 1976).

It is the primacy of the role of mother—together with the associated role of wife—that is the foundation for sex-typed expectations regarding the behavior of men and women. A woman can spend time working in a job outside the home so long as she keeps the house clean and her husband and children well tended. To the extent to which women are confined to the domestic sphere by the linkage of biological and social functions (and hence blocked from direct access to material and social resources in the larger community), women become dependent on those who participate in the public sphere: men (Dixon, 1976).

The fact that women are expected to give priority to domestic and childcare roles weakens their position both inside and outside the home. The sociologist Laurel R. Walum cites a number of reasons for this:

> First, in terms of society's values, child-caring is not a high-prestige occupation. In fact it has low status, is vacationless, pensionless, isolated, full-time on-call, and financially uncompensated. Although childrearing may be a superior activity to many of those available in the labor market it is not viewed as real work, because it is outside the market economy.

> Second, full-time child-rearing limits what else one can do. It especially diminishes one's ability to pursue a professional career. The 70 or so hours required for a high-level business or professional career are not available to the full-time child-rearer; nor are the 50 hours for middle-management success....
>
> Moreover, the spouse who takes care of the children forfeits bargaining power within the marital union. Once a formal or informal pact has been made allocating child-rearing to the wife, she becomes even more disadvantaged in future negotiations. (1977, p. 181)

The separation between public and domestic roles also has costs for men. Not the least of these is that men are denied many of the satisfactions of childcare and in some instances experience emotional estrangement from their children. One forty-six-year-old college professor whose wife died when one child was an infant and the other a toddler observes:

> Judged by the standards of the academic world, my career has been a successful and fruitful one. I have authored thirteen books and found many satisfactions in teaching. But of all my roles, none have been more fulfilling or rewarding than that of rearing my sons. For the past eleven years I have raised them as a single parent and I've really enjoyed them. Believe me, these have been Golden Years. I've gotten to know the kids in a way I never would had I followed the traditional "man-away-from-home" pattern.

This man, of course, was not limited to a domestic role. He was able to integrate his academic responsibilities and writing with childcare. By virtue of his professional position and stature, he could largely arrange his hours to suit his convenience. The situation is otherwise for many women who work outside the home and find that the workplace clock is not calibrated with that of the public school. Most parents can rarely arrange their work schedules so that they can care for their children. Family roles would not pose as great a barrier to the full participation of both parents if part-time employment, staggered work hours, and paid parental leaves could be available to facilitate and equalize the access of men and women to positions in the public sphere.

Jessie Bernard (1973) notes that men and women often inhabit different worlds although they live in the same physical location. There are two marriages, "his" marriage and "her" marriage. Bernard (1972) claims that marriage in the United States tends to be much more beneficial for husbands than for wives. She reviews mental health literature which suggests that married women are more likely to experience symptoms of mental illness than single women. The reverse is true of men—single men are more likely to experience psychological problems than married men.

Myra M. Ferree (1976) also cites evidence showing that women who are fulltime homemakers are more dissatisfied and feel themselves to be worse off than women who have jobs outside the home. The relationship between marital status and mental illness, however, remains clouded by conflicting findings. Some researchers like Walter R. Gove and his associates (Gove, 1972; Gove and Tudor, 1973, 1977; Gove and Clancy, 1976; Gove and Geerken, 1977) maintain that there is a firm relationship between the two variables. Others find no relationship (Dohrenwend and Dohrenwend, 1976; Meile, Johnson, and Peter, 1976; Warheit, Holzer, Bell, and Arey, 1976). Accordingly, it would seem advisable that we keep an open mind on the matter and await further research.

THE WAGE ECONOMY

A women has to be twice as good as a man to go half as far.
Fannie Hurst, Reader's Digest, *October 1958*

High levels of sex discrimination and segregation characterize the American wage economy. Women who worked at fulltime jobs in 1974 earned only 57 cents for every dollar earned by men (the average woman has to work nearly nine days to gross the same earnings which the average man realizes in five days). Perhaps even more shocking, the earnings differential between men and women has been *increasing*. When the absolute difference between the earnings of men and women is expressed in constant dollars (allowing for the deflated purchasing power of the dollar), the disparity between the sexes increased more than seventy-nine percent between 1955 and 1974 (U.S. Department of Labor, 1976).

Although the proportion of women in the labor force has steadily increased (it now includes about half of all women sixteen years of age or older), two major factors have contributed to the widening income gap between men and women. First, despite the fact that many women are securing higher level and better paying jobs, there is still a predominance of women in the less prestigious occupations (primarily as clerks and secretaries). Second, the dramatic rise in women's participation in the labor force has resulted in a large proportion of women who are in or near the entry level.

Despite recent changes in the composition of the labor force, historical patterns concerning "men's jobs" and "women's jobs" still persist. Physicians, lawyers, judges, engineers, accountants, college educators, and architects are most likely to be men while noncollege teachers, nurses, librarians, dietitians, and health technologists are usually women (U.S. Department of Labor, 1976). Even in "female fields," such as nursing, social work, librarianship, and school teaching, men are disproportionately represented in the administrative phases of the profession (Grimm and Stern, 1974). and, alarmingly, women appear to be losing ground in some cases. For instance, in the 1940s forty-one percent of school principals were women; today the figure has dropped to less than twenty percent (Dullea, 1975).

When women are found in the same professions as men, they are likely to earn less. For example, men's earnings in sales positions exceed women's earnings by 142 percent (men are more often in high-paying commissioned nonretail jobs while women work primarily in retail trade). See Tables 10.2 and 10.3. Further, women who work year round earn substantially less than fully employed men who have the same number of years of education (in 1974, women with four years of college had on the average lower incomes then men who had only completed the eighth grade and fifty-nine percent of the income of men with four years of college).

TABLE 10.2

Total Money Earnings of Civilian Year-Round Full-Time Workers, by Occupation Group and Sex, 1974

(Persons 14 years of age and over)

Occupation Group	Women	Men	Dollar Gap	Women's Earnings as a Percent of Men's	Percent Men's Earnings Exceeded Women's
Total	$6,772	$11,835	$5,063	57.2	74.8
Professional, technical, and kindred workers	9,570	14,873	5,303	64.3	55.4
Managers and administrators	8,603	15,425	6,822	55.8	79.3
Sales workers, total	5,168	12,523	7,355	41.3	142.3
Retail trade	4,734	9,125	4,391	51.9	92.8
Other sales workers	8,452	13,983	5,531	60.4	65.4
Clerical workers	6,827	11,514	4,687	59.3	68.7
Craft and kindred workers	6,492	12,028	5,536	54.0	85.3
Operatives (including transport)	5,766	10,176	4,410	56.7	76.5
Service workers (except private household)	5,046	8,638	3,592	58.4	71.2
Farmers and farm managers	*	5,459	—	—	—
Farm laborers and supervisors	*	5,097	—	—	—
Nonfarm laborers	5,891	8,145	2,254	72.3	38.3
Private household workers	2,676	*	—	—	—

* Base less than 75,000.

Source: U.S. Department of Labor (1976) *The Earnings Gap between Women and Men.* Washington, D.C.: Government Printing Office, Table 3, p. 8.

TABLE 10.3
Median Salaries of Full-Time Employed Civilian Scientists, by Sex and Field, 1970

Field	Median Salary Women	Median Salary Men	Percent Men's Salary Exceeded Women's
All fields	$11,600	$15,200	31.0
Chemistry	10,500	15,600	48.6
Earth and marine sciences	10,500	15,000	42.9
Atmospheric and space sciences	13,000	15,200	16.9
Physics	12,000	16,000	33.3
Mathematics	10,000	15,000	50.0
Computer sciences	13,200	16,900	28.0
Agricultural sciences	9,400	12,800	36.2
Biological sciences	11,000	15,500	40.9
Psychology	13,000	15,500	19.2
Statistics	14,000	17,100	22.1
Economics	13,400	16,500	23.1
Sociology	11,000	13,500	22.7
Anthropology	12,300	15,000	22.0
Political sciences	11,000	13,500	22.7
Linguistics	11,300	13,000	15.0

Source: U.S. Department of Labor (1976) *The Earnings Gap between Women and Men.* Washington, D.C.: Government Printing Office, Table 4, p. 9.

Because the power structure of our society is largely dominated by men, most institutions are designed to reflect male values and to accommodate male needs:

> When men say . . . that women can have any job they want, "provided they have the qualification," they do not mean . . . merely having the same facts and figures at her fingertips as her male colleague, but that she must have the same *spirit,* the same *posture,* and the same *value system.* (Kellen, 1972, p. 63).

A woman may handle a job somewhat differently than a man would, but since a man is probably the one evaluating her performance, he may judge her to be incompetent when she is merely different (Kreps, 1973; Zellman, 1976; Hennig and Jardim, 1976). Women in managerial positions commonly find it necessary to evolve a style of work that does not come across as too "masculine" (hard, tough, and aggressive) or too "feminine" (not tough enough, overemotional, and too hesitant).

Workplace rules and hours are designed to be compatible with men's but

The politics of touch. Inequality is expressed in male-female interaction in that it is the male that commonly initiates touching. Should women initiate touching, the act is often construed as a sexual invitation.

Patrick Reddy

not women's family responsibilities (Zellman, 1976). Women have difficulty shedding the roles of homemaker and mother in the work setting and often experience role conflict on at least two levels (Terborg, 1977). First, to the extent to which home and family duties are placed primarily in the domain of the "feminine role," working women experience pressures from many quarters to sacrifice their careers for family responsibilities. Second, the taking on of additional roles often creates role overload (it is difficult to allocate sufficient time and energy to all the multiple roles). A Detroit survey revealed that three out of four women physicians said that they took care of all their families' cooking, shopping, childcare, and money management in addition to their patients' health (*New York Times,* November 3, 1976:24). And women often find that they are kept off the ladder of upward job mobility because social norms define child-rearing as women's responsibility (the expectation is that sooner or later a woman of childbearing age will have a baby).

Women also frequently encounter sexual harassment on the job by male bosses and coworkers. The problem has long been whispered about but only

SEXISM

OBSERVATION Today I applied for a position as a security officer. A young woman was there before me and I overheard her being interviewed by the personnel officer. The personnel officer began by asking her a rather standard set of questions. I recall he asked her the date of her birth because he replied, "Oh, you're not 21, are you?" In the course of the interview he told her about the duties of a security officer: "You know it gets cold out there in winter when you have to check and make certain that all the stores have locked doors!" He went on, "You know you have to be on call on weekends and holidays!" to which she disappointedly replied, "Yes, I guess so." "If there is any trouble in a store you must be able to stop it" and "If you run into a big Black guy shoplifting, you gotta arrest him." The whole interview was quite negative and he painted a grim picture of what it was like to be a security officer. I was thinking of leaving, but before I actually did the personnel officer called me. My interview went differently. When he asked me my birthday he said, "Well you aren't 21, but that doesn't matter 'cause you're a well-built guy." He then got around to describing the job. He said that I would have to check the locks on stores but I wouldn't get too cold in winter because it only takes a few minutes. He explained that I would be on call on weekends but that "it shouldn't be too bad because you can easily find a replacement who wants to make the extra money." He noted that if I ran into difficulty it would be "better not to mess with it and just call the police." Well, to make a long story short, I got the job and the woman didn't.

PRINCIPLE Although the security company is technically conforming to the letter of the law and opening security positions to both men and women, in reality subtle and not so subtle practices prevail that result in sex discrimination. The job portrayed to the young woman was quite different and grim compared with that depicted to me shortly later. This is a good example of institutional sexism.

in the past several years have women felt able to speak out about it. Among the difficulties cited by women are constant leering and ogling of their bodies, continual brushing against their bodies, sexual squeezing or pinching, outright sexual propositions backed by a threat of losing a job, and forced sexual relations. Women have been reluctant to speak out against their tormentors since they run the risk of being seen as crazy, a weirdo, or a woman who actually invites sexual advances (Nemy, 1975; Crittenden, 1977).

SEXUAL INEQUALITY, EXPLOITATION, AND ABUSE

I deny that anyone knows, or can know, the nature of the two sexes, as long as they have only been seen in their present relation to one another.

John Stuart Mill

The expectation that men and women should perform different functions finds expression in the legal code. American law has been premised on the notion that men enjoy a "natural right" to dominate women (Kanowitz, 1969). Prior to the Civil War, women were defined in common law as committing "civil death" on marriage. In the eyes of the law, women became "incorporated and consolidated" with their husbands. This legal and social submersion of women is dramatically symbolized by the requirement that a wife surrender her surname and take that of her husband.

Perhaps in no area of the law has a double standard been more prevalent than in our society's handling of rape (LeGrand, 1973; Rose, 1977). Rape is a critical offense because it is a violent sexual encounter in which a male imposes his will on a female. As such it expresses and symbolizes the differential power of men and women within society and the historical commitment of social institutions. Feminists argue that rape laws are essentially property laws protecting male interests rather than protecting women from sexual assault. They point out that a woman's virginity has been viewed historically as the property of her father and her sexuality as the property of her husband. Defined in this traditional manner rape is less a crime perpetuated by a man against a woman than a crime perpetuated by one man against another man (LeGrand, 1973).

Much of society's attitude toward rape has been premised on the sexist notion that the victim precipitated the sexual encounter. The raped woman is frequently perceived as a kind of criminal in her own right (Scarpitti and Scarpitti, 1977). This attitude was reflected in a 1977 decision by Judge Archie Simonson of Madison, Wisconsin, who held that a male who raped a student in a high school stairwell was reacting "normally" to contemporary sexual standards and women's provocative clothing: "This community is well-known to be sexually permissive. Should we punish a 15- or 16-year-old boy who reacts to it normally?" (*New York Times,* May 27, 1977:9)

In rape trials much questioning is designed to find out if the woman "merits" the protection of the law. She is thought to forfeit the right if she is not "chaste" and "well-behaved" and falls into the category of a prostitute, a "sexual libertine," a divorced woman, a common-law wife, or an "adulterer." Further, it is not uncommon for state legal codes to require some corroboration for the charge of rape (usually a witness), ostensibly to protect innocent men from unwarranted accusations by women. Through the years rape victims have been subject to the indifference, disbelief, and brutality of police, doctors, attorneys, judges, and jurors.

Much the same legal double standard also prevails in other areas of behavior. The law often frees the male customer and punishes the prostitute. It allows men but not women the unwritten law of defense in the case of marital infidelity and permits intercourse of underage boys with older women but not vice versa (Kanowitz, 1969). Further, wife beating is not commonly processed as criminal assault. Victimized wives report that calling the police only serves to escalate their husbands' violence since husbands are either not arrested or released and simply given a date for their future appearance in court (Goodman, 1975).

GENDER ROLES AND SOCIAL CHANGE

> [In] the new code of laws which I suppose it will be necessary for you to make, I desire you would remember the ladies and be more generous and favorable to them than your ancestors. Do not put such unlimited power into the hands of the husbands. Remember, all men would be tyrants if they could. If particular care and attention is not paid to the ladies, we are determined to foment a rebellion, and will not hold ourselves bound by any laws in which we have no voice or representation.
>
> Abigail Adams in a letter to her husband, John, in 1777

Vast changes have occurred over the past decade in the roles of Americans, especially women. Eli Ginzberg, a Columbia University economist and head of the National Commission for Manpower Policy, describes what is happening as

> a revolution in the roles of women [that] will have an even greater impact than the rise of Communism and the development of nuclear energy. It is a worldwide phenomenon, an integral part of a changing economy and a changing society. (Quoted by Dullea, 1977, p. 28)

Today a record forty million women are in the national work force, accounting for nearly forty-six percent of all nonhousehold workers. The expansion of the female work force can be traced to many factors: the increasing availability of contraceptive methods and legalized abortion; a growing preference for smaller families; inflationary pressures giving rise to the two-paycheck family; the high divorce rate which has made many mothers the family breadwinner; a growing number of female college graduates who desire careers; the expansion of the retail sales and service industries which have spurred the employment of women; changing attitudes toward careers for women outside the home; and anti-sex discrimination legislation that has increased women's employment opportunities (Van Dusen and Sheldon, 1976; Mason, Czajka, and Arber, 1976; Dullea, 1977). Although much has changed in the past decade, the relationship between men and women still remains distant from the ideal espoused over a century ago by John Stuart Mill, who called for "a principle of perfect equality, admitting no power or privilege on one side nor disability on the other."

THE WOMEN'S MOVEMENT

The rising of us women means the rising of us all.

From Bread and Roses, 1920s suffrage song

In recent years no social movement has had a more substantial impact on the way people think and act than the women's movement. Women's movements have arisen throughout human history, especially within the context of social revolutions and movements for national independence. At first women tend to be caught up in the same broad currents that engulf a society and breed collective behavior. In the course of their immersion in such movements, women begin to extend the ideology of equality and social justice to their gender and question existing institutional arrangements that hold them in a disadvantaged status. They find, however, that the movement to which they have committed themselves does not adequately meet their concerns and needs. The bonds and communication networks which they establish with other women in the revolutionary or independence movement then serve as a base for a women's political organization (Krauss, 1974).

The suffragist movement is a good illustration of this, beginning in the 1830s and succeeding nearly a century later in securing the enfranchisement of American women. That movement, like the current women's liberation movement, developed out of Black civil rights efforts when women abolitionists in the 1800s (like women "radicals" in the 1960s) discovered strong parallels between their own circumstances and that of the group they originally aimed to help (Freeman, 1973).

The revival of feminist activity in the late 1960s was characterized by a wide diversity of groups. Some, like NOW (the National Organization for Women), were primarily "top-heavy" organizations (arising as national structures and having little initial community base—indeed, NOW's initiators were on the whole public figures who lacked the time or patience for the slow, unglamorous, and tedious work of constructing a mass organization). Others were grassroots groups—having at best tenuous contact with each other; they engaged in a variety of activities (compaigns for abortion reform or welfare rights; the promotion of the interests of gay or professional women; or the sponsorship of consciousness-raising rap sessions).

The Women's Liberation Movement was set in motion in 1961 when President John F. Kennedy established the President's Commission on the Status of Women (chaired by Eleanor Roosevelt); in turn, this commission led to the establishment of fifty state commissions. The activities of the federal and state commissions brought together many knowledgeable, politically active women on matters of direct concern to them as women; they unearthed evidence of women's economic and legal difficulties; and they created a climate of expectations that something needed to be done. Two other developments further fed the movement: the publication in 1963 of Betty Friedan's book, *The Feminine Mystique* (a bestseller that stimulated many women to question the status quo) and the addition of "sex" to Title VII of the 1964 Civil Rights Act. These strands of incipient feminism were knotted together in 1966 with the formation of NOW.

Simultaneously, on the grassroots level, many younger women began organizing. Civil rights, peace, and student power projects had attracted many women who found themselves shunted into traditional roles and faced with the contradiction of working in a "freedom movement" without being free (for instance, Stokely Carmichael of the Student Nonviolent Coordinating Committee had suggested in 1964 that "the only position for women in SNCC was prone"). These women tended to think of themselves as part of the "radical community" and to conceive of themselves as "movement people." They employed the infrastructures of the radical community, the underground press, and the free universities to disseminate ideas on women's liberation. These grassroots groups encouraged women to change their identities and attitudes. Their structure was loose and informal, proliferating horizontally without creating new organizational vehicles.

Both the Commission on the Status of Women and the "radical community" created a *communications network* through which women concerned with women's rights could easily reach others. Prior to the 1960s, a viable network had not existed (the nineteenth-century suffragist organizations were either dead or pallid ghosts of their former selves). In addition the network was *co-optable. Infrastructures* were available which provided a social base for the movement—an indispensable element in the formation of social movements. In parallel instances, the civil rights movement of the early 1960s was built on the infrastructure of the Southern Black church, and early SDS (Students for a Democratic Society) organizers made ready use of the National Student Association.

By 1970 NOW had grown to 3000 members and by 1978 to 70,000 members. The women's movement has had a profound impact on American society, particularly with respect to work, education, and men-women relationships, and has contributed a great deal to changing the climate for women. Consider, for instance, that when NOW was formed in 1966, United Airlines promoted its executive "men only" flights to Chicago, high schools packed off boys to shop classes and girls to home economics courses, newspapers classified ads into helped wanted "male" and "female," and busines*smen* had their "Gal Fridays" and husbands their "little women" (Bralove, 1977).

ANDROGYNOUS ROLES

What is most beautiful in virile men is something feminine; what is most beautiful in feminine women is something masculine.

Susan Sontag, Against Interpretation

The women's movement has held that both men and women pay a high price for restrictive and artificially polarized gender roles. Men are expected to be tough, assertive, and independent while women are supposed to be tender, nurturant, and dependent. Yet an accumulating body of evidence suggests that "male" and "female" characteristics are present in both men and women (Mead, 1935; Bem, 1975a,1975b; Rosenblatt and Cunningham, 1976). Accordingly, there are those who insist that people should

THE SEX-TYPED WORLD OF TOYS

OBSERVATION For the past several years I have worked in a large toy store. The toys are arranged by categories—games, dolls, domestic playthings, toy cars, trucks, and airplanes, building materials and blocks, science and educational toys, and so on. My coworkers and I tend to think of these categories in sex-typed terms and we encounter no difficulty when parents ask us the location of "boys' toys" or "girls' toys."

PRINCIPLE "Boys' toys" are those playthings that are related to economic-provider roles and "girls' toys" to domestic and family roles. By supplying children with sex-typed toys we are communicating to them definitions regarding their gender placements and our behavioral expectations for them. It is of interest that women are our principal customers since they tend to be segregated into domestic roles. By modeling for their children sex-typed roles and in turn buying for their children sex-typed toys, these mothers are perpetuating sexist traditions, ensuring the transmission of these traditions to future generations.

no longer be socialized to conform to outdated standards of masculinity and femininity. Rather, it is argued, individuals should be encouraged to be **androgynous**—capable of expressing the full range of human emotions and role possibilities without being restricted by gender stereotypes.

Feminists have pointed out how men benefit from male supremacy. Far less attention has been given to the price men pay for their power. Yet, as any number of men have noted, they too are trapped within the same system as women; the male prison may be much bigger and more luxurious but it is a prison nonetheless (Gitlin, 1971). Marc F. Fasteau (1974) notes that the attempt to live up to male stereotypes affects almost every area of men's lives. Friendships between men are frequently made shallow by the constant overtone of competition and the need to project a tough, impersonal front. Warmth, compassion, sensitivity, and tenderness are seen as weakness, even in relationships with women and one's own children. And by making women sex objects, men become vulnerable to mechanical sex and, when pushed to extremes, impotence.

Sandra Lipsitz Bem (1975a;1975b), a psychologist, has undertaken a series of studies with her students at Stanford University. She finds that semester after semester about fifty percent adhere to sex-typed stereotypes, fifteen percent are cross-sex-typed, and thirty-five percent are androgynous. In experimental settings, masculine men do "masculine" things very well but they are not adept at "feminine" things. They lack the ability to express warmth and playfulness toward infants and concern for people who are experiencing difficulty. Similarly, feminine women are restricted in tasks requiring independence in judgment or the assertion of their own preferences. In contrast, androgynous men and women can be warm and responsive or independent and assertive in appropriate situations.

358 Social Inequality

Further, masculine men and feminine women feel much worse than do androgynous individuals about doing a cross-sex task. Traditional men feel threatened, uncomfortable, and less attractive when they have to prepare a baby bottle; traditional women when they have to nail boards together. Bem's research suggests that sex-typed stereotypes and behaviors lock both men and women into roles that rob them of many of their potentialities. Androgynous men and women, in contrast, have available to them a wider range of responses and behaviors by which to cope with widely diverse situations.

Courtesy of AT&T

Changing social definitions of men's and women's work. Under agreement between the Bell System and the federal government's Equal Opportunity Commission, steps have been undertaken to end job discrimination based on gender within the telephone industry. Men are returning to Bell System switchboards for the first time since 1878 when the first woman was hired to the previously all-male job of operator; and women are finding employment in traditionally male jobs in the Bell System.

SUMMARY

1. Apparently all societies have seized on the biological dichotomy between men and women for the assignment of gender roles. These are sets of expectations that provide guidelines for the behavior of men and women. They specify which sex does what, when, and where.

2. Although social scientists acknowledge the biological basis for the differences between the sexes, they have viewed with skepticism claims that biological differences between the sexes are the principal source of behavioral differences. The wide variety found in the behavior patterns of men and women from one society to another, and the changes observed from one time to another in sex-linked behavior patterns within the same society point to a social foundation for a great many such differences.

3. We become male or female by stages. The human body appears to differentiate as a female except where the secretions of the embryonic testes push the organism in a male direction. Research with hermaphrodites points to the important part played by environmental factors in shaping individuals' gender identities.

4. Gender identities are the conceptions that individuals have of themselves as being male and female. Psychoanalytic theorists indicate that children acquire their gender identities as they resolve their Oedipal attachments for the parent of the opposite sex. Cultural transmission theorists argue that individuals are essentially neutral at birth and develop those ways of thinking, feeling, and acting characteristic of males or females through socialization processes. Labeling theorists claim that children categorize themselves as "boys" or "girls" and then cultivate those behaviors that fit their gender stereotypes.

5. An underlying theme in popular and scientific literature is that men and women differ in certain achievement-related characteristics. Matina S. Horner suggests that women have a "fear of success," a stable personality characteristic that leads them to reject achievement in competitive situations. Many social scientists, however, now accept the view that such qualities as competitiveness, assertiveness, and competence are not sex-linked either on the basis of genetics or early socialization. Some of what is termed "fear of success" simply reflects realistic expectations about the negative

consequences of deviance from norms of what constitutes sex-appropriate behavior.

6. The term sexism is applied to institutional arrangements that maintain a gender order of inequality and justify it by an ideology of male biological superiority and female biological inferiority. Sexism infects the entire social fabric. By virtue of sexism, the question of who shall get what, when, and how is usually answered in terms that favor males.

7. Sexual inequality is sustained by assigning the economic-provider role to men and the child-rearing role to women. The dichotomy between the public and domestic spheres has been a compelling one. Public labor has been rewarded with power, money, and prestige whereas labor in the domestic realm is generally isolated and undervalued.

8. High levels of sex discrimination and segregation characterize the American wage economy. Women generally earn less than men and are relegated primarily to "female jobs." Because the power structure of our society is largely dominated by men, most institutions are designed to reflect male values and to accommodate male needs.

9. The expectation that men and women should perform different functions finds expression in the legal code. American law has been premised on the notion that men enjoy a "natural right" to dominate women.

10. In recent years no social movement has had a more substantial impact on the way people think and act than the women's movement. It has had a profound impact on American society, particularly with respect to work, education, and men-women relationships.

11. The women's movement has held that both men and women pay a high price for restrictive and artificially polarized gender roles. Research by Sandra Lipsitz Bem suggests that sex-typed stereotypes and behaviors lock both men and women into roles that rob them of many of their potentialities. Androgynous men and women, in contrast, have available to them a wider range of responses and behaviors by which to cope with widely diverse situations.

PART FOUR

INSTITUTIONS

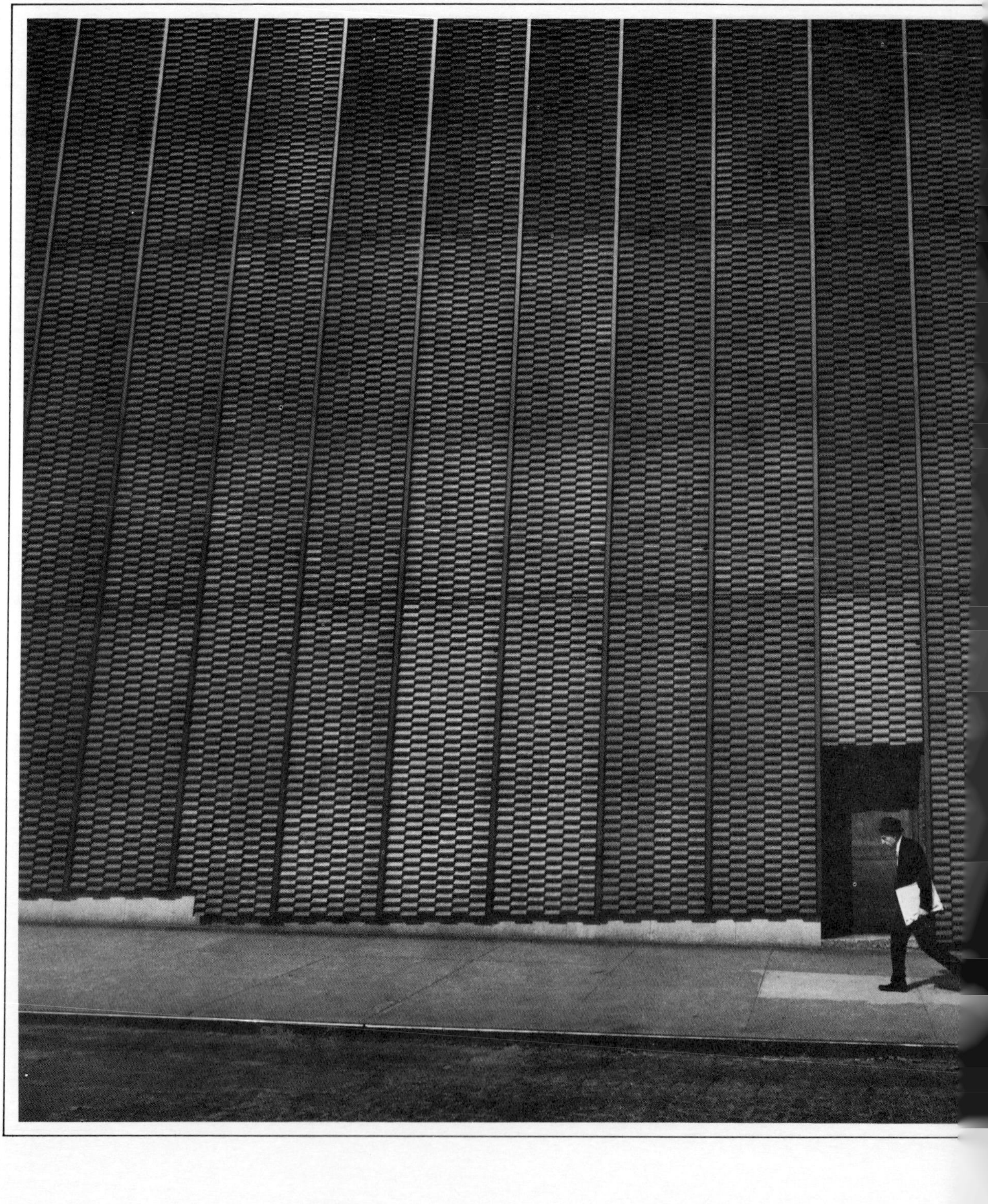

11
INSTITUTIONAL PROCESSES AND CHANGE

INSTITUTIONS IN EVERYDAY LIFE
  The Importance of Institutions: The Case of the Pitcairn Islanders
  Interrelationships Among Institutions
  Systems
  Functions and Dysfunctions
  Manifest and Latent Functions

INSTITUTIONAL CHANGE
  Rate of Change
  Processes of Institutional Change
  Innovation
  Diffusion
  Reworking and Reinterpretation
  Social Change Under Pressure
  Resistance to Change

OBSERVATION This year my family wanted to do something extra nice for my grandmother on Mother's Day. We decided to get her an automatic dishwasher. My dad thought we better play it safe, however, and first check out the idea with grandma. Well, when we approached her with the idea she flipped. She said that if we got her a dishwasher she would send it right back and that she didn't want such a thing in her house. She told us that a dishwasher would run up her electric and water bills, that a machine can't get her dishes as clean as she can by hand, that a dishwasher would chip her good china and wreck the paint design on it, and that you can never trust a machine ("They always are breaking down"). She further said she likes washing her dishes, she has done it all her life, and it gives her something to do. So that took care of that —no dishwasher for grandma.

PRINCIPLE Grandma provides a good illustration of resistance to change. She does not view the innovation as affording her an advantage relative to her current situation. The machine also conflicts with her values regarding the importance of work (she feels that if she doesn't keep busy with housework that she is being "lazy"). She regards the machine as too complex and troublesome—it will use excessive electricity and water and continually break down. And probably most important of all, she finds security, comfort, and a sense of well-being in continuing with her habitual way of doing dishes.

At the time of the assassination of President John F. Kennedy, when the nation was collectively shocked, grieved, and even dazed, James Reston of *The New York Times* wrote:

> This is not a bad time to remember that the Government of the United States has a life of its own. It is a permanent institution. It cannot be assassinated by anything less than the destruction of the nation. . . . (November 27, 1963, p. 18)

Reston's commentary is most perceptive. Institutions endure beyond the lifetime of one individual, even an individual as important as the President of the United States.

Eleven years later, at the time of President Richard M. Nixon's resignation in the face of his impending impeachment, Reston's colleague, Clifton Daniel, made a somewhat similar point:

> Watergate has now joined Teapot Dome, Credit Mobilier and the Whisky Ring in the lexicon of political infamy. Yet, in millions of minds it also symbolized the finest hour of American democracy. A President has been deposed, but the Republic endures. Its institutions have survived, and some are saying they have been strengthened as well. (August 10, 1974:1)

Institutions, then, have remarkable resiliency. They constitute an indispensable element within human life. Should, however, they be destroyed, society itself perishes.

INSTITUTIONS IN EVERYDAY LIFE

> We do not make a world of our own, but fall into institutions already made, and have to accommodate ourselves to them to be useful at all.
>
> Ralph Waldo Emerson, Journals, 1832

Our existence as social beings confronts us with a variety of perennial problems. How are we to produce and distribute the goods and services necessary for the sustenance of a society's members? How are we to realize order and protection? How are we to arrange for the reproduction, socialization, maintenance, and social placement of children? How are we to provide meaning for life, care for the sick and elderly, and in general meet the other requirements of social life?

Institutions afford the established answers to these recurring problems. They are the principal structures whereby the essential tasks of social living are organized, directed, and executed. Each institution is built about a standardized solution to a set of problems and we classify institutions on this basis: the economic institution has as its focus the production and distribution of goods and services; the family institution, the reproduction, socialization, maintenance, and positional placement of children; the political institution, the protection of citizens from one another and from foreign enemies; the religious institution, the enhancement of social solidarity and consensus; and the educational institution, the transmission of the cultural heritage from one generation to the next. Sociologists employ the concept of institutions as a shorthand term that refers to these standardized solutions. Of course, such a classification oversimplifies matters, since several institutions may contribute to the performance of the same function and a particular institution may perform more than one function.

THE IMPORTANCE OF INSTITUTIONS: THE CASE OF THE PITCAIRN ISLANDERS

We gain an appreciation of just how important institutions are for our daily living when we reflect on the experiences of the British mutineers and the Tahitians who settled Pitcairn Island (Shapiro, 1936; Nicolson, 1965; Silverman, 1967).* As most of us probably know, a mutiny occurred aboard the

---

*The author is endebted to Brewton Berry for suggesting this illustration.

Bounty in 1789 shortly after the ship had departed from Tahiti where, under the command of Lieutenant William Bligh, she had been sent to collect breadfruit plants. The leader of the mutiny was Fletcher Christian, one of Bligh's officers. The mutineers seized the *Bounty*, put Bligh and eighteen of his men adrift in a small cutter, and returned to Tahiti. Sixteen of the mutineers elected to stay on Tahiti, while another nine, including Christian, decided to seek another island where they might escape British retribution. Hence, together with six Tahitian men and twelve Tahitian women, the nine mutineers sailed for Pitcairn Island.

Imagine the great number of problems that confronted the English men and Tahitians on their arrival on Pitcairn. How would they eat? How would they apportion the produce? How would they provide for shelter? How would they regulate human behavior and institute social control? How would they make provision for the satisfaction of sexual needs—a matter of no small concern since there were fifteen men and twelve women? How would they guarantee that children would be reproduced, socialized, maintained, and placed within various social positions? How would provision be made for social consensus and solidarity? These and a variety of other requirements had to be met if the colonists were not to perish.

In solving these problems, the mutineers and the Tahitians could not rely on organic instinct. Whereas other animal forms generally have "built-in" biological responses to given stimuli and carry their whole equipment about with them as parts of their bodies, humans for the most part do not. Instead of an organic and instinctive adaptation, the human adapts through culture and social organization. The Pitcairn Islanders, therefore, had to evolve clusters of cultural patterns and networks of stable relationships whereby they could organize, direct, and execute the essential tasks of social living—in brief, institutions.

Fortunately for the Pitcairn colonists, they had the combined heritage of two cultures to fall back on. Their ancestors in England and Tahiti had been faced with similar problems of group living. As might be expected, the institutions that emerged were a blend of their combined heritage. How the Pitcairn Islanders handled the problem of subsistence is illustrative. Since Pitcarin was more like Tahiti than England in its resources, food patterns tended to follow those of the Tahitians: yams, taros, sweet potatoes, pumpkins, peas, bananas, breadfruit, and coconuts. However, the tools—metal hoes, spades, and mattocks—were an English contribution. Fish supplemented Pitcairn diet; the colonists fashioned fishhooks of European style but picked up spear-fishing with torchlight from the Tahitians. Since the women took charge of the preparation and cooking of food, Tahitian household practices came to prevail as did the Tahitian pattern of preparing meals twice a day (once in the late morning and once in early evening).

For the first eighteen years of its existence, the Pitcairn settlement re-

Residence of *Bounty* mutineer John Adams, on Pitcairn Island. After ten years of strife, the settlers of Pitcairn Island established a viable, functioning community.

The Bettmann Archive

mained unvisited by any ship. Even after 1808, when their existence became known, callers were rare and their visits brief. In time, the islanders came to constitute, in the words of a Captain Freemantle in 1833, "a well-disposed, well-behaved, kind, hospitable people." Their numbers grew. They developed deep attachments to their mountainous island and strong bonds of social cohesion. In a word, comparatively stable institutions emerged through which the Picairners came to meet the requirements of social living.

Nonetheless, we should not overlook the fact that the early years on Pitcairn were difficult ones. Intermittent strife in particular threatened the colony's survival. Apparently, things went along rather peaceably and prosperously for about two years, until the English men compelled one of the Tahitian men to bestow his wife on one of their number who had lost his wife in a fall from a precipice. The Tahitian men, outraged at this act and their general oppression and ill-treatment, made common cause with their companion, and formulated a plan to kill all the English men. The women betrayed the plot, and as a result two of the Tahitian men were murdered. Continued strife in the next eight years resulted in even more bloodshed. Yet despite considerable conflict in the early years, an underlying cooperation and institutional functioning still prevailed. For the most part, the members lived rather peaceably together, building their homes, fencing in and cultivating their grounds, fishing, catching birds, and constructing pits for entrapping hogs, which had become numerous and wild, as well as injurious to the yam crops. Had the hand of every human been turned against that of every other human, Pitcairn society could never have developed or survived.

INTERRELATIONSHIPS AMONG INSTITUTIONS

The social "totality" is composed of an interaction of social elements that, unlike interacting billiard balls, do not remain the same; they change not only their positions but also their character. The social system must be seen as an historical product, as a thing made and fashioned by men as active "subjects," as continually remade and daily enacted by the ongoing doings of men, and hence as capable of being undone or redone by their future actions.

Alvin Gouldner, Reivew of George Lukács, History and Class Consciousness, *1971*

The essence of life is the interrelatedness of its various components and their ties to the larger whole. A particular plant cannot be understood by simply describing its properties in terms of size, color, texture, leaf shape, root form, and so on. It must be understood in terms of the relationships among its parts, its connections with its environment, and its development over time (Lauer, 1977). Similarly, we cannot fully understand a phenomenon in the social world without considering it in terms of its internal and external relationships and its developmental history.

Institutions, for instance, do not exist in isolation from one another. They are bound together within a complex web of interrelationships. Hence, a change in one institution has consequences for the other institutions and for the society or community as a whole. This fact is vividly highlighted by the history of Caliente, a small Nevada community. Caliente's fortunes were closely linked with technological innovations, each of which had consequences for Caliente's economic institution and in turn for the community's other institutions (Cottrell, 1951).

Caliente was a community built at a division point on a railroad. At the turn of the century, the technological requirements of the steam engine necessitated the removing of the engine from the train at intervals of roughly 100 miles for servicing. Based on the "certainty" of the railroad's need for Caliente, people built their homes; established a water system; erected substantial buildings for their businesses and schools; established churches, a park, and a hospital; formed a variety of organizations including the Rotary, Chamber of Commerce, Masons, Odd Fellows, and the American Legion — in a word, they founded a community.

The tempo of Caliente's life was set by the daily arrival and departure of trains. As many other small communities in America, it stressed all the virtues regarded as "solid" and "sound."

Immediately following World War II, high tensile steels developed for war armaments were used for locomotives. The "ideal distance" between divisions now became 200 or even 300 miles. It was Caliente's good fortune that it was located midway between terminals and thus survived. In fact, Caliente gained and became even more important because fewer stops meant increased services for long-range travel.

But Caliente's good fortune did not last. The diesel engine was soon introduced. It required infrequent, highly skilled service. The railroad abandoned Caliente as a division point. Boilermakers and others no longer found their skills needed and had to become unskilled laborers. Operating employees found that diesels required about a fourth of the laborers needed to haul the same tonnage as steam engines; three out of four of them had to start anew at something else. Work had to be sought elsewhere because Caliente had no other industry. Merchants lost customers, churches lost congregations, government lost taxpayers, and schools lost pupils. Friendships ended as neighborhoods disintegrated.

This tragic portrayal of the vast consequences of dieselization for Caliente points to the interrelationship among institutions. Within the United States as a whole, we also find many illustrations of the complex network of interchanges that occur between institutions. The political institution, for instance, exerts numerous controls over the economic institution—it sets minimum wage-scales, collects taxes, prevents monopolies, regulates money and credit, offers facilities for settling labor disputes, and the like. In turn, the economic institution influences the political institution through the state of the national economy (the size of the tax base, the prevalence of unemployment, and the extent of inflationary tendencies), its commercial and financial transactions with foreign businesses and governments, and the prevalence of labor turmoil. In the case of the family institution, the government issues licenses to wed, determines which marriages can be legally dissolved, seeks to protect the rights of parents and children in relation to one another, and regulates the care of orphans. In turn, the family institution influences the political institution through its birth rates, its social incubation of political behavior, and its patterns of "disorganization" (with consequences for welfare and taxation policies).

SYSTEMS

The most general and fundamental property of a system is the interdependence of parts or variables. Interdependence consists in the existence of determinate relationships among the parts or variables as contrasted with randomness of variability. In other words, interdependence is order in the relationship among the components which enter into a system.
          Talcott Parsons and Edward A. Shils, Toward a General Theory of Action, 1951

The interrelatedness of social life finds expression in many theories, including the structure-function and Marxist approaches (van den Berghe,

1963; Friedrichs, 1970; Sztompka, 1974). Not uncommonly such interlocking is described and analyzed in terms of a **system**. A system is a complex of elements or components that are related to each other in a more or less stable fashion through a period of time. Viewed in these terms, society is a system that is made up of interrelated institutions. We also find considerable use made of system analysis within many other academic disciplines. Biologists view the organism as a system, as involving some sort of delimited, definite arrangement between its component parts (organs). Astronomers view celestial bodies as making up a stellar system, of which the sun is a part; in turn, the sun's system—the solar system—is made up of planets, including the earth. Similarly, chemists conceive of the atom as a system; economists, the market as a system; physicists, gravity as a system; and so on. In essence, such concepts as "atom," "market," "gravity," and "society" are models—mental constructs—that enable us to visualize something. By treating a phenomenon as a system, we derive a mental picture of "how it is put together and how it works." In this fashion, we reduce the phenomenon to manageable size and order generalizations about it in a meaningful manner.

System analysis focuses on *the particular association or mode of interaction* that occurs between the parts of a substance or entity (for instance, the interchanges between the institutions comprising society). It is the distinctive interaction that takes place between the lower-level components that gives a substance or entity its unique properties or characteristics. Accordingly, it is this interaction that ceases to exist or is initiated when, for instance, a nuclear particle is "annihilated" and another "created," or table salt is built up from sodium and chlorine atoms, or a living cells dies and becomes nothing but its constituent molecules, or a society breaks down because of widespread institutional malfunctioning. Hence, when we say that "the whole [the system] is more than the sum of its parts," the "more than" points to the fact of *organization;* organization imparts to the whole characteristics that are not only *different* from but often not found in the components alone (Buckley, 1967). Émile Durkheim eloquently expressed this idea as follows:

> A whole is not identical with the sum of its parts. It is something different, and its properties differ from those of its component parts. . . . By reason of this principle, society is not a mere sum of individuals. Rather, the system formed by their association represents a specific reality which has its own characteristics. . . . We must seek the explanation of social life in the nature of society itself. (1933, pp. 102–103)

In sum, the bringing together of an aggregate's constituent parts is often associated with an entity that is *qualitatively* different in kind from its separate parts.

FUNCTIONS AND DYSFUNCTIONS

I would define the social function of a socially standardized mode of activity . . . as its relation to the social structure to the existence and continuity of which it makes some contribution. Analogously, in a living organism, the physiological function of the beating of the heart, or the secretion of gastric juices, is its relation to the organic structure.
  A. R. Radcliffe-Brown, Presidential Address, Royal Anthropological Institute, 1940

Within system analysis, considerable attention is frequently paid to the various **functions** performed by a system's parts, especially among structure-function oriented sociologists. Functions are those observed consequences that permit the adaptation or adjustment of a given system (for instance, those observed consequences that the family institution, a particular cultural pattern, or a given group have for the maintenance of society). From this point of view, the survival of a system necessitates the meeting of a variety of requirements; should provision not be made for the meeting of these requirements, the system fails to maintain itself—it perishes. In the case of society, certain essential tasks have to be performed if it is to exist, let alone flourish. Institutions are the principal vehicles by which such functions are performed.

Our concern with the functions of the various parts of society should not lead us to overlook their **dysfunctions** (Merton, 1968). Whereas functions are those observed consequences that allow for the adaptation or adjustment of a given system, dysfunctions are those observed consequences that lessen the adaptation or adjustment of the system. A unit of a system—for in-

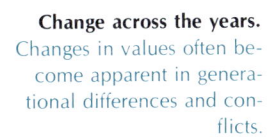

Change across the years. Changes in values often become apparent in generational differences and conflicts.

Patrick Reddy

stance, a norm, value, symbol, role, or institution — frequently has multiple consequences; some may be functional, others dysfunctional, and still others both functional and dysfunctional. There is also the possibility that a part may simply be *nonfunctional*. The concept of dysfunction suggests that a given part may hinder the fulfillment of one or more of the system's essential requirements — that it may be disharmonious with the ends to which the arrangement is presumably oriented.

Take religion. Religion is *functional* to the extent to which it encourages the members of a society to adopt common values and ends. As such, it promotes social solidarity and cohesion — it functions as an ideological and emotional glue, a social stabilizer. By the same token, it may make human suffering more bearable and aid in the emotional adjustment to disappointment, death, and disaster. But religion may also be *dysfunctional*. Where different religions coexist in the same society, there often occurs deep conflict between them that impairs social integration. Similarly, religious doctrines and values may clash with certain nonreligious values, for example, a desire to regulate family size as opposed to prohibitions against birth control or abortion. Of course, intense religious conflict can also rupture a social system, even destroy it. This is what occurred in 1947 with the division of the Indian subcontinent between Hindu and Moslem areas to form India and Pakistan; in this case, conflict gave rise to two new social systems.

In the discussion of functions and dysfunctions above, we intentionally used an illustration from our society that is heavily value-laden and emotionally charged. Readers with an anti-religious orientation probably experienced some resentment when reading the treatment of the functions of religion; on the other hand, the pro-religious may have had somewhat similar feelings when reading the account of its dysfunctions. Accordingly, by virtue of the emotions we attach to important values, it is necessary that we exercise special care when scientifically considering a system so as not to interject notions of "good" or "bad" into our analysis. We may be inclined to assume that "function" means "good" and "dysfunction" means "bad." Within a scientific context, no value judgment — no appraisal of desirability or undesirability — is associated with the notion of function or dysfunction. Admittedly, we find it easier to examine the atoms within an element from this point of view than we do society. When we note that certain patterns are functional for societies characterized by polygyny (families made up of plural wives), the statement is not meant to indicate approval of the patterns or of polygyny.

MANIFEST AND LATENT FUNCTIONS

Sociologists have also found it useful to distinguish between *manifest* functions and *latent* functions. **Manifest functions** are those consequences that are intended and recognized by the participants in a system; **latent functions** are those consequences that are neither intended nor recognized (Merton, 1968). This distinction points to the fact that individuals' *conscious* motivations for behavior may not be identical with the behavior's *objective consequences*. The Hopi Indians, for instance, have a number of ceremonials designed to produce abundant rainfall. Science tells us, however, that the manifest function of these ceremonials is not realized; they simply do not produce rain. With the concept of latent function, we find it possible to continue our inquiry, examining the consequences of the ceremonies not for the rain gods or for meteorological phenomena but for the Hopi themselves.

The ceremonials may fulfill a number of latent functions. First, they provide a periodic occasion on which the scattered members of the society assemble to engage in a common activity. As such, the ceremonials afford a means of collective expression that serves as a basic source of social unity. Second, the ceremonials provide for the "management" of emotional tension and stress that might otherwise be associated with a drought. The ceremonials enable the Hopi to believe that they can control the otherwise uncontrollable and potentially destructive forces of nature. Hence, the ceremonials give the Hopi reassurance and help to overcome their sense of helplessness. The ceremonials provide still another source for the management of tension: they offer a periodic escape from reality; they permit individuals to immerse themselves within a collectivity of ecstasy and exuberance in which daily cares and frustrations are temporarily forgotten. These, then, constitute latent functions of the rain ceremonies—functions that are neither intended nor recognized by the Hopi.

MANIFEST AND LATENT FUNCTIONS

OBSERVATION

Mother's Day is coming up and I'm going home for the day. Today I got my mother a card. They all say about the same thing: "I love you"; "You're the best mother in all the world"; and "I appreciate all the things you do for me."

PRINCIPLE

The manifest function of Mother's Day is to show appreciation for all the devotion a mother gives her family during the year. But the Day also has latent functions. It brings the family together for a special occasion which serves to rejuvenate family bonds and ties. It exalts motherhood as a desirable and honored position at a time when a mother's position of raising children is sometimes seen as pretty dull in comparison with a job in the workaday world. And it generates business for florists, card makers, jewelers, and others.

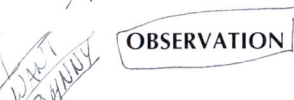

INSTITUTIONAL CHANGE

> Nothing remains what, where and as it was, but everything moves, changes, comes into being and passes out of existence.
>
> *Frederick Engels,* Anti-Duhring

In order to avoid drowning in a sea of facts, we create "models"—ways of looking at things which we then tend to assume are "true." We draw meridians and parallels on the face of the globe, and then proceed "as if" these lines have a counterpart in reality. We determine the zero point on a Fahrenheit scale and then behave "as if" it actually existed. Sociologists often do something of this sort in their treatment of institutions; for some purposes we find it useful to "shut off" all social processes and describe certain social behaviors at a given point in time. An anatomist does much the same thing when examining a cell under a microscope or a cadaver in a laboratory.

Yet such a procedure does not tell us the whole story; indeed, it distorts reality for, in the case of institutions, we fail to grasp the never ending flow of action—the activated relationships—among people. In brief, we lose *process*—interaction. The real world consists of transition and flux. The concept of institution, when viewed in static terms (as a sort of photograph or snapshot of social behavior), is a sociological tool or construct but nonetheless a fiction. For some descriptive and analytical purposes it is a useful fiction; our thinking apparatus demands that we be furnished with discrete and identifiable "things"—in a great welter of facts our sanity depends on it. But this requirement should not lead us to overlook process. To do so is to rob life of its essential dynamic quality. When we speak of an "institution," we refer not to something distinct from the ongoing interactive process but rather at best to a temporary, accommodative representation at a give time. A structure, such as an institution, is simply process that takes place in essentially the same fashion over a given period of time.

As the philosopher Alfred North Whitehead points out, change is inherent "in the very nature of things" (1925:179). Every phenomenon of which we are aware—from galaxies to electrons, from humans to amoeba, from societies to families—exists in a state of continual "becoming":

> Our human bodies change from day to day; certain external appearances of them are the same, but change is constant and sometimes visible. The constellations do not appear to change at all, though we know that they do. . . . Whether the change occurs in a minute or in billions of years, is merely a matter of human measurement. . . . Change is constant, whether we measure it by minutes or millennia; we ourselves are a part of it. (Whitehead, 1954, pp. 209–210)

There are, then, no fixed entities; change is an ultimate fact (Whitehead, 1929; Olsen, 1968). For its part society is a complex, multifaceted, fluid interplay of widely varying degrees and intensities of association and dissocia-

Institutional Processes and Change

tion. As we observed in Chapter 9, social life is characterized by opposing tendencies—by an interplay of forces advancing, retreating, converging, or diverging in patterns of greater or lesser stability. Hence, change is not something incidental, alien, or extraneous to society; rather, change is intrinsic to it. Although social systems are characterized by structure-maintaining forces (and in this sense we may speak of a "strain toward equilibrium"—a tendency for a system to achieve a balance among its parts and among the forces operating within and on it), social systems are also characterized by structure-changing forces.

In sum, sociologists employ multiple models for studying social life. For some purposes, they find it useful to focus on "being," that is, on an "instantaneous snapshot" or cross section of a phenomenon in time (for instance, institutions and social organization). A structure-function model is well-suited to this purpose. For other purposes, they focus on "behaving," that is, on those transient and reversible—often repetitive—aspects of life (for instance, social stability and order). A system's model appears well suited to this purpose. For still other purposes, they focus on "becoming," that is, on the irreversible, developing, and changing aspects of life. For this purpose a process model seems to be a particularly useful tool. Each model calls our attention to problems and data that might be overlooked by the other models (Vander Zanden, 1973).

RATE OF CHANGE

Life is never a material, a substance to be molded.... Life is the principle of self-renewal, it is constantly renewing and remaking and changing and transfiguring itself.
Boris Pasternak, Doctor Zhivago, 1958

Continuous change occurs in all societies. However, the rate of change varies a great deal from one society to another, and even from one period to another within any given society. One of the most important aspects of the twentieth century is the rapidity of change. The eminent economist, Kenneth Boulding, observes, "The world of today . . . is as different from the world in which I was born as that world was from Julius Caesar's. I was born in the middle of human history, to date, roughly. Almost as much has happened since I was born as happened before" (quoted by Toffler, 1970:13). And Dr. Robert Hilliard, a specialist with the Federal Communications Commission notes: "At the rate at which knowledge is growing, by the time the child born today graduates from college, the amount of knowledge in the world will be four times as great. By the time that same child is fifty years old, it will be thirty-two times as great, and 97 percent of everything known in the world will have been learned since the time he was born" (quoted by Toffler, 1970:137).

Alvin Toffler (1970) considers this acceleration of change and its effects in *Future Shock,* a book that has commanded considerable interest. In it Toffler argues that a new society is emerging—not a changed society or an extended, larger-than-life version of present society, but a new society; a super-industrialism. He notes that in economic development alone, the United States has gone within a single lifetime from the dominancy of agriculture at the turn of the century to industrialism and then to the world's first service economy (the latter transition occurring in 1956 when for the first time workers in "white collar" occupations—retail trade, communications, and education—came to outnumber nonfarm "blue-collar" workers). Other technologically advanced societies such as Great Britain, Canada, and Sweden have moved in the same direction.

This acceleration of change has social and psychological consequences, a phenomenon Toffler labels "future shock." It refers to the shattering stress and disorientation people experience when they are subjected to too much change in too short a time. He believes that as the super-industrialism advances, people will find themselves increasingly incapable of coping with the rapidity of change, giving rise to massive adaptational problems within society.

Toffler, however, vastly overstates the impact that social and technological change has on people. Various researchers have shown that broad and even sudden change need not be experienced as stressful where people welcome or deliberately initiate it (Lauer, 1974; Vinokur and Selzer, 1975; Rosen, 1976). Under these circumstances, it is those unable to effect change—rather than those subjected to it—who are mostly likely to experience stress. The perceived desirability or undesirability of change is the crucial factor influencing whether or not change generates psychic disorder (Lauer, 1977). Hence, we confront life only as we mediate our experience through symbols and meanings. "Things" do not simply "happen" to us. We sort experiences into categories and interpret them in ways that are critical for our sense of well-being.

Sociologists also point out that the rate of change in various segments of a society may be uneven and result in social dislocation. William F. Ogburn termed this process **cultural lag.**

> The thesis is that the various parts of modern culture are not changing at the same rate, some parts are changing much more rapidly than others; and that since there is a correlation and interdependence of parts, a rapid change in one part of our culture requires readjustments through other changes in the various correlated parts of culture. (1922, p. 200)

Cultural lag. The automobile has fostered a whole host of changes. It spawned such secondary industries as oil refineries, tire and glass conglomerates, and the giant accident insurance industry. It induced massive investments in single-family homes and in extensive road systems that move traffic from the central city to outer suburban rings. But in so doing the automobile has contributed to a despoiling of the natural environment and to an exodus of the central city's more affluent population.

Patrick Reddy

The growth of cities provides a good illustration of cultural lag. Urbanization brought together large numbers of people who simply disposed of their raw sewage in open gutters. This resulted in typhoid epidemics. Only in relatively recent times have sanitary engineers developed systems for handling and treating sewage and applying chlorine to drinking water.

Perhaps the most pervasive form of cultural lag at the present time is the lag of institutions behind changing technology. Social institutions for dealing with the menace of war have lagged behind the accelerating growth and development of weapons of mass destruction. The advances in the ability of medical science to save human life have not been accompanied by comparable institutions for handling the ensuing "population explosion." Automotive engineering has created cars that can travel faster than most highway systems can accommodate while superhighways, seat belts, and other safety features have lagged behind. Many city streets were laid out for horse-and-buggy transportation, and contribute to modern traffic congestion. Yet prohibitions against on-street parking and the institution of one-way streets have found only tardy acceptance. Further, the introduction of modern, streamlined, rapid transit systems, called for by many city planners to alleviate parking and congestion problems, have yet to pass beyond the engineer's drawing board in most urban areas.

PROCESSES OF INSTITUTIONAL CHANGE

As Christmas approaches, children in many different lands write Santa Claus letters with messages for Rudolph, the Red-Nosed Reindeer. Some even remember Rudolph in their prayers, and prepare holiday snacks of hay and vegetables for him. Yet as Christmas folklore goes, the bright-nosed, sleigh-guiding reindeer is a relative newcomer. The story of Rudolph began as a promotional device for Montgomery Ward & Company back in 1939. The company asked Robert L. May, one of its employees, to write a little booklet that could be given away to create goodwill—"a children's story on the order of Ferdinand the Bull" (May, 1963).

May pondered the matter and came up with a story patterned after *The Ugly Duckling*. The story told of a small, shy reindeer, an underdog shunned by others, who is finally vindicated. But the idea of a reindeer with a big, red nose so bright that it actually glowed met resistance. May's boss objected. "We can't do it! A reindeer with a nose like that would be a monstrosity!" Others also expressed strong reservations. Some questioned the red nose, suggesting it had alcoholic connotations. However, the proposal won a sympathetic reception from Carl Hacker, the company's display manager, and in 1939 some 2.4 million free copies of the story, cleverly illustrated, were distributed in Montgomery Ward & Company stores throughout the country.

During World War II Rudolph went into hibernation, only to be revived again in 1946, when the company reissued the story. A large record firm made a "story" record of Rudolph, and a publisher brought it out as a hardcover book. Then in 1949, Johnny Marks, a composer, wrote his now-famous song. Several vocalists turned down chances to record it, but Gene Autry liked it and recorded it for Columbia Records. The record rocketed to the top of the hit parade. Since then more than 300 different arrangements of the hit song have been recorded; millions have seen Rudolph as an animated cartoon and in a comic strip that became syndicated in twenty-five countries.

In capsule form the story of how Rudolph came to Christmas is the story of social change, even to the matter of encountering resistance. A new item or behavior is introduced to a group—an **innovation**. The trait then spreads from one social unit to another—**diffusion**.

INNOVATION

If the works of the great poets teach anything, it is to hold mere invention somewhat cheap. It is not the finding of a thing, but the making something out of it after it is found, that is of consequence.

James Russell Lowell, My Study Windows, 1871

In earlier chapters, we observed that people develop and acquire common understandings or definitions of how to act in this or that situation—culture. These understandings or definitions provide sets of ready-made blueprints for action. Yet in all societies—especially modern societies—it is common for situations to arise in which cultural guideposts are absent, ill-defined, or even in conflict with one another. For instance, by virtue of our involvement in a great variety of different groups—with their associated subcultures and countercultures—we often differ in our perceptions and interpretations of a situation (sales taxes, abortion, high defense budgets, and so on); we cut out different things in the situation, or give different weight to the things we note, or piece things together in different patterns (Blumer, 1962). Moreover, in the course of social interaction we continually arrive at new working arrangements. Each arrangement is never a total replica of that which went before, if only because of "the something that went before." Hence, for one reason or another, existing culture does not always provide an effective map for carrying out action. Social change often results when new situations compel people to construct new forms of action.

Cultural Base. Innovations generally are not a single act but a cumulative series of transmitted increments plus a series of new elements. Thus, the invention of the automobile involved a new combination of six old elements: a liquid gas engine, a liquid gas receptacle, a running-gear mechanism, an

Figure 11.1. Mechanical invention as a combination of known elements.

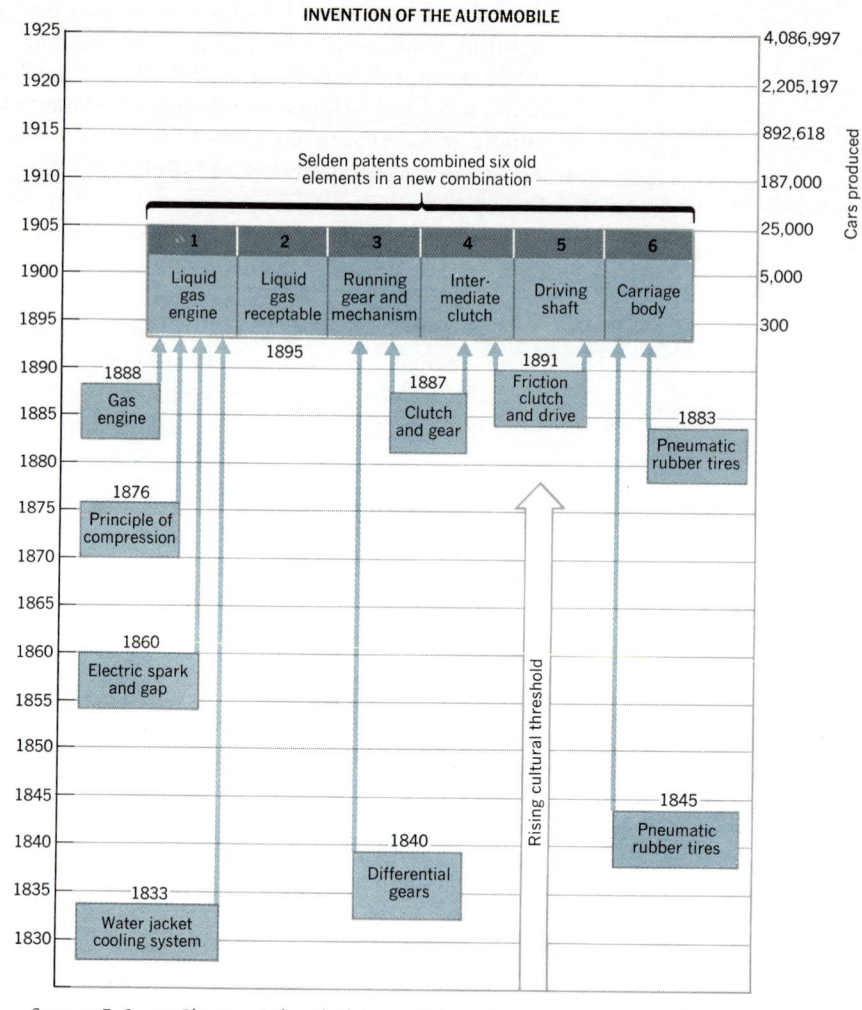

INVENTION OF THE AUTOMOBILE

[Chart showing timeline from 1830 to 1925 on left axis, and Cars produced on right axis: 300, 5,000, 25,000, 187,000, 892,618, 2,205,197, 4,086,997]

Selden patents combined six old elements in a new combination:

1. Liquid gas engine
2. Liquid gas receptacle
3. Running gear and mechanism
4. Intermediate clutch
5. Driving shaft
6. Carriage body

1895
1891 Friction clutch and drive
1888 Gas engine
1887 Clutch and gear
1883 Pneumatic rubber tires
1876 Principle of compression
1860 Electric spark and gap
1845 Pneumatic rubber tires
1840 Differential gears
1833 Water jacket cooling system

Rising cultural threshold

Source: F. Stuart Chapin, *Cultural Change* (New York: Appleton-Century-Crofts, Inc., 1928), 336. By permission.

intermediate clutch, a drive shaft, and a carriage body. (See Figure 11.1) The same holds true with regard to nonmaterial aspects of culture such as the commission form of government. (See Figure 11.2)

The greater the number of cultural elements on which innovators may draw, the greater the frequency of discovery and invention. The more elements within the cultural repertory, the more combinations of old elements or the more reapplications of old elements become possible:

> The "cave-man inventor" had at his command only a limited number of elements—his own body, with his hands, its sense organs, its brain

Figure 11.2. Social invention as a combination of known elements. The commission form of government, invented in Galveston in 1900, was a combination of previously existing elements. It evolved into the Houston plan in 1905, and into the Des Moines plan in 1908.

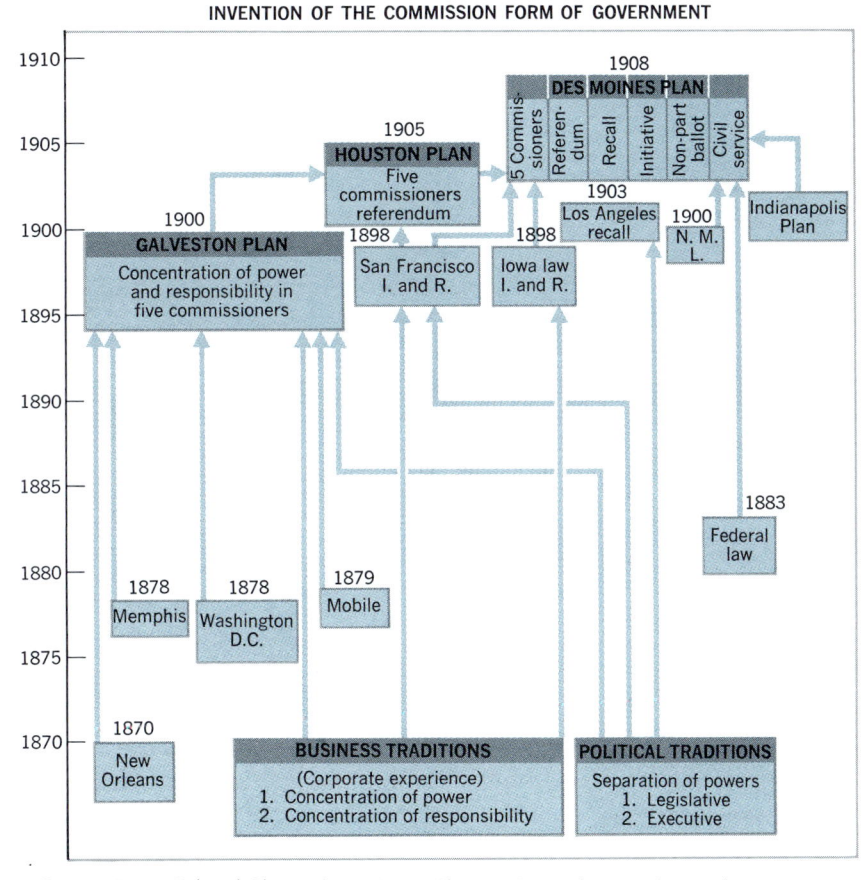

INVENTION OF THE COMMISSION FORM OF GOVERNMENT

Source: From *Cultural Change* by F. Stuart Chapin. Copyright 1928 by Appleton-Century-Crofts, Inc. Reprinted by permission of the publisher.

and the like. He had also clay, water, branches of trees, and stones of various kinds. . . . Now let us jump suddenly from the cave-man inventor to the modern research team at work in its laboratory. Instead of a limited variety of sticks, stones, hides, and mud, the modern man has at his command practically all the chemical elements in purified form and a nearly endless variety of chemical compounds, plastics, textiles, metal alloys, cutting tools, machines to control temperature, sources of almost limitless energy, and instruments for almost unlimited magnification of his sensory powers. (Hart, 1957, p. 49)

Further, modern inventors have access to written language and hundreds of thousands of elaborately indexed books and scientific articles.

The importance of the cultural inventory is seen in the fate of innovations that lacked necessary antecedents. The Greeks of the Hellenistic period knew the principle of the steam engine, but it was used only in a toy. Since

Institutional change. Industrialization has been a major source of change throughout the world. This worker is employed in a large textile mill in Khartoum, Sudan.

United Nations

they lacked industrialization, there was no background in their culture to which it might be referred. Leonardo da Vinci in the late fifteenth century sketched many machines that were quite workable in principle, but the technology of his day was inadequate for building them. One of these was the airplane, but the subsidiary inventions that go with the airplane were lacking—for instance, the internal combustion engine, metal alloys, fuels, and lubricants.

As the cultural base increases, its possible uses tend to grow in geometric ratio—the *exponential principle*. Glass, for instance, gave birth to costume jewelry, drinking goblets, windowpanes, lenses, test tubes, X-ray tubes, light bulbs, radio and television tubes, mirrors, and many other products. Lenses in turn gave birth to eyeglasses, magnifying glasses, telescopes, cameras, searchlights, and so on. Just as a prolific couple gives birth to descendants who may multiply geometrically, so a pregnant invention may bring forth a geometrically increasingly number of progeny (Hart, 1957).

Individual Genius. The role of the "great man or woman" in history has been debated many times. Writers like Carlyle and Nietzsche never tired of praising the "hero" in the unfolding drama of human life. Indeed, what would the world be like had there not been a Thomas Jefferson, a Karl Marx, a Catherine the Great, a Sigmund Freud, a Thomas Edison, or a William Shakespeare? This raises the intriguing question as to whether a given person makes history or history makes the person. It has been noted, for instance, that America's most renowned presidents—Washington and Lincoln, not to mention others—have been war presidents and it has been asked whether they would have been equally great if they had lived during another period. Others point out that ideas are not self-innovating and technology is not self-inventing. Somehow the innovator disturbs the stream of culture and, like a stone tossed into a pond, its ripples continue endlessly.

Still others have taken a different position and have argued that a culture contains the germs of a future that unrolls with little regard for the will of its carriers. William F. Ogburn and Dorothy Thomas (1922) have attempted to document the hypothesis of the inevitability of cultural change with an impressive list of discoveries and inventions within many fields. Their study and a number of others make this point—if a given invention or discovery had not been made by the person or persons who actually did make it, the logic of the developing culture would have resulted in someone else having made it. The multiplicity of duplicate inventions and discoveries is cited as evidence of the fact. Ogburn argues that the accumulated evidence for a theory of biological evolution was readily at hand in the middle of the nineteenth century: "So also the theory of evolution and natural selection would have been developed even if Wallace and Darwin had never lived" (Ogburn, 1926: 233). Drawing on the histories of astronomy, mathematics, chemistry, physics, electricity, physiology, biology, psychology, and practical mechanical inventions during the last few centuries, Ogburn (1922) found 148 examples of multiple inventions, including the following:

Discovery of the planet Neptune	By Adams (1845)
	Leverrier (1845)
Discovery of oxygen	By Scheele (1774)
	Priestley (1774)
Logarithms	By Napier-Briggs (1614)
	Burgi (1620)
Photography	By Daguerre-Niepe (1839)
	Talbot (1839)
Kinetic theory of gases	By Clausius (1850)
	Rankine (1850)

Discovery of sunspots	By Galileo (1611)
	Fabricius (1611)
	Scheiner (1611)
	Harriott (1611)
Laws of heredity	By Mendel (1865)
	DeVries (1900)
	Correns (1900)
	Tschermak (1900)
Reaper	By Hussey (1833)
	McCormick (1833)
Telegraph	By Henry (1831)
	Morse (1837)
	Cooke-Wheatstone (1837)
	Steinheil (1837)
Balloon	By Montgolfier (1783)
	Rittenhouse-Hopkins (1783)

The matter of the duplication of inventions and discoveries is not simply a matter of history, but an ever present, living reality. Scientists, sharing as they do a common cultural base and exposed to the common demands of the age in which they live, continuously find themselves working in situations where, after they have started work on a problem, another scientist "scoops" them and publishes the problem's solution. As a consequence scientists find themselves in a highly competitive situation. Research Study 17 deals with this matter, detailing data on the frequency with which scientists find themselves anticipated by other scientists and the consequences that the ensuing competition has for scientific advancement.

RESEARCH STUDY 17

COMPETITION IN SCIENCE*
Warren O. Hagstrom

Problem. Physical and biological scientists conduct their research in a highly competitive setting. They are confronted with being anticipated—"scooped." This happens on occasion when a scientist undertakes research on a problem only to find—perhaps when he or she has essentially solved it—that another scientist publishes a solution before he or she does. Warren O. Hagstrom considers this matter of scientific competition, addressing himself to a number of issues, including the following:

1. How often (with what frequency) do scientists find that after they have undertaken research on a problem, another scientist publishes its solution (scoops them)?
2. What is the likelihood of a scientist getting a work published if it has been anticipated?
3. Is the experience of being scooped more common in disciplines characterized by logically rigorous empirical theories and the wide diffusion of research skills and equipment than in disciplines lacking these characteristics?
4. What (if any) relationship exists between scientists' research productivity and the frequency with which they are anticipated?
5. What are some of the consequences of competition for science?

Method. Hagstrom derived probability samples of mathematicians and statisticians, physicists, chemists, and biologists in American universities offering graduate degrees in these fields. Probability samples are designed so that those selected are chosen automatically (for instance, every third name in a directory of scientists) with no personal discretion being exercised by the investigator. Mailed questionnaires and follow-up telephone interviews resulted in an 89 percent response, providing a sample of 1947 scientists. Additional information on careers and the frequency with which scientists' professional papers were cited was gained from *American Men and Women of Science* and the *Science Citation Index*.

Findings. Scientists in the sample were asked: "Scientists are sometimes anticipated by others in the presentation of research findings. That is, after they have started work on a problem, another scientist publishes its solution. How often has this happened to you in your career?" The data con-

Continued on next page.

---

* Adapted from Warren O. Hagstrom, "Competition in Science," *American Sociological Review,* 39 (1974), 1–18.

Figure 11.3. Frequency with which scientists report having been anticipated in a scientific discovery in entire career, by field.

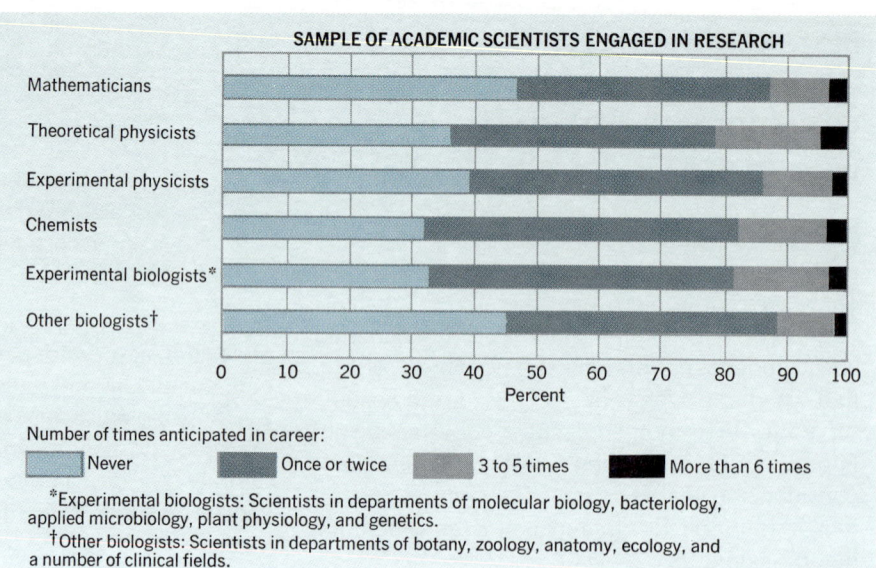

SAMPLE OF ACADEMIC SCIENTISTS ENGAGED IN RESEARCH

Number of times anticipated in career:
Never | Once or twice | 3 to 5 times | More than 6 times

*Experimental biologists: Scientists in departments of molecular biology, bacteriology, applied microbiology, plant physiology, and genetics.
†Other biologists: Scientists in departments of botany, zoology, anatomy, ecology, and a number of clinical fields.

Source: Adapted from Warren O. Hagstrom, "Competition in Science," *American Sociological Review*, 39 (1974), 3, Table 1.

tained in Figure 11.3 reveal that over three-fifths of the scientists had been anticipated—17 percent, more often than twice.

One index of the severity of scientific competition is whether a paper is published if it has been anticipated. The data reveal that in at least a majority of cases, the work is accepted for publication, although the chances are less in mathematics and theoretical physics—disciplines in which the experimental replication of studies is less important. One reason a paper is published even if it has been anticipated is that competitors seldom approach a problem in an identical manner; moreover, when a discovery occurs, those who have been anticipated see the implications of the discovery in somewhat different terms.

Hagstrom speculated that the incidence of competition would be most marked in fields where scientists agree on the relative importance of scientific problems and where many of them are able to solve these problems. It followed, he believed, that the experience of being scooped would be most common in fields characterized by logically rigorous empirical theories and a wide diffusion of research skills and equipment, for instance, physics and chemistry. (Mathematics, in contrast, is characterized by an infinite number of possible mathematical systems and vague and noncompelling criteria for calling some systems more important than others.) He found, however, that his data lent little support for this speculation. Nor did he find support for the hypothesis that mathematicians and theoretical physicists (scientists in fields in which an individual is less likely to find a publisher for a paper if anticipated and hence fields where competition would be most intense) would be more concerned with being anticipated than scientists in other fields.

Which scientists are most likely to be anticipated? Large correlations existed between measures of research productivity (those who published a good deal and whose publications were cited often) and frequency of anticipation. On the other hand, concern with being anticipated was most frequent among young scientists and those who previously had been anticipated.

Figure 11.4. Secretive behavior by concern about anticipation among a sample of scientists engaged in research.

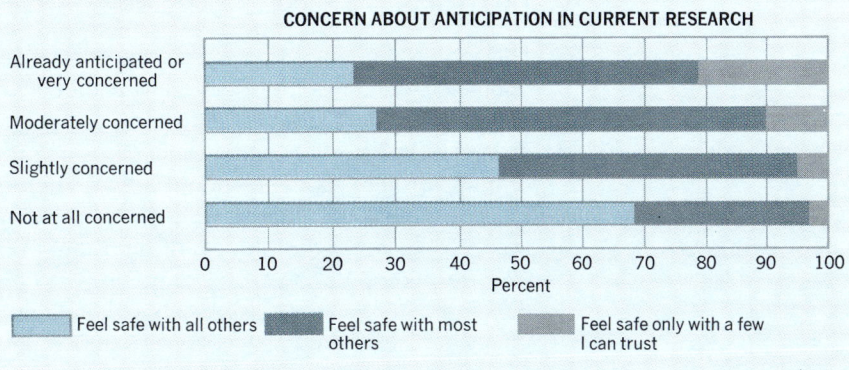

CONCERN ABOUT ANTICIPATION IN CURRENT RESEARCH

[Bar chart showing percent distribution across four categories: Already anticipated or very concerned; Moderately concerned; Slightly concerned; Not at all concerned. Horizontal axis: Percent, 0 to 100. Legend: Feel safe with all others; Feel safe with most others; Feel safe only with a few I can trust.]

Source: Adapted from Warren O. Hagstrom, "Competition in Science," *American Sociological Review*, 39 (1974), 9, Table 6.

What are the consequences of competition for science? The competitive environment places many scientists under stress. Some respond by publishing their partial findings quickly, rather than dropping the bombshell of a totally solved problem on their colleagues at a later time. Others (6 percent) said they switched specialties because they felt too many scientists were conducting research in their area (among those very or moderately concerned with being anticipated, 26 percent considered change; in comparison, among those not at all concerned, only 10 percent considered switching specialties). Still others gravitate to the most competitive specialties since these are often the very ones that offer promise of the greatest recognition (they provide the potential for discoveries deemed most important in the scientific community). In this latter regard, Hagstrom asked respondents, "How do most scientists in your discipline regard your primary specialty with respect to its importance for the future development of the discipline?" and took the proportion who responded that their specialty was more important than the others. The measures of importance had a correlation of .37 with the incidence of anticipation; the correlation of .37, while not large, was in the expected direction (correlation coefficients vary from no relationship, .00, to a direct and total relationship, 1.00).

Still another consequence of competition was secrecy. Hagstrom asked scientists in his sample, "Would you feel quite safe in discussing your current research with other persons doing similar work in other institutions?" Although most indicated they would feel safe with all others, this proportion was greatly reduced as concern with being scooped increased (see Figure 11.4). To the extent competition breeds secrecy, it tends to isolate the scientist, take some of the fun out of science, and impair the receipt of valuable feedback from other scientists. Moreover, it results in duplication of effort and a decline in solidarity in the scientific community.

Conclusion. Although one might conclude that competition results in inefficient operation within the scientific community, Hagstrom concludes this is not so. He argues the competition leading to anticipation and cases of independent multiple invention are functional since they assure that discoveries vital to scientific growth will in fact be made. Moreover, independent multiple invention speeds the process—shortens the time—whereby the new discovery is incorporated into the body of scientific knowledge. And it may also speed the publication of new discoveries: the world may have had to wait many years for Charles Darwin to publish his findings on natural selection had he not been moved to publish in 1858 by the competition of Alfred Wallace.

DIFFUSION

Diffusion is the process by which culture traits spread from one social unit to another. Sometimes a distinction is made between the circulation of a trait within a society—primary diffusion—and circulation between societies—secondary diffusion. In either event diffusion ordinarily refers to a movement of traits through space. It should not be confused with the transmission of traits through time—that is, from one generation to the next. The spread of tobacco illustrates the process of diffusion. Tobacco spread from the New World to Europe and Africa, from Europe to the South Seas and Asia, and then from Siberia into Alaska. Although Indians 1000 miles away had native tobacco, it had to travel some 15,000 miles around the world before Eskimos acquired it.

Each culture contains a minimum of traits and patterns unique to it or actually invented by it. It is easy, for example, to minimize America's debt to other cultures. We point with pride to what other people have acquired from us, yet we often neglect to note what we gained from them. As an illustration, consider the following account of the cultural content of a "100 percent" American written as satire by a distinguished anthropologist, Ralph Linton:

> . . . dawn finds the unsuspecting patriot garbed in pajamas, a garment of East Indian origin; and lying in a bed built on a pattern which originated in either Persia or Asia Minor. He is muffled to the ears in un-American materials: cotton, first domesticated in India; linen, domesticated in the Near East; wool from an animal native to Asia Minor; or silk whose uses were first discovered by the Chinese. . . .
>
> If our patriot is old-fashioned enough to adhere to the so-called American breakfast, his coffee will be accompanied by an orange, domesticated in the Mediterranean region. . . . He will follow this with a bowl of cereal made from grain domesticated in the Near East. . . . As a side dish he may have the egg of a bird domesticated in Southeastern Asia or strips of the flesh of an animal domesticated in the same region. . . . (Linton, 1937, pp. 427–429)

We frequently overlook the fact that diffusion is a two-way process. Many think this inconceivable, as in the case of the American Indian. Yet we owe to the Indian our knowledge of the potato, the tomato, the peanut, chocolate, squash, maple sugar, the pineapple, the avocado, and about thirty-five other food plants. Had Indians not domesticated these plants it is doubtful whether Whites would have, for they would probably have introduced the crops with which they were already familiar in the Old World. But these contributions do not exhaust the list. From Indians, Whites learned much about the art of woodcraft, various medicinal plants (cascara, witch hazel, cocaine, quinine), canoes, snowshoes, toboggans, moccasins, hammocks, and rubber. Moreover, no less than 500 words in the English language were appropriated from Indian tongues (Berry, 1958).

Factors Influencing Diffusion. Much of what we have said for innovation holds true for diffusion. Take the matter of an adequate cultural base. Obviously the automobile cannot be introduced to a society in the absence of adequate roads, gasoline stations, skilled repair personnel, complex repair equipment, parts for replacement, and the like.

Everett M. Rogers (1962; Rogers and Burdge, 1972) has studied the diffusion and adoption of a wide variety of innovations ranging from new drugs to hybrid corn to new educational programs. He identifies five characteristics of innovations that influence whether or not people will adopt them. First, people must view the innovation as affording some advantage relative to their current situation (Hamblin and Miller, 1976). Second, people are more likely to adopt an innovation if it is compatible with their existing value system (for instance, a new method of birth control is unlikely to be accepted if it runs counter to religious tradition). Third, people are influenced by the notions that they have regarding the complexity of the innovation (for example, the IUD has found greater acceptance in India as a method of birth control than the rhythm method because it demands little attention from users). Fourth, people initially prefer to adopt innovations on a trial basis (for instance, farmers are more likely to try a new seed variety if they first can try it out on a limited portion of their acreage). And fifth, adoption rates are influenced by the extent to which people can readily observe the effects of an innovation (for example, the more easily an innovation can be demonstrated or explained, the more likely it is to be adopted).

Networks of Relationships. In considering the process of diffusion, it is also important that we consider the network of relationships that exists among people. Factors that affect people's relationships have vast consequences for the fate of new patterns (Lin and Burt, 1975; Brieger, 1976; Hunt and Chambers, 1976; Mullins, Hargens, Hecht, and Kick, 1977). The significance of this matter is highlighted by a study undertaken by James Coleman, Elihu Katz, and Herbert Menzel (1957, 1959), which deals with the diffusion of a new drug among physicians (summarized in Research Study 18). The researchers found that those physicians who were most involved in interpersonal relations with their local colleagues typically introduced the new drug into their practices a number of months before their relatively isolated colleagues. The evidence suggests that this outcome was the product of a contagion-like process in which use of the new drug was passed from doctor to doctor.

RESEARCH STUDY 18

THE DIFFUSION OF AN INNOVATION AMONG PHYSICIANS*

James Coleman, Elihu Katz, and Herbert Menzel

Problem. In recent decades, the practice of medicine has undergone profound changes. During this period, there has appeared a large variety of new diagnostic techniques, new laboratory tests, new drugs, new forms of anesthesia, new surgical procedures, and new principles of patient management. Some of these innovations have been short lived or quickly superseded; others have constituted milestones in medical science. Yet observations such as these merely provide us with a historical record of change. They tell us nothing about the actual pathways by which a successful innovation spreads through the medical profession. Accordingly, James Coleman, Elihu Katz, and Herbert Menzel undertook the present study as a contribution to our understanding of the process whereby physicians adopt a medical innovation.

Method. The researchers investigated the fate of a single innovation in four Midwestern cities, a new variant in a well-established family of drugs. The data for the study came from two sources:

1. The researchers conducted interviews with 125 general practitioners, internists, and pediatricians, 85 percent of the doctors who were practicing in these fields in the four cities. Each of the doctors was asked three sociometric questions: To whom did he/she most often turn for advice and information? With whom did he/she most often discuss his/her cases in the course of an ordinary week? Who were the friends, among his/her colleagues, whom he/she saw most often socially? In answer to each of these questions, the researchers requested the names of three doctors. On the basis of the doctors' responses, it was possible to construct sociograms of the discussion networks, friendship networks, and advisor networks existing among the doctors of each city (see Figure 11.5).

2. Coleman, Katz, and Menzel secured data on the prescriptions written by these 125 physicians from local pharmacies. The prescription data covered a period of sixteen months beginning with the release date of the new drug. In this manner, the researchers were able to determine the month during which each doctor first used the drug.

Findings. The broad question that Coleman, Katz, and Menzel had investigated was this: How does the social structure existing among the physicians of a city facilitate or inhibit the diffusion of a new drug? Probably the simplest question that could be asked in this connection was what was the difference in the rate of drug adoptions between doctors who have contact with many and with few colleagues? More specifically: What is the difference in the rate of drug adoptions between doctors who are named as advisors (or as discussion partners or as friends) by many of their fellow doc-

---

*Adapted from James Coleman, Elihu Katz, and Herbert Menzel, "The Diffusion of an Innovation Among Physicians," *Sociometry*, 20 (1957), 253–70, and "Social Processes in Physicians' Adoptions of a New Drug," *The Journal of Chronic Diseases*, 9 (1959), 1–19.

Figure 11.5. Sociogram of the discussion network among physicians in City D. Each circle represents a physician, who is identified by a code number. An arrow pointing from Circle 10 to Circle 21 means that Dr. 10 named Dr. 21 as one of his three most frequent discussion partners. The double-headed arrow connecting Circle 31 and Circle 27 means that Dr. 31 and Dr. 27 each named the other as a frequent partner in the discussion of cases. The fact that seven arrows point to Circle 31 indicates that seven different doctors named Dr. 31 as a frequent discussion partner.

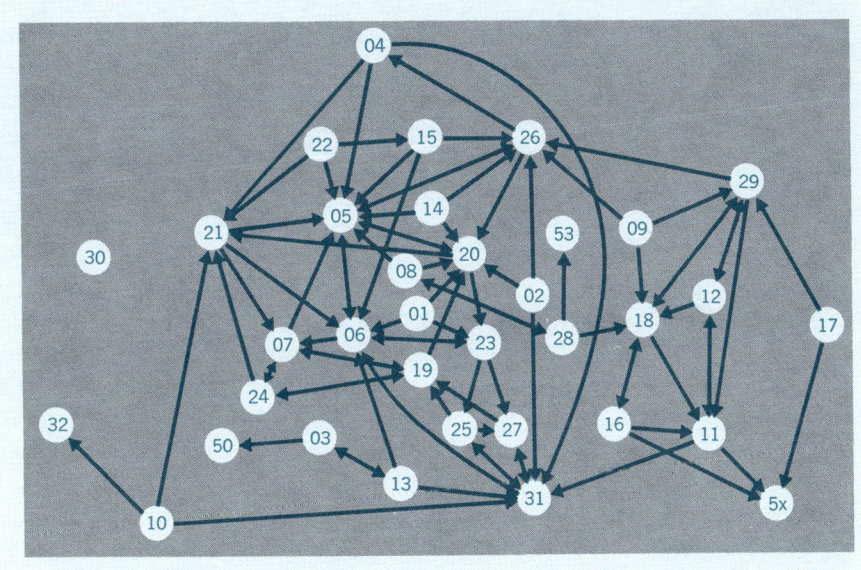

Source: Adapted from James Coleman, Elihu Katz, and Herbert Menzel, "The diffusion of an innovation among physicians," *Sociometry,* 20 (1957): 230–270, and "Social processes in physicians' adoptions of a new drug," *The Journal of Chronic Diseases,* 9 (1959): 1–19.

tors and those who are not named by any? The first group were considered to be socially integrated doctors; the second group, socially isolated doctors. Highly integrated doctors (those named four times or more as advisors or three times or more as discussion partners or friends) were much quicker to introduce the new drug than the more isolated doctors. Doctors frequently mentioned as advisors introduced the new drug on the average 3.1 months before those never named as advisors. Similarly, highly integrated discussion partners introduced the new drug on the average 4.1 months before isolated doctors; highly integrated friends, on the average 4.3 months before isolated doctors. Hence, the researchers found that doctors who maintained a variety of contacts with a large number of colleagues typically introduced the new drug into their practices a number of months before their relatively isolated colleagues.

Other evidence served to reinforce the above finding. Among the integrated doctors, the new drug spread at an accelerating rate (for instance, if one doctor introduced the new drug and converted a colleague to it during the first month,

Continued on next page.

there then would be two doctors—double the previous number—to convert other doctors during the second month; these new converts in turn would convert still other doctors during the third month, and so on in a snowballing fashion). This fact indicated that an *interpersonal process of diffusion* had occurred among the integrated doctors. In contrast, the use of the new drug spread among isolated doctors at a constant rate (the number of doctors introducing the new drug each month remained a relatively constant percentage of those who had not already adopted the drug). This suggested that there occurred among the isolated doctors largely individual responses to constant stimuli (advertising from drug companies, professional journals, and the like) outside the immediate community of doctors.

The greatest effectiveness in contacts with colleagues occurred during the *early* months, after which interpersonal relations played at best a minimal part in a doctor's adoption of the new drug. Coleman, Katz, and Menzel explain this fact in these terms: It is in the early months after a drug's appearance that doctors especially need the support and judgment of their colleagues. At this time, the drug is new, and doctors seek from their colleagues confirmation of their own judgment. Moreover, doctors can feel that, if their decision to use the new drug proves to be wrong, their responsibility is shared with other doctors. In this early period, familiarity with the new drug is minimal, and doctors find themselves in an uncertain situation. Other experiments—such as that by Muzafer Sherif with the autokinetic effect (reported in Chapter 6)—shows that it is precisely in objectively unclear situations that people need and seek a validation of their own judgment. The first months following the release of a new drug apparently confronts doctors with this kind of unstructured situation. This interpretation was confirmed by further data from another aspect of the study, which revealed that pairs of sociometrically related doctors were more likely to follow similar treatments in uncertain situations (diseases that allow many kinds of treatment and where their success can be gauged only slowly and with difficulty, for example, hypertension) than in clear-cut situations (diseases that allow few alternatives of treatment and where their success or failure becomes quickly apparent, for instance, respiratory infections).

Conclusions. This study by Coleman, Katz, and Menzel demonstrates how social structure (the web of social relationships existing among a group of people) affects the diffusion of an innovation.

REWORKING AND REINTERPRETATION

He who desires or attempts to reform the government of a state, and wishes to have it accepted and capable of maintaining itself to the satisfaction of everybody, must at least retain the semblance of the old forms; so that it may seem to the people that there has been no change in the institutions, even though in fact they are entirely different from the old ones.

Niccolò Machiavelli, Discourses on the First Ten Books of Titus Livius

Culture is not an indiscriminate mixture of cultural traits. Many early anthropologists made the error of viewing culture as so loosely knit together that the main theoretical task of cultural analysis consisted in disentangling the various elements from their matrix and showing whence they came. Culture was seen as just so many patches and shreds. Increasingly we have come to realize that the parts comprising culture are closely interwoven in such a fashion that a change in one part has consequences for other parts and for the whole. Hence in viewing diffusion it is essential that we view the units of transformation not as single traits but as larger systems or institutions.

The modification of a cultural trait may take the form of **syncretism**—the blending or fusing of the trait with an analogous element in a culture. Thus the Malagasy of Madagascar had to convert Christian saints into the ancestor-idols of their own religion before they could accept them:

> When Catholic missionaries first began to work in Madagascar the natives were much puzzled by the phenomenon of saints. Supernatural associations were at once established, partly by the missionaries' observed attitudes and behavior toward the saintly images, partly because the Malagasy themselves had images which were associated with their ancestor worship. However, the Christian concept of the nature and function of saints had no native parallel. The Malagasy finally concluded that the new figures represented the ancestors of the Europeans. These ancestors were, of course, primarily interested in the well-being of their descendants, but would help non-relatives in return for a suitable fee. Having thus rationalized and brought within the scope of native concepts of the supernatural, their worship was taken up with considerable enthusiasm. (Linton, 1940, p. 477)

As long ago as the year 601, Pope Gregory I recognized the importance of linking old cultural forms with new cultural forms in order to initiate new patterns of behavior. At that time, the Church had been attempting to convert the "heathen" Britons, and two of the missionaries, finding that they were encountering little success, wrote to Rome for advice. The Pope responded:

> We must refrain from destroying the temples of the idols. It is necessary only to destroy the idols, and to sprinkle holy water in these same temples, to build ourselves altars and place holy relics therein. If the construction of these temples is solid, good, and useful, they will pass from the cult of demons to the service of the true God; because it will come to pass that the nation, seeing the continued existence of its old places of devotion, will be disposed, by a sort of habit, to go there to adore the true God.
>
> It is said that the men of this nation are accustomed to sacrificing oxen. It is necessary that this custom be converted into a Christian rite. . . . They shall bring to the churches their animals, and kill them, no longer as offerings to the devil, but for Christian banquets in name and honor of God. (Quoted by Whyte, 1961, p. 36)

Similarly, the Church Fathers, rather than fighting "pagan" festivals, often sought to adapt them to the new faith. Hence the feast of Christmas is observed on December 25, not because this is the actual birthday of Jesus, but because December 25 was already held sacred throughout the Roman Empire as the Birthday of the Unconquered Sun.

SOCIAL CHANGE UNDER PRESSURE

Implicit in much of our discussion of institutional change has been the assumption that a people are relatively free to accept or reject a new pattern or trait. What happens, however, when this is not the case? It is to this matter that we now turn our attention, with a consideration of social change under pressure among the Hausa of Nigeria.

In 1928, a British medical team investigating the Anchau area of northern Nigeria discovered that sleeping sickness had reached epidemic proportions. In some areas, up to 40 percent of the people suffered from the disease.

> Interesting, the epidemic was an indirect result of the advent of *Pax Britannica*. Before the conquest of northern Nigeria in 1903, the area was in a state of turbulence as a result of incessant slave raids. Towns were heavily walled and the working of fields at any distance from the towns involved considerable risk. Large areas of the countryside were uninhabited and communication was limited. Although there was an area of endemic sleeping sickness to the south and tsetse flies [the vehicle by which the disease is often transmitted] were prevalent all over the North at this time, the disease remained localized. With the establishment of peace, farmers moved out into the bush and mobility increased generally. The increased fly-man contact soon produced the epidemic. (Miner, 1960, p. 154)

Entomologists discovered that the tsetse fly can only live in a relatively cool environment such as that generally prevailing along shaded banks of streams. Tests revealed that, if the brush were chopped down along the streams, the fly could not persist in the area. On the basis of these findings, British officials, ruling "indirectly" through local emirs, ordered that the job be undertaken. In turn, the emirs issued commands to their subordinates. And then the trouble began.

The British overlooked certain features of Hausa culture: the peasants believed that malevolent spirits inhabited certain patches of brush; sacred spirits in still others. They did not share with the British the same definition of sleeping sickness; they identified the illness solely with its most severe form, total somnolence, rather than with its more common symptoms of sporadic fever, headache, edema of the face and limbs, and persistent weak-

A Southeastern Asian employing an outboard motor with a traditional native craft. Items of material culture generally find more ready acceptance than nonmaterial items since their use is more readily seen and they are viewed as having fewer implications for other areas of life.

Courtesy of Exxon Corporation

ness. The peasants believed that evil spirits caused the disease and that it was highly contagious. Further, individuals afflicted with the disease were completely isolated, even from their families; consequently, the victims were loath to admit they had the disease.

Because they did not take the Hausa beliefs into account, the British failed in their attempts to educate the peasantry. In some cases, the people refused to cut down the flies' shelter along the streams. Finally, the British imported non-Hausa natives from the French Sudan to cut the sacred brush. Once the streams were cleared, annual slashings thereafter were secured through stringent measures: headmen who did not cooperate were removed from office, and fines were imposed on noncooperative peasants. After years of struggle, the British seemingly won, and sleeping sickness disappeared from Anchau.

Yet, even in 1957, when sociologist Horace Miner (1960) returned to the region and questioned villagers, he found basic attitudes unchanged. The Hausa continued to cut down the flies' cover, but only under orders from the emirs, now freed of British rule. A quarter of the village headmen had no idea whatsoever why the emirs wanted them to do the work. When Miner asked the headmen if they would continue to clear the streams if they were not forced to do so, *every* headman replied, "No." Both the British and Nigerian elites had failed to integrate effectively the new program of stream clearance with the local problems and beliefs of the Hausa. Coercion produced compliance without any fundamental cultural alteration. Again and again, those concerned with modernization in the new nations of Asia and Africa encounter replicas of the Hausa situation, not just in the field of health, but also in agricultural change, industrialization, and the initiation of new fiscal policies.

RESISTANCE TO CHANGE

It is demonstrable that many of the obstacles to change which have been attributed to human nature are in fact due to the inertia of institutions and the voluntary desire of powerful classes to maintain the existing status.

John Dewey, Monthly Review, March, 1950

As we noted earlier in the chapter, no sociocultural system is static or constant; change is continuous. Yet even while culture changes, in whole or part, it persists as a recognizable entity over long periods of time. This fact of cultural tenacity has intrigued many sociologists and anthropologists (Zucker, 1977).

Anthropologists report many instances of cultural persistence. Laura Thompson (1948) found that, although Dakota Indian rituals were officially banned from 1881 to 1933, a period during which far-reaching changes occurred in the technology and social life of the Dakotas, in 1942, 100 percent of the adolescents in one community and 92 percent in another retained the traditional Dakota cosmological dogma. The aboriginal Dakotas had conceived of the world as pervaded by a great and mysterious power. In order to win this power, they had to humble themselves ritually in supplication. Sixty years after the official banning of Dakota rituals, the children still believed that a principle of immanent justice operated in the world. But lacking rituals to supplicate this power, the children displayed much insecurity and anxiety and perceived the world as a dangerous place.

Closely associated with cultural persistence is resistance to change. But resistance should not be confused with persistence; the former is not simply a product of the latter. **Resistance** implies behavior on the part of some or all of the members of society, either passive or active, that is directed toward the rejection or circumvention of change.

That innovations often meet with opposition is well known. There were, for instance, many precursors of the modern automobile that failed to survive the opposition and apathy of their times. A three-wheeler carriage driven by two steam cylinders was invented by Joseph Cugnot in 1769 and actually moved a load in addition to its own weight. By 1860, by virtue of further developments, it appeared that mechanical transportation had come to stay in England. But the opposition of horse breeders and railroads stood in the way. They secured passage of an act of Parliament in 1861 that practically made it impossible for horseless vehicles to operate. The act provided that tires had to be at least 3 inches wide, that engines had to consume their own smoke, that each vehicle had to have at least two drivers, and that no vehicle was to exceed 10 miles an hour in the country and 5 miles an hour in towns. In 1865, the act was made even more drastic. Three drivers were required for each vehicle, one of whom had to precede the carriage at a distance of 60 yards, carrying a red flag by day and a red lantern by night. Speed was reduced to 4 miles an hour in the country and 2 miles an hour in towns, and local communities were given the right to tax the operation of vehicles and to prescribe hours of operation, which they did in a discriminatory manner. These restrictions doomed the steam-driven vehicle until their repeal in 1896 (Stern, 1937).

SUMMARY

1. Our existence as social beings confronts us with a variety of perennial problems. Institutions afford the established answers to these recurring problems. They are the principal instruments whereby the essential tasks of social living are organized, directed, and executed. Each institution is built about a standardized solution to a set of problems and we classify institutions on this basis.

2. The essence of life is the interrelatedness of its various components and their ties to the larger whole. We cannot fully understand a phenomenon in the social world without considering it in terms of its inner and external relationships and its developmental history. Thus institutions do not exist in isolation from one another. Rather they are bound together within a complex web of interrelationships.

3. The interrelatedness of social life finds expression in many theories, including the structure-function and Marxist approaches. Not uncommonly such interlocking is described and analyzed in terms of a system. A system is a complex of elements or components that are related to each other in a more or less stable fashion through a period of time. System analysis focuses on the particular association or mode of interaction that occurs between the parts of a substance or entity. It is the distinctive interaction that takes place between the lower-level components that gives a substance or entity its unique properties or characteristics.

4. Within system analysis, considerable attention is frequently paid to the various functions performed by a system's parts. Functions are those observed consequences that allow for the adaptation or adjustment of a given system. Our concern with the functions of the various parts of society should not lead us to overlook their dysfunctions. Dysfunctions are those observed consequences that lessen the adaptation or adjustment of the system.

5. Sociologists have also found it useful to distinguish between manifest functions and latent functions. Manifest functions are those consequences that are intended and recognized by the participants in a system; latent functions are those consequences that are neither intended nor recognized.

6. Sociologists employ multiple models for studying social life. For some purposes, they find it useful to focus on "being," that is, on an "instantaneous snapshot" or cross section of a phenomenon in time. A structure-function model is well-suited to this purpose. For other purposes, they focus on "behaving," that is, on those transient and reversible—often repetitive—aspects of life. A system's model appears well suited to this purpose. For still other purposes, they focus on "becoming," that is, on the irreversible, developing, and changing aspects of life. For this purpose a process model seems to be a particularly useful tool. Each model calls our attention to problems and data that might be overlooked by the other models.

7. Continuous change occurs in all societies. However, the rate of change varies a great deal from one society to another, and even from one period to another within any given society. Alvin Toffler believes that as super-industrialism advances, people experience "future shock"—they find themselves increasingly incapable of coping with the rapidity of change. However, other social scientists point out that the perceived desirability or undesirability of change is the crucial factor influencing whether or not change generates psychic disorder. Sociologists also note that the rate of change in various segments of a society may be uneven resulting in social dislocation, a process termed cultural lag.

8. Social change is associated with innovation

and diffusion. Innovation involves the introduction of a new item or behavior to a group. Diffusion is the process by which traits spread from one social unit to another. Among the factors influencing innovation and diffusion are the size of the cultural base, values and norms that permit or inhibit new cultural patterns, and the network of relationships that exists among people.

9. Culture is not an indiscriminate mixture of cultural traits. In viewing diffusion it is essential that we view the units of transformation not as single traits but as larger systems or institutions. The modification of a trait may take the form of syncretism—the blending or fusing of the trait with an analogous element in a culture.

10. Even while culture changes, in whole or part, it persists as a recognizable entity over long periods of time. This fact of cultural tenacity has intrigued many social scientists. Closely associated with cultural persistence is resistance to change. Resistance implies behavior on the part of some or all of the members of society, either passive or active, that is directed toward the rejection or circumvention of change.

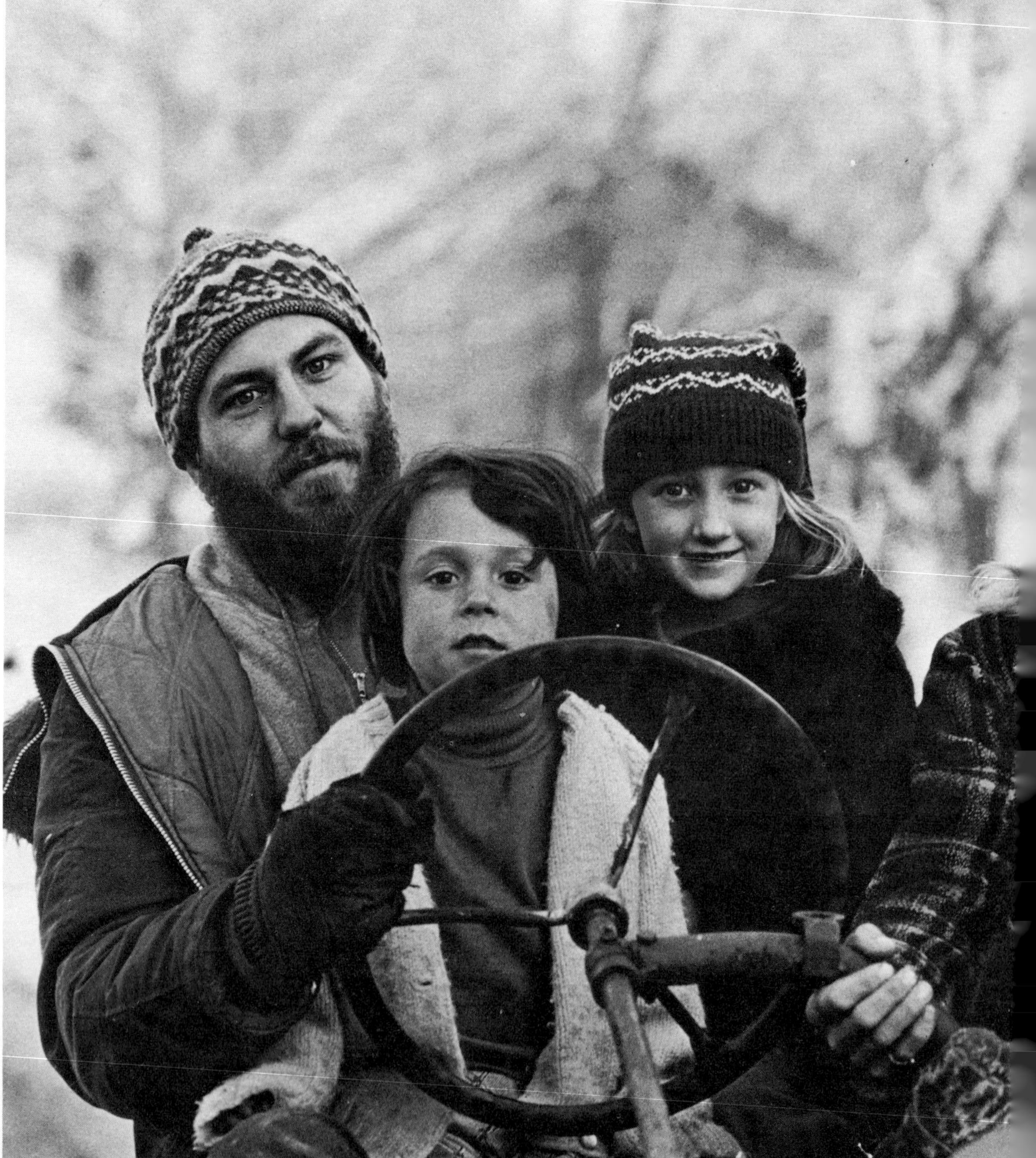

12 THE FAMILY

FUNCTIONS
    Sexual Regulation
    Reproduction
    Socialization
    Maintenance
    Social Placement
    Personal Needs

FAMILY AND MARRIAGE PATTERNS
    Cross-Cultural Variation in Family Organization
    Advantages and Disadvantages of Consanguine and Conjugal Patterns
    Forms of Marriage

MATE SELECTION
    Social Aspects of Love
    The Social Regulation of Mate Selection
    Factors in Mate Selection

MARITAL SATISFACTION

SOCIAL CHANGE: SOME RECENT TRENDS
    One-Person Households
    Unmarried Cohabitation
    Single-Parent Families
    Communes
    Homosexual Relationships

OBSERVATION It seems that in the past I have always dated girls who are very talkative, assertive, and outgoing. I am a rather quiet person and I find I need someone who can carry on most of the conversation. In truth, I am a much better listener than talker. I have noticed that whenever I have gone out with a retiring or shy girl that nothing ever got said and the date bombed. I have been going with my present girlfriend for a year now. My dad is always complaining to me about her. He says she drives him nuts, that all she does is talk, talk, talk, and that she is much too pushy. Actually we work out real well together. She is able to pull me out of my shell and she makes me feel comfortable in social situations.

PRINCIPLE As Robert F. Winch points out in his complementary need theory of mate selection, we look for persons who provide us with the maximum gratification of our needs. We generally feel most comfortable when one person has one personality trait and the other person has its counterpart so that when the traits are joined they produce a sense of completeness. In this way the two people mutually supply each other's lack and supplement one another.

We hear a good deal nowadays that the family is an "endangered" institution, one that is buffeted on every side by destructive forces with which it can scarcely cope. We have an image that in the "good old days" the traditional family was a ship held fast to its moorings, with one set of cables binding it to surrounding kin, another set to the wider community, and still another set to generations past and future (Shorter, 1975). It was a family of love, warmth, generosity, and self-sacrifice, a noble institution providing a united front against a hostile environment while affording its members a refuge against the stormy trials and tribulations of life.

Such a picture, however, is largely a myth. It is a fictitious view of family organization, portraying a stability and order that seldom existed. Lawrence Stone (1977), a historian, tells us that marriages in seventeenth century England and New England were based on family and property needs, not on choice by affection. Families were riddled by death to an unimaginable degree. The nonaffectionate marriage, the overwhelming authority of the husband, high mortality rates for parents and children, and severe discipline, beating, and abuse of children lead us to a rather stark image.

Myths are not the only problem we encounter in studying the family institution. Difficulty also arises in specifying just what the family is. The sphere of action of other institutions is generally restricted by a single function or range of functions: economic, religious, political, or educational. Family life, in contrast, frequently spans the entire range of human activities.

Throughout the world the family exhibits a great many forms and functions. We can identify certain broad tendencies regarding the structuring and functioning of the family, yet these are at best tendencies and not necessarily universals. On the basis of a cross-cultural survey of 250 societies, George Peter Murdock (1949), an eminent and respected anthropologist, could distinguish a number of features that commonly characterize the family—it tends to be a co-residential group that consists of a husband, wife, and children and that performs four basic functions: (1) it permits sexual access between at least some of the adult members; (2) it makes legitimate provision for the reproduction of children; (3) it cares for and socializes children; and (4) it collectively satisfies economic needs (at least in terms of the consumption of goods and services).

Yet the family is not everywhere a co-residential group, nor does it everywhere perform these four functions. Melford Spiro (1954), on the basis of field work in a kibbutz community (an agricultural collective farm) in Israel, found that the husband-wife unit does not raise or instruct its children; instead, the care of children is turned over to communal nurseries and schools where trained nurses and teachers assume many of the duties usually carried out by parents or other relatives. Commonly, parents spend only Saturdays and an hour or two on weekday evenings with their children. Nor is the family the basic economic unit:

> Each mate works in some branch of the kibbutz economy, and each . . . receives his equal share of the goods and services that the kibbutz distributes. Neither, however, engages in economic activities that are exclusively directed to the satisfaction of the needs of his mate. Women cook, sew, launder, etc., for the entire kibbutz, and not for their mates exclusively. Men produce goods, but the economic returns from their labor go to the kibbutz, not to their mates and themselves, although they, like all members of the kibbutz, share in these economic returns. (1954, p. 840)

Thus, the kibbutz as a whole, not the family, is the unit of economic cooperation. It is important to note, however, that the kibbutz is exceptional in these respects.

In view of such considerable cross-cultural variability, it is hardly surprising that sociologists have not as yet succeeded in defining the family in an entirely satisfactory manner. William N. Stephens, setting himself the task of defining "family" from the perspective of a large number of cultures, notes with discouragement:

> "Family" is really terribly hard to define properly. We all use this term. Doubtless, we all have the illusion that we know what we mean by it. But when one sets about trying to separate families from nonfamilies, he begins to realize how very hard it is to say just exactly what a "family" is.
>
> To make a long story short, I failed in my task of getting a good definition of the family. . . . (1963, p. 4)

However, for our purposes in this book we shall view the **family** as a social arrangement united by ties of marriage, ancestry, or adoption which community members recognize as constituting a single household and having the responsibility for bringing up children.

FUNCTIONS

> Marriage was instituted by God himself for the purpose of preventing promiscuous intercourse of the sexes, for promoting domestic felicity, and for securing the maintenance and security of children.
>
> Noah Webster, An American Dictionary of the English Language, 1828

In the previous chapter, we noted that, if a society is to survive and operate with some degree of effectiveness, a variety of functions have to be met. The performance of the activities associated with these functions cannot be left to chance—to do so would run the risk that they simply would not be carried out. Institutions are the principal instruments whereby these essential tasks of social living are organized, directed, and executed. In this respect, the family is an institution. Although the family exhibits considerable diversity throughout the world, we nonetheless can identify certain broad tendencies regarding the functions it performs. For our purposes here, we shall note six such functions: sexual regulation, reproduction, socialization, maintenance, social placement, and gratification of personal needs.

SEXUAL REGULATION

> To avoid fornication, let every man have his own wife, and let every women have her own husband.
>
> Corinthians, I:7, 2

All societies undertake to regulate the sexual behavior of their members. Social norms specify the classes of individuals that are and are not permissible sexual partners. Incest taboos afford a good illustration of this. All societies bar sexual relations among certain relatives. Although the taboo is universal, considerable variation exists among societies as to which relatives are covered by the prohibition. In clan arrangements, such as those that prevailed in traditional China, all individuals bearing the same clan name were excluded as sexual partners even though they were cousins a thousand times removed. In contrast, the norms of ancient Egypt and Hawaii provided for the marriage of brothers and sisters of the royal family (Middleton, 1962). Incest taboos are commonly explained by sociologists as social mechanisms that prevent the development of potentially disruptive sexual rivalries within the family and link together different families by marriage (thus promoting overall societal integration and solidarity).

Still another tendency found widely throughout most — perhaps even in all — societies is what has been termed the **norm of legitimacy** (like other norms, this one is occasionally violated, and those who violate it are generally punished in some way). Although perhaps some 70 percent of the world's societies permit some form of sexual license, even in these societies, childbirth outside of marriage is not approved. Legitimacy focuses on social placement, on *descent,* on the location of the child in the kinship network — that is, it regulates both the social relations of members with the newborn and the rights of the newborn to care, succession, inheritance, and instruction (Goode, 1960; Malinowski, 1964; Rodman, 1966; Hartley, 1970).

The weak link in the family group is of course the father–child bond; there is no necessary association and no easy means of identification between the two. Yet, according to Bronislaw Malinowski, a leading anthropologist, societies everywhere make provision for "fatherhood," *if only by social definition.* This he terms the principle of legitimacy — the rule that "no child should be brought into the world without a man — and one man at that — assuming the role of sociological father, that is, guardian and protector, the male link between the child and the rest of the community" (1964:13). Hence, among the Tallensi (a people of the African Sudan), if a woman is married, any child she bears is the property of, and a member of, the descent group of her husband (Fortes, 1949). If she has an adulterine child, it is easily absorbed into a legal relationship. The genitor (the agent of conception) does not feel any fatherly emotions at all, but the pater, who is the woman's husband, does feel the emotions of a father, even though he knows he is not the genitor. He also receives all the credit that is given to a father in that society, and the child is not stigmatized or deprived of any legal rights. However, when the norm of legitimacy is violated, when an unwed woman has a child, the child is not as easily absorbed (such a child receives only part of his legal rights and is stigmatized as inferior in status).

REPRODUCTION

Birth, and copulation, and death.
That's all the facts when you come to brass tacks;
Birth, and copulation, and death.
                                                T.S. Eliot

New members have to be created if a society is to be perpetuated. Some may think us naïve for even raising the matter, arguing that the biological realities of sex will guarantee that humans will reproduce themselves. But the matter is not this simple. Within many societies, people are familiar with the fact that sexual needs can be satisfied in the absence of procreation — the "pill," withdrawal, abortion, the rhythm method, and other techniques have

"INCEST" TABOOS

OBSERVATION — Before I moved into a co-ed dormitory I wondered about the relationships between the guys and girls in the same dorm. Having lived in a co-ed dorm for a while now it has turned out differently from what I had expected. Very few of the guys date girls in our dorm. Rather we date girls from "outside." With girls from our dorm we become "friends"—more a "brother-sister" relationship. I was surprised that so little sexual promiscuity occurred among the members of the opposite sexes in the same co-ed dormitory.

PRINCIPLE — A semi-incest taboo operates within a co-ed dormitory. I think the reason for this is that romantic and sexual involvement would complicate our relationships. Romantic ties might fragment our relationships and pose barriers in relating to other people. A guy involved with a particular girl wouldn't like her associating on a day-by-day, close basis with the other guys he lived with (and vice versa); you would come to resent or feel suspicious of your roommates. And if the relationship with a particular girl broke up, it would be sort of a strain living in the same dorm together and continually coming in contact with one another.

enabled people to separate sexual enjoyment from reproduction. Hence, societies have to motivate their members to have children.

Among peasant peoples, children are commonly viewed as an economic asset; at harvest time, each pair of hands becomes important since most crops are quite perishable. Within the post-Civil-War South, plantation owners traditionally inquired of prospective tenants the size of their families; those with large families received priority. Societies may have recourse to still other sources of motivation. Where other institutional provision is not made for the care of the aged—golden age villages, social security, retirement programs, and the like—children may offer the guarantee that one will be provided for in old age. Or religious considerations may prevail—for example, in China, where ancestor worship constituted the foundation of religious life, the only way one's comfort in the hereafter could be assured was to have many sons. Here in the United States, a good many people still define marriage and children as constituting the "good life"; indeed, for some, the absence of children is viewed as a misfortune. Although most societies do not confine sexual life to the marriage situation, all societies accord sexual privileges to married spouses and attempt to guarantee that reproduction takes place within a family framework.

SOCIALIZATION

Children are born social blanks. Hence, provision has to be made for their acquisition of those aspects of culture essential for competent social participation. Children must learn what is and is not appropriate—norms. They

The Family

PRINCIPLE OF LEGITIMACY

OBSERVATION A friend of mine is seven months pregnant. Her boyfriend (the baby's father) refuses to marry her. He is a junior in college, wants to graduate, and expects to "make it big" someday. My friend decided against an abortion and definitely wants the baby. Her parents and some of her relatives and friends are in an uproar. They say that the child must have a father and "a name," something it will not have if born "illegitimately." Her parents feel genuinely disgraced by the whole episode and view my friend as stigmatized. They say she is "ruined" and has lost all chance of "getting a nice husband."

PRINCIPLE The principle of legitimacy is a social rule that no child should be brought into the world without a man assuming the role of its father. My friend is violating this rule and is being hassled as a result. Because she is pregnant and not married, her baby is socially defined as a "bastard" and both she and the child are disgraced.

must acquire standards telling them what is and is not desirable, worthwhile, beautiful, and good—values. They must secure conceptions of the world about them, how it operates, and their place in it—beliefs. They must gain mastery of the means for communicating with others—symbols. Generally, the family is the chief culture-transmitting agency; family groups are the intermediary between the larger society and the individual. It is also within the family that children acquire the chief facets of their personalities—their attitudes, manners, and emotional responses.

MAINTENANCE

By virtue of the relatively long period of pregnancy, the rigors of childbirth, and the extended lactation period, the mother is quite dependent for a fairly long period and in need of protection and sustenance. Similarly, the prolonged period of human infancy necessitates that the child be fed, clothed, and provided with shelter. Throughout the world, societies have assigned the family the responsibility for shielding, protecting, sustaining, and otherwise maintaining children and dependent community members.

SOCIAL PLACEMENT

All societies are confronted with a constant stream of raw material in the form of new babies who need to be placed within the social structure. This task may be accomplished by assigning some roles to an individual on the basis of family membership. The family confers roles that (1) orient the individual to a variety of relationships, including those involving parents (e.g., mother-child), siblings (e.g., brother-sister), and parents' relatives (e.g., uncle-nephew); and that (2) orient the individual to other socially established groups (e.g., national, ethnic, religious, class, caste, and community relationships). Such roles are ascribed.

PERSONAL NEEDS

The happiest moments of my life have been the few which I have passed at home in the bosom of my family.

Thomas Jefferson, Letter to Francis Willis, 1790

People are social beings. Both as children and as adults, they have a variety of social and emotional needs that can only be met through interaction with other humans. The cases of Anna and Isabelle (see Chapter 3) provide stark evidence of this. Indeed, the family is the breeding ground for those qualities most characteristic of us as human beings. A number of studies emphasize that children reared in foundling homes suffer high mortality rates, developmental retardation, and personality impoverishment (Spitz, 1945, 1946; Goldfarb, 1945, 1947, 1949; Dennis, 1973; Rutter, 1974). Many writers, especially those influenced by the Freudian psychoanalytic tradition, hold that children's early relationships serve as prototypes for their later relationships (Erikson, 1963; White, 1973, 1975). When children fail to develop ties to one or a few significant persons, or when these ties are disrupted, children are thought to be impaired in developing close relationships in adulthood (Bowlby, 1969; Fraiberg, 1977). And regardless of age, the intimate, rapportful, face-to-face contact characteristic of healthy family relationships affords companionship, ego worth, love, security, and a general sense of well-being.

The family as a nurturing institution. Children require the warmth, affection, and security afforded by close social bonds if they are not to experience developmental retardation and personality impoverishment. Under the strong influence of the psychoanalytic tradition, American social scientists focused almost exclusively on the mother-child tie. Over the past decade, however, an accumulating body of research is pointing to the importance of the father in child-rearing.

FAMILY AND MARRIAGE PATTERNS

> For this cause shall a man leave his father and mother, and shall be joined unto his wife, and they two shall be one flesh.
>
> *Ephesians, 5:31*

Social relationships between adult males and adult females can be organized on a conjugal or a consanguine basis. If a society stresses the **conjugal** arrangement, the family consists of a nucleus of spouses and their offspring; blood relatives are functionally marginal and peripheral. If a society emphasizes the **consanguine** arrangement, the family consists of a nucleus of blood relatives; spouses are functionally marginal and peripheral. Conjugal systems stress the *spouse* relationship; consanguine systems stress *kin* ties. Sociologists also refer to conjugal families (those characterized by husband-wife-children units) as *nuclear families* and consanguine families as *extended families*. The conjugal family is basically a transitory group; it comes into being with marriage, increases in size with the coming of children, and ends with the death of the married couple. The consanguine family is long-lived—it enjoys continuity from one generation to the next.

CROSS-CULTURAL VARIATION IN FAMILY ORGANIZATION

> An exclusive relation of one or more men to one or more women, based on custom, recognized and supported by public opinion, and where law exists, by law.
>
> *Lord Avebury,* Marriage, Totems, and Religion, *1911*

Americans usually have little difficulty grasping the nature of conjugal arrangements since this is the preferred pattern of family life among the middle class. Indeed, in the course of their lives, most Americans find themselves members of two nuclear families. First, a person belongs to a nuclear family consisting of oneself and one's father, mother, and siblings. This is termed the **family of orientation**. Second, since over 90 percent of Americans marry at least once, the vast majority of the population are members of a nuclear family consisting of oneself and one's spouse and children. This is termed the **family of procreation**. However, one out of three marriages currently ends in divorce. In most cases (four out of five), divorced people remarry (Glick, 1975). Consequently, many Americans are members of multiple nuclear families over their life spans.

Probably the most extreme case of consanguine kinship was that found in the pre-British period of southwestern India, among the Nayar (a soldiering caste group) who virtually eliminated conjugal bonds (Gough, 1959, 1965; Dumont, 1970; Fuller, 1976). Shortly before puberty, a woman ritually "married" a man chosen for her by a neighborhood assembly and, after three ceremonial days, ritually "separated" from him. The woman was then free to take on a series of "visiting husbands" or "lovers." These lovers gave her regular gifts at festivals, but in no sense did they provide her with support. When the woman had a child, one of the men—not necessarily the genitor—paid a fee to the midwife, thereby establishing the child's legitimacy; this man, however, had no economic, social, legal, or ritual rights in, nor obligations to, the child. Instead, the mother's brother assumed the primary responsibility for the child's upbringing. It was to the mother's brother and not the father that a child owed allegiance; property and privileged positions were not transmitted from father to son but from maternal uncle to nephew. The father enjoyed similar duties and privileges in relation to his sister's children. Hence the Nayar family was structured around the brother-sister relation.

Since the Nayar reckoned descent solely through the line of the mother, sociologists term the Nayar **matrilineal**. In contrast, societies that trace descent through the father's line while ignoring the mother's line are referred to as **patrilineal**. Some people, such as Americans, are **bilineal**—we reckon descent through both the father and mother (however, surname is transmitted in a patrilineal manner).

Although conjugal bonds existed among the Nayar, such ties were greatly overshadowed by consanguine relationships. We should not assume that a people are necessarily characterized either by conjugal or consanguine patterns; rather, it is usually a matter of the degree to which one pattern prevails over the other. We can think of each of the consanguine and conjugal arrangements as being extremes or polar types, with cultures distributed along a continuum between the poles in accordance with the emphasis assigned to each. Thus, we would place the Hopi Indians (a Southwest Pueblo people) somewhere near the center of the continuum (see Figure 12.1). Among the Hopi, the husband moves on marriage into his wife's dwelling, and it is here that he eats and sleeps. The husband provides food and clothing for his wife and children, but the fields and the produce from them belong to the wife's group. Similarly, children belong to the mother and her clan. Nonetheless, the father is the head of the household, though he shares his authority over the children with their maternal uncle.

Figure 12.1. Continuum of family types.

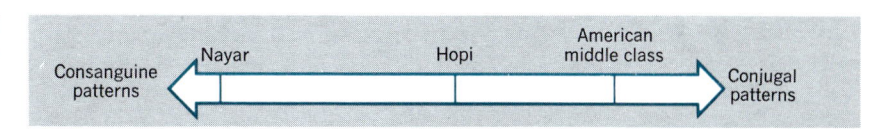

ADVANTAGES AND DISADVANTAGES OF CONSANGUINE AND CONJUGAL PATTERNS

Appraised from a perspective of societal efficiency, both the conjugal and the consanguine systems have some advantages and disadvantages. Interestingly enough, the advantages of the one are generally the disadvantages of the other.

Advantages of Consanguine Arrangements. The consanguine arrangement offers a number of advantages. First, death, divorce, or illness works less havoc within extended kinship groups than in nuclear families. Children do not form an exclusive attachment for the father and mother since intimate relationships exist with the relatives of at least one of the parents. Nor is the sexual division of labor disrupted or the provision of male and female gender models impaired by death or divorce.

Second, some tasks can be more adequately performed where recourse can be had to larger numbers of people. In the consanguine system, the economic and psychological burden of caring for the aged and infirm is distributed over many individuals. Where protection against parasitic or predatory enemies assumes importance, the consanguine group, being larger, is more capable of rendering defense than is the conjugal.

Third, where the family functions as a unit of economic production, brothers and sisters have been trained since infancy to habits of mutual adaptation; an integration of economic activities is already realized. The consanguine system enables a functioning unit to continue its cooperation. A conjugal system temporarily disrupts these cooperative work patterns and necessitates that a new unit be established; the married couple must evolve new patterns of mutual adaptation. During the transitional, adjustive period, the members of the conjugal unit are as yet unable to function with collective efficiency.

Finally, the consanguine family is better equipped to acquire material wealth and keep it in the family—property can accumulate. Since conjugal families are of relatively short duration, less time exists during which to acquire wealth and property, and provision must be made for redistributing it every generation.

Advantages of Conjugal Arrangements. The conjugal arrangement also offers a number of advantages. First, since incest taboos prevail among blood relatives, the consanguine family functions asexually; it cannot harness the motivation inherent in the sex drive for the performance of other social tasks. The conjugal system, on the other hand, offers the potential of linking sexual satisfactions to the assumption of other responsibilities, for example, maintaining and socializing children.

Conjugal patterns. Western countries place considerable emphasis on conjugal as opposed to consanguine arrangements.

Patrick Reddy

Second, the conjugal arrangement is better adapted to the dictates of an industrial society than is the consanguine arrangement. William J. Goode (1963), on the basis of a review of the evidence on modern changes in the family in the West, in Arab Islam, in sub-Saharan Africa, and in India, China, and Japan, suggests that industrialization influences the development of conjugal patterns in a number of ways: (1) Industrialism requires geographic mobility (movement in search of new job and professional opportunities) — a requirement that cannot be met if kin obligations involve frequent, intimate, and considerable interdependence among relatives. (2) Industrialism facilitates social mobility, which serves to weaken consanguine ties by virtue of differential social mobility among kin. (3) Industrialism substitutes formal, non-kin agencies for large kin groups in the handling of common problems of political protection, education, military defense, money lending, and the like. (4) Industrialism emphasizes achievement over birth (ascription), reversing the traditional pattern and thereby lessening individuals' dependence on their families (although by no means totally destroying this dependence). Hence, the conjugal system appears better suited in some ways to the demands of modern industrial society than does the consanguine (Coale et al., 1965; Gordon, 1970).

FORMS OF MARRIAGE

Marry such women as seem good to you, two, three or four, but if you fear you will not be equitable, then only one.

The Koran

In no society may individuals marry whomever they wish; culture dictates that marriage take place within certain groups, while it bars marriage within certain others. The rule of **endogamy** prescribes that individuals marry within certain groups of which they are members—in-group marriage. Within American society, cultural patterns press us to marry within our own class, religious faith, race, and nationality group. The rule of **exogamy** forbids individuals from marrying within certain groups of which they are members—outgroup-marriage. Generally, exogamy rests on the incest taboo, which bars marriage between specified kinfolk. Where clans prevail, an individual may be forbidden to marry anyone who bears the same clan name, no matter how distant the relationship.

Conjugal relationships may be structured in four ways: *monogamy,* one husband and one wife; *polygyny,* one husband and two or more wives; *polyandry,* two or more husbands and one wife; and *group marriage,* two or more husbands and two or more wives. Monogamy appears in all societies, although other forms may not only be permitted but preferred. Of 238 societies included in Murdock's sample (1949), only about 20 percent were strictly monogamous.

Polygyny has enjoyed a wide distribution throughout the world. The Old Testament, for example, records polygynous practices among the Hebrews: Gideon had many wives who bore him seventy sons; King David had several wives as did King Solomon; King Solomon's son Rehoboam had eighteen wives and sixty concubines; and Rehoboam's sons in turn had many wives. Of the 238 societies in Murdock's sample, 193 permitted husbands to take plural wives. In one-third of these polygynous societies, however, fewer than 20 percent of the married men actually had more than one wife. Generally, it is only the economically advantaged males who can afford to support more than one woman—for example, in China, India, and the Mohammedan countries, polygyny usually is the privilege of the wealthy few.

Whereas polygyny has a wide distribution, polyandry is exceedingly rare. Polyandry usually does not represent freedom of sexual choice for women. Often, it involves the right or the opportunity of younger brothers to have access to the wife of an older brother; where a man cannot afford wives or marriages for each of his sons, he may get a wife for the eldest son only. W. H. R. Rivers describes polyandrous practices among the Todas, a non-Hindu tribe in India:

> The Todas have a completely organized and definite system of polyandry. When a woman marries a man, it is understood that she becomes the wife of his brothers at the same time. When a boy is married

to a girl, not only are his brothers usually regarded as also the husbands of the girl, but any brother born later will similarly be regarded as sharing his older brother's rights. . . . The brothers live together, and my informants seemed to regard it as a ridiculous idea that there should even be disputes or jealousies of the kind that might be expected in such a household. . . . Instead of adultery being regarded as immoral . . . according to the Toda idea, immortality attaches rather to the man who grudges his wife to another. (1906, p. 515)

Social scientists are far from agreement on whether group marriage has ever existed as a cultural norm. There is some evidence that it does occur among the Kaingang of Brazil, the Marquesans of the southern Pacific, the Chukchee of Siberia, and the Todas of India. At times, as among the Todas, polyandry appears to slip into group marriage where a number of brothers share more than one wife (Stephens, 1963).

MATE SELECTION

A sympathetic foreign observer, Raoul de Roussy de Sales, once observed: "America appears to be the only country in the world where love is a national problem" (1938:645). Pulp literature, glamour magazines, scandel newspapers, movies, television, radio serials, and popular music reverberate with themes of romantic ecstasy. How-to-do-it books tell us how to conduct our love relations, how to persuade others to succumb to our love wishes, and how to excite and satisfy our sexual partners. Notions concerning romantic love play an important part in our spouse selection and in our conceptions of married life.

A number of components are typically associated with **romantic love** (Rubin, 1970; Katz, 1976). First there is the element of *attention*—the lover is absorbed and preoccupied with the loved one. Second, the lover desires physical and psychological *intimacy*—a yearning for a kind of personality fusion. And third, the lover derives special pleasure from doing things for and making gifts for the loved one—a selfless and unconditional *generosity* and even *sacrifice*.

SOCIAL ASPECTS OF LOVE

Love is the strange bewilderment which overtakes one person on account of another person.
E. B. White and James Thurber, Is Sex Necessary? 1929

Although it seems that all societies recognize that some individuals of opposite sexes may form an occasional violent, emotional attachment for one another, we Americans have capitalized on these feelings and elevated them to a highly exalted place in our national life. In sharp contrast to our American pattern, consider these words of the elders of an African tribe who, in discussing the problems of "runaway" marriages and illegitimacy, complained to the 1883 Commission on Native Law and Custom: "It is all this thing called love. We do not understand it at all. This thing called love has been introduced . . ." (quoted by Gluckman, 1955:76). To these African elders, romantic love was viewed as a disruptive force. For them, marriage traditionally had implied no particular attachment for the spouse-to-be, marriage was not the free choice of the couple marrying, and considerations other than love played a critical part in the selection of a mate.

William J. Goode (1959) suggests that the cultural distribution of romantic love can be best understood not in terms of a "romantic love–no romantic love" dichotomy but as a continuum or range between polar types. At one

Romantic love. Is romantic love a tragic, laughable aberration or the only proper, morally acceptable foundation for marriage? Different societies have answered this question differently.

Patrick Reddy

pole, a society views a strong love attraction as a laughable or tragic aberration; at the other, it defines marriage without love as mildly shameful. The American middle class falls toward the pole of positive approval, while Japan and China fall toward the pole of low institutionalization; Greece after Alexander and Rome of the Empire fall toward the center.

Ellen Bercheid and Elaine Walster (1974) emphasize the important part that *labeling* plays in determining the presence of romantic love. Love does not exist unless a person defines it as love. Accordingly, the behavior that a person interprets as love at one time will have different *meanings* at other times. The wife who interprets a gift of flowers as an expression of love will very likely define that gift differently after receiving a bouquet every Sunday for four years, after an intense and unresolved fight, after she catches her spouse with another woman, or after she has developed an allergy to pollen. Flowers in their own right mean nothing (Katz, 1976).

Bercheid and Walster note that passionate love, as with other emotional states, requires arousal and the assignment of a particular label to that arousal. They suggest that intense attraction is most likely to occur when people are in a situation in which they experience some kind of strong physiological arousal, for instance, during an exciting football game, the bombardment of a city, or a frightening storm. For example, Donald G. Dutton and Arthur P. Aron (1974) found that when men were individually interviewed by a young woman on a frightening suspension bridge high above a canyon, they evidenced sexual arousal (as revealed by the content of a story they wrote) and half of them were sufficiently attracted to the researcher to telephone her afterward (she had given each subject her name and telephone number in the event he desired more information). Such responses did not occur when another group of men were interviewed by the same woman as they crossed a solid, sturdy bridge over a small creek further upstream. In brief, an unrelated frightening event appeared to be related to increased sexual attraction.

THE SOCIAL REGULATION OF MATE SELECTION

Apparently in all societies, there are certain established ways by which mate selection is patterned and controlled. At times, special living quarters are designed to make it easy for marriageable girls to attract a husband: the Bontok of the Philippines, for instance, keep their girls in a special house where lovers call, sex play is free, and marriage is supposed to result. The Ekoi of Nigeria, who prefer women plump, send them away to be specially fattened for marriage. Others, such as the Yao of central Africa and the aborigines of the Canary Islands, send their daughters away to "convents" where old women teach them the special skills and mysteries that a wife needs to know (Scott, 1965).

Consequences of Mate Selection for the Larger Kin Group. Whatever system they use, a child's kin have more in mind generally than just getting the child married. They want the child married to the *right* spouse, especially where marriage has consequences for their larger kin group. These consequences tend to be of two kinds. First, the choice of a mate itself has an effect on the kinship group. Where consanguine families are important, marriage is often conceived as an alliance between two lineages, not simply as a relation between two individuals. Further, where the kinship unit functions as a unit of stratification, so that a "poor" marriage reflects on the honor of the whole family, a powerful incentive is added to protect the family name. Marriage may also involve significant economic interests, reflected for instance in marriage payments or "bride price." Frequently, a people view the payment of a bride price as a remuneration to the wife's parents for the expenses incurred in rearing her and a compensation for the loss of her future services. The practice further serves to assure that the wife will not be mistreated. Among the natives of East Africa, the cattle "paid" are actually held in escrow by her kinsmen. If she is ill treated and judged justified in leaving her husband, her kin group retain the cattle. If she is ruled at fault, the cattle are returned to her husband's group. Men, too, are protected since it is often customary to refund the bride price if a man must divorce his wife "for good reason," for example, if she is barren. In any event, contrary to popular opinion, the payment of a bride price does not make the woman a chattel, nor does it give the husband absolute control over his "property."

The second kind of consequence that a marriage has for the kin group derives from the conflict between the conjugal bond and the consanguine bond. The greater the solidarity of the husband and wife, the more the interests of the larger kinship group are threatened. Among the Nayar, for instance, if a man showed particular fondness for a "wife," the woman's kin were likely to suspect that the man's kin would then hire sorcerers against them—the man's kin were likely to fear that the "visiting husband" might secretly convey to the woman gifts and cash that belonged rightfully to his kin. This suspicion was especially rife if the "visiting husband" was the legal guardian of the kin group and hence controlled extensive property (Gough, 1959).

The Social Control of Love. Since marriage has consequences for the larger kin group, a child's relatives have a stake in the person who is to be a spouse. Random mating would jeopardize these interests. Love, allowed to run its course, would result at times in the child choosing the *wrong* mate. Mate choice, therefore, is too important a matter to be left to the child; love must be controlled. There are a number of ways by which societies undertake to accomplish this end—that is, to "contain" love (Goode, 1959):

1. *Child marriage.* One way of coping with the "problem of love" is child marriage. If children are betrothed, married, or both before they have a chance to interact intimately as adolescents with other children, then they have no resources with which to oppose the marriage—they are as yet unable to earn a living, they are physically weak, and they are socially dominated by elders. This pattern used to prevail in India, where the young bride went to live with her husband in a marriage that was not physically consummated until much later.
2. *Seclusion of women.* A society can prevent the widespread development of adolescent love relationships by socially isolating young people from potential mates. Social segregation is difficult, however, unless it is supported by physical segregation. Hence, the Manus of the Admiralty Islands (Melanesia) removed a girl, when she experienced her first menstruation, from her playmates and kept her at "home"—on stilts over a lagoon—under the close supervision of elders.
3. *Supervision.* In some societies, couples are closely supervised by chaperons or parents; and, if possible, whom the adolescent meets is controlled by relatives. Often, a high value is placed on female chastity, viewed either as the product of self-restraint, as among the seventeenth century Puritans, or as a "marketable" commodity, as among traditional Italians (lack of virginity was grounds for immediate separation on the wedding night).
4. *Informal group pressures.* Where love relationships are encouraged and mate choice is formally free, informal peer and parental pressures nonetheless commonly serve to narrow and limit the potential field of eligibles. In our society, for instance, parents threaten, cajole, wheedle, bribe, and persuade their children to "go with the right people." They seek to control love relationships by influencing the informal social contacts of their children: moving to appropriate neighborhoods and schools, giving parties and helping to make out invitation lists, alerting their children that certain individuals have ineligible traits (race, religion, manners, and tastes), and so on. The net result is that mate selection is socially regulated, but primarily in an informal manner.

FACTORS IN MATE SELECTION

Many Americans are averse to finding in science an explanation of why people fall in love. Love, we are sometimes told, is "too precious and sacred" to subject to scientific scrutiny. Nevertheless, love and marriage are behavior and like any other human behavior are subject to observation and study. We are confronted with this question: "Why is it that we fall in love with and marry this person and not another?" Social scientists suggest that at least five principal factors influence mate selection: (1) propinquity, (2) homogamy, (3) matching, (4) complementary needs, and (5) social exchange. Let us examine each of these in turn.

Propinquity. **Propinquity** refers to the fact that people who live near one another and go to school and work together tend to marry one another. Several studies made in recent decades have noted the effect of residential propinquity—nearness in place—on mate selection (Peach, 1974; Kahn and McGaughey, 1977). Alfred C. Clarke (1952), for example, on the basis of interviews with 431 applicants for marriage licenses over a three-month period in Columbus, Ohio, found that, at the time of the couple's first date, some 54 percent of the mates resided within sixteen standard city blocks of each other. This tendency, however, was more pronounced in some groups than others. In terms of occupation, males in skilled labor jobs selected spouses closer to home than did men in the clerical and sales group; similarly, men in professional and managerial categories were less affected by propinquity than those in unskilled jobs. Overall, though, it appears that "Cupid may have wings, but apparently they are not adapted for long flights" (Bossard, 1932:222).

Homogamy. **Homogamy** refers to the tendency of "like to marry like." More than a hundred studies have been made on homogamy. They have dealt with such characteristics as age, race, religion, nationality, social class, social attitudes, education, previous marital status, intelligence, emotional stability, health, stature, and related matters. With few exceptions, individuals who are similar to one another marry to a degree greater than would be expected by chance (Rockwell, 1976). Homogamy appears to be particularly operative on the level of social variables, but the evidence is less clear on psychological variables—personality or temperament components. One problem faced by homogamy studies is that the observed similarity between spouses may be the result of marriage (reciprocal socialization) rather than a cause of it (Kerckhoff, 1964).

Matching Hypothesis. The **matching hypothesis** states that individuals tend to pair off with one another on the basis of their physical attractiveness. Bernard I. Murstein (1972) found support for the hypothesis in a study of ninety-nine couples who were either engaged or "going together." The individuals perceived their partners as roughly comparable to themselves in physical attractiveness. Independent judges likewise rated photographs of the couples as more similar in physical attractiveness than photographs of randomly matched couples. Murstein suggests that individuals fear less rejection and greater promise of success in the "mating and dating game" when they direct their efforts toward others of approximately equal physical attractiveness.

Complementary Needs. We feel comfortable with people who have certain personality traits, while individuals with other traits "rub us the wrong way."

Robert F. Winch (1958) has formulated the **complementary needs** theory of mate selection based on this proposition. He suggests that we typically seek within the field of eligibles a person who gives the greatest promise of providing us with the maximum gratification of our needs. Winch indicates that a good many of our needs are met in a complementary fashion. A person with a strong desire for recognition might love and be loved by a deferential person who prefers to bask in the accomplishments of another; within such a relationship, each finds his own need satisfied. A feeling of completeness—a mutual supplying of reciprocal elements—produces a sense of satisfaction and well-being. A wide range of traits tend to be complementary: an individual who has a nurturance need—a need to sympathize with or help a person in need—finds a complementary relationship with a person with a succorance need—a need to be helped and taken care of; a dominant person finds a complementary relationship with a submissive person; a sadist—one who derives unconscious satisfaction by inflicting suffering—finds a complementary relationship with a masochist—one who derives unconscious satisfaction from suffering. We should note, however, a word of caution. Although some studies support the theory (Kerckhoff and Davis, 1962; Rychlak, 1965), others have contradicted it (Shellenberg and Bee, 1960; Moss, Apolonio, and Jensen, 1971). Hence, we may want to reserve judgment on the theory until more evidence is available.

Social Exchange. **Social exchange theory** suggests that we are attracted to people who supply us with more rewards than costs in the course of interaction with them (Blau, 1967; Homans, 1974; Lott and Lott, 1974). Rewards include the pleasures, benefits, and gratifications we gain from a relationship. Costs refer to those problems, anxieties, and difficulties we experience in a relationship. Thus, a couple are likely to find a relationship satisfying so long as the desired expressions of love, gratitude, recognition, and security outweigh painful disagreements, frustrations, and slights.

MARITAL SATISFACTION

> Marriage enlarges the scene of our happiness and miseries. A marriage of love is pleasant; a marriage of interest easy; and a marriage where both meet, happy. A happy marriage has in it all the pleasures of friendship, all the enjoyments of sense and reason; and indeed all the sweets of life.
>
> *Joseph Addison, The Spectator, December 29, 1711*

In recent decades, it has become quite common to substitute the word "cherish" for "obey" in the marriage vows of women. This change reflects the fact that we no longer think of marriage and the family primarily in terms of a well-defined set of duties and rights. Today, family relationships are much less formal, strict, and rigid than they were only a few generations ago. Increasingly, family living is viewed in terms of personality fulfillment, the satisfaction of emotional needs, and the realization of overall happiness and personal growth.

A good many Americans believe that marriages that do not result in divorce begin with passionate love and evolve into cooler but closer companionship and even greater intimacy. Sociological researchers find, however, that there is initially a decrease in marital satisfaction and adjustment during the early years of marriage. The speed and intensity of this decline in satisfaction varies from one study to another. In the middle and later stages of the family life cycle, the evidence is less clear (Spanier, Lewis, and Cole, 1975). Some researchers find a continual decline (Blood and Wolfe, 1960; Pineo, 1961; Paris and Luckey, 1966). More usually, however, they report a U-shaped curve, with a decline in satisfaction during the early years, a leveling off during the middle years, and an increase in satisfaction during the later years (Gurin, Verhoff, and Feld, 1960; Bradburn and Coplovitz, 1966; Burr, 1970; Smart and Smart, 1975; Glenn, 1975). Research Study 19 summarizes data from a study by Boyd C. Rollins and Harold Feldman that found a U-shaped relationship between stages in the family life cycle and marital satisfaction.

Children are generally born during the early stages of a marital career and are launched following a period of intense parental responsibilities. Any number of sociologists have noted that the presence of children in the home tends to coincide with the depression in the U-shaped curve of marital satisfaction (Blood and Wolfe, 1960; Hill, 1970; Miller, 1976). A common explanation for this finding is that parenthood requires heavy role commitments and is commonly a source of role overload and strain (Rollins and Cannon, 1974). It also appears that children interfere with the amount of communication that takes place between spouses and with the time which they have available for companionable activities (Miller, 1976; Marini, 1976; Thornton, 1977). And children often create new sources of conflict while intensifying existing sources (Urdy, 1971).

In gaining perspective on the matter of children and marital satisfaction, it is important to note that dissolution rates tend to be highest among couples without children (Thornton, 1977). Further, children can be an important source of gratification and satisfaction for their parents (Russell, 1974). Factors other than children also play a part. A family's socioeconomic level has a direct effect on the amount of companionship a couple report. The more education both the husband and wife have and the higher the husband's occupational ranking, the more companionable activities the couple share regardless of the number or spacing of children. And the more companionship activities a couple share, the greater tends to be their marital satisfaction (Miller, 1976).

RESEARCH STUDY 19

MARITAL SATISFACTION OVER THE FAMILY LIFE CYCLE*

Boyd C. Rollins and Harold Feldman

Problem. Marriage is less a state than a process. Through time, marriages and families undergo change. Indeed, sociologists have identified the existence of a family life cycle having vast consequences for marital interaction. A fairly simple scheme identifies eight stages in the cycle:

Stage I.   Beginning (the childless family)
Stage II. Infant (oldest child, birth to 2 years, 11 months)
Stage III. Preschool (oldest child, 3 years to 5 years, 11 months)
Stage IV. Schoolage (oldest child, 6 years to 12 years, 11 months)
Stage V.   Teenage (oldest child, 13 years to 20 years, 11 months)
Stage VI. Launching (first child gone to last child's leaving home)
Stage VII. Empty Nest (children gone)
Stage VIII. Retirement (retirement to death of spouse)

Just what happens over the course of marriage? More particularly, what is the nature of marital satisfaction over the family cycle? It is to these matters that Rollins and Feldman addressed themselves in the present study.

Method. Every third house in two top socioeconomic sections of Syracuse, New York, was selected as a target dwelling. Fieldworkers stopped at each of the households, dropped off a questionnaire for each spouse to complete, and made a later appointment to pick them up. The questionnaire asked for information regarding marital history, occupation, marital satisfaction, communication, decision-making, and the like. For instance, each spouse was asked: "In general, how often do you think that things between you and your wife (husband) are going well? All the time; most of the time; more often than not; occasionally; rarely; never." Some 85 percent of the husbands and wives completed the questionnaires (a high response rate), producing a sample of 799 couples (53 others who were married for more than five years and were still childless were eliminated from analysis since they were considered atypical in terms of the stages of the family life cycle under study). The couples were then classified into one of eight stages of the family life cycle.

Findings. Some 80 percent of both husbands and wives indicated that things were going well in their marriage either most of the time or all of the time. Nonetheless, the pattern of general marital satisfaction for the wives revealed a steady decline from the "beginning" to the "schoolage" stage, followed by a leveling-off and then a rapid increase from the "empty nest" to the "retired"

Continued on next page.

---

* Adapted from Boyd C. Rollins and Harold Feldman, "Marital Satisfaction Over the Family Life Cycle," *Journal of Marriage and the Family,* 32 (1970), 20–28.

Figure 12.2. Percentage of individuals at each stage of the family life cycle reporting their marriage was going well "all the time."

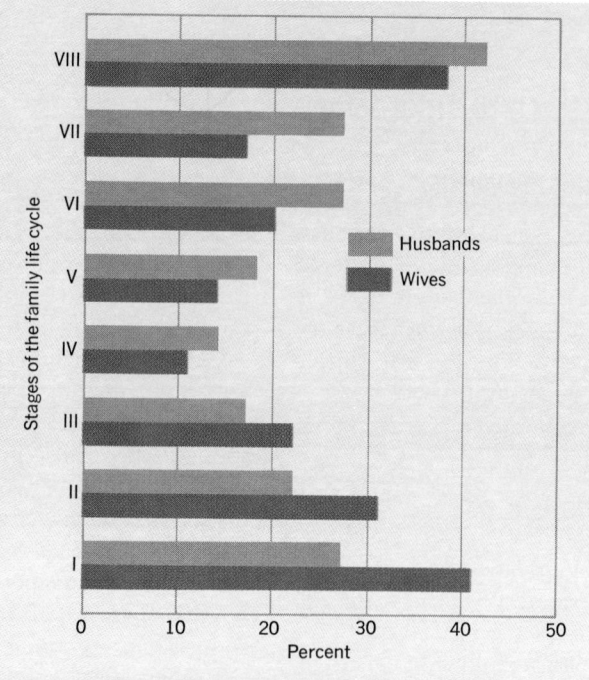

Source: Adapted from Boyd C. Rollins and Harold Feldman, "Marital Satisfaction Over the Family Life Cycle," *Journal of Marriage and the Family,* 32 (1970), 24, Tables 2 and 3.

stage. Husbands, in contrast, showed a slight decline from the "beginning" to the "schoolage" stage followed by a slight increase to the "empty nest" stage and then a rapid increase to the "retired" stage. (See Figure 12.2.)

With regard to positive companionship (laughing together, discussions with each other, having a stimulating exchange of ideas, and working together on a project), both husbands and wives reported a substantial decline from the "beginning" to the "preschool" stage, with a leveling-off in later stages, as shown in Figure 12.3. The wives also reported (although husbands revealed no consistent pattern) a sharp increase in negative feelings about their marriage with the arrival of the first child; this was followed by a leveling-off period, and then by a substantial drop in negative feelings with the "launching" stage.

Figure 12.3. Percentage of individuals in each stage of the family life cycle reporting "positive" companionship experiences with their spouse at least "once a day" or more often.

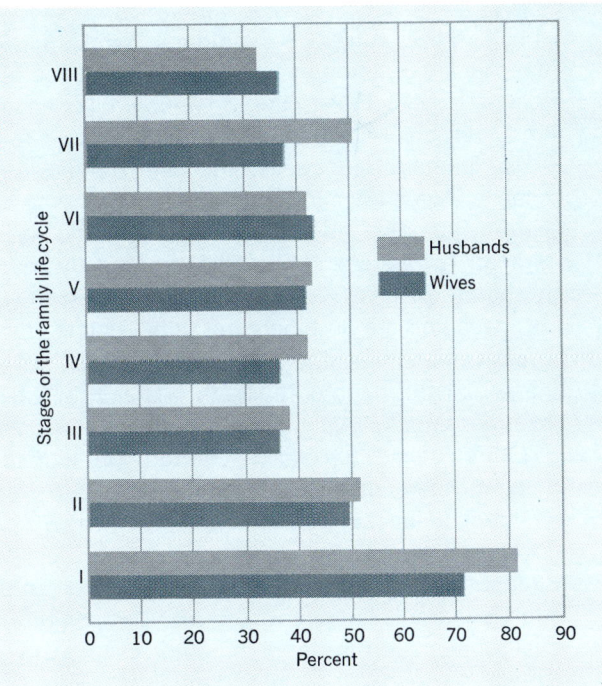

Source: Adapted from Boyd C. Rollins and Harold Feldman, "Marital Satisfaction Over the Family Life Cycle," *Journal of Marriage and the Family,* 32 (1970), 24, Tables 2 and 3.

Conclusions. The study suggests that the experiences of child-rearing have a rather profound and negative effect on marital satisfaction, particularly for wives. Overall, marital satisfaction appears to take a downward course until children leave home; then the pattern is reversed, with a marked increase in satisfaction occurring, especially during retirement.

SOCIAL CHANGE: SOME RECENT TRENDS

A good many long-held assumptions regarding marriage have increasingly given way in recent years. One of these is that women *must* marry in order to be fulfilled. The traditional role of a woman was assumed to be that of a homemaker and mother. Indeed, a woman who did not follow this course was considered to be defective as a woman—for instance, the stereotype of the prudist schoolmarm, the uptight librarian, or the masculine businesswoman. Moreover, the homemaker was seen as a woman who did not work (despite the fact that she performed an incredible variety of jobs demanding special skills); and since she did not "work" (in a society where one's job is the primary criterion for worth and status), the homemaker was at the bottom of the social heap. But as we noted in Chapter 9, the Women's Liberation Movement has done much to combat such assumptions.

Traditional notions regarding family authority have likewise undergone change. A century ago, American families were highly patriarchal, with superior authority and prestige vested in the husband—indeed, a married woman's property and earnings were legally beyond her control and at her husband's disposal. Recent marriage studies reveal that highly patriarchal arrangements are no longer the rule (Centers, Raven, and Rodrigues, 1971; Cromwell and Olson, 1975). Today perhaps only some 10 percent of marriages are husband-dominated; 4 percent wife-dominated; and the remainder broadly equalitarian (Centers, Raven, and Rodrigues, 1971).

Other changes have also occurred. Traditionally marriage was seen as a *state;* it was devoted to economic survival and the procreation and raising of children. In the play *Fiddler on the Roof,* when Tevye asks his wife, "Do you love me?," her answer is an incredulous shriek: "Do I *what?*" This was the strangest question he could have asked her. In the new world of Tevye's grandchildren, marriage is seen as a *companionship relation.* It implies mutual participation in the giving and receiving of affection, in confiding, in common experiences, and in family decisions. Couples increasingly ask of marriage that it meet a wide variety of personal needs—that they should enjoy intellectual companionship, warm intimate moments, shared values, deep romantic involvement, great sexual pleasures, in brief, "peak experiences" of all kinds.

Perhaps one of the most striking aspects about American society since World War II has been the rapid expansion in life-styles. Indeed, much of the conflict and turmoil of the late 1960s had to do with anxiety and uncertainty engendered by massive increases in the range of choices available to people. From the various liberation movements (Black, Chicano, Red, women, gay, youth) has come a wider acceptance (even institutionalization) of a set of pluralistic standards that legitimate a far wider range of styles than previously was the case. The ability to pursue a life-style more tailored to individual choice (and less constrained by standards of what a "respectable" person should be like) has been enhanced by increases in material affluence and cultural sophistication. Here we shall examine a number of these alternative life styles.

ONE-PERSON HOUSEHOLDS

I would be married, but I'd have no wife; I would be married to a single life.
Richard Crashaw, The Delights of the Muses, 1646

People living alone account for 21 percent of all American households and the figure is expected to reach 26 percent by 1985. Since 1970, the number of one-person households grew by 43 percent while the number of households with both a husband and wife increased by only 6 percent (Kronholz, 1977). One factor contributing to the increase in single households is that Americans are marrying later and less often. The median age of first marriage is up a year from a decade ago. In 1977, 45 percent of all women between ages twenty and twenty-four had never married, up from 28 percent in 1960. For men the figure rose to 64 percent from 53 percent. Another factor contributing to the increase in people living alone has been the doubling of the divorce rate during the past decade. Still another factor has been the increasing number of widows who are choosing to live by themselves (widows account for one-third of all one-person households). Whereas widows once moved in with their children, now only about ten percent do so (Lopata, 1973).

As Roger W. Libby notes, there are degrees of singleness:

> One may be more single one month than another but still not move outside the single status. Or, one may be single, choose to cohabit or marry, and perhaps choose to later divorce and become single again. In this sense singlehood and other choices are *reclaimable* statuses or identities. One has the option of repudiating a current identity or reclaiming an earlier status. (1977, p. 40)

In sum, singlehood (like marriage) is not a lifelong commitment for many people.

Although not so long ago single men and women were stereotyped as life's failures and dour and pathetic misfits, many Americans now question whether all individuals must marry to achieve happiness and well-being. Singles communities have arisen in many metropolitan areas. Moreover, single individuals can move into a singles apartment complex, go to a singles bar, take a singles trip, and, if they choose, lead an active sex life without acquiring an unwanted marital partner, child, or reputation. Unfortunately, we know little about singlehood, but what we do know seems best summarized by Libby: "Between the extreme images of the swinging and always elated single and the desperately lonely, suicidal single lies a continuum of single people with joys and sorrows similar to those of people electing other life-styles" (1977:49).

UNMARRIED COHABITATION

Census officials estimate that there are about one million unmarried couples currently living together and that the number will triple over the next decade (Kronholz, 1977). Richard R. Clayton and Harwin L. Voss (1977), based on a national sample of 2510 American males born in the decade from 1944 to

COHABITATION

OBSERVATION I guess you would say I am cohabiting with my boyfriend. He lives in an apartment off-campus and I "technically" live in a dorm. We first started seeing one another in just a casual way. But as time went on and we went to plays, football games, and basketball games together, we got more involved. Occasionally on weekends after a game there would be a party at his place. The parties lasted quite late and usually everyone got drunk and some even passed out. At first I always went back to the dorm but one night I was just too drunk and stayed overnight. As time went by I started staying over on weekends. Then we started adding other nights during the week so that now I just stay with him most of the time. I still have my room back at the dorm and I think my parents know what I'm up to, but we both pretend that nothing is amiss. I do the cooking and cleaning up around the place, much as in married arrangements.

PRINCIPLE Apparently most couples drift into cohabitation as we have done (Cole, 1977). We never made a conscious decision to live together but just kept increasing the amount of time we spent together. We don't consider ourselves married. We just feel it is natural for us to live together; we like it this way. We still maintain our separate residences and I go back to the dorm a couple of times during the week to get my mail and belongings and to see my friends.

1954, found that 18 percent of the men had at some time lived with a woman for six months or longer without being married (of the men, 64 percent had done so with only one partner). On major college campuses, about one-quarter to one-third of the students report that they are either currently living with or have lived with someone of the opposite sex (Henze and Hudson, 1974; Macklin, 1974; Peterman, Ridley, and Anderson, 1974; Bower and Christopherson, 1977). Further, a late 1977 *New York Times*-CBS News poll, based on a cross section of adult Americans, found that whereas nearly three-fourths of the population over 65 believed unmarried cohabitation "always wrong," an equal proportion of those under 30 believed it was "okay" or did not matter (Meislin, 1977). On the whole, the stigma associated with unwed living together has faded over the past decade.

In most cases, cohabiting college students do not view living together as a replacement for marriage or even as a "trial marriage." Rather than rejecting marriage, they appear merely to be adding a new form of courtship to traditional patterns (Bower and Christopherson, 1977). Living together without marriage satisfies needs for intimacy without the binding legal restrictions. In many respects, however, cohabitation is not radically different from marriage except that the participants generally acknowledge that they are *not* married. The partners easily fall into traditional gender roles and share many of the same functions as married couples (Macklin, 1974; Cole, 1977). Further, the emotional trauma of breaking up is often every bit as severe as among divorced couples undergoing divorce.

The growing popularity of unwed cohabitation is associated with the substantial changes that have occurred in the past ten years in sexual behavior, especially among young people. This is the second major period of rapid change that has taken place in this century, with the other occurring around the time of World War I. Prior to 1915, approximately 75 percent of all first-time brides were virgins; by 1920 the figure had dropped to around 50 percent (Terman, 1938; Kinsey et al., 1953; Burgess and Wallin, 1953). This decrease in virginity among women was largely associated with the increasing proportion of women having premarital relations with their future husbands. Between 1920 and 1965, little overall change occurred in *actual* premarital sexual behavior. However, in the post-World War II period, *attitudes* became more permissive (Clayton, 1975; Reiss, 1976).

Dramatic changes in sexual behavior showed up again in the latter 1960s (especially among women), with liberalization accelerating in the early 1970s (Urdy, Bauman, and Morris, 1975; Schulz, Bohrnstedt, Borgatta, and Evans, 1977). Due to the greater liberalization in female premarital sexual attitudes and behavior, the traditional double standard (allowing men but not women premarital sexual experience) was severely undermined. Taken as a whole, the evidence suggests that among the younger generation a single premarital sexual standard is coming to prevail (King, Balswick, and Robinson, 1977).

SINGLE-PARENT FAMILIES

Over the past two decades there has been a sharp rise in single parent families in the United States. Single-parent families have increased seven times more rapidly than the traditional two-parent family. As a result, approximately two out of every five children born in the 1970s have lived in a single-parent home for at least part of their youth. Currently one out of every three schoolchildren lives in a home headed by only one parent or relative (Nordheimer, 1977). The vast majority of children in single-parent families are reared by their mothers; less than nine percent by their fathers.

Single-parent homes are produced by unwed parenthood, divorce, desertion, marital separation, death, and, in a small but growing number of instances, adoption. In the mid-1970s, 14.2 percent of all births in the United States were to unwed mothers. And Washington, D.C., became the first major city in the nation with more children born out of wedlock than were born to married women (Kihss, 1977). However, divorce still accounts for

Figure 12.4. Marriage and divorce trends.

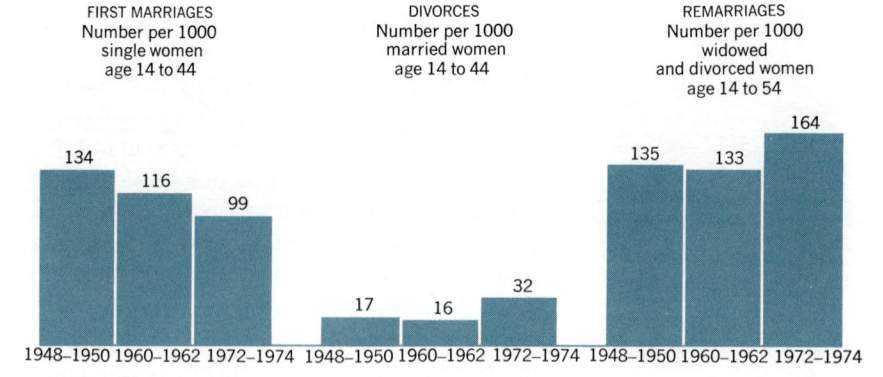

FIRST MARRIAGES Number per 1000 single women age 14 to 44	DIVORCES Number per 1000 married women age 14 to 44	REMARRIAGES Number per 1000 widowed and divorced women age 14 to 54
134 / 116 / 99	17 / 16 / 32	135 / 133 / 164
1948–1950 1960–1962 1972–1974	1948–1950 1960–1962 1972–1974	1948–1950 1960–1962 1972–1974

Source: *Pocket Data Book: USA 1976.* Washington, D.C.: Government Printing Office, 1977.

the largest number of single-parent homes, in part the product of the doubling of the divorce rate over the past decade (see Figure 12.4).

Many single-parent families experience economic difficulties. Slightly more than half of American children under eighteen years of age (and 62 percent under the age of six) who are living in homes with a female head also have a family income that falls below the poverty level. Single parents find that the responsibilities for family living fall on one adult rather than two and often calls for a good deal of juggling of time and energy. Their circumstances are frequently made more difficult by the fact that schools and workplaces have inflexible hours, and these hours do not coincide. One divorced mother comments:

> Everything is a tradeoff, a continuing conflict. There is no one else to do anything—shopping, dentists, chores, everything has to be done in evenings and week ends. I need the job, so I can't tell the boss to go to hell and take time off. (Brown, Feldberg, Fox, and Kohen, 1976, p. 123)

Until relatively recently it was widely believed that one-parent homes were defective and pathological. Increasingly, however, social scientists are coming to recognize that they are a viable family form (Billingsley and Giovannoni, 1971; Brandwein, Brown, and Fox, 1974). E. E. LeMasters observes:

> If one wishes to debate the number of adults required to socialize children properly the question can be raised: who decided that *two* parents are the proper number? Biologically this is natural enough, but this does not prove its social rightness.
>
> As a matter of fact, a good family sociologist, [Bernard] Farber, has asked the question—"Are two parents enough? . . . In almost every human society *more* than two adults are involved in the socialization of the child. (1974, p. 528)

Divorce on the rise. The Census Bureau indicates that there were 75 divorced persons for every 1000 married persons in the United States in 1976. In 1970, the ratio was only 47 per 1000. The bureau estimates that one-third of all married persons between 25 and 35 will eventually end their first marriage in divorce. About 40 percent of those who divorce and remarry will also have their second marriage end in divorce.

Patrick Reddy

Further, researchers find that differences are small or nonexistent between children from one- and two-parent homes of comparable social status with respect to school achievement, social adjustment, and delinquent behavior (Burchinal, 1964).

COMMUNES

The social unrest and change of the late 1960s gave rise to an estimated two to three thousand communes. Although there are various types of communes, most tend to be household arrangements of three or more persons for whom the chief bond is some form of sharing as opposed to ancestral or legal ties (Fairfield, 1972). The American version of the movement has a long historical tradition going back to such nineteenth century utopian communities as the Shakers, Fourierists, Zoarites, and Perfectionists (Kanter, 1972, 1973). For the most part, both the old and contemporary communes have been fragile institutions. This has been particularly true of those stressing personal freedom and a "do your own thing" ethic, an orientation clashing with the requirements of an integrated, cohesive, collective enterprise (Fairfield, 1972; Shey, 1977).

Rosabeth Moss Kanter has studied a number of urban communes in the Boston area. She finds that many people are attracted to communes in response to a life crisis:

> Young people who are out of school, new to a city, not attracted to marriage or perhaps divorced, find in communal living a way to create a family, live in a nice house, and lead a full, rich, family-like life. The recently separated and the single parent find communes a way to ease the pain of transition, to share the burdens, to develop a new life. People in mid-life, perhaps part of a couple, perhaps divorced, with grown or nearly grown children, find in communal living an opportunity to open their horizons, to start a new set of adventures, to focus on self-development instead of the narrower responsibilities of running a nuclear family. (1974, p. 44)

Kanter notes, however, that contemporary urban communes have frequently posed emotional difficulties for both children and their parents (Kanter, Jaffe, and Weisberg, 1975). Children experience confusion from rapid demands or corrections simultaneously emanating from a number of unrelated adults, what she terms the "Cinderella effect." The sharing of children also creates problems for their parents, until eventually parents tend to reserve for themselves the right to protect and punish their children. Other researchers also report stress in communal child-rearing (Berger, Hackett, and Millar, 1972). Rearing a child involves obligations for which most communes are not prepared since it necessitates a futuristic orientation, planning, and some status distinctions among adults.

HOMOSEXUAL RELATIONSHIPS

Conservative estimates place the number of adult Americans who are exclusively homosexual at about five million. Politically militant homosexual activists, who consider themselves a minority group like Blacks, place the number at nearer twenty million. Some twenty-five years ago, the distinguished sex researcher, Alfred Kinsey (1953), reported that by age forty about 37 percent of males and 13 percent of females had reached homosexual orgasm at least once in their lives. However, depending on the population sampled, only 3 to 16 percent of the men and 1 to 3 percent of the women were exclusively homosexual. Over the past decade homosexuals have become more vocal on such issues as job discrimination but the vast majority apparently still find it necessary to lead a "double life," concealing for most purposes their homosexual preferences. Most large and medium-sized cities in the United States have several bars catering to homosexuals, and many have at least one men's bath, a homosexual community center, and gay political groups and newsletters.

Despite setbacks, homosexuals have in recent years been winning greater public acceptance of their rights. Some major corporations—including AT&T, IBM, NBC, and the Bank of America—and the Federal Civil Service Commission have declared themselves equal opportunity employers with respect to homosexuals. A 1977 Gallup Poll revealed that 56 percent of those Americans questioned answered "yes" when asked, "In general do you think homosexuals should or should not have equal rights in terms of job opportunities?" When asked about specific jobs, however, 65 percent were against homosexuals as elementary school teachers. In contrast, 51 percent said homosexuals should be allowed in the armed forces and 68 percent approved of homosexuals as sales persons (Lichtenstein, 1977a). The population split, 43 percent each way, on whether "homosexual relations should or should not be legal." Fourteen percent had no opinion (Lichtenstein, 1977b).

For a quarter of a century the American Psychiatric Association listed homosexuality as a form of mental illness in its official diagnostic manual. In December 1973, the organization's board of directors voted to remove the label. The board explained: "For a mental condition to be considered a psychiatric disorder, it should either regularly cause emotional distress or regularly be associated with generalized impairment of social functioning: homosexuality does not meet those criteria." The following spring the organization's membership voted 5854 to 3810 to endorse the change (*Time*, September 8, 1975).

Liberalizing attitudes regarding alternative life styles. Although homosexuals still encounter considerable prejudice and discrimination, American society is becoming more willing to allow them freedom to express their sexual preferences. This gay couple has established a home with one another.

Patrick Reddy

SUMMARY

1. Throughout the world the family exhibits a great many forms and functions. We can identify certain broad tendencies regarding the structuring and functioning of the family, yet these are at best tendencies and not necessarily universals. For our purposes, we have viewed the family as a social arrangement united by ties of marriage, ancestry, or adoption that community members recognize as constituting a single household and having the responsibility for bringing up children. Six functions commonly performed by the family are sexual regulation, reproduction, socialization, maintenance, social placement, and gratification of personal needs.

2. Social relationships between adult males and adult females can be organized on a conjugal or a consanguine basis. If a society stresses the conjugal arrangement, the family consists of a nucleus of spouses and their offspring; blood relatives are functionally marginal and peripheral. If a society emphasizes the consanguine arrangement, the family consists of a nucleus of blood relatives; spouses are functionally marginal and peripheral. Both arrangements have certain advantages and disadvantages.

3. In the course of their lives, most Americans find themselves members of two nuclear families. First, a person belongs to a nuclear family consisting of oneself and one's father, mother, and siblings. This is termed the family of orientation. Second, since over 90 percent of Americans marry at least once, the vast majority of the population are members of a nuclear family consisting of oneself and one's spouse and children. This is termed the family of procreation.

4. Societies that trace descent through the father's line while ignoring the mother's line are referred to as patrilineal. Those that ignore the father's line are termed matrilineal. Some people are bilineal — descent is reckoned through both the father and the mother.

5. The rule of endogamy prescribes that individuals marry within certain groups of which they are members. The rule of exogamy forbids individuals from marrying within certain groups of which they are members. Conjugal relationships may be structured in four ways: monogamy, one husband and one wife; polygyny, one husband and two or more wives; polyandry, two or more husbands and one wife; and group marriage, two or more husbands and two or more wives.

6. A number of components are typically associated with romantic love. First there is the element of attention — the lover is absorbed and preoccupied with the loved one. Second, the lover desires physical and psychological intimacy — a yearning for a kind of personality fusion. And third, the lover derives special pleasure from doing things for and making gifts for the loved one — a selfless and unconditional generosity and even sacrifice. The cultural distribution of romantic love can best be viewed as a continuum between polar types. At one pole, a society views a strong love attraction as a laughable or tragic aberration; at the other, it defines marriage without love as mildly shameful.

7. Apparently in all societies, there are certain established ways by which mate selection is patterned and controlled. Whatever system they use, a child's kin have more in mind generally than just

getting the child married. They want the child married to the right spouse, especially where marriage has consequences for their larger kin group. There are a number of ways by which societies undertake to "contain" love: child marriage, seclusion of women, supervision of children, and informal group pressures.

8. Social scientists suggest that at leave five principal factors influence mate selection: (1) propinquity, (2) homogamy, (3) matching, (4) complementary needs, and (5) social exchange.

9. Sociologists find that there is initially a decrease in marital satisfaction and adjustment during the early years of marriage. In the middle and later stages of the family cycle, the evidence is less clear. Some researchers find a continual decline. More usually, however, they report a U-shaped curve, with a decline in satisfaction during the early years, a leveling-off during the middle years, and an increase in satisfaction during the later years.

10. A good many long-held assumptions regarding marriage have increasingly given way in recent years. One of these is that women must marry to be fulfilled. Traditional notions regarding family authority have likewise undergone change. Perhaps one of the most striking aspects about American society since World War II has been the rapid expansion in life-styles. Among these have been one-person households, unmarried cohabitation, single-parent families, communes, and homosexual relationships.

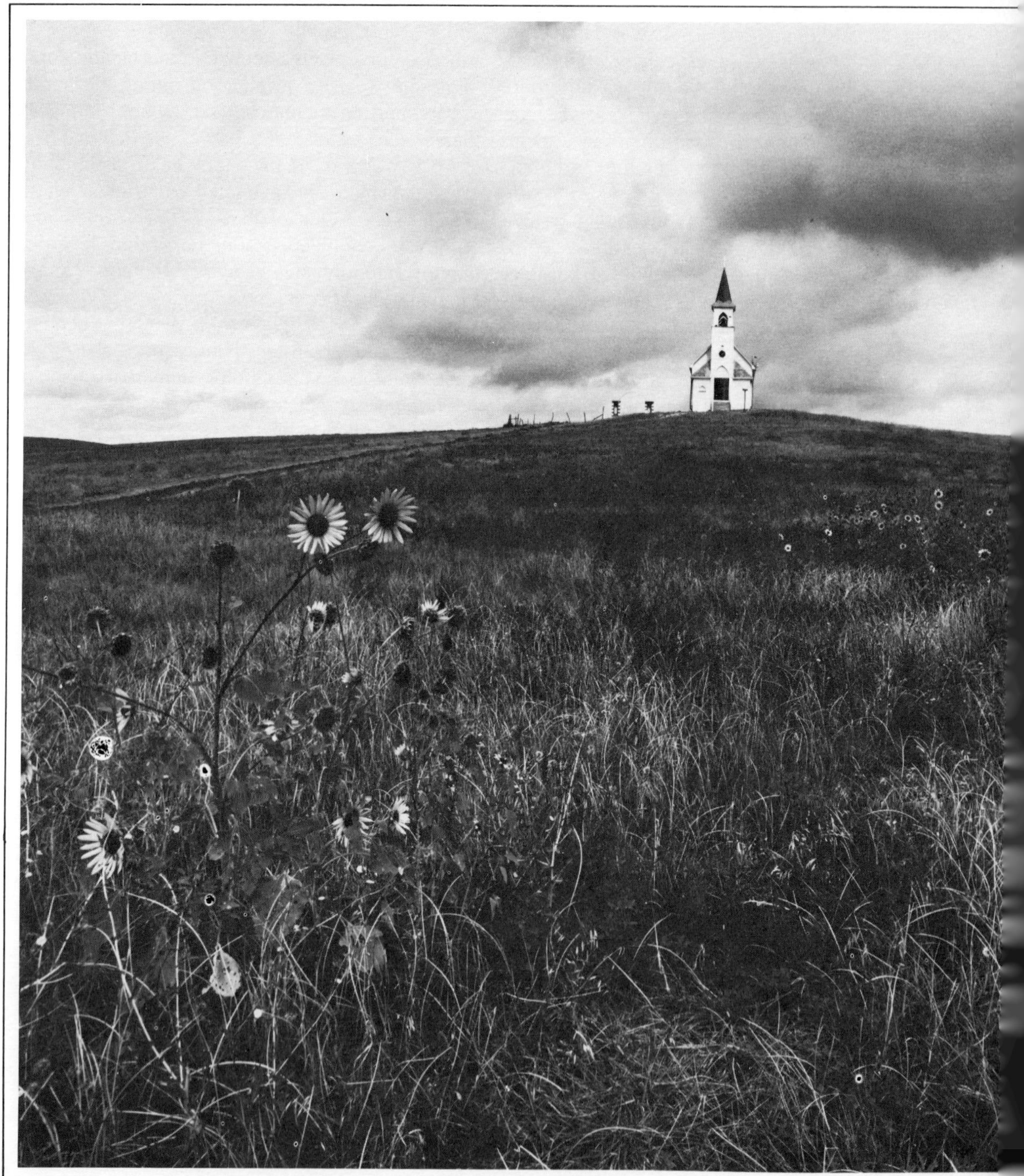

13 RELIGION

THE NATURE OF RELIGION
Secular and Humanistic Religions
Religion and Magic

FUNCTIONS
Dealing with the "Breaking Points"
An Integrator of Society
Opiate or Inspiration?

TYPES OF RELIGIOUS ORGANIZATION
Church
Sect
Denomination
Cult
The Emergence of Sects: The Black Muslims
Critique of the Church-Sect Typology

THE PROTESTANT ETHIC
The Weber Thesis
Critique of the Weber Thesis
Religious Preference and Worldly Success

SOCIAL CHANGE: SOME RECENT TRENDS
Secularization
Countercultural Religions
Catholic Pentecostalism

440 Institutions

OBSERVATION My friend, Jan, asked me to go to church with her today. It is in an area of small stores, many of them no longer used. We entered the door and were in a small musty room that looked as if it once had been an upholstery shop. There were about seventeen people there and no special person was in charge of the service. It was like a meeting of the Christians of the First Church told about in Acts (the New Testament). Another girl was there who besides myself was the only one new to the group. She wanted to know just what and why the group believed as they did. They answered her questions, showing her how the Scriptures supported the answers. I found it thrilling—just so amazing. When she would get an answer to her questions concerning the Lord Jesus Christ she said she felt electric shocks go through her. The joy of the group was contagious. I and the others felt our hearts brimming over, our beings radiating the joy of the Lord. What peace, what wonder, what sheer contentment!

PRINCIPLE This group was a religious sect. It did not have an established ministry but rather relied on lay inspiration. Rigid formal patterns of worship were absent and emphasis fell on spontaneous, emotional involvement of the fellowship. The service was characterized by fervor and active participation as opposed to passive listening. Considerable concern revolved about evangelism and conversion and not upon religious education.

Among both social scientists and the public the subject of "religion" has been gaining popularity in recent years (Wallis, 1975; Glock and Bellah, 1976; McCready and Greeley, 1976; Wuthnow, 1976a, 1976b). Indeed, the 1960s and 1970s have been decades of religious ferment, turmoil, and change. The 1960s opened with the nation electing its first Roman Catholic President and in 1976 Americans elected a "born again" Southern Baptist as their President. During the 1960s clergy and religious activists hurried South in civil rights marches and later North to antiwar protests. The Second Vatican Council of world bishops in the 1960s inaugurated major changes in Catholicism and launched controversial movements including those promoting the ordination of women priests, giving priests the option of marrying, and fostering neo-Pentecostalism (the Charismatics). And thousands of youth joined Hare Krishna, the Children of God, the Jesus People, and Sun Myung Moon's Unification Church.

By virtue of ethical and practical considerations, experimental studies involving religion have been exceedingly rare (Batson, 1977). Further, there have always been those who have viewed with distrust sociological studies of religion. It is the conviction of some thoughtful people that the objective study of religion is at best impossible, and at worst dangerous (Yinger, 1970). How is it possible, they ask, to "see" a stained-glass window from the outside? Its whole meaning only becomes apparent as the light shines through, just as the true meaning of religion is visible only to one on the inside. What can be the consequences of an objective study of religion, based as religion is on faith, but the weakening of that very faith? And some would add: At a time when humans so desperately need courage to face the crises that beset the world, is not the weakening of faith disastrous?

Yet, by the same reasoning, we could also argue that only monogamists should study monogamy; only confirmed democrats, democracy; and only dedicated capitalists, capitalism. Of course, some things can be said about religion only by the practitioner, and the sociologist will need to take the statements and actions of the practitioner into account. But some kinds of observations can be made by people who share another faith, and still others by doubters, all of whose observations may provide the sociologist with fruitful insights. Further, as Kingsley Davis observes:

> . . . whether or not religious ideas are true is probably the least important question for social science. Religious behavior includes many things besides statements of purported fact. Much more important for social science is the role of ritual and belief, of the clergy and the church, of symbols and taboos, in the social system. (1951, p. 12)

In other words, sociology is primarily interested in exploring the part religion plays in human behavior. Indeed, if religious beliefs and practices are found in every known society, as does seem to be the case, then no study of society would be complete that neglected religion.

THE NATURE OF RELIGION

The propitiation or conciliation of powers superior to man which are believed to control the course of nature or of human life.
James G. Frazer, The Golden Bough, I, 1890

As with the family, sociologists have had difficulty finding a definition of religion that is at once neither so narrow as to exclude much behavior that we commonly take to be religious nor so broad as to encompass all human behavior (Berger, 1974; Weigert, 1974; Machalek and Martin, 1976; Machalek, 1977). For our purposes, we shall define **religion** as those ways of thinking, feeling, and acting by which people undertake to deal with the ultimate problems of life. Religion is concerned with those aspects of experience that transcend the mundane events of everyday existence—with those comparatively vague and intangible features of life.

Religion is not limited to doctrine, dogma, church attendance, devotion, or ritual but encompasses people's conception of the Real. It involves behaviors that pertain to some kind of "beyond" or "otherness." It is the way humans struggle with the ultimate questions of the meaning and purpose of

Behavior that pertains to some kind of "beyond" or "otherness". Religion deals with ultimate questions having to do with the meaning and purpose of life. In the photo a Hindu Holy Man holds a replica of the trident of Shiva.

United Nations/Jongen

life. As such, religion provides interpretations for the most complex problems such as suffering, death, injustice, evil, and uncertainty. In brief, it saves people from having to live with a pervasive and debilitating chaos (McCready and Greeley, 1976). Hence, as with other realms of life, humans in their religious behavior are creatures suspended in webs of meaning which they themselves spin.

Common to most religions is a complex of beliefs and practices that pertain to *superhuman* beings. In Buddhism, for instance, Buddha is seen as a superhuman being, who, unlike ordinary humans, acquired the power to attain Enlightenment (a totally transformed state of consciousness) and hence Buddhahood. Moreover, he showed the Way for its attainment. Without

Buddha's teachings, humans could not, unassisted, have discovered the way to Enlightenment and Final Release. Whereas in the Judeo-Christian-Islamic tradition God is living, Buddha is viewed as dead. Nonetheless, for the Buddhist and the Western religionist alike, the Way to salvation was revealed by a superhuman being, and salvation can be attained only if one follows this revealed Way. In the one case, compliance with the Way leads directly to the ultimate goal because of the very nature of the world; in the other, compliance leads to the goal only after divine intercession. Similarly, superhuman beings generally have the power to assist (or hinder) people in their attempts to realize mundane as well as supermundane goals. For example, Buddha—or, according to more sophisticated believers, his power—is believed to protect people from harm. Hence, Burmese peasants recite Buddhist spells and perform rites before certain Buddha images that are believed to have the power of protecting them from harm, to cure snake bites, and the like (Spiro, 1966).

SECULAR AND HUMANISTIC RELIGIONS

Religion is like the fashion: one man wears his doublet slashed, another laced, another plain; but every man has a doublet; so every man has a religion. We differ about the trimming.
John Selden, Table Talk, 1689

At times we overlook the religious overtones in behavior that is otherwise thought of as nonreligious and even anti-religious. The search for a doctrine that reveals the meaning of existence and answers the fundamental questions that are set by life may lead one person to God while another to "the party," nationalism, science, or some other agency. It is a mistake to disregard the differences that these choices indicate, but it is equally a mistake to overlook certain similarities.

Communism. Arthur Koestler describes the religious quality that communism had for him in quite vivid terms:

> By the time I had finished with *Feuerbach* and *State and Revolution* [books by Marx and Lenin], something had clicked in my brain which shook me like a mental explosion. To say that one had "seen the light" is a poor description of the mental rapture which only the convert knows (regardless of what faith he has been converted to). The new light seems to pour from all directions across the skull; the whole universe falls into pattern like the stray pieces of a jigsaw puzzle assembled by magic at one stroke. There is now an answer to every question, doubts and conflicts are a matter of the tortured past—a past already remote, when one had lived in dismal ignorance in the tasteless, colorless world of those who *don't know*. (1949, p. 23)

Many social scientists have noted the similarities between communism and Christianity (Grossman, 1975; O'Toole, 1975). Communism offers a world view; a promise of a Messianic Era (a communist utopia); a detailed program for personal conduct; a priesthood; inspired revelators; saints; martyrs; missionaries; heresies; inquisitions; sacred shrines (Lenin's and Mao's tombs); and ikons (statues of Marx, Lenin, Mao, and others). Indeed, Santiago Carillo, leader of the Spanish Communist party, has recently noted that he considers the new movement of Western European Communists against Moscow's dominance comparable to Martin Luther's rejection of Rome:

> We had our pope, our Vatican, and we thought we were predestined to triumph.... And why not make a comparison with Luther? Nowadays he wouldn't be burned by the Inquisition. Heretics usually turn out to be all right. (Quoted by Lewis, 1976, p. 2)

Of course within the Soviet Union and other Communist nations, Marxism has become very much a state religion (Zeldin, 1969).

National and Civil Religions. Contemporary nationalism has also taken on many religious qualities:

> The cult of nationalism has its high priests, its rituals, and its theology no less than other cults.... The patriot has learned reverence for the land of his ancestors—for merrie England, America the beautiful, *la Patrie,* or *das Vaterland*. This involves both ancestor worship and territorial fetishism.... Living political leaders are judged by the degree to which they appear to come up to or fall short of the traditional standards set by the departed figures of national myths and legend.
> Similarly, the patriot worships the land of his nation—the hallowed soil, watered by the blood of heroes.... The national flag is everywhere a peculiarly sacred symbol, always to be respected and never to be defiled. (Schumann, 1933, pp. 287–288)

Indeed, any number of writers have observed that nationalism within many of the new nations of Africa and Asia can be best understood as a political religion (Apter, 1963).

Social and political philosophers beginning with Jean Rousseau (1712–1778) have identified and discussed the role of **civil religion** in nation-states (Thomas and Flippen, 1972; Richey and Jones, 1974; Wimberley et al., 1976). More recently, Robert N. Bellah (1967, 1975) has outlined a number of components of American civil religion. Its central ideas include the notion that Christianity is the national faith and the premise that the real religion of Protestants, Catholics, and Jews is the "American Way of Life." Although it has Biblical parallels (the United States as the "New Israel," George Washington as Moses, and Abraham Lincoln as the suffering Christ figure), American civil religion remains at a diffuse and abstract level, providing a guiding vision. While American religious pluralism prevents any one denomination from being used by all people as the lone source of meaning, civil religion compensates by affording an overarching sacred canopy (Cole and Hammond, 1974). The beliefs, symbols, and rituals of the American civil religion find expression in the statements and documents of the Founding Fathers, Presidential inaugural addresses, national holidays, historic shrines, and patriotic expressions in times of crisis and peril.

Science and Humanism as Religions. For some science has come to take on certain attributes of religion (science viewed as a way of life and not as a method). Many modern intellectuals find that a supernatural view of the world has become meaningless to them, yet they are also repelled by doctrinaire political faiths and by boastful and worshipful nationalism. They feel quite comfortable with a quiet kind of scientific secularism, motivated by curiosity and perhaps coupled with a nudge from a desire to help solve some human problem. In brief, science has become a way of life for them, one that provides them with answers to such questions as "salvation" (how humanity can be saved from its most difficult problems), the nature of reality, and evil (why do people suffer). Perhaps "secular religion" would be an appropriate term for such phenomena as this (along with communism and nationalism) — as distinct from "religion" unqualified, as defined earlier (Yinger, 1957).

There is the further question as to what to call such beliefs as Humanism:

> Religion for the Humanists is almost identical with ethics. They discard all theological beliefs about God, heaven, hell, and immortality. Substituted for God are the supreme values, the good in human life which man himself must strive to increase. Heaven is the ideal society here on earth and hell the society in which war, disease, and ignorance flourish. The soul is the human personality and immortality is one's influence on other personalities, both during one's life and after it has ended. (Vernon, 1962, p. 57)

The superhuman element is obviously missing from Humanism, although it does concern itself with the ultimate problems of life. Humanism, Ethical Culture, and other such faiths, then, might appropriately be labeled "humanistic religion" to take account of this fact.

RELIGION AND MAGIC

Religion is not removed by removing superstition.
    Cicero, De Divinatione, II, 78 B.C.

Certain broad similarities exist between religion and magic. Both share the conception of "beyond" — the idea of a "nonempirical" reality, a faith in processes and powers whose effectiveness cannot be established simply by

MAGIC

OBSERVATION While I played football in high school I had a number of superstitious rituals that I would go through before every game. First, the night before the game and immediately after our team meeting, I would go out to get something to eat with my friend, Danny, who played guard. We always had the same thing to eat and always went together. The day of the game I would always go over to the football field on Madison Street rather than Monroe which would have been the more normal way to go. As long as we were winning I would never change my shoelaces and if one broke I would just retie it in a knot. And I wouldn't get a haircut during football season.

PRINCIPLE These procedures were forms of magic involving mechanical manipulation of superhuman power. I just didn't want to test the fates or break my luck. We did win eight out of nine games and the conference championship but the magic wasn't all that good as I got hit in the sixth game and broke my leg.

observation. They differ, however, in a number of respects. First, religion is primarily concerned with fundamental issues of human existence—such things as salvation, life's meaning, and death—while magic revolves around specific, concrete, and detailed problems—such things as control of the weather, assurance of a good crop, and victory in battle (Malinowski, 1944). In other words, magic is employed primarily to reach "here-and-now" goals; it provides something like an old-fashioned book of recipes or a home medical manual.

Second, magic and religion differ in the means they commonly employ in dealing with the nonempirical or the superhuman. Religionists pray and sacrifice; they use techniques similar to those they have found useful in dealing with other persons. Love, punishment, reverence, and command have all been means used for dealing with superhuman spirits—cajolery, bribery, and false pretenses may be viewed as effective as awe. There is probably no customary behavior toward one's fellows that is not found somewhere as a religious technique. In contrast with religion, magic employs *mechanistic manipulation*. It involves the *compulsion* of superhuman power; no submission or conciliation is necessary. Thus, the mere fact of carrying a rabbit's foot compels its inherent supernatural power to bring good luck—this quality of bringing good luck is as much an attribute of the object as is color and weight. One does not talk to the rabbit's foot or offer it gifts; no spirit is involved (Benedict, 1938).

Although the beliefs and practices of some societies fall quite clearly in the category of religion or magic, others do not permit rigid categorization.

In Tikopia, for instance, when a man is fishing with a rod and line on the reef, he recites a formula commanding the fish to come to bite on the hook. He addresses the fish alone and brings in no spirit being. But he does not merely order the fish to obey. . . . He talks to the fish as he would to a human being, he cajoles them with tempting offers. He believes that they hear and appreciate his words. . . . But he also calls upon spiritual beings, his ancestors and guardian dieties, to assist in bringing the fish to him. Here command and entreaty, belief in his own power of "spellbinding," and in the power of his spirit helpers are so closely intertwined with his practical situation, that to separate out the magical and religious elements involved would be to tear the formula apart, phrase by phrase, and almost word by word. (Firth, 1958, pp. 133–135)

Since some practices do not permit a clear-cut placement in either a religious or magical category, it seems advisable to avoid a rigid dichotomy. Instead, religion and magic can be viewed as two polar types on a continuum, with many shades of difference in between (Benedict, 1938; Hammond, 1970):

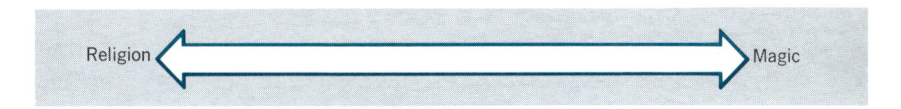

Religion ⟵⟶ Magic

FUNCTIONS

The prevalence of religion in societies throughout the world raises the question of the contributions it makes to social life. Since all societies have something known as religion, its presence can hardly be dismissed as accidental (Davis, 1949). There is good reason for considering the functions of religion.

DEALING WITH THE "BREAKING POINTS"

If I were personally to define religion I would say that it is a bandage that man has invented to protect a soul made bloody by circumstance.

Theodore Dreiser

In their lives, people confront conditions of uncertainty and insecurity; some events of critical significance to their safety and welfare are *beyond* their plan, design, and control. Humanity is confronted with more or less recurrent crises and certain haunting perplexities—the holocausts of nature, flood, epidemic, drought, famine, war, accident, sickness, vast and sudden social change, personal defeat and humiliation, conflict and dissension, injustice, the nature and meaning of life, the mystery of death, and the enigma of the hereafter:

RELIGION AND LIFE'S BREAKING POINTS

OBSERVATION My grandmother died today. It is a big upset for our family and especially me. I always have been very close to grandma. Until she had gotten sick a few months ago, she had been a person who was full of life and liked to travel a lot. Every summer since Grandpa died six years ago, she and I went on a trip—one year to Europe, another to the Far East and Japan, still another to Latin America, and so on. She was a very bright, creative, and talented woman, and I found her quite stimulating. I truly learned a lot from her and I find I'm like her in many ways (my family and friends say the same thing). I've really been extremely sad and I've been crying a lot. My main comfort is my religion and my belief that our family will be reunited in an afterlife.

PRINCIPLE My religion is helping me through a breaking point in my life. It is filling the gap that I am experiencing now that grandma is dead. In this case my religion is providing me with an answer to some of the questions I am asking revolving about grandma's death.

> Man is so perplexed, so helpless in such an inscrutable, frustrating world, the uncertainties, obscurities, and solicitudes of which are for him very real, that he feels the necessity of some sort of explanation, some sort of security and certainty against mischance and the unknown in all its innumerable forms; he wants cosmic peace, positive affirmations of stability and continuity, spiritual serenity, some assurance of a mode of reconciliation as a policy of welfare, some adjustment to, and identity with, the ultimates and absolutes. (Hertzler, 1961, pp. 464–465)

We live under conditions of uncertainty—human ventures, no matter how carefully planned or expertly executed, go awry. Further, our capacity to control and affect the conditions of our lives, although technologically increasing, are limited; in some respects, we seem powerless. In brief, the human condition brings us face-to-face with situations in which established, mundane techniques and prescriptions are simply inadequate. Why, for instance, should we have to die? Why should a loved one die, and in unfulfilled youth? Why should this venture on which I set my heart go amiss? Why must I be ill? At these "breaking points" beyond ordinary, daily experience, religion can fulfill a real social need. It provides "answers" and offers the prospect of hope—of spiritual intercession or magical control (O'Dea, 1966; Geertz, 1966). Thus, J. Milton Yinger (1977) finds in a religious survey conducted in five countries (Japan, Korea, Thailand, New Zealand, and Australia) that religions, in all their diversity, rest on a common base: the persistent experience of injustice, suffering, and meaninglessness and the conviction that, despite the enduring quality of these problems, they can be dealt with by our own beliefs and actions.

AN INTEGRATOR OF SOCIETY

Religion is the basis of civil society, and the source of all good and of all comfort.
Edmund Burke, Reflections on the Revolution in France, *1790*

An abiding proposition of sociology has been that religion serves the central and critical function in society of supporting what has been variously called social integration, social solidarity, and social cohesion (Glock and Stark, 1965; Nottingham, 1971). Underlying this proposition is a still more general one: In order to maintain itself, every society must realize some degree of consensus around a set of basic values—in brief, an agreement on ultimate meaning that affords a foundation for social organization and common action. This view constituted the central thesis of a book by Émile Durkheim, the eminent French sociologist (1858–1917), entitled *The Elementary Forms of Religious Life*. Durkheim viewed religion as "a unified system of beliefs and practices relative to sacred things [that] . . . unite[s] into one single moral community . . . all those who adhere to them" (1947:47).

A social integrator. Rituals play an important part in providing people with a social sense of oneness. Here Jews celebrate Simchath Torah (Rejoicing in the Law—the Gift of the Bible).

Israel Government Tourist Office

According to this view, religion makes a number of significant contributions to social integration. First, its *belief system* affords support to basic societal values. Second, its system of *supernatural rewards and punishments* often helps to insure the translation of societal values into everyday behavior. And third, its *ritual* provides for the periodic reinforcement of, identification with, and commitment to these values.

Durkheim was particularly impressed by the part rituals play in recharging people's sense of collective solidarity. Festivities, marriage and funeral ceremonies, flag salutes, church services, singing the national anthem in unison, holiday parades, and public gatherings symbolize the reality of the group and people's relation to it. By uttering the same words or performing the same gesture, people inform one another that they share a common unity and harmony. And simultaneously, the rituals fuse people within a fellowship of sentiment, a shared mental state. Thus, rituals are mechanisms by which individuals *reveal* to one another that they share a common mental state while serving to *create* among themselves a collective consciousness.

OPIATE OR INSPIRATION?

Religious distress is at the same time the *expression* of real distress. Religion is the sigh of the oppressed creature, the heart of a heartless world, just as it is the spirit of an unspiritual situation. It is the opium of the people.
Karl Marx, Introduction, Critique of the Hegelian Philosophy of Right, *1844*

A recurring theme in sociological literature is that religious involvement serves to accommodate people to existing social arrangements, producing a highly otherworldly focus and little concern with thisworldly social change. J. Milton Yinger states the matter in these terms:

> If a society is to exist at all, it must find some means for distributing its scarce goods and values in such a way that the great majority accept the outcome or protest against it only by means approved by the social system itself. And it must find a way to control the expression of hostility generated by frustration, pain, and guilt. . . . Insofar as it is accepted religion, by rite and symbol, gives emotional support to the fundamental values of a society; it softens the hardness of the struggle for scarce values by emphasizing values that can be achieved by all (e.g., salvation); and it lessens the tension of those who have failed to achieve a desired level of a society's values by approved means by emphasizing supra-mundane values. (1957, pp. 63–65)

Charles Y. Glock, Benjamin B. Ringer, and Earl R. Babbie set forth a somewhat similar "comfort thesis":

Contrasting views regarding religion. Karl Marx (the photo on the left) considered religion a tool by which a ruling class keeps the masses in check by offering them nextworldly salvation in return for thisworldly subservience. Émile Durkheim (the photo on the right) took quite a different position. He viewed religion as a critical instrument for promoting social integration and solidarity.

The attributes which a society values most, it is also most likely to reward. Such rewards appear in different forms: money, power, status, attention, a sense of belonging, and so forth. People who lack the valued attributes, are to some extent, deprived of the concomitant rewards. The church, then becomes an alternative source of rewards for those who cannot fully enjoy the fruits of secular society. Parishioners who feel outside the mainstream of society by virtue of being famililess find a surrogate family in the church. Elderly parishioners who may feel cast out of the youth-oriented secular society find acceptance within the church. Lower class parishioners are taught that secular status is ultimately irrelevant. Women who are denied serious consideration for the responsible positions in secular society find they can be very important to the life of the church. In sum, the church offers a refuge for those who are denied access to valued achievement and rewards in everyday American life. (1967, p. 107)

Culver Pictures

The Bettmann Archive

It was this aspect of religion that was the basis for Marx's angry comment that religion is "the opium of the people," a painkiller for frustration and deprivation that interferes with the masses' attainment of "true class consciousness." From this viewpoint, the explosive tensions of society are kept in check by religion, but this is done for the benefit of the elite. A number of early socialist leaders, including Marx and Engels, noticed that radical political parties of the left *competed* with the churches in offering opposite solutions to the deprived, the one calling for change, the other for acceptance. Leon Trotsky (Russian revolutionist) was so aware of the similarity of revolutionary Marxism to religious sectarianism that in the late 1890s he successfully recruited the first working-class members of the South Russian Workers' Union among adherents to religious sects.

Religion, however, does not always function in the conservative manner depicted by Yinger, Glock, and Marx nor does it necessarily attract those

Religion — an opiate? Marxists argue that religious involvement drains away the explosive tensions associated with social inequality. Religious occasions such as Palm Sunday offer the disadvantaged hope in a nextworldly life.

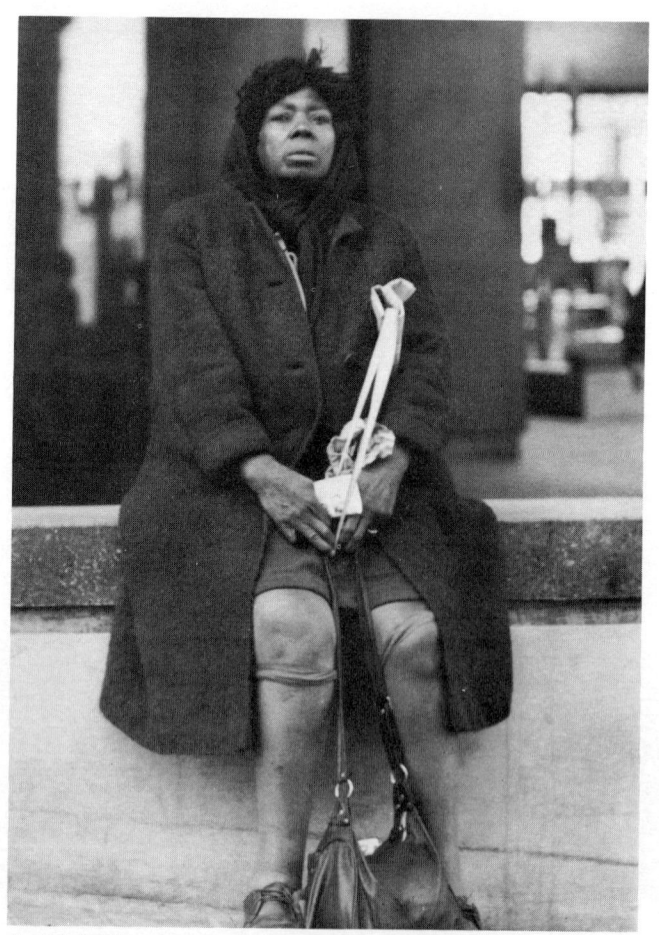

Patrick Reddy

who find their lot a difficult one (Stark, 1972; Hobart, 1974; Carr and Hauser, 1976). Black religion has historically made a significant contribution to the mobilization of protest as evidenced in the 1960s by the civil rights movement identified with Rev. Martin Luther King, Jr. Although a sectarian, otherworldly emphasis corroded civil rights militancy, a churchlike orientation associated with the established Black denominations made for greater militancy (Nelsen, Madron, and Yokley, 1975; Hunt and Hunt, 1977). Similarly, Bryan R. Wilson (1973) finds that religious movements have frequently had a strong protest theme among tribal and third-world peoples including the Delaware Prophet movement (associated with the Pontiac Indian uprising), the Ghost Dances of 1870 and 1890 (among Pacific Coast and Plains Indians), and the Mau Mau (an anti-colonial movement in Kenya during the 1950s).

TYPES OF RELIGIOUS ORGANIZATION

A prevalent interest among sociologists studying religion has been a concern with classifying different religious organizations. A typology that appears rather frequently in sociological writings has involved a fourfold division (Niebuhr, 1929; Troeltsch, 1931; von Wiese and Becker, 1932; Pope, 1942): (1) church, (2) sect, (3) denomination, and (4) cult. Let us examine each of these types in turn.

CHURCH

I contemplate with sovereign reverence that act of the whole American people . . . [of] building a wall of separation between church and state.
Thomas Jefferson, To Baptists of Danbury, Conn., 1802

. . . the fatal theory of the separation of Church and State.
Pope Leo XIII

The model often used for describing the church is Roman Catholicism during the Middle Ages. The aim of the church is professedly universal, and membership is frequently compulsory. The phrase, "Come out from among them and be ye separate," has no place in the ideology of a church—indeed the theme "Force them to come in" better characterizes its thinking. Thus, in the Middle Ages, populations were often "converted" and baptized *en masse*—by "fire and sword." Members are *born into* the church; they do not have to *join* it. All children of members born within a territory are automatically, through birth, defined as members.

454 Institutions

The church. The church is an institution that has established itself across many generations. It commonly views itself as an integral part of the larger society rather than as a select group set apart from and at odds with the broader community.

Patrick Reddy

The church usually makes its peace with the secular aspects of social life; it compromises the more radical teachings of Jesus and accepts many features of the larger world as at least relatively good. It tends to be a conservative body and customarily allies itself with the upper classes. Generally, it does not champion "new causes" or social reform—in fact, it often longs for an earlier way of life. The church attaches a high importance to the means of grace that it administers, to a system of doctrine that it has formulated, and to the administration of sacraments that it controls through an official clergy. It strives to dominate all elements within society, to teach and guide them, and to dispense to them saving grace. In the Middle Ages, the ideal of church supremacy came close to realization; the doctrine that the king (the state) was subordinate to the pope (the church) was virtually unchallenged.

The Anglican Church of England, the Roman Catholic Church in Spain, and the Lutheran Church in the Scandinavian countries represent close approximations to national churches. However, as changes occur within a society, a church may gradually be reduced to the status of a denomination. In contemporary England, groups other than the Anglican are increasing their importance and thereby diminishing the influence of the Church of England. By virtue of the special conditions existing within the United States, the Roman Catholic Church functions within this country more like a denomination than a church.

SECT

Come unto me, all ye that labor and are heavy laden, and I will give you rest.

Matthew, 11:28

The sect is a small, voluntary fellowship of converts, most usually drawn from the lower class, who seek to realize the divine law in their own behavior. The sect has abandoned the attempt to win the whole world over to its doctrines; it follows literally the phrase, "Come out from among them and be ye separate"; exclusiveness is stressed. Those who entertain heretical opinions or commit moral misdemeanor are subject to expulsion. Its self-conception is of an elect—*the* religious elite. Religious interpretations other than its own are seen as in error—it alone possesses special enlightenment. It rejects the social environment in which it exists; at times, it may even discourage its members from extensive participation in the "ways of the world" —for example, the sect may prescribe specific patterns of dress (as among the Old Order Amish) or speech (as among the early Quakers); it may prohibit smoking and drinking (as among the Mormons) or forbid the use of automobiles, telephones, and cameras, the bearing of arms, the taking of oaths, and participation in litigation (as among the Old Order Amish).

The sect frequently requires a definite type of religious experience as a prerequisite of acceptance. Through the conversion experience, individuals "know" they are "saved" and are "on the right path." A sharp distinction between clergy and laity is not drawn; the sect prefers to trust for guidance to lay inspiration rather than to theological expertness. Emotional demonstrations during services are common; rigid formal patterns of worship are avoided, since it is felt that they hinder the free expression of the "manifestations of the spirit." Liston Pope describes a typical Holiness sect service in North Carolina:

> The service begins at eight o'clock or thereabouts. Rather, the actions of the congregation become more intense and concerted in character; there is almost nothing by way of formal announcement. The choir, in cooperation with the pastor, breaks into a rhythmic hymn, and the congregation follows suit. . . . The stanzas are punctuated with loud shouts of "Hallelujah," "Thank you, Jesus," "Glory," and the rhythmic clapping of hands and tapping of feet. Almost immediately, various members of the congregation begin to "get the Holy Ghost" (as a teenage boy awesomely remarks). One young woman leaves the front row of the choir and jerks about the pulpit, with motions so disconnected as to seem involuntary, weird. A man's head trembles violently from side to side. Another man, tieless and red-faced, laughs boomingly at odd moments, in a laugh resembling that of intoxication.
>
> Half a dozen songs follow in succession. Then comes a prayer, with everybody kneeling on the floor and praying aloud at the same time, each in his own way. Some mutter with occasional shouts; others chant, with frequent bendings backward and forward; the volume of sound rises and falls, without unified pattern or group concentration. The pastor's voice booms out occasionally above all the others. Then, as if by a prearranged but unobservable signal, the prayer abruptly ends; the onlooker is amazed to see emerging from the confusion a concerted return to a sitting position. The cacophony of prayer is ended as suddenly as it began.
>
> Then the pastor reads "the Scripture." . . . Having finished the Scripture lesson, the preacher takes up a collection. . . . Then the service moves toward a climax; the taking of the collection has been an emotional interlude. The preacher begins a sermon; more precisely, he enunciates verbal symbols that arouse immediate response from the congregation. Such motifs play through his shoutings as "sanctification," "the Second Coming," "the world despises and misunderstands and lies about the Church of God," "Jesus can heal your body and soul." . . . Then there is a testimony meeting in which a large number of the more faithful testify to their personal experience and joy in religion, some mutteringly, some loudly, fervidly. . . .

The sect. The sect calls on people to join a select group who conceive of themselves as a religious elite.

Patrick Reddy

All the while waves of ecstatic rhythm have been sweeping over the congregation, with the actions of the preacher setting the pace. There are patterns to the rhythmic actions: running around the pulpit, holding trembling hands to the sky, very fast clogging of the feet, swinging the arms in sharp, staccato motions.

About ten o'clock the pastor calls for sinners to come to the front and kneel around the altar (constructed of a bench quickly placed before the pulpit). About ten come, including one five-year-old boy. A hundred members of the congregation gather about, and a tremendous tumult ensues as they attempt to "pray and shout the sinners through," interspersed with wild demonstrations of joy as one is "saved."

It is nearly 11 P.M., but one stays and wonders. They cry out, and cry; they are drunken, but not with wine; they stagger, but not with strong drink.*

* Reprinted by permission of the Yale University Press from *Millhands & Preachers* by Liston Pope. Copyright © 1942 by Yale University Press.

DENOMINATION

Church and sect may be viewed as polar types on a continuum. Near the center of the continuum between the poles of church and sect falls the denomination:

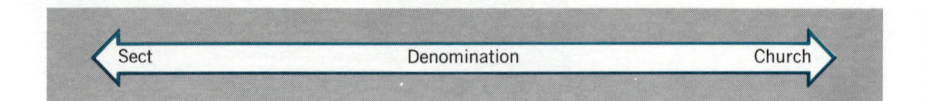

⟵ Sect   Denomination   Church ⟶

Denominations are simply sects in an advanced stage of development and adjustment to the secular world. The membership of the denomination comes mainly from the middle class. The moral rigor and religious fervor of the sect are relaxed. Spontaneous demonstrations by congregation members are discouraged and shunned as vulgar displays; services are formal, the congregation participating only in prescribed ways. The clergy have undergone specialized training to prepare them for their positions, usually at a theological seminary. Although conversions still occur, most new members are born into the denomination. Consequently, church officials are especially concerned with developing a training program to prepare the children of members to become adult adherents of their creed. Denominational members often view church-going as one of the duties of an upstanding member of the community; religion is only one among many interests and involves a segmental commitment rather than the totalitarian commitment of the sect. The denomination is content to be one movement among others, all of which are thought to be acceptable in the sight of God. Present-day denominations include the Presbyterians, Baptists, Congregationalists, Methodists, and Unitarians.

CULT

Cults are a special type of religious organization, characterized by a very amorphous, loosely textured structure. They generally lack rigid, sharply defined creeds and well-formulated criteria for membership. They are "open" rather than "closed" groups—inviting all to come freely rather than admitting only a select few who can pass strict doctrinal tests. Further, they lack tight discipline imposed by rank-and-file members who are preoccupied with holding one another "up to the mark." Cult leadership is informal and often built about the considerable emotional appeal of a leader. Generally, cults are primarily concerned with the problems of individuals, appealing to people who are confronted with loneliness, fear, inferiority, tension, and kindred troubles. Some cults are built about a single function

Figure 13.1.
Types of religious organization.

	Culturally respectable	Culturally deviant
Claims lone legitimacy	CHURCH	SECT
Accepts pluralistic legitimacy	DENOMINATION	CULT

Source: Adapted from Roy Wallis, *Sectarianism: Analyses of Religious and Non-Religious Sects.* New York: John Wiley, 1975, p. 41.

such as spiritual healing or spiritualism. Others, like various "New Thought" cults, attempt to combine elements of conventional religion with ideas and practices that are essentially nonreligious. Still others direct attention toward the attainment of "self-awareness" or "self-realization," wisdom, or insight, for instance, Vedanta, Subud, Soto Zen, the Human Potential Movement, and Transcendental Meditation (Eister, 1972).

Whereas church and denomination embody culturally approved forms of religious belief and organization, cults and sects are deviant when viewed against churchly and denominational respectability. However, cults differ from sects in that cults are conceived by their members to be pluralistically legitimate, one of a variety of paths to truth or salvation. In this respect, cults resemble denominations. In contrast, the sect, like the church, views itself as being uniquely legitimate, it alone possessing access to truth or salvation (Wallis, 1975). See Figure 13.1.

THE EMERGENCE OF SECTS: THE BLACK MUSLIMS

Islam dignifies the Black man, and it gives him the desire to be clean, internally and externally, and to have for the first time a sense of dignity.

Elijah Muhammad

Sociologists point out that most sects are a product of the stresses and tensions that come to bear on particular groups within a society. Change renders existing patterns inadequate for orienting the members of these groups to the larger world. People feel deprived of a meaningful orientation—a "rootedness"—within their lives. Frequently, such people have been caught up in a web of insecurity and anxiety produced by steadily advancing urbanization and industrialization. The foundations of their traditional way of life crumble; belief in the efficacy of the old ways declines; new values and desires are taken over. Yet disadvantaged class position or minority group status bars them from fully accepting the new ways.

The Black Muslim sect grew out of conditions such as these. Sometime in the midsummer of 1930, a peddler—variously known as Mr. Farrad Mohammad, Mr. F. Mohammad Ali, Professor Ford, Mr. Wali Farrad, and W. D. Fard—made his appearance in the Black community of Detroit. Apparently, he was an Arab, but his racial and national identity remains undocumented. In addition to peddling his silks and artifacts, he expounded a doctrine that was a hodgepodge of Christianity, Mohammedanism, and his own personal prejudices. Fard described himself to his followers as having been sent to awaken the "Black Nation" to the full range of its possibilities in a world temporarily dominated by Whites—"blue-eyed devils" (Lincoln, 1961).

Fard and later Elijah Muhammad, Fard's lieutenant who took over the movement, preached a doctrine of Black racial supremacy. Whites were seen as an inferior race, comparatively low in physical and moral stamina. Muhammad declared: "The human beast—the serpent, the dragon, the devil, and Satan—all mean one and the same; the people or race known as the white or Caucasian race, sometimes called the European race" (Quoted by Lincoln, 1961:77).

Through the years, the Black Muslims have recruited their members primarily from among urban low-income groups with little schooling, many of them migrants from the rural South. Black nationalism has its roots in the frustrations, anxieties, and disillusionments of contemporary urban life that are complicated by segregation, discrimination, and poverty—by life within Black ghettos at the periphery of White society. Its members are often strangers not only to the White society but also to the urbanized Black community. The vast majority are the "unwanted from Dixie," who find themselves rejected by both the White society and by upward mobile and middle-class Blacks who resent, fear, and despise the migrants as a threat to an improved "Black image." The result is a dual alienation giving rise to a sense of apathy, futility, and emptiness of purpose. E. U. Essien-Udom, a Nigerian who studied the movement, asserts:

> In a psychological sense, many are lonesome within and outside their own group. They are rootless and restless. They are without an identity, i.e., a sense of belonging and membership in society. In this situation, there is neither hope nor optimism. In fact, most lower-class Negroes in these large cities see little or no "future" for themselves and posterity. This is partly because they have no faith in themselves or in their potential as black men in America and especially because important decisions which shape their lives appear entirely beyond their control. (1964, pp. 354–355).

Black nationalism offers its members a way out. Converts to the movement are no longer members of a despised minority. They belong, at least spiritually, to a larger whole where people are "dark, proud, and unapologetic." The movement combines the attractions of religion and nationalism with a sense of belonging and self-esteem.

On the death of Elijah Muhammad in 1975, his son, Wallace D. Muhammad, assumed leadership of the movement. The younger Muhammad changed the organization's name to the World Community of Al-Islam in the West and reshaped its philosophy to one of working with Whites toward improving Black conditions. He also disbanded the Fruit of Islam, the semimilitary arm of the movement, and relaxed the strict dress code for followers. In the process, the organization is moving toward accommodation with the larger society and losing many of its more distinctive sectlike characteristics.

These developments have resulted in a split in the movement and its ideological polarization. Orthodox followers of Elijah Muhammad oppose the liberalizing tendencies introduced by his son and have established a rival organization led by Abdul Haleem Farrakhan (Sheppard, 1978). During Elijah Muhammad's later years the Black Muslims claimed 250,000 members (law enforcement authorities say it was never larger than 25,000). The factionalism of recent years has contributed to a sharp drop in the movement's membership. It is important to remember, however, that the Black Muslims, especially through the influence of the late Malcolm X, had an enormous impact on the Black Power and Black nationalism movements within the United States.

CRITIQUE OF THE CHURCH-SECT TYPOLOGY

Although many sociologists have attempted to order various forms of religious behavior in terms of the church-sect typology, efforts to develop the scheme have not been entirely satisfactory (Johnson, 1963; Swatos, 1976; Robertson, 1977; Welch, 1977). As is generally true of classificatory approaches, the types tend to be arbitrary — they "oversimplify" the data by disregarding what are held to be minor differences in order to emphasize what are thought to be major similarities. Accordingly, the descriptions associated with them do not portray total "reality." Any concrete case provides its own unique exceptions — for example, we often find instances of the coexistence of sectlike and churchlike tendencies within the typical Christian church. Even the most enthusiastic sects within the United States quickly develop a rather elaborate organizational structure and the most formal churchlike organizations have room for enthusiastic small groups

(McCready and Greeley, 1976). Further, the approach has often implied that sects necessarily move in the direction of accommodation to the larger world (Redekop, 1974). Yet this has not been true for all sects including the Old Order Amish and Jehovah's Witnesses (Yinger, 1963; Hostetler, 1968; Beckford, 1975).

Critics have pointed out that virtually all attempts to develop the church-sect typology have employed Judeo-Christian materials; the applicability of the scheme to nonWestern religions needs to be tested. Moreover, although the approach is valid for many Western religions, it falls short of providing a general theory of the origin and evolution of all Western religious groups. Not all religious groups emerge as sects; some resemble churches in their original form, for example, Reform Judaism in Europe, Conservative Judaism in the United States, and many Protestant groups. And as Roger O'Toole (1975, 1976) has pointed out, religious sects have many features in common with some political groups such as the American Maoists and De Leonists. Although these criticisms alert us to the shortcomings of the church-sect typology, we should not lose sight of the fact that the typology nonetheless provides us with a useful tool for ordering religious phenomena. As with any tool, however, we need to employ it with care and be continuously aware of its limitations.

THE PROTESTANT ETHIC

Be ashamed to catch yourself idle.
Sloth makes all things difficult, but industry all things easy.
Early to bed and early to rise makes a man healthy, wealthy and wise.
But dost thou love life? Then do not squander time, for that's the stuff life is made of.
God helps them that help themselves.
Women and wine, game and deceit, make the wealth small and the wants great.
For age and want, save while you may; no morning sun lasts a whole day.
Beware of little expenses; a small leak will sink a great ship.
Remember that money is of a prolific, generating nature. Man can beget money, and its offspring can beget more, and so on.
A sleeping fox catches no poultry.

Benjamin Franklin, Poor Richard's Almanac, *1757*

Many individuals conceive of religion as a conservative force that serves to retard social change. As is true of any set of ideas, religion of course may prove an obstacle to change under some circumstances. But religion may also be a powerful agent for social change (Bellah, 1957; 1958; Wilson, 1973). By serving to redefine for people various aspects of their lives or the environment about them, religion may impel people to inaugurate new lines of action. The significance of religion in providing people with a new worldview and bringing about new behavior is set forth by Max Weber in his now famous study of the **Protestant ethic**, a body of ideas reflected in Benjamin Franklin's *Poor Richard's Almanac*. In essence, Weber believed that the Protestant ethic served to liberate individuals from the domination of tradition and created a perception of the world that was a stimulus for innovation and rationalized economic activity.

THE WEBER THESIS

The Puritan sects are the most specific bearers of the inner-worldly form of asceticism. . . . For Puritanism, that conduct was a certain methodical, rational way of life which — given certain conditions — paved the way for the "spirit" of modern capitalism.
Max Weber, The Protestant Sects and The Spirit of Capitalism, *1906*

Weber (1864–1920; an eminent German sociologist), in an essay that has become a classic, *The Protestant Ethic and the Spirit of Capitalism* (1905/1930), asserted that it was not accidental that Protestantism and modern capitalism appeared on the historical scene at roughly the same time. He undertook to demonstrate that, without Protestantism, modern capitalism would not have developed. Once capitalism is established, Weber argued, it carries on in a self-perpetuating fashion. But the critical problem is to discover its origin in precapitalist society. Only by discovering the source of the spirit (ideology) of capitalism, Weber asserted, can we discover the source of modern capitalism itself.

Weber based his thesis regarding a causal connection between Protestantism and capitalism on a number of observations. First, capitalism attained its highest development in Protestant countries, for example, the United States and England; in contrast, Catholic countries, for example, Spain and Italy, lagged behind in capitalist development. Second, in countries containing both Protestant and Catholic regions, like Germany, Weber found that the Protestant — not the Catholic — regions pioneered in capitalist development. Third, Weber sought to demonstrate that by and large it was the Protestants, not the Catholics, who became the capitalist entrepreneurs. And fourth, Weber found that in Protestant countries capitalism was more marked in Calvinist than in Lutheran-Evangelist states. On the basis of these observations, Weber concluded that the chief source of modern capitalism was Protestantism, and more especially Calvinism and Puritanism. The spirit of capitalism — the Protestant ethic — Weber maintained, was distinguished by three main tenets: each person is predestined for heaven or hell; work is a

Figure 13.2. The Protestant ethic and the spirit of capitalism.

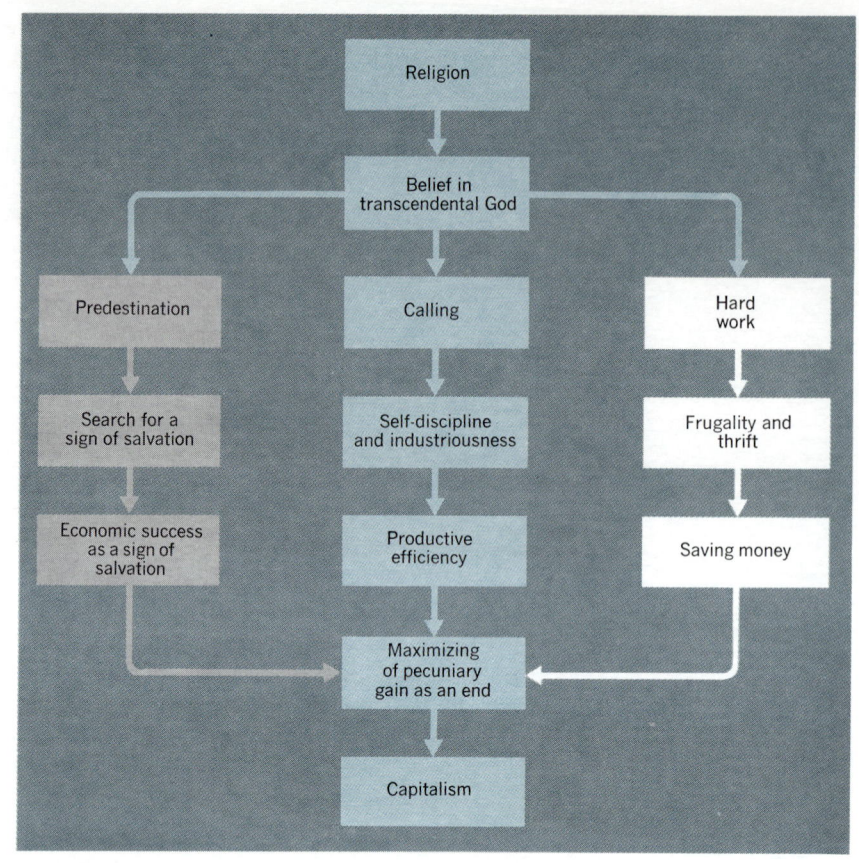

Source: Adapted from Takie Sugiyama Lebra, "Religious Conversion as a Breakthrough for Transculturation: A Japanese Sect in Hawaii," *Journal for the Scientific Study of Religion*, 9 (1970), 183.

virtue; and people should select their own calling in life. See Figure 13.2. Let us examine each of these matters in turn.

Weber drew attention to the fact that the followers of John Calvin rejected an idea prevalent in Catholicism during the Middle Ages, namely, that an individual's status in the afterlife is determined and influenced by the type of life led here on earth. Instead, Calvin taught that at birth every soul is predestined for heaven or hell—*the doctrine of predestination*. This was a particularly disquieting and anxiety-producing doctrine since people did not know what their fate was to be. As a consequence, Weber suggested, Calvin's followers, searching for some reassurance, in time came to accept certain earthly symbols as testifying to their salvation—the "saved" were believed to give evidence of their salvation through their industry, sobriety, thrift, restraint, and avoidance of fleshly pleasures. And as people are wont to do, the

Calvinists, concerned with their fate, subtly began to cultivate these very traits. Weber concluded that self-discipline and the willingness to defer gratification are qualities that contribute to economic success in the capitalist system (strong *asceticism* allowed the poor to amass capital by reducing their expenditures on vices and luxuries). In brief, Calvinism fostered the search for economic success through the pursuit of business and private economic gain, and, in so doing, promoted practices that constituted the essence of capitalism.

But this was not the entire story. Calvinists believed that each individual is created solely to glorify God through labor and hard work in His universe. Hence, industry, sobriety, thrift, restraint, and avoidance of fleshly pleasures also contribute in their own right to the greater glory of God. This view was in sharp contrast with that of Catholicism which accorded leisure, not work, the highest place: God, in driving Adam and Eve from Paradise, ordained that henceforth Eve and her daughters would bear their children in pain and Adam and his sons would earn their bread by the sweat of their brows. Labor, then, came to be seen not as a virtue but as a punishment—a reminder of original sin. The followers of John Calvin disputed this view. By being the vigilant shepherds of God's gifts and resources they fulfilled their duty to God. Within this ethic, work was something to be done for its own sake, a viewpoint that Weber held was consistent with capitalism.

The Calvinists also introduced the notion of the "calling." Unlike Catholicism and other Reformation faiths like Lutheranism, Calvinism taught its adherents to exercise selectivity in their choice of vocations. Individuals were expected to employ those unique talents provided by God in a manner that would produce the greatest achievement and hence the greatest glory for God. This exhortation differed from that of medieval Christianity which held that people should accept their position in life as part of God's social creation. Thus the Calvinist notion of the calling increased people's flexibility and freedom in undertaking worldly action while simultaneously making such action an overriding motivation (Stokes, 1975).

CRITIQUE OF WEBER'S THESIS

Historical controversy is the life-blood of historical writing. Without it, history becomes dogma. ... Whatever may have happened to Max Weber's theories about the influence upon economic life of Protestantism in general and Puritanism in particular, nobody could say they were dead or claim that they had passed unchallenged or unsupported. ... For in spite of much damaging criticism, of refutations and counter-refutations, the belief in some sort of influence wielded by Puritanism on capitalism is still strong and pervasive.
    D. C. Coleman, Introduction, Kurt Samuelsson, Religion and Economic Action, *1961*

In the seven decades since Weber published his study, numerous scholars have investigated the same problem only to arrive at very different conclusions. H. M. Robertson (1933) maintained that capitalism and the "capitalist spirit" existed long before the ideas of the Reformation began to assert themselves. But far from rejecting Weber's formulation, Robertson turned it about and argued that it was economic activity that engendered religious change, not religion that transformed economic life. Similarly, Marxists have insisted that basic changes in the economic realm gave birth to new classes who in turn developed religious creeds to harmonize with their vested interests. Halfway between Weber and such inversions of Weber stands R. H. Tawney (1926) who spoke in highly general terms of the interplay between economic and religious changes, of the ability of economics to transform religious doctrine, and in turn of the capacity of a transformed religious doctrine to deepen and nurture the spirit of capitalism.

Others, including the noted Catholic scholar and four-time Italian premier, Amintore Fanfani (1955), suggest that the spirit of capitalism is foreign to every kind of religion—to the extent that Protestantism had any effect, it divorced labor from religious life and thereby released economic activity from the inhibitions of religion. Still others, such as Werner Sombart (1913), advance the argument that it was another religious group—the Jews—who pioneered the spirit of capitalism. And even more recently, Richard L. Means (1966) indicates that, although Weber was on the right track, it was chiefly Protestant views on education, liberty and freedom, and social reform, and Protestantism's own minority status that played a critical part in transforming economic life.

Kurt Samuelsson (1961), a Swedish economic historian, took a far different approach. In contrast with the critics mentioned above who contented themselves merely with advancing new or modified explanations for the connection between Protestantism and economic development, Samuelsson asked, "Did such a clear correlation exist between Protestantism and economic progress that there is any reason to inquire into cause and effect at all?" His answer, a resounding "No!" Instead of just tinkering with the Weber hypothesis, Samuelsson sought to demolish it. Re-examining the regions in Europe cited by Weber, Samuelsson found that none of them was characterized by such symmetry in terms of religious faith and economic progress that a meaningful correlation could be arrived at. Moreover, by the time Calvin was born, the Low Countries and the northern and western districts of Germany had already been characterized by exceptionally brisk economic activity for at least three to four centuries: textile manufacturing and commerce in the Netherlands and Flanders; and iron-founding, salt-drying, and international trade in the Hanseatic territories. Further, many of the largest merchants in Amsterdam were Catholics, and it was among the better-off sections of the community that Catholicism maintained its grip the longest; it was among the poorest classes that Calvinism first spread. Finally, Samuelsson reanalyzed the data Weber had used to assert that Protestants were more likely than Catholics to be entrepreneurs and found it to be wanting; little difference existed between the two groups.

Randall G. Stokes (1975) has recently taken a somewhat different approach to the Weberian thesis. He shows that those beliefs comprising the Protestant ethic do not inevitably lead people to engage in behavior that results in economic development. Calvinism did not produce the same results it had in Europe when it was transplanted by Dutch and French Huguenot settlers (Afrikaners) to South Africa. Although Afrikaner Calvinism was theologically identical to European Calvinism, it had a conservative rather than innovative economic impact.

Stokes suggests that the South African Calvinists came to regard themselves as a Chosen People by virtue of their identification with the ancient Israelites and their long series of confrontations with the indigenous Black population. This led them to conceive of the Elect in collective rather than individual terms. As such they did not suffer the same kind or degree of anxiety about salvation that plagued the Europeans and motivated them to seek thisworldly success as a mark of otherworldly salvation. Further, the Afrikaners defined themselves as a sacred society, and, accordingly, they came to uphold traditional ways with a passion while viewing innovations with suspicion. Thus, the same religion can have quite different consequences in differing social contexts.

If Weber's thesis concerning Protestantism and the rise of capitalism has fallen on hard times, why have we dealt with it at such length? We have done so, first, because few general hypotheses in the social sciences have aroused more interest, and in recent years won wider acceptance, than that of Max Weber regarding the rise of capitalism. Second, the questioning of Weber's thesis demonstrates anew that we should not view previous findings, even those of the most eminent authorities, as the final word on a matter; new evidence needs to be pursued and analyzed—in brief, young scholars need not stand in awe of established authorities and works but should be prepared to challenge them when evidence so warrants.

RELIGIOUS PREFERENCE AND WORLDLY SUCCESS

In the above discussion, we examined Weber's *historical hypothesis* concerning the relationship between Protestantism and capitalism. Sociologists have also sought to extract from Weber's many writings on religion a basic underlying assumption—namely, that each of the major religions of the world develops its own distinctive orientation toward various phases of human activity, and thus comes to exercise an influence on them. One aspect in particular has attracted the interest and research of sociologists—the relationship between religious affiliation and worldly success in contemporary America.

Most studies dealing with the issue have revealed a rather consistent patterning in the rankings of religious groups on various measures of socioeconomic achievement. With regard to educational attainment, occupational status, and income, Jews, Episcopalians, Congregationalists, and Presbyterians traditionally have ranked at the top; Baptists and Catholics (with the exception of those with Northwestern European origins) at the bottom; and Methodists and Lutherans in the middle (Mayer and Sharp, 1962; Warren, 1970). But whether these differences are the product of religious affiliation is problematic (Bouma, 1973). Several studies suggest that factors other than those that are strictly religious account for many of the differences found among religious groups in socioeconomic achievement. David Featherman's study, summarized in Research Study 20, is one example. Further, it is questionable whether American Catholics any longer fit Weber's image (Greeley, 1977).

It is not particularly surprising that researchers should find that religious affiliation currently plays at best but a minor part in worldly success within the United States. The beliefs comprising the Protestant ethic have become widely diffused throughout American life. Any study that investigates at this late date differences in capitalist spirit between Protestants and Catholics cannot fairly be said to test Weber's thesis (Hammond and Williams, 1976). Indeed, Weber himself warned against judging his work in this manner:

> Since asceticism [the Protestant ethic] undertook to remodel the world and to work its ideals in the world, material goods have gained an increasing and finally an inexorable power over the lives of men. . . . Today the spirit of religious asceticism . . . has escaped from the cage. But victorious capitalism, since it rests on mechanical foundations, needs its support no longer. (1930, pp. 181–182)

Hei C. Kim (1977) recently undertook a study involving a randomly selected sample of 252 men in a small midwestern community. Kim found only a minimal relationship between religious affiliation and occupational status. However, Kim did find that individuals' responses with respect to an index of Calvinist beliefs and values did correlate with both their occupational status and educational achievement. In sum, the study suggests that religious affiliation no longer provides a measure of the Protestant ethic although adherence to the ethic's tenets appears to be associated with worldly success.

RESEARCH STUDY 20

THE SOCIOECONOMIC ACHIEVEMENT OF WHITE RELIGIO-ETHNIC SUBGROUPS: SOCIAL AND PSYCHOLOGICAL EXPLANATIONS*

David L. Featherman

Problem. Do major religious groups differ in the relative occupational and income attainments of their members? If such differences exist, can they be explained in other than strictly religious terms, for instance, social origins (the higher or lower overall occupational status of their members' fathers), number of siblings (various studies have revealed that smaller numbers of siblings are positively associated with educational, occupational, and economic achievements), and urban versus rural residential origins? Are members of major religious groups distinguished from one another in terms of their motivational orientations toward work? If so, do these differing orientations account for the differences in the socioeconomic achievements of the various groups? These, then, were the major matters interesting Featherman in the present study.

Method. In 1957 the Princeton Fertility Study obtained data from a stratified sample of 715 native White males with two-child families who resided in seven large American cities. Researchers conducted follow-up interviews in 1960 and again between 1963 and 1967. Featherman found that he could employ data from the Princeton study to secure answers to the above questions. For purposes of his study, he employed six religious categories: (1) Jewish; (2) Anglo-Saxon Protestant; (3) Protestant, Other; (4) Roman Catholic, except Italian and Mexican; (5) Italian and Mexican Roman Catholics; and (6) None or Other Religion.

Featherman then compared the groups in terms of the average education, level of occupational prestige, and income of their members. Recognizing that all groups are not equally favored with backgrounds conducive to economic success, he next ran some statistical tests that sought to control (to allow) for differences in father's occupation, number of siblings, and extent of rural origins—in brief, the groups were rendered equivalent in each of these respects through statistical measures. In this manner he undertook to determine whether it was religion in its own right that was influencing socioeconomic achievement or whether one (or more) of these other factors was intervening to account for group differences in economic success.

Having considered the process of status attainment for various religious groups, Featherman then asked how factors associated with motivation enlarged our understanding of the achievement of a religious group's members. Three indexes of motivational orientations toward work had been included in the 1957 interviews. The first, "Primary

---

* Adapted from David L. Featherman, "The Socioeconomic Achievement of White Religio-Ethnic Subgroups: Social and Psychological Explanations," *American Sociological Review*, 36 (1971), 207–222.

Work Orientation," sought to measure the extent to which an individual regarded work as rewarding in its own right (noneconomic qualities)—a sample question: "The work I do is one of the most satisfying parts of my life." The second index, "Materialistic Orientation," emphasized the material goals achieved through work—a sample question: "Getting money and material things out of life is very important to me." The third, "Subjective Achievement Evaluation," indicated an individual's sense of relative deprivation (the gap between his actual status and what he had come to expect or hope for)—a sample question: "I would be satisfied if my children, when they reach my age, have the same income and live the same way as I." Using these indexes, Featherman hoped to determine through statistical tests whether members of various religious groups differed in their orientations toward achievement, and, if so, if these differences accounted for their differential socioeconomic attainments.

Findings. The major religious groups differed in the relative occupational and income attainments of their members. Jews surpassed all other religious groups, followed by Protestants and Roman Catholics, in that order. When Featherman equated the groups through statistical controls for differentials in father's occupation, the range of differences between the groups was reduced by about one-third in educational achievement, 40 percent in occupational achievement, and 20 percent in income achievement. Further, by the time of the third interview (the 1963–1967 interval), virtually all the variation in occupational and income attainment among religious groups was explained by differentials in social origins (father's occupation), education, and earlier career achievements. The direct impact of religion on achievement thus appeared to be negligible. An individual's religous origins, however, did have a direct impact on how many years of school he completed; education in turn had a direct impact on achievement:

$$\text{Religion} \rightarrow \text{Education} \rightarrow \text{Occupational Attainment} \rightarrow \text{Economic Achievement}$$

Indirectly, then, via its influence on education, religion had some impact on achievement.

But what about factors associated with motivation—are members of major religious groups distinguished from one another in terms of their motivational orientations toward work? Featherman found that Jews showed positive motivations toward work both as an intrinsically rewarding activity (a noneconomic quality) and as an activity with material payoff. Anglo-Saxon Protestants responded more strongly to the intrinsically rewarding aspects of work than to its materialistic elements. Roman Catholics, like the Jews, shared in a materialistic approach toward work; but unlike the Jews, they had a less positive sense of socioeconomic achievement (the Catholics experienced a stronger sense of relative deprivation). Do these differing orientations account for the differences in the socioeconomic achievements of the various groups? The data and statistical tests revealed that the achievement-related motivations of adult males played at best a modest part in socioeconomic attainment; in belief, they did not constitute a primary or major factor.

Conclusion. On the whole, Featherman's study does not lend support to the Weberian thesis that religious affiliation has significant and meaningful consequences for worldly success within contemporary America.

SOCIAL CHANGE: SOME RECENT TRENDS

The United States is very likely the most religiously diverse nation of any society in human history. Central to the American religious scene has been the element of change, from the earliest settlement of the colonies by persecuted European religious minorities through the Great Awakening in the 1730s and 1740s (led by such evangelists as Jonathan Edwards, George Whitefield, and John Wesley) on through the turbulent 1960s to the present time. In the post-World War II period, religious indicators reveal that a growth in religious commitment took place during the 1950s followed by a decline or substantially slower growth during the 1960s and early 1970s, with another upturn in commitment occurring in the later 1970s (Wuthnow, 1976).

During the 1970s the more evangelical and conservative Protestant churches registered the biggest membership gains. Included were the Southern Baptists, the Assemblies of God, and the Seventh-Day Adventists, up respectively 18, 37, and 34 percent over the decade. In contrast, the more "mainline" and liberal churches experienced slippage, the United Methodists, Episcopalians, and United Presbyterians down respectively 10, 15 and 10 percent during the same period. To some extent these changes have been part of a larger contemporary drift toward privatism and self-concern, with many Americans seemingly searching for a personal religious experience and authenticity.

Roman Catholicism has also undergone significant changes during the past decade. Recent statistics from the National Opinion Research Center, an institute affiliated with the University of Chicago, suggest that a dual church may be evolving, one in which the lay members differ markedly from the leadership on doctrine and discipline. According to the Center's findings, 83 percent of American Catholics now approve of artificial birth control (by 1974, the proportion of married women using the pill for contraception was the same for Catholics and non-Catholics, 34 percent) and 72 percent would allow for the abortion of a malformed fetus, positions in clear conflict with those of the church hierarchy (Deedy, 1976; Brody, 1977). Further, only 42 percent agree that the Pope holds his authority in direct line from Jesus (clearly in opposition to the doctrine of papal infallibility) and only 54 percent attend mass weekly (despite the church's requirement that members do so).

Jews likewise have found the past decade one of change. A particularly significant statistic has been the rapid increase in the intermarriage rate among Jews. Between 1960 and 1972, Jewish-Gentile marriages jumped from 5.9 percent to 31.7 percent, and some Jewish leaders say the figure now is close to 40 percent. On the whole Jewish leaders have been concerned with the passive erosion of the practice of Judaism. Although many

Jews continue to identify themselves with their faith, they often do not take an active part in religious activities. However, one force that has given psychological unity to American Jews has been the Jewish community's commitment to the survival of Israel. Though American Jews generally do not view Israel as their homeland, many nonetheless see that nation as the embodiment of their heritage.

SECULARIZATION

Secularism is not a synonym for atheism but merely describes those aspects of life that are "of the world," finite, civil, and nonecclesiastical. It refers to the relative ascendancy of nonreligious over sacred and religious considerations. Evidence for secularization within the United States seemingly abounds. Although public opinion surveys show that 94 percent of Americans believe in God (compared with 76 percent in Britain, 72 in France and West Germany, 88 in Italy, 63 in Scandinavia, and 98 in India) and 69 percent in Afterlife (compared with 43 percent in Britain, 72 in France, 33 in West Germany, 46 in Italy, 35 in Scandinavia), only 35 percent can name four gospels, and 54 percent admit that religion does not have any effect on the way they conduct their daily business. A 1975 Gallup Poll reported that 40 percent of American adults of all faiths attend a place of worship in a typical week (54 percent of Catholics, 38 percent of Protestants, and 21 percent of Jews). And frequently the joining of many middle-class churches is not sharply different from joining Kiwanis or related community organizations.

Such findings lead some religious observers to suggest that, in contemporary America, religious motives generally have little relevance for other aspects of life; they scarcely affect the course of most daily developments, including suburbanization, school desegregation, the transformation of sexual morals, business activities, and political decision-making. Contemporary religion often simply affirms the "O.K. World." Other evidence of secularization is the conversion of holy days into commercialized holidays—Easter, for example, focuses on the latest Fifth Avenue fashions and Christmas on merchandise bartering involving informal, but nevertheless somewhat strict, accounting methods.

There is little in the sociological literature, however, that constitutes a serious and systematic defense of the secularization hypothesis. Some sociologists note that in 1947, 94 percent of the American population indicated that they believed in God, a statistic identical to that in 1975. Similarly, in 1947, 68 percent of the population said that they believed in life after death, a statistic quite comparable to the 69 percent who indicated a like belief in 1975 (Sigelman, 1977). Still other observers of the American scene argue that it is not so much that the nation is becoming secularized as that national life is becoming "religious"—national culture and religion are

Professional football: New national religion? Some argue that the fervor, passions, and loyalties excited by professional football constitute a major unifying force that acts like religion to bind people together. They describe our gigantic stadiums as the cathedrals of our contemporary age.

Courtesy of the Green Bay Press-Gazette

becoming intermingled into a kind of civil religion. As noted earlier in the chapter, civil religion is not a state religion; rather civil religion recognizes national values, national heroes, national history, and national ideals. The dollar bill, for example, contains on the Great Seal of the United States an unfinished pyramid under the eye of God, with the Latin motto, "*Annuit Coeptis*" ("He, God, has smiled upon our beginnings"), and with it another motto, "*Novus Ordo Seclosrum*" ("A new order of the ages"). This fuses national and religious visions. George Washington and Abraham Lincoln have been elevated to a kind of sainthood. And in our Presidential Inaugural ceremonies—just as in the ancient Athenian processions—the warriors and the priests unite in a powerful enactment of a civil religion (Herberg, 1973:58).

COUNTERCULTURAL RELIGIONS

The late 1960s and early 1970s were a period of considerable experimentation in politics, family styles, and living arrangements. The so-called counterculture consumed the imaginations and energies of a good many young people. During this same period a variety of youth-oriented religious sects sprang into existence. These included a number of Christian groups (Children of God and the Christian World Liberation Front), Eastern-influenced groups (Transcendental Meditation, Zen Buddhism, Hare Krishna, and yoga groups), and mystical sects. A 1976 Gallup survey found that 12 percent of those polled had participated in at least one of such groups (Briggs, 1977). The largest number, four percent, had been involved in transcendental meditation, three percent in yoga, two percent in charismatic renewal, two percent in mysticism, and one percent in Eastern religions. The heaviest concentration of participants were among youths between 18 and 24 years.

Robert Wuthnow (1976) suggests that this experimentation with new religious forms reflects changes in the cultural meaning systems by which many young people make sense of their lives. He bases his conclusion on survey data collected in 1973 among a random sample of 1000 youth in the San Francisco Bay area. Wuthnow found that for many young Americans both theism and individualism have eroded, losing much of their plausibility. Theism is an understanding of life that identifies God as the creator of the universe and director of history. Individualism views each person as shaping his or her own destiny while simultaneously extolling those qualities embedded within the Protestant ethic.

As theism and individualism decline, a "new consciousness" espousing mystical and social scientific definitions of reality is emerging. Mysticism emphasizes intense personal experiences and intuitively grasped reality. Social scientific interpretations focus on the precarious nature of all existing structures and the relativity of morality as viewed from a cross-cultural perspective. Only time will tell how permanent and deep-seated these countercultural patterns will be. Evangelical Christian movements with a traditional emphasis appear to be capturing the mood of far more youth today than was the case in the early days of the 1970s (Roof, 1977).

CATHOLIC PENTECOSTALISM

GLENDOWER: I can call spirits from the vastly deep.
HOTSPUR: Why, so can I, or so can any man; But will they come when you do call them?
William Shakespeare, Henry IV, Part 1

In 1967 the first Roman Catholic Pentecostal prayer groups appeared on the campuses of Duquesne, Notre Dame, and Michigan universities. Initially the movement attracted college students and other youth, but its following has since expanded to middle-class adults and many nuns and some priests (Harrison, 1974; Briggs, 1978). The Pentecostalists (also known as Charismatics) share the belief that one's life can be dramatically changed by an infusion of the Holy Spirit of God, a process known as "Baptism in the Holy Spirit" (McGuire, 1977). This has led the Pentacostalists to a number of practices that they contend allow them to heal the sick, utter prophecies, and speak in tongues (a practice also known as "glossolalia" in which the Spirit is believed to speak through the person in unknown languages). The movement derives its inspiration from the miraculous events that occurred to the twelve apostles on Pentecost Sunday (fifty days after Christ's Resurrection) as described in the New Testament:

> And when the day of Pentecost was fully come, they were all with one accord in one place. And suddenly there came a sound from heaven as of a rushing mighty wind, and it filled all the house where they were sitting. And there appeared unto them cloven tongues like as of fire, and it sat upon each of them. And they were all filled with the Holy Ghost, and began to speak with other tongues, as the Spirit gave them utterance. (The Acts, 2)

The movement has become a major element in American Catholicism. The church's hierarchy, although viewing Pentacostalism with a certain degree of wariness, has cautiously endorsed it (Fichter, 1975; Laurentin, 1977). It appears that most Pentecostal Catholics have retained and even increased their loyalty to Catholicism, combining frequent mass attendance with weekly attendance at Pentecostal prayer meetings (Harrison, 1974). Thus far, the Pentecostal Catholics have not demonstrated strong separatist tendencies. Rather, they state their goal as one of "building a new society in the shell of the old." Some clergy and laity distrust the movement because they believe it attracts a "kooky" element. Research suggests, however, that glossolalics do not differ from nonglossolalics in psychological pathology (Lovekin and Malony, 1977). Nor do the Pentecostal Catholics seem to experience a higher incidence of psychological stress and difficulties than do non-Pentecostal Catholics (Harrison, 1974; Heirich, 1977). The Pentecostal movement appears to have been fed by many of the same currents of political disillusionment and religious experimentation that have bred a variety of political and religious movements among Americans during the same historical period.

SUMMARY

1. Religion encompasses those ways of thinking, feeling, and acting by which people undertake to deal with the ultimate problems of life. It is concerned with those aspects of experience that transcend the mundane events of everyday existence — with those comparatively vague and intangible features of life.

2. At times, we overlook the religious overtones in behavior that is otherwise thought of as nonreligious and even anti-religious. The search for a doctrine that reveals the meaning of existence and answers the fundamental questions that are set by life may lead one person to God while another to "the party," nationalism, science, or some other agency.

3. Religion and magic are similar in that both share a conception of a nonempirical reality whose existence cannot be established simply by observation. They differ, however, in a number of respects. First, religion is primarily concerned with fundamental issues of human existence. Second, they differ in the means they employ in dealing with the supernatural world.

4. The prevalence of religion in societies throughout the world raises the question of the contributions it makes to social life. Since all societies have something known as religion, its presence can hardly be dismissed as accidental. Religion helps individuals deal with "the breaking points" of life, fosters social integration, and, depending on the historical circumstances, facilitates or hinders social change.

5. Sociologists commonly distinguish among four types of religious organization: church, sect, denomination, and cult. Churches and sects claim lone legitimacy whereas denominations and cults accept pluralistic legitimacy. Churches and denominations tend to be perceived by the members of a society as culturally respectable whereas sects and cults are commonly viewed as culturally deviant. The church-sect typology has shortcomings; nonetheless, if we employ it with care and are aware of its limitations, it can serve as a useful tool for ordering religious phenomena.

6. The significance of religion in providing people with a new worldview and bringing about new behavior is set forth by Max Weber in his now famous study of the Protestant ethic. Weber believed that the Protestant ethic served to liberate individuals from the domination of tradition and created a perception of the world that was a stimulus for innovation and rationalized economic activity. He maintained that the Protestant ethic was distinguished by three main tenets: each person is predestined for heaven or hell; work is a virtue; and people should select their own calling in life.

7. In the seven decades since Weber published his study, numerous scholars have investigated the same problem only to arrive at very different conclusions. Randall G. Stokes, for instance, shows that the beliefs comprising the Protestant ethic do not inevitably lead people to engage in behavior that results in economic development. Calvinism did not produce the same results it had in Europe when it was transplanted by Dutch and French Huguenot settlers to South Africa.

8. Researchers find that religious affiliation currently plays at best but a minor part in worldly success within the United States. The beliefs comprising the Protestant ethic have become widely diffused throughout American life. Nonetheless, adherence to the ethic's tenets appears to be associated with worldly success.

9. The United States is very likely the most religiously diverse nation of any society in human history. Central to the American religious scene

has been the element of change. In the post-World War II period, religious indicators reveal that a growth in religious commitment took place during the 1950s followed by a decline or substantially slower growth during the 1960s and early 1970s, with another upturn in commitment occurring in the later 1970s.

10. Secularism is not a synonym for atheism but merely describes those aspects of life that are "of the world," finite, civil, and nonecclesiastical. Evidence of secularization within the United States seemingly abounds. Yet there is little in the sociological literature that constitutes a serious and systematic defense of the secularization hypothesis.

11. The late 1960s and early 1970s were a period of considerable experimentation in politics, family styles, and living arrangements. The so-called counterculture consumed the imaginations and energies of a good many young people. During this same period a variety of youth-oriented religious sects sprang into existence.

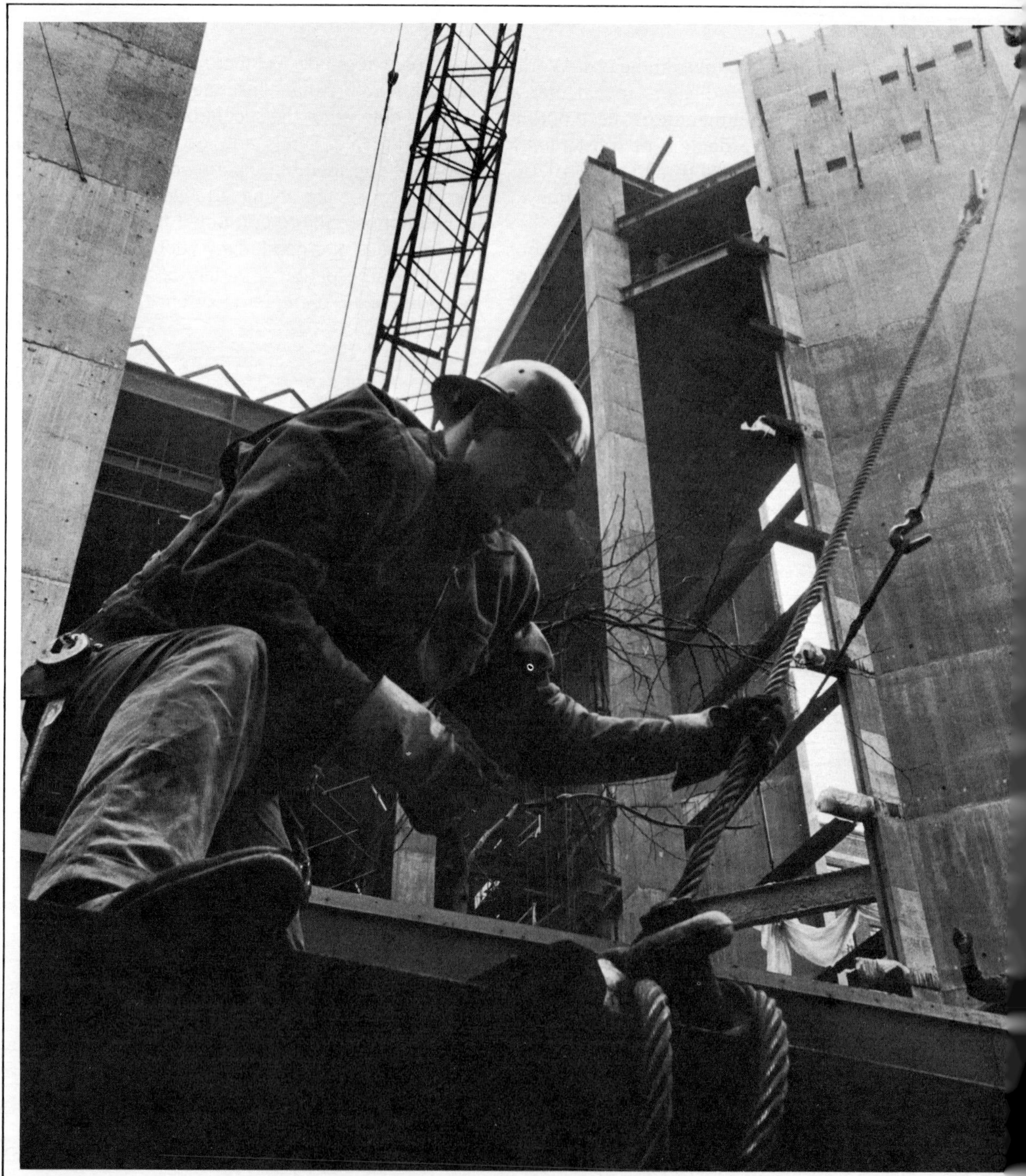

14
THE ECONOMY AND THE STATE

THE ECONOMY
    Functions
    Work
    National Development

THE STATE
    Functions
    Power and Authority
    Power in America
    Democracy

SOCIAL CHANGE: SOME RECENT TRENDS
    Poverty
    American Voting Behavior

OBSERVATION   Last summer I worked in a tomato canning plant where I stood on an assembly line and with a machine put lids on cans. I found the work extremely ungratifying and downright boring. I did the same job as all the other girls in my unit. I couldn't add any personal touch to the job; no one even knew what I contributed to the product: all the cans at the end looked alike. I did the same thing every day and watched the clock. All I was really interested in was getting off of work and getting paid. I felt no loyalty to the company or to the job. Since nobody could trace what I had done, I started finding shortcuts and ways to pass the time while still turning out the cans. I didn't care if I did sloppy work because no one cared so long as the production rate was maintained.

PRINCIPLE   This is a good illustration of alienation—I was estranged and separated from the work setting. I really didn't give a damn. All that was important was the pay check. I couldn't have cared less about the job or about the canned tomatoes.

In modern societies few aspects of our lives are not touched by economic and political institutions. Indeed, to many observers of the American scene the economy and the state seem to be the most conspicuous features of the social structure. President Calvin Coolidge may not have been far from the mark when he told the Society of Newspaper Editors in 1925 that "The business of America is business."

THE ECONOMY

All humans are biological beings. As such, they are confronted with the realities posed by physical survival and maintenance. The economic institution has its roots in this elemental fact. But people are not only biological beings; they are also social beings. Accordingly, human "needs" are seldom simply biological cravings. Thus, consumer goods not only provide for the satisfaction of sustenance needs but they also communicate status information to others. But whether human wants derive from biological or social sources, people are confronted with the fact that many things are not available in unlimited amount; they are *scarce*.

FUNCTIONS

The fact of human wants and the scarcity of goods and services must be faced by every society. Hence, social life confronts us with three functional imperatives. We must provide for the (1) production, (2) distribution, and (3) consumption of goods and services.

Production. Production involves the assemblying and applying of human and natural resources in the creation of goods and services. Many of nature's resources are unusable in their natural state. Hence, they have to be removed from nature, combined, and re-formed into useful forms and substances. For analytical purposes, the extractive–transformative function can be broken down into three processes: (1) primary industry or production—the extracting or gathering of undeveloped natural resources from nature through agriculture, mining, fishing, and forestry (for example, cotton is seeded, cultivated, and harvested); (2) secondary industry or production—the processing or converting of raw materials in a fashion that enhances their final consumption value (for example, at this level, cotton is transformed into cloth and then into garments, linens, and other items); and (3) tertiary industry or production—service activities of one sort or another (for example, marketing, entertainment, industrial engineering, banking, medical care, barbering, television repair, and secretarial work).

Distribution. Distribution involves channeling inputs (natural resources and labor) to producing agencies, and outputs (goods and services) to consuming agencies. This function derives from certain unavoidable conditions. Human and natural resources are only rarely found in immediate physical proximity to one another. Some essential elements—the work force or materials—need to be transferred to spatial locations where they add form and quality to the goods and services being produced. Further, humans are not self-sufficient isolates in the manner of Robinson Crusoe. A division of labor and specialization—differences among members of a population in their sustenance activities—requires that goods and services be channeled to individuals or producing facilities (such as an industrial plant) other than the initial producer (Gibbs and Poston, 1975; Freidson, 1976).

Distribution requires social mechanisms by which goods and services are exchanged. In no society is exchange purely haphazard or left to chance. One such mechanism is money—some form of common denominator or medium of exchange that facilitates the exchange of goods and services. A commodity—socially recognized as possessing value—is accepted in exchange for a variety of other commodities. Many commodities, varying with the time and society, have served as money—precious metals, beads, trinkets, shells, cows, fine mats, rice, coconuts, and the like. The advantage of money is that it widens the possible market for the goods and services that one wishes to dispose of. One does not have to encounter another who wants what one has to dispose of and in turn has exactly what one wishes; one sells for money, then proceeds to buy from another the goods or services desired. Commodities cannot become money except in group relations. This can be seen most clearly in the case of engraved paper and bank checks. Without *social definitions* as to their special quality, they would be little more than bits of paper.

Property is another aspect of exchange, the distributive aspect of the economy in its static aspect (Davis, 1949). Property consists of the rights and duties of one individual or group (the owner) as against all other persons and groups with respect to some scarce object. The concept of property appears to be a cultural universal—all societies have rules regarding the possession, handling, and disposition of property. Societies differ, however, in the emphasis they place on individual "private property" rights as opposed to the "communal" or "collective" holding of property by families, clans, communities, or nation-states. No society carries individual ownership to the point where no one but the person concerned has jurisdiction over the objects; some limitations exist, be they in the form of building codes, taxation, auto licensing, maintenance requirements, and the like. And no society, no matter how collectivist, lacks individual ownership of certain objects—clothes and various personal possessions.

Property rights. Property is a social fact. It defines who may and may not have access to given objects and resources.

Patrick Reddy

We often confuse property with the object owned; property itself is not material. Since it consists of a complex of rights and duties, it is not tangible in a physical sense. Thus, property is not to be equated with an object; rather, property is always a *social fact*. It defines the claim of an individual or group to an object; conversely, it defines the conditions under which some individuals or groups are excluded from the use or enjoyment of an object (Collins, 1975).

The social nature of property finds reflection in the civil disturbances that took place in American cities between 1964 and 1970. Looting occurred in at least 122 of these events. If we view property as the shared understanding of who can do what with the valued resources within a community, then in civil disorders we witness a breakdown in that understanding. What was previously taken for granted became a matter of dispute, at least among some segments of America's Black ghettos. At the height of the outbreaks, plundering (of supermarkets, furniture stores, liquor stores, pawn shops) became the normative and socially accepted thing to do. Far from being deviant, it became the conforming behavior in the situation. Viewed from this perspective, the looting behavior was not the product of the civilized facade of humanity giving way to savage animal instincts (as viewed in some mass media accounts). Indeed, looters continued to pay attention to traffic lights — an indication of the continuous operation of traditional norms even in highly confused circumstances. Many Blacks involved in massive looting were acting on the basis of new, emergent norms that had evolved in ghetto communities with regard to some categories of property (Quarantelli and Dynes, 1970).

Consumption. Consumption involves the "using up" of goods and services. Production requires consumption while consumption necessitates production. In order for us to produce, we must consume at least a minimum of food, clothing, and shelter. At stake is our survival as an organism. And if we are to consume, generally at some time or another and to some degree, we must produce.

Some of what is produced may be consumed immediately; some may be stored for future gratification. The accumulation of surpluses over and above immediate needs may have the object of carrying people through lean periods. But it may also serve personal and social ends far beyond the immediate economic realm. The accumulation of possessions became the foundation for systems of social stratification based on wealth and property (Lenski, 1966; Prewitt and Stone, 1973). In the Neolithic period, humans came to master nature through the domestication of animals and the cultivation of crops — in brief, *agriculture*. The availability of surpluses made it possible for the community to support specialists such as a priestly class who did not directly engage in production. It was also the origin of formal government, the State. The influential British archeologist, Gordon Childe, notes: "Chiefs cannot rule over a community unless that community can produce a social surplus above the needs of domestic consumption, sufficient to support the chieftain in idleness—i.e., as full-time ruler" (1963:47).

Such an arrangement is vividly portrayed by an anthropologist who studied the Ngwato people of South Africa:

> As head of the tribe, [the chief] formerly received tribute from his subjects in corn, cattle, wild animal skins, ivory and ostrich feathers, retained most of the cattle looted in war, and kept all unclaimed stray cattle and part of the fines imposed in his court, especially for cases of assault. He could also confiscate the entire property of tribesmen conspiring against him or banished for any other serious offence. In addition, he could through the regimental system command the services of his people for personal as well as tribal purposes. He further had a large number of servants directly attached to him and doing most of his domestic work. (Schapera, 1940, p. 76)

This arrangement would not have been possible in the absence of the production of foodstuffs at a level far above subsistence. In sum, the origin of the State and thereby the division of society into rulers and ruled corresponds to the production of a social surplus.

WORK

Work keeps at bay three great evils: boredom, vice, and need.

Voltaire, Candide, *XXX, 1759*

In nonindustrial societies the family dominates the other institutional spheres. Work (the earning of a living) is not readily distinguishable from other social activities. The situation is quite different in industrial societies. First, the workplace is physically separated from the home. Second, "working time" is temporally segregated in the daily cycle from "leisure time." Third, specialized organizational structures such as businesses and industries take over the management of work activities. And finally, the productive institution has become increasingly focal for other institutions, with the family, religion, the state, and education adjusting to its dictates (Dubin, 1976).

Incentives to Work. Work has no inherent meaning but, rather, people impute meanings to their work activities (Kalleberg, 1977). Accordingly, societies have employed a good many different kinds of incentives for getting their members to engage in work. "Self-interest" in the broadest sense, however, including the interests of one's family or friends, appears to be an underlying motivation of labor in all societies. Self-interest need not be defined solely in terms of money acquisition and profit. Among the Maori of the Pa-

Incentives to work. People work primarily for money and for what money purchases. But work also offers the opportunity to be associated with other people and to derive a sense of self-respect as a contributing member of society.

Patrick Reddy

cific, the pleasure of craftsmanship, the desire for public approval, the feeling of emulation, the sense of duty toward the community, and the wish to conform to custom and tradition—all these and more find outcome in economic activity (Hsu, 1943).

Even within the United States, work cannot be understood simply as a response to economic necessity. In a study conducted more than twenty years ago (Morse and Weiss, 1955), and since replicated (Tausky, 1969; Kaplan and Tausky, 1972), 80 percent of the men in a random sample said they would continue to work even if they inherited enough money to live comfortably. This is not to deny the significance of money as a source of motivation. Money and what it purchases remains a dominant feature of working. Work involving danger, unusual hours, physically stressing activity, exceptional isolation, or other extraordinary condition is usually paid more on the presumption that it will lure otherwise reluctant workers to such jobs. And it generally does (Dubin, Hedley, and Taveggia, 1976). In modern industrial societies, whether capitalist or communist, money is the essential medium of exchange and the prerequisite for material existence (Neff, 1968). Indeed, wage incentives (for instance, piecework) have been used more extensively in the Soviet Union than in any capitalist society (Fein, 1976).

WORK HAS MANY MEANINGS

OBSERVATION When I was home over the weekend I learned our neighbor had died. He was 87 years old, and had been retired since he was about 70. When he retired he had been encouraged by his family and friends to "take it easy" but somehow he never did. He continued to be the neighborhood handyman, doing many carpenter, electrical, and plumbing jobs. He also kept a huge 20-acre garden that he worked religiously. The garden produced an incredible supply of beans, tomatoes, squash, and corn, all of which he canned at harvest time or gave away.

PRINCIPLE My mother, commenting on the neighbor's death, indicated that she didn't understand why he had continued to work after his retirement. She said that he worked himself to death. I can't help but wonder if it was not the other way around. I wonder if his good health and good frame of mind after retirement were not a product of his working. People work for reasons other than simply making money. Through work they gain self-respect as useful members of the community and they escape from boredom and monotony. The neighborhood gave this man a sense of identity as they called on him for his talents as a handyman. And in this way he also came to associate with people and to be integrated in community life.

People also work for reasons other than money (Kaplan, 1977). They may work because they enjoy it, gain a sense of self-respect, achieve a feeling of self-actualization, want to be associated with other people, and wish to keep busy (escape boredom). Moreover, money is an important incentive to many, not merely for its own sake, but because its acquisition represents power, achievement, success, safety, public recognition, and many other things. Harry Levinson observes:

> Work has many social meanings. When a man works he has a contributing place in society. He earns the right to be the partner of other men. . . . The fact that someone will pay for his work is an indication that what he does is needed by others, and therefore that he himself is a necessary part of the social fabric. He matters—as a man. . . .
>
> A man's work . . . is a major social device for his identification as an adult. Much of who he is, to himself and others, is interwoven with how he earns his livelihood. . . . (1964, p. 20)

And Daniel P. Moynihan notes: "In America what you do is what you are: to do nothing is to be nothing; to do little is to be little. The equations are implacable and blunt, and ruthlessly public" (1965:746).

Elliot Liebow in *Tally's Corner*, a study of Black streetcorner men in Washington, D.C., points out the consequences of people's job experiences for their self-conceptions:

A crucial factor in the streetcorner man's lack of job commitment is the overall value he places on the job. *For his part, the streetcorner man puts no lower value on the job than does the larger society around him.* . . . In a real sense, every pay day, he counts in dollars and cents the value placed on the job by society at large. . . . Both employee and employer are contemptuous of the job. The employee shows his contempt by his reluctance to accept it or keep it, the employer by paying less than is required to support a family. . . .

The streetcorner man wants to be a person in his own right, to be noticed, to be taken account of . . . [but] his job fails him. The job and the man are even. The job fails the man and the man fails the job. (1967, pp. 57–63)

Changing Attitudes toward Work. One of the most striking characteristics of the traditional American value system has been the tendency for people to identify themselves with their work role. Europeans often express amazement when Americans introduce themselves by saying, "I am a furniture salesman," "I'm a doctor," "I manage a department store in Cleveland," and "I'm a housewife." But during the 1960s and 1970s, an increasing number of Americans, while still valuing work, have come to make somewhat different demands on their jobs than did previous generations.

Leisure is becoming increasingly important. Public opinion surveys reveal that when work and leisure are compared as sources of satisfaction, only 21 percent say that work means more to them than leisure. Sixty percent say that while they enjoy working, it is not their major source of satisfaction. Another 19 percent cannot conceive of work as even a minor source of satisfaction (Yankelovich, 1978).

It appears that Americans, especially those of the younger generations who were raised in affluence, are taking many of the traditional benefits of work such as money for granted. Increasingly, they are demanding more psychological satisfactions: more opportunities to exercise some control over the decisions of the workplace; more freedom to set one's own pace of work and the scheduling of hours; more opportunities to learn and grow; more possibilities of accomplishing something worthwhile; and more chances to exercise their talents and skills (Renwick and Lawler, 1978).

This pursuit of self-fulfillment is placing new demands on employers to revamp incentives to bring them in line with people's work motivations. No longer does the old carrot-and-stick value system offer adequate inducements to many American workers (the carrot being money and success; the stick being the threat of economic insecurity). Hence, the issue of evolving new incentive systems and transforming the character of work is a critical matter confronting Americans as they enter the 1980s (Yankelovich, 1978).

Do the Poor Want to Work? "We are faced this year," said President Nixon in his 1972 Labor Day message, "with the choice between the 'work ethic' that built this nation's character—and the new 'welfare ethic' that could cause that American character to weaken." The one, he argued, represents the traditional American ethic of striving and sacrifice; the other a new and alien ethic of indulgence and passivity. According to this view, welfare recipients prefer welfare as a way of life; lazy, slothful, and irresponsible, they simply do not want to and refuse to work.

Leonard Goodwin (1972), in a survey of more than 4000 people, from poor to nonpoor, concludes that the poor identify their self-esteem with work as strongly as do the nonpoor. This finding runs contrary to Nixon's view and the notion of a "culture of poverty"—a subculture with different values and ethics where the poor live only for the present, are fatalistic about the future, and place little value on work. Goodwin's findings suggest that the poor are very much absorbed in the dominant values and myths embodied in the American dream. A number of other studies have reached somewhat similar conclusions (Coward, Feagin, and Williams, 1974; Davidson and Gaitz, 1974). For instance, H. Roy Kaplan and Curt Tausky (1972) found that nearly three-fourths of those enrolled in a federally sponsored job-training program in a large New England city preferred a low-ranking job to public assistance (see Table 14.1).

Among the American public as a whole, there is deep antagonism to the concept of public welfare although there is strong support for what welfare programs do. In a 1977 national poll, 58 percent of the surveyed Americans said they disapprove of "most government-sponsored welfare programs" while 32 percent approve. Similarly, by 54 to 31 percent, they agreed with the statement that "most people who receive money from welfare could get along without it if they tried." Such attitudes held across a broad range of social and economic categories, even among many of those with low incomes. However, when a series of questions were asked that omitted the word "welfare," a quite different picture emerged. For instance, 81 percent approved of governmental financial assistance for children raised in low-income homes where one parent is missing, 81 percent endorsed food stamps for the poor, and 82 percent supported the use of tax money to "pay for health care for poor people" (Reinhold, 1977).

Alienation in Work. Within recent years, a growing body of literature has appeared dealing with **alienation** in work—a pervasive sense of powerlessness, meaninglessness, isolation, and self-estrangement (Seeman, 1959, 1967). A widely heralded government report, *Work in America* (Upjohn Institute for Employment Research, 1973), finds that significant numbers of American workers are dissatisfied with the quality of their working lives. The report places heavy reliance on a University of Michigan survey that asked a sample of Americans: "What type of work would you try to get into if you

TABLE 14.1
Comparison of Blue-Collar Workers, White-Collar Workers, and Hard-Core Unemployed to Work-Related Questions

	Blue-Collar Workers (267)	White-Collar Workers (151)	Hard-Core Unemployed* (275)
Would prefer to take a job as a car washer paying the same as welfare to welfare	91%	91%	71%
Would work even if had enough money to live comfortably without work	82	89	84
Would prefer low-paid respected work to average-pay work that people look down on	67	54	57

* The subjects of the study were 275 individuals enrolled in a federally sponsored job-training program. To be eligible for the program the individual had to be "disadvantaged," for example, recieve an income below the poverty level or lack suitable employment. Sixty-two percent of the participants were Black, 24 percent Puerto Rican, and 14 percent White. Only 24 percent had graduated from high school.

Source: Adapted from H. Roy Kaplan and Curt Tausky, "Work and the Welfare Cadillac: The Function of and Commitment to Work among the Hard-Core Unemployed," *Social Problems,* 19 (1972), 479, Table 5.

could start all over again?" Only 43 percent of the white-collar workers (including professionals) would choose the same kind of work if given another chance. The figure was even lower—24 percent—for blue-collar workers (see Figure 14.1).

Work in America indicates that "dull, repetitive, seemingly meaningless tasks, offering little challenge or autonomy, are causing discontent among workers at all occupational levels" (1973:xv). The report says that the "blue-collar blues" are not limited to bored, alienated assembly-line workers. The problems of the assembly line are also mirrored in the office where work is segmented and authoritarian: for a growing number of office jobholders (keypunch operators, typists, and others), there is little to distinguish them from industrial workers.

The discontent of trapped, dehumanized workers, the report *Work in America* argues, is contributing to increasing absenteeism, high worker turn-over rates, wildcat strikes, sabotage, poor-quality products, and a reluctance by workers to commit themselves to their work tasks. Work-related prob-

Figure 14.1. Job satisfaction: Percentages in occupational groups who would choose similar work again.

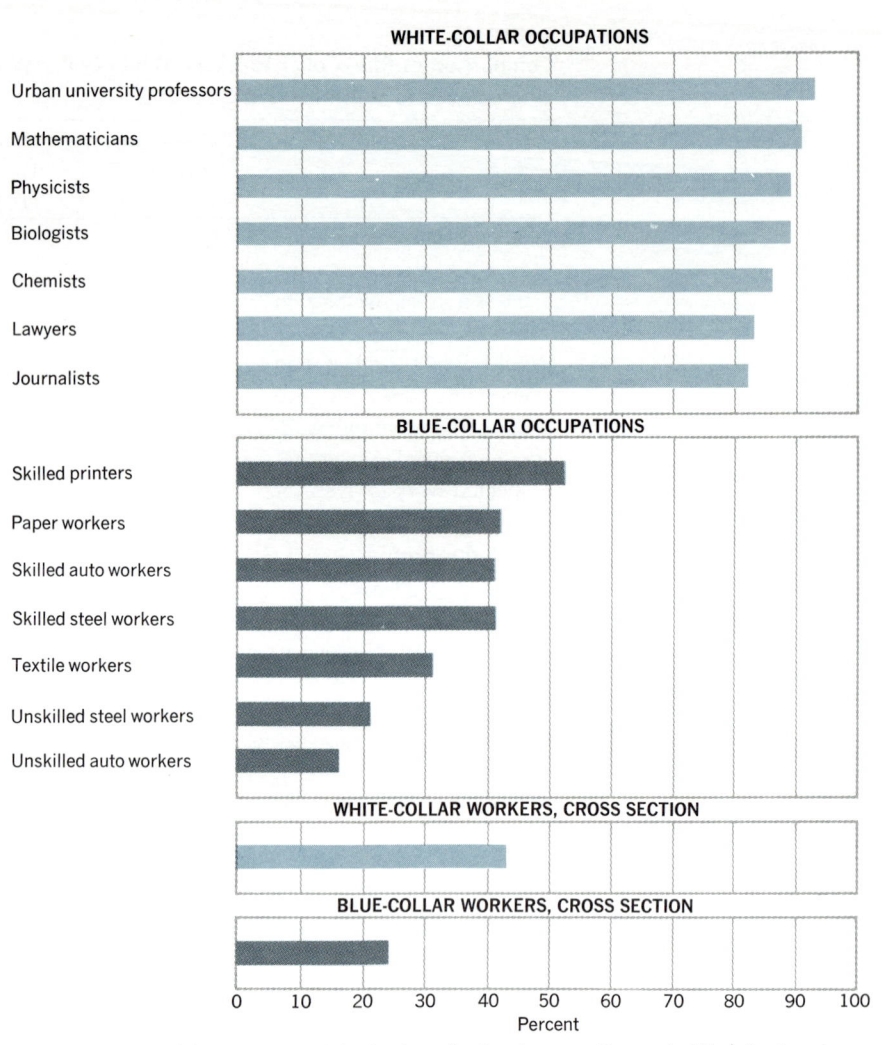

WHITE-COLLAR OCCUPATIONS
- Urban university professors
- Mathematicians
- Physicists
- Biologists
- Chemists
- Lawyers
- Journalists

BLUE-COLLAR OCCUPATIONS
- Skilled printers
- Paper workers
- Skilled auto workers
- Skilled steel workers
- Textile workers
- Unskilled steel workers
- Unskilled auto workers

WHITE-COLLAR WORKERS, CROSS SECTION

BLUE-COLLAR WORKERS, CROSS SECTION

Percent: 0, 10, 20, 30, 40, 50, 60, 70, 80, 90, 100

Source: Adapted from W. E. Upjohn Institute for Employment Research, *Work in America* (Cambridge, Mass.: The MIT Press, 1973), 16, Table 1.

lems in turn have their impact in other life spheres, contributing to problems of physical and mental health, drug abuse, alcohol addiction, less "balanced" political attitudes among workers (an increased tendency to cast ballots for extremist or "protest" candidates), and a growth in "clannishness" (a preoccupation with ethnic membership).

Work in America was sponsored by the Department of Health, Education, and Welfare, and has resulted in considerable controversy. Another government report, that of the U.S. Department of Labor (1974), came to drastically different conclusions. It based its findings on public opinion polls examining job satisfaction among American workers between 1958 and 1973:

> In spite of public speculation to the contrary, there is no conclusive evidence of a widespread, dramatic decline in job satisfaction. Reanalysis of fifteen national surveys conducted since 1958 indicates that there has not been any significant decrease in overall levels of job satisfaction over the last decade.
>
> There is no convincing evidence of the existence of a direct cause-effect relationship between job satisfaction and productivity. In reality, the contribution of job satisfaction to productivity is probably indirect and more likely to be reflected in reductions on the "cost" side of the corporate ledger than in increases on the output side. These indirect benefits are associated with reductions in turnover, absenteeism, alcohol and drug abuse, sabotage and theft — all of which have been linked to some degree with job dissatisfaction. (Quoted by Fein, 1976, p. 469)

Further, the percentage of satisfied workers rose from 81 percent in 1958 to 90 percent in 1973. Hence, two government reports have reached contradictory conclusions based on the answers to a different set of polling questions.

Sociologists find that the overall best predictor of strong work attachment and the absence of alienation is an occupation that combines high economic, occupational, and educational prestige (Blauner, 1969; Dubin, Hedley, and Taveggia, 1976). In part, this factor represents a kind of composite index since it partly subsumes a number of other factors, for example, the amount of control and responsibility associated with an occupation. Jobs with high prestige, however, tend to be valued even when "objective" aspects of the work are undesirable:

> ... the lowliness or nastiness of a job are subjective estimates. ... A doctor or a nurse, for example, or a sanitary inspector, have to do some things which would disgust the most unskilled casual laborer who did not see these actions in their social context. Yet the status and prestige of such people is generally high. ... Above all, it is the prestige of his working group and his position in it which will influence the worker's attitude to such jobs. (Brown, 1954, pp. 149–150)

Alienation. Considerable controversy exists as to whether alienation among American workers is increasing or decreasing. Different sets of questions yield differing conclusions.

Patrick Reddy

Control also represents an important factor in work satisfaction (Shepard, 1969; Israel, 1971; Kohn and Schooler, 1973; Form, 1975). Generally, the greater the control over time, physical movement, and pace of work, the greater the job satisfaction and the less the alienation. In the United States, where individual initiative has long been a cultural ideal, we find especially strong pressures for control and independence in work. Still other factors associated with low work alienation are a career that has not been blocked and chaotic, a work-setting characterized by integrated teams of people, an off-the-job environment made up of an occupational community (for example, as in coal mining), and job conditions where workers feel that their superiors and peers will support their decisions or complaints. In Research Study 21 Melvin L. Kohn explores some of these matters at greater length.

RESEARCH STUDY 21

OCCUPATIONAL STRUCTURE AND ALIENATION*

Melvin L. Kohn

> Labor . . . is external to the worker, i.e., it does not belong to his essential being; . . . in his work, therefore, he does not affirm himself but denies himself. . . . His labor is . . . merely a *means* to satisfy needs external to it. . . . It belongs to another; it is the loss of self.
>
> Karl Marx, Estranged Labour, 1844

Problem. Karl Marx held that within modern society (more particularly under the property system of capitalism) workers lose control of their labor and become commodities, objects used by capitalists for their own gain. Workers thus lose control over the *product* of their labor — what they themselves produce. They also lose control over the *process* of their labor — they are required to do work that does not engage their interests or challenge their abilities. As a consequence workers are unable to express themselves in work or find meaningful identities through it. This study by Melvin L. Kohn is designed to appraise Marx's conception of work in capitalist societies.

Hypotheses. Kohn investigates two related hypotheses suggested by Marx's analysis of alienation. First, emphasizing loss of control over the *product* of one's labor, Marx posits that ownership and high hierarchical position (supervisory rank) are of crucial importance in minimizing feelings of alienation. Second, emphasizing loss of control over the *process* of labor, Marxist theory suggests that such determinants of occupational self-direction as being closely supervised, doing routinized work, and doing work of little substantive complexity result in feelings of alienation.

Method. The data for the study came from a sample survey of 3101 men, representative of all

Continued on next page.

---

* Adapted from Melvin L. Kohn (1976) Occupational Structure and Alienation. *American Journal of Sociology,* 82:111–130.

men employed in civilian occupations in the United States, who were interviewed by the National Opinion Research Center. Kohn conceived of alienation in terms of three dimensions: powerlessness—a feeling that one is at the mercy of uncontrollable, external forces; self-estrangement—a negative evaluation of one's own worth and a sense of being adrift; and normlessness—a high expectancy that socially unacceptable behavior is required to achieve given goals (for instance, "if something works it doesn't matter whether it's right or wrong"). In addition to securing responses to questions measuring these aspects of alienation, Kohn also asked respondents detailed questions about the closeness of their supervision, the routinization of their work, and the substantive complexity of the tasks they performed.

Findings. Kohn found that both control over the product of one's labor (ownership and high hierarchical position) and control over the process of one's labor (closeness of supervision, routinization, and the substantive complexity of work) are related to feelings of powerlessness, self-estrangement, and normlessness. However, the pivotal occupational conditions are those that determine self-direction in one's work. Insofar as ownership and hierarchical rank affect alienation, it is mainly because owners and supervisors are able to be self-directed in their work.

Kohn also statistically examined other factors that may affect alienation and "wash out" the effects of self-direction (he ran some statistical tests in which he sought to control or allow for these other factors). Among these additional factors were education, wages (or salary), job security, age, race, social class origins, and religious background. Adding these variables to the package of statistical controls did not appreciably change the picture.

Conclusion. Kohn concludes:

In sum, there is substantial evidence that doing work of little substantive complexity is not only associated with, but actually results in, feelings of alienation. It seems a fair presumption that closeness of supervision and routinization also have a causal impact on alienation. In their principal thrust, then, the findings are entirely consonant with the basic Marxian analysis of the alienating effects of workers' loss of control over their essential job conditions. In this large-scale, capitalist economy, the type of control that is most important for alienation, though, is control, not over the product, but over the process, of one's work. Ownership, hierarchical position, and division of labor have less effect on workers' feelings of alienation than do closeness of supervision, routinization, and substantive complexity. (pp. 126–127)

NATIONAL DEVELOPMENT

Economic growth without social progress lets the great majority of the people remain in poverty, while a privileged few reap the benefits of rising abundance.
John F. Kennedy, message to Congress on the Inter-American Fund for Social Progress, March 14, 1961

Following World War II, Western social scientists introduced a number of concepts to deal with the transformations occurring in the nations of Asia, Africa, and Latin America. These concepts included "development," "the Third World," and "modernization." "Third World" nations, long-labeled as "backward" or "undeveloped," were portrayed as "developing" or "modernizing." The cultural standard against which they were judged was

The absence of the application of inanimate power in agriculture. Here peasants plant rice in central Java. Sociologists who view development as social differentiation view this subsistence activity as taking place at a relatively undifferentiated level in the division of labor.

Patrick Reddy

that of the United States and Western Europe. Sociologist Immanuel Wallerstein notes the implicit ethnocentrism of this view:

> The new terms replaced older, distasteful ones. Backward nations were only underdeveloped. The Yellow Horde became instead the Third World. And progress no longer involved Westernization. Now one could antiseptically modernize. (1976, p. 131)

The growing realization among Western social scientists that many of their concepts are ethnocentric has produced considerable controversy. And it has served to highlight three contrasting viewpoints regarding the transformations occurring in non-Western nations (Portes, 1976). Let us consider and critically examine each of these perspectives.

Development as Social Differentiation. A number of sociological theories have adopted a "before-and-after" model describing beginning and end "stages" in social development (Émile Durkheim's "mechanic" and "organic" solidarities; Ferdinand Toennies's "community" and "society"; and Robert Redfield's "folk" and "urban" cultures). Transformation is portrayed as progression from "lower" to "higher" social forms. According to these formulations, a society experiences pressures at some point. It undertakes to deal with these stresses by specialization and social differentiation which in turn give rise to new forms of functional interdependence. These "adaptive features" include a money economy, urbanism, industrialism, and formal bureaucratic structures characterized by rational organization.

Critics point out that the approach fails to explain why such transformations occur (the interpretations are excessively general) and why they take place at different rates and in different forms in different societies. Further, growth is depicted as an automatic, gradual, and irreversible process. As such the formulation does not adequately reflect the twists, turns, sudden thrusts, convulsions, and reversals associated with change. It portrays those societies that ultimately "make it" (the "winners") as structurally resembling the advanced capitalist nations but fails to note the impact that these powerful nations have on the less powerful ones.

Development as an Enactment of Values. The starting point for this perspective is the psychological characteristics of a society's members, not the nature of the society itself. The critical element is thought to be people's "value orientations"—the "spirit" that impels individuals to promote and accept social change (McClelland, 1967; Inkeles and Smith, 1974). This perspective is a continuation of Max Weber's thesis regarding the influence of the Protestant ethic in promoting capitalism. Ideas are seen as more important in shaping history than technological and economic forces. Alex Inkeles and David H. Smith (1974) suggest that "becoming modern" leads to a variety of new characteristics in individuals including openness to new experience and to new ways of doing things; being oriented to the present and the future rather than the past; believing that people can exert control over the environment; being able to plan; valuing technical skill; and being informed regarding the wider world.

Critics dispute the view that social life can be understood by merely understanding the psychological characteristics of a society's members. Social arrangements (including networks of political and economic interests) serve to limit, contain, shape, and channel people's behavior. Further, it is ethnocentric to assume that transformations in non-Western societies will lead them to become reproductions of Western societies and their members miniature-thinking Westerners. Social change occurs within the context of vastly different traditions and hence needs to be studied in terms of the unique historical processes operating in each nation.

Development as Liberation from Dependency. Some sociologists, especially those influenced by Marxist formulations, view development as occurring within a "world system." Centers of advanced capitalism are seen as exploiting the hinterlands (Chase-Dunn, 1975). Direct colonial control of the peripheral areas is said to have been replaced by neocolonial mechanisms of foreign investment and credit and the operations of multinational corporations (like Exxon, Gulf Oil, Royal Dutch Shell, and British Petroleum). The result is uneven development, structural distortion (economies specializing in raw materials such as oil or copper), unequal exchange, vulnerability to the vicissitudes of the international market, and the suppression of autonomous policies (alliances between elites of the core nations and the periphery nations). Thus, dependence is fostered not through an "army of occupation" but through the operation of political and economic controls from the outside that are implemented by willing local elites.

Critics contend that the theory of dependency contains more rhetoric than a system of logically interrelated and testable propositions. In the hands of some writers, dependency becomes an explanation for everything that is wrong or malfunctioning within Asian, African, and Latin American nations. The approach often leads to denunciations of imperialism without considering variations among nations. Thus, some countries like Canada are profoundly "dependent," in the sense that their economies are heavily penetrated by foreign-owned concerns, and yet they exhibit a relatively high per capita income and provide relatively efficient health and educational services. And sight is lost of various internal dynamics that provide certain "degrees of freedom" for national governments, permitting them to carry out fairly drastic programs of internal transformation (Portes, 1976). All of this brings us to a consideration of the State.

THE STATE

It is evident that the State is a creation of nature, and that man is by nature a political animal. And he who by nature and not by mere accident is without a State is either above humanity or below it; he is the "tribeless, lawless, heartless one," whom Homer denounces. . . . Man alone has any sense of good and evil, of just and unjust; and the association of living beings who have this sense makes a family and a State.

Aristotle, Politics, Book 1, Chapter 2

The **state** — the political institution — is that social agency that exercises a supreme monopoly of authority within a given territory. In the final analysis this authority rests on the right to apply physical coercion. Two views have prevailed regarding the State. The first explains the State as a social contract; the second, as an organization of violence that serves the interests of elites.

The social contract perspective derives from seventeenth and eighteenth century social philosophers who argued that humans in their "natural" condition are a perverse and destructive lot. In order to escape from circumstances of brutality, rampant violence, and discomfort, they voluntarily enter into a social agreement that provides for their common rule and collective defense. Thus according to John Locke (1632–1704), self-love "will make men partial to themselves and their friends; and [their] ill-nature, passion and revenge will carry them too far in punishing others; and hence nothing but confusion and disorder will follow; and that therefore God hath certainly appointed government to restrain the partiality and violence of men." Thomas Hobbes (1588–1679) took an even more dismal view; he stated that "during the time men live without a common power [government] to keep them in awe, they are in that condition which is called war; and such a war, as is of every man, against every man." To escape from this "natural" condition of the war of all against all, Hobbes said humans voluntarily established the State.

Another eighteenth century social philosopher, Jean Rousseau (1712–1778), set forth a view in sharp contrast to that of Locke and Hobbes. "Man is born free," he writes in *The Social Contract* (1762), "and everywhere he is in chains." In the "natural" condition, Rousseau said, the human was a "noble savage"—spontaneous, outgoing, loving, kind, and uncorrupted. Civilization brought corruption, and now humans have to obey commands that they know do not stem directly from within themselves.

Marxists and conflict sociologists give a somewhat different twist to Rousseau's formulation. They view society as a social arena in which groups compete for wealth, power, and status. Those groups that control the State are able to effect their will in the course of human affairs and answer the distributive question (who shall get what, when, and how) in their own favor. Randall Collins, a conflict sociologist, asserts:

> What we mean by the state is the way in which violence is organized. The state consists of those people who have the guns or the other weapons and are prepared to use them; in the version of political organization found in the modern world, they claim monopoly on this use. The state *is,* above all, the army and the police, and if these groups did not have weapons we would not have a state in the classical sense. This is a type of definition much disputed by those who like to believe that the state is a kind of grade-school assembly in which people get together to operate for their common good. . . . I believe it can be shown that . . . we can deal with all questions that might arise about politics. Who will fight or threaten whom and who will win what? (1975, pp. 351–352)

Perhaps we can gain additional insight regarding these matters by examining the functions of the State.

FUNCTIONS

Every society is confronted with the general requirement of maintaining order and effecting control over its members. This requirement, however, has far different implications for large, modern societies, such as the United States, than it has for societies in which there are no community bonds or permanent leaders beyond those supplied by family and friends (as was the case, for instance, among the Western Shoshoni Indians of the United States). Among larger, more complex societies, some norms generally require formal enforcement; cultural heterogeneity and an elaborate division of labor usually necessitate overall planning and direction; conflicting interests among individuals and groups seeking scarce values commonly demand final arbitration; and, externally, a people often require protection against the peoples of other societies. These, then, are functions that may be performed by the political institution.

Enforcement of Norms. George Peter Murdock, an eminent anthropologist, tells us that

> ... for 99 per cent of the approximately one million years that man has inhabited this earth, he lived, thrived, and developed without any true government whatsoever, and that as late as 100 years ago half the peoples of the world—not half the population but half the tribes or nations—still ordered their lives exclusively through informal controls without benefit of political institutions. (1950, p. 716)

INFORMAL ENFORCEMENT OF NORMS

OBSERVATION While waiting to get gas this afternoon in an unusually long line a funny thing happened. A woman who apparently felt she didn't have to wait in line like the average citizen pulled her car ahead of the line, backed up to the pumps, and refused to move until she was sold some gas. Needless to say, everyone in line was rather upset (including myself). However, the man in front of me (mad as hell) took action. He got out of his car, removed his locking gas cap, and locked it onto the woman's tank. He then dropped the gas cap key down a gutter. Everyone clapped.

PRINCIPLE Not all norms are enforced by formal political institutions. People at times take the law into their own hands. In extreme cases, especially when people lose confidence in the ability of government to enforce the law or where law is for the most part absent, vigilantism may spring up. Although this was not technically a case of vigilantism, it does show how an enraged citizenry could come to respond on its own when it becomes dissatisfied.

Where people lack formal political institutions, the folkways and mores are enforced through the spontaneous and collective action of the community. No judicial or police system is necessary. The Crow Indians, for instance, subjected violators of certain of their mores to scathing ridicule, and the Ibans of Borneo handled dishonesty through erecting "liars' heaps" that thoroughly disgraced the wrongdoer. In circumstances such as these, the community as a whole acts to enforce the norms; nonpolitical institutions serve as agencies for social control.

In still other societies, a specialized political structure may come to assume responsibility for social control (although other institutions may simultaneously continue to function as regulators of human behavior). In brief, a special body or organization within a society comes to be invested with the right of applying physical coercion for the enforcement of certain norms. These norms are *laws*. Laws, in contrast with folkways and mores, do not rest for their enforcement on the spontaneous and collective action of a society's members. Laws may be customary—arising in a more or less gradual, unplanned, and nondeliberative fashion—or enacted—arising in a planned and deliberative fashion through the action of an authoritative group or organization within the society. In either case, they are enforced by a special organization that enjoys the right of applying physical coercion.

Planning and Direction. Where a society is continuously confronted with major social change, folkways, mores, and customary laws often are no longer capable of providing people with functioning guideposts for carrying on their daily activities. New norms become indispensable. The folkways of fairness that regulated traffic in horse and buggy days are no longer suitable for the congested traffic posed by contemporary automobiles at major street and road intersections. Nor are the laws enacted for automobiles adequate for handling congested air traffic over airports. Where critical shortages develop in petroleum and vital metals, where segments of the population become permanently unemployed, where rivers and lakes become polluted with industrial wastes, in these and other situations, old ways no longer provide effective answers and solutions. Enacted law, since it is planned and deliberate, is highly adaptable to new conditions. The political institution offers the possibility for planning and directing human activities in accordance with the dictates of new circumstances.

Moreover, the sheer complexity and scope of certain operations requires some overall coordination and integration. Informal and personal arrangements no longer suffice. People acting by themselves on the basis of traditional procedures are simply incapable of providing a variety of essential services. Highways, fire and police protection, public sanitation (street cleaning, garbage collection, insect and rodent elimination, and so on), the safeguarding of public health (the control and prevention of both endemic and epidemic diseases), the provision of fiduciary money, these and many other activities necessitate the control, direction, and coordination of the activities of many individuals performing different tasks.

Further, in times of crisis when the ordinary equilibrium is upset, as in cases of war, financial panics, and natural disasters, the multitude cannot usually act in mass to cope with the situation. The efficient and effective channeling of human endeavor requires planning and direction. This can be performed by only one or at most a few individuals. And these few must enjoy the power and authority to implement their plans (Davis, 1949).

Arbitration of Conflicting Interests. Society is confronted with the fact that individuals, in seeking to realize their goals, often come into conflict with one another. Not all goods and services are found in unlimited amount; some are scarce. If no bonds except the pursuit of immediate self-interest unite individuals, society becomes a jungle in which every person's hand is turned against that of every other person. Of course, disruptive conflict may be minimized by social consensus that formulates the "rules of the game." But in the face of rapid normative change, social anonymity, and cultural heterogeneity, not all people are likely to agree on the common rules for playing the game. Where conflict between segments or strata within a society becomes deep and intense, the entire social fabric may be weakened and jeopardized. Hence, some body is needed that is strong enough to contain conflict within tolerable limits (Goode, 1972).

Moreover, the larger goals of the society must take precedence over those of smaller groups and individuals. The political institution performs this balancing and adjudicating function. This can be seen in the realm of civil rights. Within the past two decades, Blacks have raised, with considerable militancy, demands for new rights, opportunities, and privileges. Many Whites feel that they must give up something of value if Blacks are to gain their demands. Hence, Black movement has bred White countermovement. Within this setting, the federal government has stepped in as an arbitrator—for example, through judicial decisions, presidential executive orders relating to governmental employment, and Congressional enactment of civil rights laws.

Protection Against Other Societies. Societies throughout human history have felt the need to protect themselves and their interests against outside groups, and to engage in what they have felt to be necessary acts of aggression against other groups. The two chief means for accomplishing these ends have been war and diplomacy. Each demands centralized control and authority if a society is to bring to bear its full weight against an adversary. The political institution meets this requirement.

POWER AND AUTHORITY

> The great question which, in all ages, has disturbed mankind, and brought on them the greatest part of those mischiefs which have ruined cities, depopulated countries, and disordered the peace of the world, has been, not whether there be power in the world, not whence it came, but who should have it.
>
> *John Locke,* Treatises on Government, *1690*

Power has acquired a bad name. It is associated with tyranny, dictators, and totalitarianism. However, as commonly used in the social sciences, the term is devoid of sinister connotations. Rather, it refers to the capacity of an individual or group to control or influence the behavior of others, even in the absence of their consent. Power is a very general and comprehensive concept. It includes control realized through the physical threats of an armed robber or a rapist. It includes influence wielded by the shaman, priest, or doctor. And it includes control gained through indirect manipulation, as for example by means of oversolicitousness or putting people under obligation.

Since power may be either legitimate or illegitimate, sociologists find it useful to introduce another concept—**authority**—to refer to *legitimate power*. When people possess authority, Robert M. MacIver writes, they possess "the established *right,* within any social order, to determine policies, to pronounce judgments on relevant issues, and to settle controversies, or, more broadly, to act as leader or guide to other[s]" (1947:83). Legitimacy—the social justification of power—may take any number of forms. Max Weber proposed a three-fold classification of authority based on the manner in which power is socially legitimated: legal–rational, traditional, and charismatic. Although his classification has been criticized and modified by some, it remains a useful tool for considering leadership.

Legal–Rational Authority. In the legal–rational type, governmental officials claim obedience on the ground that their commands fall within the impersonal, formally defined scope of their office. The authority inheres in the position. Obedience is owed not to a person but to a set of impersonal principles; authority derives from a belief in the supremacy of law. People accept the exercise of power because the formulation of policies and orders follows rules to which they subscribe. Ideally, legal–rational authority is "a government of laws, not of people." Within the United States, citizens accept the authority of a newly elected President regardless of the bitterness with which the previous campaign had been waged. The failure of an appreciable number of Americans to accept these rules as "the rules of the game" would impair the exercise of governmental power. This is precisely what happened in 1861 when the southern states rejected Abraham Lincoln and federal authority. And it was the public's perception of the failure of the Nixon Administration to play by "the rules of the game" that led to its downfall.

Traditional Authority. In traditional authority, power is legitimated by the sanctity of custom. The ruler's power is often viewed as eternal, inviolable, and sacred. Many Roman Catholics invest the Pope with infallibility stemming from divine guidance when acting in matters pertaining to the Church. The Tibetan Dalai Lama traditionally exercised both spiritual and temporal authority that was associated with a belief in his divine nature. Medieval kings ruled in the name of "a divine right" ordained by God. Considerable moral force stands behind this type of authority. Claim to traditional authority commonly rests on birthright; it is usually inherited—royal blood is thought to be somehow different from the blood of commoners. Although the ruler's power is limited by tradition, in practice the ruler enjoys considerable leeway—in fact, a certain amount of arbitrariness may come to be expected.

Charismatic Authority. Charisma, meaning literally "gift of grace," is used by Weber to characterize leaders whose followers believe them to be endowed with extraordinary, superhuman, or supernatural powers and qualities. Founders of world religions, prophets, and military and political heroes are the archetypes of the charismatic leader. Miracles, revelations, heroic feats, valor, and baffling success are their characteristic marks. They are the Christs, Cromwells, Napoleons, Caesars, Hitlers, Stalins, Castros, and Joan of Arcs that dot the pages of history. And they are also lesser people who gathered together in a band devoted followers or disciples for a new cause. They usually have a sense of being "called" to spread the new word, a sense of rejecting the past and heralding the future as symbolized in Christ's declaration, "It is written . . . , but I say unto you. . . ."

These three types of authority are not necessarily mutually exclusive. England's Richard the Lionhearted possessed both traditional and charismatic authority. Magnetic personalities may attain legal office and remain there so long that their authority becomes in part traditional, as in the case of Franklin Delano Roosevelt. The leadership of Presidents Dwight D. Eisenhower and John F. Kennedy was also characterized by certain charismatic qualities.

Authority in New Nations. Seymour Martin Lipset notes that a basic problem faced by all new nations and postrevolutionary societies is the crisis of legitimacy. An old order is abolished and with it the set of beliefs that justified its system of authority. Hence, as in postrevolutionary America, France, and much of contemporary Asia and Africa, traditional authority is absent; legitimacy can be developed only through reliance on legal and/or charismatic authority. Legal–rational authority, however, is often weak since the law has been identified with the interests of an imperial exploiter. Charismatic authority, in contrast, is well suited to the needs of newly developing nations:

It requires neither time or a rational set of rules, and is highly flexible. A charismatic leader plays several roles. He is first of all the symbol of the new nation, its hero who embodies in his person its values and aspirations. But more than merely symbolizing the new nation, he legitimizes the state, the new secular government, by endowing it with his "gift of grace." (1963, p. 18)

Lipset makes the interesting observation that the early American Republic, like many contemporary new nations, was legitimized by charisma. It is easy to forget that, in his time, George Washington was idolized as much as many of the contemporary leaders of new states. Marcus Cunliffe, the author of an able biography of the first President, points out:

In the well-worn phrase of Henry Lee, he was *first in war, first in peace and first in the hearts of his countrymen*. . . . He was the prime native hero, a necessary creation for a new country. . . . Hence . . . the comment . . . made by the European traveler Paul Svinin, as early as 1815: "Every American considers it his sacred duty to have a likeness of Washington in his home, just as we have the image of God's saints." For America, he was originator and vindicator, both saint *and* defender of the faith, in a curiously timeless fashion, as if he were Charlemagne, Saint Joan and Napoleon Bonaparte telescoped into one person. . . . (1960, pp. 20–21)

POWER IN AMERICA

The problem of power is how to achieve its responsible use rather than its irresponsible and indulgent use — of how to get men of power to live *for* the public rather than *off* the public.
Robert F. Kennedy, The Pursuit of Justice, 1964

In both popular and sociological literature, we encounter two prevalent views regarding the nature of power within the United States. One is the power elite thesis which holds that a small number of individuals make the important decisions affecting the lives and welfare of Americans. The other, the pluralist thesis, says that power is widely dispersed within the United States and that policy is formulated by numerous interest groups acting on behalf of their respective memberships. Let us consider each of these views in turn.

The Power Elite Thesis. A good many people believe that "they" run things: America's "Sixty Families," the bankers, the generals, Wall Street, or some other power lurking behind the scene. As Robert A. Dahl, a leading political scientist, observes, this kind of view has a good deal of appeal:

It is simple, compelling, dramatic, "realistic." It gives one standing as an inside-dopester. For individuals with a strong strain of frustrated idealism, it has just the right touch of hard-boiled cynicism. Finally, the hypothesis has one very great advantage over many alternative explanations: It can be cast in a form that makes it virtually impossible to disprove.... If the overt leaders of a community do not appear to constitute a ruling elite, then the theory can be saved by arguing that behind the overt leaders there is a set of covert leaders who do. If subsequent evidence shows that this covert group does not make a ruling elite, then the theory can be saved by arguing that behind the first covert group there is another, and so on. (1958, p. 463)

The theme of conspiracy has long haunted the mind of the political left. Leftists talk about the "machinations of Wall Street," about the behind-the-scenes dealings and operations within government of wealthy interest groups, particularly those of Big Business. In support of this notion proponents like to cite Dwight D. Eisenhower's Presidential Farewell Address of January 17, 1961. In that speech, the late General–President warned against a new phenomenon in American life that he indicated had not existed earlier. He identified it as the "conjunction of an immense military establishment and a large arms industry" (a military–industrial complex). He said the total influence of it "... is felt in every city, every state house, every office of the Federal Government," and that "only an alert and knowledgeable citizenry" can so manage this complex that "security and liberty may prosper together." The political right has likewise been preoccupied with conspiracy, but in somewhat different terms, viewing the matter as one of an international communist conspiracy.

The late sociologist, C. Wright Mills, in his controversial book, *The Power Elite* (1956), develops the thesis of behind-the-scenes control of government by powerful interest groups. In essence, Mills argues that the major decisions affecting Americans and others—especially those having to do with the possibilities of war and peace—are made not by the people through the formal structures of government but through the deliberate action of a very small number of persons and groups whom he terms the "power elite." The real rulers of America, according to his theory, come from three groups: corporation executives, military men, and high-ranking politicians. They are subject to little control by others, and particularly by the ordinary citizen. More often than not, they act in "immoral" ways and are often "irresponsible" in the exercise of their power.

Writers like Mills contend that one result of this elite domination of governmental policymaking has been oversized defense budgets and overly aggressive foreign policies. Many fateful decisions are made without public debate or consultation which the American public is then asked to support in the name of "patriotism." Illustrations include the Bay of Pigs invasion of Cuba, the bombing of North Vietnam and the subsequent American invasion of Cambodia, the invasion of Santo Domingo, the 1954 overthrow of the Guatemalan government, President Nixon's visit to China, and so on.

Figure 14.2. Percentage of cabinet members with business interlocks by administration.

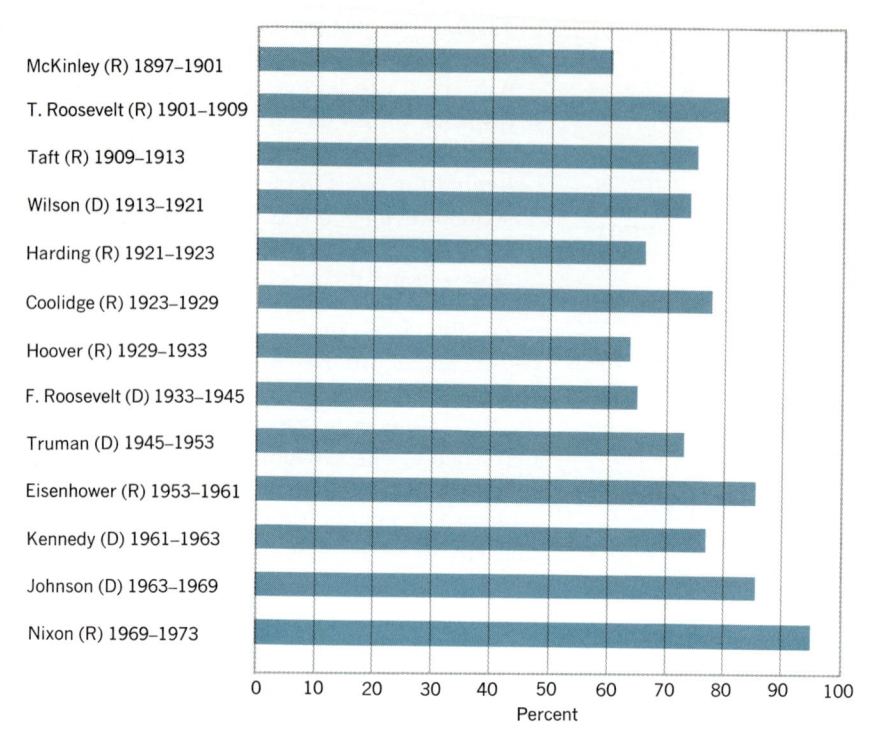

Administration	
McKinley (R) 1897–1901	
T. Roosevelt (R) 1901–1909	
Taft (R) 1909–1913	
Wilson (D) 1913–1921	
Harding (R) 1921–1923	
Coolidge (R) 1923–1929	
Hoover (R) 1929–1933	
F. Roosevelt (D) 1933–1945	
Truman (D) 1945–1953	
Eisenhower (R) 1953–1961	
Kennedy (D) 1961–1963	
Johnson (D) 1963–1969	
Nixon (R) 1969–1973	

Source: Adapted from Peter J. Freitag (1975) "The cabinet and big business: A study of interlocks," *Social Problems,* 23: Table 2, p. 142.

Power elite theorists take particular note of the linkage between the military and their corporate arms' suppliers. In 1958, for example, the 100 largest primary military contractors employed some 768 former military officers who had retired with the rank of at least colonel or naval captain; by 1968, the linkage had increased to 2072 former military officers. The interlock between suppliers and the military suggests a community of interest between the two sectors of the society (for instance, in recent years at least seven high-ranking former military officers, some of them four-star generals, have been employed by the Northrop Corporation, a major producer of military aircraft). Personal contacts between high-ranking officers and their former colleagues can affect negotiations, especially if the military officers may shortly be seeking corporate employment after their military retirement. Military contracts may be negotiated in any number of ways to maximize the contractor's gain: alloting a contract to a favored corporation, research and development advantages, patent rights, and shoddy procedures for cost accounting (Lieberson, 1971).

Peter J. Freitag (1975) has studied the business interlocks of United States Cabinet Secretaries from 1897 to 1973. He finds support for Mills's contention that there is a high degree of interchange of personnel between the elites of the corporate and political institutions. Of the 205 Cabinet officers during this seventy-six year period, at least 76.1 percent came from big corporations (see Figure 14.2). Republican administrations had only a slightly higher proportion of interlocks (78.1 percent) than Democratic administrations (73.6 percent). Eighty-four of the 205 Cabinet officers served in elite business positions both prior to *and* after their stay in the Cabinet. Freitag takes this interlocking of business and government as an indication of a unified elite within American life.

The Pluralist Thesis. A "pluralist" theory of national power—a formulation in sharp contrast with the power elite thesis—has also won favor with some sociologists. According to this view, expressed for instance by David Riesman in *The Lonely Crowd* (1953), no one group really runs the government, although many groups have veto power to stop things inimical to their perceived interests. Instead, important decisions about policy are made by a good many different groups—business organizations, labor organizations, farm blocs, racial and ethnic groups, and religious groups. These interest groups allegedly engage in a struggle for allies among the more or less unorganized public. Moreover, in sharp contrast with power elite formulations, Riesman does not believe that the same group or coalition of groups sets all major policies. Instead, he argues that the exercise of power varies with the issue at stake: the great majority of groups are inoperative on most issues and mobilize their resources only on those issues that impinge on their central interests. Stanley Lieberson (1971) advances a somewhat similar "hypothesis of compensating strategies" in which interest groups are seen as concentrating their efforts in areas that benefit them most directly.

Pluralists see military–industrial relations as only one of many powerful influences on government policy. They reject the power elite formulations that view the linkage between the military and industry as a dominant and pervasive force related to an inherent necessity of the capitalist system. Pluralists insist that only a relatively small minority of large American businesses are deeply dependent on military spending—of the largest fifty industrial companies, only one-fifth have more than a quarter of their sales stemming from military contracts. Further, the vast majority of merchandising companies (department stores, supermarkets, drug store chains) do not enjoy any direct benefits from military contracts. And it is estimated that a 20 percent cut in armament expenditures accompanied by a compensating increase in nonmilitary expenditures would mean a reduction in total output and employment in only ten of the nation's 56 industrial sectors (Lieberson, 1971).

Whereas C. Wright Mills sees a power elite as deriving from a *coincidence* of interests among elitist groups, pluralist theorists stress instead the *diversity* of interests among organized groups—the issues that serve to *divide* them. If the "power elite" is really as cohesive and unitary as Mills maintains, then pluralists insist unity must prevail among the three groups constituting the elite (corporate executives, military men, and high-ranking politicians), as well as within each of the groups themselves. Yet pluralists argue this is hardly the case (Rose, 1967). The pluralists note the continuous, running controversies that take place, for example, between high civilian officials and the Pentagon. During the Kennedy and Johnson administrations, Defense Secretary Robert S. McNamara forcefully overrode Pentagon wishes on any number of occasions: the awarding of the contract for building the TFX (a supersonic aircraft, since renamed the F-111) to the General Dynamics Corporation (the military leaders favored the model produced by the Boeing Company, and Congressional leaders—especially the Senate Permanent Investigation Subcommittee—took the position that the military leaders had the better arguments); the downgrading of the RS-70 bomber; the cancellation of the Air Force's Skybolt missile and Dyna-Soar space projects; the closing of nearly four hundred obsolete military bases; and the institution of a "weak" rather than a "heavy" antiballistic missile (ABM) system. During the Nixon Administration, government agencies and departments found themselves at odds over the Trident missile-carrying submarine, and the F-14 and F-15 fighter planes. Moreover, investigations of the Watergate Scandal that rocked the Nixon Administration revealed deep divisions within the federal government, for instance, the rift in the White House staff between the forces of John Mitchell and those of H. R. Haldeman and John Ehrlichman, the conflict between the President and Congress (including its Republican members), friction between the FBI and the CIA, and Henry Kissinger's distrust of aides and officials whom he allowed the FBI to wiretap. And the Carter Administration overrode the Joint Chiefs of Staff on the B-1 bomber and the phased withdrawal of American ground forces from South Korea.

Is a Synthesis Possible? What conclusions can we reach regarding the contrasting elitist and pluralist views of American political life? It may well be, as William Kornhauser (1966) implies in his examination of the two formulations, that the truth lies somewhere between both points of view. It is perhaps a fine point whether a "military–industrial complex" is precisely the best phrase for describing the relationship of the American armed forces to the war materiels industry. But it is beyond doubt that there does exist an intense dependency on military contracts among some very large corporations and this fact exerts enormous influence in the shaping of national policy. However, to attribute our high level of defense spending simply to the schemings of a "power elite" overlooks the very real fear in post-World War II America of communism, be it the Russian or Chinese variety. Nor does the evidence substantiate the power elite view of some sort of national, monolithic power structure.

The pluralists, for their part, tend to overstate the case for the countervailing force of multiple power centers. Overlooked are the power differentials among the various interest groups in our society; some are simply stronger than others. And in some cases the tendency toward power aggrandizement in one center is not checked by other countervailing interest blocks. The Central Intelligence Agency (CIA), for instance, enjoys a quasi-independent position within the government and has taken on some aspects of an "invisible government." Moreover, the governmental system of checks and balances does not always operate as it was designed — for instance, on Capitol Hill the Senate and House Armed Services Committees are supposed to oversee the Defense Department, but it is questionable whether these "watchdogs really bark," whether they themselves are not part of the same "military–industrial complex."

DEMOCRACY

Every government degenerates when trusted to the rulers of the people alone. The people themselves therefore are its only safe depositories.
Thomas Jefferson, Notes on the State of Virginia, 1784-1785

Democracy is a political system that provides regular constitutional avenues for changing governing officials; it permits the population a considerable voice in decision-making through their right to choose among contenders for political office (Lipset, 1963). Quite clearly, democratic government is not distinguished from other kinds of government — for instance, oligarchic or totalitarian regimes — by an absence of powerful officials. Nor is democracy characterized by the rule of the people themselves. "Government by the people," in the sense in which democratic folklore thinks of it, is an illusion — except of course for rare instances of direct democracy involving face-to-face relations among citizens. What distinguishes democracy is the accountability of officials to the public; periodic elections either confirm officials in power or else replace them with new ones.

A number of conditions seemingly favor a stable democracy. One of these is conflict and cleavage associated with a struggle over ruling positions, challenges to incumbents, and shifts in the parties holding office. Ideally this struggle should occur across multiple group identities and loyalties. A single clear-cut political cleavage serves to polarize society into rigidly hostile groups incapable of accepting compromise. Where class lines ossify — where allegiance to one's class becomes a paramount concern — militant class struggle may jeopardize democratic existence.

Likewise, deep-rooted racial or ethnic cleavages jeopardize national unity and make a stable democracy difficult. Contemporary Canada, for instance, finds itself caught within the currents of deep, unsettling ferment deriving from the divergent ethnic loyalties and sentiments of its English- and French-speaking citizens. Sharp regional conflicts in interest, such as those which culminated in the American Civil War, similarly impair democratic functioning. Where political issues cut so deeply across a population, are felt so keenly, and are so fully reinforced by other social identifications (class, ethnic, racial, religious, or other group membership), basic consensus is jeopardized.

Multiple loyalties serve to prevent the polarization of society into rigidly hostile groups. Under such circumstances, there are multiple groups, with membership in one cutting across membership in others. By way of illustration, American Catholics are found in both the lower and the middle classes, and the same holds true of Protestants. Hence, in terms of religious membership, Catholics and Protestants find themselves counterposed to one another; simultaneously, lower-class Catholics and Protestants are linked together (as are middle-class Catholics and Protestants) by class membership and set apart by their class membership from middle-class Catholics and Protestants. In brief, loyalties cleave along plural axes. Such criss-crossing of ties—pluralistic allegiances—appears to present an optimum condition for the development and maintenance of democracy.

Countervailing interest groups are a second condition favoring a stable democracy. The presence of many large, well-integrated groups that represent significant divisions of interests and values operates as a check against one another. Each group is limited in power by the fact that it must take into account the interests of other groups. Hence, within a democracy, individuals have the protection of many institutions and groups against the encroachment of any one of them. No institution or group can attain a monopoly of power. In contrast, the totalitarian society destroys all independent groups and autonomous opinion. Isolated and vulnerable individuals face the full power of an omnipotent Leviathan state.

A third condition of a stable democracy is an underlying consensus among the population that democratic government is desirable and valid. The various groups within the society must recognize the legitimacy of the political institution. When groups are convinced that they can realize their aims within the existing organizational framework, they are likely to hold the belief that democracy is worthwhile and appropriate.

Voting is a key mechanism for realizing this sort of consensus in democracies. Studies reveal that within the United States the institution of elections enjoys a broad base of popular support. Further, most people *believe* that elections make the government pay attention to what the people think (Dennis, 1970). Although election campaigns may be waged with considerable fury and fervor, when the election returns are in, the population and the can-

Socialist and radical parties: Absence of a mass base within the United States. Political movements calling for a fundamental restructuring of capitalist society have failed to win a mass following. America's democratic system has allowed discontented groups to enter the political arena and win major concessions. Further, the massive nature of the American electorate requires alliances and compromises between diverse interests that serve to "water down" orthodox political programs.

Patrick Reddy

didates accede to the results. Losing candidates and parties recognize the legitimacy of the process and do not have recourse to extralegal means. Instead, they criticize the incumbents in office and prepare to "throw the rascals out" at the *next election.*

A fourth condition favoring a democratic order is a relatively stable economic and social structure. As we observed in the chapter on collective behavior, major institutional failure confronts people with stressful circumstances that make them vulnerable to extremist social movements. For instance, within pre-Hitler Germany, ruinous inflation and economic dislocation made the middle classes susceptible to the appeal of Nazism. Coupled with their economic difficulties, the middle classes felt that their status was eroding and collapsing before the onslaught of large-scale capitalism and a powerful labor movement. Precariously situated in a world that seemed increasingly incomprehensible and that was threatening to swallow them up in a torrent of social change, they viewed the Nazi cause as the road to salvation. In so doing, they sounded the death knell to Germany's fragile democratic institutions. Similarly, in 1917 Russia and post-World War II China, social and economic chaos made the people vulnerable to the revolutionary slogans of communism.

SOCIAL CHANGE: SOME RECENT TRENDS

As with the other institutions we have considered, change is an ever-present feature of the economy and the state. Indeed, it is questionable whether the word "change" is adequate for depicting the dynamic flow of social life. Change implies a shift from one static "state" to another, yet much of life is process, a continual "becoming." Admittedly, the English language does not help us in formulating these matters since the nouns that provide the subjects of most of our sentences largely refer to static objects, not to ongoing process (Olsen, 1968).

POVERTY

Poverty is very good in poems, but it is very bad in a house. It is very good in maxims and in sermons, but it is very bad in practical life.

Henry Ward Beecher, *Proverbs from Plymouth Pulpit,* 1887

In 1958, the prominent economist John Kenneth Galbraith, in his well-known book that he significantly titled *The Affluent Society,* wrote that poverty in this country was no longer "a massive affliction [but] more nearly an afterthought." Yet within two years "poverty" had become a political issue in the 1960 presidential campaign, when John F. Kennedy won a crucial primary election in West Virginia by highlighting the depressed economic conditions of Appalachia. And in early 1964 President Johnson declared "unconditional war on poverty in America."

Usually we think of poverty in economic terms, although even as measured by such a thing as monetary income the concept is an elusive one. The Census Bureau, for instance, defines poverty as comprising all those families below a particular income figure (see Figure 14.3), a figure it continually redefines. Viewed in this fashion, the poverty problem becomes analogous to the mechanical rabbit at the race track: no matter how fast the dogs run, they will never catch the rabbit. From this perspective, the poverty line is always relative to time, place, and possibilities; hence, in this sense, "ye have the poor always with you."

A widely publicized study by the University of Michigan's Institute for Social Research portrays the poverty population as a kind of pool with people flowing in and out (Reinhold, 1977b). The findings are based on a survey of 5000 families chosen in 1967 and followed over a seven-year period. The study cast doubt on the "culture of poverty" thesis that being poor at one time means being poor always. Only one-fifth of the sample were actually poor all seven years. Nonetheless, three-quarters were poor four years or more (they were poor for at least half the time of the study).

Critics of census procedures point out that the people the Census Bureau considers poor are the prime beneficiaries of many types of nonmoney in-

Patrick Reddy

Poverty among the aged. Many elderly people with fixed incomes experience economic problems, especially as the purchasing power of their money is decreased by inflation. Although older people represent 10 percent of the total population of the United States, they represent 25 percent of the poor. And the majority are women.

Figure 14.3. Family income in the United States.

WHO THE POOR ARE

Based on official poverty level — $5815 annual income for a nonfarm family of four, $4950 for a farm family of four:

Of this group	This share is poor
All Americans	11.8%
Whites	9.1
Blacks	31.1
People of Spanish origin	24.7
People 65 and older	15.0
Families in central cities	15.8
Farm families	15.9

INCOME DISTRIBUTION

Based on median family income in 1976

Income	Income bracket
More than $50,000	Top 2%
$25,000 or more	Top 18
$20,000 or more	Top 31
$15,000 or more	Top 50
Less than $12,000	Bottom 38
Less than $10,000	Bottom 30
Less than $8,000	Bottom 22
Less than $6,000	Bottom 14
Less than $4,000	Bottom 7

WHEN EARNINGS HIT A PEAK

Age of family head	Median family income, 1976
Younger than 25	$ 9,439
25–34	$14,790
35–44	$17,389
45–54	$19,037
55–64	$16,118
65 and older	$ 8,721

Source: U.S. Census Bureau, news release of October 4, 1977.

come, including food stamps, housing subsidies, and Medicaid. All of this points up the fact that the term "poverty" cloaks many differing, even conflicting, conceptions as well as strategies for combating it. Let us consider five of these (Rein and Miller, 1967; Spilerman and Elesh, 1971; Williamson and Hyer, 1975).

Poverty and Social Decency. According to this conception, people have a *right* not only to freedom from want but also to adequate housing, medical care, and recreation. The lack of these amenities is defined as poverty. Proponents of this view argue that the government should reduce poverty through programs that strengthen and enrich the quality of life — such things as public housing, child care facilities, medical care, and recreation centers. If the poor have these things, they are less poor in the sense that they enjoy such services.

Poverty and Equality. Poverty, according to this view, exists as long as the bottom fifth or tenth of the population receives a stable or shrinking share of a growing economic pie. The concern of the proponents of this view is with inequality — the position of the lowest income groups (sometimes termed the "underclass") *relative* to the rest of the people. Policy, then, should be guided by a commitment to the more equitable distribution of benefits — who gets what, where, why, and how. Proposals for a guaranteed annual income (for instance, a negative income tax), children's allowances, and various cash subsidies are illustrative of this strategy; they call for programs that redistribute income outside the marketplace through cash transfers to the poor.

Poverty and Mobility. By this conception, poverty is the lack of opportunity to alter one's income, occupation, or social class. In a rigidly stratified social order, those at the bottom cannot escape upward. Reducing poverty would call for a "structural strategy," one that would facilitate the capacity of the poor to earn decent incomes. The emphasis would fall on breaking down the barriers to equality of opportunity (for instance, civil rights legislation banning discrimination against Blacks), job training programs, and the creation of new jobs.

Poverty and Social Control. For some, poverty is seen primarily in terms of delinquency, illiteracy, alcoholism, illegitimacy, and mental illness. According to this view, the remedy to poverty is to change people, to restore their social functioning through "rehabilitation"—usually by psychological means ranging from guidance and counseling, through casework, to psychotherapy and psychoanalysis. In brief, the aim is to overcome poverty by overcoming personal and family "disorganization" and deviancy—to get the poor to behave according to accepted standards ("accepted" = "middle class"). Hence, the aim is not to change society but the individual, to realize "effective" social control over individuals.

Poverty and Social Inclusion. Poverty, according to this conception, means that people cannot participate in major institutions of society, especially the institutions that affect their lives—when they have little or nothing to say about schools, employment, law enforcement, and welfare services. Poverty, consequently, is a lack of power, dignity, and self-respect. The answer proposed by proponents of this view is to engage the participation of the poor in institutional life—to involve them in policy-making functions through neighborhood boards, community action programs, economic opportunity councils, and the like. To the extent to which such programs have been inaugurated as part of the "war on poverty," they have often been viewed by local officials as threatening the status quo. "Poverty power" has meant "political power," and hence strong attempts have been made to keep it "safe," that is, to maintain "city hall control" (in effect, emasculating "poverty power").

AMERICAN VOTING BEHAVIOR

Traditionally the Democratic party has been viewed as the party of working people; the Republican party, the party of business. Although a simplistic view, opinion polling has revealed in recent decades that white-collar workers and their families have been much more likely than blue-collar workers to identify with the Republican party and to vote for Republican candidates (See Table 14.2). But a good many political observers argue that

TABLE 14.2
Presidential Voting among Various Social Categories*

	1972		1976	
	McGovern (Dem.)	Nixon (Rep.)	Carter (Dem.)	Ford (Rep.)
Family income				
High income	34%	66%	38%	62%
Middle income	38	62	52	48
Low income	46	54	61	39
Sex				
Men	36%	64%	51%	49%
Women	38	62	52	48
Race/Ethnic				
Whites	32%	68%	48%	52%
Blacks	82	18	82	18
Spanish-speaking	74	26	82	18
Religion				
Protestants	28%	72%	46%	54%
Catholics	44	56	54	46
Jews	65	35	68	32
Age				
First-time voters†	50%	50%	49%	51%
Others under 30	42	58	55	45
30–44 years	35	65	52	48
45–59 years	35	65	48	52
60 and older	30	70	48	52
Residence				
Large-city dwellers	49%	51%	61%	39%
Smaller-city dwellers	39	61	51	49
Suburbanites	37	63	46	54
Rural, small-town residents	33	67	50	50

* Percentages based only on votes for two major candidates, excluding votes for minor party candidates.

† 18–24 in 1972; 18–21 in 1976

Source: CBS News.

all this is changing—that America is undergoing a major political realignment with the Democratic party becoming the voice of a college-educated elite while the Republican party is becoming the party of blue-collar Whites. Indeed, some have ventured the notion that the history of the Kennedy–Johnson administrations on the domestic front could be written in terms of a coalition of the top and the bottom against the middle, while the 1968 and 1972 elections represented a counterrevolution of the middle strata against the pressures from both of the other two (Glenn, 1973; 1975).

Yet predictions of big changes in the partisan balance have often been made during the past twenty-five years, only to be quickly proved wrong. In the 1950s, politicians, journalists, and scholars alike saw the Republican party riding to ascendancy on the growth of middle-class suburbs. In 1952, the late Senator Robert A. Taft argued that "the Democratic party will never win another national election until it solves the problem of the suburbs." And Harvard urbanologist Edward Banfield predicted that the Democrats' electoral advantage would disappear with suburban growth so that the Republicans would become numerically the strongest party. By the 1960s, new prophets were in turn sounding the virtual death knell of the Republican party. After the 1964 election, James Reston of the *New York Times* wrote that "he [Senator Barry Goldwater] had wrecked his party for a long time to come. . . ." Angus Campbell, a keen student of electoral politics (after examining 1964 election data), similarly concluded that the United States was entering "a period of party realignment which will increase the prevailing Democratic advantage in the party balance." But within four years political commentators were telling us a quite different story; they were saying that the Democratic majority was disintegrating and that a new "Republican majority" was emerging (Ladd, Hadley, and King, 1971).

What has frequently led political observers astray is their failure to reckon with the depth of political loyalties. People develop emotional ties to political parties as part of the process of self-definition; "Who am I?" is answered not only in terms of family, ethnic group, and occupation, but also in terms of being a "Republican" or a "Democrat." Many Americans vote not for principle but "for" a group to which they are attached—*their* group (religious, ethnic, racial, class, regional). An individual's political preference tends to be group-anchored. Within the group, various favorable and unfavorable attitudes prevail toward given political parties. As part of his or her acceptance of a group, an individual tends to accept its political attitudes; the group's views become his or her views.

All this is not to suggest that people do not change their party identities—the Survey Research Center of the University of Michigan has found that about 20 percent of the electorate has changed from one party to another. Yet such shifting is not done easily (Ladd, Hadley, and King, 1971; Nie, Verba, and Petrocik, 1976). Research within the United States suggests that the basic division of party loyalties is not *seriously* disturbed even in a "deviating election." Election outcomes tend to vary according to nonvoting, the cast of the independent vote, and the differential vote of the temporary "defectors" from their party, nearly all of whom vote thereafter and think of themselves even during defection as loyal to their original party affiliation.

Although people vote for a President on a given November day, their choice is not made simply on the basis of what has happened in the preceding months or even four years. Some people are in effect voting on the depression issues of 1932, others on the Korean War issue of 1952 or that of Vietnam of 1968 and 1972, and some, indeed, on the slavery issue of 1860. Hence, the vote is a kind of "moving average" of reactions to the political past. Voters carry over to each election remnants of issues and loyalties that are the product of earlier elections. Thus, there is an overlapping of old and new decisions and loyalties that gives cohesion and stability to the political system.

If any major trend is occurring among American voters, it is that the importance of political parties is declining. Further, the electorate appears to be developing a more coherent set of issue positions that guide its voting behavior (Nie, Verba, and Petrocik, 1976). The weakening of partisanship seems to be most prevalent among the younger generation of voters (Abramson, 1975).

SUMMARY

1. The fact of human wants and the scarcity of goods and services must be faced by every society. Hence, social life confronts us with three functional imperatives. We must provide for the (1) production, (2) distribution, and (3) consumption of goods and services. Production involves the assemblying and applying of human and natural resources in the creation of goods and services. Distribution entails channeling inputs to producing agencies, and outputs to consuming agencies. Consumption involves the "using up" of goods and services.

2. Work has no inherent meaning but, rather, people impute meanings to their work activities. Accordingly, societies have employed a good many different kinds of incentives for getting their members to engage in work. Work cannot be understood simply as a response to economic necessity. People may also work because they enjoy it, gain a sense of self-respect, achieve a feeling of self-actualization, want to be associated with other people, and wish to keep busy.

3. Within recent years, a growing body of literature has appeared dealing with alienation in work—a pervasive sense of powerlessness, meaninglessness, isolation, and self-estrangement. Controversy prevails regarding the extent of job alienation within the United States. Sociologists find that the overall best predictor of strong work attachment and the absence of alienation is an occupation that combines high economic, occupational, and educational prestige. Control also represents an important factor in work satisfaction.

4. The growing realization among Western social scientists that many of their conceptions for dealing with the transformations occurring in the nations of Asia, Africa, and Latin America are ethnocentric has produced considerable controversy. Three perspectives prevail regarding these transformations: development as social differentiation, development as enactment of values, and development as liberation from dependency.

5. The State—the political institution—is that social agency that exercises a supreme monopoly of authority within a given territory. In the final analysis this authority rests on the right to apply physical coercion.

6. Every society is confronted with the general

requirement of maintaining order and effecting control over its members. In larger and more complex societies these functions are performed by the State. More particularly, this involves the enforcement of norms, planning and direction, the arbitration of conflicting interests, and protection against other societies.

7. Power refers to the capacity of an individual or group to control or influence the behavior of others, even in the absence of their consent. Since power may be either legitimate or illegitimate, sociologists find it useful to introduce another concept — authority — to refer to legitimate power. Max Weber proposed a three-fold classification of authority based on the manner in which power is socially legitimated: legal-rational, traditional, and charismatic.

8. In both popular and sociological literature we encounter two prevalent views regarding the nature of power within the United States. One is the power elite thesis which holds that a small number of individuals make the important decisions affecting the lives and welfare of Americans. The other, the pluralist thesis, says that power is widely dispersed within the United States and that policy is formulated by numerous interest groups acting on behalf of their respective memberships.

9. A number of conditions seemingly favor a stable democracy. These include multiple loyalties which serve to prevent the polarization of society into rigidly hostile groups, countervailing interest groups, an underlying consensus among the population that democratic government is desirable and valid, and a relatively stable economic and social structure.

10. Poverty cloaks many differing, even conflicting, conceptions as well as strategies for combating it. These include the following notions: poverty as social decency, poverty as inequality, poverty as the lack of opportunity, poverty as deviance, and poverty as powerlessness.

11. If any major trend is occurring among American voters, it is that the importance of political parties is declining. Further, the electorate appears to be developing a more coherent set of issue positions that guide its voting behavior. The weakening of partisanship seems to be most prevalent among the younger generation of voters.

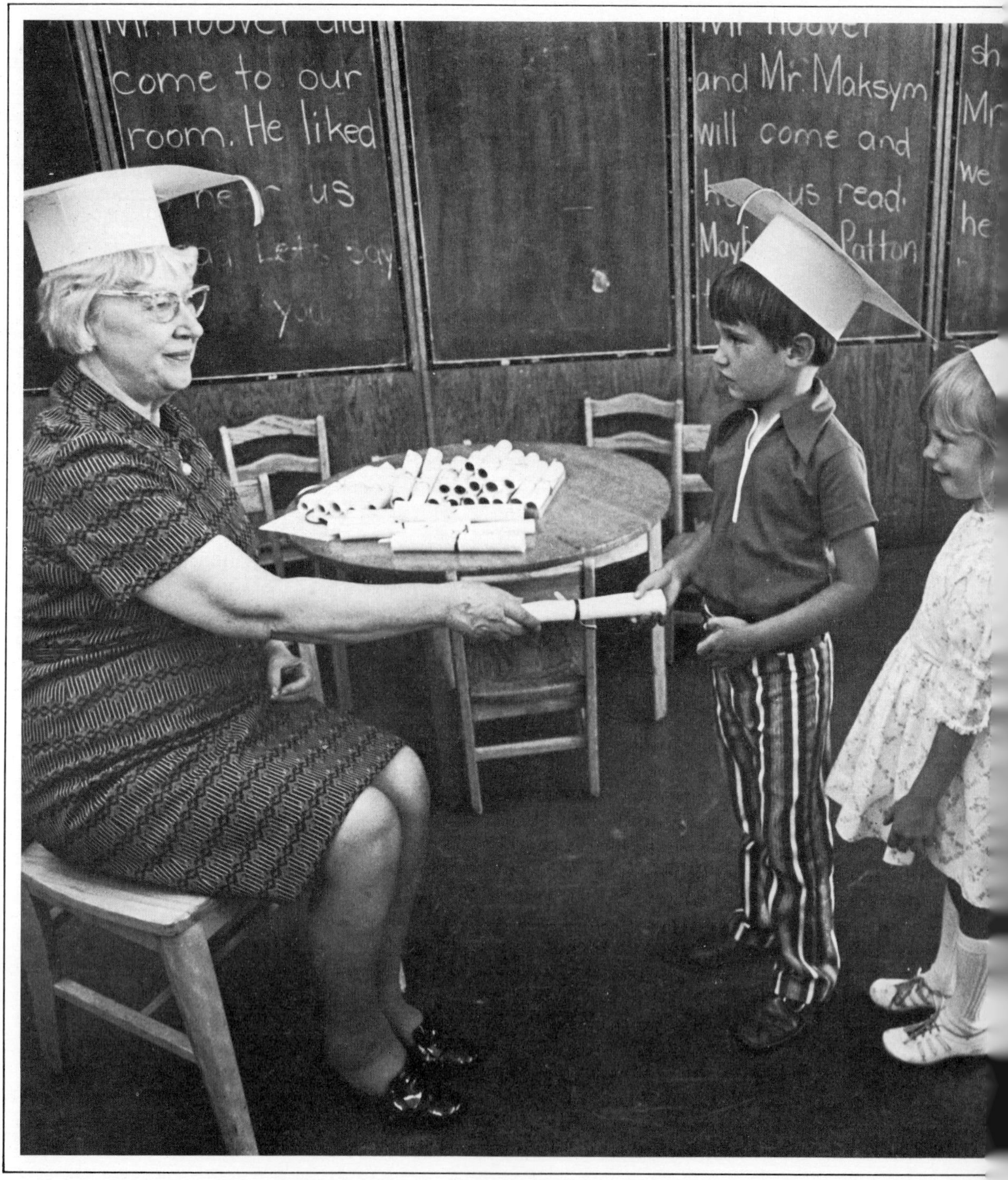
come to our
room. He liked
and Mr. Maksym
will come and

15
EDUCATION

FUNCTIONS
   Completing Socialization
   Transmission of Specialized Skills
   Reproducing the Social Relations of Production
   Research and Development
   A "Sorting and Sifting" Agency
   Latent Functions

THE SCHOOL AS A SOCIAL SYSTEM
   Classroom Life
   Bureaucratic Organization
   Informal Organization
   School Effectiveness

SOCIAL CLASS AND EDUCATION
   Alienation of Inner-City Children
   Subcultural Differences
   Educational Self-Fulfilling Prophecies

SOCIAL CHANGE: SOME RECENT TRENDS
   School Desegregation
   The "Back to Basics" Movement

OBSERVATION I just got back from tutoring and felt I must write this now. One of the boys I tutor in elementary school had been giving me some trouble at the beginning of the year. I feel I am finally making a breakthrough with this boy. He is in the third grade, and I tutor him in reading and writing skills. He was tested at the beginning of the year and "supposedly" was doing first grade work. Today I was very proud of him as he did his work with no problems and is certainly not behind his grade (class) at all. Yet after I finished working with him I found out that in class he has been doing poorer work than ever, yet when he is with me he has been steadily improving.

I went to talk with his teacher and I was amazed. This woman was not only a super bitch to me, she "teaches" (?) by yelling at the kids in her class constantly. I asked her about my student and she went on about how his family life is very bad, he is a problem child, he never behaves, he doesn't care to learn and probably never will, he is lazy, and I only disrupt her class by coming to get him which is a waste of time, etc., etc., etc. I was ready to spit on her, really!

PRINCIPLE I think it is interesting how this middle-class teacher handles the lower-class kids. She simply assumed my student wouldn't do well and in fact he did respond with resentment and rebellion. His attitude has spread beyond the classroom and he assumes that role with other new people he meets. I do feel good though because he has become comfortable with me and he has shown he can do the work under positive conditions.

An extremely rapid expansion of educational enrollments has occurred throughout the world since 1950 (Meyer, Rubinson, Ramirez, and Boli-Bennett, 1977). Schools are seen as a means for solving national problems and securing the national welfare. This has entailed turning over some of the tasks associated with the socialization of the young to specialized agencies. As we noted in Chapter 3, socialization refers to the broad and encompassing process by which people become humanized — by which they acquire those ways of thinking, feeling, and acting essential for effective participation within society. Viewed in this fashion, socialization is the process whereby society recreates itself in the young. Socialization, then, is an *inclusive* concept. Education, in contrast, is only one aspect of this many-sided process. We commonly think of **education** as denoting *formal, conscious, systematic training*. Blaine E. Mercer and Edwin R. Carr observe: "Its [education's] emphasis seems to be on teaching rather more than on learning, and, while its objects may be clearly outlined or vaguely envisioned, there is always a degree of consciousness of the process on the part of teacher or learner or both" (1957:31).

FUNCTIONS

> We have entered an age in which education is not just a luxury permitting some men an advantage over others. It has become a necessity without which a person is defenseless in this complex, industrialized society. . . . We have truly entered the century of the educated man.
> Lyndon B. Johnson, Commencement Address, Tufts University, June 9, 1963

Schools came into existence several thousand years ago to prepare a select few for leadership and certain professions. A century or so ago, public schools became the vehicle whereby the masses were taught the three R's, providing them with the literacy required by an industrial–urban world. Today, we are in the midst of still a third educational revolution in which education has become a weapon of national survival. Accordingly, let us turn to a consideration of the functions that the educational institution commonly performs within modern societies.

Enrollments up in nursery schools. By 1978, an estimated 42 percent of American mothers of preschool children were in the work force as compared with 14 percent in 1950. This has given a considerable boost to nursery school enrollments. It is now estimated that over half of all American children between three and five years of age are enrolled in some nursery school or child care program outside the home.

Patrick Reddy

COMPLETING SOCIALIZATION

All education indoctrinates.

Robert M. MacIver, Politics and Society, *1969*

What are our schools for if not indoctrination against Communism?

Richard M. Nixon

The family gets children first and maintains an intensive and continuous relationship with them until they reach maturity. As such, no other institution seriously rivals the family in its molding of the child. In fact, it is a matter of debate whether other institutions including the school can do more than support trends of character already formed in the home. Christopher Jencks, in his controversial study, *Inequality,* writes:

> It is true that schools have "inputs" and "outputs" . . . that one of their nominal purposes is to take human "raw material" . . . and convert it into something more "valuable" [the factory metaphor]. . . . Our research suggests, however, that the character of a school's output depends largely on a single input, namely the characteristics of the entering children. Everything else—the school budget, its policies, the characteristics of the teachers—is either secondary or completely irrelevant. (1972, p. 256)

Nevertheless, mounting pressure is being laid on the school to perform a task once considered the more or less exclusive province of the family. Increasingly, Americans have come to look to the school as making up for any deficiencies in home training of manners and morals. The school is expected to do everything the rest of the world lets undone. Hence, schools have come to share with the family the responsibility for transmitting those aspects of culture essential for competent social participation. In this respect, schools are conservative institutions that seek to instill in students the traditional patterns of their culture.

TRANSMISSION OF SPECIALIZED SKILLS

Some societies have no schools. In preliterate and peasant societies, education is carried out by the same "natural process" by which parents teach their children to walk or talk. Farley Mowat, an anthropologist, describes the process among the Ihalmiut, an Eskimo people. If an Ihalmiut boy indicates he wishes to become a hunter, a great hunter, all at once, his parents do not make him feel foolish nor do they condescend to his childish fancy. Instead, his father sets to work to make a small bow that is not a toy but an efficient weapon on a reduced scale. The father then presents the boy with the bow and the boy

Completing socialization. American schools are expected to do much of what other social agencies fail to get done. The net result is that schools often become tradition-ridden instititions producing boredom among the pupils.

Patrick Reddy

> . . . sets out for his hunting grounds—a ridge, perhaps, a hundred yards away, with the time-honored words of good luck ringing in his ears. These are the same words which are spoken by the People to their mightiest hunter when he starts on a two-month trip for musk ox. . . . There is no distinction, and this lack of distinction is not a pretense; it is perfectly real. The boy wants to be a hunter? Very well, he shall be a hunter—not a boy with toy bow! . . . When he returns at last with hunger gnawing at his stomach, he is greeted gravely as if he were his father. The whole camp wishes to hear about his hunt. He can expect the same ridicule at failure, or the same praise if he managed to kill a little bird, which would come to a full-grown man. (1952, pp. 156–157)

In this fashion, the Ihalmiut socialize the boy. The content of culture in such societies is very much the same for everyone, and it is acquired mostly in an unconscious manner through daily living. Except in "coming of age" and other special ceremonies, "education" in a technical sense is absent. Socialization is carried on as an undifferentiated activity of the family and community.

In a world of rapid change—of urbanism and industrialism—the transmission of knowledge and skills can no longer take place on the informal basis of the Ihalmiut. Adults cannot afford to shape their children in their own image. Adults often find themselves with obsolete skills, trained for jobs that are passing out of existence. They are "out of touch with the times" and unable to understand, much less inculcate, the standards of a social order that has changed so much since their youth (Coleman, 1961).

Modern living confronts us with the fact that we shall not live all of our lives in the world into which we were born nor shall we die in the world in which we worked in our maturity (Rothman and Perrucci, 1971). We need only read the "help wanted ads" in our newspapers to recognize the stark reality of the new age—for instance, recent advertisements in *The New York Times* ask for applications from persons with experience in inertial guidance–missiles, gyrodynamics–supersonic aircraft, shielding design–atomic power, microminiaturization, data telemetry, and the like. The technical and scientific personnel needs of contemporary industrial society cannot be satisfied by the more or less automatic "natural" process found among the Ihalmiut. Rather, a specialized agency is required that can transmit to the youth the skills and attitudes necessary for their placement within society.

REPRODUCING THE SOCIAL RELATIONS OF PRODUCTION

Industry places a high value on the college degree, not because it is convinced that the four years of schooling insure the individuals acquire maturity and technical competence, but rather because it provides an initial starting point of division between those more trained and those less trained; those better motivated and those less motivated; those with more social experience and those with less.

Robert A. Gordon and James E. Howell, *Higher Education for Business, 1959*

In recent years a number of neo-Marxist social scientists have argued that the schools are agencies for reproducing among the youth the social relations of production found in capitalist nations (Althusser, 1971; Squires, 1977; Collins, 1977). Probably the best known proponents of this view are Samuel Bowles and Herbert Gintis. In *Schooling and Capitalist America* (1976) they set forth what they term the "correspondence principle": the social relations of work are reflected in the social relations of the school. According to Bowles and Gintis, the schools mirror the workplace and hence on a day-to-day basis prepare children for their future lives in the occupational sphere. Not only does the school curriculum teach the skills required by employers, but the authoritarian structure of the school reproduces the bureaucratic hierarchy of the corporation (diligence, submissiveness, and compliance being rewarded in both contexts). Similarly, parallels exist between the wages used to motivate workers and the grades employed to motivate students. In sum, the schools are seen as socializing a docile labor force for the capitalist economy.

Randall Collins (1976) takes the argument a step further and says that minority ethnic groups pose the greatest threat to dominant groups. In large, conflict-ridden, multi-ethnic societies, like the United States and the Soviet Union, the schools are vehicles to "Americanize" or "Sovietize" minority peoples. In the hands of dominant groups, education is a mechanism that erodes ethnic differences and loyalties and transmits to minorities the values of the dominant group.

Collins points out, however, that groups who engage in schooling also evolve their own vested interests in the educational enterprise. School teachers, administrators, intellectuals, book publishers, and media professionals elaborate technical jargons and procedures into their own independent fiefs. The educational institution provides such groups with direct economic payoffs. Hence, they systematically undertake to carve out professional monopolies over lucrative educational services.

RESEARCH AND DEVELOPMENT

The principal goal of education is to create men [and women] who are capable of doing new things, not simply of repeating what other generations have done — men [and women] who are creative, inventive, and discoverers.
Jean Piaget, Swiss developmental psychologist

Why should we subsidize intellectual curiosity?
Ronald Reagan

Thus far we have considered how education functions as a conservative institution. On the whole, schools are designed to produce people who fit into society, not people who set out to change society. But the schools — especially at higher levels — may not merely transmit culture; they may add to the cultural heritage, so long as they do not seriously question a people's cherished institutions and values. Contemporary American society, for instance, places considerable emphasis on the development of new knowledge, especially in the physical and biological sciences.

The launching of the first Soviet sputnik (an artificial satellite) in 1957 had a major impact on American government support for research. Between 1955 and 1965, funds from both private and governmental sources for research and development increased nearly four times (since 1968, however, some leveling-off in expenditures had occurred). Even in the social sciences the federal government has been the chief source of research funds.

Federal outlays for social research stood at $6 million annually in 1951, but increased to $421 million in 1971. Much of these monies is allocated for research useful for government policy formation (Useem, 1976). This fact has raised concern in some quarters regarding the nature and objectivity of research conducted under governmental auspices (Broadhead and Rist, 1976).

Over the past two decades the nation's leading universities have increasingly become centers of research—some of them in fact becoming primarily "contract research factories." Stanford, for example, appropriated $5000 for all research in 1935—and the largest grant, to the physics department, was $500. In contrast, sponsored research at Stanford in 1970 came to $57 million, plus an annual outlay of $25 to $30 million for the Stanford Linear Accelerator Center. And in this period, more than two-thirds of the operating income of Johns Hopkins, MIT, and the California Institute of Technology came from the federal government through research activities. Further, new industries have shown a predilection for locating around major universities from which scientific and engineering talent can be drawn.

This emphasis on research in the universities has led to the prevalent practice of judging professors not primarily in terms of competence as teachers but as researchers. Promotions, salary increases, and other benefits may be contingent on research and publication—"publish or perish" and "publish and prosper." Although most faculty members are hired to teach students and bear their share of academic responsibilities, there is a tendency for university officials to punish successful performance of these tasks. Academic success is most likely to come to those who have learned to "neglect" their assigned duties in order to have more time and energy to pursue their private research interests (Caplow and McGee, 1958; van den Berghe, 1970).

A "SORTING AND SIFTING" AGENCY

The schools must sort all the human material that comes to them, but they do not subject all children to the same sorting process. Other things being equal, the schools tend to bring children at least up to an intellectual level which will enable them to function in the same economic and social structure as their parents.

Willard Waller, The Sociology of Teaching, 1932

Within every society, some roles are assigned to individuals independent of their unique qualities or abilities. Still others are realized by individuals through choice and competition. No society ignores individual differences; all societies make recognition of individual accomplishment and failure. Hence, societies must select certain of their youth for those positions requiring special qualities and abilities. The educational institution may serve as an agency for this "sorting and sifting." In this sense, it functions as a sys-

Figure 15.1. Relation of intelligence to college attendance.

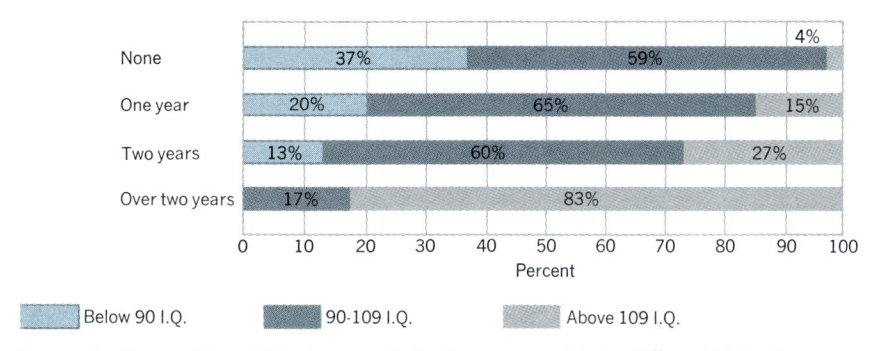

College	Below 90 I.Q.	90-109 I.Q.	Above 109 I.Q.
None	37%	59%	4%
One year	20%	65%	15%
Two years	13%	60%	27%
Over two years	17%	83%	

Source: Problems of Youth (Washington, D.C.: Government Printing Office, 1964), 46.

tem of allocation, conferring success on some and failure on others (Karabel and Astin, 1975; Meyer, 1977).

Within the United States, one of the major functions of the educational system is to select out youth for upward mobility—to make it possible for able, industrious children to ascend the social ladder. Although we seldom witness the amassing of great private fortunes as in the nineteenth century, opportunity has not come to an end. Opportunity merely lies in different areas and is fulfilled by different means. A whole new field for "opportunity to rise in the world" has been opened by the astonishing expansion of technical, managerial, and professional employment—careers open to talents. Since advanced education is a common prerequisite for these positions, the schools play a considerable part in selecting out those youth who come to occupy higher status positions. The schools function as "mobility escalators." The sorting is done with respect to two quite different characteristics: (1) the children's ability, and (2) their social-class background.

Our schools treat children of high ability differently from those of low ability and keep those of high ability in school for a longer period (see Figure 15.1). About one in three of those who drop out of school prior to high school graduation are in the bottom fifth of their class (as measured by I.Q. tests), while about one in twenty are in the top fifth (Havighurst and Neugarten, 1975).

Schools also sort out students with respect to their social-class background. Youth from higher-status families are more likely to be placed in a college-curriculum track (rather than a vocational track) in high school than are youth from lower-status families, even when they have equal ability (Alexander and McDill, 1976; Alexander, Cook, and McDill, 1978). Youth from higher-status families are more likely to go to college even though they have only average ability, while youth from lower-status families have less

TABLE 15.1
Probability of a Male Entering College Within Five Years After High School

Academic Aptitude	SOCIOECONOMIC STATUS				
	Lowest Quarter	Second Quarter	Third Quarter	Highest Quarter	Total
Highest quarter	.81	.81	.95	.96	.91
Second quarter	.59	.65	.78	.90	.74
Third quarter	.34	.45	.47	.76	.48
Lowest quarter	.14	.29	.35	.42	.25
Total	.32	.53	.69	.86	.58

Source: Project Talent.

chance of entering college, even when they have high ability. See Table 15.1. We shall shortly return to a consideration of the factors underlying class selection.

LATENT FUNCTIONS

An institution may function in a manner that is neither recognized nor intended — it may have latent functions. Within the United States, the educational institution performs a number of such functions. First, the schools have a custodial function — in essence, they provide a babysitting service that keeps children out from under the feet of adults and from under the wheels of automobiles. Second, the schools function as a marriage market — they afford opportunity for selective mating on the basis of similar class and educational status. Third, schools widen the individual's circle of acquaintances and facilitate various alignments that help in launching a subsequent career — that is, making "contacts." Fourth, formal compulsory education keeps younger children out of the labor market and thus out of competition with adults for jobs, and it further protects children against economic exploitation.

THE SCHOOL AS A SOCIAL SYSTEM

> The school is a social organism.... As a social organism the school shows an organismic interdependence of its parts; it is not possible to affect a part of it without affecting the whole.
> Willard Waller, The Sociology of Teaching, 1932

Since John Dewey (1928), the preeminent figure in shaping educational thinking during the first half of the twentieth century, it has been fashionable to view the school as a small community. The school is seen as an organization that brings together a variety of activities which, at least in theory, are directed toward training the young. The integration of these activities within a larger whole gives shape to a rather unique institution, a social system having identifiable characteristics.

CLASSROOM LIFE

Schools should be places where people go to find out the things they want to find out and develop the skills they want to develop.... What is most shocking and horrifying about public education today is that in almost all schools the children are treated, most of the time, like convicts in jail. Like black men in South Africa, they cannot move without written permission.... And yet, on second thought, this is not what shocks me most. What shocks me most is that the students do not resist this, do not complain about it, do not mind it, even defend it as being necessary and for their own good.

John Holt, contemporary critic of American schools

Within the United States school environments are remarkably standardized in both physical and social characteristics. Moreover, physical objects, social relations, and major activities are experienced by both pupils and teachers as remaining much the same from day to day, week to week, and even from year to year (Jackson, 1968). Most classrooms feature but a single teacher and a group of 25 to 40 students of approximately equal age. Pupils and teachers begin and end their days in private pursuits and only enter the school for a period of from four to eight hours. At the primary level a single teacher and a group of students remain together in a particular classroom for a nine-month period. At the secondary level "lessons" are conducted by specialist teachers, each occupying a classroom, with pupils moving from teacher to teacher and classroom to classroom at the ringing of the bell. Despite innovations in classroom architecture, most classrooms are rectangular, contain a desk for the teacher and smaller desks for the pupils, are surrounded by chalkboards and bulletin boards, and display a flag, patriotic pictures, and exhibits of work by pupils or of pertinent teaching materials (Dunkin and Biddle, 1974).

Time is highly formalized. Activities are organized into a schedule—the pledge of allegiance is followed by reading at 8:35, which is follwed by arithmetic at 9:15, which is followed by recess, and so on. The art teacher comes for forty-five minutes on Tuesday mornings, the music teacher on Thursdays, and gym is on Friday. Although the details vary from school to school and class to class, the basic structure of the "daily grind" is common to most. Indeed, there is an almost holy aura about the schedule so that it takes an event of crisis proportions to change it. In addition to the overall rigidity of the schedule, each individual activity has its own rules—no loud talking during seat work, raise your hand to talk during discussion, and keep your eyes on your own paper during tests.

Philip W. Jackson, an educator, observes:

School is a place where tests are failed and passed, where amusing things happen, where new insights are stumbled upon, and skills acquired. But it is also a place in which people sit, and listen, and wait, and raise their hands, and pass out paper, and stand in line, and sharpen pencils. School is where we encounter both friends and foes, where imagination is unleashed and misunderstanding brought to ground. But it is also a place in which yawns are stifled and initials scratched on desktops, where milk money is collected and recess lines are formed. (1968, p. 4)

The adult personnel of the school enjoy considerable authority; children clearly occupy subordinate positions. The physical layout of the school reflects this fact. Generally, certain rooms are set aside for the exclusive use of teachers. Cloakrooms and lunchrooms may be divided with special space reserved for the teachers and separate space for the children. And the teacher's desk commonly occupies a special part of the classroom. Not only is space differentially assigned, but other privileges are accorded teachers and denied children—for instance, the teacher may inspect the child's desk and possessions at will, but the child is denied a similar privilege. This overall system fosters student passivity. The "good" student listens to the teacher, follows direction and instructions generally, does not disturb the class by speaking out of turn, and is otherwise receptive to *being taught*. (Boocock, 1973).

Teacher-centered education. American education is primarily teacher-centered with the teacher controlling the pace, the content, and direction of the educating process. Experiments during the late 1960s and early 1970s with informal classroom arrangements that were student-centered have largely given way once more to traditional practices in the face of mounting pressures from the back to basics movement.

Patrick Reddy

BUREAUCRATIC ORGANIZATION

A school system is made up of a network of positions that are functionally interrelated for the purpose of achieving given educational objectives. Generally, four main categories of roles can be identified in the formal organization of schools: (1) the trustees or board of education, (2) administrators (superintendents, principals, chancellors, and deans), (3) teachers, and (4) students. Much sociological analysis has been concerned with specifying the similarities and dissimilarities between schools and bureaucratic organizations (Katz, 1964; Corwin, 1965; Pellegrin, 1976).

Representative of these efforts is the approach of Charles E. Bidwell (1965). He finds that schools have the following bureaucratic characteristics:

1. A functional division of labor as found in the allocation of instructional tasks to teachers and coordinating tasks to administrators
2. The definition of staff roles as offices: recruitment is conducted according to merit and competence; positions are held after an initial trial period by tenure; tasks are specified in terms of a rather formal set of duties and responsibilities; and relationships with a client are kept sufficiently free of emotional involvement so as to best meet the client's needs
3. A hierarchical ordering of offices, providing a chain-of-command and regularized lines of communication
4. Operation according to rules of procedure that set limits on the discretion that individuals may display in performing their work.

Ronald G. Corwin also notes bureaucratic elements that limit the professional authority of teachers:

> Teachers have virtually no control over their standards of work. They have little control over the subjects to be taught; the materials to be used; the criteria for deciding who should be admitted, retained, and graduated from training schools; the qualifications for teacher training; the forms to be used in reporting pupil progress; school boundary lines and the criteria for permitting students to attend; and other matters that affect teaching. Teachers have little voice in determining who is qualified to enter teaching. Nonprofessionals control the state boards which set standards for teaching certificates. (1965, p. 241)

Despite such bureaucratic features, there is noteworthy "structural looseness" in schools and school systems (Pellegrin, 1976). Individual schools evolve their own unique styles and traditions. Further, classrooms are for many purposes self-contained units. The interaction patterns of teachers and students, shaped by the dictates of interpersonal relations, serve as countervailing forces to bureaucratic operations. Accordingly, many factors intervene to frustrate the implementation of bureaucratic procedures: the characteristics of the staff and students vary from school to school; the demands of various publics differ depending on neighborhood and residential patterns; a teacher's role performance is relatively invisible to outsiders; and there is low interdependence associated with a school's internal division of labor. Hence, it would be a gross distortion to regard schools as bureaucratic in the same way in which the military, the postal service, or certain commercial and industrial organizations are bureaucratic.

INFORMAL ORGANIZATION

... at Madison Junior High School, if you cooperated with the teacher and did your homework, you were a "kook." At Levi Junior High School, if you don't cooperate with the teacher and don't do your homework, you are a "kook." ... At Madison we asked a question, "Are you going to college?" At Brighton the question always is "What college are you going to?" ...

What the pupils are learning from one another is probably just as important as what they are learning from the teachers. This is what I refer to as the hidden curriculum. It involves such things as how to think about themselves, how to think about other people, and how to get along with them. It involves such things as values, codes, and styles of behavior.

U.S. Commission on Civil Rights

Formal organizations beget informal organizations. Hence, a knowledge of the formal role expectations constitutes only a part of the interpersonal relationships of the school. Teachers of course have a variety of formal duties both within and outside the classroom. They may serve on committees, supervise study halls and lunchrooms, patrol toilets every noon hour to guard against smoking and obscene wall art, and be required to do a goodly number of other activities, many of which they view as onerous nuisance tasks. In elementary schools, one teacher is likely to serve as an assistant to the principal and enjoy an added measure of authority and prestige. In those high schools divided into departments according to subject matter, one teacher usually acts as a department head.

But this is only one side of the picture. An informal organization also operates within most schools and influences the social interaction that develops among teachers. A teacher's ranking among colleagues may be relatively unrelated to official school duties. More prestige generally goes to the teacher who has longer experience, who teaches a higher rather than a lower grade, who teaches "academic" and college-preparatory subjects rather than vocational subjects (bookkeeping, typing, shop, home economics, and the like), and who teaches in the "better" neighborhoods. Cliques and friendship groups likewise form within the faculty and serve to channel social interaction. These groups often develop among teachers on the basis of common interests, similarity in age, marital status, religious or ethnic

INFORMAL ORGANIZATION

OBSERVATION In high school there were different cliques of students: "brains," "jocks," and "dope-heads." I think though the group that was disliked the most were the "brains." These "brown-nosers" studied a lot, didn't run around much, made friends with the teachers, and were on the honor roll every 9 weeks. The rest of us considered them "goody-goodies."

PRINCIPLE Various subcultures existed among the students in my high school at the informal level. Although the purpose of high school is supposed to be education, by the time most kids got to be sophomores they downgraded getting good marks. We were more concerned with popularity, and athletics counted for a lot more than doing well in the classroom.

background, and so on. At times, one group will seem to dominate school politics, and sometimes considerable friction develops among groups.

Likewise, within the formal organization of the school there arise among the students informal organizations—systems that are more or less self-contained and separate from those of adults. Hence, it is not uncommon that students and teachers should have different views of the social "reality" of the classroom. Many times, the informal definition of what constitutes a good student differs from that of the formal organization. Students often feel that they should not be too successful academically, that they should have a strong identification with the world of their peers, and that they should take on the values of the informal peer group rather than those of the adult-teacher world.

The prevalence of these attitudes is attested to by James S. Coleman's (1961) study based on a sample of 7500 students in ten midwestern high schools. Although Coleman expected to find that secondary schools in small towns, working-class suburbs, well-to-do suburbs, and university settings differed in their social climates regarding academic achievement, he found instead that they were quite similar in their nonintellectual—even anti-intellectual—traditions. Regardless of the setting, student norms were directed toward holding down effort. Moreover, every high school tends to have several "crowds" that frequently are mutually exclusive and even antagonistic to one another (Kerckhoff, 1972). Distinctions such as "brains," "goodies," "jocks," "hoodies," "freaks," and "swingers" are commonly encountered in most high schools.

SCHOOL EFFECTIVENESS

Schools bring little influence to bear on a child's development that is independent of his background and general social context.

The Coleman Report, 1966

Both educators and the American public have assumed that "good" schools—as measured by small classes, experienced teachers, instructional hardware, and school expenditures—lead to improved student performance. Doubt regarding the validity of this belief was provided by the Coleman Report (1966), a study named after its principal author, James S. Coleman, a prominent sociologist. The study, funded by Congress, involved tests and surveys of 645,000 pupils and 60,000 teachers in 4000 schools.

The data of the Coleman Report have been widely interpreted as revealing that school differences have little impact on achievement. This interpretation is derived from the fact that only about 10 percent of the variance in test scores was associated with differences between schools while about 90 percent was associated with differences between individuals. In other words, the researchers found that children who went to well-funded, well-equipped public schools with low teacher-pupil ratios did no better on intelligence and achievement tests than children who went to poorly funded schools with poorly trained teachers, dilapidated buildings, and crowded classrooms, once statistical allowance was made for the initial differences in intelligence and social background of the children attending the two types of schools.

Doubts regarding the effectiveness of the schools were intensified by the publication in 1972 of *Inequality* by Christopher Jencks and his Harvard University associates. These researchers found that school resources have little effect on either test scores or educational attainment; the general effect of variations in total money spent, per-pupil expenditures, teachers' salaries, and student-teacher ratios on a pupil's verbal and nonverbal test performance is either slight or unpredictable.

Jencks and his associates also challenge a number of assumptions regarding poverty and inequality. It long has been believed that the basic reason poor children fail to escape from poverty is that they cannot read, write, calculate, or articulate, and, lacking these skills, they cannot get or keep well-paying jobs. Further, the best way for breaking this vicious circle is to teach poor children basic skills in school through making sure they attend the same schools as middle-class children, giving them extra compensatory programs in school, and giving their parents a voice in the running of schools.

Jencks's finding run contrary to these assumptions. Although children born into poverty have an above-average chance of ending up poor, nonetheless an enormous amount of economic mobility occurs from one generation to the next. Brothers reared in the same family are apt to end up with incomes almost as far apart as two individuals picked randomly. Among men born in the most affluent fifth of the population, fewer than half will be part of this same elite when they grow up; very few will be in the bottom fifth, but often at least one of their children will end up there.

According to Jencks and his associates, people do not end up poorer than others primarily because they lack skills relating to reading, writing, calculating, or articulating. Although children who read well, get the right answers to problems in arithmetic, and articulate their thoughts clearly are somewhat more likely than others to get ahead, other factors are also involved. Indeed, there is virtually as much economic inequality among those who score high on standardized tests as in the population-at-large. It follows that equalizing people's reading scores would not appreciably reduce the incidence of economic failure.

If such factors as heredity, home background, intelligence quotient, differences in schooling, and all the other factors that have commonly been thought to explain why some people are rich and others are poor are rather inconsequential (accounting for only about a quarter of the variation in Americans' incomes), what then accounts for the other three-quarters of the variation? Economic success, Jencks argues, depends on varieties of competence, such traits as "the ability to hit a ball thrown at high speed, the ability to type a letter quickly and accurately, the ability to persuade a customer that he wants a larger car than he thought he wanted, the ability to look a man in the eye without seeming to stare, and so forth." So, he indicates, do countless unpredictable accidents such as "chance acquaintances who steer you to one line of work rather than another, the range of jobs that happen to be available in a particular community when you are job hunting, . . . whether bad weather destroys your strawberry crop, [and] whether the new super highway has an exit near your restaurant." Put more simply, economic success is a matter of "luck" (1972:227).

Admittedly such findings are controversial and contradict dozens of prior studies that have stressed the importance of education and family background as determinants of income. And they fly in the face of common observation. As economist Alice Rivlin observes: "What most of us think we see around us is a world in which people with a lot of education earn substantially more, on the average, than those with little education and a world in which children from middle and upper income families tend to get not only more and better schooling, but better jobs and higher incomes than those from poor families" (1973:70).

Critics of American education have used the Coleman and Jencks findings to support their arguments against spending additional funds to upgrade the nation's schools. They insist that such expenditures are useless since educa-

School effectiveness. Although there are some research findings that suggest that school differences bear little relationship to student achievement, many argue that sympathetic, understanding, and caring teachers do make a difference.

Patrick Reddy

tors can do little to increase school effectiveness. But the matter is not as simple as such critics would have us believe (Good, Biddle, and Brophy, 1975). Various researchers have challenged the Coleman and Jencks studies on the representativeness of their samples, the reliability of their data, the validity of their measures, the way they aggregated their data, their choice of statistics, and the ways they went about interpreting their statistics (Taylor, 1973; Hauser and Dickinson, 1974; Carver, 1975; Hurn, 1976).

There is also a body of literature that suggests that schools *do* make a difference (Pedersen, Faucher, and Eaton, 1978). Herbert H. Hyman, Charles R. Wright, and John S. Reed (1975) assembled data from 54 surveys undertaken by leading research organizations. They then examined the degree to which the amount of education a respondent had received was associated with correct answers to questions dealing with national and foreign affairs, literature, historical and geographical facts, sports, health, and the like. Their findings point to the enduring effects of education, with the more educated at every age interval being the more knowledgeable. Data from other countries similarly show that education is closely associated with political information, attitudes, and participation (Almond and Verba, 1963; Kohn, 1969; Inkeles and Smith, 1974). And research by Herbert J. Walberg and Sue P. Rasher (1974) revealed that high pupil-teacher ratios, low rates of per pupil expenditures, and low rates of age-eligible children enrolled in public schools were associated with high rates of test failure among men examined by the Selective Service (during the period prior to 1974 when the draft was operative).

SOCIAL CLASS AND EDUCATION

The social-class affiliation of families affects how far youth will go in schooling and how well they will perform in school (Boocock, 1972; Matras, 1975; Sewell and Hauser, 1976). On the average, youth whose parents enjoy more prestigious positions go farther in the formal school grades and perform better than those whose parents occupy lower socioeconomic positions. This holds true even for youth of above average ability. Consider, for instance, those high school graduates who rank in the top one-fifth in academic aptitude. If the parents of these relatively able youth are from the top socioeconomic quarter of the population, 95 percent of them will go on to college. But if their parents come from the bottom socioeconomic quarter, *only 50 percent* will go on to college. Even high school graduates from the top socioeconomic quarter who are in the middle ability group are more

Figure 15.2. Entrance to college, by ability and socioeconomic status (within five years after high school graduation).

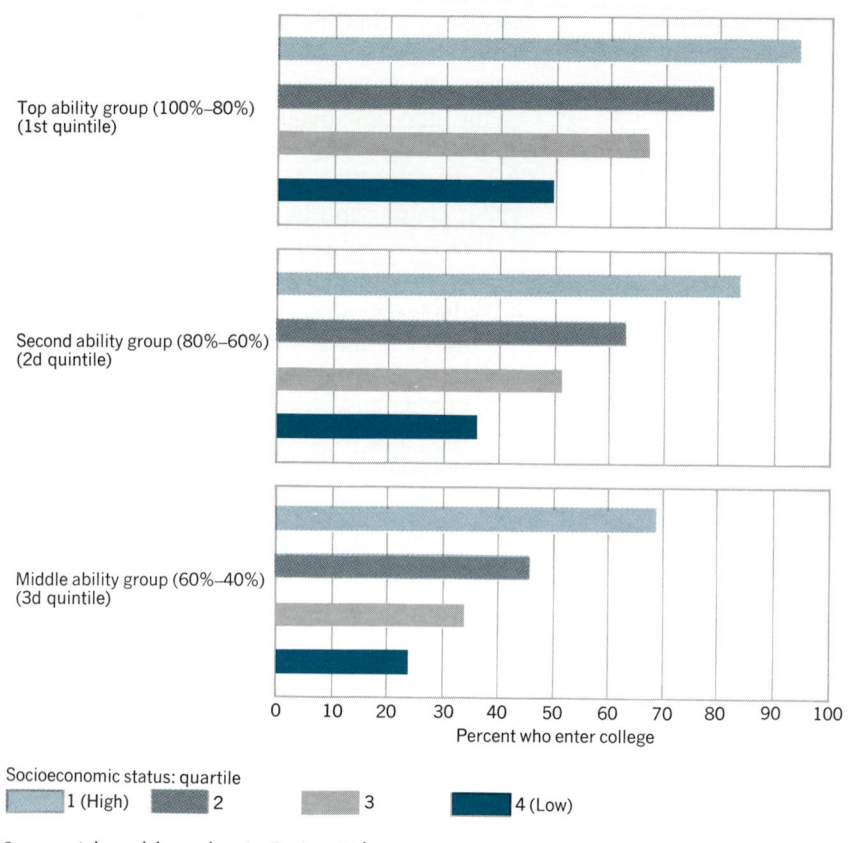

Top ability group (100%–80%) (1st quintile)

Second ability group (80%–60%) (2d quintile)

Middle ability group (60%–40%) (3d quintile)

Percent who enter college

Socioeconomic status: quartile
1 (High)   2   3   4 (Low)

Source: Adapted from data in Project Talent.

likely to enter college than the top ability group from the bottom socioeconomic quarter. See Figure 15.2.

Further, five years after high school graduation, those high school graduates in the top fifth by ability are *five times* more likely to be in a graduate or professional school if their parents were in the top socioeconomic quarter than if their parents were in the bottom socioeconomic quarter. Other measures also show that the higher the socioeconomic status of students' families, the more academic honors and awards the children are likely to receive, the more elective offices they are likely to hold, and the greater the children's participation in extracurricular activities is likely to be.

Why are children from more prestigious families generally more successful in their studies? Why do inner-city children often drop out of school at younger ages than middle-class youngsters? Any number of hypotheses have been advanced to explain these facts. Let us look at three of these: first, teachers are middle class in their values and consequently alienate inner-city youth; second, important subcultural differences distinguish middle-class from inner-city families, and hence children of differing social classes are differentially exposed to those attitudes and skills making for academic success; and third, inner-city children are the victims of educational self-fulfilling prophecies.

ALIENATION OF INNER-CITY CHILDREN

Most American teachers, regardless of their social-class origins, fit into middle-class life and share its outlook on such things as thrift, cleanliness, punctuality, respect for property and authority, ambition, sexual morality, and neatness. The identical values are not necessarily shared by all children. Hence, the middle-class teacher, without necessarily being aware of the fact, may find less affluent students unacceptable.

By way of illustration, middle-class teachers often find the aggressive behavior of inner-city children quite discomforting. One inner-city teacher observes:

> The formal organization rules set up by traditionalist teachers and administrators relate to order in the classroom, quietness, things like that. However, the rules that are *really* running the school are the informal organizational rules created by lower-class black male street-corner behavior. The student challenges and tests teachers by playing games [the dozens,* woofing,† and shucking and jiving**]. Because the average teacher or administrator doesn't understand the games and can't cope with them in a positive way, chaos and disorder result. These games—I call them games, but they're manifestations of the street-corner culture—are a product of social class behavior, not color. They're survival techniques. . . . The teacher has to be able to best him [the student] to the satisfaction of the "audience". . . . (Quoted by Cole, 1974, p. 171)

Further, inner-city sex norms and values may conflict with the middle-class teacher's sense of morality. Many teachers report shock on finding that words that are "innocent" to them have obscene meanings to their inner-city students:

> I decided to read them a story one day. I started reading them "Puss and Boots" and they just burst out laughing. I couldn't understand what I had said that had made them burst out like that. . . . [Later another teacher "enlightened" her on the matter.] It seems that Puss means something else to them. It means something awful—I wouldn't even tell you what. It doesn't mean a thing to us. (Becker, 1952, p. 454)

---

* The dozens—saying insulting things about another's mother, wife, sister, or grandmother, usually with the connotation of their sexually satisfying 10 to 15 other men.

† Woofing—combining physical aggression and rhetoric to intimidate Whites.

** Shucking and jiving—playing up to an authority figure's stereotyped notion of how the subservient Black ought to act.

MIDDLE-CLASS BIAS

OBSERVATION I do my student teaching at a lower-class elementary school. Today a child came to class complaining of the terrible bug bites he received in his bed. I don't think he ever brushes his teeth; his front teeth are crooked and clipped. He wears a tattered, stained T-shirt. His tennis shoes are all beat up and worn, with his unsocked feet visible at the toes and on the sides. His speech isn't the best. Frankly, the kid gives me the creeps. Whenever I'm around him I worry that I'll catch lice or some other bugs from him; I just get itchy when I see him. When I have to work with him I get it over with as quickly as possible; I really don't think he is going to learn too much in school anyway. He couldn't care less.

PRINCIPLE I know I shouldn't feel and act toward Jerry the way I do but I really can't help it. I just find his appearance disgusting and depressing. I could lie about it but the truth is I just feel extremely uncomfortable around the kid. My middle-class ways conflict with what I observe in Jerry. And the pay-off is that Jerry is alienated from school because his regular teacher feels toward him the same way I do. We'll just pass him on to the next grade to get rid of him but he really should repeat fourth grade.

Many middle-class teachers are unaware of the class bias and ethnocentrism of their values. But in one way or another, they frequently communicate to inner-city children the attitude and feeling that they are somehow unacceptable. Disgust, horror, fear, and discomfort are not easily hidden. Some sociologists and educators have advanced the hypothesis that inner-city students acquire a sense of rejection and respond with resentment and rebellion. Their attitude becomes, "If you don't like me, I won't cooperate" (Davis and Havighurst, 1947).

SUBCULTURAL DIFFERENCES

...the things outside the schools matter even more than the things inside the schools, and govern and interpret the things inside.

M. E. Sadler (writing in 1900)

Another hypothesis—also seeking to explain why middle-class children generally stay in school longer and perform better than do inner-city children—looks to the experiences and attitudes that children of the different classes bring with them to the school situation. Allison Davis observes:

> Whereas the middle-class child learns a socially adaptive fear of receiving poor grades in school, of being aggressive toward the teacher, of fighting, of cursing, and of having early sex relations, the slum child learns to fear quite different social acts. His gang teaches him to fear being taken in by the teacher, of being a softie with her. To study homework seriously is literally a disgrace. Instead of boasting of good

Education

marks in school, one conceals them, if he ever receives any. The lower-class individual fears not to be thought a street-fighter; it is a suspicious and dangerous social trait. He fears not to curse. If he cannot claim early sex relations his virility is seriously questioned. (1950, p. 30)

But not all inner-city children have a hostile orientation to school. This leads Jackson Toby (1957) to ask: "Why should middle-class children 'take to' school so much better?" He makes a number of interesting observations. First, middle-class parents make it quite clear to children that they are not to trifle with school. Parents, friends, and friends' parents *expect* that they will apply themselves to studies. They are caught within a neighborhood pattern of academic achievement in much the same manner that some inner-city youth are caught within a neighborhood pattern of truancy and delinquency. Further, middle-class parents continuously reinforce the authority

Do schools alienate inner-city youth? Some educators argue that the American school system is unrelated and unresponsive to the needs of inner-city youth. As a consequence, it alienates many of them.

Patrick Reddy

and prestige of the teacher. They urge children to value the gold stars that are given out and the privilege of being a monitor. They impress on them that scholastic competition as reflected in good marks is similar to the social and economic competition in which they themselves participate as adults.

Second, middle-class children probably "take to" school better because they typically come to school already possessing a variety of skills that many inner-city children lack—for instance, conceptions regarding books, crayons, pencils, paper, and numerals. Robert J. Havighurst, on the basis of a survey of Chicago schools, observes:

> These [ghetto] children come to school pitifully unready for the usual school experiences, even at the kindergarten level. Teachers remark that some don't even know their own names and have never held a pencil. Their speech is so different from that of the teachers and the primer that they almost have a new language to learn. They have had little practice in discriminating sounds, colors or shapes, part of the everyday experiences of the middle-class preschool child, whose family supplies educational toys and endless explanations. (Quoted by Star, 1965, p. 59)

Third, middle-class children are further advantaged in the competitive race by their greater verbal facility since their parents generally manipulate symbols rather than concrete objects in their occupational roles (Pozner and Saltz, 1972). Moreover, middle-class parents are usually better educated than inner-city parents and hence are more capable of helping their children with schoolwork should this be necessary. In this and many other ways, middle-class children generally enjoy advantages. Further, minority-group children who speak Spanish or "Black English" may find themselves handicapped in schools where "standard" English is employed (Harber and Bryen, 1976; Simões, 1976; Marwit, 1977).

EDUCATIONAL SELF-FULFILLING PROPHECIES

If men [people] define . . . situations as real, they are real in their consequences.
W. I. Thomas, The Relation of Research to the Social Process, *1931*.

A third hypothesis that seeks to explain social-class differences in the performance of schoolchildren suggests that inner-city children are the victims of educational "self-fulfilling" prophecies." Kenneth B. Clark, a distinguished Black psychologist, makes the following charge.

> [Ghetto] children, by and large, do not learn because they are not being taught effectively and they are not being taught because those who are charged with the responsibility of teaching them do not believe that they can learn, do not expect that they can learn, and do not act toward them in ways which help them to learn. (1965, p. 131)

Robert Rosenthal and Lenore Jacobson, in *Pygmalion in the Classroom* (1968), undertook to demonstrate that a teacher's expectations can markedly affect a student's performance, regardless of the student's actual abilities. Teachers at a South San Francisco elementary school (the first grade through the sixth grade) were falsely told that I.Q. tests (previously administered to the children) showed which pupils were due to "spurt ahead" academically. The teachers were given the names of 20 percent of the students, randomly selected from all grades and all three tracks ("slow," "medium," and "fast" tracks), and were told that every pupil so listed would improve dramatically within a year. For ethical reasons, it was not predicted that any children would turn out dull. A year later, when the children were retested, there were average I.Q. gains of 12.22 points among the children for whom a learning "spurt" was predicted, compared with 8.42 for a control group representing the rest of the student body. The most dramatic gains, however, came from the first- and second-graders—increases of 27.4 points were registered in the first grade and 16.5 points in the second grade for the predicted "spurters." In comparison, the first-grade control group rose only 12 points, and that of the second grade only 7 points.

The widespread publicity received by *Pygmalion in the Classroom* had a far-reaching effect on educational thinking. It was not long, however, before critics pointed out that the data-gathering methods, the techniques of analysis, and the data presentation were not sufficiently rigorous to warrant the generalizations that the report contained (Thorndike, 1968; Snow, 1969; Dusek, 1975; Braun, 1976). More recent research has yielded mixed results (West and Anderson, 1976; Wilkins, 1976; Cooper and Baron, 1977). Rosenthal reports that

> 242 studies have been done from which 84 found the experimenters' or teachers' expectations made a difference in subjects' or students' performance . . . the proportion of significant results is about the same for experiments conducted in the field as in the laboratory, some 37 percent for the field and 34 percent for the laboratory. (1973, p. 59)

It would seem, then, that teacher expectations do not always produce performance differences in students, yet the effect is observed often enough that its importance cannot be discounted. Research Study 22 summarizes a study that sheds additional insight on educational self-fulfilling prophecies.

RESEARCH STUDY 22

TEACHER-STUDENT INTERACTIONS*
Glenn Firestone and Nathan Brody

Problem. A prevalent assumption among educators and social scientists is that children's interactions with their teacher communicate to them various expectations. Some research suggests that students who are perceived by their teacher as being "bright" enjoy an "interactional advantage" over children who are perceived as being "dull"—they receive more attention, more chances to respond, more praise, and more verbal cues. In this study, Glenn Firestone and Nathan Brody seek to specify the role that teacher-student interactions play in academic achievement.

Hypothesis. The researchers hypothesized that the quality of interactions that children experience in the classroom influences their academic performance.

Method. Seventy-nine children in four kindergarten classes in an inner-city school were observed once every three weeks for two hours. They were observed again during the first half year of first grade. A time-sample approach was employed. At the end of every five-second interval, an observer decided which among eleven categories best represented the nature of the teacher-student interaction. The observer wrote down the number of that category and the student who was involved in the interaction (such categories as praises or encourages, accepts or uses ideas of student, asks questions, lecturing, giving directions, criticizes, and so on). In February of the kindergarten year, the students were administered an IQ test. Fifteen months later in first-grade, the children were given an academic achievement test measuring their word, reading, and math skills.

Findings. The interactions that occurred between teachers and children were related to academic performance. Children who experienced the highest proportion of negative interactions with their kindergarten teacher were also the children who did more poorly on the first-grade achievement tests. Since these results persisted when IQ was statistically controlled (allowed for), it removed the possibility that unfavorable interactions related negatively to achievement solely because the "duller" students were also those receiving most of the unfavorable interactions. Further, the total number of times students were chosen to demonstrate something in class was positively related to their word knowledge and reading scores.

Conclusion. These findings lend themselves to several alternative explanations. The first involves the self-fulfilling prophecy—students internalize their teacher's expectations of them and then perform in a manner consistent with this image. A second possibility is that the teacher's reactions to a student were governed by one or more personality or temperamental characteristics that were unrelated to IQ—the negative interactions did not cause the poor academic performance but were themselves caused by characteristics of the child that also independently led to poor academic performance. The study cannot provide a definitive answer as to which explanation best fits the data. But even if one is inclined to reject the first explanation, the study makes clear that knowing how a child interacts within the classroom provides significant information, apart from IQ, about how well he or she performs academically.

* Adapted from Glenn Firestone and Nathan Brody, "Longitudinal investigation of teacher-student interactions and their relationship to academic performance." *Journal of Educational Psychology,* 67 (1975):544–550.

SOCIAL CHANGE: SOME RECENT TRENDS

To many it seems that schooling changes little from one generation to the next. Elementary school children still learn the 3 R's under much the same circumstances as did their grandparents and daily school routines have remained essentially the same. Although the architecture of a building dates its vintage, the arrangement and outfitting of the individual classrooms has not appreciably changed since the turn of the century. Indeed, many educational practices seem somewhat faddish, coming in and going out of style in a cyclical manner. Nonetheless, as in all areas of human life, change does occur.

SCHOOL DESEGREGATION

The desegregation of America's schools has been a source of great controversy since the Supreme Court declared school segregation unconstitutional in 1954. In its ruling (347 U.S. 483:1954), the nation's highest court declared that racial segregation in the schools generates feelings of inferiority among Black children and "may affect their hearts and minds in ways unlikely ever to be undone." However, ten years after the ruling, the year in which the Civil Rights Act of 1964 was enacted, 98 percent of Southern Black children were still in all Black schools. By 1974, twenty years later, this picture had changed: more than 44 percent of Black pupils in the South were in schools whose enrollments were less than half Black. In sharp contrast, Northeastern and Middle Western schools have remained largely segregated with 81 percent of Black children in predominantly Black schools.

With the publication in 1966 of the findings contained in the Coleman Report, educators concluded that the academic performance of Blacks increased as the proportion of White students in a school increased. This relationship was credited to the higher levels of educational motivation and background present in predominantly White student bodies. From this a "lateral transmission of values" hypothesis was formulated. It held that the superior performance of Blacks in predominantly White schools was the result of Black students acquiring the achievement-related values held by Whites. The hypothesis has been a major assumption underlying many school desegregation policies (Bradley and Bradley, 1977).

Over 120 studies have been undertaken since 1954 to determine whether school desegregation helps children in some direct way (Carithers, 1970; St. John, 1975; Hunt, 1977). Taken as a whole, however, the evidence is inadequate, inconclusive, and often contradictory. It has not been established with any certainty that a causal relationship exists between the racial composition of a school and the academic achievement of its Black

School desegregation. Today northern schools remain more segregated than southern schools.

Patrick Reddy

and White pupils. Nonetheless, one major finding does stand out: desegregation has rarely lowered academic achievement for either racial group. Those studies designed with the greatest sophistication suggest little or no change occurs in Black children's performance in desegregated settings. Even where gains are found, it is not entirely clear whether they result from desegregation or some other factor such as the quality of the school or the teachers. It does appear, however, that new theories of achievement motivation are called for that take into account various situational factors so as to better understand the achievement of both Black and White students.

The effects of desegregation on the self-esteem of Black students is also not clear. Some evidence suggests that Black pupils in segregated schools have higher aspirations and self-conceptions than those in desegregated schools (St. John, 1975). Again, many individual and situational factors appear to be operative. The same holds for the effects of desegregation on prejudice. For instance, research by Louise C. Singleton and Steven R. Asher (1977) points to positive patterns of classroom interaction. Other research by Harold B. Gerard and Norman Miller (1975) suggests that elementary-school children in desegregated settings become increasingly ethnocentric in their friendship choices as they grow older. However, the fact that students have even some friendship choices among students of other racial groups represents more integration than would have resulted had the schools remained segregated.

In hindsight it appears that a naive optimism led educators and social scientists to believe that school desegregation would automatically improve students' academic achievement and intergroup relationships. It is unrealistic to expect the schools to undo in a few years what has been accomplished by centuries of racial segregation and intergroup tensions (Schofield and Sagar, 1977; Patchen, Davidson, Hofmann, and Brown, 1977). Indeed, schools mirror the racial system of the larger society. They cannot be expected to eliminate behaviors that the large society continually re-creates in its day-by-day functioning.

THE "BACK TO BASICS" MOVEMENT

In the crudest cost-benefit terms, the more the parents have spent on schools, the less their children have learned. Scores on academic achievement tests, administered to all grades in most states, reveal that the academic ability of schoolchildren declined almost unremittingly in the second half of the 1960's and the first half of the 1970's.

Frank E. Armbruster, Our Children's Crippled Future, 1977

The 1960s were a decade of experimentation in which educators explored new avenues for enriching and broadening the scope of conventional education—open classrooms, racial balance, community control of schools, compensatory education, and so on. Concern centered on making the curriculum relevant and subjects interesting while keeping the students happy. Nonetheless, the problems of American education remained and in many instances deepened. Pressed by budget considerations, demands for accountability, and, above all, a growing concern for "the basics," schools are re-examining many of their innovations of the 1960s and are returning to earlier premises and policies. This has meant renewed attention to multiplication tables, spelling lists, grammar, and composition.

Reflecting this renewed emphasis on learning is a pamphlet entitled *Learning is Hard Work* (1977) issued by the NEA (National Educational Association), whose 1.8 million members form the nation's largest teacher organization:

> School is a place of learning. It is not a place of entertainment or relaxation, like a theater or like the beach. That means that school is essentially a work place and that the pleasure to be derived from school is integrally related to the satisfaction derived from accomplishing a hard job. That means too, that a day at school can sometimes be routine and tiresome. . . . Learning is hard work. And the future of all of us—students, parents, teachers, the community at large—depends on it.

The "back to basics" movement has been fed by a number of developments. Since 1963 average scores on the Scholastic Aptitude Tests (SAT) given to college-bound juniors and seniors by the College Entrance Board have been falling steadily and significantly (Harnischfeger and Wiley, 1976). The decline has been unrelated to socioeconomic background, race, or geographical location; not only has performance in city schools declined, but so has that in suburban and rural schools. Further, a 1977 report of the National Assessment of Educational Progress found that 13 percent of American seventeen-year-olds are functionally illiterate (most alarmingly, the illiteracy rate among Black youth approached 42 percent). Functional illiteracy means that the individuals are unable to read newspaper advertisements, add up bills, write grocery lists, or complete a job application form. And colleges and universities, plagued by growing numbers of students unable to write coherent sentences or handle simple arithmetic, are compelled to devote increasing resources to remedial programs teaching basic skills.

Many critics blame the schools for these failures (Armbruster, 1977). They charge that the schools are neglecting the 3 R's and are attempting to satisfy all the requests made of them, especially in areas not directly related to traditional education—physical fitness, drug and alcohol abuse, sex education, driver training, energy conservation, vaccinations, school lunchrooms, bilingualism, psychological counseling, and career selection. Others suggest that increased television viewing cuts down on the time students spend doing homework and in cultivating reading and literary skills. Still others point to various social trends, including a "breakdown" in family life (more working mothers and more single parent families), social unrest, youth involvement with drugs, and "a decade of distractions."

All of this has led educators to begin again emphasizing basic skills and specific standards for the nation's youth. Increasingly, states are requiring high-school seniors to pass a test for competency in basic skills before they can get a diploma. And the practice of automatic promotions is being reviewed. At another pull-back from the earlier permissiveness, school officials are taking aim at student misbehavior, including truancy, drug offenses, vandalism, and class disruption.

Perhaps not surprisingly, many educators are alarmed by these developments. They fear that the atmosphere of the schools may become needlessly coercive. Like all trends, they are concerned that the "back to basics" in the schools can suffer from extremism (Weber, 1978).

Back to basics movement. Confronted with falling test scores on national achievement tests, schools have been under increasing pressure to emphasize the 3'Rs.

Patrick Reddy

SUMMARY

1. Socialization involves the process by which we become humanized—by which we acquire our society's cultural patterns. Socialization is an inclusive concept. Education is more limited—it denotes a formal, conscious, systematic training.

2. Educational institutions and groups commonly aid in the completion of children's socialization, transmit a variety of specialized skills, reproduce among the young the social relations of production, add to the cultural heritage through research and discovery, "sort and sift" youth for various achieved roles, and perform a number of latent functions.

3. Within the United States school environments are remarkably standardized in both physical and social characteristics. Moreover, physical objects, social relations, and major activities are experienced by both pupils and teachers as remaining much the same from day to day, week to week, and even from year to year.

4. A school system is made up of a network of roles that are functionally interrelated for the purpose of achieving given educational objectives. Schools share many similarities with other bureaucratic organizations. Despite such bureaucratic features, there is noteworthy "structural looseness" in schools and school systems. Individual schools evolve their own unique styles and traditions.

5. Formal organizations beget informal organizations. Hence, a knowledge of the formal role expectations constitutes only a part of the interpersonal relationships of the school. An informal organization also operates within most schools and influences the social interaction of both teachers and pupils.

6. Both educators and the American public have assumed that "good schools"—as measured by small classes, experienced teachers, instructional hardware, and school expenditures—lead to improved student performance. Doubt regarding the validity of this belief has been provided by the Coleman Report and the research of Christopher Jencks and his associates. Such findings, however, remain controversial and contradict a number of other studies.

7. The social-class status of families affects how far youth will go in schooling and how well they will perform in school. Any number of hypotheses have been advanced to explain these facts: first, teachers are middle class in their values and consequently alienate inner-city youth; second, important subcultural differences distinguish middle-class from inner-city families, and hence children of differing social classes are differentially exposed to those attitudes and skills making for academic success; and third, inner-city children are the victims of educational self-fulfilling prophecies.

8. Over 120 studies have been undertaken since 1954 to determine whether school desegregation helps children in some direct way. Taken as a whole, however, the evidence is inadequate, inconclusive, and even contradictory. It has not been established with any certainty that a causal relationship exists between the racial composition of a school and the academic achievement of its pupils. It needs to be emphasized, however, that it is unrealistic to expect the schools to undo in a few years what has been accomplished by centuries of racial segregation and intergroup tensions.

9. The 1960s were a decade of experimentation in which educators explored new avenues for enriching and broadening the scope of conventional education. Nonetheless, the problems of American education remained and in some instances deepened. Pressed by budget considerations, demands for accountability, and, above all, a growing concern for the "basics," schools are reexamining many of their innovations of the 1960s and are returning to earlier premises and policies.

PART FIVE

DEMOGRAPHY AND URBANIZATION

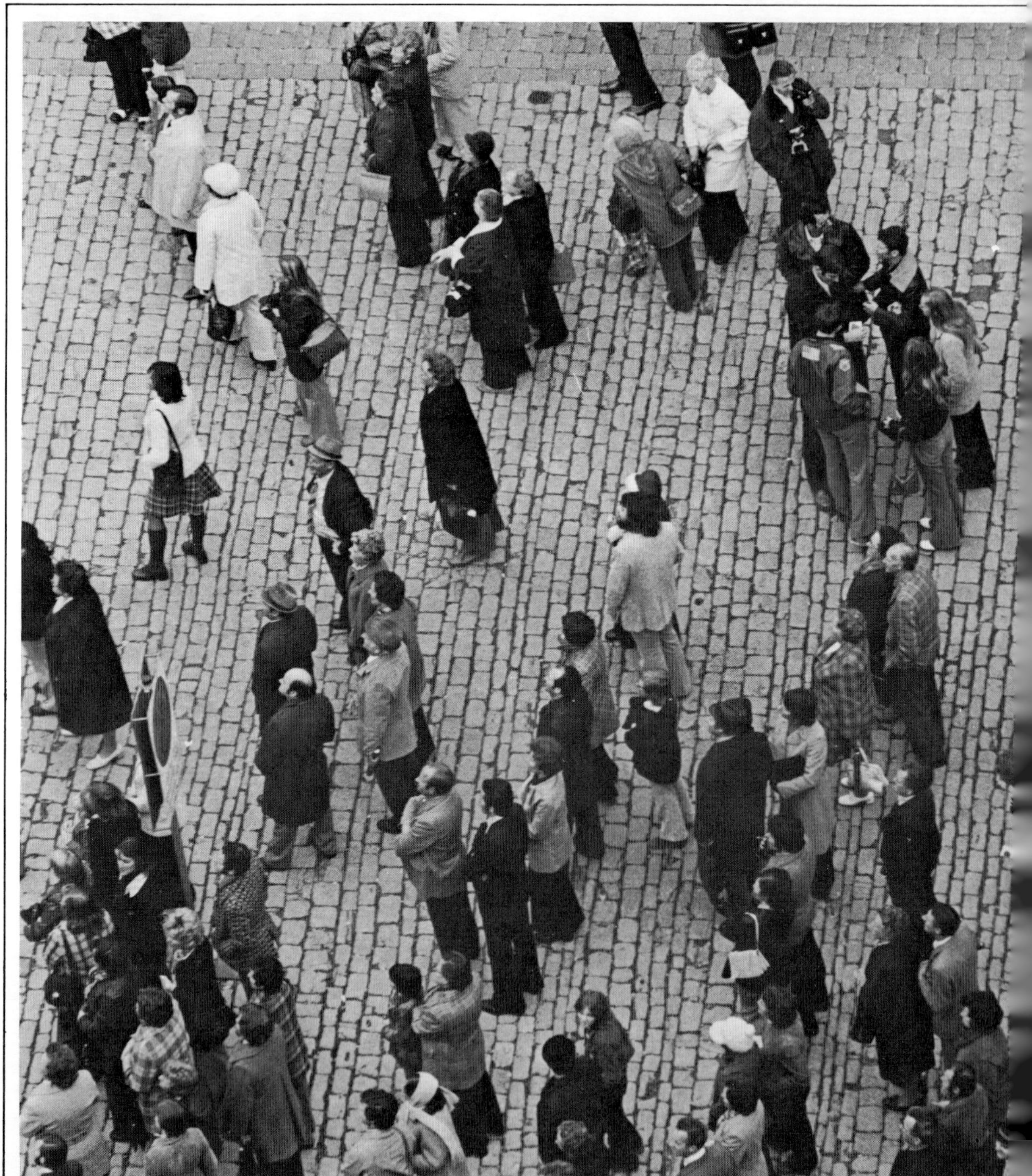

16 POPULATION

POPULATION OF THE UNITED STATES
  Determinants of Population Size
  Spatial Distribution
  Composition

WORLD POPULATION
  Population, Food, and Theory
  Food Supply
  Birth Control

OBSERVATION Three weeks ago my grandfather died of a heart attack. Today, exactly three weeks later, my grandmother suddenly died of some sort of coronary problem that neither she nor we knew she had. She seemed in good health although she emotionally deteriorated after grandpa's death. Much of her life centered about grandpa. She was very proud of him and would talk constantly about how tough grandpa was and recount his youthful exploits—how he could hold his own with his fists against anyone in town and how he could wrestle young bulls on the farm. She told me once or twice recently that she would be "leaving" us for good soon and be "joining grandpa in heaven." And then on the third-week anniversary of grandpa's death she too just up and died.

PRINCIPLE I think grandma's case illustrates very well the part that social factors play in death. Her most important social relationship was terminated with grandpa's death and it had a profound psychological impact on her. Very likely this activated physiological changes that resulted in her death. At least that is what the doctor said.

We hear a good deal nowadays about the "population explosion." Some population experts tell us that if the post-World War II rate of increase continues, there would be a population of one person per square foot of the earth's land surface in less than 800 years. A major computer study of world trends by an MIT research team (Meadows, Meadows, Randers, and Behrens, 1972), *The Limits to Growth,* has concluded that either civilization or population growth must end, and soon. Continued population and industrial growth will exhaust the world's minerals and bathe the biosphere in fatal levels of pollution. The MIT researchers assert:

> If the present growth trends in world population, industrialization, pollution, food production, and resource depletion continue unchanged, the limits to growth on this planet will be reached sometime within the next one hundred years. The most probable result will be a rather sudden and uncontrollable decline in both population and industrial capacity. (p. 29)

Even if we adjust only one of the trends—a new discovery of minerals, a technical advance, or a sharp increase in agricultural output—the catastrophe will still occur since other destructive or wasteful trends continue. A subsequent report to the Club of Rome (which also sponsored *The Limits to Growth* study) maintained much the same attitude as the earlier work, although its conclusions were somewhat less pessimistic (Mesarovic and Pestel, 1976).

Such prospects seem none too cheerful. Some population experts, however, argue that the MIT researchers are unnecessarily alarmist. They note that the principle of exponential growth retrospectively applied to the

557 Population

chewing-tobacco and horse "crisis" in New York in 1850 would arrive at the prediction that by today New York City would be buried under 170 feet of brown spit in the gutters and the same level of horse manure in the streets (reaching 14 stories high). Our imaginary study, however, would have failed to take into account the falling off in popularity of tobacco-chewing and the vanishing of the horse from the city streets. Had this not happened, we perhaps would have recycled horse manure and tobacco juice as fertilizer—in brief, social feedback may occur to deal with social imbalance. Proponents of this view reject the idea that the world's resources are fixed; rather, they see an expanding potential in better use and recycling of existing resources and development of new ones as the world progresses economically and technologically. And they find encouragement in the substantial decline in fertility in some portions of the less-developed world during the 1970s (Schmeck, 1978).

Population explosion or social inequality? Some population experts contend that the problem confronting the world is not so much one of an exploding population but one of an inequality in the distribution of resources. The child on the right suffers from kwashiorkor, a condition of malnutrition characterized by skin disorders and a protuberant belly (due to an enlargement of the liver and water retention in the abdomen).

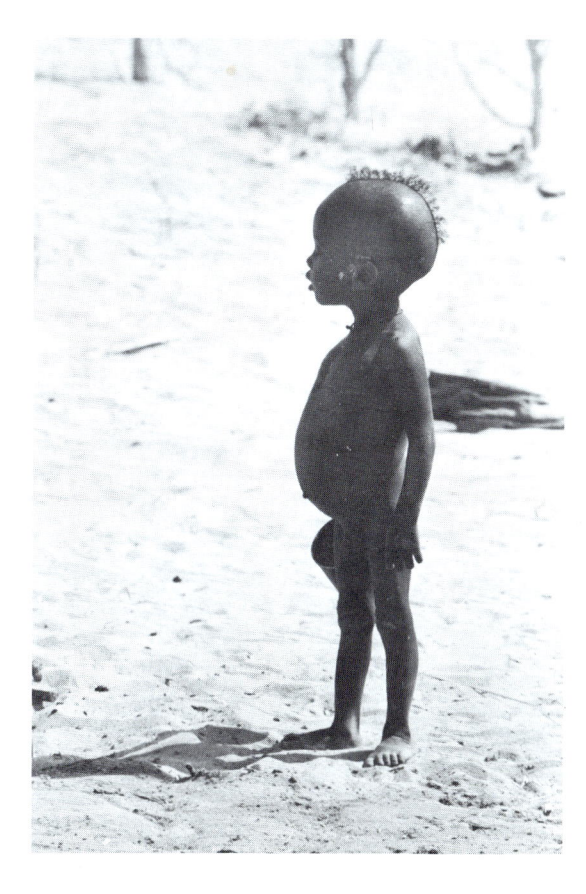

Patrick Reddy

Agency for International Development

Figure 16.1. World population growth. Confronted by the prospect or world population tending to grow in a geometric ratio, some population experts suggest that humankind has but a short time — perhaps less than a hundred years — to avert global disaster. They suggest that by virtue of exponential growth, the final point may occur with seeming suddenness. Suppose, by way of analogy, that we own a pond on which a water lily is growing. The lily plant doubles its size each day. If unchecked, it will completely cover the pond in 30 days, choking off all other forms of water life. For a long time the lily plant seems small, and there appears little cause for alarm. On the 25th day it covers only 1/32 of the pond, on the 26th day 1/16, on the 27th day 1/8 — even by the 28th day it covers only 1/4 of the pond. But by the 29th day the pond is one-half covered and by the 30th day completely covered. A number of population experts warn that a similar fate awaits humanity and that the collapse will come with awesome suddenness, with no way of stopping it, unless immediate remedial action is taken. Others, as the text points out, view such thinking as extreme and only too likely to breed a spirit of defeatism.

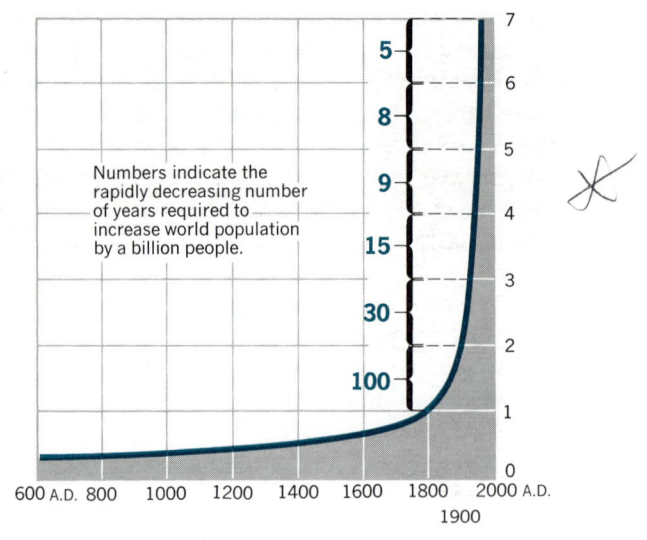

Numbers indicate the rapidly decreasing number of years required to increase world population by a billion people.

Source: United Nations data.

There are also those who argue that the main risks of environmental damage on a global scale and the greatest pressures on natural resources stem from the economic activities of the rich nations and the exploding appetites of their inhabitants. According to this view, there is not an overall shortage of foodstuffs but an inequality in their distribution: "hunger is caused by plunder and not by scarcity" (Barraclough, 1975:25). These population experts note that the consumption of beef per person doubled in the United States since 1940 (not to mention the wastefulness of food consumption by the some 75 million American cats and dogs and the extensive use of fertilizer for lawns). In West Germany meat consumption has risen by one-third since 1960, in Italy, it has almost doubled, and in Japan is has increased over three and a half times. Further, for the past century tropical countries have put practically all their efforts into export crops like cocoa, tea, coffee, and rubber and little to food production.

We do not possess accurate figures on the world's current population, but it is estimated to be about four billion (China is the world's largest nation with between 925 million and 1.1 billion). As we go backward in time, the available statistics become increasingly fragmentary and unreliable, so that the earliest figures represent only informed guesses. It is estimated that *Homo sapiens* has inhabited the earth anywhere from 50,000 to 1,000,000 years. It took humanity thousands upon thousands of years to reach a global total of one-quarter of a billion people, the estimated population of the world A.D. 1. Another 1650 years passed before the population doubled, reaching a half-billion. Within 200 years, by the time of the American Civil War, it had doubled again, reaching the one billion mark; by 1930, it had doubled once more. Hence, the rate of world population growth has progressively accelerated. If the present rate of growth is maintained (which is by no means a certainty) it will reach 7 billion around A.D. 2000; by A.D. 2023, it will have doubled to 14 billion (see Figure 16.1).

In continuing with our discussion of population, it would seem useful to focus our attention initially on one nation and then later to examine the broader matter of world population. This is the approach that we shall follow in the chapter, opening with a consideration of the population of the United States.

POPULATION OF THE UNITED STATES

A few years ago the United States seemed blessed by an absence of severe "population problems." Indeed, we felt quite smug as the world's wealthiest nation. We had come to see ourselves occupying a wide continent, rich in natural resources. And far from having a food problem, we actually faced an embarrassment of agricultural riches; although there did exist "pockets of poverty" in the midst of our affluence, we nonetheless paid farmers subsidies to withhold agricultural land from production lest wheat, corn, and other grains glut the market.

As the 1970s unfolded, however, Americans came face-to-face with very real population problems, especially as they were tied to ecological and environmental resources. Although we make up only 6 percent of the world's population, we account for nearly a third of the world's energy consumption. And as America's seemingly insatiable appetite for energy has grown more ravenous, especially for petroleum, harsh reality has struck in the form of brownouts during summers, unheated schools and powerless factories in winter, and emptying gasoline pumps across the nation. But it is not alone petroleum—we are now almost completely dependent on foreign sources for 22 of the 74 non-energy mineral commodities considered essential to a modern industrial society.

The population crisis was seen in other areas as well, as ecological resources became overtaxed. Lake Erie approached the state of a "dead sea" and Lake Michigan was not far behind; Yellowstone Park, drawing more than 50,000 campers on summer days, was rapidly becoming an "outdoor slum"; and during times of drought, wildlife in Florida's Everglades became endangered because of the diversion of water to farms and subdivisions. Further, it is estimated that each American has roughly 50 times the negative impact on the earth's life-support systems as the average citizen of India (in terms of eco-system destruction, adding 70 million more Americans—an es-

Despoiling nature? As Americans take to nature in growing numbers, are they impairing the ecological balance and reducing it to an "outdoor slum"?

Patrick Reddy

timate of the increase in the American population by the year 2000 — would be equivalent to adding 3.7 billion Indians to the world population). Let us turn then to a more detailed consideration of the population within the United States.

DETERMINANTS OF POPULATION SIZE

In late 1967, the United States reached a new bench mark, a population of 200 million. It took the country until 1915 to reach its first 100 million, and until 1950 to reach 150 million. The next big step — 250 million — may come as early as 1990. All such population change can be reduced to four variables:

1. Fertility (births)
2. Mortality (deaths)
3. Immigration (movement to an area)
4. Emigration (movement away from an area)

Any factor that affects the size of population does so by influencing one or more of these demographic variables. The size of a population is somewhat analogous to the amount of water in a bathtub. The water comes into the tub through two faucets, comparable to births and immigration. The water leaves, in this case, through two drains, comparable to deaths and emigration. Hence, the future population (P_2) of any given area is the result of the present population (P_1) plus natural increase or decrease (births minus deaths) plus net migration (immigrants minus emigrants):

$$P_2 = P_1 + (\text{births} - \text{deaths}) + (\text{immigrants} - \text{emigrants})$$

Fertility. Fertility refers to the *actual* reproduction of a people; **fecundity** on the other hand, refers to *potential* reproduction—that is, the birth rate if every woman of childbearing age bore all the children she possibly could. Clearly, a population's fertility constitutes only a part of its fecundity. One common way to measure fertility is to calculate the number of births per 1000 of the total population at a given period. This gives us the **crude birth rate**:

$$\text{Crude birth rate} = \frac{\text{number of births per year}}{\text{total population}} \times 1000$$

or substituting 1977 figures:

$$\text{U.S. crude birth rate} = \frac{3.3 \text{ million}}{216 \text{ million}} \times 1000 = 15.3$$

Figure 16.2 reflects the crude birth *rate* of the United States since 1900. From 1910 to 1933, the birth rate fell steadily. In 1920, it stood at 27.7 births

Figure 16.2. Birth rate in the United States per 1000 population: 1900–1976.

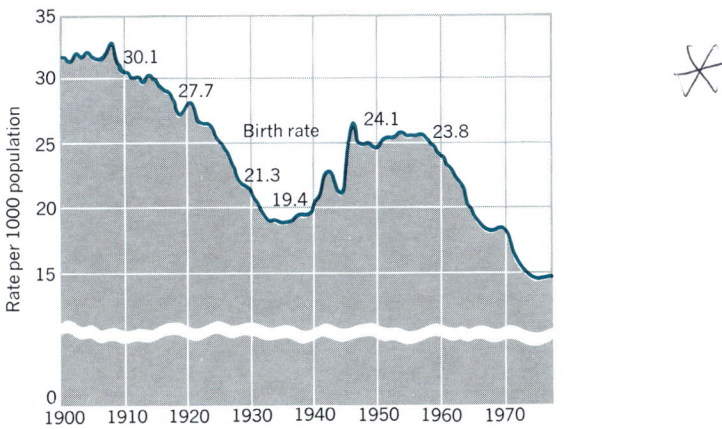

Source: Statistical Abstract of the United States, 1977 (Washington, D.C. Government Printing Office.)

per 1000 persons, but within thirteen years it had dropped to 18.4, a decline of 35 percent. However, there was no appreciable decline in the annual *number* of births until 1926–1927; then the number of births also fell but not as sharply as the birth rate. The less drastic decline in the annual number of births resulted because the declining rate was applied to a base of women of childbearing age (fourteen to forty-four years of age) that was still growing— that is, although on the average each woman had fewer children, there were more women to have children than in the earlier period.

Beginning in 1939, an appreciable rise occurred in the nation's birth rate; it leveled off in the decade between 1947 and 1956, but started falling again in 1957. Today's decline in the birth rate (15.3 in 1977) has surpassed the previous low of 16.9 reported in 1935. Between 1957 and 1961, the *number* of births within the United States held at about 4.3 million annually. About 1961, the number began falling, reaching 3.25 million in 1972 (a matter of no small interest to manufacturers of toys, Pablum, disposable diapers, and baby furniture). The number of births held to 3.1 to 3.3 million between 1973 and 1976. In 1977 the nation's birth rate rose for the first time since 1970. This upswing reflects an increase in the number of women of childbearing age and an increase in the rate of childbearing. The trend is expected to continue over the next five to ten years (a contributing factor is that some women who postpone having children reach their thirties, and recognize that their chances for motherhood will soon end).

Of even greater interest perhaps, in 1972 the fertility rate (children per family) fell for the first time below the 2.1 level, the figure required for the population *eventually* to no more than replace itself (the goal of ZPG, the zero population growth movement). The figure is 2.1 rather than merely 2 in order to account for girls who die before reaching childbearing age. Population experts warn against excessive optimism, however, since fertility can be quite volatile (Blake, 1974; Sklar and Berkov, 1975). In 1950, 35,405,000 women of childbearing age had 3,632,000 births; in 1974, 48,310,000 potential mothers (36 percent more) had 3,160,000 babies (13 percent less).

BIRTH RATES AND MARKETING

OBSERVATION I have been noticing a good many advertisements on TV and in the newspapers promoting many baby products for use by adults—baby oil, baby powder, and baby shampoo. I have even seen ads in the newspaper encouraging adult consumption of baby foods. The ads point out various delicious desserts that can be made using baby food.

PRINCIPLE Over the past decade or so birth rates in the United States have declined. Accordingly, various businesses specializing in items and food for babies are hurting. In order to expand their markets beyond infant needs, they have undertaken campaigns to appeal to older generations.

But it is the presence of so many potential mothers in the population that is the source of concern; even a small upward rise in fertility could turn the trend lines up again (Gibson, 1977). Moreover, zero population growth can come only if low fertility rates continue for some 65 or so years. The reason is this: there are 1.1 million women who are now 44 years old but 2.1 million who are 18. Even if the 18-year-olds merely replace themselves as they pass through the childbearing years, they will be producing twice as many babies as the 44-year-olds did, continuing to increase the population.

Why have birth rates fallen in recent years? Some people suggest the answer lies with the growing popularity of contraception, especially the "pill" (the first widespread medical trials with the pill took place in Puerto Rico in 1956). Recent surveys reveal that at least 70 percent of American married couples are using some method of contraception. During the 1970s, sterilization (laparoscopies in women and vasectomies in men) displayed a sharp rise. A 1973 survey revealed that nearly one in four married couples using contraception relied on sterilization and current estimates place the figure at one in three (Stokes, 1977).

Yet new innovations in contraception are not the entire story. It is of interest to note that a sharp decline occurred in the 1920s and 1930s (see Figure 16.2) before the advent of oral contraception. Clearly, we also have to look to other factors, most particularly to the motivation people have for regulating family size. Indeed, there appears to be a growing disenchantment among Americans with the idea of large families. The Gallup Poll revealed that the proportion of Americans believing four or more children to be the "ideal" number declined from 40 percent in 1967 to 13 percent in 1977 (when the Gallup Poll first asked the question in 1936, the figure was 34 percent; it received a high of 49 percent in 1945). Moreover, today's young women are tending to delay the first child and space out the other children. Yet the longer a couple postpones its first child, the greater the chance that it will not have any. And "spacing" of children after the first one tends to reduce the number of children in the family.

The above discussion raised but did not answer the question, "Why do many contemporary American couples want to limit their family size?" One consideration appears to be economic. It is estimated that it costs a middle-income family $53,605 to raise a child to age 18, a figure that rises to $64,215 if the expense of a four-year education at a state university is included. This means it costs parents $214,420 to bring up four children to college age ($256,860 to college graduation). Further, the fertility of young adults corresponds closely to their relative affluence, that is, the level of living they actually have compared with the standard of living they would like to have. The baby boom following World War II was partly a response of young adults to the fact that they were able to achieve income quite high in relation to their expectations. In recent years, in contrast, large numbers of young adults entering the marketplace have found it increasingly difficult to meet their economic goals. Indeed, young people today are experiencing more economic stress than their counterparts in the 1950s and 1960s and seemingly have responded by having smaller families (as did parents during the Great Depression).

But the reasons for smaller families are not all economic. Some young couples fear that a large family would deprive their children of individual attention. The increasing mobility of families—taking weekend trips, camp outings, moving from one city to another because of company transfers—similarly encourages couples to limit the size of their families. And some parents with several children report that large families seem to carry something of a social stigma.

Other factors also have contributed to the drop in birth rates. Women are getting married later and divorced more, both factors operating to depress fertility. Another particularly important factor is the increase in the proportion of women at work, providing women with roles and interests that are alternative or supplementary to childbearing (Waite and Stolzenberg, 1976; Stolzenberg and Waite, 1977). This latter factor has been coupled with the rise of the women's liberation movement. Still another factor has been the steady liberalization of abortion laws (in 1976 there were an estimated 1,115,000 abortions, accounting for about one out of every four pregnancies). And then of course there has been a rise in social awareness that unchecked population growth may outstrip natural resources.

Mortality. *Mortality* refers to the termination of life within a population as measured by the death rate. One common way to measure mortality is to calculate the number of deaths per 1000 of the total population at a given period. This gives us the **crude death rate**

$$\text{Crude death rate} = \frac{\text{number of deaths per year}}{\text{total population}} \times 1000$$

or substituting 1976 figures:

$$\text{U.S. crude death rate} = \frac{1.9 \text{ million}}{219 \text{ million}} \times 1000 = 8.8$$

Since 1915, the death rate has dropped from about 13.2 per 1000 to 8.8 per 1000 in 1976. The rate rose markedly in 1918 to 18.1 as a result of an influenza epidemic, but in 1919 it fell again to 12.9. Spectacular gains have been registered in the reduction of the death rate in all age categories, especially among infants (see Table 16.1). Advances in medical science and public health practice, improvement in nutrition and the overall standard of living, and the easing of the costs of medical care through the growth of insurance programs have contributed to these gains.

TABLE 16.1
Death Rate per 1000 Population by Age

Age	1900	1974
Under one year	162.4	15.3
1–4	19.8	.7
5–14	3.9	.3
15–24	5.9	.6
25–34	8.2	.9
35–44	10.2	2.0
45–54	15.0	4.7
55–64	27.2	10.5
65–74	56.4	23.6
75–84	123.3	63.3
85 years and over	260.9	153.9

Source: Pocket Data Book, USA 1976. Washington, D.C.: Government Printing Office. Table 53, p. 73.

The control of many communicable diseases during the past century has dramatically increased our chances of survival. The death rate has been lowered more in the early ages than for the years over sixty. Medical science has had less success in attacking the degenerative diseases (diseases generally associated with age such as cancer and cardiovascular disorders) than it has had with communicable diseases. Although the probability of living to be seventy is much greater today than it was a hundred years ago, the probability of living to be a hundred is no greater at all, and may even be less.

We would be seriously amiss, however, if we were to overlook the part that social and cultural factors play in mortality. Consider the following illustrations:

- A survey of cancer mortality reveals that male residents of counties in the United States where the petroleum industry is most heavily concentrated experience significantly higher rates for cancers of the lung, the nasal cavity, and sinuses and the skin compared to male residents of nonpetroleum counties similar in other population characteristics (Blot, Brinton, Fraumeni, and Stone, 1977).
- A California study discloses that 29.7 percent of pregnant nurses working in operating rooms where they are exposed to anesthetic gases have spontaneous miscarriages. This compares with 8.8 percent among pregnant general-duty nurses. Further, oral surgeons and dentists who are exposed to anesthetic gas for three hours or more per week have wives with a 78 percent higher incidence of spontaneous abortions than do wives of other such practitioners (Bronson, 1977).

Figure 16.3. Cancer mortality rates by county for White males, 1950–1969.

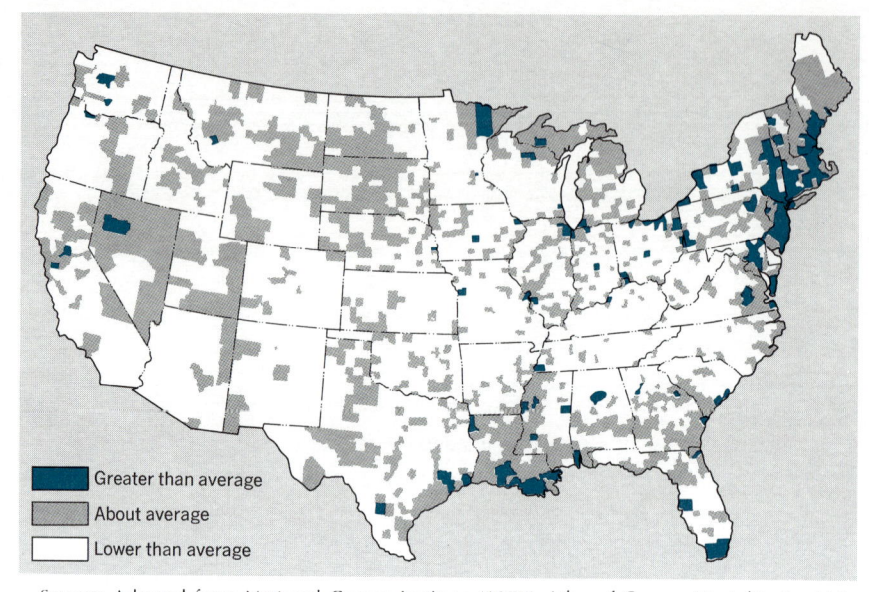

- Greater than average
- About average
- Lower than average

Source: Adapted from National Cancer Institute (1975) *Atlas of Cancer Mortality for U.S. Countries: 1950–1969.* Washington: Government Printing Office.

- Finland, particularly the province of North Karelia, had the worst rate for heart disease of all developed nations. A five-year program of preventive medicine was inaugurated that reduced the heart attack rate for males by 40 percent. The program involved eliminating smoking and the reduction of high cholesterol foods in the diet.
- The National Cancer Institute reports regional differences in cancer patterns within the United States. Rates of bladder cancer are unusually high among New Jersey Whites (where the large chemical industry traditionally barred Blacks) and of the cervix among Southern Black women with less ready access to health care (Mason, McKay, Hoover, Blot, and Faumeni, 1976). See Figure 16.3.

Perhaps most striking of all are the findings of David P. Phillips and Kenneth A. Feldman that point to the part that social and cultural processes play in causing people to postpone their death so as to participate in meaningful ceremonies. This research is summarized in Research Study 23.

RESEARCH STUDY 23

A DIP IN DEATHS BEFORE CEREMONIAL OCCASIONS*

David P. Phillips and Kenneth A. Feldman

Problem. Émile Durkheim (1858–1917), a pioneer French sociologist and a profound student of social organization, suggested that individuals who are integrated within their society are necessarily involved with its religious (e.g., Christmas and Easter) and political (e.g., July 4th) ceremonies. Through celebrations, reunions, assemblies, and special events, individuals are bound together within the social fabric as they express and reaffirm in common their shared sentiments. Further, Durkheim equated individuals' integration within society with the obligation they felt to participate in its ceremonies. The strength of this integration and obligation ranges between two extremes. At one extreme are those persons so lacking in social integration—so detached from society—that they prematurely die by committing suicide. At the other extreme (extending Durkheim's argument) are those persons so highly integrated—so attached to society—that they postpone death in order to participate in ceremonies. It is to this matter that the researchers direct their attention in this paper.

Hypothesis. The notion that a dip in deaths occurs before important ceremonies is termed by the researchers "the death-dip hypothesis."

Method. Phillips and Feldman investigated whether there are fewer deaths than expected before three ceremonial occasions: a person's birthday, Presidential elections, and the Jewish Day of Atonement (Yom Kippur). Let us consider the method the researchers employed in seeking to establish whether a death-dip occurred before the birthday. They examined the deaths of famous people only (the data are readily accessible and a famous person's birthday is often publicly celebrated, providing tangible recognition). The month of birth and the month of death for famous people from all periods in America were derived from *Four Hundred Notable Americans* (the sample consisted of 348 Americans since some had not yet died or the month of birth and/or death was not known).

Phillips and Feldman tested the hypothesis that the deathmonth is *independent* of the birthmonth—in brief, the deaths of those born in any given month are distributed throughout the year in the *same* way as the deaths of those born in any other month. Note that the researchers state the hypothesis in terms *opposite* to what in fact they actually postulate. This is termed a *null hypothesis.*

Since in employing statistical methods for testing a hypothesis we can come nearer to proving

Continued on next page.

---

* Adapted from David P. Phillips and Kenneth A. Feldman, "A Dip in Deaths before Ceremonial Occasions," *American Sociological Review*, 38 (1973), 678–696.

Rituals. Parades are staged public occasions by which people can fuse themselves within a collective consciousness. They afford a communion of patriotic fervor as citizens reenact their "sacred past" through the symbolic mechanism of rituals.

Patrick Reddy

that something is *not* true than that something is true, we often use a negativistic approach. If we want to establish one hypothesis, we do not test it directly but formulate the opposite hypothesis, a null hypothesis, and test it on the basis of our data (in this sense the null hypothesis becomes a target). In this particular case, the researchers believe that the deathmonth is *dependent* on the birthmonth (the occurrence of the ceremony). Made into a null hypothesis, it beomes: the deathmonth is *independent* of the birthmonth.

If 1/12 of all sample deaths (12 months constituting a year) fall in the month before the birthmonth, then the null hypothesis cannot be rejected. If on the other hand, fewer than 1/12 of the deaths occur in the month before the birthmonth, then the null hypothesis can be rejected (and by implication the researchers have demonstrated their expected postulate). The researchers calculated that 29 (348/12) deaths would occur in the month before the birthmonth if the deaths were distributed equally over the months of the year. The number of *actual* deaths falling in the month before the birthmonth was 16. Moreover, whereas 116 deaths (348 × 4/12) would have been expected in the birthmonth and in the three months thereafter (4 months; 4/12 of a year), 140 deaths *actually* occurred. Both a statistically significant death-dip *and* a statistically significant death-peak occurred. Thus, the findings of 16 deaths in the month before the birthmonth (as opposed to 29 deaths) and 140 deaths in the birthmonth and in the three months thereafter (as opposed to 116 deaths) could have occurred by *chance* only twenty-five times in ten thousand (statistical significance of .00025).* Accordingly, the researchers *rejected* the null hypothesis of independence between birthmonth and deathmonth.

Despite the statistical significance of the finding, the results could have occurred by chance (twenty-five times in ten thousand). So as to be more confident that the death-dip and the death-peak were not the product of chance fluctuations,

---

* The approach is analogous to playing a game of craps with loaded dice in which the chance of a given combination coming up is only twenty-five in ten thousand throws.

Phillips and Feldman undertook to see whether the phenomenon could be replicated in four other samples of famous people. They found that it could, lending additional confirmation to the death-dip hypothesis.

Findings. In our treatment of method above, we indicated that the data lent support to the death-dip hypothesis. What were some of the other findings? Evidence revealed that fewer deaths than expected occurred for Americans before Presidential elections (the mortality level was lower than expected in September and October before thirteen out of seventeen elections between 1904 and 1968) and for New York City and Budapest Jews before the Jewish Day of Atonement (Yom Kippur was used since it is possible to separate the effect of the occasion from the effect of the *season* of the year for those annual occasions that occur at a *different* date each year; it is not possible to separate the seasonal effect from ceremonies occurring once a year at exactly the *same* date, for example, Christmas and Independence Day).

Conclusion. The death-dip phenomenon reveals the impact of social and cultural processes on population dynamics. Phillips and Feldman observe:

The size of the death-dip before a ceremony appears to reflect the degree to which people are involved within that ceremony, and consequently the degree to which they are attached to that segment of the culture which is symbolized by the ceremony. (p. 692)

Immigration and Emigration. Migration—both immigration and emigration—is the product of "push" and "pull," or, more precisely, two sets of forces: (1) one set of forces tends to produce movement away from the habitat already occupied, and (2) one set of forces attracts the prospective migrant toward an alternative habitat. Before migration actually takes place, a period normally occurs in which individuals compare the relative opportunities offered by the present and the anticipated habitat. If the balance is on the side of the anticipated habitat the person or group generally migrates unless prevented, as for example, by the Berlin wall, immigration quotas, or lack of financial resources. In the 1840s the "push" of the potato famine in

TABLE 16.2
The Changing Flow of Immigrants from Abroad: Ten Leading Nations Supplying Immigrants

1951		1976	
Country of Birth	Percent of 1951 Immigrants	Country of Birth	Percent of 1976 Immigrants
1. Poland	18.2%	Mexico	14.5%
2. Germany	12.8	Philippines	9.4
3. Canada	10.1	Korea	7.7
4. Britain	6.1	Cuba	7.3
5. U.S.S.R.	5.8	China (including Taiwan)	4.7
6. Latvia	5.1	India	4.4
7. Yugoslavia	4.0	Dominican Republic	3.1
8. Italy	3.6	Britain	2.9
9. Mexico	3.1	Portugal	2.6
10. Hungary	2.4	Jamaica	2.3

Source: United State Department of Justice.

Ireland and the "pull" of employment opportunities in the United States made this country seem attractive to many Irish; similarly, the "push" ensuing from the failure of the 1848 Revolution and the "pull" of American political freedom led many Germans to seek their fortunes in America. Currently, both "push" and "pull" factors are contributing to the entry into the United States of large numbers of illegal aliens from Mexico: low Mexican agricultural productivity, commodity prices, and investments in agriculture serve as "push" factors while wages in the United States which are twice as high or higher than those in Mexico are the "pull" factor (Jenkins, 1977). Table 16.2 reflects the changing flow of immigrants to the United States over the past 25 years.

SPATIAL DISTRIBUTION

We have considered how fertility, mortality, immigration, and emigration affect population *size*. Sociologists are also interested in how a people are *distributed* in space. Depending on the sociologist's purpose, the "where" may be a large area such as a continent, or a small area such as a city block. Between these extremes are world regions, countries, intracountry regions, states, cities, and rural areas. Changes in numbers and proportions of people living in various areas are the cumulative effect of differences in fertility, mortality, and net migration rates.

Within the contemporary United States, internal migration has resulted in a dramatic geographical redistribution of population. Indeed, the physical mobility of our population is such that one out of every five of our citizens changes his or her place of residence every year. Among the most important shifts in the distribution of our population are the following:

1. The exodus of Americans from farms continued in the 1970s despite a large increase in agricultural production over the same period. Fewer than one American in 25 now lives on a farm; in 1935 one in four did. In part this has to do with the increasing mechanization of agriculture and the preference of many farm owners and hired workers to live in town and commute to the fields. Simultaneously, the output of crops and livestock products has swelled since 1970 by 20 percent.
2. Whereas the nation's population grew by 5.6 percent between 1970 and 1976, the growth of 278 metropolitan areas — the biggest cities and their suburbs — lagged behind at a 4.7 percent rate. Eight of the largest metropolitan areas actually lost people despite suburban growth. The greatest population increase occurred in rural areas and small towns due to the migration of industry rather than a resurgence in farming.
3. Both the South and the West have been growing in the 1970s at about double the national growth rate. By 1978, the South's population was up 11.2 percent and that of the West, 12.7 percent. The Northeast lagged behind, up 0.4 percent (New York, Pennsylvania, and Rhode Island actually lost population), while the Midwest grew by only 2.4 percent.
4. At the turn of the century the Black population was predominantly rural and Southern. Today it is more urban than the White population (Census officials estimate that in 1977 the number of Blacks living on farms was less than 500,000). In 1970 little more than half the Black population was living in the South (as recently as 1950 it was about two-thirds). The Black population in our large cities has continued to grow. The increase in the Black population in large cities is only partially due to migration from other areas; two-thirds of the increase has resulted from an excess of births over deaths.

The point of these statistics is that some of the most significant changes in population are changes in population distribution. The very fact of such changes brings a demand for still other changes. For instance, every change in population distribution means that new facilities have to be provided in the areas that are growing, and that existing facilities in areas of outmigration are likely to be underused. This holds for housing, schools, roads, hospitals, shopping facilities, and all other things that people need and use. And in turn, the derivative changes range far and wide. In order to construct new public facilities, new tax sources often have to be sought and existing taxes raised.

Population distribution also has consequences for the relative political strength of the various regions within the United States. If present trends continue to 1982 when Congress is reapportioned, New York will lose three members in Congress, Ohio two, and Illinois, Michigan, Pennsylvania, and South Dakota one each; Florida and Texas will stand to qualify for two more seats and Arizona, California, Oregon, Tennessee, and Utah will add one. In turn the political muscle of Congressional delegations is related to the allocation of federal monies to the individual states and the distribution of defense bases, jobs, and contracts.

For the devoted follower of a given college football team, a population growth in southern, southwestern, and west coast states means that more high schools are built in these areas. There are also more talented and well-coached prep gridders available for Southeastern, Southwestern, and Pacific Coast teams. Accordingly, the fortunes of the college teams in these regions improve. Likewise, those of the Northeast and Midwest (including the Big Ten) appear to deteriorate, especially in intersectional contests.

COMPOSITION

We are interested not only in the size and spatial distribution of a population but also in its *composition* or characteristics. A variety of traits distinguish individuals from one another and are useful for classifying populations into basic categories. Among these characteristics are age, sex, rural or urban residence, race, education, income, marital status, occupation, religion, and national origin. For our purposes here, we shall single out age and sex characteristics for special consideration.

The Sex Composition. The sex composition of a population is measured by the sex ratio–the number of males per 100 females:

$$\text{Sex ratio} = \frac{\text{males}}{\text{females}} \times 100$$

At birth, for every 100 females, there are roughly 105 males born (Markle, 1974). Within the United States, the male death rate exceeds that of females so that by age 19 women outnumber men. As people grow older, the increase of women over men accelerates so that at age 65-and-older the ratio is 72 men per 100 women (the life expectancy of a male born in 1977 was 69.4 years; for a female, 77.2 years). Mythology has it that men die earlier on the average than women because they allegedly work harder. Yet newborn and one-year-old boys do not work harder than newborn and one-year-old girls. Rather, it appears that the female is simply a more durable organism than the male.

Within the United States, Alaska has the highest sex ratio (119), while the District of Columbia has the lowest (87). For the nation as a whole, the sex ratio reached an all-time low of 94.8 in 1970. Generally, frontier, mining, cattle-raising, and lumbering areas attract a disproportionate number of males. Females, on the other hand, are found in greatest numbers in cities characterized by commercial and clerical activities (for example, Hartford, Connecticut, and Washington, D.C.) and light industry (for example, textile manufacturing and small equipment assembly centers). Hence, on the whole, modern cities tend to have lower sex ratios than do rural areas.

Age Composition. One of the most important characteristics of any population is its age composition. A population heavily concentrated in the years from 20 to 69 has a large labor force relative to its nonproductive population. Hence, its dependency burdens are likely to be light. On the other hand, a population concentrated at either extreme of the age distribution — either under 20, over 65, or both — has a heavy dependency ratio, that is, a large number of nonproductive individuals in relation to its productive population.

If people aged 20 through 69 are regarded as the working population, and people below and above these ages are regarded as nonproducing but consuming dependents, then the changes in the age distribution of the United States during the 1950s and 1960s alone have served to alter the nation's production picture. In 1950, dependents constituted 42 percent of the total population; by 1970, they were 48 percent. However, this rise in the proportion of dependents is unlikely to result in scarcities of goods and services since technological advances have contributed to a rising level of productivity. Nevertheless, the responsibility of the family wage earner, employer, and taxpayer for these dependents is becoming increasingly complex. Many of the requirements for schools, hospitals, special housing, and welfare services derive from the needs of the people in the younger and older age groups. This puts considerable pressure on government to supply these facilities.

We can gain a clearer picture of the age and sex composition of a population by constructing a **population pyramid**, often referred to as the "tree of ages." The population pyramid may be based either on absolute numbers or

Figure 16.4. Population pyramids, United States, 1900, 1940, and 1970, based on proportions.

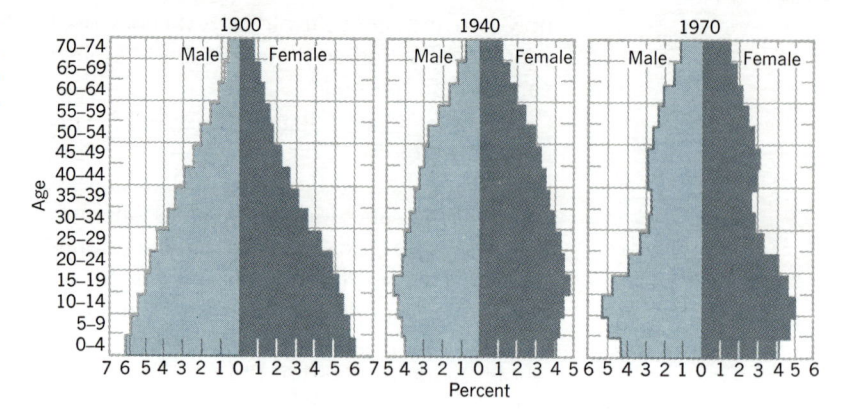

Figure 16.5. Population pyramid, United States, 1970, based on absolute numbers.

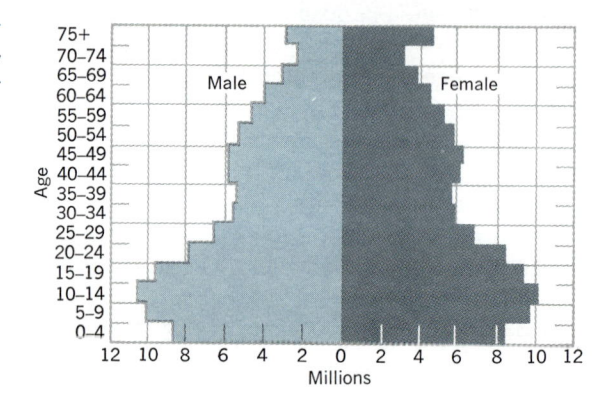

proportions (see Figures 16.4 and 16.5). Age groupings are placed in order on a vertical scale, with the youngest age group located at the bottom and the oldest age group at the top of the diagram. On the horizontal axis are plotted the numbers or percentages that each specified age group constitutes of the total, with the sum or portion corresponding to the male segment placed to the left of the central dividing line and that representing the female segment placed to the right of it. The pyramid itself represents the entire group.

Figure 16.4 shows the population pyramids for the United States in 1900, 1940, and 1970 based on proportions. The pyramid for 1900 has the shape of a true pyramid, typical of a population that is increasing by virtue of a high birth rate and a declining death rate. The 1940 pyramid reveals a different picture. It is the product of a decline in both the birth rate and the death rate. Compared with 1900, the productive portion of the population had increased relative to dependents (although the relative proportion of the aged increased, that of the children declined sharply). The 1970 pyramid with its contracted base reflects the decline in the birth rate. By the same token, the short bars in the middle of the pyramid reflect the lower birth rates of the 1930s—those occupying the base bars in the 1940 pyramid have now moved up into the middle-age range. Hence, overall the percentage of the dependent population has increased relative to those in the working population.

Figure 16.5 shows the population pyramid for the United States in 1970 based on absolute numbers. Such pyramids are of particular value for those engaged in planning for the future, for example, educators, public officials, and investors. From these pyramids, it is possible to project the age structure of the population at various intervals in the future. Hence, the 1970 population pyramid contained in Figure 16.5 foretold that the boom in kindergarten, elementary, and secondary school enrollments that occurred during the 1960s would end during the 1970s. As can readily be seen from Figure 16.5, a major feature of the development of the population is the large number of people who have reached marriage and childbearing age during the 1970s (a trend continuing into the early 1980s). In the early 1970s there were about 43 million persons between 20 and 34 years old. By 1980, that number will be about 58 million—an increase of more than one-third in a decade.

These changes should trigger a whole new set of side effects. The number of crimes against property and persons is expected to decline since youths— aged 12 to 21—commit more of these crimes than do other age groups. Prevailing tastes may change in such diverse fields as music and fashion, long dominated by young people. The emphasis on youth may gradually give way to an emphasis on "singles" and young married couples. The demand for housing is obvious and this might focus on high-rise and garden apartments since, if birth rates stay low, families will become gradually smaller. However, the postwar "boom" group of young adults is moving into an overcrowded job market. Many of these younger workers will find career ladders blocked by the glut of senior employees.

The proportion of the elderly is also growing. In 1960, 9.2 percent of Americans were 65 years or older, a figure increasing to 10.8 percent in 1977. In 1990, they are expected to constitute 12.2 percent of the population. This rise has serious implications for the financial solvency of the Social Security system and has dictated continually rising taxes to cover mounting deficits. Within 50 years, one beneficiary will be receiving social security benefits for every two workers paying into the system, instead of one for every three, as it stands today. With the growth in the proportion of the elderly, it is likely that demands will also accelerate for the government to play a larger role in providing housing, recreation, health care, and income maintenance for the elderly (in numbers, the elderly have overtaken the nation's 22.5 million labor-union members and constitute a substantial political force as they are more likely to vote than people in almost any other age category).

WORLD POPULATION

> Famine seems to be the last, the most dreadful resource of nature. The power of population is so superior to the power of the earth to provide subsistence . . . that premature death must in some shape or other visit the human race. The vices of mankind are active and able ministers of depopulation. . . . But should they fail in this war of extermination, sickly seasons, epidemical pestilence, and plague advance to terrible array, sweep off their thousands and tens of thousands. Should success still be incomplete, gigantic inevitable famine stalks in the rear, and with one mighty blow, levels the population with the food of the world.
>
> Thomas Robert Malthus, Essay on the Principle of Population, 1798

World population growth and food shortages are a major concern for all contemporary nations and play a part in their policy considerations. The United States is no exception. A 1974 State Department policy memorandum said:

> Excessive global population growth widens the gap between rich and poor nations; distorts international trade; increases the likelihood of famine in the relatively near future; adds to environmental problems; produces unemployment; enlarges the danger of civil unrest; and promotes aggressions endangering peace. (Hill, 1974, p. 2)

And a C.I.A. research report concludes that world grain shortages

> could give the United States a measure of power it had never had before—possibly an economic and political dominance greater than that of the immediate post-World War II years. . . . In bad years, when the United States could not meet the demand for food of most would-be importers, Washington would acquire virtual life-and-death power over the fate of the multitudes of the needy. (Weinstein, 1975, p. 13)

Clearly matters of population and food have moved center stage on governmental agendas.

POPULATION, FOOD, AND THEORY

> Population, when unchecked, increases in a geometrical ratio. Subsistence only increases in an arithmetical ratio.
>
> Thomas Robert Malthus, Essay on the Principle of Population, 1798

The relationship between population growth and the level of a nation's welfare has long enjoyed a central concern for those interested in population problems, especially since 1798 when Thomas Robert Malthus (1766–1834) first published his *Essay on the Principle of Population*. Malthus took an extremely pessimistic view, asserting that humans confront two unchangeable and antagonistic natural laws: (1) the "need for food," and (2) the "passion between the sexes." He argued that, whereas agricultural production tends to increase in arithmetical progression (1-2-3-4-5-6-7), population has a tendency to increase in geometrical progression (1-2-4-8-16-32-64). Based on this formulation, Malthus took a dim view of the future, considering famine, war, and pestilence as the chief deterrents to excessive population growth. He also noted that preventive checks might operate to reduce the birth rate; he thought, however, that the postponement of marriage was and would remain the primary preventive check.

Many questions have since been raised regarding the Malthusian thesis. There is no clear evidence that food always and everywhere can increase only in an arithmetic ratio—within the United States, for instance, the application of technology (farm machinery, irrigation, fertilizers, pesticides, hybrid plants and animals) has resulted in subsistence growing as fast and even faster than the population. And whereas world population increased by less than 50 percent between 1951 and 1971, world production of cereals doubled (Barraclough, 1975). However, the bulk of the surplus went to the peoples of affluent nations. In North America, consumption of cereals per person rose from 1000 pounds to nearly 1900 pounds. This increase was associated with the acceleration in meat-eating among North Americans and Europeans (whereas in 1940 each American ate 55 pounds of beef, in 1972 consumption more than doubled to over 120 pounds). Although American farmers produce 4800 kilograms of grain for every person in the United States, only about 300 kilograms of this is directly consumed as cereal and bread products. Some is exported, but most of the bulk is fed to animals to produce meat, milk, and eggs.

Some social scientists have even turned Malthus upside-down and have argued that population growth leads to agricultural and technological innovation. For instance, anthropologist Mark N. Cohen (1977) points out that incipient agriculture is not an "invention" but an accumulation of refinements of existing horticultural techniques. Hence, under population pressure, peoples on all major continents (except Australia) progressively abandoned foraging economies for more productive agricultural techniques. And finally there are those who note that Malthus overlooked the part that voluntary control of conception (contraception) can play as a preventive check on population growth. Nonetheless, there remains genuine concern in many quarters that Malthus may have been basically right but merely overstated his case; hence, the world cannot be complacent but must confront and deal with the grave Malthusian issue of whether continued growth in population will outrun the world's food supply.

FOOD SUPPLY

The world average per capita diet is expected to improve slightly between 1970 and 1985 (Berg, 1975; Chancellor and Goss, 1976). Still, the food situation is precarious in some parts of the world, especially Asia (which has 20

578 Demography and Urbanization

Figure 16.6. Birth and death rates: Selected countries.

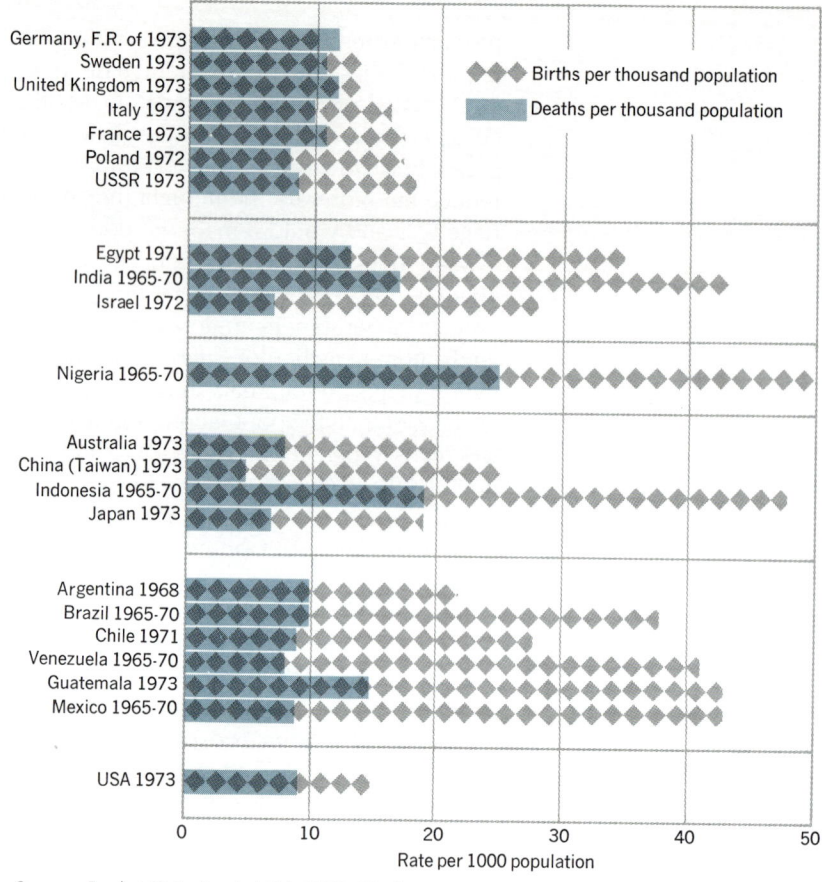

[Figure 16.6: Bar chart showing births and deaths per thousand population for selected countries, Rate per 1000 population from 0 to 50]

Countries shown:
- Germany, F.R. of 1973
- Sweden 1973
- United Kingdom 1973
- Italy 1973
- France 1973
- Poland 1972
- USSR 1973
- Egypt 1971
- India 1965-70
- Israel 1972
- Nigeria 1965-70
- Australia 1973
- China (Taiwan) 1973
- Indonesia 1965-70
- Japan 1973
- Argentina 1968
- Brazil 1965-70
- Chile 1971
- Venezuela 1965-70
- Guatemala 1973
- Mexico 1965-70
- USA 1973

Legend: Births per thousand population; Deaths per thousand population

Source: Pocket Data Book, USA 1976. Washington, D.C.: Government Printing Office. Figure 5, p. 9.

percent of the world's potentially arable land and 57 percent of the world's population). See Figure 16.6. Further, when we look closely at the developing nations, we find a variety of handicaps to sustained rises in agricultural productivity:

1. Widespread illiteracy hampers the introduction of new ideas and techniques to agriculturalists.
2. Low per-capita income prevents the farmers from acquiring the machinery, pesticides, fertilizers, and other products that they need. Further, the new high-yield varieties of rice and wheat (the so-called "Green Revolution" described below) are up to ten times as costly as using the old.
3. Incentives to increased productivity are often lacking, for example, if the resulting increased income merely goes to wealthy landlords, as in some Latin

American countries. Thus, in Brazil the country's gross national product per capita grew by 3.1 per cent per year in the decade 1960–1970. But the share of the national income received by the poorest 40 percent of the population declined from 10 percent in 1960 to 8 percent in 1970 whereas the share of the richest 5 percent grew from 29 percent to 38 percent.

4. Farmers do not get sufficient cash prices for their produce to buy the yield-increasing machinery and chemicals they need; frequently they raise just enough for subsistence and hence do not produce a surplus that they can sell for cash on the market.
5. Needed farm services, such as research, credit, and transportation, are often lacking.

Yet the more closely we examine the balance of food and population, the more difficult it is to come to an unequivocal conclusion. Long-term projections of food resources have been quite reliable. Just what the future holds in terms of developments in agricultural technology and organization remains to be seen. A case in point has been the development in recent years of high-yield varieties of rice and wheat—the "Green Revolution," perhaps the most significant breakthrough in agricultural technology in this century—that eased for a time the specter of mass famine. In India alone, the Green Revolution made possible an expansion of wheat production from 11 million to 27 million tons between 1965 and 1972. Still, Norman E. Borlaug, the Nobel Prize-winning father of high-yield wheat, observes that "this is just a modest step. This damned monster of population growth wipes out most of the gains. And what is the most frustrating are these continual political problems that won't let us implement the technology we have."

Some scientists predict that a breakthrough will be made in the next decade or so in the development of new strains of plants or bacteria. All plants require nitrogen. Most of them fail to get enough to fully realize their growth potentials without large additions of nitrogen fertilizer. However, some plants, especially legumes like alfalfa and soybeans, obtain nitrogen from the air through the work of "nitrogen fixing" bacteria in the soil. Scientists are attempting to breed bacteria that can do the same thing for other plants like corn. They are also seeking to produce new plant varieties that can utilize nitrogen directly from the air without bacterial intermediaries.

BIRTH CONTROL

One of the best things people could do for their descendants would be to sharply limit the number of them.

Olin Miller, as quoted in Reader's Digest, *November 1971*

With the exception of increased food production, there are only three possible solutions to the problem of population pressure: a rise in the death rate, a drop in the birth rate, or emigration. If we are thinking of the entire world, emigration is obviously not a solution. On the other hand, few people want to see a rise in the death rate. Nonetheless, although not adopted as a population policy, a rise in the death rate may prove to be an unintended and unwanted solution should new epidemics or thermonuclear warfare occur (Davis, 1976).

The above considerations bring us to the prospects for reducing the birth rate. In seeking to reduce birth rates, the governments of developing countries have often fallen into the "technological fallacy" that has long marked Western thinking on the matter. They have adopted a kind of blind faith in the gadgetry of contraception (for example, intrauterine coils, reversible vasectomy, "foolproof" contraceptive pills) without fully appreciating the *social* changes that may first be required; even the best technique will not be used unless people *want* to use it (Schnore, 1966; Davis, 1976). The simple truth is that people in wide areas of the world do *not* want to limit the number of children. For many, children are their chief protection against the buffetings of life. Where Social Security and state-financed health care are absent, children may constitute insurance that one will be provided for in old age. One New Delhi family-planning specialist observes:

> Look, if I were a poor man in India there's no reason on earth why I should limit my family. You want to have a son to look after you in old age, and you want a couple of them just to make sure. In event of any disaster, like being unemployed or getting old or sick, you fall back on the family. If you don't have a family, you just die. No one else is going to take care of you. (Quoted by Weinraub, 1975, p. 5)

Nor is there reason to believe that nations with the problem of population pressure are overpopulated because the people lack the know-how to have fewer children. Many societies have evolved social mechanisms for regulating population size where their people have seen a need for such regulation. In the Middle Ages, primogeniture (inheritance by the eldest son only) served to reduce population pressures in various parts of Europe (the device ensured that the farmland was not divided into even smaller and less economically viable parcels); excess sons went off on Crusades to kill heathens for Christ, ending up getting killed themselves or dying of disease. Eskimos used to "expose" excess female babies and old people to the elements, thereby inducing death; similarly, the English in the last century introduced infanticide under the euphemism "baby farming":

> When socioeconomic changes occur that make fewer children seem desirable, birth rates always start to come down *before* family planners [professionals] and birth control devices arrive on the scene. It happened in almost all of today's industrialized countries in the last century; it happened in Taiwan and South Korea recently. People just aren't all that ignorant and unenterprising—and scientists are beginning to realize it. Today, for instance, natural-products chemists are scouring

the world for "folk contraceptives," many of which are now suspected of being fairly effective and having possible commercial value. (Ehrlich and Ehrlich, 1974, p. 9)

One population expert, Kingsley Davis, suggests a number of social reforms that would reduce fertility by rewarding low fertility and penalizing high fertility:

> ... the most effective social changes would be those that offer opportunities and goals that compete with family roles. For instance, giving advantages in housing, taxes, scholarships, and recreation to single as compared to married people, would discourage early marriage. Giving special educational and employment opportunities to women would foster career interests and therefore lessen motherhood as a woman's sole commitment.... Discontinuing the custom of family names, giving more complete control over children to nursery and elementary schools while holding parents responsible for the costs.... As for methods of birth control, including abortion, these could be provided free of charge. (Davis, 1971, p. 403)

SOLVING ONE PROBLEM MAY CREATE NEW PROBLEMS

OBSERVATION Until recently my family consisted of two parents and two kids. In the past year my maternal grandmother has moved in with us. She isn't healthy enough to live by herself. She can't walk very well, her hearing is poor, and her nose runs constantly. She tries to be part of the family but she just doesn't fit in. She just belongs to another era in terms of her views, attitudes, and living style. And some of her health problems make us uncomfortable. Today grandma wanted to help mom make the turkey but my mom and the rest of us didn't want her to—we didn't want her nose dripping on the turkey, the rest of the meal, or the dishes. Maybe this seems cruel, but a progressive and gradual erosion is taking place in her welcome in our home. Nobody in our family wants her living with us but nevertheless we feel obligated to take care of her.

PRINCIPLE This situation with my grandmother highlights a problem within contemporary America. Medical science has made great strides in prolonging human life. But our society does not have a role where old people can play a significant part in human affairs. Rather they have to retire when they are 65 and then there is really not too much for them to do but mark time until they die. Further, as they get older they are more likely to develop chronic health problems and disabilities since aging takes its toll in effective bodily functioning. Yet they are not too ill to die. This has consequences for the rest of us since our society views us as having obligations toward aged relatives. And this may be quite disruptive of conjugal family functioning as in our case. Society in solving one population problem creates still another population problem. In this case the problem of a high mortality rate is solved among the younger generations but creates a new problem: what do you do with so many surviving aged people?

Of 120 developing nations, about 30 have policies aimed at limiting population; another 30 have family-planning programs nominally aimed only at social welfare; and 50 or so nations are either "neutral" or hostile to ideas of population limitation. Probably the most dramatic decline in birth rates over the last several years has come in China. The pronounced fall-off, from 32 to 19 per thousand, has resulted from family planning services (including abortion) and the reshaping of economic and social policies to encourage small families (Brown, 1976). In India, under Mrs. Indira Gandhi, a carrot and stick approach to family planning (including sterilizations coerced by the police, making employment conditional on sterilization, and cash incentives for sterilization) resulted in upwards of one million sterilizations per month (Borders, 1978). Perhaps not surprisingly, the program politically backfired, contributing to the defeat of the Gandhi government in the 1977 elections. Since then family planning has been returned to a voluntary basis.

In some nations, concern is being expressed regarding the *drop* in birth rates. Some leaders such as French President Valéry Giscard d'Estaing link national grandeur to population size. In a 1976 New Year's Eve speech, Giscard d'Estaing warned that no country with a middle-sized population could realistically aspire to grandeur: "In 1800 France was three times more populous than Britain and nearly as populated as Russia. But now!" (Now France's population stands at 52.7 million, Britain's at 56 million, and the Soviet Union's at 245 million). And Argentina, as part of a program to double its population by the end of this century, decreed in 1974 a ban on oral contraceptives (to be sold only with a prescription signed by three medical authorities) and prohibited the dissemination of birth control information.

SUMMARY

1. Three major views prevail regarding the world's population: (1) continued population and industrial growth will soon exhaust the world's minerals and bathe the biosphere in fatal levels of pollution; (2) the world's resources can expand through better use, the recyclings of existing resources, and the development of new ones; and (3) the main risks of environmental damage and the greatest pressures on natural resources stem from the economic activities of the rich nations and the exploding appetites of their inhabitants.

2. Population change can be reduced to four variables: (1) fertility (births); (2) mortality (deaths); (3) immigration (movement to an area); and (4) emigration (movement away from an area). Any factor that affects the size of population does so by influencing one or more of these demographic variables.

3. Fertility refers to the actual reproduction of a people; fecundity refers to potential reproduction. One common way to measure fertility is to calculate the number of births per 1000 of the total population in a given period. This provides the crude birth rate.

4. Mortality refers to the termination of life within a population as measured by the death rate. One common way to measure mortality is to calculate the number of deaths per 1000 of the total population at a given period. This provides the crude death rate.

5. Migration—both immigration and emigration—is the product of "push" and "pull," or, more precisely, two sets of forces: (1) one set of forces tends to produce movement away from the habitat already occupied, and (2) one set of forces attracts the prospective migrant toward an alternative habitat.

6. Sociologists are interested in how a people are distributed in space. Depending on the sociologist's purpose, the "where" may be a large area such as a continent, or a small area such as a city block. Changes in numbers and proportions of people living in various areas are the cumulative effect of differences in fertility, mortality, and net migration rates.

7. Sociologists are interested not only in the size and spatial distribution of a population but also in its composition or characteristics. A variety of traits distinguish individuals from one another and are useful for classifying populations into basic categories. Among these characteristics are age, sex, rural-urban residence, race, education, income, marital status, occupation, religion, and national origin.

8. Thomas Robert Malthus argued that agricultural production tends to increase in arithmetical progression whereas population has a tendency to increase in geometrical progression. Based on this formulation, Malthus took a dim view of the future, considering famine, war, and pestilence as the chief deterrents to excessive population growth. Many questions have been raised through the years regarding the Malthusian thesis. There is no clear evidence that food always and everywhere can increase only in an arithmetic ratio. Critics also note that Malthus overlooked the part that contraception can play as a preventive check on population growth.

9. The world average per capita diet is expected to improve slightly between 1970 and 1985. Still, the food situation is precarious in some parts of the world. Further, when we look closely at the developing nations, we find a variety of handicaps to sustained rises in agricultural productivity. However, long-term projections of food resources have been quite unreliable. Just what the future holds in terms of developments in agricultural technology and organization remains to be seen.

10. In seeking to reduce birth rates, governments of developing countries have often fallen into the "technological fallacy" that has long marked Western thinking on the matter. They have adopted a kind of blind faith in the gadgetry of contraception without fully appreciating the social changes that may first be required; even the best technique will not be used unless people want to use it.

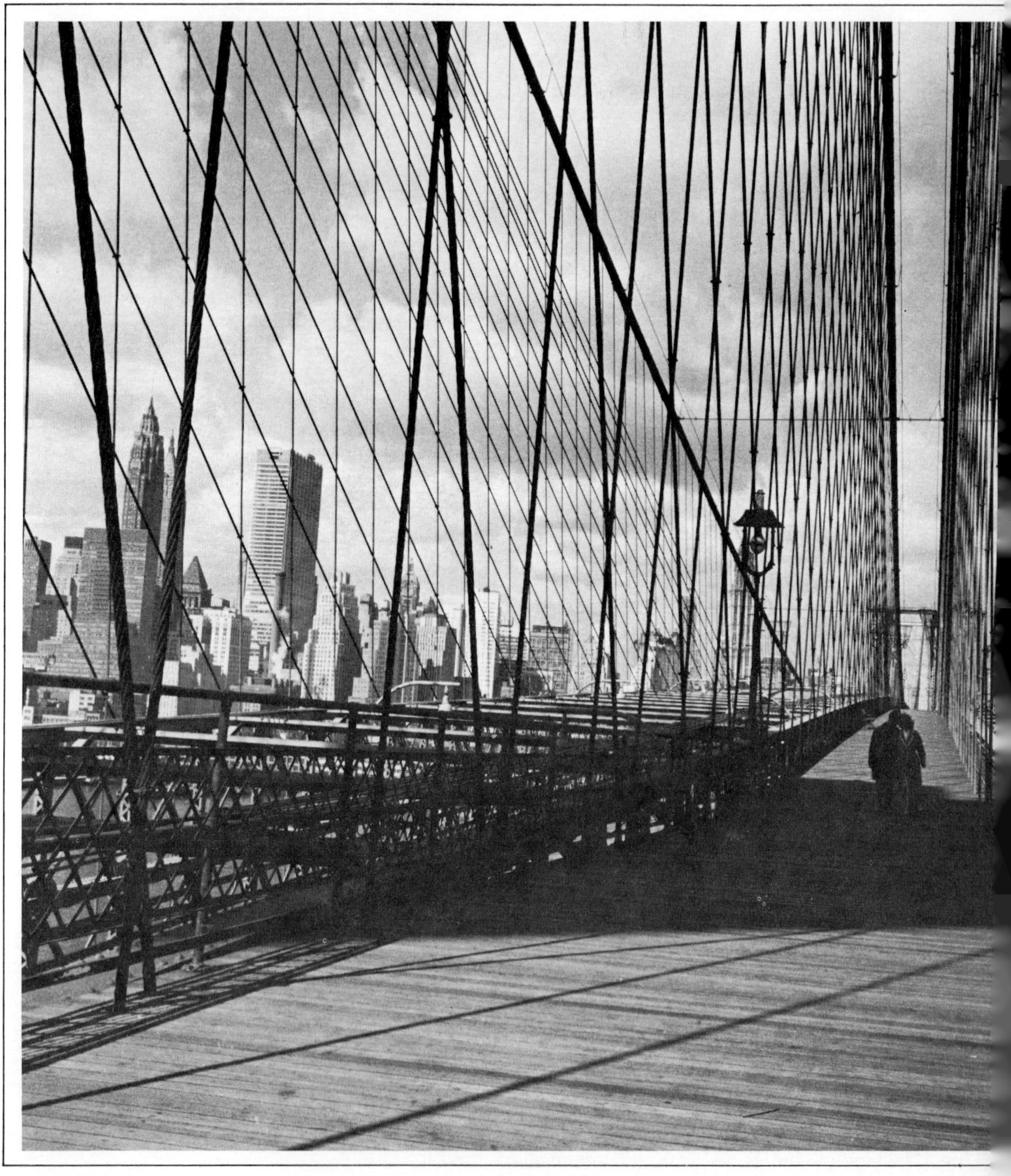

17
URBAN SOCIETY

ECOLOGY

ORIGIN AND EVOLUTION OF CITIES
　The Preindustrial City
　The Industrial-Urban Center
　The Metropolitan City

URBAN TRENDS AND PATTERNS IN THE UNITED STATES
　Suburbanization
　Central Cities in Difficulty
　Patterns of Urban Growth
　Ecological Processes
　Social Consequences of Urbanism

586 Demography and Urbanization

OBSERVATION I generally park on one of the side streets east of campus on Monday and Wednesday since I find that I can usually park closer to the building housing my 8 o'clock class than if I park in one of the student parking facilities on campus. I have observed that many of the large houses and apartments in this area are coming to be occupied by Blacks. Originally these dwellings housed university faculty members and others of the middle class. As the years passed, the newer faculty made their homes in the suburbs. In time most of these homes were turned into rooming houses and apartments for students. Now the area is shifting again toward a nonstudent population.

PRINCIPLE "Invasion" is occurring as a new type of people encroaches on an area occupied by a different type. The area appears to be undergoing a third phase in transitional use. Soon succession will likely occur and the "invasion" will be complete. The process won't stop. It seems probable that a new "invasion" of some other sort will occur. It may be, for instance, that university buildings will encroach on the area as the university expands outside its current boundaries.

Although *Homo sapiens* has inhabited the earth anywhere from 50,000 to 1,000,000 years, humans did not begin to live in cities until some 5500 years ago. Urbanized societies are an even more recent development and represent a new phase in human social evolution. "The large and dense agglomerations comprising the urban population," writes Kingsley Davis, ". . . exceed in size the communities of any other large animal; they suggest the behavior of communal insects rather than of mammals" (1967:4). Indeed, before 1850 no society could be described as predominantly urbanized, and by 1900 only Great Britain could be so regarded. Today, all industrialized nations are highly urbanized, and throughout the world the process of urbanization is accelerating rapidly. United Nations experts predict that by the year 2000, some 50 percent of the world's population will live in urban areas. This compares with 39 percent now. There will be at least 60 cities with 5 million or more people, compared with the current 21 cities. Mexico City, now third-ranking in size, is expected to swell to the world's largest metropolitan area with 32 million inhabitants.

In the world's developing nations the mass movement to cities has been largely chaotic and unorganized, creating severe problems. Calcutta, India, provides a good illustration of this. The city's sewerage system was dug between 1896 and 1905 to serve a population of 600,000. Little has since been added to the system and its operating effectiveness has been seriously impaired by the accumulation of seven million tons of silt. Uncollected "night-soil" from the city's 40,000 public privies pollutes the air and frequently overflows into the public water supply. Further, sewage seeps into cracks in the 700 miles of Calcutta's crumbling water mains. Streetcar service is deteriorating and is now capable of carrying only three-quarters as many passengers as twenty years ago when the population was only half its current size. The threat of breakdown in essential services is constant. The unemployment rate exceeds 30 percent, a problem aggravated by the drop in factory jobs since 1965. Nonetheless, Calcutta's population continues to grow, swollen by a high Indian birth rate and by peasants fleeing from rural poverty. In 1985, the United Nations projects a population of 12 million for the city (Wilsher, 1975).

ECOLOGY

> Man can improve the quality of his life, not by imposing himself on nature as a conqueror, but by participating in the continuous act of creation in which all living things are engaged. Otherwise, he may be doomed to survive as something less than human.
>
> René Dubos, as quoted in Life, July 28, 1970

In considering urban life, we find it useful to view humanity within the context of its habitat (Catton and Dunlap, 1978). Humans, among other things, are physical beings. As such, their very nature requires that they be located within space in some sort of physical environment—within an ecological complex. In its broadest sense, the concept of **ecology** refers to the mutual relations between organisms and their environment—in brief, to the total web of life wherein all plant and animal species (including humans) *reciprocally* interact with one another and with the physical features of their habitat.

By way of illustration, consider the links that bind together fish and their marine environment. In surface waters fish excrete organic waste that is converted by marine bacteria to inorganic products; in turn, the latter are nutrients for algal growth; the algae then are eaten by the fish, completing the cycle. Such a cyclical process achieves the self-purification of the environmental system, in that wastes produced in one step in the cycle become the necessary raw materials for the next step. But if sufficiently stressed by an external agency, a cycle may eventually go haywire and be strangled. Thus, if the water cycle is overloaded with sewage and industrial effluents, the amount of oxygen needed to support waste decomposition by the bacteria of decay may be greater than the oxygen available in the water. Lacking the needed oxygen, the marine bacteria die and this phase of the cycle stops, halting the cycle as a whole. In this fashion pollution has made Lake Erie virtually a "dead sea." Similarly, sewage, industrial wastes, and oil pollutants are killing all the oceans of the world, although the size of the job has prevented us from killing the seas as fast as we killed Lake Erie.

Illustrations abound of the reciprocal impact that exists between human beings and their physical environment. For instance, a United Nations report indicates that human misuse of land has converted to desert 6.7 percent of

588 Demography and Urbanization

Asphalt jungles? Critics often charge that contemporary cities are barren, asphalt jungles that have destroyed many of the positive bonds existing between human beings and nature.

Patrick Reddy

the earth's surface, an area larger than Brazil (Hill, 1976). In Asia, Africa, and Latin America, about 60 million people live directly on the interfaces of deserts and arable land. The destructive overworking of these marginal lands for crops, grazing, and firewood has resulted in "desert creep." Much of this "desertification" is not attributable to basic climatic changes (for instance, North African weather records reveal no evidence of a decline in rainfall over the past century). Rather a vicious circle operates in which people intensify their exploitation of the land so as to compensate for desert creep, only to compound their problems as this misuse in turn feeds new desert expansion. Much the same thing is happening in the highlands of Asia, Africa, and Latin America where fragile mountain ecosystems are irreversibly destroyed by woodcutting, excessive cropping, and grazing (Eckholm, 1975).

Otis Dudley Duncan (1959; 1961), a sociologist, provides us with a good illustration of how each element in the ecological system is tied to and influences the others in his consideration of air pollution in Los Angeles. He distinguishes four elements in the ecological complex: population, (social) organization, environment, and technology (P, O, E, T). Let us consider his illustration more carefully.

During the 1940s, residents of Los Angeles began experiencing episodes of a bluish-gray haze in the atmosphere that reduced visibility and produced irritation in the eyes and respiratory tract (E→P); the smog also damaged growing plants (E→E) and cracked rubber, accelerating automobile tire deterioration (E→T). In response to the smog problem, various civic movements were organized, abatement officers were designated in the city and county health departments, and a control ordinance was promulgated (E→O). The California legislature established the Los Angeles County Air Pollution Control District (APCD), which was authorized to conduct research and to exercise broad regulatory powers. At the instance of the APCD, a variety of abatement devices were installed in industrial plants (O→T). Meanwhile, chemists and engineers developed and confirmed the "factory in the sky" theory of smog formation. Combustion and related processes release unburned hydrocarbons and oxides of nitrogen into the atmosphere that, when subjected to strong sunlight, form smog (T→E). Also implicated in the problem is the frequent occurrence of temperature inversion in the southern California area, which serves to prevent polluted air from rising very far above ground level (E→E). The problem was accentuated by the rapid growth of population in the Los Angeles area, spreading out over a wide territory (P→E), and thereby heightening the population's dependence on the automobile as the primary means of local movement (T→O). Duncan concludes: "Where could one find a more poignant instance of the principle of circular causation, so central to ecological theory, than that of the Los Angelenos speeding down their freeways in a rush to escape the smog produced by emissions from the very vehicles conveying them?" (1961:146). Let us continue our examination of our urban environment by turning to a consideration of the origin and evolution of cities.

ELEMENTS IN THE ECOLOGICAL COMPLEX

After reading the chapter on Urban Society, it occurred to me how the four elements in the ecological complex — population, social organization, environment, and technology (POET) — can be seen as operating in the current energy crisis. The United States has a large population that has ruthlessly exploited environmental resources (P→E) and depleted many traditional sources of energy. Due to the crisis, the federal government issued restrictions on driving (mandatory 55 mile speed limit, closing gas stations on Sundays), setting thermostats at 68 degrees, and conserving electricity (O→T). The government is also frantically working on new techniques to harness new sources and forms of energy (O→T→E). The population has to change its lifestyle in order to cope with the new situation of energy curtailment (E→T). Thus one can see that no one element exists independently of the others but rather they act on one another.

ORIGIN AND EVOLUTION OF CITIES

Perhaps the two most significant phenomena of human history have been first, the tendency of man to expand into an existing niche and second, his tendency to expand the niche itself once an old niche has become tight. This is what has brought us from the paleolithic to the neolithic to civilization, and now to post-civilization.

Kenneth E. Boulding, Zoom, Gloom, Doom, and Room, *1973*

We tend to take our cities for granted. Certainly one of the most striking aspects of the modern era is urbanization. The urban mode of life extends far beyond the immediate boundaries of metropolitan areas. Many of the characteristics as well as the problems of modern societies are rooted in an urban existence. Yet, as we noted earlier, cities constitute a relatively recent development in human history.

THE PREINDUSTRIAL CITY

It was not until the Neolithic Period that technological conditions became ripe for the existence of settled communities. Although it is difficult for us today to imagine a world without agriculture and animal husbandry, it must be emphasized that these were nonetheless innovations, and critical innovations at that. With these innovations, humans became a partner with nature instead of a parasite on nature. Humans derived the ability to "produce" food, augmenting their own food supply and providing the foundation for population expansion. This new aggressive approach toward the environment did not stop short at producing new food supplies. Other hallmarks of the Neolithic Period were pottery, weaving, and an enlarged assortment of stone tools (Childe, 1941; 1942).

Yet Neolithic population density was hardly a matter of town concentration but rather a matter of small villages scattered over the land. What then had to be added to the Neolithic complex to make possible the first towns? Between 6000 and 4000 B.C., additional inventions, such as the ox-drawn plow and the wheeled cart, the sailboat, metallurgy, irrigation, and the domestication of new plants, facilitated—when taken together—a more intensive and more productive use of Neolithic innovations. When this enriched technology was employed in certain unusual regions where climate, soil, water, and topography were most favorable, the result was a sufficiently productive economy to make possible the concentration in one place of people who did not grow their own food. Such favoring conditions prevailed in broad river valleys with alluvial soil not exhausted by successive use, with a dry climate that minimized soil leaching, with plenty of sunshine, and with sediment-containing water for irrigation from the river itself, such as was found in Mesopotamia, the Nile Valley of Egypt, the Indus Valley of India, and the Yellow River Basin of China (Davis, 1955).

A productive economy, however, though necessary, is not sufficient for the growth of cities. Instead of producing a surplus for city dwellers, the cultivators can, at least in theory, multiply on the land until they end up producing just enough to sustain themselves. Hence, the rise of towns and cities also required a form of social organization in which certain strata could appropriate for themselves part of the produce grown by the cultivators, for instance, religious personnel, government officials, traders, and artisans (Davis, 1955).

It is important to stress that preindustrial cities were at best generally feeble prototypes of contemporary cities. In areas where cities existed, usually no more than 10 percent, and perhaps less than 5 percent, of the population were able to live in the urban settlements. Cities of 100,000 or more were rare, though under certain favorable social and economic conditions, some surpassed this size. Rome in the second century A.D., Constantinople as the later political successor to Rome, Baghdad before A.D. 1000, the cities of Sung China between A.D. 1100 and 1300, and Tokyo, Kyoto, and Osaka in seventeenth- and eighteenth-century Japan all had populations well above 100,000, and in some cases, possibly even 1,000,000. However, most preindustrial cities, including many important ones, had populations of 5000 to 10,000 (Sjoberg, 1960).

The size of preindustrial cities was generally restricted by a number of factors. First, transportation (both vehicles and roads) was a limiting factor, being ill-equipped to bear food, fibers, and other bulky materials for long distances to cities and nonadapted to the preservation of perishable commodities (e.g., foodstuffs). Second, early cities had difficulty securing their hinterlands; they were constantly threatened and frequently conquered by neighboring towns and nonurban peoples—indeed, mighty Rome in due course itself succumbed to foreign invaders. Third, in the absence of modern

Wall surrounding preindustrial city. In medieval cities, such as Langres, France, walls surrounded a portion of the community and the gates were closed at night.

Courtesy of Exxon Corporation

medicine and sanitation, urban living was often deadly (its water supply was frequently polluted by sewage wastes, and, as commercial centers, cities attracted transients who often served as carriers of contagious diseases). And fourth, the fixity of the peasant on the land (through caste, serf, and slave arrangements) minimized rural–urban migration. These and other factors served to make early cities small affairs (Davis, 1955).

What were preindustrial cities like? Gideon Sjoberg (1955), an authority on the matter, tells us that their streets were usually mere passageways for people and for animals used in transport. Crowded conditions prevailed, fostering serious sanitation problems. Even more significant, rigid social segregation typically led to the formation of "quarters" or "wards." In some cities (e.g., Fez, Morocco, and Aleppo, Syria), these sectors were sealed off from each other by walls and their gates were locked at night. The quarters reflected the sharp local social divisions of ethnic and occupational groupings, each group typically residing apart from others. Lower-class and "outcaste" groups lived on the city's periphery. Despite rigid ecological segregation, however, there was no real specialization of land use such as is functionally necessary in industrial–urban communities. In medieval Europe, for instance, city dwellings often served as workshops, and religious structures were used as schools or marketing centers. Finally, the "business district" did not enjoy the position or dominance found in the industrial–urban community (for example, in the Middle East the principal mosque and in medieval Europe the cathedral usually served as the focal point of the community).

THE INDUSTRIAL-URBAN CENTER

Urbanization has proceeded much faster and reached proportions far greater during the past 160 years or so than at any previous time in world history. It is estimated that between 1800 and the present, the percentage of the world's population living in cities increased from about 2 percent to 39 percent. In 1800, there were fewer than 50 cities with 100,000 or more inhabitants; by 1950, there were close to 900 such cities.

Both technological and social factors contributed to the accelerated growth of cities. That complex series of events termed "the Industrial Revolution" enabled humans to use steam as a source of energy, making possible for the first time the widespread introduction of machines. The introduction of power-driven machines drew manufacturing out of the home and placed it in a centralized location, the factory. As the factory system expanded, more workers were required; to the factories flocked rural people, attracted not only by the novelty of city life but by the possibilities of greater economic rewards. Urban development, however, advanced not only as a response to industrialization but as a consequence of transformations in the social structure. In Europe, city growth was stimulated by the demise of feudal systems of government and the emergence of nation-states. Under the impetus of nationalism, large areas were consolidated, making for larger internal markets, integrated transportation sytems, common coinage and weights, and an absence of frequent duties on goods, all developments favoring commerce and hence city growth (Gist and Fava, 1964).

THE METROPOLITAN CITY

During the industrial–urban phase, cities for the most part were widely scattered centers that, although politically and militarily dominating the hinterlands, had only tenuous economic and social relations with them. In place of this pattern, there emerged in the metropolitan phase a multiplicity of interrelated cities embracing every aspect of the political, economic, and social lives of the citizenry. The technological base for the metropolitan phase of urbanism is found in the great increase in the application of science to industry, the widespread use of electric power (freeing industry from the limitations imposed on plant location by steam and belt-and-pulley modes of power), and the advent of modern forms of transportation (the automobile and rapid transit released cities from the limitations imposed by foot and hoof travel, which had more or less restricted city growth to a radius of 3 miles from the center). This third phase does not represent a sharp break with the second (industrial–urban centers), but rather a widening and deepening of technical influences in every aspect of life.

The tendency for the urban agglomeration to cling to the industrial base under steam and belt-and-pulley power had, by the beginning of the twentieth century, produced great congestion in urban areas. But, increasingly, a number of factors built up to buck the centripetal pressures, such as rising city taxes, increased land values, traffic and transport problems, and decayed and obsolescent inner zones. These and other forces served to accelerate the centrifugal movement made technologically possible by electric power, rapid transit, the automobile, and the telephone. The result was the development of satellite and suburban areas, in brief, the growth of large metropolitan complexes (Hauser, 1957).

URBAN TRENDS AND PATTERNS IN THE UNITED STATES

Our national flower is the concrete cloverleaf.
Lewis Mumford, quoted in Quote, *October 8, 1961*

As the United States enters its third century, the nation is experiencing major population shifts with fundamental consequences for its cities. The largest population increases are occurring in the South and the West. In the East and portions of the industrial Midwest, urban growth is slowing and in some cases the population is actually declining (in New York, Pittsburgh, Detroit, Newark, and Cleveland). These shifts are bringing with them basic changes in national economic and political power patterns, with a weakening of the position of the Northern states that have been the base of population and power since the nation's infancy.

SUBURBANIZATION

Following World War II, when the trickle of people out of central cities became a tide, the stereotype of suburbia arose. Despite their diversity, the suburbs became framed in the American mind as the land of green velvet lawns, two-car garages, swimming pools, the bridge-club set, picture windows, and Republicanism. Yet such a stereotype is unreal. The homogenized, split-level image makes up only a fragment of the new America of 84 million people that has grown up around the nation's inner cities. Although most Americans still speak of suburbs, they are no longer just bedroom communities. Indeed, they are no longer *sub*. The contemporary suburb differs from its earlier namesake in both function and form (Rosenthal, 1971a; 1971b; Weaver, 1977).

They are broad, ballooning bands, interlinked by beltways, that constitute cities in their own right. In population, jobs, investment, construction, and stores they rival the old inner cities. They are the sites of industrial plants, fine stores, independent newspapers, theaters, restaurants, corporate offices and office towers, superhotels, and big-league stadiums. Although once characterized by tract homes, schools, and flat shopping centers, some suburbs are now the scene of industrial parks and high-rise office buildings, apartments, and condominiums. By 1977, 39.1 percent of Americans lived in suburbs, 28.5 percent in central cities, and 32.4 percent elsewhere.

A common American image is that of the radial city, in which residents go downtown to work in the morning and return home at night. But former "bedroom towns" are being transformed into places where residents both sleep and work. Increasingly, more people who live in suburbs also work in them. For instance, none of the New York counties surrounding New York Citys' five boroughs now sends even half of its workers to jobs in the city. Nassau County has less than 40 percent of its residents traveling to New York City to earn a living. Westchester has less than 32 percent and Suffolk County less than 20 percent. The picture is not too different for other of the nation's large cities. Indeed, between 1960 and 1970, most of the nation's largest cities lost jobs while their suburbs gained: New York City lost 9.7 percent of its jobs, while its suburbs gained 24.9 percent; Los Angeles lost 10.8 percent, while its suburbs gained 16.2 percent; Chicago lost 13.9 percent, while its suburbs gained 64.4 percent; Detroit lost 22.5 percent, while its suburbs gained 61.5 percent. Although San Francisco and Oakland made a minute gain of 0.4 percent, their suburbs gained 22.7 percent. Washington, D.C., gained 1.9 percent in jobs, but its suburbs gained a spectacular 117.9 percent. Preliminary figures for the 1970s suggest that these trends have continued, and, in some cases, accelerated.

The movement of industrial and commercial employment away from central cities has influenced the process of suburban growth. It has contributed to new patterns of suburban differentiation. This has found expression in stratification by both social class and fiscal wealth. Generally "industrial" suburbs enjoy lower social status than do "residential" suburbs. Some suburbs (such as Beverly Hills, Sands Point, West Palm Beach, and Lake Forest) have attempted to restrict industrial and commercial development through zoning and land-use controls so as to maintain "quality" communities (Molotch, 1976; Logan, 1976).

Currently an estimated 70 cents of every retail dollar is spent in the suburbs. Houston is not untypical. Sakowitz' downtown department store had 70 percent of the company's sales in 1962 while its only suburban store did 30 percent of the business. Ten years later the downtown store accounted for only 30 percent of the trade, and three suburban stores contributed 70 percent of the sales. Foley's department store had a similar pattern. And Neiman-Marcus, once a pillar of Houston's downtown business district, moved to a suburban location in 1969. The story is not too different elsewhere. More and more people say that they no longer go downtown to shop. Increasingly, residents of the suburbs relate to the central city as a place to visit and enjoy, much in the fashion of tourists—to see an annual parade, to take in a play, and to go to a museum or gallery. There is even a strong trend for stadiums to move to the suburbs—thus the professional football New York Giants are the "Hackensack" Giants and the Detroit Lions are the "Pontiac" Lions. And other avenues of entertainment—theaters and restaurants—are migrating to the outer cities.

A common trait of outer cities is a tendency to turn inward, a determination to shut out the "decay" and "social problems" of the central city. Many of the people of the outer cities have formed unfavorable stereotypes of inner-city life. They feel threatened by what they view as a haven of crime and drugs, pollution, high density, substandard schools, and "alien" people.

The Black population is growing in suburban rings (Roof and Spain, 1977). However, Blacks often encounter resistance to their movement into the suburbs. This resistance is couched in new terminology and techniques that nonetheless mean "keep out," such as opposition to "high density" developments, "low-income" housing, and "forced integration." For the larger share of Blacks who technically make it to "suburbia," the movement has been to municipalities that are just a political dividing line from the central city's ghetto. More often than not it has meant little more than exchanging one hand-me-down neighborhood for another.

The broad multilane beltways and expressways that ring most large cities have in their own way become the new main streets of the outer cities. The sleek new highways, begun under the Eisenhower Administration, make an interlinked outer city literally possible. In many cases the residents use the suburbs collectively as a city, a centerless city. One California woman observes: "I live in Garden Grove, work in Irvine, shop in Santa Ana, go to the dentist in Anaheim, my husband works in Long Beach, and I used to be president of the League of Women Voters in Fullerton" (Rosenthal, 1971a:28). And in New York, a Nassau County woman indicates: "We live in East Meadow. I work in Garden City. My husband works in Syosset. We shop for clothes in Hempstead. My husband's Phythias Lodge meets in Great Neck. Our temple is in Merrick. The children's doctor is in Westbury. And we pay our parking tickets in Mineola" (Rosenthal, 1971b:35).

Overall, there is a Balkanization of government and authority—a tendency toward fragmentation and centerlessness. In the four New York counties closest to the city of New York—Nassau, Suffolk, Rockland, and Westchester—there are 548 governmental units, including municipal, town, and village governments and a variety of "special districts," such as school, hospital, cemetery, sewage, park, and library districts. Each of these is administratively and fiscally independent, and 545 of them have taxing power.

As the population of our metropolitan centers has grown, the space consumed by urban development has progressively expanded. Many people have sought to escape the mounting congestion of the central cities through movement to satellite and suburban areas. But the effort to escape mounting congestion simply creates more congestion; it is self-defeating. Families want ranch houses on half-acre plots; retailers want one-floor supermarkets and acres for parking; manufacturers want one-floor factories and parklike grounds; and motorists want eight-lane superhighways and cloverleaf turns. As each new area fills us, the quest for space takes the suburbs farther out. In time, the home that once was "in the country" or in "a pleasant suburb" becomes a dot in a continuous sea of housing developments and shopping centers.

Loss of rural areas to urbanization. As urban areas spread outward merging with one another, rural interstices are devoured by the urbanizing process.

Patrick Reddy

598 Demography and Urbanization

As a result of these trends, the rural interstices between metropolitan centers fill up with urban development, making for a "strip city" or "megalopolis." The Northeastern Seaboard is a good illustration of this. The "Bos-Wash Megalopolis" lies along a 600 mile axis from southern New Hampshire to northern Virginia, covering 10 states, 117 counties, 32 cities larger than 500,000, and embracing some 38 million people (Miller, 1975). Population projections suggest that by the year 2050, another urbanized strip will extend from New York State through Pennsylvania, Ohio, northern Indiana and Illinois to Green Bay, Wisconsin, and Minneapolis-St. Paul. Farther South, a continuous urban belt will link much of Florida and the Gulf Coast states through Alabama to eastern Texas. In the Far West, a similar strip will stretch from Arizona through most of California, with a gap before picking up again in the Northwest all the way to Seattle. Figure 17.1 depicts urban population projections for year 2000, only thirty years from now.

Figure 17.1. Megalopolises, year 2000. Population projections suggest that the urban strips depicted in the map above will characterize many parts of the United States in the year 2000.

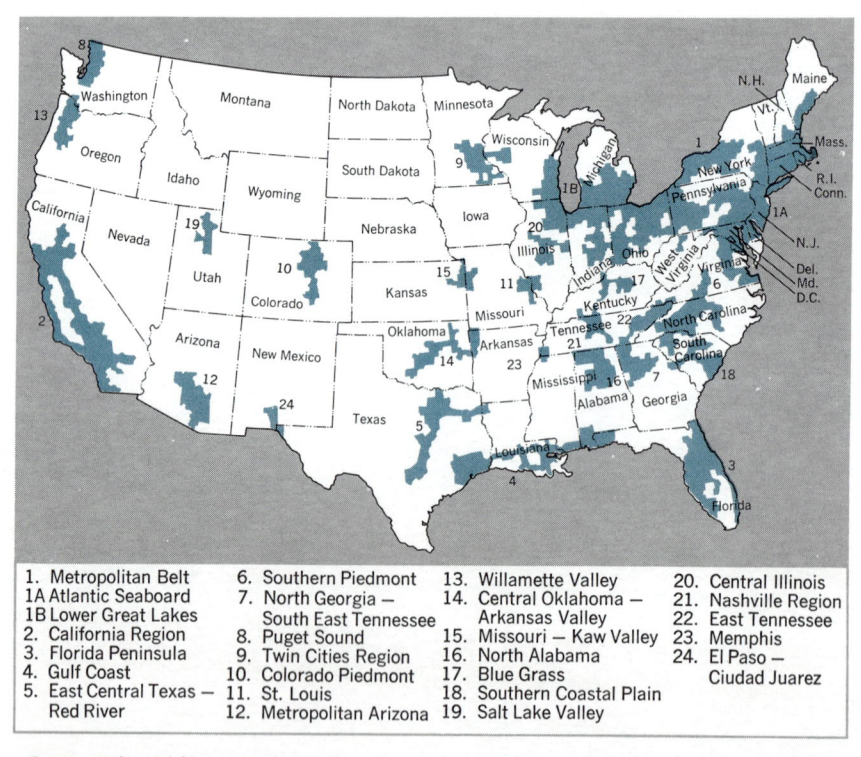

1. Metropolitan Belt
1A. Atlantic Seaboard
1B. Lower Great Lakes
2. California Region
3. Florida Peninsula
4. Gulf Coast
5. East Central Texas — Red River
6. Southern Piedmont
7. North Georgia — South East Tennessee
8. Puget Sound
9. Twin Cities Region
10. Colorado Piedmont
11. St. Louis
12. Metropolitan Arizona
13. Willamette Valley
14. Central Oklahoma — Arkansas Valley
15. Missouri — Kaw Valley
16. North Alabama
17. Blue Grass
18. Southern Coastal Plain
19. Salt Lake Valley
20. Central Illinois
21. Nashville Region
22. East Tennessee
23. Memphis
24. El Paso — Ciudad Juarez

Source: Adapted from *Population Growth and American Future.* Washington, D.C.: Government Printing Office.

CENTRAL CITIES IN DIFFICULTY

We will neglect our cities to our peril, for in neglecting them we neglect the nation.
John F. Kennedy, message to Congress, January 30, 1962

We hear a good deal nowadays about the problems of American cities. The continuing fiscal plight of New York City is perhaps the best known. But other cities, especially those comprising the older Northern crescent from Maine to the Great Lakes, are also losing population, industry, jobs, payrolls, bank deposits, credit ratings, and tax bases (Wooten, 1976). In some respects the officials of these cities find themselves in circumstances paralleling those of the manager of an aging mansion who must keep up all the rooms while the inhabitants dwindle in number and affluence.

Indeed, for some the weather-beaten plywood board is increasingly replacing the gleaming steel and glass skyscraper as a symbol of the American city (Flint, 1971). The suburbs have pirated from the city many of its functions and people. Some functions are still left to the inner city as rapid high-rise office development in many cities testifies; insurance companies, banks, investment firms, and government complexes have found it juridically difficult to leave. But other institutions are virtually deserting the central cities. For those remaining in the central cores—the Black ghettos and the poor and even middle-class areas around them—it is harder to buy food as the big supermarkets are going and the old "mom-and-pop" grocery, candy, and drug stores, barber shops, meat markets, and neighborhood bakeries are boarded up or torn down; it is harder to find a dentist or doctor (in the last ten years Newark has lost half its physicians); harder to buy a newspaper; call a taxi; find a pleasant park, a good restaurant, or a first-run theater (in Newark, there is not a single first-run theater left in the entire city of 400,000). And some argue that the cities are no longer capable of fulfilling one of their historic functions—assimilating immigrants into the economic mainstream. This assimilation occurred in entry-level jobs in a variety of industries, such as New York City's garment district. But many of these jobs have now been exported to South Korea, Hong Kong, and Taiwan and new industries are not being incubated to replace them.

There are those who press the moral argument of unfairness. A city planner in Baltimore complains: "The city of Baltimore makes the suburbs possible because we carry the burdens of the old, poor, black and deviants. Why should we keep carrying the burden" (Rosenthal, 1971a:28). Suburbs must, they argue, take their share of the social welfare task now being left almost entirely to impoverished—indeed bankrupted—central cities. They criticize those suburbanites who quote with unabashed candor the old troopship cry, "Pull up the ladder, Jack, I'm on board." Taking the argument a step further, there are those who criticize the city for functioning as a reservation for the poor, the deviant, the unwanted, and those who make a business or career on managing them (Keeping them "safe") for the rest of society — the model of inmates and keepers, people economically dependent on transfer payments from the outside society made in consideration of custodial services rendered. These critics call for a politics of colonial emancipation, self-help, and the development of a viable internal economy (Long, 1971).

The difficulty experienced by the inner city are not merely the product of middle-class Americans fleeing from the poor and the Blacks to the suburbs (Weaver, 1977). The aging downtowns of hundreds of smaller cities have been quietly deteriorating and declining. In the downtowns of Janesville (Wisconsin), Portland (Maine), Selma (Alabama), and Rochester (Minnesota) the streets and buildings are often antiquated and unable to cope with today's traffic and merchandising needs:

> People do not really flee from the Janesvilles of America. They may leave in search of greater opportunity, more excitement or a different quality of life, but they're not running away from high crime rates, exorbitant rents, and noise and crush of the city or a tide of minority-group immigration. Most of them, in fact, do not leave: they merely spread out a bit. (Kneeland, 1972, p. 1)

But the net result is that the old downtowns, once the primary shopping and service centers for wide areas, are losing businesses and office users just as surely as their metropolitan cousins.

Many of this nation's urban policies and programs have had unforeseen detrimental consequences and in some cases have contributed to the very

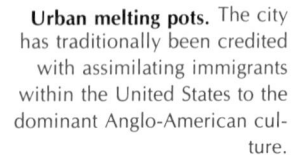

Urban melting pots. The city has traditionally been credited with assimilating immigrants within the United States to the dominant Anglo-American culture.

Patrick Reddy

problems they were supposed to cure. Federal water and sewer grants have encouraged development in the suburbs and not in cities. Federal mortgage insurance has lured homebuyers outside central cities. Superhighway systems have knifed through residential neighborhoods, weakening their social fabric, while expediting the movement of suburbanites between homes and jobs. And a Civil Service Commission survey reveals that in seven major metropolises, the proportion of the federal jobs that were located in the central city fell to 56 percent in 1975 from 65 percent in 1967; the percentage in the suburbs rose during this same period to 44 percent from 35 percent (Hyatt, 1977).

PATTERNS OF URBAN GROWTH

A clash of doctrines is not a disaster—it is an opportunity.
  Alfred North Whitehead

A number of theories have been advanced in an attempt to explain observed regularities in the spatial distribution of people and their institutions within the modern metropolis. Three theories dealing with the ecological patterns of urban growth have gained particular attention: (1) the "concentric zone theory" of Ernest W. Burgess and his associates at the University of Chicago, (2) the "sector theory" of Homer Hoyt, and (2) the "multiple nuclei theory" of C. D. Harris and Edward L. Ullman. Figure 17.2 graphically depicts these approaches. Let us examine each of them in turn.

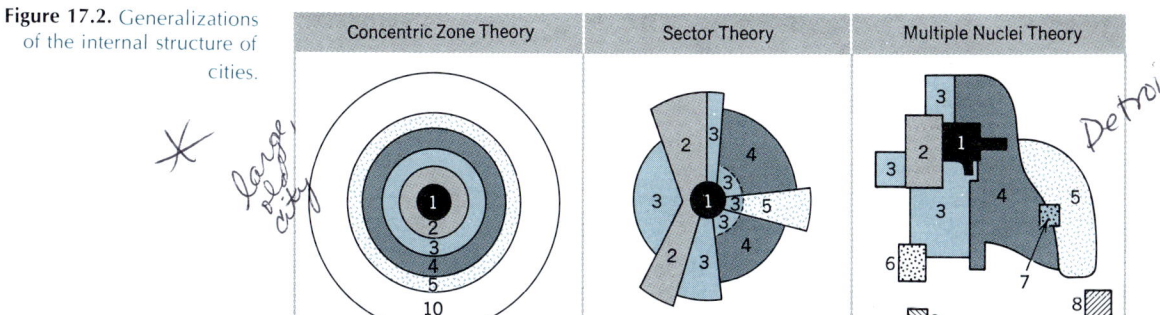

Figure 17.2. Generalizations of the internal structure of cities.

Three generalizations of the internal structure of cities
Districts:

1. Central Business District
2. Wholesale Light Manufacturing
3. Low-Class Residential
4. Medium-Class Residential
5. High-Class Residential
6. Heavy Manufacturing
7. Outlying Business District
8. Residential Suburb
9. Industrial Suburb
10. Commuters' Zone

Source: Reprinted from "The Nature of Cities" by Chauncey D. Harris and Edward L. Ullman in Volume 242 of *The Annals of The American Academy of Political and Social Science.* © 1945 by The American Academy of Political and Social Science.

The "Concentric Circle Theory." In the period between World Wars I and II, the University of Chicago occupied a dominant position within American sociology. Prominent in the scholarly enterprise of the Chicago sociologists was the study of Chicago itself. Chicago was viewed as a "social laboratory," and was subjected to intensive and systematic study. Included in these studies were investigations of juvenile gangs, immigrant ghettos, wealthy Gold Coast and slum life, taxi-dance halls, prostitution, and mental disorders. The concentric circle theory enjoyed an important place in a good deal of this work (Park, Burgess, and McKenzie, 1925). The Chicago group help that the modern city assumes a pattern of concentric circles, each with certain distinguishing characteristics:

1. *Zone 1: the central business district.* At the center of the city is situated the main business district, containing retail stores, financial institutions, hotels, theaters, and other businesses that cater to the needs of downtown shoppers. In the upper floors of skyscrapers are the offices of the most important business organizations and professional people. In Chicago, this area is called the "Loop"; in New York, the "Midtown" and "Downtown" areas; and in Pittsburgh, the "Golden Triangle."

2. *Zone 2: the zone in transition.* Surrounding the central business district is an area of residential deterioration caused by the encroachment of business and industry. In bygone days, this section usually contained the pretentious homes of the city's most wealthy and prominent people. In later years these dwellings came to be used as rooming houses and offices for persons and businesses that could not afford the rentals of the central business district. Warehouses, light industries, and a variety of marginal business establishments (pawnshops, secondhand stores, and more modest restaurants and taverns) tended to cluster here. Usually a slum area, it contained the city's Chinatown, Little Poland, and Black ghetto, and the residences of social outcasts including prostitutes and criminals, and resorts of gambling, and bootlegging, and sexual vice.

3. *Zone 3: the zone of workingmen's homes.* The zone in transition shades into this zone, which consists largely of a residential area of low to medium rentals. The homes are superior to those of the second zone but fall short of the residential districts of the middle classes. Two-flat, old single dwellings, and inexpensive apartments are typical of this zone. As its names implies, it is an area populated largely by workers.

4. *Zones 4 and 5: residential zones.* Beyond the zone occupied by the working classes is a broad area populated mainly by small business proprietors, professional people, and clerical and managerial personnel. Here the homes are generally of the single-dwelling variety.

5. *Zone 10: the commuters' zone.* Out beyond the areas of better residence is a ring of encircling small cities, towns, and hamlets. These towns and hamlets often bear the names of "brook," "park," "hills," and "heights" — for instance, Meadowbrook, Oak Park, Yorkshire Hills, and Walnut Heights.

The zone in transition. According to the Chicago group of sociologists, a belt surrounds the central business district, which is occupied by marginal businesses and minority ghettos.

Patrick Reddy

Burgess noted that these zones constitute ideal types; no city conforms absolutely to the overall scheme. Rather, the approach provides a frame of reference and theory—a model in which there is a direct relationship between social status and distance of residence from the center of the city. Topography, rivers, lakes, hills, and escarpments serve to distort the actual zonal pattern of a city. In the case of Chicago, the city borders on Lake Michigan so that concentric semicircular rather than circular areas prevail.

Critics, however, note that the concentric circle theory is less applicable today to the direction in which cities are evolving than in earlier decades of the twentieth century. And some critics contend that even then the theory was not applicable to a sizable number of American cities: Maurice R. Davie (1937) found that the theory clearly did not apply to New Haven, and Howard W. Green (1932) indicated that the same held true of Greater Cleveland. Further, a number of sociologists and others who have done ecological research on cities in Latin America, Asia, and Africa have noted the following ecological features that differ from what would be expected on the basis of American urban patterns: (1) the center of the city is more often the hub of administrative, governmental, and religious activity than of business; (2) where there is an approximation to a central business district, it lacks the dominance found within the United States; (3) there is less specialization in land use than in the United States—residences and shops often occupy the same buildings, both are scattered throughout the city, and a site often serves religious, educational, business, and residential uses concurrently; and (4) the higher socioeconomic status groups tend to live in or near the center of the city, while the poorer strata live at or near the periphery (Marsh, 1967).

The "Sector Theory." Homer Hoyt (1939) views the large city as made up of a number of sectors rather than concentric circles. He holds that high-rent areas tend to locate on the outer fringes of one or more sectors (wedge-shaped areas) of the city. In some sectors, the low-rent districts assume the shape of a cut of pie and extend from the center of a city out to its periphery (see Figure 17.2). As a city grows in population, the high-rent areas move outward within one sector—that is, they move toward the fringes of the city but remain in their original sector. Districts within a sector that are abandoned in this fashion by upper-income groups become obsolete and often deteriorate as lower-income groups move in. Instead of forming a concentric zone around the periphery of the city, Hoyt suggests that the high-rent areas ordinarily locate on the outer edge of one or more sectors. Moreover, industrial areas develop along river valleys, water courses, and railroad lines instead of forming a concentric circle around the central business district. But like the Burgess theory, Hoyt's sector theory has also come in for criticism. Walter Firey (1947), for example, on the basis of his study of Boston, concludes that adjacent areas in a sector do not necessarily represent a "gradation," and that some Boston working-class sectors do not conform to the theory.

The "Multiple Nuclei Theory." Still a third theory, that of C. D. Harris and Edward L. Ullman, postulates that a city does not have one center, but several. Harris and Ullman view the city as divided into a number of specialized areas, each of which exerts a dominant influence over a certain type of activity in the surrounding area (see Figure 17.2). The downtown business area, for instance, dominates commercial and financial activities within the city and in surrounding communities. The "bright lights" (theater and recreation) area, "automobile row," government centers, wholesaling districts, heavy manufacturing districts, and medical centers—each tends to have a distinct nucleus that sets it apart from other districts.

Multiple centers develop for a variety of reasons: (1) Certain activities require specialized facilities—for example, the retail district needs to be near the point of greatest intracity accessibility; the port district, along a suitable waterfront; manufacturing districts, in areas of large blocks of land and near water or rail connections. (2) Certain like activities group together because they profit from cohesion—for example, retail districts benefit from grouping that increases the concentration of potential customers; and financial districts, from grouping that facilitates communication between offices. (3) Certain unlike activities are detrimental to each other—for example, the antagonism between factory development and affluent residential development. (4) Certain activities are unable to afford the high rents of the most desirable sites—for example, bulk wholesaling and storage activities require considerable room. In many respects, the multiple nuclei theory is less useful for discovering universal spatial patterns of cities than in describing the unique patterns and variations found in given communities. One final word of caution is necessary regarding these theories of urban growth: they rest on studies of North American cities and are not necessarily applicable to cities in other parts of the world.

ECOLOGICAL PROCESSES

We find it useful to identify a number of basic ecological processes operating within urban areas. Each of these involves changes in the spatial patterning of ecological units. Let us examine a number of these processes.

Concentration, Centralization, and Decentralization. **Concentration** refers to the massing of people, while **centralization** refers to the massing of services in a given area. Urbanization involves both of these processes. Certain advantages accrue to people through concentration and centralization. Not the least of these is a more elaborate division of labor. Specialization generally promotes efficiency and competence since specialists are usually faster and more skillful than generalists. Large urban centers, for example, can provide an individual with a variety of medical specialists (for example, neurosurgeons, gynecologists, and orthopedists) who possess skills and knowledge regarding given health problems unknown to the general practitioner. Moreover, concentration may in its own right offer the advantage of numbers in those circumstances in which group size assumes importance, for instance, in providing for defense, security, and the common welfare and in providing a large enough market to support a variety of special services (large department stores, many specialty shops, opera houses, art galleries, theaters, sports stadiums, and the like).

DECENTRALIZATION

OBSERVATION As I drove through my hometown, I noticed that the downtown area is progressively sliding downhill as decay sets in. The old J.C. Penney's store is vacant and boarded up. The Sears and Ward's stores have been torn down, all replaced by new stores in the malls at the outskirts of the city. Even lawyers' offices, insurance offices, doctors' offices, and other service type businesses (for instance, banks) have moved out of the downtown area and are now locating nearer to residential areas where they are more convenient.

PRINCIPLE Decentralization is occurring in the town as the massing of services and even people is moving away from, rather than toward, a central point. It is a result of concentration (the massing of people) and centralization (the massing of services) having reached their limits. Traffic congestion and the lack of ample parking facilities have all reduced the gains associated with earlier concentration and centralization.

A limit is reached, however, beyond which concentration and centralization may entail definite dysfunctions. This may give rise to **decentralization**—namely, the tendency to move away from, rather than toward, a central point. We see this process at work in the development of shopping centers in or near residential areas. Since traffic congestion within large cities often reduces many of the gains to be derived from concentration and centralization, decentralization ensues.

Segregation. **Segregation** involves a process of clustering wherein individuals and groups are sifted and sorted out in space on the basis of sharing certain common characteristics or activities. This clustering may occur deliberately and voluntarily when individuals or groups find close spatial proximity an advantage. The multiple nuclei theory of city growth, for example, noted that certain like activities profit from the cohesion provided by a segregated area—for instance, the business district, the bright lights area, automobile row, and the wholesaling and storage district. Similarly, some nationality and cultural groups prefer to live in close proximity to one another. Cultural homogeneity facilitates communication, understanding, and rapport that foster a sense of "we-group" membership. Moreover, a segregated neighborhood may offer protection against the intrusion of strange beliefs, values, and norms, while affording political leverage at City Hall through bloc-voting.

But segregation may also be involuntary. Residential areas often take great pains to exclude a variety of commercial and industrial activities through zoning ordinances. Likewise, some cultural, nationality, and racial groups may rather systematically exclude certain other groups, for instance, Jews and Blacks. The fact that our major residential areas tend to follow class, religious, ethnic, and racial lines is by no means accidental. Yet slums and exclusive suburbs, Black Belts, Chinatowns, and Little Italys are also, as we have noted, the product of groups seeking to live with others like themselves. Hence, we often find that both voluntary and involuntary factors simultaneously operate to produce segregation. In some cities (such as Boston, Cleveland, and Seattle), patterns of ethnic segregation remain strong, although overall ethnic ties appear to weaken as a group's members become upwardly mobile in the status hierarchy (Guest and Weed, 1976; Simkus, 1978).

Invasion and Succession. Invasion and succession are closely related yet nevertheless distinct processes. **Invasion** occurs when a new type of people, institutional organization, or activity encroaches on an area occupied by a different type. If the invasion continues until the encroaching type displaces the other, **succession** is said to have occurred. Common examples of these processes include residential areas invaded by business or industry and neighborhoods invaded by new occupational, ethnic, or racial groups.

Urban renewal. Critics charge that urban renewal programs have often been "Black removal" programs. At times it has created new slums by pushing relocatees into areas that then have become overcrowded and deteriorated rapidly. Small retail merchants have lost their businesses. In many cases the land had been converted to well-financed commericial developments primarily benefiting the middle and upper classes.

Patrick Reddy

We commonly think of invasion and succession as changing the nature of an area, and indeed this is often the case. Although a neighborhood's ecological function may remain unchanged (for example, housing a segment of the population), it usually becomes less desirable as a place to live, and neighborhood blight may become common. Yet occasionally the reverse process occurs. Georgetown, in Washington, D.C., was an abject slum in the 1920s. Gradually, private individuals restored the crumbling homes, many of them pre-Civil War mansions. Currently, parts of Georgetown afford expensive and very attractive neighborhoods in which many government, business, and professional leaders live. Recently, a somewhat similar process has been occurring in the Adams-Morgan section near downtown Washington, in the South End of Boston, the Park Slope section of Brooklyn, German Village in Columbus, and Queens Village in Philadelphia. Young middle-class couples seem to have acquired a renewed taste for city life, with its nearness to work, entertainment, and ethnic diversity. Further, many young people are forgoing marriage and children, which means that they are not particularly concerned about good schools and large yards (Reinhold, 1977).

Residential succession has far-reaching consequences for a community and its organizations. Local businesses are a case in point. Over a period most neighborhoods experience a moderate degree of turnover in business establishments as their proprietors retire, die, experience health problems, or encounter financial difficulties. In racially changing areas the reason for the decline in the proportion of White-owned businesses is not so much that Whites *leave* (the best predictor of whether a business survives during a neighborhood transition is whether it is profitable) but that Whites do not *enter* these areas as *new* business owners. Simultaneously, minorities lack both the capital requirements and the business experience to fill all the opportunities opened to them by the withdrawal of Whites. Thus, the proportion of vacant sites tends to increase over time. The net result of this change is a loss of jobs, forcing local residents to seek employment elsewhere. And neighborhood consumers find they have to go outside of their own communities for various retail goods and services (Aldrich and Reiss, 1976).

SOCIAL CONSEQUENCES OF URBANISM

One of the most penetrating and insightful attempts to relate the basic characteristics of the urban environment to the larger social order is to be found in Louis Wirth's classic statement of "Urbanism as a Way of Life" (1938). Emphasizing *size, density,* and *heterogeneity* as three basic characteristics of the city, Wirth attempted to show how these features influence social relationships and individual psychology and behavior. Regarding the first characteristic, the sheer size of the population agglomeration, Wirth stressed the "atomization" of relationships that takes place within urban settings:

> Characteristically, urbanites meet one another in highly segmental roles. They are, to be sure, dependent upon more people for the satisfaction of their life-needs than are rural people and thus are associated with a greater number of organized groups, but they are less dependent upon particular persons, and their dependence upon others is confined to a highly fractionalized aspect of the other's round of activity. This is essentially what is meant by saying that the city is characterized by secondary rather than primary contacts. The contacts of the city may indeed be face to face, but they are nevertheless impersonal, superficial, transitory, and segmental. The reserve, the indifference, and the blasé outlook which urbanites manifest in their relationships may thus be regarded as devices for immunizing themselves against the personal claims and expectations of others. (p. 5)

The second characteristic, the density of urban populations, both flows from and generates differentiation and specialization. This may be noted in any number of spheres. Place of work, for example, tends to become dissociated from place of residence. Similarly, different parts of the city acquire specialized functions, reflected in residential, business, industrial, warehouse, and related districts. And diverse population elements—racial, ethnic, and status groupings—tend to become segregated from one another to the degree to which their modes of life are incompatible with and antagonistic to one another. Consequently, the city comes to resemble a mosaic of social worlds in which the transition from one to the other is often abrupt.

In the third of the urban characteristics, heterogeneity, Wirth found the source of the breaking down of caste lines, the appearance of new and complicating forms of class structure, and the emergence of the mass society. Heightened geographical and social mobility purportedly immerses the individual in an unstable and insecure social milieu. No single group commands a person's allegiance; the individual lives a segmented life, moving from one compartmentalized social sphere to another.

Wirth's ideas regarding the consequences of city life have been challenged and modified by sociologists in the forty years that have intervened since his paper was first published. A growing body of evidence points to the fact that urbanization is not a simple, unitary, or universally similar process. Instead, urbanization assumes different forms and meanings, depending on a variety of historic, economic, social, and cultural factors. For one thing, researchers studying cities in the United States, Latin America, Asia, and Africa find a wealth of personal ties and thriving primary groups even in the innermost recesses of the largest cities (Lewis, 1952; Bruner, 1959; 1961; Gans, 1962; Gulick, 1973; Hunter, 1975). Urban societies do not necessarily become secularized, individuals do not become isolated, kinship organizations do not break down, nor do social relationships in the urban environment become impersonal, superficial, and utilitarian (Fischer, 1976).

Nor should we assume, as Wirth suggests, that the small, rural American town necessarily takes notice of its people; here too we find indifference, aloofness, and unconcern. Rural people often refer to their "less advantaged" residents as "animal-like," hardly suggesting a more "human" outlook than the city (Wilheim, 1971). And Claude S. Fischer's research, summarized in Research Study 24, brings into question Wirth's formulation that urbanism *directly* (in its own right, unfettered by other covarying factors) leads to more tolerant and universalistic attitudes.

All of this is not to say that urbanism is of no social consequence. City residents are more likely than rural residents to behave in ways that diverge from the central or traditional norms of their common society (Fischer, 1975a; 1975b). Cities, especially large areas, are fertile environments for the spawning of various subcultures and countercultures. Overall, cities do have effects on social organization and individual behavior, but these effects are neither as simple nor as dramatic as Wirth implied (House, 1977).

RESEARCH STUDY 24

URBANISM AND TOLERANCE*

Claude S. Fischer

Problem. Based on Louis Wirth's theory of city life, sociologists have viewed residence in large cities as directly leading to greater ethnic tolerance and universalism (evaluating people and relating to them on the basis of identical standards of individual merit rather than on standards associated with ascribed status—race, religion, sex). According to Wirth, urbanism breeds "impersonality," "rationality," judging people in terms of their "utility," and a breakdown in "traditional bases of solidarity," all of which foster the development of universalistic attitudes. Fischer undertakes to determine the accuracy of this portrayal.

Hypotheses. From Wirth's formulation, Fischer deduces the following hypothesis:

The more urban a person's place of residence, the more likely he is to be tolerant of racial and ethnic differences (especially in regard to decisions calling for universalistic criteria).

Wirth further holds that the effect of the city is *direct*. Tolerance, then, is not the product, for instance, of greater educational opportunities in urban areas but, rather, the direct effect of city life on the individual. The second hypothesis becomes:

Size of community will be related to tolerance independent of other covarying factors.

Method. Between 1958 and 1965, five Gallup polls asked a total sample of 7714 persons (the samples being combined for purposes of this analysis) the question: "If your party nominated a generally well-qualified man for president and he happened to be a _____, would you vote for him?" The blank would be filled with the name of an ethnic minority—a Black, a Jew, or a Catholic. These items appear especially relevant for testing tolerance in an area of life presumably calling for the evaluation of an individual in terms of universalistic criteria. Sample data were available from the American Institute of Public Opinion (Gallup) for communities of different size and location.

In testing the second hypothesis, Fischer was interested in determining the direct impact of city size upon tolerance unfettered by other associated factors. In other words, the effect of the city may not be direct, but the product of some other factor or factors that convary (fluctuate in a manner parallel) with urbanism: the racial composition of a city, its religious composition (Protestant, Catholic, Jewish), its regional location (South or non-South), and its occupational distribution (professional and business; white collar; blue collar; service, labor, and farm). Using statistical techniques measuring covariance, Fischer was able to cancel out each of these latter factors in turn by subtracting its effect from city life.

Continued on next page.

---

* Adapted from Claude S. Fischer, "A Research Note on Urbanism and Tolerance," *American Journal of Sociology*, 76 (1971), 847–856.

TABLE 17.1
Community Size and Universalism

	Farm or Country (N = 2279)	Under 25,000 (N = 1342)	25,000 to 500,000 (N = 1701)	Over 500,000 (N = 2392)
Would vote for all three	26.2%	36.0%	43.4%	55.5%
Would vote for two of the three	30.7	29.5	31.5	28.6
Would vote for one of the three	21.8	20.3	14.2	9.2
Would vote for none	21.3	14.2	10.9	6.7

Source: Adapted from Claude S. Fischer, "A Research Note on Urbanism and Tolerance," American Journal of Sociology, 76 (1971), 849, Table 2.

Findings. The data contained in Table 17.1 reveal a strong association between tolerance (universalism) and place of residence. This confirmed the hypothesis that greater tolerance exists in urban settings.

What about the second hypothesis—urban size is related to tolerance *independently* of other factors? Figure 17.3 provides data for evaluating the hypothesis. The mean difference in percentage tolerant between large communities and small communities (percentage tolerant in large communities minus percentage tolerant in small communities) is 20 percent. When the impact of the racial variable is statistically subtracted from that of city size, the impact of urbanism on tolerance is increased. When, however, the impacts of region, religion, and occupation are each in turn subtracted, the effect of city size is progressively "washed out"—the effect of city size constantly decreases with the entry of other variables (covariants). Since controlling for covariants causes the relationship between city size and tolerance to approach zero, Fischer rejects the second hypothesis.

Conclusion. Fischer considers four possible explanations for his findings:

1. Louis Wirth's theory that city life directly leads to greater tolerance and universalistic attitudes is wrong.

Figure 17.3. Mean difference in percentage tolerant between large and small communities at each step in the entry of control variables.

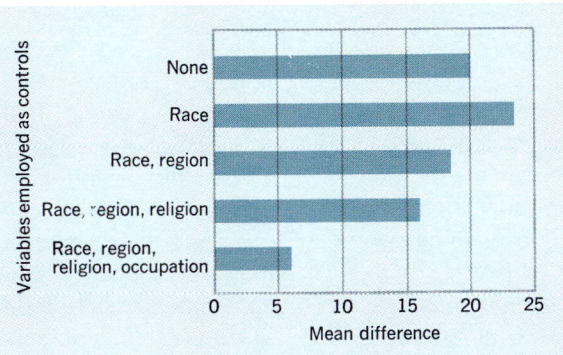

Variables employed as controls:
- None: ~20
- Race: ~23
- Race, region: ~18
- Race, region, religion: ~16
- Race, region, religion, occupation: ~6

Mean difference
(Percent tolerant in large communities minus percent in small communities)

Source: Adapted from Claude S. Fischer, "A Research Note on Urbanism and Tolerance," American Journal of Sociology, 76 (1971), 852, Figure 1.

2. Other forces within the city operate to counteract those producing greater tolerance. Interracial and interethnic competition for jobs and housing in larger cities may increase prejudice.
3. Large numbers of urban citizens gravitate to their "own kind"—race, religion, social class—insulating themselves from other people and minimizing the cosmopolitan impact of city life.
4. The distinct social–psychological mind-set of the "countryside" (rural and small-city areas) may be disappearing as the impact of the megalopolis (through mass communication and an all-embracing economic fabric) comes to encompass the entire nation.

Fischer suggests that all these explanations are pausible but he lacked the data necessary for evaluating the latter three. Other research, especially cross-cultural, is required. On the basis of this study, however, Fischer concludes that although urbanites are less likely to be prejudiced than rural residents, Wirth's formulation that urban life *directly* leads to universalistic attitudes is not supported.

SUMMARY

1. Throughout the world the process of urbanization is accelerating. United Nations experts predict that by the year 2000, some 50 percent of the world's population will live in urban areas. This compares with 39 percent now. There will be at least 60 cities with 5 million or more people, compared with the current 21 cities.

2. Ecology refers to the mutual relations between organisms and their environment, in brief, to the total web of life wherein all plant and animal species (including humans) reciprocally interact with one another and with the physical features of their habitat. Otis Dudley Duncan distinguishes four elements in the ecological complex: population, social organization, environment, and technology.

3. It was not until the Neolithic Period that technological conditions became ripe for the existence of settled communities. Preindustrial cities, however, were at best generally feeble prototypes of contemporary cities. Urbanization has proceeded much faster and reached proportions far greater during the past 160 years or so than at any previous time in world history. This initially gave rise to the industrial-urban center and more recently to the metropolitan city.

4. As the United States enters its third century, the nation is experiencing major population shifts with fundamental consequences for its cities. The largest population increases are occurring in the South and the West. In the East and portions of the industrial Midwest, urban growth is slowing and in some cases the population is actually declining. These shifts are bringing with them basic changes in national economic and political power patterns.

5. Although Americans still speak of suburbs, they are no longer just bedroom communities. The contemporary suburb differs from its earlier namesake in both function and form. Former "bedroom towns" are being transformed into places where residents both sleep and work. The movement of industrial and commercial employment away from central cities has influenced the process of suburban growth. It has contributed to new patterns of suburban differentiation. As the population of our metropolitan centers has grown, the space consumed by urban development has progressively expanded. As a consequence, the rural interstices between metropolitan centers fill up with urban development, making for a "strip city" or "megalopolis."

6. The suburbs have pirated from the city many of its functions and people. This has contributed to a host of urban problems. For those remaining in the central cores, it is harder to buy food, retail goods, and services. The aging downtowns of America's smaller cities are also quietly declining and deteriorating.

7. A number of theories have been advanced in an attempt to explain observed regularities in the

spatial distribution of people and their institutions within the modern metropolis. Three theories dealing with the ecological patterning of urban growth have gained particular attention: (1) the "concentric zone theory" of Ernest W. Burgess, (2) the "sector theory" of Homer Hoyt, and (3) the "multiple nuclei theory" of C. D. Harris and Edward L. Ullman. Each theory has certain limitations and advantages, and draws our attention to somewhat different dimensions of urban life.

8. We find it useful to distinguish between six ecological processes: (1) concentration—the massing of people in physical space; (2) centralization—the massing of services in a given area; (3) decentralization—the tendency to move away from, rather than toward, a central point; (4) segregation—a process of clustering wherein individuals and groups are sifted and sorted out in space on the basis of sharing certain common characteristics or activities; (5) invasion—a process wherein a new type of people, institutional organization, or activity encroaches on an area occupied by a different type; and (6) succession—the end result of invasion wherein a new type of people, institutional organization, or activity displaces another type.

9. Louis Wirth indicated that size, density, and heterogeneity are the three basic characteristics of the city. He attempted to show how these features influence social relations and individual behavior, stressing the "atomization" of relationships, social differentiation and specialization, and the emergence of new forms of social organization. However, his ideas have been challenged and modified by sociologists. Overall, cities have effects on social organization and people's behavior, but these effects are neither as simple nor as dramatic as Wirth implied.

GLOSSARY

Accommodation. A process in which individuals or groups seek to reach an adjustment whereby conflict can be temporarily or permanently suspended.
Achieved status. Roles allocated to an individual on the basis of his or her unique talents or characteristics.
Acting crowd. An excited, volatile collection of people who are engaged in rioting, looting, or other forms of aggressive behavior in which established norms carry little weight.
Alienation. A pervasive sense of powerlessness, meaninglessness, isolation, and self-estrangement.
Analysis. The search for meaningful links between the facts that have emerged in the course of research.
Androgynous. Capable of expressing the full range of human emotions and role possibilities without being restricted by gender stereotypes.
Anomie. A condition within a society or group in which there exists a weakened repect for some of the norms.
Ascribed status. Roles assigned to an individual independent of his or her unique talents or characteristics.
Assimilation. A process in which groups with diverse behavior patterns become fused together in a social unity and a common culture.
Authority. Legitimate power.
Avoidance rituals. Individuals or groups attest to their regard, awe, or respect for superiors through maintaining distance from them.
Belief. An idea concerning the universe or any of its component parts, including people.
Bilineal. A cultural pattern tracing descent through both the father's and mother's groups.
Bureaucracy. A hierarchical arrangement among the parts of an organization in which the pyramiding order is based on division of function and authority.

Glossary

Caste. A system of stratification based on inherited inequality.

Casual crowd. A collection of people who have little in common with one another except that they may be viewing a common event.

Centralization. An ecological process that involves the massing of services in physical space.

Church. A religious organization whose aim is professedly universal and membership is frequently compulsory.

Civil religion. Nationalism and patriotism take on the properties of a religion.

Class. A system of stratification based on equality of opportunity.

Collective behavior. Relatively spontaneous and unstructured ways of thinking, feeling, and acting that develop among a large number of people.

Communication. The process by which individuals transmit information, ideas, and attitudes to one another.

Community. A collectivity of interacting people who share a limited territorial area as the base for carrying on the greater part of their daily activities.

Compartmentalization. Individuals subdivide their lives, so to speak, and within a given context act in accordance with the dictates of one role while ignoring the other.

Competition. A process in which individuals or groups seek to realize their goals through established rules that strictly define what constitute "fair tactics."

Complementary needs. The theory of mate selection that holds that people typically seek within the field of eligibles a person who gives the greatest promise of providing them with the maximum gratification of their needs.

Concentration. An ecological process that involves the massing of people in physical space.

Conflict. A process in which individuals or groups seek to realize their goals through neutralizing, injuring, or eliminating their rivals.

Conjugal. A family arrangement consisting of a nucleus of spouses and their offspring; blood relatives are functionally marginal and peripheral.

Consanguine. A family arrangement consisting of a nucleus of blood relatives; spouses are functionally marginal and peripheral.

Consensus. A social oneness deriving from the fact that people perceive themselves as being socially and culturally alike.

Consumption. The using up of goods and services.

Conventional crowd. A group of people who have assembled for some specific purpose and who act in accordance with prevailing norms.

Cooperation. A process in which individuals or groups seek to realize their goals through mutual aid.

Counterculture. A set of distinctive ways of thinking, feeling, and acting that characterizes the behavior of a group's members and that is opposed to and clashes with those of the larger society.

Crazes. Fads that become all-consuming passions.

Crowd. A temporary, relatively unorganized gathering of people who are in close physical proximity.

Crude birth rate. The number of births per 1000 of the total population at a given period.

Crude death rate. The number of deaths per 1000 of the total population at a given period.

Cult. A special type of religious organization, characterized by a very amorphous, loosely textured structure.

Cultural lag. One part of culture may change more rapidly than another, with the result that a disbalance or dislocation occurs between the parts.

Cultural universals. Common denominators or constants found in the behavior patterns of all societies.

Culture. The socially standardized ways of feeling, thinking, and acting that an individual acquires as a member of society.

Culture of poverty. The view advanced by Oscar Lewis that the poor share a distinctive social ethos of defeatism, dependence, and a present-time orientation that is transmitted to successive generations through socialization processes.

Decentralization. An ecological process involving the tendency to more away from, rather than toward, a central point.

Deference. The ritual or ceremonial dramatizing of an individual's or group's priority.

Definition of situation. Preliminary to any self-determined act of behavior there is always a stage of examination and deliberation. We mentally define each path of contemplated behavior in terms of what we anticipate will result if we follow one path and not another.

Demography. The science dealing with the size, distribution, and composition of population.

Denomination. A sect in an advanced stage of development and adjustment to the secular world.

Deviance. Behavior that is viewed by a considerable number of people as reprehensible and beyond the tolerance limit.

Diffusion. The spread of a trait from one social unit to another.

Discrimination. Overt action in which members of a group are accorded unfavorable treatment by others on the basis of their group membership.

Distribution. Channeling inputs (natural resources and labor) to producing agencies, and outputs (goods and services) to consuming agencies.

Dysfunctions. Those observed consequences that lessen the adaptation or adjustment of a system.

Ecology. The mutual relations between organisms and their environment; the total web of life wherein all plant and animal species reciprocally interact with one another and with the physical features of their habitat.

Education. Formal, conscious, systematic training.

Enacted laws. Laws that arise in a planned and deliberative fashion through the action of an authoritative party or organization within the society.

Endogamy. A cultural pattern prescribing in-group marriage.

Environment. The sum total of the external factors that affect the organism.

Equilibrium. The tendency of a system to achieve a balance among its various parts and among the forces that are operating within and on it.

Ethnic groups. Populations differing in their cultural practices.

Ethnocentrism. The tendency for a people to put their own group in a central position of priority and worth.

Ethnomethodology. A sociological school of thought that seeks to expose the taken-for-granted and background expectancies of life.

Exogamy. A cultural pattern prescribing out-group marriage.

Experiment. A study in which the researcher manipulates or varies one or more variables (termed the independent variables) and measures other variables (termed the dependent variables).

Exponential principle. Growth occurs in geometric ratio.

Expressive crowd. An aggregate of people who have gotten together for self-stimulation and personal gratification.

Extended families. An arrangement consisting of a nucleus of blood relatives; spouses are functionally marginal and peripheral.

Facts. Empirically verifiable observations.

Fad. A behavior that endures for a short time and enjoys acceptance among a limited segment of a society.

Family. A social arrangement united by ties of marriage, ancestry, or adoption that community members recognize as constituting a single household and having the responsibility for bringing up children.

Family of orientation. The family consisting of oneself and one's father, mother, and siblings.

Family of procreation. The family consisting of oneself and one's spouse and children.

Fashion. A behavior that endures for a short time and enjoys widespread acceptance within a society.

Fecundity. The potential reproduction rate if every woman of childbearing age bore all the children she possibly could.

Formal organizations. Associations that arise when individuals deliberately construct a social unit to seek specific objectives.

Front. The communications that serve to define the situation for an audience.

Gatekeeping. The decision-making process by which members of a society are admitted to positions of power, privilege, and status.

Gender identities. The conceptions that individuals have of themselves as being male or female.

Gender roles. Sets of expectations that provide the guidelines for the behavior of men and women.

Generalized other. A concept introduced to sociology by George Herbert Mead that suggests that individuals internalize the norms of their group and make these norms the standards regulating their own behavior.

Gestures. Symbols that involve the movement and positioning of the body,

Glossolalia. The Holy Spirit is believed to speak through a person in unknown languages.

Group. A collection of people with certain common attributes.

Groupthink. A decision-making process in which group consensus is so paramount that an individual's critical facilities become ineffective.

Heredity. That which is inherent and inborn; that which is genetically transmitted from parents to offspring.

Hermaphrodites. Individuals whose reproductive structures are sufficiently ambiguous that they cannot be defined as exclusively male or female.

Hypothesis. A proposition that can be tested to determine its validity; a tentative guess or hunch that is employed as a guide to investigation.

Ideal type. A model or description created by a sociologist. It is derived by abstracting the most characteristic aspects that are present in a real phenomenon.

Identity. Our answer to the question, "Who am I?"

Ideology. A set of ideas providing people with conceptions of a social movement's purpose, its rationale for existence, its indictment of existing arrangements, and its design for action.

Imitation. Individuals do what they see other people doing.

Impression management. The process by which we undertake to define the situation for others by generating words, gestures, and actions that will lead them to act in accordance with our wishes.

In-group. A social unit of which an individual is a part or with which he or she identifies.

Informal organizations. Networks of personal and social relations that arise within a formal organization but which are not defined or prescribed by it.

Innovation. A new item or behavior.

Institution. The principal instrument whereby the essential tasks of social living are organized, directed, and executed; social structures.

Institutional racism. People of one racial group are systematically oppressed or exploited by the institutions of a society controlled by another racial group.

Integration. A state of being whole or entire.

Interaction. The mutual and reciprocal influencing by two or more people of each other's feelings, attitudes, and actions.

Interview. A meeting of persons face to face, especially for the purpose of formal conference on some point.

Invasion. An ecological process wherein a new type of people, institutional organization, or activity encroaches on an area occupied by a different type.

Iron law of oligarchy. The view of Robert Michels that bureaucratic organizations inevitably lead to the concentration of power in the hands of the few who in turn use their positions to advance their own fortunes and self-interests.

Labelling theory of deviance. The sociological perspective that holds that no act by itself is inherently criminal or noncriminal but rather is the product of social definitions and meanings.

Language. A socially structured system of sound patterns (words and sentences) with standardized meanings.

Latent functions. Those consequences that are neither intended nor recognized by the participants in a system.

Law. A norm that is externally guaranteed by a special body or organization which enjoys the right of applying physical coercion to bring about conformity or avenge violation.

Life-chances. The typical probability that an individual or group will possess a given level of (1) goods and services, (2) external conditions of life, and (3) subjective satisfaction or frustration.

Looking-glass self. A mental process described by Charles Horton Cooley involving three separable phases: perception, interpretation, and response.

Magic. The use of mechanistic manipulation and the compulsion of superhuman power.

Manifest functions. Those consequences that are intended and recognized by the participants in a system.

Mass. A relatively large number of separate individuals, each of whom responds independently to the same stimulus in the same fashion.

Mass communication. The relatively simultaneous exposure of large heterogeneous audiences to symbols transmitted by impersonal means from an organized source for whom audience members are anonymous.

Matching hypothesis. Individuals tend to pair off with one another on the basis of their physical attractiveness.

Matrilineal. A cultural pattern tracing descent through the mother's group.

Money. Some form of common denominator or medium of exchange that facilitates the exchange of goods and services.

Monogamy. A cultural pattern prescribing the marriage of one husband and one wife.

Mores. Norms that are looked on by members of a society (or a group within the society) as being extremely important and that, when violated, result in severe punishment.

Mortality. The termination of life within a population as measured by the death rate.

Nation. A collectivity of people who feel that they belong together in the double sense that they share deeply significant elements of a common heritage and that they have a common destiny for the future.

Negotiated order. People construct a sense of social reality as they repeat, reaffirm, and recreate their social acts.

Norms. Rules that specify appropriate and inappropriate behavior.

Nuclear families. An arrangement consisting of a nucleus of spouses and their offspring; blood relatives are functionally marginal and peripheral.

Null hypothesis. The stating of a hypothesis in terms opposite to what the researcher actually postulates.

Object permanence. The awareness that things continue to exist when one is not perceiving them.

Objective approach to social stratification. A technique for studying social class employing such yardsticks as education, occupation, and income.

Observational learning. Behavior that is acquired by watching that of another individual.

Oedipal complex. A concept coined by Sigmund Freud to refer to the sexual love boys experience for their mothers and the hostile rivalry they feel toward their fathers.

Out-group. A social unit of which an individual is not a part or with which he or she does not identify.

Participant observation. A rather casual, uncontrolled research technique in which the investigators do not reveal their true professional identity so as to be accepted as members of a group.

Path analysis. A set of classificatory or quantitative measurements taken at successive stages.

Patrilineal. A cultural pattern tracing descent through the father's group.

Perception. A process by which an individual selects, organizes, and interprets sensory stimuli so as to realize a meaningful and coherent picture of the world.

Period of concrete operations. The third stage in cognitive development described by Jean Piaget. It spans the elementary school years. During the period children gain the ability to solve conservation problems. They come to recognize that the quantity or amount of something remains the same regardless of changes in its shape or position.

Period of formal operations. The final stage in Piaget's system of cognitive development. It occurs during adolescence. Individuals become capable of engaging in logical and abstract thought.

Peter Principle. In a hierarchy every employee tends to rise to his or her level of incompetence.

Pluralism. A process whereby people with differing cultural backgrounds live together harmoniously and peacefully, permitting the expression of their distinctive ways of life within a range consonant with the national welfare.

Polyandry. A cultural pattern prescribing the marriage of two or more husbands and one wife.

Polygyny. A cultural pattern prescribing the marriage of one husband and two or more wives.

Population pyramid. A diagram showing the age and sex composition of a people.

Power. The ability of an individual to realize his or her will even if it involves the resistance of others.

Power elite. A concept introduced by C. Wright Mills that refers to the control of government by powerful interest groups acting in unison.

Prejudice. A state of mind characterized by negative conceptions, feelings, and action-orientations regarding the members of a particular group.

Preoperational period. The second stage in cognitive development described by Jean Piaget. It spans the ages from two to seven. The chief achievement of this period is the developing capacity of children to employ symbols, especially language.

Presentation rituals. Individuals or groups attest to their regard, awe, or respect for superiors through symbolic acts.

Primary group. Two or more people who enjoy an intimate, personal, cohesive relationship with one another.

Principle of legitimacy. The rule providing for fatherhood if only by social definition.
Privilege. The control and possession of goods and services that contribute to physical and psychological comfort.
Production. The assemblying and applying of human and natural resources in the creation of goods and services.
Property. The rights and duties of one individual or group (the owner) as against all other persons and groups with respect to some scarce object.
Propinquity. People who live near one another and go to school and work together tend to marry one another.
Protestant ethic. A body of ideas embodying a methodical, rational way of life that is conducive to capitalism.
Public. A collection of people who are divided on an issue and who, by virtue of their interest, are engaged in direct or indirect communication about it.
Public opinion. The attitude of a public.
Questionnaire. An interview taking a written form.
Races. Populations that differ in the incidence of certain genes but which are capable of producing fertile hybrid offspring.
Reference group. A group that provides the standards and perspective regulating an individual's behavior within a given context, regardless of whether he or she is a member of the group or not.
Reinforcement. Learning that takes place as behavior is strengthened by its consequences.
Relative deprivation. A gap between what people actually have and what they have come to expect and feel to be their just due.
Religion. Those ways of thinking, feeling, and acting by which people undertake to deal with the ultimate problems of life.
Reputational approach to social stratification. A technique for studying social class that involves asking people how they classify others.
Resistance. Behavior on the part of some or all of the members of society, either passive or active, that is directed toward the rejection or circumvention of change.
Rights. The actions that we can legitimately insist that others perform.
Role. Who does what, when, and where; a category we employ for placing people in terms of their common attributes, their common behavior, or the common reactions other people make to them.
Role-set. A number of linked, interdependent, and complementary roles.
Role strain. Circumstances in which people experience difficulties in meeting the demands and expectations associated with a role.
Role-taking. The process by which we devise our performance based on our interpretation of people's behavior.
Romantic love. A lover is absorbed and preoccupied with the loved one and yearns for some kind of personality fusion.
Schemas. Mental models for coping with the world.
Science. A systematic way of organizing knowledge about empirical phenomena and a method of objective observation through which systematic and accurate knowledge is acquired.

Secondary group. Relationships characterized by their touch-and-go and impersonal nature.

Sect. A small, voluntary fellowship of converts who seek to realize the divine law in their own behavior.

Segregation. A process (or state) whereby people are separated or set apart.

Self. The conception that individuals acquire of themselves through social interaction with others (the qualities that individuals attribute to themselves). It involves the system of concepts we employ in attempting to define ourselves.

Self-conception. An overriding view of onself through time—"the real me," or "I myself as I really am.".

Self-fulfilling prophecy. A false definition of the situation that evokes behavior that makes the originally false state of affairs come true.

Self-image. A mental conception or picture we have of ourselves that is relatively temporary; it is subject to change as we move from one situation to another.

Sensorimotor period. The first stage in cognitive development described by Jean Piaget. It lasts from birth to about two years of age. The major task of this stage revolves around infants' coordination of their motor activities with their sensory inputs.

Sexism. Institutional arrangements that maintain a gender order of inequality and justify it by an ideology of male biological superiority and female biological inferiority.

Significant other. A concept introduced to sociology by George Herbert Mead that suggests that children in play take the role of one person at a time and seek to act out the behavior associated with this role.

Social categories. A group characterized by a consciousness of kind but not by social interaction or formal organization.

Social exchange theory. People are viewed as ordering their relationships with others in terms of a sort of mental bookkeeping that entails a ledger or rewards, costs, and profits.

Social control. A process whereby a group or a society secures its members' conformity to norms.

Social differentiation. A process whereby individuals are sorted out as occupants of various positions.

Social groups. A collection of people who share a consciousness of kind and who are characterized by social interaction, but who lack formal organization.

Social mobility. The movement of individuals or groups from one social stratum to another.

Social movement. A more or less persistent and organized effort on the part of a relatively large number of people to bring about or resist change.

Social organization. Organization denotes both structure and process; social denotes organization among people.

Social stratification. The process whereby people come to be ranked in a hierarchical arrangement or to the state of being so ordered.

Social structure. A configuration in which different categories of people are bound together within a network of relationships.

Socialization. A process of social interaction in which the individual acquires those ways of thinking, feeling, and acting essential for effective participation within society.

Society. The network or web of social relationships that exists among a plurality of individuals, constitutes a more or less self-sufficient unit for its members, and possesses continuity through successive generations.

Sociobiology. The study of the biological basis of all social behavior.

Sociology. The scientific study of human interaction.

Split labor market. A large difference exists in the price of labor between groups at the same occupational level.

State. The social agency that exercises a supreme monopoly of authority within a given territory.

Statistical categories. Groups formed, not by the members themselves, but by sociologists, statisticians, demographers, and others. The individuals making up statistical categories are not characterized by consciousness of kind, social interaction, or formal organization.

Status. A sense of worth and respect, particularly the extent to which individuals feel themselves admired and thought well of.

Stereotype. An unscientific and hence unreliable generlization that people make about other people as persons or as groups.

Structural conduciveness. Social conditions that permit collective behavior of a particular sort to take place.

Style of life. The mode of living shared by people of a similar social rank.

Subculture. A set of distinctive ways of thinking, feeling, and acting that set the members of a group apart from the larger society.

Subjective approach to social stratification. A technique for studying social class that involves self-classification or self-placement.

Succession. The end result of the ecological process of invasion wherein a new type of people, institutional organization, or activity displaces another type.

Symbol. Any act or object that has socially come to be accepted as standing for something else.

Symbolic interactionism. A sociological school of thought that stresses the part communication plays in human life. Language and gestures are seen as the foundation of the mind, self, and society. Through symbols, humans fit their acts to those of others, mapping, testing, suspending and revising their behavior in response to the behavior of other people.

Syncretism. The blending or fusing of a trait with an analogous element in culture.

System. A complex of elements or components that are related to each other in a more or less stable fashion through a period of time.

Taboos. Mores stated negatively as "thou shall not's."

Theory. A way of binding together a great number of facts so that we might comprehend them all at once.

Values. The criteria or conceptions used in evaluating things (including objects, ideas, acts, feelings, and events) as to their relative desirability or merit.

White collar crime. Violations of the law committed by persons of affluence, often in the course of their business activities.

References

Abercrombie, C. L., III. (1977) *The Military Chaplain.* Beverly Hills, Calif.: Sage Publications.

Abramson, P. R. (1975) *Generational Change in American Politics.* Lexington, Mass.: Lexington Books.

Adamek, R. and Lewis, J. (1973) Social control, violence and radicalization: The Kent State case. *Social Forces,* 51:342–347.

Ajzen, I. and Fishbein, M. (1973) Attitudinal and normative variables as predictors of specific behaviors. *Journal of Personality and Social Psychology,* 27:41–57.

Aldrich, H. and Reiss, A. J., Jr. (1976) Continuities in the study of ecological succession: Changes in the race composition of neighborhoods and their businesses. *American Journal of Sociology,* 81:846–866.

Allen, E., (1975) Against "Sociobiology." *New York Review of Books* (November 13):43–44.

Alexander, K. L., Cook, M., and McDill, E.L. (1978) Curriculum tracking and educational stratification: Some further evidence. *American Sociological Review,* 43:47–66.

Alexander, K. L. and McDill, E. L. (1976) Selection and allocation within schools: Some causes and consequences of curriculum placement. *American Sociological Review,* 41:963–980.

Almond, G. A. (1954) *The Appeals of Communism.* Princeton, N.J.: Princeton University Press.

Almond, G. A. and Verba, S. (1963) *The Civic Culture.* Princeton, N.J.: Princeton University Press.

Althusser, L. (1971) *Lenin and Philosophy and Other Essays.* New York: Monthly Review Press.

Ambedkar, B. R. (1955) *Thoughts on Linguistic States.* Delhi, India: B. R. Ambedkar.

American Anthropological Association. (1973) *Professional ethics.* Washington, D.C.: American Anthropological Association.

American Political Science Association Committee on Professional Standards and Responsibilities. (1968) Washington, D.C.: American Political Science Association.

American Psychological Association. (1973) *Ethical principles in the conduct of research on human participants.* Washington, D.C.: American Psychological Association.

American Sociological Association. (1971) *Code of ethics.* Washington, D.C.: American Sociological Association.

Anastasi, A. (1958) Heredity, environment, and the question "how?" *Psychological Review,* 65:197–208.

Anderson, C. H. (1971) *Toward a New Sociology.* Homewood, Ill.: The Dorsey Press.

Anderson, L. S., Chiricos, T. G., and Waldo, G. P. (1977) Formal and informal sanctions: A comparison of deterrent effects. *Social Problems,* 25:103–114.

Anderson, N. (1923) *The Hobo.* Chicago: The University of Chicago Press.

Andrew, R. J. (1966) Precocious adult behaviour in the young chick. *Animal Behaviour,* 14:485–500.

Angrish, S., Lefton, M., Dinitz, S., and Pasamanick, B., (1968) *Women After Treatment.* New York: Appleton-Century-Crofts.

Antonovsky, A. (1972) Social class, life expectancy, and overall mortality. In Jaco, E. G., Ed. *Patients, Physicians, and Illness.* 2nd ed. New York: Free Press.

Appelbaum, R. P. (1978) Marx's theory of the falling rate of profit: Towards a dialectical analysis of structural social change. *American Sociological Review,* 43:67–80.

Apter, D. E. (1963) Political religion in the new nations. In Geertz, C., Ed. *Old Societies and New States.* New York: The Free Press.

Archer, J. (1976) Biological explanations of psychological sex differences. In Lloyd, B. and Archer, J., Eds. *Exploring Sex Differences.* New York: Academic Press.

Argyle, M. (1975) *Bodily Communication.* New York: International Universities Press.

Armbruster, F. E. (1977) *Our Children's Crippled Future.* New York: Quadrangle.

Aronoff, J. and Crano, W. D. (1975) A Re-examination of the cross-cultural principles of task segregation and sex role differentiation in the family. *American Sociological Review,* 40:12–20.

Aronson, E. and Carlsmith, J. M. (1962) Performance expectancy as a determinant of actual performance. *Journal of Abnormal and Social Psychology,* 65:178–82.

Asch, S. E. (1952) *Social Psychology.* Englewood Cliffs, N.J.: Prentice-Hall.

Asch, S. E. (1965) Effects of group pressure upon the modification and distortion of judgements. In Proshansky, H. and Seidenberg, B., Eds. *Basic Studies in Social Psychology.* New York: Holt, Rinehart & Winston, Inc.

Averitt, R. (1968) *The Dual Economy.* New York: W. W. Norton.

Bagehot, W. (1875) *Physics and Politics.* New York: Appleton-Century-Croft, Inc.

Ball, D. W. (1966) An abortion clinic ethnography. *Social Problems,* 14:293–301.

Bandura, A. (1965) Influence of models' reinforcement contingencies on the acquistion of imitative responses. *Journal of Personality and Social Psychology,* 1:589–595.

Bandura, A. (1967) The role of modeling processes in personality development. In Hartup, W. W. and Smothergill, N. L., Eds. *The Young Child: A Review of Research.* Washington, D.C.: National Association for the Education of Young Children.

Bandura, A. (1971) *Social Learning Theory.* Morristown, N.J.: General Learning Corporation.

Bandura, A. (1973) *Aggression: A Social Learning Analysis.* Englewood Cliffs, N.J.: Prentice-Hall.

Barash, D. P. (1977) *Sociobiology and Behavior.* New York: Elsevier Scientific Publishing.

Barraclough, G. (1975) The great world crisis I. *The New York Review* (January 23):20–29.

Bartley, R. L. (1976) Mao: The romantic revolutionary. *Wall Street Journal* (October 20):20.

Batson, C. D. (1977) Experimentation in psychology of religion: An impossible dream. *Journal for the Scientific Study of Religion,* 16:413–418.

Becker, H. S. (1951) The professional dance musician and his audience. *American Journal of Sociology,* 57:136–44.

Becker, H. S. (1952) Social-class variations in the teacher-pupil relationships. *Journal of Education Sociology,* 25:451–465.

Becker, H. S. (1963) *Outsiders: Studies in the Sociology of Deviance.* New York: The Free Press.

Becker, H. S. (1967) Whose side are we on? *Social Problems,* 14:239–247.

Becker, H. S. and Horowitz, I. L. (1972) Radical politics and sociological research: Observations on methodology and ideology. *American Journal of Sociology,* 78:48–66.

Beckford, J. A. (1975) *The Trumpet of Prophecy: A Sociological Study of Jehovah's Witnesses.* New York: Halsted Press.

Bellah, R. N. (1957) *Tokugawa Religion.* New York: The Free Press.

Bellah, R. N. (1958) Religious aspects of modernization in Turkey and Japan. *American Journal of Sociology,* 64:1–5.

Bellah, R. N. (1967) Civil religion in America. *Daedalus*, 96:1–21.

Bellah, R. N. (1975) *The Broken Covenant: American Civil Religion in Time of Trial*. New York: Seabury Press.

Bem, S. L. (1975a) Sex role adaptability: One consequence of psychological androgyny. *Journal of Personality and Social Psychology*, 31:634–643.

Bem, S. L. (1975b) Androgyny vs. the tight little lives of fluffy women and chesty men. *Psychology Today*, 9 (September):58–62.

Benedict, R. (1938) Religion. In Boas, F., Ed. *General Anthropology*. Boston: D.C. Heath & Co.

Benedict, R. (1940) *Race: Science and Politics*. New York: Modern Age Books.

Benedict, R. (1946) *Patterns of Culture*. New York: Mentor Books.

Benson, J. K. (1977) Innovation and crisis in organizational analysis. *The Sociological Quarterly*, 18:3–16.

Bercheid, E. and Walster, E. (1974) A little bit about love. In Huston, E. L., Ed. *Foundations of Interpersonal Attraction*. New York: Academic Press.

Berelson, B., Lazarsfeld, P. F., and McPhee, W. N. (1954) *Voting: A Study of Opinion Formation in a Presidential Campaign*. Chicago: University of Chicago Press.

Berg, A. (1975) The trouble with triage. *New York Times Magazine* (June 15):26+.

Berger, B., Hackett, B., and Millar, R. M. (1972) The communal family. *The Family Coordinator*, 21:419–428.

Berger, P. L. (1963) *Invitation to Sociology: A Humanistic Perspective*. Garden City, N.Y.: Doubleday & Co.

Berger, P. L. (1974) Some second thoughts on substantive versus functional definitions of religion. *Journal for the Scientific Study of Religion*, 13:125–133.

Berk, B. (1977) Face-saving at the singles dance. *Social Problems*, 24:530–544.

Berk, R. A. (1974) A gaming approach to collective behavior. *American Sociologial Review*, 39:355–373.

Berkowitz, L. (1975) *A Survey of Social Psychology*. Hinsdale, Ill.: The Dryden Press.

Berman, G. S. and Haug, M. R. (1975) Occupational and educational goals and expectations: The effects of race and sex. *Social Problems*, 23:166–181.

Bernard, J. (1966) Marital stability and patterns of status variables. *Journal of Marriage and the Family*, 28:421–439.

Bernard, J. (1972) *The Future of Marriage*. New York: Bantam Books.

Bernard, J. (1973) My four revolutions: An autobiographical history of the ASA. *American Journal of Sociology*, 78;773–791.

Bernstein, I. N., Kelly, W. R., and Doyle, P. A. (1977) Societal reaction to deviants: The case of criminal defendants. *American Sociological Review*, 42:743–755.

Berreman, G. D. (1960) Caste in India and the United States. *American Journal of Sociology*, 66:120–127.

Berreman, G. D. (1971) Speech to Council. *Newsletter of the American Anthropological Association*, 12 (January):19.

Berry, B. (1958) *Race and Ethnic Relations*. New York: Houghton Mifflin.

Berry, B. (1965) *Race and Ethnic Relations*. 3rd ed. Boston: Houghton Mifflin.

Bertenthal, B. I. and Fischer, K. W. (1978) Development of self-recognition in the infant. *Developmental Psychology*, 14:44–50.

Bevan, W. D., Daves, W. F., and Levy, F. W. (1960) The relation of castration, androgen therapy and pre-test fighting experience to competitive aggression in male C57BL/10 mice. *Animal Behaviour*, 8:6–12.

Biblarz, A. (1969) On the question of objectivity in sociology. *Et Al.*, 2:3–6.

Biddle, B. J. and Thomas, E. J., Eds. (1966) *Role Theory: Concepts and Research*. New York: Wiley.

Bidwell, C. E. (1965) The school as a formal organization. In March, J. G., Ed. *Handbook of Organizations*. Chicago: Rand McNally.

Bierstedt, R. (1948) The sociology of majorities. *American Sociological Review*, 13:700–713.

Bierstedt, R. (1963) *The Social Order*. 2nd ed. New York: McGraw-Hill.

Bigner, J. J. (1974) A Wernerian developmental analysis of children's description of siblings. *Child Development*, 45:317–323.

Billingsley, A. and Giovannoni, J. M. (1971) One parent family. In Morris, R., Ed. *Encyclopedia of Social Work* (16th Issue). Vol. 1. New York: National Association of Social Workers.

Blackwell, J. E. (1976) The power basis of ethnic conflict in American society. In Coser, L. A. and Larsen, O. N., Eds. *The Uses of Controversy in Sociology.* New York: The Free Press.

Blake, J. (1974) Can we believe recent data on birth expectancies in the United States? *Demography,* 11:131–142.

Blau, P. M. (1967) *Exchange and Power in Social Life.* New York: Wiley.

Blau, P. M. (1973) *The Organization of Academic Work.* New York: Wiley.

Blau, P. M. and Duncan, O. D. (1967) *The American Occupational Structure.* New York: Wiley.

Blau, P. M. and Duncan, O. D. (1972) *The American Occupational Structure.* 2nd Ed. New York: Wiley.

Blau, P. M. and Schoenherr, R. A. (1971) *The Structure of Organization.* New York: Basic Books.

Blauner, R. (1969) Internal colonialism and ghetto revolt. *Social Problems,* 16:393–408.

Blauner, R. (1969) Work satisfaction and industrial trends. In Etzioni, A., Ed. *A Sociological Reader on Complex Organizations.* New York: Holt, Rinehart and Winston.

Blood, R. O., Jr. and Wolfe, D. M. (1960) *Husbands and Wives.* New York: The Free Press.

Bloom, B. S. (1977) Affective outcomes of school learning. *Phi Delta Kappan,* 59:193–198.

Blot, W. J., Brinton, L. A., Fraumeni, J. F., Jr., and Stone, B. J. (1977) Cancer mortality in U.S. counties with petroleum industries. *Science,* 198:51–53.

Blumer, H. (1946) Collective behavior. In Lee, A. M., Ed. *New Outline of the Principles of Sociology.* New York: Barnes & Noble.

Blumer, H. (1962) Society as symbolic interaction. In Rose, A. M., Ed. *Human Behavior and Social Processes.* Boston: Houghton Mifflin Co.

Blumer, H. (1964) Collective behavior. In Gould, J. and Kolb, W. L., Eds. *A Dictionary of the Social Sciences.* New York: The Free Press.

Blumer, H. (1966) Sociological implications of the thought of George Herbert Mead. *American Journal of Sociology,* 71:535–544.

Blumer, H. (1969) *Symbolic Interactionism: Perspective and Method.* Englewood Cliffs, N.J.: Prentice-Hall.

Blumer, H. (1971) Social problems as collective behavior. *Social Problems,* 18:298–306.

Blumer, H. (1977) Comment on Lewis' "The classic American pragmatists as forerunners to symbolic interactionism. *Sociological Quarterly,* 18:285–289.

Bonacich, E. (1972) A theory of ethnic antagonism: The split labor market. *American Sociological Review,* 37:547–549.

Bonacich, E. (1975) Abolition, the extension of slavery, and the position of free Blacks: A study of split labor markets in the United States, 1830–1863. *American Journal of Sociology,* 81:601–628.

Bonacich, E. (1976) Advanced capitalism and Black/White relations in the United States: A split labor market interpretation. *American Sociological Review,* 41:34–51.

Boocock, S. S. (1972) *An Introduction to the Sociology of Learning.* Boston: Houghton Mifflin.

Boocock, S. S. (1973) The school as a social environment for learning: Social organization and microsocial process in education. *Sociology of Education,* 46:15–50.

Booth, A., Johnson, D. R., and Choldin, H. M. (1977) Correlates of city crime rates: Victimization surveys versus official statistics. *Social Problems,* 25:187–197.

Borders, W. (1978) Birth control slows in India: targets put back by years. *New York Times* (February 6):2.

Borke, H. (1972) Chandler and Greenspan's "Ersatz Egocentrism": A rejoinder. *Developmental Psychology,* 7:107–109.

Borke, H. (1973) The development of empathy in Chinese and American children between three and six years of age: A cross-cultural study. *Developmental Psychology,* 9:102–108.

Bossard, J. H. S. (1932) Residential propinquity in mate selection. *American Journal of Sociology,* 38:219–224.

Bottomore, T. B. (1966) *Classes in Modern Society.* New York: Pantheon Books.

Bottomore, T. B. (1975) *Marxist Sociology.* New York: Holmes & Meier Publishers.

Bouma, G. D. (1973) Beyond Lenski: A critical review of recent "Protestant ethic" research. *Journal for the Scientific Study of Religion.* 12:141–155.

Bower, D. W. and Christopherson, V. A. (1977) University student cohabitation: A regional comparison of selected attitudes and behavior. *Journal of Marriage and the Family,* 39:447–452.

Bowers, W. J. and Salem, R. G. (1972) Severity of formal sanctions as a repressive response to deviant behavior. *Law and Society Review,* 6:427–441.

Bowlby, J. (1969) *Attachment.* New York: Basic Books.

Bowles, S. and Gintis, H. (1976) *Schooling in Capitalist America.* New York: Basic Books.

Bradburn, N. M. and Caplovitz, D. (1965) *Reports on Happiness.* Chicago: Aldine.

Bradley, L. A. and Bradley, G. W. (1977) The academic achievement of Black students in desegregated schools: A critical review. *Review of Educational Research,* 47:399–449.

Bralove, M. (1977) NOW and then: The feminists after 10 years. *Wall Street Journal* (April 1):8.

Brandwein, R. A., Brown, C. A., and Fox, E. M. (1974) Women and children last: The social situation of divorced mothers and their families. *Journal of Marriage and the Family,* 36:498–514.

Braun, C. (1976) Teachers expectation: Sociopsychological dynamics. *Review of Educational Research,* 46:185–213.

Brewer, M. B. and Campbell, D. T. (1976) *Ethnocentrism and Intergroup Attitudes: East African Evidence.* New York: Halsted Press.

Brieger, R. L. (1976) Career attributes and network structure: A blockmodel study of a biomedical research specialty. *American Sociological Review,* 41:117–135.

Briggs, K. A. (1977) New spiritual organizations considered likely to last. *New York Times* (June 22):13.

Briggs, K. A. (1978) Educated Catholics remaining in church. *New York Times* (March 3):8.

Brim, O. G., Jr. (1966) Socialization through the life cycle. In Brim, O. G., Jr. and Wheeler, S., Eds. *Socialization after Childhood.* New York: Wiley.

Brinton, C. (1958) *The Anatomy of Revolution.* New York: Vintage Books, Inc.

Broadhead, R. S. and Rist, R. C. (1976) Gatekeepers and the social control of social research. *Social Problems,* 23:325–336.

Brody, J. E. (1975) Chiropractic, long ignored as "unscientific," now is increasingly scrutinized by health specialists. *New York Times* (October, 1):25.

Brody, J. E. (1977) Fewer Catholics aid to meet church rule on birth control. *New York Times,* September 26:18.

Bronson, F. H. and Desjardins, C. (1971) Steroid hormones and aggressive behavior in mammals. In Elefthrious, B. E. and Scott, J. P., Eds. *The Physiology of Aggression and Defeat.* New York: Plenum.

Bronson, G. (1977) Long exposure to waste anesthetic gas is peril to workers, U.S. safety unit says. *Wall Street Journal,* 57 (March 1):10.

Brooks, C. H. (1975) The changing relationship between socioeconomic status and infant mortality: An analysis of state characteristics. *Journal of Health and Social Behavior,* 16:291–303.

Broom, L. and Cushing, R. G. (1977) A modest test of an immodest theory: The functional theory of stratification. *American Sociological Review,* 42:157–169.

Broverman, D. M., Klaiber, E. L., Kobayashi, Y., and Vogel., W. (1968) Roles of activation and inhibition in sex differences in cognitive abilities. *Psychological Review,* 75:23–50.

Brown, C. A., Feldberg, R., Fox, E. M., and Kohen, J. (1976) Divorce: Chance of a newlifetime. *Journal of Social Issues,* 32:119–33.

Brown, J. C. (1954) *The Social Psychology of Industry.* Baltimore: English Pelican Edition.

Brown, J. K. (1969) Female initiation rites: A review of the current literature. In Rogers, D., Ed. *Issues in Adolescent Psychology.* New York: Appleton-Century-Crofts.

Brown, J. V., Bakeman, R., Snyder, P. A., Fredrickson, W. T., Morgan, S. T., and Hepler, R. (1975) Interactions of Black inner-city mothers with their newborn infants. *Child Development,* 46:677–86.

Brown, L. R. (1976) The growth of population is slowing down. *New York Times* (November 21):8E.

Bruner, E. M. (1959) Kinship organization among the urban Batak of Sumatra. *Trans-actions,* The New York Academy of Sciences, 22:118–125.

Bruner, E. M. (1961) Urbanization and ethnic identity in North Sumatra. *American Anthropologist,* 63:508–521.

Buckley, W. (1967) *Sociology and Modern Systems Analysis.* Englewood Cliffs, N.J.: Prentice-Hall.

Bunce, R. (1976) *Television in the Corporate Interest.* New York: Praeger Publishers.

Burchard, W. W. (1954) Role conflicts in military chaplains. *American Sociological Review,* 19:528–535.

Burchinal, L. G., (1964) Characteristics of adolescents from unbroken, broken, and reconstituted familes. *Journal of Marriage and The Family,* 26:44–51.

Burgess, E. and Wallin, P. (1953) *Engagement and Marriage.* Philadelphia: Lippincott.

Burns, H. (1963) *The Voices of Negro Protest in America.* Fair Lawn, N.J.: Oxford University Press.

Burr, W. R. (1970) Satisfaction with various aspects of marriage over the life cycle: A random middle class sample. *Journal of Marriage and the Family,* 26:29–37.

Cantor, N. L. and Gelfand, D. M. (1977) Effects of responsiveness and sex of children on adults' behavior, *Child Development,* 48:232–238.

Cantril, H. (1941) *The Psychology of Social Movements.* New York: Wiley.

Caplan, F. and Caplan, T. (1973) *The Power of Play.* Garden City, N.Y.: Anchor Books.

Caplow, T. and McGee, R. J. (1958) *The Academic Marketplace.* New York: Basic Books, Inc.

Carey, A. (1967) The Hawthorne studies: A radical criticism. *American Sociological Review,* 32:403–416.

Carithers, M. W. (1970) School desegregation and racial cleavage, 1954–1970: A review of the literature. *Journal of Social Issues,* 26:25–47.

Carlsmith, J. M., Ellsworth, P. C., and Aronson, E. (1976) *Methods of Research in Social Psychology.* Reading, Mass.: Addison-Wesley.

Carmichael, S. and Hamilton, C. V. (1967) *Black Power.* New York: Random House.

Carpenter, E. (1965) Comments. *Current Anthropology,* 6:55.

Carr, L. G., and Hauser, W. J. (1976) Anomie and religiosity: An empirical re-examination. *Journal for the Scientific Study of Religion,* 15:69–74.

Cartwright, D. (1949) Some principles of mass persuasion: Selected findings of research on the sale of United States war bonds. *Human Relations,* 2:253–267.

Carver, R. P. (1975) The Coleman report: Using inappropriately designed achievement tests. *American Educational Research Journal,* 12:77–86.

Catton, W. R., Jr. and Dunlap, R. E. (1978) Environmental sociology: A new paradigm. *The American Sociologist,* 13:41–49.

Centers, R. (1949) *The Psychology of Social Classes.* Princeton, N. J.: Princeton University Press.

Centers, R., Raven, B. H., and Rodrigues, A. (1971) Conjugal power structure: A re-examination. *American Sociological Review,* 36:264–278.

Cerf, B. A. and Klopfer, D. S. (1963) *The Complete Plays of Gilbert and Sullivan.* New York: The Modern Library, Inc.

Chambliss, W. (1974) The state, the law and the definition of behavior as criminal or delinquent. In Glaser, D., Ed. *Handbood of Criminology.* Indianapolis: Bobbs-Merrill.

Chambliss, W. J. and Seidman, R. B. (1971) *Law, Order and Power.* Reading: Addison-Wesley.

Chancellor, W. J. and Goss, J. R. (1976) Balancing energy and food production, 1975–2000. *Science,* 192:213–218.

Chandler, M. J. and Greenspan, S. (1972) Ersatz egocentrism: A reply to H. Borke. *Developmental Psychology,* 7:104–6.

Chapin, S. (1928) *Cultural Change.* New York: Appleton-Century-Crofts.

Chase-Dunn, C. (1975) The effects of international economic dependence on development and inequality: A cross-national study. *American Sociological Review,* 40:720–738.

Chasin, B. (1977) Letter to the Editor. *Contemporary Sociology,* 6:525–526.

Childe, G. (1941) *Man Makes Himself.* London: Watts & Co., Ltd.

Childe, G. (1942) *What Happened in History.* Middlesex: Penguin Books, Ltd.

Childe, G. (1963) *Social Evolution.* New York: Meridian

Chiricos, T. G. and Waldo, G. P. (1970) Punishment and crime: An examination of some empircal evidence. *Social Problems,* 18:200–217.

Chiricos, T. G. and Waldo, G. P (1975) Socioeconomic status and criminal sentencing: An empirical assessment of a conflict proposition. *American Sociological Review,* 40:753–772.

Chodorow, N. (1974) Family structure and feminine personality. In Rosaldo, M. Z. and Lamphere, L., Eds. *Woman, Culture, and Society*. Stanford, Calif.: Stanford University Press.

Cicourel, A. V. (1964) *Method and Measurements in Sociology*. New York: Free Press.

Cicourel, A. V. (1968) *The Social Organization of Juvenile Justice*. New York: Wiley.

Cicourel, A. V. (1970) Basic and normative rules in the negotiation of status and role. In Dreitzel, H. P., Ed. *Recent Sociology No. 2 Patterns of Communicative Behavior*. New York: Macmillan.

Cicourel, A. V. (1974) *Cognitive Sociology*. New York: Free Press.

Clarity, J. F. (1977) Arson for profit reported on rise, with cost of $2 billion last year. *New York Times* (May 23):1+.

Clark, J. P. and Tifft, L. L. (1966) Polygraph and interview validation of self-reported deviant behavior. *American Sociological Review*, 31:516–23.

Clark, K. B. (1964) *Youth in the Ghetto*. New York: Haryou Associates.

Clark, K. B. (1965) *Dark Ghetto*. New York: Harper & Row.

Clark, K. B. (1965) The wonder is there have been so few riots. *New York Times Magazine* (September 5):10+

Clarke, A. C. (1952) An examination of the operation of residential propinquity as a factor in mate selection. *American Sociological Review*, 17:17–22.

Clausen, J. A. (1965) Drug use. In Merton, R. K. and Nisbet, R., Eds. *Contemporary Social Problems*. 4th ed. New York: Harcourt Brace Jovanovich.

Clayton, R. R. (1975) *The Family, Marriage, and Social Change*. Lexington, Mass.: D. C. Heath and Company.

Clayton, R. R. and Voss, H. L. (1977) Shacking up: Cohabitation in the 1970s. *Journal of Marriage and the Family*, 39:273–283.

Coale, A. J., Fallers, L. A., Levy, M. J., Jr., Schneider, D. M., and Tomkins, S. S. (1965) *Aspects of the Analysis of Family Structure*. Princeton, N.J.: Princeton University Press.

Cohen, A. K. (1965) The sociology of the deviant act: Anomie theory and beyond. *American Sociological Review*, 30:5–14.

Cohen, A. K. (1966) *Deviance and Control*. Englewood Cliffs, N.J.: Prentice Hall, Inc.

Cohen, M. N. (1977) *The Food Crisis in Prehistory: Overpopulation and the Origins of Agriculture*. New Haven: Yale University Press.

Cole, C. L. (1977) Cohabitation in social context. In Libby, R. W. and Whitehurst, R. N., Eds. *Marriage and Alternatives*. Glenview, Ill.: Scott, Foresman and Company.

Cole, R. W., Jr. (1974) Ribbin', jivin', and playin' the dozens. *Phi Delta Kappan*, 56:171–175.

Cole, S. (1975) The growth of scientific knowledge: Theories of deviance as a case study. In Coser, L., *The Idea of Social Structure: Papers in Honor of Robert K. Merton*. New York: Harcourt Brace and Jovanovich.

Cole, W. A. and Hammond, P. E. (1974) Religious pluralism, legal development, and societal complexity: Rudimentary forms of civil religion. *Journal for the Scientific Study of Religion*, 13:177–189.

Coleman, J., Katz, E., and Menzel, M. (1957) The diffusion of an innovation among physicians. *Sociometry*, 20:253–270.

Coleman, J., Katz, E., and Menzel, H. (1959) Social processes in physicians' adoptions of a new drug. *The Journal of Chronic Diseases*, 9:1–19.

Coleman, J. S. (1961) *The Adolescent Society*. New York: The Free Press.

Coleman, J. S. (1966) *Equality of Educational Opportunity*. Washington, D.C.: Government Printing Office.

Coleman, J. S. (1973) *The Mathematics of Collective Action*. Chicago: Aldine.

Colfax, J. D. (1970) Knowledge for whom? *Sociological Inquiry*, 40:73–83.

Collins, R. (1975) *Conflict Sociology*. New York: Academic Press.

Collins, R. (1976) Review of "Schooling in Capitalist America." *Harvard Educational Review*, 46:246–251.

Collins, R. (1977) Some comparative principles of educational stratification. *Harvard Educational Review*, 47:1–27.

Colombotos, J. (1969) Physicians and medicare. A before-after study of the effects of legislation on attitudes. *American Sociological Review*, 34:318–334.

Commager, H. S. (1947) *America in Perspective*. New York: Random House.

Comte, A. (1871) *Positive Philosophy.* Vol. 2. Trans. Marineau, H. New York: Longmans, Green & Co.

Condry, J. and Dyer, S. (1976) Fear of success: Attribution of cause to the victim. *Journal of Social Issues,* 32:63–83.

Conger, J. J. (1977) *Adolescence and Youth.* 2nd ed. New York: Harper & Row.

Conrad, P. (1955) The discovery of hyperkinesis: Notes on the medicalization of deviant behavior. *Social Behavior,* 23:12–21.

Cony, E. and Kann, P. (1977) In China, equality is elusive. *Wall Street Journal* (December 1):16.

Conyers, J. E. and Wallace, W. L. (1976) *Black Elected Officials: A Study of Black Americans Holding Governmental Office.* New York: Russell Sage.

Cook, K. S. (1977) Exchange and power in networks of interorganizational relations. *The Sociological Quarterly,* 18:62–82.

Cook, S. W. (1976) Ethical issues in the conduct of research in social relations. In Selltiz, C., Wrightsman, L. S., and Cook, S. W. *Research Methods in Social Relations.* 3rd ed. New York: Holt, Rinehart and Winston.

Cooley, C. H. (1902) *Human Nature and the Social Order.* New York: Scribner.

Cooley, C. H. (1909) *Social Organization.* New York: Scribner.

Coombs, R. H. (1969) Social participation, self-concept and interpersonal valuation. *Sociometry,* 32:273–286.

Cooper, H. M. and Baron, R. M. (1977) Academic expectations and attributed responsibility as predictors of professional teachers' reinforcement behavior. *Journal of Educational Psychology,* 69:409–418.

Coopersmith, S. (1967) *Antecedents of Self-Esteem.* San Francisco: W. H. Freeman and Company.

Corwin, R. G. (1965) *A Sociology of Education.* New York: Appleton-Century-Crofts.

Coser, L. A. (1962) Some functions of deviant behavior and normative flexibility. *American Journal of Sociology,* 68:172–181.

Coser, L. A. (1965) The sociology of poverty. *Social Problems,* 13:140–8.

Cottrell, W. F. (1951) Death by dieselization: A case study in the reaction to technological change. *American Sociological Review,* 16:358–365.

Couch, C. J. (1968) Collective behavior: An examination of some stereotypes. *Social Problems,* 15:310–322.

Coward, B. E., Feagin, J. R., and Williams, J. A., Jr. (1974) The culture of poverty debate: Some additional data. *Social Problems,* 21:621–634.

Cressey, D. R. (1960) Epidemiology and individual conduct: A case from criminology. *Pacific Sociological Review,* 3:49–53.

Critchfield, R. (1978) The culture of poverty. *Human Behavior,* 7 (January): 65–69.

Crittenden, A. (1977) Women tell of sexual harassment at work. *New York Times* (October 25):35.

Cromwell, R. E. and Olson, D. H. (1975) *Power in Families.* New York: Halsted Press.

Crossman, R. (1952) *The God That Failed.* New York: Bantam Books.

Cunliffe, M. (1960) *George Washington, Man and Monument.* New York: Mentor Books.

Cutright, P. (1968) Occupational inheritance: A cross-national analysis. *American Journal of Sociology,* 73:400–416.

Dahl, R. A. (1958) A critique of the ruling elite model. *The American Political Science Review,* 52:462–485.

Dahrendorf, R. (1959) *Class and Class Conflict in Industrial Society.* Stanford, Calif.: Stanford University Press.

D'Andrade, R. G. (1966) Sex differences and cultural institutions. In Maccoby, E. E., Ed. *The Development of Sex Differences.* Stanford, Calif.: Stanford University Press.

Daniel, C. (1974) Gains of Watergate. *New York Times,* August 10:1, 7.

Darley, S. A. (1976) Big-time careers for the little woman: A dual-role dilemma. *Journal of Social Issues,* 32:85–98.

Davidson, C. and Gaitz, C. M. (1974) "Are the poor different?" A comparison of work behavior and attitudes among the urban poor and nonpoor. *Social Problems,* 22:229–245.

Davie, M. R. (1937) The pattern of urban growth. In Murdock, G. P., Ed. *Studies in the Science of Society.* New Haven: Yale University Press.

Davis, A. (1950) *Social-Class Influences upon Learning* Cambridge: Harvard University Press.

Davis, A., Gardner, B. B., and Gardner, M. R. (1941) *Deep South*. Chicago: University of Chicago Press.

Davis, A. and Havighurst, R. J. (1947) *Father of the Man*. Boston: Houghton Mifflin Co.

Davis, K. (1947) Final note on a case of extreme isolation. *American Journal of Sociology*, 52:432–37.

Davis, K. (1949) *Human Society*. New York: Macmillan.

Davis, K. (1951) Introduction. Goode, W. J. *Religion among the Primitives*. New York: Free Press.

Davis, K. (1955) The origin and growth of urbanization in the world. *American Journal of Sociology*, 60:429–437.

Davis, K. (1967) The urbanization of the human population. In *Cities*. New York: Alfred A. Knopf.

Davis, K. (1971) The world's population crisis. In Merton, R. K. and Nisbet, R. A., Eds. *Contemporary Social Problems*. 3rd ed. New York: Harcourt Brace Jovanovich.

Davis, K. (1976) The world's population crisis. In Merton, R. K. and Nisbet, R., Eds. *Contemporary Problems*. 4th ed. New York: Harcourt Brace Jovanovich.

Davis, K. and Moore, W. E. (1945) Some principles of stratification. *American Sociological Review*, 10:242–249.

Daw, N. W., Berman, N. E. J., and Ariel, M. (1978) Interaction of critical periods in the visual cortex of kittens. *Science*, 199:565–566.

Dawkins, R. (1976) *The Selfish Gene*. New York: Oxford University Press.

Day, R. and Day, J. V. (1977) A review of the current state of negotiated order theory: An appreciation and a critique. *Sociological Quarterly*, 18:126–42.

Deedy, J. (1976) American flock strays beyond Catholicism. *New York Times*, May 23:11.

DellaCava, F. A. (1975) Becoming an ex-priest: The process of leaving a high commitment status. *Sociolocial Inquiry*, 45:41–49.

Dellinger, R. W. (1977) Keeping tabs on the Joneses. *Human Behavior*, 6 (November):22–30.

Dennis, J. (1970) Support for the institution of elections by the mass public. *American Political Science Review*, 64:819–835.

Dennis, W. (1973) *Children of the Crèche*. New York: Appleton-Century-Crofts.

Denzin, N. K. (1970) Symbolic interactionism and ethnomethodogy. In Douglas, J. D., Ed. *Understanding Everyday Life*. Chicago: Aldine.

Denzin, N. K. (1972) The genesis of self in every childhood. *Sociological Quarterly*, 13:291–314.

de Sales, R. R. (1938) Love in America. *The Atlantic* (May):645+.

Deutsch, M. and Krauss, R. M. (1965) *Theories in Social Psychology*. New York: Basic Books.

Dewey, J. (1928) *Democracy and Education*. New York: Macmillan.

Dixon, R. R. (1976) Measuring equality between the sexes. *Journal of Social Issues*, 32:19–32.

Djilas, M. (1957) *The New Class*. New York: Frederick A. Praeger.

Dohrenwend, B. P. and Dohrenwend, B. S. (1976) Sex differences and psychiatric disorders. *American Journal of Sociology*, 81:1447–1454.

Dowdall, G. W. (1974) White gains from Black subordination in 1960 and 1970. *Social Problems*, 22:162–183.

Dragastin, S. E. and Elder, G. H., Jr. (1975) *Adolescence in the Life Cycle*. New York: Wiley.

Dubin, R. (1976) Work in modern society. In Dubin, R., Ed. *Handbook of Work, Organization, and Society*. Chicago: Rand McNally.

Dubin, R., Hedley, R. A., and Taveggia, T. C. (1976) In Dubin, R., Ed. *Handbook of Work, Organization, and Society*. Chicago: Rand McNally.

Dullea, G. (1975) Women in classrooms, not the principal's office. *New York Times* (July 13):8E.

Dullea, G. (1977) Vast changes in society traced to the rise of working women. *New York Times* (November 29):1, 28.

Dumont, L. (1970) *Homo Hierarchicus: The caste system and its implications*. London: Weidenfeld and Nicolson.

Duncan, O. D. (1959) Human ecology and population studies. In Hauser, P. M. and Duncan, O. D., Eds. *The Study of Population*. Chicago: The University of Chicago Press.

Duncan, O. D. (1961) From social system to ecosystem. *Sociological Inquiry*, 31:140–149.

Duncan, O. D., Featherman, D. L., and Duncan, B. (1972) *Socioeconomic Background and Achievement.* New York: Seminar Press.

Duncan, S., Jr., (1972) Some signals and rules for taking speaking turns in conversations. *Journal of Personality and Social Psychology,* 23:283–292.

Dunkin, M. J. and Biddle, B. J. (1974) *The Study of Teaching.* New York: Holt, Rinehart and Winston.

Durkheim, E. (1933) *The Division of Labor in Society.* Trans. Simpson, G. New York: Macmillan.

Durkheim, E. (1933) *The Rules of Sociological Method.* New York: The Free Press.

Durkheim, E. (1947) *The Elementary Forms of Religious Life.* New York: The Free Press.

Durkheim, E. (1897) *Suicide.* Trans. Simpson, G. New York: The Free Press. Reprinted 1951.

Dusek, J. B. (1975) Do teachers bias children's learning? *Review of Educational Research,* 45:661–684.

Dutton, D. G. and Aron, A. P. (1974) Some evidence for heightened sexual attraction under conditions of high anxiety. *Journal of Personality and Social Psychology,* 30:510–517.

Eaton, W. W., Jr. (1974) Residence, social class, and schizophrenia. *Journal of Health and Social Behavior,* 15:289–299.

Eckholm, E. P. (1975) The deterioration of mountain environments. *Science,* 189:763–770.

Ehrlich, P. R. and Ehrlich, A. H. (1974) Misconceptions. *New York Times Magazine* (June 16):9+.

Eister, A. W. (1972) An outline of a structural theory of cults. *Journal for the Scientific Study of Religion,* 11:319–333.

Ekeh, P. P. (1974) *Social Exchange Theory: Two Traditions.* Cambridge, Mass: Harvard University Press.

Ellis, L. (1977) The decline and fall of sociology. *American Sociologist,* 12:56–66.

Empey, L. T. and Rabow, J. (1961) The Provo experiment in delinquency rehabilitation. *American Sociological Review,* 26:679–96.

Erbe, W. (1964) Social involvement and political activity: A replication and elaboration. *American Sociological Review,* 29:198–215.

Erickson, F. (1975) Gatekeeping and the melting pot: Interaction in counseling encounters. *Harvard Educational Review,* 45:44–70.

Erikson, E. H. (1963) *Childhood and Society.* New York: W. W. Norton.

Erikson, E. H. (1968) *Identity: Youth and Crisis.* New York: W. W. Norton.

Erikson, K. (1962) Notes on the sociology of deviance. *Social Problems,* 9:307–314.

Erikson, K. (1964) Notes on the sociology of deviance. In Becker, H. S., Ed. *The Other Side.* New York: The Free Press.

Erlanger, H. S. (1974) Social class and corporal punishment in childrearing: A reassessment. *American Sociological Review,* 39:68–85.

Essien-Udom, E. U. (1964) *Black Nationalism.* New York: Dell.

Etzioni, A. (1964) *Modern Organizations.* Englewood Cliffs, N.J.: Prentice-Hall.

Fairfield, R. (1972) *Communes USA.* Baltimore: Penguin Books.

Fanfani, A. (1955) *Catholicism, Protestantism and Capitalism.* New York: Sheed & Ward, Inc.

Faris, R. E. L. (1964) The discipline of sociology. In Faris, R. E. L., Ed. *Handbook of Modern Sociology.* Chicago: Rand McNally & Co.

Farrell, R. A. and Nelson, J. F. (1976) A causal model of secondary deviance: The case of homosexuality. *Sociological Quarterly,* 17:109–120.

Fast, J. (1970) *Body Language.* New York: M. Evans and Company.

Fasteau, M. F. (1974) *The Male Machine.* New York: McGraw-Hill.

Feather, N. T. and Simon, J. G. (1972) "Luck and the unexpected outcome," *Australian Journal of Psychology,* 24:113–117.

Featherman, D. L. and Hauser, R. M. (1976) Changes in the socioeconomic stratification of the races, 1962–73. *American Journal of Sociology,* 82:621–651.

Fein, M. (1976) Motivation for work. In Dubin, R., Ed. *Handbook of Work, Organization, and Society.* Chicago: Rand McNally.

Fendrich, J. M. (1977) Keeping the faith or pursuing the good life: A study of the consequences of participation in the civil rights movement. *American Sociological Review,* 42:144–157.

Ferree, M. M. (1976) Working-class jobs: Housework and paid work as sources of satisfaction. *Social Problem,* 23:431–441.

Festinger, L. (1957) *A Theory of Cognitive Dissonance.* New York: Harper & Row.

Fichter, J. H. (1971) *Sociology.* 2nd ed. Chicago: University of Chicago Press.

Fichter, J. H. (1975) *The Catholic Cult of the Paraclete.* New York: Sheed and Ward.

Firestone, G. and Brody, N. (1975) Longitudinal investigation of teacher-student interactions and their relationship to academic performance. *Journal of Educational Psychology,* 67:544–550.

Firey, W. (1947) *Land Use in Central Boston.* Cambridge: Harvard University Press.

Firth, R. (1958) *Human Types.* Rev. ed. New York: Mentor Books.

Fischer, C. S. (1971) A research note on urbanism and tolerance. *American Journal of Sociology,* 76:847–856.

Fischer, C. S. (1975a) The effect of urban life on traditional values. *Social Forces,* 53:420–432.

Fischer, C. S. (1975b) Toward a subcultural theory of urbanism. *American Journal of Sociology,* 80:1319–1341.

Fischer, C. S. (1976) *The Urban Experience.* New York: Harcourt Brace Jovanovich.

Fisher, J. (1947) *Why They Behave Like Russians.* New York: Harper & Row.

Fisher, S. and Greenberg, R. P. (1977) *The Scientific Credibility of Freud's Theories and Therapy.* New York: Basic Books.

Flavell, J. H. (1974) The development of inferences about others. In Mischel, T., Ed. *Understanding Other Persons.* Oxford: Blackwell.

Flint, J. M. (1971) Inner-city decay causes business to wither. *New York Times* (July 19):18.

Foote, N. N. and Hart, C. W. (1953) Public opinion and collective behavior. In Sherif, M. and Wilson, M. O., Eds. *Group Relations at the Crossroads.* New York: Harper & Row.

Form, W. H. (1975) The social construction of anomie: A four-nation study of industrial workers. *American Journal of Sociology,* 80:1165–1191.

Fort, J. and Cory, C. T. (1975) *American Drugstore: A (Alcohol) to V (Valium).* Boston: Little, Brown.

Fortes, M. (1949) *The Web of Kinship Among the Tallensi.* Fair Lawn, N.J.: Oxford University Press.

Fraiberg, S. (1977) *Every Child's Birthright.* New York: Basic Books.

Franklin, R. S. and Resnik, S. (1973) *The Political Economy of Racism.* New York: Holt, Rinehart and Winston.

Franks, D. R. and Marolla, J. (1976) Efficacious action and social approval as interacting dimensions of self-esteem: A tentative formulation through construct validation. *Sociometry,* 39:324–341.

Frazier, C. E. (1976) *Theoretical Approaches to Deviance: An Evaluation.* Columbus, Ohio: Charles E. Merrill.

Freeman, H. and Simmons, O. (1961) Feelings of stigma among relatives of former mental patients. *Social Problems,* 8:321–332.

Freeman, J. (1973) The origins of the women's liberation movement. *American Journal of Sociology,* 78:792–811.

Freidson, E. (1976) The division of labor as social interaction. *Social Problems,* 23:304–313.

Freitag, P. J. (1975) The cabinet and big business: A study of interlocks. *Social Problems,* 23: 137–152.

Freud, S. (1948) *Some psychical consequences of the anatomical distinction between the sexes.* Collected Papers. Vol. V. London: Hogarth Press.

Friedl, E. (1975) *Women and Men: An Anthropologist's View.* New York: Holt, Rinehart and Winston.

Friedrichs, R. W. (1970) *A Sociology of Sociology.* New York: The Free Press.

Fuller, C. J. (1976) *The Nayars Today.* Cambridge: Cambridge University Press.

Funck-Brentano, F. (1939) *Luther.* London: Jonathan Cape, Ltd.

Galbraith, J. K. (1958) *The Affluent Society.* Boston: Houghton Mifflin Co.

Galliher, J. F. and McCartney, J. L. (1977) *Criminology: Power, Crime and Criminal Law.* Homewood, Ill.: Dorsey Press.

Gans, H. J. (1962) *The Urban Villagers.* New York: Free Press.

Gardner, B. T. and Gardner, R. A. (1974) Comparing the early utterances of child and chimpanzee. In Pick, A., Ed. *Minnesota Symposium in Child Psychology.* Vol. 8. Minneapolis: University of Minnesota Press.

Gardner, M. (1978) The third coming. *New York Review of Books* (January 26):21–22.

Garfinkel, H. (1964) Studies of the routine grounds of everyday activities. *Social Problems,* 11:225–250.

Garfinkel, H. (1967) *Studies in Ethnomethodology.* Englewood Cliffs, N.J.: Prentice-Hall.

Garrett, C. S. and Cunningham, D. J. (1974) Effects of vicarious consequences and model and experimenter sex on imitative behavior in first-grade children. *Journal of Educational Psychology,* 66:940–947.

Garvey, C. and Hogan, R. (1973) Social speech and social interaction: Egocentrism revisited. *Child Development,* 44:562–8.

Gasson, R. M., Haller, A. O., and Sewell, W. H. (1972) *Attitudes and Facilitation in the Attainment of Status.* Washington, D.C.: American Sociological Association.

Gecas, V. (1971) Parental behavior and dimensions of adolescent self-evaluation. *Sociometry,* 34:466–482.

Gecas, V. (1972) Parental behavior and contextual variations in adolescent self-esteem. *Sociometry,* 35:332–345.

Gecas, V. and Nye, F. I. (1974) Sex and class differences in parent-child interaction: A test of Kohn's hypothesis. *Journal of Marriage and the Family,* 26:742–749.

Geertz, C. (1966) Religion as a cultural system. In Banton, M., Ed. *Anthropological Approaches to the Study of Religion.* New York: Frederick A. Praeger.

Geis, G. and Meier, R. F., Eds. (1977) *White-Collar Crime: Offenses in Business, Politics, and the Professions.* New York: The Free Press.

Gerard, H. B. and Miller, N. (1975) *School Desegregation.* New York: Plenum Press.

Gergen, K. J. (1965) Interaction goals and personalistic feedback as factors affecting the presentation of self. *Journal of Personality and Social Psychology,* 1:413–424.

Gergen, K. J. (1967) The significance of skin color in human relations. *Daedalus,* 96:387–421.

Gergen, K. J. (1968) Personal consistency and presentation of the self. In Gordon, C. and Gergen, K. J., Eds. *The Self in Social Interaction.* New York: Wiley.

Gergen, K. J. (1971) *The Concept of Self.* New York: Holt, Rinehart and Winston.

Gergen, K. J. (1972) Multiple identity. *Psychology Today,* 5 (May, 1972):31–35;64–66.

Germain, A. (1975) A major resource awaiting development: Women in the third world. *New York Times* (August 26):8E.

Gerth, H. H. and Mills, C. W. (1953) *Character and Social Structure.* New York: Harcourt, Brace.

Gibbs, J. P. (1975) *Crime, Punishment, and Deterrence.* New York: Elsevier.

Gibbs, J. P. and Poston, D. L., Jr. (1975) The division of labor: Conceptualization and related measures. *Social Forces,* 53:468–476.

Gibson, C. (1977) The elusive rise in the American birthrate. *Science,* 196:500–503.

Gillespie, D. L. (1971) Who has the power? The marital struggle. *Journal of Marriage and the Family,* 33:445–458.

Gist, N. P. and Fava, S. F. (1964) *Urban Society.* 5th ed. New York: Thomas Y. Crowell Co.

Gitlin, T. (1971) The price men pay for supremacy. *New York Times* (December 11):31.

Glaser, B. and Strauss, A. (1971) *Status passage:* A formal theory. Chicago: Aldine.

Glass, B. (1965) The ethical basis of science. *Science,* 150 (December 3):1254–61.

Glenn, N. D. (1973) Class and party support in the United States: Recent and emerging trends. *Public Opinion Quarterly,* 37:1–20.

Glenn, N. D. (1975) Class and party support in 1972. *Public Opinion Quarterly,* 39:117–122.

Glenn, N. D. (1975) Psychological well-being in the postparental stage: Some evidence from national surveys. *Journal of Marriage and the Family,* 37:105–110.

Glenn, N. D. and Alston, J. P. (1968) Cultural distances among occupational categories. *American Sociological Review,* 33:365–382.

Glick, P. C. (1975) A demographer looks at American families. *Journal of Marriage and the Family,* 37:15–26.

Glock, C. Y. and Bellah, R. N. (1976) *The New Religious Consciousness.* Berkeley: University of California Press.

Glock, C. Y., Ringer, B. B., and Babbie, E. R. (1967) *To Comfort and to Challenge: A Dilemma of the Contemporary Church.* Berkeley: University of California Press.

Glock, C. Y. and Stark, R. (1965) *Religion and Society in Tension.* Chicago: Rand McNally & Co.

Gluckman, M. (1955) *Custom and Conflict in Africa.* Oxford: Blackwell.

Goffman, E. (1959) *The Presentation of Self in Everyday Life.* Garden City, N.Y.: Doubleday.

Goffman, E. (1961) *Asylums: Essays on the Social Situation of Mental Patients and Other Inmates.* Garden City, N.Y.: Doubleday Anchor Books.

Goffman, E. (1961) *Encounters.* Indianapolis: Bobbs-Merrill.

Goffman, E. (1962) *Asylums.* Chicago: Aldine.

Goffman, E. (1963) *Stigma: Note on the Management of Spoiled Identity.* Englewood Cliffs, N.J.: Prentice-Hall.

Goffman, E. (1967) *Interaction Ritual.* Garden City, N.Y.: Doubleday Anchor Books.

Goffman, E. (1974) *Frame Analysis.* Cambridge: Harvard University Press.

Goldfarb, W. (1945) Psychological privation in infancy and subsequent adjustment. *American Journal of Orthopsychiatry,* 15:247–255.

Goldfarb, W. (1947) Variations in adolescent adjustment of institutionally reared children. *American Journal of Orthopsychiatry,* 17:449–457.

Goldfarb, W. (1949) Rorschach test differences between family-reared, institution-reared, and schizophrenic children. *American Journal of Orthopsychiatry,* 19:624–633.

Goldman, P. and Van Houten, D. R. (1977) Managerial strategies and the worker: A Marxist analysis of bureaucracy. *The Sociological Quarterly,* 18:108–125.

Good, T. L., Biddle, B. J., and Brophy, J. E. (1975) *Teachers Make a Difference.* New York: Holt, Rinehart and Winston.

Goode, E. (1975) On behalf of labeling theory. *Social Problems,* 22:570–583.

Goode, W. J. (1956) *Women in Divorce.* New York: The Free Press.

Goode, W. J. (1959) The theoretical importance of love. *American Sociological Review,* 24:38–47.

Goode, W. J. (1960) Illegitimacy in Caribbean social structure. *American Sociological Review,* 25:21–31.

Goode, W. J. (1963) *World Revolution and Family Patterns.* New York: The Free Press.

Goode, W. J. (1972) The place of force in human society. *American Sociological Review,* 37:507–519.

Goodenough, W. H. (1963) *Cooperation in Change.* New York: Russell Sage Foundation.

Goodman, E. J. (1975) Abused by her husband—and the law. *New York Times* (October 7):18.

Goodwin, L. (1972) *Do the Poor Want to Work?* Washington, D.C.: Brookings Institution.

Gordon, D., Edwards, R., and Reich, M. (1975) *Labor Market Segmentation.* Lexington, Mass.: Heath.

Gordon, D. N. (1970) Societal complexity and kinship: Family organization or rules of residence? *Pacific Sociological Review,* 13:252–262.

Gordon, L. (1970) Functions of the family. In Tanner, L. B., Ed. *Voices from Women's Liberation.* New York: New American Library.

Gornick, V. and Moran, B. K. (1971) *Woman in Sexist Society.* New York: New American Library.

Gough, E. K. (1959) The Nayars and the definition of marriage. *Journal of the Royal Anthropological Institute,* 89:23–24.

Gough, E. K. (1965) A note on Nayer marriage. *Man,* 65:8–11.

Gouldner, A. W. (1955) Metaphysical pathos and the theory of bureaucracy. *American Political Science Review,* 49:496–507.

Gouldner, A. W. (1962) Anti-minotaur: The myth of a value-free sociology. *Social Problems,* 9:199–213.

Gouldner, A. W. (1976) The dark side of the dialectic: Toward a new objectivity. *Sociological Inquiry,* 46:3–15.

Gouldner, A. W. (1977) Letter to the Editor. *New York Review of Books,* 24 (November 10):42.

Gove, W. R. (1970) Societal reaction as an explanation of mental illness: An evaluation. *American Sociological Review,* 35:873–884.

Gove, W. R. (1972) The relationship between sex roles, mental illness and marital status. *Social Forces,* 51:34–44.

Gove, W. R. Ed. (1975) *The Labelling of Deviance: Evaluating a Perspective*. New York: Halsted Press.

Gove, W. R. (1976) Deviant behavior, social intervention, and labeling theory. Coser, L. A. and Larsen, O. N., Eds. *The Uses of Controversy in Sociology*. New York: The Free Press.

Gove, W. R. and Geerken, M. R. (1977) The effect of children and employment on the mental health of married men and women. *Social Forces*, 56:66–76.

Gove, W. R. and Tudor, J. (1973) Adult sex roles and mental health. *American Journal of Sociology*, 78:812–835.

Gove, W. R. and Tudor, J. (1977) Commentary and debate. *American Journal of Sociology*, 82:1327–1336.

Grandjean, B. D. (1975) An economic analysis of the Davis-Moore theory of stratification. *Social Forces*, 53:543–552.

Gray, J. A. (1971) Sex differences in emotional behavior in mammals, including man: Endocrine bases. *Acta Psychologica*, 35:29–46.

Greeley, A. M. (1977) *The American Catholic*. New York: Basic Books.

Green, H. W. (1932) Cultural areas in the city of Cleveland. *American Journal of Sociology*, 38:356–367.

Grimm, J. W. and Stern, R. N. (1974) Sex roles and internal labor market structures: The "female" semi-professions. *Social Problems*, 21:690–705.

Groombridge, B. (1975) *Television and the People: A Programme for Democratic Participation*. Baltimore, Md.: Penguin Books.

Gross, N., Mason, W. S., and McEachern, A. W. (1958) *Explorations in Role Analysis*. New York: Wiley.

Grossman, N. (1975) On Peter Berger's definition of religion. *Journal for the Scientific Study of Religion*, 14:289–292.

Guardo, C. (1969) Sociometric status and self-concept in sixth graders. *Journal of Educational Research*, 62:320–2.

Guest, A. M. and Weed, J. A. (1976) Ethnic residential segregation: Patterns of change. *American Journal of Sociology*, 81:1088–1111.

Guhl, A. M. (1964) Psychophysiological interrelations in the social behavior of chickens. *Psychological Bulletin*, 61:277–285.

Gulick, J. (1973) Urban anthropology. In Honigman, J. J., Ed. *Handbook of Social and Cultural Anthropology*. Chicago: Rand McNally.

Gurin, G., Verhoff, J., and Feld, S. (1960) *Americans View Their Mental Health*. New York: Basic Books.

Gurwitz, S. B. and Dodge, K. A. (1975) Adults' evaluations of a child as a fuction of sex of adult and sex of child. *Journal of Personality and Social Psychology*, 32:822–828.

Hacker, A. (1975) What rules America? *The New York Review of Books* (May 1):9–13.

Hagan, J. and Leon, J. (1977) Rediscovering delinquency: Social history, political ideology and the sociology of law. *American Sociological Review*, 42:587–598.

Hagstrom, W. O. (1974) Competition in Science. *American Sociological Review*, 39:1–18.

Hall, E. T. (1973) *The Silent Language*. Garden City, N.Y.: Anchor Books.

Hallowell, A. I. (1951) Cultural factors in the structuralization of perception. In Roher, J. H. and Sherif, M., Eds. *Social Psychology at the Crossroads*. New York: Harper & Row.

Hamblin, R. L. (1962) The dynamics of racial discrimination. *Social Problems*, 10:103–120.

Hamblin, R. L. and Miller, J. L. L. (1976) Reinforcement and the origin, rate and extent of cultural diffusion. *Social Forces*, 54:743–759.

Hammond, D. (1970) Magic: A problem in semantics. *American Anthropologist*, 72:1349–1359.

Hammond, K. R. and Adelman, L. (1976) Science, values, and human judgment. *Science*, 194 (October 22):389–96.

Hammond, P. E. and Williams, K. R. (1976) The Protestant ethic thesis: A social-psychological assessment. *Social Forces*, 54:579–589.

Hansen, S. B. (1975) Participation, political structure, and concurrence. *American Political Science Review*, 69;1181–1199.

Harber, J. R. and Bryen, D. N. (1976) Black English and the task of reading. *Review of Educational Research*, 46:387–405.

Hardin, G. (1974) *Mandatory Motherhood: The True Meaning of "Right to Life."* Boston: Beacon Press.

Harkey, J., Miles, D. L., and Rushing, W. A. (1976) The relation between social class and functional status: A new look at the drift hypothesis. *Journal of Health and Social Behavior,* 17:194–204.

Harnischfeger, A. and Wiley, D. E. (1976) *Achievement Test Score Decline: Do We Need To Worry?* St. Louis: Cemrel, Inc.

Harper, D. and Emmert, F. (1963) Work behavior in a service industry. *Social Forces,* 42:216–225.

Harris, A. R. (1976) Race, commitment to deviance, and spoiled identity. *American Sociological Review,* 41:432–442.

Harris, C. D. and Ullman, E. L. (1945) *The nature of cities.* The Annals of the American Academy of Political and Social Science, 242:7–17.

Harris, M. (1975) *Culture, People, Nature.* 2nd ed. New York: Thomas Y. Crowell.

Harris, M. (1977) Why men dominate women. *New York Times Magazine* (November 13):46+.

Harrison, M. I. (1974) Sources of recruitment to Catholic Pentecostalism. *Journal for the Scientific Study of Religion,* 13:49–64.

Hart, H. (1957) Acceleration in social change. In Allen, E. R., Hart, H., Miller, D. C., Ogburn, W. F., and Nimkoff, M. F., Eds. *Technology and Social Change.* New York: Appleton-Century-Crofts.

Hartley, S. F. (1970) The decline of illegitimacy in Japan. *Social Problems,* 18:78–91.

Hartnagel, T. F., Teevan, J. J., Jr., and McIntyre, J. J. (1975) Television violence and violent behavior. *Social Forces,* 54:341–351.

Hauser, P. M. (1957) *Urbanization in Asia and the Far East.* Calcutta: UNESCO.

Hauser, R. M. (1973) Disaggregating a social-psychological model of educational attainment. In Goldberger, A. J. and Duncan, O. D., Eds. *Structural Equation Models in the Social Sciences.* New York: Seminar Press.

Hauser, R. M. and Dickinson, P. J. (1974) Inequality on occupational status and income. *American Educational Research Journal,* 11:161–168.

Hauser, R. M., Dickinson, P. J., Travis, H. P., and Koffel, J. N. (1975) Structural changes in occupational mobility among men in the United States. *American Sociological Review,* 40:585–598.

Havighurst, R. J. and Neugarten, B. L. (1975) *Society and Education.* 4th ed. Boston: Allyn and Bacon, Inc.

Hawley, A. H. (1963) Community power and urban-renewal success. *American Journal of Sociology,* 68:422–431.

Hayes, C. (1951) *The Ape in Our House.* New York: Harper & Row.

Hazelrigg, L. E. and Garnier, M. A. (1976) Occupational mobility in industrial societies: A comparative analysis of differential access to occupational ranks in seventeen countries. *American Sociological Review,* 41:498–511.

Heath, A. (1976) *Rational Choice and Social Exchange: A Critique of Exchange Theory.* New York: Cambridge University Press.

Heirich, M. (1977) Change of heart: A test of some widely held theories about religious conversion. *American Journal of Sociology,* 83:653–680.

Hennig, M. and Jardim, A. (1976) *The Managerial Woman.* Garden City, N.Y.: Doubleday & Co.

Henze, L. F. and Hudson, J. W. (1974) Personal and family characteristics of cohabiting and noncohabiting college students. *Journal of Marriage and the Family,* 36:722–6.

Herberg, W. (1973) Interview. *U.S. News & World Report,* June 4:58.

Hertzler, J. O. (1961) *American Social Institutions.* Rockleigh, N.J.: Allyn & Bacon, Inc.

Hewitt, J. P. (1976) *Self and Society.* Boston: Allyn and Bacon, Inc.

Heydebrand, W. (1977) Organization contradictions in public bureaucracies: Toward a Marxian theory of organizations. *The Sociological Quarterly,* 18:83–107.

Hill, G. (1974) U.N. population talks to open in Bucharest. *New York Times* (August 18):2.

Hill, G. (1976) United Nations study says spreading deserts are caused by man's misuse of the land. *New York Times* (February 25):17.

Hill, R. (1970) *Family Development in Three Generations.* Cambridge: Schenkman Publishing Company.

Hinkle, R. C., Jr. and Hinkle, G. J. (1954) *The Development of Modern Sociology.* New York: Random House.

Hobart, C. W. (1974) Church involvement and the comfort thesis in Alberta. *Journal for the Scientific Study of Religion,* 13:463–470.

Hodge, R. W., Siegel, P. M., and Rossi, P. M. (1966) Occupational prestige in the United States: 1925–1963. In Bendix, R. and Lipset, S. M., Eds. *Class, Status and Power.* New York: Free Press.

Hodge, R. W. and Treiman, D. J. (1968) Class identification in the United States. *American Journal of Sociology,* 73:535–547.

Hodges, H. M., Jr. (1964) *Social Stratification.* Cambridge: Schenkman Publishing Co.

Hoebel, E. A. (1958) *Man in the Primitive World.* 2nd ed. New York: McGraw-Hill.

Hoffer, E. (1951) *The True Believer.* New York: Harper & Row.

Hoffman, L. W. (1972) Early childhood experiences and women's achievement motives. *Journal of Social Issues,* 28:129–155.

Hoffman, M. L. (1975) Developmental synthesis of affect and cognition and its implications for altruistic motivation. *Developmental Psychology,* 11:607–22.

Hollingshead, A. B. (1949) *Elmtown's Youth.* New York: Wiley.

Holter, H. (1973) *Sex Roles and Social Structure.* Oslo: Universitetsforlaget.

Homans, G. C. (1974) *Social Behavior: Its Elementary Forms.* Rev. ed. New York: Harcourt.

Horner, M. S. (1968) Sex differences in achievement motivation and performance in competitive and non-competitive stituations. Unpublished doctoral dissertation. University of Michigan, 1968.

Horner, M. S. (1972) Toward an understanding of achievement related conflicts in women. *Journal of Social Issues,* 28:157–175.

Horowitz, I. L. and Liebowitz, M. (1968) Social deviance and political marginality: Toward a definition of the relation between sociology and politics. *Social Problems,* 15:280–296.

Horowitz, A. (1977) Marxist theories of deviance and teleology: A critique of Spitzer. *Social Problems,* 24:362–363.

Hostetler, J. A. (1968) *Amish Society.* Rev. Ed. Baltimore: The Johns Hopkins University Press.

House, J. S. (1977) The three faces of social psychology. *Sociometry,* 40:161–177.

Hout, M. and Morgan, W. R. (1975) Race and sex variations in the causes of the expected attainments of high school seniors. *American Journal of Sociology,* 81:363–393.

Howard, J. and Holman, B. L. (1970) The effects of race and occupation on hypertension mortality. *The Milbank Fund Quarterly,* 47:263–270.

Howells, W. W. (1973) *Evolution of the Genus Homo.* Reading, Mass.: Addison-Wesley.

Hoyt, H. (1939) *The Structure and Growth of Residential Neighborhoods in American Cities.* Washington, D.C.: Federal Housing Administration.

Hraba, J. and Richards, R. O. (1975) Race relations, social science, and social policy: A comment on two articles. *American Journal of Sociology* 80: 1438–1447.

Hsu, F. L. K. (1943) Incentives to work in primitive communities. *American Sociological Review,* 8:638–642.

Huaco, G. A. (1963) A logical analysis of the Davis-Moore theory of stratification. *American Sociological Review,* 28:801–804.

Huaco, G. A. (1966) The functionalist theory of stratification: Two decades of controversy. *Inquiry,* 9:215–240.

Hummon, N. P., Doreian, P., and Teuter, K. (1975) A structural control model of organizational change. *American Sociological Review,* 40:813–824.

Humphreys, L. (1972) *Out of the Closets.* Englewood Cliffs, N.J.: Prentice-Hall.

Hunt, J. G. (1977) Assimilation or marginality? Some school integration effects reconsidered. *Social Forces,* 56:604–610.

Hunt, L. G. and Chambers, C. D. (1976) *The Heroin Epidemics: A Study of Heroin Use in the United States, 1965–75.* New York: Spectrum Publications.

Hunt, L. L. and Hunt, J. G. (1977) Black religion as both opiate and inspiration of civil rights militance: Putting Marx's data to the test. *Social Force,* 56:1–14.

Hunter, A. (1975) The loss of community: An empirical test through replication. *American Sociological Review,* 40:537–552.

Hurn, C. J. (1976) Theory and ideology in two traditions of thought about schools. *Social Forces,* 54:848–865.

Hutt, C. (1972a) Neuroendocrinological, behavioural and intellectual aspects of sexual differentiation in human development. In Ounsted, C. and Taylor, D. C., Eds. *Gender Differences: Their Ontogeny and Significance.* London: Churchill.

Hutt, C. (1972b) Sexual dimorphism: Its significance in human development. In Monks, F. J., Hartup, W. W., and de Wit, J., Eds. *Determinants of Behavioral Development.* New York: Academic Press.

Hyatt, J. C. (1977) The administration's urban 'tilt.' *The Wall Street Journal* (December 5):24.

Hyde, J. S. and Rosenberg, B. G. (1976) *Half the Human Experience.* Lexington, Mass.: D. C. Heath and Company.

Hyde, J. S., Rosenberg, B. G., and Behrman, J. A. (1974) Tomboyism: Implications for theories of female development. Paper presented at Western Psychological Association Meetings, April 1974.

Hyde, J. S., Rosenberg, B. G., and Behrman, J. A. (1977) Tomboyism. *Psychology of Women Quarterly,* 2:73–75.

Hyman, H. H. and Sheatsley, P. (1973) Some reasons why information campaigns fail. In Schramm, W., Ed. *Men, Messages and Media.* New York: Harper & Row.

Hyman, H. H. and Singer, E. (1968) Introduction. In Hyman, H. H. and Singer, E., Eds. *Readings in Reference Group Theory and Research.* New York: Free Press.

Hyman, H. H., Wright, C. R., and Reed, J. S. (1975) *The Enduring Effects of Education.* Chicago: The University of Chicago Press.

Inkeles, A. and Smith, D. H. (1974) *Becoming Modern: Individual Changes in Six Developing Countries.* Cambridge, Mass.: Harvard University Press.

Israel, J. (1971) *Alienation: From Marx to Modern Sociology.* Boston: Allyn & Bacon.

Jackson, E. F. (1962) Status consistency and symptoms of stress. *American Sociological Review,* 27:469–480.

Jackson, E. F. and Crockett, H. J., Jr. (1964) Occupational mobility in the United States: A point estimate and trend comparison. *American Sociological Review,* 29:5–16.

Jackson, P. W. (1968) *Life in Classrooms.* New York: Holt, Rinehart and Winston, Inc.

Janis, I. L. (1972) *Victims of Groupthink.* Boston: Houghton Mifflin.

Jencks, C. (1972) *Inequality: A Reassessment of the Effect of Family and Schooling in America.* New York: Basic Books.

Jenkins, J. C. (1977) Push/pull in recent Mexican migration to the U.S. *International Migration Review,* 11:178–189.

Jensen, A. R. (1973a) Race, intelligence and genetics: The differences are real. *Psychology Today,* 7 (December):80–86.

Jensen, A. R. (1973b) *Educatability and Group Differences.* New York: Harper & Row.

Jensen, M. C. (1976) Companies' payoffs in U.S. come under new scrutiny. *New York Times* (March 16):1+.

Johnson, B. (1963) On church and sect. *American Sociological Review,* 28:539–549.

Johnson, M. P. and Sell, R. R. (1976) The cost of being Black: A 1970 update. *American Journal of Sociology,* 82:183–190.

Johnson, N. R. and Feinberg, W. E. (1977) A computer simulation of the emergence of consensus in crowds. *American Sociological Review,* 42:505–521.

Judah, J. S. (1974) *Hare Krishna and the Counterculture.* New York: Wiley.

Kahn, A. and McGaughey, T. A. (1977) Distance and liking: When moving close produces increased liking. *Sociometry,* 40:138–144.

Kalleberg, A. (1977) Work values and job rewards: A theory of job statisfaction. *American Sociological Review,* 42:124–143.

Kanowitz, L. (1969) *Women and the Law, The Unfinished Revolution.* Albuquerque: University of New Mexico Press.

Kanter, R. M. (1972) *Commitment and Community: Communes and Utopias in Sociological Perspective.* Cambridge, Mass.: Harvard University Press.

Kanter, R. M. (1973) *Communes: Creating and Managing the Collective Life.* New York: Harper & Row.

Kanter, R. M. (1974) Communes in cities. *Working Papers,* 2 (Summer):36–44.

Kanter, R. M. (1977) Some effects of proportions on group life: Skewed sex ratios and responses to token women. *American Journal of Sociology,* 82:965–990.

Kanter, R. M., Jaffe, D., and Weisberg, D. K. (1975) Coupling, parenting and the presence of others: Intimate relationships in communal households. *The Family Coordinator*, 24:433–452.

Kaplan, H. R. (1977) Introduction. In Kaplan, H. R., Ed. *American Minorities and Economic Opportunity.* Itasca, Ill.: F. E. Peacock Publishers, Inc.

Kaplan, H. R. and Tausky, C. (1972) Work and the welfare Cadillac: The function of and commitment to work among the hard-core unemployed. *Social Problems*, 19:469–483.

Karabel, J. and Astin, A. W. (1975) Social class, academic ability, and college "quality." *Social Forces*, 53:381–398.

Katcher, A. (1955) The discrimination of sex differences by young children. *Journal of Genetic Psychology*, 87:131–143.

Katz, F. E. (1964) The school as a complex formal organization. *Harvard Educational Review*, 34:428–455.

Katz, J. M. (1976) How do you love me? Let me count the ways. *Sociological Inquiry*, 46:17–22.

Kaufman, M. T. (1976) Detention of hundreds under South African security laws becoming focus of dissent. *New York Times* (November 28):3.

Kellen, K. (1972) *The Coming Age of Woman Power.* New York: Peter Wyden.

Keller, H. (1908) *The Story of My Life.* Garden City, N.Y.: Doubleday & Co.

Keller, H. (1938) *The World I Live In.* New York: Appleton-Century-Crofts, Inc.

Kellogg, W. N. and Kellogg, L. A. (1933) *The Ape and the Child.* New York: McGraw-Hill.

Kelly, G. A. (1955) *The Psychology of Personal Constructs.* New York: W. W. Norton.

Kemper, T. D. (1974) On the nature and purpose of ascription. *American Sociological Review*, 39:844–853.

Kemper, T. D. (1976) Marxist and functionalist theories in the study of stratification: Common elements that lead to a test. *Social Forces*, 54:559–578.

Kerckhoff, A. C. (1964) Patterns of homogamy and the field of eligibles. *Social Forces*, 42:289–297.

Kerckhoff, A. C. (1972) *Socialization and Social Class.* Englewood Cliffs, N.J.: Prentice-Hall, Inc.

Kerckhoff, A. C. and Back, K. W. (1968) *The June bug: A case of hysterical contagion.* New York: Appleton-Century-Crofts.

Kerckhoff, A. C. and Davis, K. E. (1962) Value consensus and need complementarity in mate selection. *American Sociological Review*, 27:295–303.

Kihss, P. (1977) 30% of all New York City births prove illegitimate. *New York Times*, September 29:39.

Killian, L. M. (1952) The effects of southern white workers on race relations in northern plants. *American Sociological Review*, 17:327–331.

Killian, L. M. (1953) The adjustment of southern White migrants to northern urban norms. *Social Forces*, 33:66–69.

Killian, L. M. (1964) Social movements. In Faris, R. E. L., Ed. *Handbook of Modern Sociology.* Chicago: Rand McNally.

Killian, L. M. (1975) *The Impossible Revolution II: Black Power and the American Dream.* New York: Random House.

Kim, H. C. (1977) The relationship of protestant ethic beliefs and values to achievement. *Journal for the Scientific Study of Religion*, 16:255–262.

Kim, O., Petrocik, J. R., and Enokson, S. N. (1975) Voter turnout among the American states: Systemic and individual components. *American Political Science Review*, 69:107–123.

King, K., Balswick, J. O., and Robinson, I. E. (1977) The continuing premarital sexual revolution among college females. *Journal of Marriage and the Family*, 39:455–459.

King, M. L., Jr. (1965) Civil right no. 1 — The right to vote. *New York Times Magazine* (March 14):26+.

Kinsey, A. C., Pomeroy, W. B., Martin, C. E., and Gebhard, P. H. (1953) *Sexual Behavior in the Human Female.* Philadelphia: Saunders.

Klapper, J. T. (1960) *The Effects of Mass Communication.* New York: The Free Press.

Klockars, C. B. (1974) *The Professional Fence.* New York: The Free Press.

Kluckhohn, C. (1960) *Mirror for Man.* Greenwich, Conn.: Fawcett Publications, Inc.

Kluckhohn, C. and Kelly, W. H. (1945) The concept of culture. In Linton, R., Ed. *The Science of Man in the World Crisis.* New York: Columbia University Press.

Kluegel, J. R., Singleton, R., Jr., and Starnes, C. E. (1977) Subjective class identification: A multiple indicator approach. *American Sociological Review*, 42:599–611.

Kneeland, D. E. (1972) Quiet decay erodes downtown areas of small cities. *New York Times* (February 8):1+.

Koestler, A. (1949) The God that failed. In Crossman, R., Ed. *The God That Failed.* New York: Harper & Row.

Kohlberg, L. (1966) A cognitive-developmental analysis of children's sex-role concepts and attitudes. In Maccoby, E. E., Ed. *The Development of Sex Differences.* Stanford, Calif.: Stanford University Press.

Kohlberg, L. (1969) Stage and sequence: The cognitive-developmental approach to socialization. In Goslin, D. A., Ed. *Handbook of Socialization Theory and Research.* Chicago: Rand McNally.

Kohlberg, L. (1976) Moral stages and moralization. In Lickona, T., Ed. *Moral Development and Behavior: Theory, Research and Social Issues.* New York: Holt, Rinehart and Winston.

Kohlberg, L. and Gilligan, C. F. (1971) The adolescent as philosopher: The discovery of the self in a postconventional world. *Daedalus,* 100:1051–86.

Kohlberg, L. and Ullian, D. Z. (1974) Stages in the development of psychosexual concepts and attitudes. In Friedman, R. C., Richart, R. N., and Vande Wiele, R. L., Eds. *Sex Differences in Behavior.* New York: Wiley.

Kohn, M. L. (1969) *Class and Conformity: A Study in Values.* Homewood, Ill.: Dorsey Press.

Kohn, M. L. (1975) Occupational structure and alienation. *American Journal of Sociology,* 82:111–130.

Kohn, M. L. and Schooler, C. (1973) Occupational experience and psychological functioning: An assessment of reciprocal effects. *American Sociological Review,* 38:97–118.

Kolata, G. B. (1975) Behavioral development: Effects of environment. *Science,* 189 (July 18):207–209.

Koluchová, J. (1972) Severe deprivation of twins: A case study. *Journal of Child Psychology and Psychiatry,* 13:107–14.

Koluchová, J. (1976) A report on the further development of twins after severe and prolonged deprivation. In Clarke, A. M. and Clarke, A. D. B., Eds. *Early Experience: Myth and Evidence.* London: Open Books.

Kornhauser, W. (1966) "Power elite" or "veto groups"? In Bendix, R. and Lipset, S. M., Eds. *Class, Status, and Power.* 2nd ed. New York: The Free Press.

Krauss, W. R. (1974) Political implications of gender roles: A review of the literature. *American Political Science Review,* 68: 1706–1723.

Kraut, R. E. (1976) Deterrent and definitional influences on shoplifting. *Social Problems,* 23:358–368.

Kreps, J. (1973) Sources of inequality. In Ginzberg, E. and Yohalem, A., Eds. *Corporate Lib: Women's Challenge to Management.* Baltimore: Johns Hopkins University Press.

Kretch, D. and Crutchfield, R. (1973) Perceiving the world. In Schramm, W., Ed. *Men, Messages and Media.* New York: Harper & Row.

Kristol, I. (1969) Blacks are the last immigrant group. In Moynihan, D. P., Ed. *On Understanding Poverty: Perspectives from the Social Sciences.* New York: Basic Books.

Kristol, I. (1974) Taxes, poverty, and equality. *The Public Interest,* 37 (Fall):3–28.

Kroeger, N. (1975) Bureaucracy, social exchange, and benefits received in a public assistance agency. *Social Problems,* 23:182–196.

Kronholz, J. (1977) A living-alone trend affects housing, cars and other industries. *Wall Street Journal,* November 16:1 and 27.

Kuhn, M. H. (1960) Self-attitudes by age, sex, and professional training. *Sociological Quarterly,* 1:39–55.

Labovitz, S. and Hagedorn, R. (1975) A structural-behavioral theory of intergroup antagonism. *Social Forces,* 53:444–448.

Ladd, E., Jr., Hadley, C., and King, L. (1971) A new political realignment? *The Public Interest,* 23:46–63.

Lang, K. and Lang, G. E. (1961) *Collective Dynamics.* New York: Thomas Y. Crowell Co.

Langman, L. (1971) Dionysus—Child of tomorrow. *Youth and Society,* 3:84–87.

LaPiere, R. T. (1934) Attitudes vs. Actions. *Social Forces,* 13:230–37.

Larsen, O. N. (1964) Social effects of mass communication. In Faris, R. E. L., Ed. *Handbook of Modern Sociology.* Chicago: Rand McNally & Co.

Lauderdale, P. (1976) *Deviance and moral boundaries.* American Sociological Association, 41:660–676.

Lauer, R. H. (1974) Rate of change and stress: A test of the "Future Shock" thesis. *Social Forces,* 52:510–516.

Lauer, R. H. (1977) *Perspectives on Social Change.* 2nd ed. Boston: Allyn and Bacon, Inc.

Laurentin, R. (1977) *Catholic Pentecostalism.* Trans. O'Connell, M. J. Garden City, N.Y.: Doubleday & Company.

Lazarsfeld, P. F., Berelson, B., and Gaude, H. (1948) *The People's Choice.* New York: Columbia University Press.

Lazarsfeld, P. F. and Reitz, J. G. (1975) *An Introduction to Applied Sociology.* New York: Elsevier Scientific Publishing Co.

Leacock, E. B. Ed. (1971) *The Culture of Poverty: A Critique.* New York: Simon & Schuster.

Le Bon, G. (1896) *The Crowd: A Study of the Popular Mind.* London: Ernest Benn, Ltd.

Lebra, T. S. (1970) Religious conversion as a breakthrough for transculturation: A Japanese sect in Hawaii. *Journal for the Scientific Study of Religion,* 9:181–196.

Lee, A. M. (1944) The social dynamics of the physician's status. *Psychiatry,* 7:371–377.

Lee, A. M. (1973) *Toward Humanist Sociology.* Englewood Cliffs, N.J.: Prentice-Hall.

Lee, A. M. (1976) Sociology for whom? *American Sociological Review,* 41:925–36.

Leger, R. R. (1977) South Africans assert foreign pressures only stiffen their resolve. *Wall Street Journal* (November 14):1, 23.

LeGrand, C. E. (1973) Rape and rape laws: Sexism in society and law. *California Law Review,* 61:919–941.

LeMasters, E. E. (1974) Parents without partners. In Skolnick, A. and Skolnick, J. H., Eds. *Intimacy, Family, and Society.* Boston: Little, Brown and Company.

Lemert, E. M. (1972) *Human Deviance, Social Problems and Social Control.* 2nd ed. Englewood Cliffs, N.J.: Prentice-Hall.

Lemert, E. M. (1976) Response to critics: Feedback and choice. In Coser, L. A. and Larsen, O. N., Eds. *The Uses of Controversy in Sociology.* New York: The Free Press.

Lenney, E. (1977) Women's self-confidence in achievement settings. *Psychological Bulletin,* 84:1–13.

Lenski, G. E. (1966) *Power and Privilege: A Theory of Social Stratification.* New York: McGraw-Hill.

Lenski, G. E. (1976) Review of *Sociobiology. Social Forces,* 55:530–531.

Leopold, L. (1913) *Prestige: A Psychological Study of Social Estimates.* London: T. Fisher Unwin.

Lerner, R. M. (1976) *Concepts and Theories of Human Development.* Reading, Mass.: Addison-Wesley Publishing Co.

Lerner, R. M. (1978) Nature, nurture, and dynamic interactionism. *Human Development,* 21:1–20.

Lever, J. (1976) Sex differences in the games children play. *Social Problems,* 23:478–487.

Levine, A. and Crumrine, J. (1975) Women and the fear of success: A problem in replication. *American Journal of Sociology,* 80:964–974.

Levinson, H. (1964) Money aside, why spend life working? *National Observer,* March 9:20+.

Lewis, F. (1976) Spanish Red likens revolt against Moscow to Luther. *New York Times,* July 7:2.

Lewis, J. M. (1972) A study of the Kent State incident using Smelser's theory of collective behavior. *Sociological Inquiry,* 42:87–96.

Lewis, M. (1977) The busy, purposeful world of a baby. *Psychology Today,* 10:53–6.

Lewis, M. and Brooks, J. (1975) Infants' social perception: A constructivist view. In Cohen, L. B. and Salapatek, P., Eds. *Infants Perception: From Sensation to Cognition.* Vol. II. New York: Academic Press.

Lewis, O. (1952) Urbanization without breakdown. *Scientific Monthly,* 75 (July):31–41.

Lewis, O. (1959) *Five Families: Mexican Case Studies in the Culture of Poverty.* New York: Basic Books.

Lewis, O. (1961) *The Children of Sanchez.* New York: Random House.

Lewis, O. (1966) *La Vida: A Puerto Rican Family in the Culture of Poverty: San Juan and New York.* New York: Random House.

Lewis, O. (1968) The culture of poverty. In Moynihan, D. P., Ed. *On Understanding Poverty: Perspectives from the Social Sciences.* New York: Basic Books.

Libby, R. W. (1977) Creative singlehood as a sexual lifestyle: Beyond marriage as a rite of passage. In Libby, R. W. and Whitehurst, R. N., Eds. *Marriage and Alternatives.* Glenview, Ill.: Scott Foresman.

References

Lichtenstein, G. (1977a) Homosexuals are moving toward open way of life as tolerance rises among the general population. *New York Times,* July 17:34.

Lichtenstein, G. (1977b) Poll finds public split on legalizing homosexual acts. *New York Times,* July 19:17.

Lickona, T. Ed. (1976) *Moral Development and Behavior: Theory, Research, and Social Issues.* New York: Holt, Rinehart and Winston.

Lieberson, S. (1971. An empirical study of military-industrial linages. *American Journal of Sociology,* 76:562–584.

Liebow, E. (1967) *Tally's Corner, A Study of Negro Streetcorner Men.* Boston: Little, Brown & Co.

Limber, J. (1977) Language in child and chimp. *American Psychologist,* 32:280–95.

Lin, N. and Burt, R. S. (1975) Differential effects of information channels in the process of innovation diffusion. *Social Forces,* 54:256–274.

Lincoln, E. E. (1961) *The Black Muslims in America.* Boston: Beacon Press, Inc.

Lindesmith, A. R., Strauss, A. L., and Denzin, N. K. (1978) *Social Psychology.* 5th Ed. Hinsdale, Ill.: The Dryden Press.

Lindgren, E. J. (1938) An example of culture contact without conflict: Reindeer Tungus and Cossacks of Northwestern Manchuria. *American Anthropologist,* 40:605–621.

Lindsay, P. H. and Norman, D. A. (1977) *Human Information Processing.* 2nd ed. New York: Academic Press.

Linton, R. (1936) *The Study of Man.* New York: Appleton-Century-Crofts.

Linton, R. (1937) One hundred per cent American. *The American Mercury,* 40:427–429.

Linton, R. (1940) *Acculturation in Seven American Indian Tribes.* New York: Appleton-Century-Crofts.

Linton, R. (1945) *The Cultural Background of Personality.* New York: Appleton-Century-Crofts.

Lipset, S. M. (1963) *The First New Nation.* New York: Basic Books, Inc.

Lipset, S. M. (1963) *Political Man.* Garden City, N.Y.: Doubleday & Co., Inc.

Lipset, S. M. (1972) Social mobility and equal opportunity. *The Public Interest,* 29:90–108.

Lipset, S. M. (1976) The wavering polls. *The Public Interest,* 43 (Spring):70–89.

Lipset, S. M. and Bendix, R. (1959) *Social Mobility in Industrial Society.* Berkeley: University of California Press.

Lipset, S. M. and Seabury, P. (1965) The lesson of Berkeley. In Lipset, S. M. and Wolin, S. S., Eds. *The Berkeley Student Revolt.* Garden City, N.Y.: Doubleday & Co.

Lipset, S. M., Trow, M. A., and Coleman, J. S. (1956) *Union Democracy.* Garden City, N.Y.: Doubleday & Co.

Liska, A. E. (1974) Emergent issues in the attitude-behavior consistency controversy. *American Sociological Review,* 39:261–72.

Livesley, W. J. and Bromley, D. B. (1973) *Person Perception in Childhood and Adolescence.* New York: Wiley.

Lofland, J. (1967) Role management. Mimeographed paper No. 30 of the Center for Research in Social Organization. University of Michigan, June, 1967.

Logan, J. R. (1976) Industrialization and the stratification of cities in suburban regions. *American Journal of Sociology,* 82:333–348.

Loman, L. A. and Larkin, W. E. (1976) Rejection of the mentally ill: An experiment in labeling. *Sociological Quarterly,* 17:555–560.

Long N. E. (1971) The city as reservation. *The Public Interest,* 25 (Fall):22–38.

Lopata, H. Z. (1973) *Widowhood in an American City.* Cambridge, Mass.: Schenkman.

Lott, A. J. and Lott, B. E. (1974) The role of reward in the formation of positive interpersonal attitudes. In Huston, T. L., Ed. *Foundations of Interpersonal Attraction.* New York: Academic Press.

Lovekin, A. and Malony, H. N. (1977) Religious glossolalia: A longitudinal study of personality changes. *Journal for the Scientific Study of Religion,* 16:383–393.

McAuliffe, W. (1975) Beyond secondary deviance: Negative labelling and its effect on heroin addiction. In Gove, W., Ed. *Labelling Deviant Behavior: The Evaluation of a Perspective.* New York: Halsted.

McCarthy, J. D. and Zald, M. N. (1977) Resource mobilization and social movements: A partial theory. *American Journal of Sociology,* 82:1212–1241.

McClelland, D. G. (1967) *The Achieving Society.* New York: The Free Press.

McClendon, M. J. (1976) The occupational status attainment processes of males and females. *American Sociological Review,* 41:52–64.

McClosky, H. and Dahlgren, H. E. (1959) Primary group influence on party loyalty. *American Political Science Review,* 53:757–776.

Maccoby, E. E. and Jacklin, C. N. (1974) *The Psychology of Sex Differences.* Stanford, Calif.: Stanford University Press.

Maccoby, E. E. and Maccoby, N. (1954) The interview: A tool of social science. In Lindzey, G., Ed. *Handbook of Social Psychology.* Reading, Mass.: Addison-Wesley.

McCready, W. C. and Greeley, A. M. (1976) *The Ultimate Values of the American Population.* Beverley Hills, Calif.: Sage Publications.

McGuire, M. B. (1977) Testimony as a commitment mechanism in Catholic Pentecostal prayer groups. *Journal for the Scientific Study of Religion,* 16:165–168.

Machalek, R. (1977) Definitional strategies in the study of religion. *Journal for the Scientific Study of Religion,* 16:395–401.

Machalek, R. and Martin, M. (1976) "Invisible" religions: Some preliminary evidence. *Journal for the Scientific Study of Religion,* 15:311–321.

Machonin, P. (1970) Social stratification in contemporary Czechoslovakia. *American Journal of Sociology,* 75:725–741.

McHugh, P. (1968) *Defining the Situation.* Indianapolis: Bobbs-Merrill.

MacIver, R. M. (1947) *The Web of Government.* New York: Macmillan.

MacIver, R. M. (1954) Forward. In Berger, M. *Equality By Statute.* New York: Columbia University Press.

Macklin, E. D. (1974) Going very steady. *Psychology Today,* 8 (November):53–59.

Maddox, G. L. and Wiley, J. (1976) Scope, concepts and methods in the study of aging. In Binstock, R. H. and Shanas, E., Eds. *Handbook of Aging and the Social Sciences.* New York: Van Nostrand Reinhold Company.

Malinowski, B. (1944) *A Scientific Theory of Culture and Other Essays.* Chapel Hill, N. C.: The University of North Carolina Press.

Malinowski, B. (1964) Parenthood—The basis of social structure. In Coser, R., Ed. *The Family: Its Structure and Functions.* New York: St. Martin's Press.

Mann, L., Nagel, T., and Dowling, P. (1976) A study of economic panic: The "run" on the Hindmarsh Building Society. *Sociometry,* 39:223–235.

Manning, P. K. (1977) Rules in organizational context: Narcotics law enforcement in two settings. *The Sociological Quarterly,* 18:44–61.

Maratsos, M. P. (1973) Nonegocentric communication abilities in preschool children. *Child Development,* 44:697–700.

Marcuse, H. (1972) Blue-collar revolution. *New York Times* (August 7):27.

Marecek, J. and Mettee, D. R. (1972) Avoidance of continued success as a function of self-esteem, level of esteem certainty, and responsibility for success. *Journal of Personality and Social Psychology,* 22:98–107.

Marini, M. M. (1976) Dimensions of marriage happiness: A research note. *Journal of Marriage and the Family,* 38:443–448.

Markle, G. E. (1974) Sex ratio at birth: Values, variance, and some determinants. *Demography,* 11:131–142.

Marsh, R. M. (1967) *Comparative Sociology.* New York: Harcourt Brace Jovanovich.

Martin, W. B. W. (1976) *The Negotiated Order of the School.* Toronto: Macmillan of Canada.

Martinson, R. (1974) What works?—Questions and answers about prison reform. *The Public Interest,* 35 (Spring):22–54.

Marvin, R. S., Greenberg, M. T., and Mossler, D. G. (1976) The early development of conceptual perspective taking: Distinguishing among multiple perspectives. *Child Development,* 47:511–4.

Marwit, S. J. (1977) Black and White children's use of standard English at 7, 9, and 12 years of age. *Developmental Psychology,* 13:81–82.

Marx, G. T. and Wood, J. L. (1975) Strands of theory and research in collective behavior. *Annual Review of Sociology,* 1:363–428.

Marx, K. and Engels, F. (1848/1955) *The Communist Manifesto.* Beer, S. H. (ed.) New York: Appleton-Century-Crofts.

Mason, K. O., Czajka, J. L., and Arber, S. (1976) Change in U.S. women's sex-role attitudes, 1964–1974. *American Sociological Review,* 41:573–96.

Mason, T. J., McKay, F. W., Hoover, R., Blot, W. J., and Fraumeni, J. F., Jr. (1976) *Atlas of Cancer Mortality among U.S. Nonwhites:* 1950–1969. Washington: Government Printing Office.

Matras, J. (1975) *Social Inequality, Stratification, and Mobility.* Englewood Cliffs, N.J.: Prentice-Hall.

May, R. L. (1963) How Rudolph came to Christmas. *Family Weekly,* December 22:15+.

Mayer, A. J. and Sharp, H. (1962) Religious preference and worldly success. *American Sociological Review,* 27:218–227.

Mead, G. H. (1932) *The Philosophy of the Present.* Chicago: Open Court.

Mead, G. H. (1934) *Mind, Self, and Other.* Chicago: University of Chicago Press.

Mead, M. (1935) *Sex and Temperament in Three Primitive Societies.* New York: William Morrow & Co.

Mead, M. (1950) *Sex and Temperament in Three Primitive Societies.* New York: Mentor Books.

Meadows, D. H., Meadows, D. L., Randers, J., and Behrens, W. W., III. (1972) *The Limits to Growth.* New York: New American Library.

Means, R. L. (1966) Protestantism and economic institutions: Auxiliary theories to Webers's Protestant ethic. *Social Forces:* 44:372–381.

Mechanic, D. (1972) Social class and schizophrenia: Some requirements for a plausible theory of social influence. *Social Forces,* 50:305–309.

Medalia, N. Z. and Larsen, O. N. (1958) Diffusion and belief in a collective delusion: The Seattle windshield pitting epidemic. *American Sociological Review,* 23:180–186.

Meeker, B. F. and Weitzel-O'Neill, P. A. (1977) Sex roles and interpersonal behavior in task-oriented groups. *American Sociological Review,* 42:91–105.

Mehan, H. and Wood, H. (1975) *The Reality of Ethnomethodology.* New York: Wiley.

Mehan, H. and Wood, H. (1976) De-secting ethnomethodology. *American Sociologist,* 11:13–21.

Meier, R. F. and Johnson, W. J. (1977) Deterrence as social control: The legal and extralegal production of conformity. *American Sociological Review,* 42:292–304.

Meile, R. L., Johnson, D. R., and St. Peter, L. (1976) Marital role, education, and mental disorder among women: Test of an interaction hypothesis. *Journal of Health and Social Behavior,* 17:295–301.

Meislin, R. J. (1977) Poll finds more liberal beliefs on marriage and sex roles, especially among the young. *New York Times,* November 27:75.

Meltzer, B. N., Petras, J. W., and Reynolds, L. T. (1975) *Symbolic Interactionism.* London: Routledge & Kegan Paul.

Mercer, B. E. and Carr, E. R. (1957) *Education and the Social Order.* New York: Holt, Rinehart & Winston, Inc.

Merton, R. K. (1957) The role-set: Problems in sociological theory. *British Journal of Sociology,* 8:106–120.

Merton, R. K. (1959) Conformity, deviation, and opportunity-structures. *American Sociological Review,* 24:180–182.

Merton, R. K. (1964) Anomie, anomia, and social interaction. In Clinard, M. B., Ed. *Anomie and Deviant Behavior.* New York: The Free Press.

Merton, R. K. (1968) *Social Theory and Social Structure.* Rev. ed. New York: The Free Press.

Merton, R. K. and Kitt, A. S. (1966) Reference group theory and social mobility. In Bendix, R. and Lipset, S. M., Eds. *Class, Status, and Power.* 2nd ed. New York: The Free Press.

Mesarovic, M. and Pestel, E. (1976) *Mankind at the Turning Point: The Second Report to the Club of Rome.* New York: New American Library.

Meyer, J. W. (1977) The effects of education as an institution. *American Journal of Sociology,* 83:55–57.

Meyer, J. W., Rubinson, R., Ramirez, F. O., and Boli-Bennett, J. (1977) The world educational revolution, 1950–1970. *Sociology of Education,* 50:242–258.

Michalowski, R. J. and Bohlander, E. W. (1976) Repression and criminal justice in capitalist America. *Sociological Inquiry,* 46 (1976):95–106.

Michels, R. (1966) *Political Parties.* New York: The Free Press. (First published in 1911)

Middleton, R. (1962) A deviant case: Brother-sister and father-daughter marriage in ancient Egypt. *American Sociological Review,* 27:603–611.

Mileti, D. S., Gillespie, D. F., and Haas, J. E. (1977) Size and structure in complex organizations. *Social Forces,* 56:208–217.

Milgram, S. (1977) *The Individual in a Social World*. Reading, Mass.: Addison-Wesley Publishing Company.

Miller, B. C. (1976) A multivariate developmental model of marital satisfaction. *Journal of Marriage and the Family*, 38:643–657.

Miller, D. C. (1975) *Leadership and Power in the Bos-Wash Megalopolis: Environment, Ecology, and Urban Organization*. New York: Wiley.

Miller, D. C. and Form, W. H. (1964) *Industrial Sociology*. 2nd ed. New York: Harper & Row.

Miller, S. C. (1974) *The Unwelcome Immigrants: The American Image of the Chinese, 1785–1882*. Berkeley: University of California Press.

Mills, C. W. (1956) *The Power Elite*. Fair Lawn, N.J.: Oxford University Press.

Mills, C. W. (1959) *The Sociological Imagination*. New York: Oxford University Press.

Miner, H. (1960) Culture change under pressure: A Hausa case. *Human Organization*, 19:164–167.

Mintz, S. W. (1971) Men, women, and trade. *Comparative Studies in Society and History*, 13:247–269.

Mischel, W. (1970) Sex-typing and socialization. In Mussen, P. H., Ed. *Carmichael's Manual of Child Psychology*. 3rd ed. Vol. 2. New York: Wiley.

Molotch, H (1976) The city as a growth machine: Toward a political economy of place. *American Journal of Sociology*, 82:309–332.

Molotch, H. and Lester, M. (1975) Accidental news: The great oil spill as local occurrence and national event. *Americal Journal of Sociology*, 81:235–260.

Money, J. (1977) Destereotyping sex roles. *Society*, 14 (July/August):25–28.

Money, J. and Ehrhardt, A. A. (1973) *Man and Woman, Boy and Girl*. Baltimore: Johns Hopkins University Press.

Money, J. and Tucker, P. (1975) *Sexual Signatures*. Boston: Little, Brown & Co.

Monge, R. H. (1973) Developmental trends in factors of adolescent self-concept. *Developmental Psychology*, 8:382–93.

Montemayor, R. and Eisen, M. (1977) The development of self-conceptions from childhood to adolescence. *Developmental Psychology*, 13:314–319.

Morse, N. C. and Weiss, R. S. (1955) The function and meaning of work and the job. *American Sociological Review*, 20:191–198.

Moskos, C. C., Jr. (1967) A sociologist appraises the G.I. *New York Times Magazine* (September, 24):33+.

Moskos, C. C. Jr. (1969) Why men fight. *Trans-action*, 7 (November):13–23.

Moss, J. J., Apolonio, F., and Jensen, M. (1971) The premarital dyad during the sixties. *Journal of Marriage and the Family*, 33:59–67.

Mowat, F. (1952) *People of the Deer*. Boston: Little, Brown & Co.

Moynihan, D. P. (1965) Employment, income, and the ordeal of the Negro family. *Daedalus*, 94:731–752.

Mueller, C. W. and Johnson, W. T. (1975) Socioeconomic status and religious participation. *American Sociological Review*, 40:785–800.

Muensterberger, W. (1961) The adolescent in society. In Lorland, S. and Schneer, H., Eds. *Adolescents*. New York: Paul B. Hoeber, Inc.

Mullins, N. C., Hargens, L. L., Hecht, P. K., Kick, E. L. (1977) The group structure of cocitation clusters: A comparative study. *American Sociological Review*, 42:552–562.

Murdock, G. P. (1949) *Social Structure*. New York: The Free Press.

Murdock, G. P. (1950) Feasibility and implementation of comparative community research. *American Sociological Review*, 15:713–720.

Murdock, G. P. and Provost, C. (1973) Factors in the division of labour by sex: A cross-cultural analysis. *Ethnology*, 12:203–225.

Murguia, E. (1975) *Assimilation, Colonialism and the Mexican American People*. Austin: Center for Mexican American Studies, University of Texas.

Murphy, R. J. and Watson, J. M. (1967) *The Structure of Discontent: The Relationship Between Social Structure, Grievance, and Support for the Los Angeles Riot*. Los Angeles: The University of California Institute of Government and Public Affairs.

Murstein, R. I. (1972) Physical attractiveness and marital choice. *Journal of Personality and Social Psychology*, 22:8–12.

Myers, J. K. and Bean, L. L. (1968) *A Decade Later: A Follow-up of "Social Class and Mental Illness."* New York: Wiley.

National Education Association (1977) *Learning Is Hard Work.* Washington: National Education Association.

Neff, W. S. (1968) *Work and Human Behavior.* New York: Atherton.

Nelsen, H. M., Madron, T. W., and Yokley, R. L. (1975) Black religion's promethean motif: Orthodoxy and militancy. *American Journal of Sociology,* 81:139–146.

Nelson, W. E., Jr. and Meranto, P. J. (1977) *Electing Black Mayors: Political Action in the Black Community.* Columbus: Ohio State University Press.

Nemy, E. (1975) Women begin to speak out against sexual harassment at work. *New York Times* (August 19):38C

New York Times (1926) Emperor's message to George III. February 28, 1926:15.

New York Times (1976) 75% of women physicians in Detroit survey report they do housework, too. November 3, 1976:24.

New York Times (1977) Judge in Wisconsin calls rape by boy "normal" reaction. May 27:9.

New York Times (1977) "Time theft" said to cause the economy of Canada loss of $8 billion a year. November 25 :5.

Newton, H. P. (1973) *Revolutionary Suicide.* New York: Harcourt Brace Jovanovich.

Nicolson, R. B. (1965) *The Pitcairners.* Sydney: Angus & Robertson, Ltd.

Nie, N. H., Verba, S., and Petrocik, J. (1976) *The Changing American Voter.* Cambridge, Mass.: Harvard University Press.

Niebuhr, H. R. (1929) *The Social Sources of Denominationalism.* New York: Holt, Rinehart & Winston.

Nisbet, R.A. (1970) *The Social Bond.* New York: Knopf.

Nobile, P. (1973) Uncommon conversations: Robert Welch. *The Milwaukee Journal,* August 19:45.

Noel, D. L. and Pinkney, A. (1964) Correlates of prejudice: Some racial differences and similarities. *American Journal of Sociology,* 69:609–622.

Noel, D. M. (1969) Minority responses to intergroup situations. *Phylon,* 30:367–374.

Nordheimer, J. (1977) The family in transition: A challenge from within. *New York Times,* November 27:1.

Northrop, F. S. C. (1947) *The Logic of the Sciences and the Humanities.* New York: Macmillan.

Northrup, B. (1976) The harsh machinery of apartheid touches every South African. *Wall Street Journal* (December 3):1, 13.

Nottingham, E. K. (1971) *Religion: A Sociological View.* New York: Random House.

Nowlis, H. H. (1971) Perspectives on Drug Use. *Journal of Social Issues,* 27:7–21.

Oberschall, A. (1973) *Social Conflict and Social Movements.* Englewood Cliffs, N.J.: Prentice-Hall.

Offenbacher, D. (1967) *Roles, norms and typifications in contemporary American society.* Paper presented at the annual meetings of the American Sociological Association, San Francisco.

Ogburn, W. F. (1922) *Social Change.* New York: B. W. Huebsch.

Ogburn, W. F. (1926) The great man versus social forces. *Social Forces,* 5:225–231.

Ogburn, W. F. and Thomas, D. (1922) Are inventions inevitable? *Political Science Quarterly,* 37:83–99.

Olsen, M. E. (1968) *The Process of Social Organization.* New York: Holt, Rinehart and Winston.

Olsen, M. E. (1971) The science and profession of involved sociology. *Sociological Focus,* 4:83–91.

Orcutt, J. D. (1975) Deviance as a situated phenomenon: Variations in the social interpretation of marijuana and alcohol use. *Social Problems,* 22:346–356.

O'Toole, R. (1975) Sectarianism in politics: Case studies of Maoists and DeLeonists. In Wallis, R., Ed. *Sectarianism: Analyses of Religious and Non-Religious Sects.* New York: Wiley.

O'Toole, R. (1976) "Underground" traditions in the study of sectarianism: Non-religious uses of the concept "sect." *Journal for the Scientific Study of Religion,* 15:145–156.

Overton, W. F. (1973) On the assumptive base of the nature-nurture controversy: Additive versus interactive conceptions. *Human Development,* 16:74–89.

Paris, B. L. and Luckey, E. B. (1966) A longitudinal study of marital satisfaction. *Sociology and Social Research,* 50:212–223.

Park, R. E. and Burgess, E. W. (1921) *Introduction to the Science of Sociology.* Chicago: The University of Chicago Press.

Park, R. E., Burgess, E. W., and McKenzie, R. D. (1925) *The City.* Chicago: The University of Chicago Press.

Parsons, J. E., Ruble, D. N., Hodges, K. L., and Small, A. W. (1976) Cognitive-developmental factors in emerging sex differences in achievement-related expectancies. *Journal of Social Issues,* 32:47–61.

Parsons, T. (1937) *The Structure of Social Action.* New York: McGraw-Hill.

Parsons, T. (1951) *Toward a General Theory of Action.* New York: Harper & Row.

Parsons, T. (1966) *Societies: Evolutionary and Comparative Perspectives.* Englewood Cliffs, N.J.: Prentice-Hall, Inc.

Parsons, T. (1971) *The System of Modern Societies.* Englewood Cliffs, N.J.: Prentice-Hall, Inc.

Parsons, T. and Bales, R. F. (1955) *Family, Socialization and Interaction Process.* New York: The Free Press.

Parsons, T. and Shils, E. A. (1951) *Toward a General Theory of Action.* Cambridge, Mass.: Harvard University Press.

Patchen, M., Davidson, J. D., Hofmann, G., and Brown, W. R. (1977) Determinants of students' interracial behavior and opinion change. *Sociology of Education,* 50:55–75.

Patterson, T. E. and McClure, R. D. (1976) *The Unseeing Eye: The Myth of Television Power in National Politics.* New York: G. P. Putnam's Sons.

Peach, C. (1974) Homogamy, propinquity and segregation: A re-evaluation. *American Sociological Review,* 39:636–641.

Pearlin, L. I. (1954) Shifting group attachments and attitudes toward Negroes. *Social Forces,* 33:47–50.

Pedersen, E., Faucher, T. A., and Eaton, W. W. (1978) A new perspective on the effects of first-grade teachers on children's subsequent adult status. *Harvard Educational Review,* 48:1–31.

Pellegrin, R. J. (1976) Schools as work settings. In Dubin, R., Ed. *Handbook of Work, Organization, and Society.* Chicago: Rand McNally.

Perinbanayagam, R. S. (1974) The definition of the situation: An analysis of the ethnomethodological and dramaturgical view. *Sociological Quarterly,* 15:521–41.

Peter, L. J. and Hull, R. (1969) *The Peter Principle.* New York: William Morrow & Co., Inc.

Peterman, D. J., Ridley, C. A., and Anderson, S. M. (1974) A comparison of cohabiting and noncohabiting college students. *Journal of Marriage and the Family,* 36:344–54.

Peterson, R. A. and Berger, D. G. (1975) Cycles in symbol production: The case of popular music. *American Sociological Review,* 40:158–173.

Pfohl, S. J. (1977) The "discovery" of child abuse. *Social Problems,* 24:310–323.

Phillips, D. P. and Feldman, K. A. (1973) A dip in deaths before ceremonial occasions. *American Sociological Review,* 38:678–696.

Piaget, J. (1932) *The Moral Judgment of the Child.* Trans. Gabain, M. London: Kegan Paul, Trench, Trubner and Company.

Piaget, J. (1952a) *The Origins of Intelligence in Chidlren.* Trans. by Cook, M. New York: International Universities Press, Inc.

Piaget, J. (1952b) *The Child's Conception of Number.* New York: Humanities Press.

Piaget, J. (1954) *The Construction of Reality in the Child.* New York: Basic Books.

Piaget, J. (1967) *Six Psychological Studies.* New York: Random House.

Pineo, P. C. (1961) Disenchantment in the later years of marriage. *Marriage and Family Living,* 25:3–11.

Platt, A. (1975) Prospects for a radical criminology in the U.S.A. In Taylor, I., Walton, P., and Young, J., Eds. *Critical Criminology.* London: Routledge and Kegan Paul.

Pope, L. (1942) *Millhands and Preachers.* New Haven: Yale University Press.

Portes, A. (1976) On the sociology of national development: Theories and issues. *American Journal of Sociology,* 82:55–85.

Pozner, J. and Saltz, E. (1972) Social-class, conditional communication, and egocentric speech. *Studies in Intellectual Development* (December): Report #2.

Premack, A. J. (1976) *Why Chimps Can Read.* New York: Harper & Row.

Premack, D. (1976) *Intelligence in Ape and Man.* New York: Lawrence Erlbaum Associates.

Prewitt, K. and Stone, A. (1973) *The Ruling Elites.* New York: Harper & Row.

Pufall, P. B. (1975) Egocentrism in spatial thinking: It depends on your point of view. *Developmental Psychology,* 11:297–303.

Quadagno, D. M., Briscoe, R., and Quadagno, J. S. (1977) Effect of perinatal gonadal hormones on selected nonsexual behavior patterns: A critical assessment of the nonhuman and human literature. *Psychological Bulletin,* 84:62–80.

Quarantelli, E. L. and Cooper, J. (1966) Self-conceptions and others: A further test of Meadian hypotheses. *The Sociological Quarterly,* 7:281–97.

Quarantelli, E. L. and Dynes, R. R. (1970) Property norms and looting: Their patterns in community crises. *Phylon,* 31:168–182.

Quinney, R. (1974) *Criminal Justice in America.* Boston: Little, Brown.

Quinney, R. (1975) *Criminology.* Boston: Little, Brown.

Rainwater, L. (1970) *Behind Ghetto Walls.* Chicago: Aldine.

Ransford, H. E. (1972) Blue collar anger: Reactions to student and Black protest. *American Sociological Review,* 37:333–346.

Razran, G. (1950) Ethnic dislike and stereotypes: A laboratory study. *Journal of Abnormal and Social Psychology,* 45:7–27.

Reasons, C. (1974) The politics of drugs: An inquiry in the sociology of social problems. *The Sociological Quarterly,* 15:381–404.

Redekop, C. (1974) A new look at sect development. *Journal for the Scientific Study of Religion,* 13:345–352.

Redlich, F. and Kellert, S. R. (1978) Trends in American mental health. *American Journal of Psychiatry,* 135:22–28.

Reed, M. S., Jr., Burnette, J., and Troiden, R. R. (1977) Wayward cops: The functions of deviance in groups reconsidered. *Social Problems,* 24:565–575.

Rein, M. and Miller, S. M. (1967) Poverty programs and policy priorities. *Trans-action,* 4 (September):60–71.

Reinhold, R. (1977a) Middle-class return displaces some urban poor. *New York Times* (June 5):1, 58.

Reinhold, R. (1977b) Poverty is found less persistent but wider spread than thought. *New York Times* (July 17):1+.

Reinhold, R. (1977c) Public found hostile to welfare as idea but backs what it does. *New York Times,* August 3:1, 49.

Reiss, A. J., Jr. (1961) *Occupations and Social Status.* New York: The Free Press.

Reiss, I. L. (1970) Premarital sex as deviant behavior: An application of current approaches to deviance. *American Sociological Review,* 35:78–87.

Reiss, I. L. (1976) *Family Systems in America.* 2nd ed. Hinsdale, Ill.: The Dryden Press.

Renwick, P. A. and Lawler, E. E. (1978) What you really want from your job. *Psychology Today,* 11 (May):53+.

Reston, J. (1963) Nobody can assassinate a government. *New York Times,* November 27:18.

Rheingold, H. L. (1969) The social and socializing infant. In Goslin, D. A., Ed. *Handbook of Socialization Theory and Research.* Chicago: Rand McNally.

Rheingold, H. L. and Cook, K. V. (1975) The contents of boys' and girls' rooms as an index of parents' behavior. *Child Development,* 46:459–463.

Rheingold, H. L., Hay, D. F., and West, M. J. (1976) Sharing in the second year of life. *Child Development,* 47:1148–1158.

Richey, R. E. and Jones, D. G. (1974) *American Civil Religion.* New York: Harper & Row.

Riesman, D. (1953) *The Lonely Crowd.* Garden City, N.Y.: Doubleday & Co.

Rivers, W. H. R. (1906) *The Todas.* New York: Macmillan.

Rivlin, A. M. (1973) Forensic social science. *Harvard Educational Review,* 43:61–75.

Rivlin, A. M. and Timpane, P. M., Eds. (1975) *Ethical and Legal Issues of Social Experimentation.* Washington, D.C.: The Brookings Institution.

Robertson, H. M. (1933) *Aspects of the Rise of Economic Individualism.* London: Cambridge University Press.

Robertson, R. (1977) Church-sect and rationality: Reply to Swatos. *Journal for the Scientific Study of Religion,* 16:197–200.

Robinson, D. E. (1976) Fashions in shaving and trimming of the beard. *American Journal of Sociology,* 81:1133–1139.

Rockwell, R. C. (1976) Historical trends and variations in educational homogamy. *Journal of Marriage and the Family*, 38:83–95.

Rodman, H. (1966) Illegitimacy in the Caribbean social structure: A reconsideration. *American Sociological Review*, 31:673–683.

Rodman, H. (1968) Class culture. In Sills, D. L., Ed. *International Encyclopedia of the Social Sciences*. Vol. 15. New York: Macmillan.

Roethlisberger, F. J. and Dickson, W. J. (1939) *Management and the Worker*. Cambridge: Harvard University Press.

Rogers, E. M. (1962) *Diffusion of Innovations*. New York: The Free Press.

Rogers, E. M. and Burdge, R. J. (1972) *Social Change in Rural Societies*. 2nd ed. New York: Appleton-Century-Crofts.

Rogers, J. W. and Buffalo, M. D. (1974) Fighting back: Nine modes of adaptation to a deviant label. *Social Problems*, 22:101–118.

Rogers, L. (1976) Male hormones and behavior. In Lloyd, B. and Archer, J., Eds. *Exploring Sex Differences*. New York: Academic Press.

Rollins, B. C. and Cannon, K. L. (1974) Marital satisfaction over the family life cycle: A reevaluation. *Journal of Marriage and the Family*, 36:271–282.

Rollins, B. C. and Feldman, H. (1970) Marital satisfaction over the family life cycle. *Journal of Marriage and the Family*, 32:20–28.

Roof, W. C. (1977) Counter-culture religions: Passage or passing? *Journal for the Scientific Study of Religion*, 16:328–329.

Roof, W. C. and Spain, D. (1977) A research note on city-suburban socioeconomic differences among American Blacks. *Social Forces*, 56:15–20.

Rosaldo, M. Z. (1974) Woman, culture, and society: A theoretical overview. In Rosaldo, M. Z. and Lamphere, L., Eds. *Woman, Culture, and Society*. Stanford, Calif.: Stanford University Press.

Rose, A. M. (1962) A systematic summary of symbolic interaction theory. In Rose, A. M., Ed. *Human Behavior and Social Processes*. Boston: Houghton Mifflin Co.

Rose, A. M. (1967) *The Power Structure*. Fair Lawn, N.J.: Oxford University Press.

Rose, V. M. (1977) Rape as a social problem: a byproduct of the feminist movement. *Social Problems*, 25:75–89.

Rosen, S. (1976) Wherein future shock is disputed. *New York Times*, June 18:21.

Rosenblatt, P. C. and Cunningham, M. R. (1976) Sex differences in cross-cultural perspective. In Llyod, B. and Archer, J., Eds. *Exploring Sex Differences*. New York: Academic Press.

Rosenfeld, R. A. (1978) Women's intergenerational occupational mobility. *American Sociological Review*, 43:36–46.

Rosenthal, J. (1971a) The outer city: U.S. in suburban turmoil. *New York Times* (May 30):28.

Rosenthal, J. (1971b) Suburbs shed city dominance. *New York Times* (August 16):35.

Rosenthal, R. (1973) The Pygmalion effect lives. *Psychology Today*, 7:56–63.

Rosenthal, R. and Jacobson, L. (1968) *Pygmalion in the Classroom*. New York: Holt, Rinehart & Winston, Inc.

Ross, R. and Staines, G. (1971) The politics of analyzing social problems. *Social Problems*, 20:86–112.

Rothman, R. A. and Perrucci, R. (1971) Vulnerability to knowledge obsolescence among professionals. *The Sociological Quarterly*, 12:147–158.

Roy, D. (1952) Quota restriction and goldbricking in a machine shop. *American Journal of Sociology*, 57:427–442.

Roy, D. (1953) Work satisfaction and social reward in quota achievement: An analysis of piecework incentive. *American Sociological Review*, 18:507–514.

Roy, D. (1954) Efficiency and 'the fix': Informal intergroup relations in a piecework machine shop. *American Journal of Sociology*, 60:255–266.

Rubin, Z. (1970) Measurement of romantic love. *Journal of Personality and Social Psychology*, 16:267–273.

Rumbaugh, D. M. Ed. (1977) *Language Learning by a Chimpanzee: The LANA Project*. New York: Academic Press.

Rushing, W. A. (1969) Two patterns in the relationship between social class and mental hospitalization. *American Sociological Review*, 34:533–541.

Russell, C. S. (1974) Transition to parenthood: Problems and gratifications. *Journal of Marriage and the Family*, 36:294–302.

Russo, N. F. (1976) The motherhood mandate. *Journal of Social Issues*, 32:143–153.

Rychlak, J. F. (1965) The similarity, compatibility, or incompatibility of needs in interpersonal selection. *Journal of Personality and Social Psychology*, 2:334–340.

Sacks, H. (1972) On the analysability of stories by children. In Gumperz, J. J. and Hymes, D., Eds. *Directions in Sociolinguistics: The Ethnography of Communication.* New York: Holt, Rinehart & Winston.

Safire, W. (1977) Christmas in July. *New York Times* (July 8):27.

Sagarin, E. (1973) The research setting and the right not to be researched. *Social Problems*, 21:52–64.

Sagarin, E. (1975) *Deviants and Deviance*. New York: Praeger.

Sahlins, M. (1976) *The Use and Abuse of Biology: An Anthropological Critique of Sociobiology.* Ann Arbor: University of Michigan Press.

St. John, N. (1975) *School Desegregation: Outcomes for Children.* New York: Wiley.

Samuelsson, K. (1961) *Religion and Economic Action: A Critique of Max Weber.* Trans. French, E. G. New York: Harper Torchbooks.

Sanday, P. R. (1973) Toward a theory of the status of women. *American Anthropologist*, 75:1682–1700.

Scarf, M. (1970) Brain researcher Jose Delgado Asks—"What Kind of Humans Would We Like to Construct?" *The New York Times Magazine* (November 15):46+.

Scarf, M. (1976) *Body, Mind, Behavior*. Washington, D.C.: New Republic Book Company, Inc.

Scarpitti, F. R. and Scarpitti, E. C. (1977) Victims of rape. *Society*, 14 (July):29–32.

Schaffer, R. T. (1971) The Ku Klux Klan: Continuity and change. *Phylon*, 32:143–157.

Schapera, I. (1940) The political organization of the Ngwato of Buchuanaland Protectorate. In Fortes, M. and Evans-Pritchard, E. E., Eds. *African Political Systems.* London: Oxford University Press.

Scheck, D. C. and Emerick, R. (1976) The young male adolescent's perception of early child-rearing behavior: The differential effects of socioeconomic status and family size. *Sociometry*, 39:39–52.

Scheff, T. (1966) *Being Mentally Ill*. Chicago: Aldine.

Scheff, T. (1968) The societal reaction to deviance. In Spitzer, S. and Denzin, N., Eds. *The Mental Patient*. New York: McGraw-Hill.

Schein, E. H. (1957) Reaction patterns to severe, chronic stress in American army prisoners of war of the Chinese. *Journal of Social Issues*, 13:21–30.

Schellhardt, T. D. (1977) Loosening the laws. *The Wall Street Journal* (May 26):34.

Schermerhorn, R. A. (1967) Polarity in the approach to comparative research in ethnic relations. *Sociology and Social Research*, 51:234–240.

Schiamberg, L. B. (1969) Some socio-cultural factors in adolescent-parent conflict: A cross-cultural comparison of selected cultures. *Adolescence*, 4:333–60.

Schlesinger, A., Jr. (1965) *A Thousand Days*. Boston: Houghton Mifflin.

Schlesinger, J. A. (1965) Political party organization. In March, J. G., Ed. *Handbook of Organizations.* Chicago: Rand McNally.

Schmeck, H. M., Jr. (1978) Population experts say world birth rate is declining. *New York Times* (February 15):15.

Schnore, L. F. (1966) Population problems in perspective. In Becker, H. S., Ed. *Social Problems: A Modern Approach.* New York: Wiley.

Schoenherr, R. A. and Greeley, A. M. (1974) Role commitment processes and the American Catholic priesthood. *American Sociological Review*, 39:407–426.

Schofield, J. W. and Sagar, H. A. (1977) Peer interaction patterns in an integrated middle school. *Sociometry*, 40:130–138.

Schramm, W. T., Lyle, J. and Parker, E. B. (1961) *Television in the Lives of Our Children.* Stanford: Stanford University Press.

Schreiber, E. M. and Nygreen, G. T. (1970) Subjective social class in America: 1945–68. *Social Forces*, 48:348–356.

Schulz, B., Bohrnstedt, G. W., Borgatta, E. F., and Evans, R. R. (1977) Explaining premarital sexual intercourse among college students: A causal model. *Social Forces*, 56:148–165.

Schumacher, C. F. (1961) Medical school grad: His biographical history. *Journal of Medical Education*, 36:398–406.

Schuman, F. L. (1933) *International Politics*. New York: McGraw-Hill.

Schutz, A. (1964) *Collected Papers: II*. Edited by Brodersen, A. The Hague: Nijhoff.

Scott, J. F. (1965) Sororities and the husband game. *Trans-action*, 2 (September-October):10–14.

Scott, J. W. (1976) *The Black Revolts: Racial Stratification in the U.S.A.* Cambridge, Mass.: Schenkman Publishing.

Sears, R. R. (1970) Relation of early socialization experience to self-concepts and gender role in middle childhood. *Child Development*, 41:267–89.

Sebald, H. (1977) *Adolescence: A Social Psychological Analysis*. 2nd ed. Englewood Cliffs, N.J.: Prentice-Hall.

Secord, P. F. and Backman, C. W. (1964) *Social Psychology*. New York: McGraw-Hill.

Seeman, M. (1959) On the meaning of alienation. *American Sociological Review*, 24:783–791.

Seeman, M. (1967) On the personal consequences of alienation in work. *American Sociological Review*, 32:273–285.

Selltiz, C., Wrightsman, L. S., and Cook, S. W. (1976) *Research Methods in Social Relations*. 3rd ed. New York: Holt, Rinehart and Winston.

Selznick, P. (1952) *The Organizational Weapon*. New York: McGraw-Hill.

Sewell, W. H. and Hauser, R. M. (1975) *Education, Occupation, and Earnings: Achievement in the Early Career*. New York: Academic Press.

Sewell, W. H., Haller, A. O., and Ohlendorf, G. W. (1970) The educational and early occupational attainment process: Replications and Revisions. *American Sociological Review*, 35:1014–27.

Sewell, W. H. and Hauser, R. M. (1976) Causes and consequences of higher education: Models of the status attainment process. In Sewell, W. H., Hauser, R. M., and Featherman, D. L., Eds. *Schooling and Achievement in American Society*. New York: Academic Press.

Shapiro, E. D. (1976) Death penalty. *Wall Street Journal* (December 9):20.

Shapiro, H. L. (1936) *The Heritage of the Bounty*. New York: Simon & Schuster, Inc.

Shellenberg, J. A. and Bee, L. S. (1960) A Re-examination of the theory of complementary needs in mate selection. *Marriage and Family Living*, 22:227–232.

Shepard, J. M. (1969) Functional specialization and work attitudes. *Industrial Relations*, 8:185–194.

Sheppard, N., Jr. (1978) Black Muslims movement is split in dispute over doctrinal change. *New York Times* (March 7):18.

Sherif, M., Harvey, O. J., White, B. J., Hood, W. R., and Sherif, C. W. (1961) *Intergroup Conflict and Cooperation: The Robbers Cave Experiment*. Norman, Okla.: University of Oklahoma Book Exchange.

Sherif, M. and Sherif, C. W. (1969) *Social Psychology*. New York: Harper & Row.

Sherlock, B. J. and Morris, R. T. (1972) *Becoming a Dentist*. Springfield, Ill.: Charles C Thomas.

Shey, T. H. (1977) Why communes fail: A comparative analysis of the viability of Danish and American communes. *Journal of Marriage and the Family*, 39:605–613.

Shils, E. A. and Janowitz, M. (1948) Cohesion and disintegration in the Wehrmacht in World War II. *Public Opinion Quarterly*, 12:280–315.

Shipler, D. K. (1977) In Russia, the revolutionary dream has run its course. *New York Times* (November 6):5E.

Shorter, E. (1975) *The Making of the Modern Family*. New York: Basic Books.

Siegel, P. M. (1971) Prestige in the American occupational structure. Unpublished Ph.D. dissertation. University of Chicago.

Sigelman, L. (1977) Review of the polls: Multi-nation surveys of religious beliefs. *Journal for the Scientific Study of Religion*, 16:289–294.

Silberman, M. (1976) Toward a theory of criminal deterrence. *American Sociological Review*, 41:442–461.

Silverman, D. (1967) *Pitcairn Island*. Cleveland: The World Publishing Company.

Silverman, D. (1971) *The Theory of Organizations*. New York: Basic Books.

Simkus, A. A. (1978) Residential segregation by occupation and race in ten urbanized areas, 1950–1970. *American Sociological Review*, 43:81–93.

Simmel, G. (1955) *Conflict*. Trans. Wolff, K. New York: The Free Press.

References

Simmons, R. G., Rosenberg, F., and Rosenberg, M. (1973) Disturbance in the self-image at adolescence. *American Sociological Review,* 38:553–568.

Simões, A., Jr. (1976) *The Bilingual Child.* New York: Academic Press.

Simon, J. G. and Feather, N. T. (1973) Causal attributions for success and failure at university examinations. *Journal of Educational Psychology,* 64:46–56.

Simon, W. and Gagnon, J. H. (1976) The anomie of affluence: A post-Mertonian conception. *American Journal of Sociology,* 82:356–378.

Simpson, R. L. and Simpson, I. H. (1964) Social Organization and Behavior. New York: Wiley.

Singleton, L. C. and Asher, S. R. (1977) Peer preferences and social interaction among third-grade children in an integrated school district. *Journal of Educational Psychology,* 69:330–336.

Sjoberg, G. (1955) The preindustrial city. *American Journal of Sociology,* 60:438–445.

Sjoberg, G. (1960) *The Preindustrial City.* New York: The Free Press.

Sklar, J. and Berkov, B. (1975) The American birth rate: Evidences of a coming rise. *Science,* 189:693–700.

Slaby, R. G. and Frey, K. S. (1975) Development of gender constancy and selective attention to same-sex models. *Child Development,* 46:849–56.

Slotkin, J. S. (1950) *Social Anthropology.* New York: Macmillan.

Smart, M. S. and Smart, R. C. (1975) Recalled, present, and predicted satisfaction in stages in the family life cycle in New Zealand. *Journal of Marriage and the Family,* 37:408–415.

Smelser, N. (1963) *Theory of Collective Behavior.* New York: The Free Press.

Snoek, J. D. (1966) Role strain in diversified role sets. *American Journal of Sociology,* 71:363–372.

Snow, R. E. (1969) Unfinished Pygmalion. *Contemporary Psychology,* 14:197–199.

Snyder, D. and Tilly, C. (1972) Hardship and collective violence in France. *American Sociological Review,* 37:520–532.

Sombart, W. (1913) *The Jews and Modern Capitalism.* Trans. Epstein, M. London: F. Fisher Unwin, Ltd.

Sørensen, A. B. (1975) The structure of intragenerational mobility. *American Sociological Review,* 40:456–471.

Sowell, T. (1975) *Race and Economics.* New York: David McKay Co.

Spanier, G. B., Lewis, R. A., and Cole, C. L. (1975) Marital adjustment over the family life cycle: The issue of curvilinearity. *Journal of Marriage and the Family,* 37:263–275.

Spates, J. L. (1976) Counterculture and dominant culture values: A cross-national analysis of the underground press and dominant culture magazines. *American Sociological Review,* 41:868–83.

Spector, M. and Kutsuse, J. I. (1973) Social problems: A refformulation. *Social Problems,* 21:145–159.

Spencer, H. (1877) *The Principles of Sociology.* New York: Appleton-Century-Crofts, Inc.

Spilerman, S. and Elesh, D. (1971) Alternative conceptions of poverty and their implications for income maintenance. *Social Problems,* 18:358–373.

Spiro, M. (1954) Is the family universal? *American Anthropologist,* 56:839–846.

Spiro, M. (1966) Religion: Problems of definition and explanation. In Banton, M., Ed. *Anthropological Approaches to the Study of Religion.* New York: Frederick A. Praeger, Inc.

Spitz, R. A. (1945) Hospitalism: An inquiry into the genesis of psychiatric conditions in early childhood. *Psychoanalytic Study of the Child,* 1:53–74.

Spitz, R. A. (1946) Hospitalism: A follow-up report. *Psychoanalytic Study of the Child,* 2:113–7.

Spitzer, S. (1975) Toward a Marxist theory of deviance. *Social Problems,* 22:638–651.

Squires, G. D. (1977) Education, jobs, and inequality: Functional and conflict models of social stratification in the United States. *Social Problems,* 24:436–450.

Srole, L., Langner, T. S., Michael, S. T., Kirkpatrick, P. Opler, M. K., and Rennie, T. A. C. (1962) *Mental Health in the Metropolis: The Midtown Manhattan Study.* Vol. 1. New York: McGraw-Hill.

Star, J. (1965) Chicago's troubled schools. *Look* (May 4):59+.

Stark, R. (1972) The economics of piety: Religious commitment and social class. In Thielbar, G. W. and Feldman, S. D., Eds. *Issues in Social Inequality*. Boston: Little, Brown.

Starr, P. (1974) The edge of social science. *Harvard Educational Review*, 44:393–415.

Stephens, W. N. (1963) *The Family in Cross-Cultural Perspective*. New York: Holt, Rinehart & Winston, Inc.

Stern, B. J. (1937) Resistance to the Adoption of Technological Innovations. In *Technological Trends and National Policy*. Washington, D.C.: Government Printing Office.

Stokes, B. (1977) Birth control: More people are turning to sterilization. *New York Times* (May 22):7E.

Stokes, R. G. (1975) Afrikaner Calvinism and economic action: The Weberian thesis in South Africa. *American Journal of Sociology*, 81:62–81.

Stokes, R. G. and Hewitt, J. P. (1976) Aligning actions. *American Sociological Review*, 41:838–49.

Stolzenberg, R. M. (1975) Education, occupation, and wage differences between White and Black men. *American Journal of Sociology*, 81:299–323.

Stolzenberg, R. M. and Waite, L. J. (1977) Age, fertility, expectations and plans for employment. *American Sociological Review*, 42:769–783.

Stone, G. P. (1970) Appearance and the self. In Stone, G. P. and Farberman, H. A., Eds. *Social Psychology Through Symbolic Interaction*. Waltham, Mass.: Xerox College Publishing.

Stone, L. (1977) *The Family, Sex and Marriage in England: 1500–1800*. New York: Harper & Row.

Stouffer, S. A. (1949a) *The American Soldier: Adjustment During Army Life*. Princeton, N.J.: Princeton University Press.

Stouffer, S. A. (1949b) *The American Soldier: Combat and Its Aftermath*. Princeton, N.J.: Princeton University Press.

Strathern, M. (1976) An anthropological perspective. In Llyod, B. and Archer, J., Eds. *Exploring Sex Differences*. New York: Academic Press.

Strauss, A., Schatzman, L., Bucher, R., Ehrlich, D., and Sabshin, M. (1963) The hospital and its negotiated order. In Freidson, E., Ed. *The hospital in modern society*. New York: The Free Press.

Strauss, A., Schatzman, L., Bucher, R., Ehrlich, D., and Sabshin, M. (1964) *Psychiatric Ideologies and Institutions*. New York: The Free Press.

Street, D. P. and Winstein, E. A. (1975) Problems and prospects of applied sociology. *American Sociologist*, 10:65–72.

Sudnow, D. (1967) *Passing on: The Social Organization of Dying*. Englewood Cliffs, N.J.: Prentice-Hall.

Sudnow, D. (1972) *Studies in Social Interaction*. New York: The Free Press.

Sullivan, H. S. (1947) *Conceptions of Modern Psychiatry*. Washington, D.C.: William A. White Psychiatric Foundation.

Sullivan, H. S. (1953) *The Interpersonal Theory of Psychiatry*. New York: W. W. Norton.

Sumner, W. G. (1906) *Folkways*. Boston: Ginn & Co.

Sutherland, E. H. (1949) *White-Collar Crime*. New York: The Dryden Press.

Sutherland, E. H. and Cressey, D. R. (1970) *Principles of Criminology*. 8th ed. Philadelphia: J.B. Lippincott Co.

Swatos, W. H., Jr. (1976) Weber or Troeltsch? *Journal for the Scientific Study of Religion*, 15:129–144.

Swinehart, J. W. (1963) Socio-economic level, status aspiration, and maternal roles. *American Sociological Review*, 28:391–399.

Sztompka, P. (1974) *Systems and Function: Toward a Theory of Society*. New York: Academic Press.

Szulc, T. (1977) The CIA's electric kool-aid acid test. *Psychology Today*, 11 (November):92–104+.

Szymanski, A. (1970) Toward a radical sociology. *Sociological Inquiry*, 40:3–25.

Tallman, I. (1976) *Passion, Action, and Politics: A Perspective on Social Problems and Social-Problem Solving*. San Francisco: W. H. Freeman.

Tannenbaum, A. S. (1965) Unions. In March, J. G., Ed. *Handbook of Organizations*. Chicago: Rand McNally.

Tausky, C. (1969) Meanings of work among blue collar men. *Pacific Sociological Review*, 12:49–55.

Tawney, R. H. (1926) *Religion and the Rise of Capitalism*. New York: Harcourt Brace Jovanovich.

Taylor, H. F. (1973) Playing the dozens with path analysis: Methodological pitfalls in Jencks et al., Inequality. *Sociology of Education*, 46:433–450.

Terborg, J. R. (1977) Women in management: A research review. *Journal of Applied Psychology*, 62:647–664.

Terman, L. M. (1938) *Psychological Factors in Marital Happiness.* New York: McGraw-Hill.

Thomas, M. C. and Flippen, C. C. (1972) American civil religion: An empirical study. *Social Forces,* 51:218–225.

Thomas, W. I. (1937) *The Unadjusted Girl.* Boston: Little, Brown.

Thompson, L. (1948) Attitudes and acculturation. *American Anthropologist,* 50:200–215.

Thompson, S. K. (1975) Gender labels and early sex role development. *Child Development,* 46:339–347.

Thorndike, R. L. (1968) Review of Robert Rosenthal and Lenore Jacobson, *Pygmalion in the Classroom. American Educational Research Journal,* 5:708–711.

Thornton, A. (1977) Children and marital stability. *Journal of Marriage and the Family,* 39:531–540.

Time (1975) Gays on the march. September 8:32–43.

Tiryakian, E. T. (1976) Biosocial Man, Sic Et Non. *American Journal of Sociology,* 82:701–6.

Tittle, C. R. and Logan, C. H. (1973) Sanction and deviance: Evidence and reexamining questions. *Law and Society Review,* 7:372–392.

Tittle, C. R. and Rowe, A. R. (1973) Moral appeal, sanction threat, and deviance: An experimental test. *Social Problems,* 20:488–489.

Tittle, C. R. and Rowe, A. R. (1974) Certainty of arrest and crime rates: A further test of the deterrence hypothesis. *Social Forces,* 52:455–462.

Toby, J. (1957) Orientation to education as a factor in the school maladjustment of lower-class children. *Social Forces,* 35:259–266.

Toffler, A. (1970) *Future Shock.* New York: Random House.

Townsend, J. M. (1975) Cultural conceptions, mental disorders, and social roles: A comparison of Germany and America. *American Sociological Review,* 40:739–752.

Treiman, D. J. (1977) *Occupational Prestige in Comparative Perspective.* New York: Academic Press.

Treiman, D. J. and Terrell, K. (1975) Sex and the process of status attainment: A comparison of working women and men. *American Sociological Review,* 40:174–200.

Tresemer, D. (1974) Fear of success: Popular but unproven. *Psychology Today,* 7 (March):82–85.

Troeltsch, E. (1931) *The Social Teachings of the Christian Churches.* Trans. Wyon, O. 2 Vols. New York: Macmillan.

Tucker, C. W. (1968) A comparative analysis of subjective social class: 1945–1963. *Social Forces:* 46:508–514.

Tuckman, J., Youngman, W. F., and Kreizman, G. B. (1965) Occupational level and mortality. *Social Forces,* 43:575–577.

Tullock, G. (1974) Does punishment deter crime? *The Public Interest,* 36 (Summer):103–111.

Tully, J. C., Jackson, E. F., and Curtis, R. F. (1970) Trends in occupational mobility in Indianapolis. *Social Forces,* 49:186–200.

Tumin, M. M. (1953) Some principles of stratification: A critical analysis. *American Sociological Review,* 18:387–394.

Turk, A. T. (1976) Law as a weapon in social conflict. *Social Problems,* 23:276–91.

Turk, H. (1970) Interorganizational networks in urban society: Initial perspective and comparative research. *American Sociological Review,* 35:1–19.

Turner, J. H. (1974) *The Structure of Sociological Theory.* Homewood, Ill.: The Dorsey Press.

Turner, R. H. (1962) Role-taking: Process versus conformity. In Rose, A., Ed. *Human Behavior and Social Processes.* Boston: Houghton Mifflin Company.

Turner, R. H. (1964) Collective behavior. In Faris, R. E. L., Ed. *Handbook of Modern Sociology,* Chicago: Rand McNally & Co.

Turner, R. H. (1968a) The self-conception in social interaction. In Gordon, C. and Gergen, K. J., Eds. *The Self in Social Interaction.* New York: Wiley.

Turner, R. H. (1968b) Role: Sociological aspects. In Sills, D., Ed. *International Encyclopedia of the Social Sciences.* Vol. 13. New York: The Free Press.

Turner, R. H. (1976) The real self: From institution to impulse. *American Journal of Sociology,* 81:989–1016.

Turner, R. H. and Killian, L. M. (1972) *Collective Behavior.* 2nd ed. Englewood Cliffs, N.J.: Prentice-Hall.

Turner, R. H. and Shosid, N. (1976) Ambiguity and interchangeability in role attribution: The effect of alter's response. *American Sociological Review,* 41:993–1006.

Turner, R. J. and Wagenfeld, M. O. (1967) Occupational mobility and schizophrenia. *American Sociological Review,* 32:104–113.

Turner, S. P. (1977) Blau's theory of differentiation: Is it explanatory? *The Sociological Quarterly,* 18:17–32.

Turnure, C. (1975) Cognitive development and role-taking ability in boys and girls from 7 to 12. *Developmental Psychology,* 11:202–209.

Tyree, A. and Treas, J. (1974) The occupational and marital mobility of women. *American Sociological Review,* 39:293–302.

U.S. Department of Labor (1974) *Job Satisfaction: Is There a Trend?* Manpower Research Monograph No. 30. Washington, D. C.: Government Printing Office.

U.S. Department of Labor (1976) *The Earnings Gap Between Women and Men.* Washington, D.C.: Government Printing Office.

U.S. News & World Report (1964) A police chief talks of "police brutality." August 10:33.

Upjohn Institute for Employment Research (1973) *Work in America.* Cambridge, Mass.: The MIT Press.

Urberg, K. A. and Docherty, E. M. (1976) Development of role-taking skills in young children. *Developmental Psychology,* 12:198–203.

Urdy, J. R. (1966) Marital instability by race, sex, education, and occupation using 1960 census data. *American Journal of Sociology,* 72:203–209.

Urdy, J. R. (1967) Marriage instability by race and income based on 1960 census data. *American Journal of Sociology,* 72:673–674.

Urdy, J. R. (1971) *The Social Context of Marriage.* 2nd ed. Philadelphia: J.B. Lippincott.

Urdy, J. R., Bauman, K. E., and Morris, N. M. (1975) Changes in premarital coital experience of recent decade-of-birth cohorts of urban American women. *Journal of Marriage and the Family,* 37:783–787.

Useem, M. (1975) *Protest Movements in America.* Indianapolis: Bobbs-Merrill Company.

Useem, M. (1976) Government influence on the social science paradigm. *The Sociological Quarterly,* 17:146–61.

Useem, M. (1976) State production of social knowledge: Patterns in government financing of academic social research. *American Sociological Review,* 41:613–629.

Valentine, C. A. (1968) *Culture and Poverty: Critique and Counter-Proposals.* Chicago: University of Chicago Press.

van den Berghe, P. L. (1963) Dialectic and functionalism: Toward a theoretical synthesis. *American Sociological Review,* 28:695–705.

van den Berghe, P. L. (1965) *South Africa: A Study in Conflict.* Middletown, Conn.: Wesleyan University Press.

van den Berghe, P. L. (1967) *Race and Racism.* New York: Wiley.

van den Berghe, P. L. (1970) *Academic Gamesmanship: How to Make a Ph.D Pay.* New York: Abelard-Schuman, Ltd.

van den Berghe, P. L. (1976) Review of Sociobiology. *Contemporary Society,* 5:731–33.

Van Den Haag, E. (1976) Death penalty. *Wall Street Journal* (December 9):20.

Vander Zanden, J. W. (1959) Resistance and social movements. *Social Forces,* 37:312–315.

Vander Zanden, J. W. (1965) *Race Relations in Transition.* New York: Random House.

Vander Zanden, J. W. (1972) *American Minority Relations.* 3rd ed. New York: The Ronald Press.

Vander Zanden, J. W. (1973) Sociological studies of American Blacks. *Sociological Quarterly,* 14:32–52.

Vander Zanden, J. W. (1977) *Social Psychology.* New York: Random House.

Vander Zanden, J. W. (1978) *Human Development.* New York: Random House.

Van Dusen, R. A. and Sheldon, E. B. (1976) The changing status of American women. *American Psychologist,* 31:106–116.

Vanneman, R. and Pampel, F. C. (1977) The American perception of class and status. *American Sociological Review,* 42:422–437.

Vernon, G. M. (1962) *Sociology of Religion.* New York: McGraw-Hill.

Videbeck, R. (1960) Self-conception and the reactions of others. *Sociometry,* 23:351–9.

Villemez, W. J. and Rowe, A. R. (1975) Black economic gains in the sixties: A methodological critique and reassessment. *Social Forces,* 54:181–193.

Vinokur, A. and Selzer, M. L. (1975) Desirable versus undesirable life events: Their relationship to stress and mental distress. *Journal of Personality and Social Psychology*, 32:329–337.

Vizedom, M. (1976) *Rites and Relationships: Rites of Passage and Contemporary Anthropology*. Beverly Hill, Calif.: Sage Publications.

von Wiese, L. and Becker, H. (1932) *Systematic Sociology*. New York: John Wiley.

Wagley, C. and Harris, M. (1958) *Minorities in the New World: Six Case Studies*. New York: Columbia University Press.

Waite, L. J. and Stolzenberg, R. M. (1976) Intended childbearing and labor force participation of young men: Insights from nonrecursive models. *American Sociological Review*, 41:235–252.

Walberg, H. J. and Rasher, S. P. (1974) Public school effectiveness and equality: New evidence and its implications. *Phi Delta Kappan*, 57:3–9.

Waldo, G. P. and Chiricos, T. G. (1972) Perceived penal sanction and self-reported criminality: A neglected approach to deterrence research. *Social Problems*, 19:522–540.

Wallerstein, I. (1976) Modernization: Requiescat in pace. In Coser, L. A. and Larsen, O. N., Eds. *The Uses of Controversy in Sociology*. New York: The Free Press.

Wallis, R. (1975) *Sectarianism: Analyses of Religious and Non-Religious Sects*. New York: Wiley.

Walters, J. and Stinnett, N. (1971) Parent-child relationships: A decade review of research. *Journal of Marriage and the Family*. 33:70–111.

Walum, L. R. (1977) *The Dynamics of Sex and Gender: A Sociological Perspective*. Chicago: Rand McNally.

Wanderer, J. J. (1968) 1967 Riots: A test of the congruity of events. *Social Problems*, 16:193–198.

Wardwell, W. I. (1955) The reduction of strain in a marginal social role. *American Journal of Sociology*, 61:16–25.

Warheit, G. J., Holzer, C. E., III, Bell, R. A., and Arey, S. A. (1976) Sex, marital status, and mental health: A reappraisal. *Social Forces*, 55:459–470.

Warner, L. G. and DeFleur, M. L. (1969) Attitude as an interactional concept: Social constraint and social distance as intervening variables between attitudes and action. *American Sociological Review*, 34:153–69.

Warner, W. L. (1949) *Democracy in Jonesville*. New York: Harper & Row.

Warner, W. L. (1949) *Social Class in America*. Chicago: Science Research Associates.

Warner, W. L. (1959) *The Living and the Dead*. New Haven: Yale University Press.

Warner, W. L., Havighurst, R. J., and Loeb, M. B. (1944) *Who Shall Be Educated?* New York: Harper & Row.

Warner, W. L. and Low, J. O. (1947) *The Social System of the Modern Factory*. New Haven: Yale University Press.

Warner, W. L. and Lunt, P. S. (1941) *The Social Life of a Modern Community*. New Haven: Yale University Press.

Warner, W. L. and Lunt, P. S. (1942) *The Status System of a Modern Community*. New Haven: Yale University Press.

Warner, W. L. and Srole, L. (1945) *The Social System of American Ethnic Groups*. New Haven: Yale University Press.

Warren, B. L. (1970) Socioeconomic achievement and religion: The American Case. *Sociological Inquiry*, 40:130–155.

Waterman, A. S., Geary, P. S., and Waterman, C. K. (1974) Longitudinal study of changes in ego identity status from the freshman to the senior year at college. *Developmental Psychology*, 10:387–92.

Weaver, R. C. (1977) The suburbanization of America. *Civil Rights Digest*, 9 (Spring):3–11.

Weber, G. (1978) Back to basics has its pitfalls. *New York Times* (January 8):20ED.

Weber, M. (1905/1930) *The Protestant Ethic and the Spirit of Capitalism*. Trans. Parsons, T. New York: Charles Scribner's Sons.

Weber, M. (1946) *From Max Weber: Essays in Sociology*. Trans. Gerth, H. H. and Mills, C. W. Fair Lawn, N. J.: Oxford University Press.

Weber, M. (1947) *The Theory of Social and Economic Organization*. Trans. by Henderson, A. M. and Parsons, T. New York: Oxford University Press.

Weber, M. (1958) *From Max Weber: Essay in Sociology*. Trans. by Gerth, H. H. and Mills, C. W. New York: Oxford University Press.

Weigert, A. J. (1974) Functional, substantive, or political? A comment on Berger's "Second thoughts on defining religion. *Journal for the Scientific Study of Religion,* 13:483–486.

Weinraub, B. (1975) Why the poorest nations have so many babies. *New York Times* (February 2):E15.

Weinstein, H. (1975) C.I.A. report says worsening world grain shortages could give U.S. great power. *New York Times* (March 17):13C.

Welch, M. R. (1977) Analyzing religious sects: An empirical examination of Wilson's sect typology. *Journal for the Scientific Study of Religion,* 16:125–141.

Wellford, C. (1975) Labelling theory and criminology: An assessment. *Social Problems,* 22:332–345.

West, C. K. and Anderson, T. H. (1976) The question of preponderant causation in teacher expectancy research. *Review of Educational Research,* 46:613–630.

West, C. K. and Zimmerman, D. H. (1977) Women's place in everyday talk: Reflections on parent-child interaction. *Social Problems,* 24:521–529.

Wheeler, M. (1976) *Lies, Damn Lies, and Statistics: The Manipulation of Public Opinion in America.* New York: Liveright.

Wheeler, S. (1976) Trends and problems in the sociological study of crime. *Social Problems,* 23:525–534.

White, B. L. (1973) Discussions and conclusions. In White, B. L. and Watts, J. C., Eds. *Experience and Environment.* Englewood Cliffs, N.J.: Prentice-Hall.

White, B. L. (1975) *The First Three Years of Life.* Englewood Cliffs, N.J.: Prentice-Hall.

White, R. W. (1965) The experience of efficacy in schizophrenia. *Psychiatry,* 28:199–211.

Whitehead, A. N. (1925) *Science and the Modern World.* New York: Macmillan.

Whitehead, A. N. (1929) *Process and Reality.* New York: Macmillan.

Whitehead, A. N. (1951) *The Aims of Education.* New York: The New American Library of World Literature, Inc.

Whitehead, A. N. (1954) *The Dialogues of Alfred North Whitehead.* Recorded by Lucien Price. London: Max Reinhardt.

Whyte, W. F. (1943) *Street Corner Society.* Chicago: University of Chicago Press (1955, enlarged edition).

Whyte, W. F. (1961) *Men at Work.* Homewood, Ill.: The Dorsey Press.

Wicker, A. W. (1969) Attitudes versus actions: The relationship of verbal and overt behavioral responses to attitude objects. *Journal of Social Issues,* 25:41–78.

Wicker, A. W. (1971) An examination of the "other variables" explanation of attitude-behavior inconsistency. *Journal of Personality and Social Psychology,* 19:18–30.

Wilhelm, S. M. (1971) *Who Needs the Negro?* Garden City, N.Y.: Doubleday Anchor Books.

Wilkins, W. E. (1976) The concept of a self-fulfilling prophecy. *Sociology of Education,* 49:175–183.

Williams, R. M., Jr. (1947) *The Reduction of Intergroup Tensions.* New York: Social Science Research Council.

Williams, R. M., Jr. (1970) *American Society.* 3rd ed. New York: Alfred A. Knopf.

Williamson, J. B. (1974) Beliefs about the motivation of the poor and attitudes toward poverty policy. *Social Problems,* 21:634–648.

Williamson, J. B. and Hyer, K. M. (1975) The measurement and meaning of poverty. *Social Problems,* 22:652–663.

Wilsher, P. (1975) Everyone, everywhere, is moving to the cities. *New York Times* (June 22):18.

Wilson, B. R. (1973) *Magic and the Millennium.* London: Heinemann.

Wilson, E. O. (1975) *Sociobiology: The New Synthesis.* Cambridge, Mass.: Harvard University Press.

Wilson, K. L. and Portes, A. (1975) The educational attainment process: Results from a national sample. *American Journal of Sociology,* 81:343–362.

Wilson, J. Q. (1967) The bureaucracy problem. *The Public Interest,* 6 (Winter):3–9.

Wilson, J. Q. (1975) *Thinking about Crime.* New York: Basic Books.

Wilson, J. Q. (1977) Social protest and social control. *Social Problems,* 24:469–481.

Wimberley, R. C., Clelland, D. A., Hood, T. C., and Lipsey, C. M. (1976) The civil religious dimension: Is it there? *Social Forces,* 54:890–900.

Winch, R. F. (1958) *Mate Selection: A Study of Complementary Needs.* New York: Harper & Row.

Wirth, L. (1938) Urbanism as a way of life. *American Journal of Sociology*, 44:3–24.

Wolff, B. B. and Langley, S. (1968) Cultural factors and the response to pain: A review: *American Anthropologist*, 70:494–501.

Womack, J., Jr. (1977) An American in Cuba. *New York Review of Books*, 24 (August 4):25–9.

Woodward, C. V. (1966) *The Strange Career of Jim Crow*. 2nd rev. ed. Fair Lawn, N.J.: Oxford University Press.

Wooten, J. T. (1976) Aging process catches up with cities of the North. *New York Times* (February 13):1, 14.

Wright, J. D. and Wright, S. R. (1976) Social class and parental values for children: A partial replication and extension of the Kohn thesis. *American Sociological Review*, 41:527–537.

Wrigley, E. A. (1977) Reflections on the history of the family. *Daedalus*, 106:71–85.

Wrong, D. (1961) The oversocialized conception of man in modern sociology. *American Sociological Review*, 26:183–93.

Wuthnow, R. (1976a) Recent pattern of secularization: A problem of generations? *American Sociological Review*, 41:850–867.

Wuthnow, R. (1976b) *The Consciousness Reformation*. Berkeley: University of California.

Yankelovich, D. (1978) The new psychological contracts at work. *Psychology Today*, 11 (May):46–50.

Yarrow, M., Schwartz, C., Murphy, H., and Deasy, L. (1955) The psychological meaning of mental illness in the family. *The Journal of Social Issues*, 11:12–24.

Yinger, J. M. (1957) *Religion, Society and the Individual*. New York: Macmillan.

Yinger, J. M. (1960) Contraculture and subculture. *American Sociological Review*, 25:625–35.

Yinger, J. M. (1963) *Sociology Looks at Religion*. New York: Macmillan.

Yinger, J. M. (1965) *Toward a Field Theory of Behavior*. New York: McGraw-Hill.

Yinger, J. M. (1970) *The Scientific Study of Religion*. New York: Macmillan.

Yinger, J. M. (1977) A comparative study of the substructures of religion. *Journal for the Scientific Study of Religion*, 16:67–86.

Yinger, J. M. (1977) Countercultures and social change. *American Sociological Review*, 42:833–853.

Zborowski, M. (1969) *People in Pain*. San Francisco: Jossey-Bass.

Zeldin, M. B. (1969) The religious nature of Russian Marxism. *Journal for the Scientific Study of Religion*, 8:100–111.

Zellman, G. L. (1976) The role of structural factors in limiting women's institutional participation. *Journal of Social Issues*, 32:33–46.

Zentner, J. L. (1977) Cocaine and criminal sanction. *Journal of Drug Issues*, 7:93–101.

Zimbardo, P. G., Haney, C., and Banks, W. C. (1973) A Priandellian prison. *The New York Times Magazine* (April 8):38–40+.

Zimbardo, P. G. and Ruch, F. L. (1975) *Psychology and Life*. 9th ed. Glenview, Ill.: Scott, Foresman.

Zimmerman, D. H. (1978) Ethnomethodology. *The American Sociologist*, 13:6–15.

Zimmerman, D. H. and Wieder, D. L. (1970) Ethnomethodology and the problem of order: Comment on Denzin. In Douglas, J. D., Ed. *Understanding Everyday Life*. Chicago: Aldine.

Zola, I. K. (1968) Culture and symptoms—An analysis of patients' presenting complaints. *American Sociological Review*, 31:615–630.

Zucker, L. G. (1977) The role of institutionalization in cultural persistence. *American Sociological Review*, 42:726–743.

AUTHOR INDEX

Abercrombie, C. L., III., 130
Abramson, P. R., 517
Ademek, R., 224
Adelman, L., 9
Ajzen, I., 297
Aldrich, H., 608
Alexander, K. L., 529
Allen, E., 81
Almond, G. A., 247-248, 539
Alston, J. P., 267
Althusser, L., 526
Ambedkar, B. R., 311
Anastasi, A., 78
Anderson, C. H., 265, 267
Anderson, L. S., 200
Anderson, N., 22
Anderson, S. M., 430
Anderson, T. H., 545
Andrew, R. J., 335
Angrist, S., 212
Antonovsky, A., 275
Apolonio, F., 423
Appelbaum, R. P., 16
Apter, D. E., 444
Arber, S., 274, 354
Archer, J., 333
Arey, S. A., 348
Argyle, M., 64
Ariel, M., 80
Armbruster, F. E., 550
Aron, A. P., 419
Aronoff, J., 332
Aronson, E., 27, 96

Asch, S. E., 187, 213, 230
Asher, S. R., 548
Astin, A. W., 529
Averitti, R., 302

Babbie, E. R., 450-451
Back, K. W., 221
Backman, C. W., 133
Bagehot, W., 225
Bakeman, R., 338
Bales, R. F., 341
Ball, D. W., 120
Balswick, J. O., 431
Bandura, A., 340
Banks, W. C., 31
Barash, D. P., 80
Baron, R. M., 545
Barraclough, G., 557, 577
Bartley, R. L., 256
Batson, C. D., 440
Bauman, K. E., 431
Bean, L. L., 275
Becker, H., 453
Becker, H. S., 18, 23, 35, 189, 209, 210, 541
Beckford, J. A., 462
Bee, L. S., 423
Behrens, W. W., III., 556
Behrman, J. A., 335
Bell, R. A., 348
Bellah, R. N., 440, 444, 462-463
Bem, S. L., 356, 357, 361
Bendix, R., 279

Benedict, R., 45, 294-295, 446-447
Benson, J. K., 171, 172
Bercheid, E., 419
Berelson, B., 236
Berg, A., 577
Berger, B., 434
Berger, D. G., 232
Berger, P. L., 124, 434, 441
Berghe, P. L. van den, 81, 308, 311, 312, 371, 528
Berk, B., 126
Berk, R. A., 227
Berkov, B., 562
Berkowitz, L., 267
Berman, G. S., 343
Berman, N. E. J., 80
Bernard, J., 277, 345, 347
Bernstein, I. N., 210
Berreman, G. D., 37, 280
Berry, B., 35, 36, 391
Bertenthal, B. I., 103
Bevan, W. D., 336
Biblarz, A., 36
Biddle, B. J., 110, 531, 539
Bidwell, C. E., 533
Bierstedt, R., 35, 36, 150
Bigner, J. J., 103
Billingsley, A., 432
Blackwell, J. E., 309
Blake, J., 562
Blau, P. M., 17, 165, 166, 170, 171, 267, 283, 285, 423
Blauner, R., 309-310, 491

Blood, R. O., Jr., 277, 424
Bloom, B. S., 92
Blot, W. J., 565, 566
Blumer, H., 10, 12, 17, 18, 47, 51, 116, 117-118, 219, 225, 238-242, 381
Bohlander, E. W., 205
Bohrnstedt, G. W., 431
Boli-Bennett, J., 522
Bonacich, E., 305
Boocock, S. S., 532, 539
Booth, A., 193
Borders, W., 582
Borgatta, E. F., 431
Borke, H., 103
Bossard, J. H. S., 422
Bottomore, T. B., 16, 265, 267
Bouma, G. D., 468
Bower, D. W., 430
Bowers, W. J., 200
Bowlby, J., 411
Bowles, S., 526-527
Bradburn, N. M., 424
Bradley, G. W., 547
Bradley, L. A., 547
Bralove, M., 356
Brandwein, R. A., 432
Braun, C., 545
Brewer, M. B., 294
Brieger, R. L., 391
Briggs, K., 474
Brim, O. G., Jr., 92, 104
Brinton, C., 245
Brinton, L. A., 565
Briscoe, R., 334, 335
Broadhead, R. S., 528
Brody, J. E., 137, 471
Brody, N., 546
Bromley, D. B., 104
Bronson, F. H., 336
Bronson, G., 565
Brooks, C. H., 274
Brooks, J., 103
Broom, L., 265
Brophy, J. E., 539
Broverman, D. M., 333
Brown, C. A., 432
Brown, J. C., 491
Brown, J. K., 140
Brown, J. V., 338
Brown, L. R., 582
Brown, W. R., 548-549
Bruner, E. M., 609

Bryen, D. N., 544
Bucher, R., 58-59, 172
Buckley, W., 372
Buffalo, M. D., 211
Bunce, R., 235
Burchard, W. W., 130
Burchinal, L. G., 433
Burdge, R. J., 391
Burgess, E., 76, 431, 601, 602, 603, 615
Burnette, J., 192
Burns, H., 320
Burr, W. R., 424
Burt, R. S., 391

Campbell, D. T., 294
Cannon, K. L., 424
Cantor, N. L., 338
Cantril, H., 228
Caplan, F., 339-340
Caplan, T., 339-340
Caplow, T., 528
Carey, A., 175
Carithers, M. W., 547
Carlsmith, J. M., 27, 96
Carmichael, S., 299
Carpenter, E., 76
Carr, E. R., 522
Carr, L. G., 452-453
Cartwright, D., 236
Carver, R. P., 539
Catton, W. R., Jr., 587
Centers, R., 269, 428
Cerf, B. A., 129
Chambers, C. D., 391
Chambliss, W. J., 205, 207
Chancellor, W. J., 577
Chandler, M. J., 102
Chase-Dunn, C., 497
Chasin, B., 81
Childe, G., 483-484, 590
Chiricos, T. G., 200, 207
Chodorow, N., 331
Choldin, H. M., 193
Christopherson, V. A., 430
Cicourel, A. V., 19, 112, 117
Clancy, K., 348
Clark, J. P., 26
Clark, K., 309
Clark, K. B., 231, 544
Clarke, A. C., 422
Clausen, J. A., 190
Clayton, R. R., 429-430, 431

Clelland, D. A., 444
Coale, A. J., 415
Cohen, A. K., 183, 191, 204
Cohen, M. N., 577
Cole, C. L., 424, 430-431
Cole, R. W., Jr., 541
Cole, S., 209
Cole, W. A., 445
Coleman, J. S., 17, 170, 391-394, 526, 535, 536-537, 551
Coleman, R., 274
Colfax, J. D., 35
Collins, R., 16, 56, 170, 345, 482, 498, 526, 527
Colombotos, J., 298
Commager, H. S., 61
Comte, A., 14, 311, 325
Condry, J., 342, 343
Conger, J. J., 190
Conrad, P., 238
Cony, E., 256
Conyers, J. E., 322
Cook, K. S., 172
Cook, K. V., 338
Cook, M., 529
Cook, S. W., 24, 27, 31
Cooley, C. H., 93, 94, 107, 153
Coombs, R. H., 95
Cooper, H. M., 545
Cooper, J., 95
Coopersmith, S., 95
Coplovitz, D., 424
Corwin, R. G., 533
Cory, C. T., 190
Coser, L. A., 10, 192
Cottrell, W. F., 370
Couch, C. J., 228
Coward, B. E., 488
Crano, W. D., 332
Cressey, D. R., 208
Critchfield, R., 69
Crittenden, A., 352
Crockett, H. J., Jr., 281-282
Cromwell, R. E., 428
Crumrine, J., 342
Crutchfield, R., 235
Cunliffe, M., 504
Cunningham, D. J., 336
Cunningham, M. R., 330, 331-332, 356-357
Curtis, R. F., 281-282
Cushing, R. G., 265
Cutright, P., 282

Author Index

Czajka, J. L., 354

Dahl, R. A., 504-505
Dahlgren, H. E., 155
Dahrendorf, R., 16, 258-259, 265-266
D'Andrade, R. G., 332
Daniel, C., 366
Darley, S. A., 343
Daves, W. F., 336
Davidson, C., 488
Davidson, J. D., 548-549
Davie, M. R., 603
Davis, A., 271, 542, 543
Davis, K., 15, 55, 77, 84, 86, 153, 264, 280, 288, 440, 447, 481, 501, 580, 581, 586, 591, 592
Davis, K. E., 423
Daw, N. W., 80
Dawkins, R., 80
Day, J. V., 56, 58
Day, R., 56, 58
Deasy, L., 212
Deedy, J., 471
DeFleur, M. L., 297
Delgado, J. M. R., 87, 89
DellaCava, F. A., 135-136
Dellinger, R. W., 273, 274
Dennis, J., 510
Dennis, W., 411
Denzin, N. K., 18, 63, 92, 98, 116, 191
Desjardins, C., 336
Deutsch, M., 13
Dewey, J., 530-531
Dickinson, P. J., 281-282, 539
Dickson, W. J., 175, 176
Dinitz, S., 212
Dixon, R. R., 346
Djilas, M., 258
Docherty, E. M., 103
Dodge, K. A., 338
Dohrenwend, B. P., 348
Dohrenwend, B. S., 348
Doreian, P., 166
Dowdall, G. W., 302
Dowling, P., 220
Doyle, P. A., 210
Dragastin, S. E., 138
Dubin, R., 485, 491
Dullea, G., 348, 354
Dumont, L., 412
Duncan, B., 283

Duncan, O. D., 267, 283, 285, 589, 614
Duncan, S., Jr., 64
Dunkin, M. J., 531
Dunlap, R. E., 587
Durkheim, E., 27, 201, 312, 372, 449-450, 567
Dusek, J. B., 545
Dutton, D. G., 419
Dyer, S., 342, 343
Dynes, R. R., 483

Eaton, W. W., 539
Eaton, W. W., Jr., 275
Eckholm, E. P., 589
Edwards, R., 302
Ehrhardt, A. A., 333, 334, 341
Ehrlich, A. H., 629
Ehrlich, D., 58, 172
Ehrlich, P. R., 580-581
Eisen, M., 104
Eister, A. W., 459
Ekeh, P. P., 17
Elder, G. H., Jr., 138
Elesh, D., 513
Ellis, L., 80
Ellsworth, P. C., 27
Emerick, R., 275
Emmert, F., 174-175
Empey, L. T., 38
Engels, F., 15, 258, 266, 267, 288-289, 452
Enokson, S. N., 278
Erbe, W., 278
Erickson, F., 300
Erikson, E. H., 140, 411
Erikson, K., 192, 209
Erlanger, H. S., 275
Essien-Udom, E. U., 460
Evans, R. R., 431

Fairfield, R., 433
Fallers, L. A., 415
Fanfani, A., 466
Faris, R. E. L., 11, 13
Farrell, R. A., 210
Fast, J., 64, 121, 263
Fasteau, M. F., 357
Faucher, T. A., 539
Fava, S. F., 593
Feagin, J. R., 488
Feather, N. T., 343
Featherman, D. L., 283, 301, 468, 469-470

Fein, M., 485, 491
Feinberg, W. E., 227, 230
Feld, S., 424
Feldberg, R., 432
Feldman, H., 424, 425-427
Feldman, K. A., 566, 567-569
Fendrich, J. M., 224
Ferree, M. M., 348
Festinger, L., 236
Fichter, J. H., 60, 475
Firestone, G., 546
Firey, W., 604
Firth, R., 446
Fischer, C. S., 610, 611-613
Fischer, K. W., 103
Fishbein, M., 297
Fisher, J., 246
Fisher, S., 337
Flavell, J. H., 102
Flint, J. M., 599
Flippen, C. C., 444
Foote, N. N., 237
Form, W. H., 165-166, 492
Fort, J., 190
Fortes, M., 407
Fox, E. M., 432
Fraiberg, S., 411
Franklin, R. S., 309
Franks, D. R., 95
Fraumeni, J. F., Jr., 565, 566
Frazier, C. E., 201
Fredrickson, W. T., 338
Freeman, H., 212
Freeman, J., 355
Freidson, E., 481
Freitag, P. J., 507
Freud, S., 336-337, 341-342
Frey, K. S., 341
Friedl, E., 345
Friedrichs, R. W., 371
Fuller, C. J., 412
Funck-Brentano, F., 246

Gagnon, J. H., 204
Gaitz, C. M., 488
Galbraith, J. K., 512
Galliher, J. F., 205
Gans, H. J., 609
Gardner, B. B., 271
Gardner, B. T., 83
Gardner, M., 222
Gardner, M. R., 271
Gardner, R. A., 83

Garfinkel, H., 19, 117, 118
Garnier, M. A., 282
Garrett, C. S., 336
Gaudet, H., 236
Garvey, C., 103
Gasson, R. M., 285
Geary, P. S., 140
Gebhard, P. H., 431
Gecas, V., 95, 275
Geerken, M. R., 348
Geertz, C., 448
Geis, G., 195
Gelfand, D. M., 338
Gerard, H. B., 548
Gergen, K. J., 92, 95, 122, 304
Germain, A., 332
Gerth, H. H., 259
Gibbs, J. P., 200, 481
Gibson, C., 563
Gilbert, W. S., 129
Gillespie, D. F., 166
Gillespie, D. L., 353
Gilligan, C. F., 89
Gintis, H., 526-527
Ginzberg, E., 354
Giovannoni, J. M., 432
Gist, N. P., 593
Gitlin, T., 357
Glaser, B., 138
Glass, B., 12
Glenn, N. D., 267, 278-279, 424, 516
Glick, P. C., 412
Glock, C. Y., 440, 449, 450-452
Gluckman, M., 314, 418
Gockel, G. L., 277, 278
Goffman, E., 38, 112, 115, 116, 120, 122, 126, 212, 263
Goldfarb, W., 411
Goldman, P., 172
Goldstein, S., 277
Good, T. L., 539
Goode, E., 209
Goode, W. J., 56, 277, 407, 415, 418-419, 420, 501
Goodenough, W. H., 124-125
Goodman, E. J., 353
Goodwin, L., 488
Gordon, D., 302
Gordon, D. N., 415
Gordon, L., 346
Gornick, V., 345
Goss, J. R., 577

Gough, E. K., 412, 420
Gouldner, A. W., 9, 35, 69, 170
Gove, W. R., 209, 210, 211-212, 348
Grandjean, B. D., 265
Gray, J. A., 333
Greeley, A. M., 135, 440, 442, 461-462, 468
Green, H. W., 603
Greenberg, M. T., 102
Greenberg, R. P., 337
Greenspan, S., 102
Grimm, J. W., 348
Groombridge, B., 235
Gross, N., 118
Grossman, N., 444
Guardo, C., 95
Guest, A. M., 606
Guhl, A. M., 336
Gulick, J., 609
Gurin, G., 424
Gurwitz, S. B., 338

Haas, J. E., 166
Hacker, A., 259
Hackett, B., 434
Hadley, C., 516
Hagan, J., 207
Hagedorn, R., 304
Hagstrom, W. O., 387-389
Hall, E. T., 44
Haller, A. O., 285
Hallowell, A. I., 47
Hamblin, R. L., 305, 391
Hamilton, C. V., 299
Hammond, D., 447
Hammond, K. R., 9
Hammond, P. E., 445, 468
Haney, C., 31
Hansen, S. B., 278
Harber, J. R., 544
Hardin, G., 346
Hargens, L. L., 391
Harkey, J., 275
Harnischfeger, A., 549
Harper, D., 174-175
Harris, A. R., 211
Harris, C. D., 601, 604, 615
Harris, M., 292, 293, 315, 333
Harrison, M. I., 475
Hart, C. W., 237
Hart, H., 383, 384
Hartley, S. F., 407

Hartnagel, T. F., 235
Harvey, O. J., 159-160
Haug, M. R., 343
Hauser, P. M., 594
Hauser, R. M., 281-282, 286-287, 301, 539
Hauser, W. J., 452-453
Havighurst, R. J., 271, 529, 542, 543
Hawley, A. H., 257
Hay, D. F., 102
Hayes, C., 82-83
Hayes, K., 82-83
Hazelrigg, L. E., 282
Heath, A., 16
Hecht, P. K., 391
Hedley, R. A., 485, 491
Heirich, M., 475
Hennig, M., 350
Henze, L. F., 430
Hepler, R., 338
Herberg, W., 473
Hertzler, J. O., 448
Hewitt, J. P., 53, 56, 63, 118
Heydebrand, W., 172
Hill, G., 576, 589
Hill, R., 424
Hinkle, G. J., 33
Hinkle, R. C., Jr., 33
Hobart, C. W., 452-453
Hodge, R. W., 267, 270
Hodges, H. M., Jr., 267, 276
Hodges, K. L., 341
Hoebel, E. A., 56
Hoffer, E., 246
Hoffman, L. W., 341
Hoffman, M. L., 103
Hofmann, G., 548-549
Hogan, R., 103
Hollingshead, A. B., 271, 276
Holman, B. L., 275
Holter, H., 345-346
Holzer, C. E., III, 348
Homans, G. C., 17, 423
Hood, T. C., 444
Hood, W. R., 159-160
Hoover, R., 566
Horner, M. S., 341-342, 343, 360
Horowitz, I. L., 35-36, 189, 206
Horwitz, A., 207
Hostetler, J. A., 462
House, J. S., 610
Hout, M., 285
Howard, J., 275

Author Index

Howells, W. W., 292
Hoyt, H., 601, 604, 615
Hraba, J., 31
Hsu, F. L. K., 485
Huaco, G. A., 265
Hudson, J. W., 430
Hull, R., 169
Hummon, N. P., 166
Humphreys, L., 224
Hunt, J. G., 453, 547
Hunt, L. G., 391
Hunt, L. L., 453
Hunter, A., 609
Hurn, C. J., 539
Hutt, C., 333
Hyatt, J. C., 601
Hyde, J. S., 335, 337, 340
Hyer, K. M., 10, 513
Hyman, H. H., 162, 235, 539

Inkeles, A., 496, 539
Israel, J., 492

Jacklin, C. N., 335, 341
Jackson, E. F., 133, 281-282
Jackson, P. W., 531-532
Jacobson, L., 545
Jaffe, D., 434
Janis, I. L., 162
Janowitz, M., 156-157
Jardim, A., 350
Jencks, C., 524, 536-539, 551
Jenkins, J. C., 570
Jensen, A. R., 77
Jensen, M., 423
Jensen, M. C., 195
Johnson, B., 461
Johnson, D. R., 193, 348
Johnson, M. P., 302
Johnson, N. R., 227, 230
Johnson, W. J., 200
Johnson, W. T., 277
Jones, D. G., 444
Judah, J. S., 69

Kahn, A., 422
Kalleberg, A., 484
Kann, P., 256
Kanowitz, L., 352, 353
Kanter, R. M., 343-344, 433-434
Kaplan, H. R., 485, 486, 488, 489
Karabel, J., 529
Katcher, A., 341

Katz, E., 391-394
Katz, F. E., 533
Katz, J. M., 417, 419
Kaufman, M. T., 312
Kellen, K., 350
Keller, H., 64-65
Kellert, S. R., 275
Kellogg, L. A., 82
Kellogg, W. N., 82
Kelly, G. A., 14
Kelly, W. R., 210
Kemper, T. D., 263, 280
Kerckhoff, A. C., 104, 138, 221, 422, 423, 535
Kick, E. L., 391
Kihss, P., 431
Killian, L. M., 219, 228, 243, 247, 297, 321, 322
Kim, H. C., 468
Kim, O., 278
King, K., 431
King, L., 516
King, M. L., Jr., 138
Kinsey, A. C., 431, 434
Kirkpatrick, P., 275
Kitsuse, J. I., 242
Kitt, A. S., 162
Klaiber, E. L., 333
Klapper, J. T., 235
Klockars, C. B., 196-197
Klopfer, D. S., 129
Kluckhohn, C., 45-46, 61
Kluegel, J. R., 269
Kneeland, D. E., 600
Kobayashi, Y., 333
Koestler, A., 443
Koffel, J. N., 281-282
Kohen, J., 432
Kohlberg, L., 60, 89, 340, 341
Kohn, M. L., 275, 492, 493-494, 539
Kolata, G. B., 80
Koluchová, J., 86
Kornhauser, W., 508
Krauss, R. M., 13
Krauss, W. R., 345-346, 355
Kraut, R. E., 200
Kreizman, G. B., 275
Kreps, J., 350
Kretch, D., 235-236
Kristol, I., 30-31, 309
Kroeger, N., 172
Kronholz, J., 429

Kuhn, M. H., 18

Labovitz, S., 304
Ladd, E., Jr., 516
Lang, G. E., 225
Lang, K., 225
Langley, S., 49
Langman, L., 61
Langner, T. S., 275
LaPiere, R. T., 297
Larkin, W. E., 210
Larsen, O. N., 218, 222, 233
Lauderdale, P., 192
Lauer, R. H., 51-52, 370, 378
Laurentin, R., 475
Lawler, E. E., 487
Lazarsfeld, P. F., 38, 236
Leacock, E. B., 69
Le Bon, G., 225-227
Lee, A. M., 35, 132
Lefton, M., 212
Leger, R. R., 312
LeGrand, C. E., 353
LeMasters, E. E., 432
Lemert, E. M., 189, 209
Lenney, E., 341, 343
Lenski, G. E., 81, 263, 265, 483
Leon, J., 207
Leopold, L., 261
Lerner, R. M., 77
Lester, M., 239-241
Lever, J., 340
Levine, A., 342
Levinson, H., 486
Levy, F. W., 336
Levy, M. J., Jr., 415
Lewis, F., 444
Lewis, J. M., 218, 224
Lewis, M., 103
Lewis, O., 68, 609
Lewis, R. A., 424
Libby, R. W., 429
Lichtenstein, G., 435
Lickona, T., 60
Lieberson, S., 506, 507
Liebow, E., 69, 486
Liebowitz, M., 189, 206
Limber, J., 83
Lin, N., 391
Lincoln, E. E., 460
Lindesmith, A. R., 63, 92
Lindgren, E. J., 305, 306-307
Lindsay, P. H., 12, 47

Linton, R., 111, 117, 280, 390, 395
Lipset, S. M., 19, 170, 216, 279, 281-282, 503-504, 509
Lipsey, C. M., 444
Liska, A. E., 297
Livesley, W. J., 104
Loeb, M. B., 271
Lofland, J., 112
Logan, C. H., 200
Logan, J. R., 595
Loman, L. A., 210
Long, N. E., 600
Lopata, H. Z., 429
Lott, A. J., 423
Lott, B. E., 423
Lovekin, A., 475
Low, J. O., 271
Luckey, E. B., 424
Lunt, P. S., 269, 271
Lyle, J., 235

McAuliffe, W., 211
McCarthy, J. D., 220
McCartney, J. L., 205
McClelland, D. G., 496
McClendon, M. J., 285
McClosky, H., 155
Maccoby, E. E., 24, 335, 341
Maccoby, N., 24
McCready, W. C., 440, 442, 461-462
McClure, R. D., 236
McDill, E. L., 529
McEachern, A. W., 118
McGaughey, T. A., 422
McGee, R. J., 528
McGuire, M. B., 474
Machalek, R., 441
Machonin, P., 282
McHugh, P., 51
McIntyre, J. J., 235
MacIver, R. M., 297, 502
McKay, F. W., 566
McKenzie, R. D., 602
Macklin, E. D., 430, 431
McPhee, W. N., 236
Maddox, G. L., 283
Madron, T. W., 453
Malinowski, B., 407, 446
Malony, H. N., 475
Malthus, T. R., 576-577, 583
Mann, L., 220
Manning, P. K., 172
Maratsos, M. P., 103

Marcuse, H., 266
Marecek, J., 96-97
Marini, M. M., 424
Markle, G. E., 572
Marolla, J., 95
Marsh, R. M., 603
Martin, C. E., 431
Martin, M., 441
Martin, W. B. W., 56
Martinson, R., 198
Marvin, R. S., 102
Marwit, S. J., 544
Marx, G. T., 220
Marx, K., 15-16, 258, 266, 267, 288-289, 452, 493
Mason, K. O., 354
Mason, T. J., 566
Mason, W. S., 118
Matras, J., 539
May, R. L., 380
Mayer, A. J., 468
Mead, G. H., 10, 17, 39, 94, 97-99, 100, 107, 339-340, 356-357
Mead, M., 49, 330-331
Meadows, D. H., 556
Meadows, D. L., 556
Means, R. L., 466
Mechanic, D., 210
Medalia, N. Z., 218, 222
Meeker, B. F., 343
Mehan, H., 19, 56
Meier, R. F., 195
Meile, R. L., 348
Meislin, R. J., 430
Meltzer, B. N., 17
Menzel, M., 391-394
Meranto, P. J., 322
Mercer, B. E., 522
Merton, R. K., 15, 61, 114, 162, 188, 201-204, 213, 295-296, 339, 373, 374
Mesarovic, M., 556
Mettee, D. R., 96-97
Meyer, J. W., 522, 529
Michael, S. T., 275
Michalowski, R. J., 205, 206
Michels, R., 170, 177-178
Middleton, R., 28-30, 406
Miles, D. L., 275
Mileti, D. S., 166
Milgram, S., 220, 230
Millar, R. M., 434
Miller, B. C., 424

Miller, D. C., 165, 598
Miller, J. L. L., 391
Miller, N., 548
Miller, S. C., 305
Miller, S. M., 513
Mills, C. W., 16, 37, 259, 265, 505, 508
Minor, H., 396, 397
Mintz, S. W., 331
Mischel, W., 339
Molotch, H., 239-241, 595
Money, J., 328, 333-335, 341
Monge, R. H., 140
Montemayor, R., 104
Moore, W. E., 264, 288
Moran, B. K., 345
Morgan, S. T., 285
Morgan, W. R., 285
Morris, N. M., 431
Morris, R. T., 265
Morse, N. C., 485
Moskos, C. C., Jr., 157
Moss, J. J., 423
Mossler, D. G., 102
Mowat, F., 524-525
Moynihan, D. P., 486
Mueller, C. W., 277
Muensterberger, W., 140
Mullins, N. C., 391
Murdock, G. P., 331, 332, 405, 416, 499
Murguia, E., 308
Murphy, H., 212
Murphy, R. J., 229
Murstein, B. I., 422
Myers, J. K., 275

Nagel, T., 220
Neff, W. S., 485
Nelson, H. M., 453
Nelsen, J. F., 210
Nelson, W. E., Jr., 322
Nemy, E., 352
Neugarten, B. L., 529
Newton, H. P., 148
Nicolson, R. B., 367
Nie, N. H., 516, 517
Niebuhr, H. R., 453
Nisbet, R. A., 267
Nobile, P., 244-245
Noel, D. L., 279
Noel, D. M., 318
Nordheimer, J., 431

Author Index

Norman, D. A., 11-12, 46-47
Northrop, F. S. C., 22
Northrup, B., 312
Nottingham, E. K., 449
Nowlis, H. H., 190
Nye, F. I., 275
Nygreen, G. T., 269

Oberschall, A., 224
O'Dea, T. F., 448
Offenbacher, D., 117
Ogburn, W. F., 378, 385-386
Ohlendorf, G. W., 285
Olsen, M. E., 38, 170, 376, 512
Olson, D. H., 428
Opler, M. K., 275
Orcutt, J. D., 190
O'Toole, R., 444, 462
Overton, W. F., 78

Pampel, F. C., 267
Paris, B. L., 424
Park, R. E., 76, 602
Parker, E. B., 235
Parsons, J. E., 341
Parsons, T., 15, 56, 117, 341
Pasamanick, B., 212
Patchen, M., 548-549
Patterson, T. E., 236
Peach, C., 422
Pearlin, L. I., 163
Pedersen, E., 539
Pellegrin, R. J., 533
Perinbanayagam, R. S., 51, 120
Perrucci, R., 526
Pestel, E., 556
Peter, L. J., 169
Peter, L. S., 348
Peterman, D. J., 430
Peterson, R. A., 232
Petras, J. W., 17
Petrocik, J., 278, 516, 517
Pfohl, S. J., 238
Phillips, D. P., 566, 567-569
Piaget, J., 60, 88-91
Pineo, P. C., 424
Pinkney, A., 279
Platt, A., 205
Pomeroy, W. B., 431
Pope, L., 277, 453, 456-457
Portes, A., 283, 495, 497
Poston, D. L., Jr., 481
Pozner, J., 544

Premack, A. J., 83
Premack, D., 83
Prewitt, K., 483
Provost, C., 331, 332
Pufall, P. B., 102

Quadagno, D. M., 334, 335
Quadagno, J. S., 334, 335
Quarantelli, E. L., 95, 483
Quinney, R., 205

Rabow, J., 38
Rainwater, L., 124
Ramirez, F. O., 522
Randers, J., 556
Ransford, H. E., 279
Rasher, S. P., 539
Raven, B. H., 428
Razran, G., 47
Reasons, C., 238
Redekop, C., 462
Redlich, F., 275
Reed, J. S., 539
Reed, M. S., Jr., 192
Reich, M., 302
Rein, M., 513
Reinhold, R., 488, 512, 608
Reiss, A. J., Jr., 267, 608
Reiss, I. L., 431
Reitz, J. G., 38
Rennie, T. A. C., 275
Renwick, P. A., 487
Resnik, S., 309
Reston, J., 366, 516
Reynolds, L. T., 17
Rheingold, H. L., 76, 102, 338
Richards, R. O., 31
Richey, R. E., 444
Ridley, C. A., 430
Riesman, D., 507
Ringer, B. B., 450-451
Rist, R. C., 528
Rivers, W. H. R., 416-417
Rivlin, A. M., 31, 537
Robertson, H. M., 465-466
Robertson, R., 461
Robinson, D. E., 232
Robinson, I. E., 431
Rockwell, R. C., 422
Rodman, H., 267, 407
Rodrigues, A., 428
Roethlisberger, F. J., 174-175, 176
Rogers, E. M., 391

Rogers, J. W., 211
Rogers, L., 334, 335
Rollins, B. C., 424, 425-427
Roof, W. C., 474, 596
Rosaldo, M. Z., 331, 332
Rose, A. M., 65, 508
Rose, V. M., 353
Rosen, S., 378
Rosenberg, B. G., 335, 337, 340
Rosenberg, F., 140
Rosenberg, M., 140
Rosenblatt, P. C., 330, 331-332, 356-357
Rosenfeld, R. A., 285
Rosenthal, J., 595, 596, 599
Rosenthal, R., 545
Ross, R., 238
Rossi, P. M., 267
Rothman, R. A., 526
Rowe, A. R., 200, 301
Roy, D., 174-175
Rubin, Z., 417
Rubinson, R., 522
Ruble, D. N., 341
Ruch, F. L., 49
Rumbaugh, D. M., 83
Rushing, W. A., 275
Russell, C. S., 424
Russo, N. F., 346
Rutter, M., 411
Rychlak, J. F., 423

Sabshin, M., 58-59, 172
Sacks, H., 19
Safire, W., 228
Sagar, H. A., 548-549
Sagarin, E., 201, 205, 207, 209
Sahlins, M., 81
St. John, N., 547, 548
Salem, R. G., 200
Sales, R. R. de, 417
Saltz, E., 544
Samuelsson, K., 466
Sanday, P. R., 332
Scarf, M., 87-83, 334
Scarpitti, E. C., 353
Scarpitti, F. R., 353
Schaffer, R. T., 245
Schapera, I., 484
Schatzman, L., 58-59, 172
Scheck, D. C., 275
Scheff, T., 211
Schein, E. H., 149

Author Index

Schellhardt, T. D., 190
Schermerhorn, R. A., 310
Schiamberg, L. B., 140
Schlesinger, A., Jr., 162-163
Schlesinger, J. A., 170
Schmeck, H. M., Jr., 557
Schneider, D. M., 415
Schnore, L. F., 580
Schoenherr, R. A., 135, 165, 166, 170-171
Schofield, J. W., 548-549
Schooler, C., 492
Schramm, W. T., 235
Schreiber, E. M., 269
Schulz, B., 431
Schumacher, C. F., 265
Schuman, F. L., 444
Schutz, A., 112, 113
Schwartz, C., 212
Scott, J. F., 419
Scott, J. W., 322
Seabury, P., 216
Sears, R. R., 95
Sebald, H., 138
Secord, P. F., 133
Seeman, M., 488
Seidman, R. B., 207
Sell, R. R., 302
Selltiz, C., 24, 27
Selzer, M. L., 378
Selznick, P., 170
Sewell, W. H., 285, 286-287, 539
Shapiro, E. D., 200
Shapiro, H. L., 367
Sharp, H., 468
Sheatsley, P., 235
Sheldon, E. B., 354
Shellenberg, J. A., 423
Shepard, J. M., 492
Sheppard, N., Jr., 461
Sherif, C. W., 159-160, 186-187
Sherif, M., 20, 159-160, 186, 187, 213, 230, 304, 394
Sherlock, B. J., 265
Shey, T. H., 433
Shils, E. A., 156-157
Shipler, D. K., 256
Shorter, E., 404
Shosid, N., 114
Siegel, P. M., 267
Sigelman, L., 472
Silberman, M., 200
Silverman, D., 171, 367

Simkus, A. A., 606
Simmel, G., 310
Simmons, O., 212
Simmons, R. G., 140
Simões, A., Jr., 544
Simon, J. G., 343
Simon, W., 204-205
Simpson, I. H., 204
Simpson, R. L., 204
Singer, E., 162
Singleton, L. C., 548
Singleton, R., Jr., 269
Sjoberg, G., 591
Sklar, J., 562
Slaby, R. G., 341
Slotkin, J. S., 182
Small, A. W., 341
Smart, M. S., 424
Smart, R. C., 424
Smelser, N., 220, 221, 222, 249
Smith, D. H., 496, 539
Snoek, J. D., 131
Snow, R. E., 545
Snyder, D., 220
Snyder, P. A., 338
Sombart, W., 466
Sørensen, A. B., 281
Sowell, T., 309
Spain, D., 596
Spanier, G. B., 424
Spates, J. L., 67
Spector, M., 242
Spencer, H., 14, 312
Spilerman, S., 513
Spiro, M., 405, 443
Spitz, R. A., 411
Spitzer, S., 205
Squires, G. D., 526
Srole, L., 271, 275
Staines, G., 238
Star, J., 544
Stark, R., 449, 452-453
Starnes, C. E., 269
Starr, P., 37-38
Stephens, W. N., 405, 417
Stern, B. J., 399
Stern, R. N., 348
Stinnett, N., 275
Stokes, B., 563
Stokes, R. G., 53, 56, 118, 465, 467, 476
Stolzenberg, R. M., 285, 301, 564
Stone, A., 483

Stone, B. J., 565
Stone, G. P., 120
Stone, L., 404
Stouffer, S. A., 38, 185
Strathern, M., 328
Strauss, A., 58-59, 63, 92
Street, D. P., 34
Sudnow, D., 19
Sullivan, H. S., 95
Sumner, W. G., 34, 54, 295
Sutherland, E. H., 195, 208-209
Swatos, W. H., Jr., 461
Swinehart, J. W., 275, 276
Sztompka, P., 371
Szulc, T., 31
Szymanski, A., 37

Tallman, I., 238
Tannenbaum, A. S., 170
Tausky, C., 485, 488, 489
Taveggia, T. C., 485, 491
Tawney, R. H., 466
Taylor, H. F., 539
Teevan, J. J., Jr., 235
Terborg, J. R., 351
Terman, L. M., 431
Terrell, K., 285
Teuter, K., 166
Thomas, D., 385
Thomas, E. J., 110
Thomas, M. C., 444
Thomas, W. I., 51
Thompson, L., 398
Thompson, S. K., 341
Thorndike, R. L., 545
Thornton, A., 424
Tifft, L. L., 26
Tilly, C., 220
Timpane, P. M., 31
Tiryakian, E. T., 81
Tittle, C. R., 200
Toby, J., 543
Toffler, A., 377, 378, 400
Tomkins, S. S., 414
Townsend, J. M., 210
Travis, H. P., 281-282
Treas, J., 285
Treiman, D. J., 270, 285
Tresemer, D., 342
Troeltsch, E., 453
Troiden, R. R., 192
Trow, M. A., 170
Tucker, C. W., 269

Author Index

Tucker, P., 333, 335
Tuckman, J., 275
Tudor, J., 348
Tullock, G., 198
Tully, J. C., 281-282
Tumin, M. M., 265
Turk, A. T., 56
Turk, H., 165
Turner, J. H., 14, 19
Turner, R. H., 18, 94, 96, 98, 114, 117, 118, 219, 228, 243
Turner, R. J., 275
Turner, S. P., 171
Turnure, C., 103
Tyree, A., 285

Ullian, D. Z., 340-341
Ullman, E. L., 601, 604, 615
Urberg, K. A., 103
Urdy, J. R., 277, 424, 431
Useem, M., 31, 238, 528

Valentine, C. A., 69
Van Den Haag, E., 200
Vander Zanden, J. W., 51, 66-67, 77, 88, 96, 98, 104, 112, 116, 119, 236, 244, 245, 279, 293, 321, 377
Van Dusen, R. A., 354
Van Houten, D. R., 172
Vanneman, R., 267
Verba, S., 516, 517, 539
Verhoff, J., 424
Vernon, G. M., 445
Videbeck, R., 95
Villemez, W. J., 301
Vinokur, A., 378
Vizedom, M., 138
Vogel, W., 272
Voss, H. L., 429-430

Wagenfeld, M. O., 275
Wagley, C., 293, 315
Waite, L. J., 564
Walberg, H. J., 539
Waldo, G. P., 200, 207
Wallace, W. L., 322
Wallerstein, I., 495
Wallin, P., 431
Wallis, R., 440, 459
Walster, E., 419
Walters, J., 275
Walum, L. R., 338, 346-347
Wanderer, J. J., 228

Wardwell, W. I., 136-137
Warheit, G. J., 348
Warner, L. G., 297
Warner, W. L., 267, 269, 271, 277
Warren, B. L., 468
Waterman, A. S., 140
Waterman, C. K., 140
Watson, J. M., 229
Weaver, R. C., 595, 600
Weber, G., 550
Weber, M., 34, 35, 36, 166-168, 170, 171, 177, 257, 259, 262, 463-468, 476, 502, 519
Weed, J. A., 606
Weigert, A. J., 441
Weinrauh, B., 580
Weinstein, H., 34, 576
Weisberg, D. K., 434
Weiss, R. S., 485
Weitzel-O'Neill, P. A., 343
Welch, M. R., 461
Wellford, C., 210
West, C. K., 257, 545
West, M. J., 102
Wheeler, M., 235
Wheeler, S., 195
White, B. J., 159-160
White, B. L., 411
White, L., 66
White, R. W., 95-96
Whitehead, A. N., 38, 376
Whyte, W. F., 23, 24-25, 395
Wicker, A. W., 297
Wieder, D. L., 18
Wiese, L. von, 453
Wiley, D. E., 549
Wiley, J., 283
Wilhelm, S. M., 610
Wilkins, W. E., 545
Williams, J. A., Jr., 488
Williams, K. R., 468
Williams, R. M., Jr., 188, 304
Williamson, J. B., 10, 513
Wilsher, P., 587
Wilson, B. R., 453, 462-463
Wilson, E. O., 80-81
Wilson, J. Q., 168, 191, 198-199, 200, 224
Wilson, K. L., 283
Wimberley, R. C., 444
Winch, R. F., 404, 423
Wirth, L., 608, 609, 610, 611, 615
Wolfe, D. M., 277, 424

Wolff, B. B., 49
Womack, J., Jr., 69
Wood, H., 19, 56
Wood, J. L., 220
Woodward, C. V., 320
Wooten, J. T., 599
Wright, C. R., 539
Wright, J. D., 275
Wright, S. R., 275
Wrightsman, L. S., 24, 27
Wrong, D., 56, 96
Wuthnow, R., 440, 471, 474

Yankelovich, D., 487
Yarrow, M., 212
Yinger, J. M., 67, 95, 277, 440, 445, 448, 450, 452-453, 462
Yokley, R. L., 453
Youngman, W. F., 275

Zald, M. N., 220
Zborowski, M., 49-51
Zeldin, M. B., 444
Zellman, G. L., 346, 350, 351
Zenter, J. L., 190
Zimbardo, P. G., 31, 49
Zimmerman, D. H., 18, 19, 172, 173, 257
Zola, I. K., 49
Zucker, L. G., 398

SUBJECT INDEX

Achieved status, 279-280
Achievement motivation, 341-343
Adolescence, 138-140
Alcohol, 190
Alienation, 488-494, 541
Analysis, in science, 30-31
Androgyny, 356-358
Anomie, defined, 201
  Merton's theory of, 201-205
    critique of, 204-205
    responses to, 202-204
Anti-Semitism, 28-30
Anti-war movement, 217-218, 223
Apes, 82-83
Arapesh, 331
Ascribed status, 127, 279-280, 409-410
Assimilation, 316-318
Associations, see Organization
Attitudes, changing, 163-164
  measuring, 19-20
  toward pain, 49-51
  prejudice, 296-298
Authority, defined, 502
  in new nations, 503-504
  types of, 502-503
Autokinetic phenomenon, 186-187, 230
Avoidance rituals, 263

Back-to-basics movement, 549-550
Berkeley student revolt, 216-217, 222

Bilineal descent, 413
Biological processes, 48-51, 333-336
Birth control, 563-564, 579-582
Black Muslims, 459-461
Black Power, 138, 311, 321
Blacks, civil rights movement, 137-138, 216, 221, 453
  colonialism, 308-310
  desegregation, school, 547-549
  disadvantages, 301-302
  discrimination, 296-298
  ghetto rioting, 229, 230-231, 258, 309, 483
  institutional racism, 299-302
  marital stability among, 277
  Muslims, 459-461
  NAACP, 320
  population, 571, 596, 608
  protest, 320-322
  and relative deprivation, 320-322
  responses to racism, 318-322
  role ambiguity, 137-138
  and social change, 137-138
Bureaucracy, characteristics, 166-167
  defined, 165-166
  dysfunctions, 168-170
  in education, 533-534
  functions, 168
  Iron Law of Oligarchy, 170
  Peter Principle, 169-170

Calvinism, 462-470, 496

Capitalism, 258, 493-494, 526
Caste, 279, 305
Categories, and language, 66-67
  in race situations, 303-304
  social, 152
  statistical, 151-152
Centralization, 605
Change, see Social change
Charismatic, 474
Charismatic authority, 503
Chicanos, 299, 300, 309
Chiropractor, position of, 136-137
Chromosomes, sex, 333-334
Church, 453-455
Cities, see Urban centers
Civil religion, 444-445
Civil rights movement, 137-138, 216, 221, 453
Classes, see Social class; Stratification
Coercion, 315
Cognitive development, 88-91
Cohabitation, unmarried, 429-431
Collective behavior, crowds, 225-231. See also Crowd
  defined, 219
  determinants of, 219-224
  mass, 231-236
  mass hysteria, 218-219
  public, 236
  significance of, 220
  social movements, 243-248
  social problems, 238-241

Colonialism, 308-310, 497
Communes, 433-434
Communication, 17-18, 63-67
  mass, 232-236
Communism, 222, 247-248, 258-259, 266-267, 443-444
Compartmentalization, 133
Competition, 304-306
Concentration, 605
Concentric circle theory, 602-603
Concrete operations, period of, 90-91
Conflict, contact without, 306-307
  defined, 15
  and disunity, 310
  Marxism, 15-16, 205-207, 258, 266-267, 452, 493-494
  role, 127-133
  and the state, 509-510
  stratification, 527
  theory of, 15-16, 205-207, 258, 265-267
Conformity, and anomie, 202
  Asch experiment, 187-188, 230
  brainwashing, 149
  and deviance, 183-212
  factors in, 183-185
  group forces in, 186-187
  Sherif experiment, 186-187, 230
Conjugal family, 412-415
Consanguine family, 412-415
Consciousness of kind, 150, 294
Consensus, ceremonies, 567-569
  death dip and, 567-569
  defined, 311
  in democracy, 510-511
  provided by religion, 448-451
  social unity, 311
Conservation of quantity, 90-91
Consumption, 483-484
Contagion theory of crowds, 225-227
Contraception, 391, 563-564
Control groups, 27-28
Convergence theory of crowds, 227-228
Cossacks, 306-307
Counterculture, 69-70, 473-474
Craze, 232
Crime, anomie theory of, 201-207
  labeling theory of, 209-212
  prevalence of, 193-196
  Sutherland's theory of, 208-209
  white-collar, 195-196
Crowd, acting, 225

contagion theory of, 225-227
conventional, 225
convergence theory of, 227-228
craze, 232
defined, 225
emergent norm theory of, 228-230
expressive, 225
fad, 232
fashion, 232
ghetto riots, 229, 230, 258, 309, 483
selection of targets, 230-231
Crude birth rate, 561-562
Crude death rate, 564
Cult, 458-459
Culture, acquiring, 76-106
  base, 381-384
  and biological processes, 48-51
  consensus, 311
  contact without conflict, 306-307
  counterculture, 69-70, 473-474
  defined, 45
  and ethnic groups, 49-51
  and family organization, 412-413
  folkways, 53-55
  and foreign aid programs, 44-45
  and gender roles, 330-333
  lag, 378, 380
  law, 56
  mores, 53-55
  and pain, 49-51
  and perception, 46-48
  persistence, 398
  pluralism, 316
  subculture, 67-69
  symbols, 63-67
  transmission of, 338-340
  values, 60-63
Culture of poverty, 67-69, 267

Death dip, 567-569
Decentralization, 606
Deference, 263
"Definition of situation," 51-53
Democracy, 509-511
Demography, see Population
Denominations, 458
Descriptive studies, 22
Desegregation, school, 547-548
Deterrence, 198-200
Deviance, anomie, 201-205
  defined, 188-189
  deterrence of, 198-200

differential association, theory of, 208-209
drug use, 190
functions, 191-192
labeling theory of, 209-212
marihuana, 190
Merton's theory of, 201-205
prevalence of, 193-196
rehabilitation in, 198-200
and social learning, 208
societal reaction and, 209-212
variant behavior, 188
white-collar crime, 195-196
as zone, 188
Differential association, theory of, 208-209
Diffusion, 381, 390-394
Discrimination, see Prejudice; Racism
Distribution, 481-483
Drug use, 190
Duties, 115
Dysfunctions, 373-374

Ecology, defined, 587
  elements in, 589
  and population, 556-558, 587-589
  processes in cities, 605-608
Economy, and capitalism, 462-470
  consumption, 483-484
  development, national, 494-497
  distribution, 481-483
  functions of, 480-484
  money, 481
  and poverty, 512-514
  production, 481
  property, 482-483
  and religion, 462-470
  and sexism, 348-352
  and social change, 512-517
  and work, 484-494
Education, back-to-basics movement, 549-550
  bureaucracy in, 533-534
  characteristics in U.S., 530-539
  classroom life, 531-532
  defined, 522
  desegregation, 547-548
  functions, 523-530
  social change, 547-550
  and social class, 539-546
  socialization, 524
Electra complex, 337
Emergent norm theory, 228-230

Subject Index

Endogamy, 416
Environment, 77-89
Ethics in research, 31-32
Ethnic group, 293
Ethnocentrism, 294
Ethnomethodology, 18-19, 173, 239-241
Exogamy, 416
Experiment, control groups, 27-28
  controlled, 27
  experimental groups, 27-28
  ex post facto, 28
Experimental groups, 27-28
Exploratory studies, 22
Exponential principle, 384

Fabricating impressions, 120-122
Face-saving, 126
Facts, 11
Fad, 232
Family, bilineal, 413
  cohabitation, unmarried, 429-431
  conjugal, 412-415
  consanguine, 412-415
  defined, 406
  extended, 412-415
  functions, 404-405, 406-411
  homemaking, 346-348
  life cycle, 425-427
  marital satisfaction, 423-427
  matrilineal, 413
  nuclear, 412-415
  of orientation, 412
  patrilineal, 413
  of procreation, 412
  and social change, 427-435
  and socialization, 408-409
Fashion, 232
Fatherhood, 407
Fecundity, 561
Fertility, 560-564
Folkways, 53-55
Food supply, 577-579
Force, 315
Formal operations, period of, 91
Formal organization, *see* Organization
Front, 120
Function, bureaucracy, 168
  defined, 373-374
  dysfunctions, 373-374
  of economy, 480-484
  of education, 523-530
  of family, 404-405, 406-411

latent, 375, 530
of primary groups, 153-156
of religion, 374
of state, 499-501
theory of stratification, 263-265
Functional reciprocity, 312
Future shock, 378
Gatekeeping, 300-302
Gender, and achievement motivation, 341-343
  acquiring identities, 336-341
  and androgyny, 356-358
  biology of, 333-336
  and childcare, 346-348
  and chromosomes, sex, 333-334
  and culture transmission theory, 338-340
  defined, 328
  and exploitation, 352-353
  and hermaphrodites, 334-335
  and homemaking, 346-348
  and labeling theory, 340-341
  and psychoanalytic theory, 336-337
  role, 328-343
  and social change, 354-358
  stratification, 345-353
  and wage economy, 348-352
  the Women's Movement, 354-356
Generalized other, 100
Genius, individual, 385-386
Ghetto riots, 229, 230, 258, 309, 483
Glossolalia, 474-475
Group, bureaucracy, 165-170
  control, 28
  defined, 150, 153
  experimental, 28
  formal organization, 164-176
  informal organization, 174-176, 534-535
  in-groups, 158-161
  out-groups, 158-161
  primary, 153-158
  in prisons, 148
  reference, 161-164
  secondary, 155
  social, 152-164
  social categories, 152
  as social class, 269-274
  statistical categories, 151-152
Groupthink, 162

Hare Krishna, 69-70

Health, 274-275
Heredity, 77-89, 333-336
Hermaphrodites, 334-335
Hierarchy of obligations, 133
Holiness sects, 245, 456-457
Homogamy, 422
Homosexuality, 434-435
Hospitals, order in, 58-59
Hypothesis, 21
  null, 567

Ideal type, 166
Identity, 122-125, 336-341
Ideology, 222
Imitation, 339
Immigration, 569
Impression management, 120-122
Incest, 406-407
Indians, *see* Native Americans
Individual genius, 385-386
Informal organization, 174-176, 534-535
In-groups, 158-161
Innovation, 381-389
Institution, change in, 376-399
  defined, 367
  economic, 480-497
  education, 522-551
  family, 403-435
  functions, 373-375
  importance of, 367
  interrelationships among, 370-371
  among Pitcairn Islanders, 367-370
  religion, 440-477
  the state, 497-517
  syncretism, 395
  systems, 371-372
Institutional racism, 299-302
Interviews, 25-26
Invasion, 606
Invention, 381-389
Iron Law of Oligarchy, 170
Isolation, severe, 84-86, 148

Kent State, 217-218

Labeling theory, 209-212, 340-341, 419
Language, 17, 63-67, 82-86, 97-100
Latent functions, 375, 530
Law, 56, 297-298
Leader, 246-247
Legal-rational authority, 503

Legitimacy, principle of, 407
Life-chances, 259
Looking-glass self, 92-94

Magic, 445-447
Manifest functions, 375
Marihuana, usage, 190
Marriage, cohabitation, unmarried, 429-431
 communes, 433-434
 endogamy, 416
 exogamy, 416
 group, 416-417
 mate selection, 417-423
 monogamy, 416
 polyandry, 416
 polygyny, 416
 satisfaction in, 423-427
Marxism, 15-16, 205-207, 258, 266-267, 452, 493-494
Mass, 231-236
Mass communication, 232-236
Mass hysteria, 218-219
Matching hypothesis, 422
Materialism, 60
Mate selection, complementary needs, 423
 factors in, 417-423
 homogamy, 422
 love and, 417-419, 420-421
 matching hypothesis of, 422
 propinquity, 422
 social exchange, theory of, 423
 social regulation of, 419-421
Matrilineal, 413
Mental illness, 58-59, 275
Mexican-Americans, see Chicanos
Minority groups, characteristics of, 293-294
 discrimination, 296-298
 ethnic groups, 293
 ethnocentrism, 294
 institutional racism, 299-302
 prejudice, 296-298
 races, 293
Mob, see Crowd
Money, 481
Monogamy, 416
Mores, 53-55
Mortality, 564-566
Motherhood, 346-348
Movements, see Social movements
Multiple nuclei theory, cities, 604-605

Mundugumor, 331

National Association for the Advancement of Colored People, 320
National Organization for Women, 355
Native Americans, 299, 302
Nayar, 412-413
Negotiated order, 56-59
Networks, 391-394
News, 239-241
Norms, and anomie, 201-202
 and collective behavior, 228
 conflicting, 131-132
 defined, 53
 emergent, 228-230
 folkways, 53-55
 laws, 56
 mores, 53-55
 and political institutions, 499-500
 and primary groups, 155-158
 property, 258-259, 482
 and values, 567
Null, hypothesis, 567
Nurses, position of, 114-116

Objectivity, 8-10
Object permanence, 90
Observation, 22-24
Oedipal complex, 337
Order, negotiated, 56-59
Organic solidarity, 312
Organization, formal, associations, 164-176
 characteristics of, 166-167
 defined, 150
 dysfunctions of, 168-170
 functions of, 168
 informal, 174-176
Out-groups, 158-161

Pain, experience of, 49-51
Participant observation, 22-24
Path analysis, 283
Patrilineal, 413
Pentecostalism, 474-475
Perception, 46-48
Peter Principle, 169-170
Physician, roles of, 131-132
Pitcairn Islanders, 367-370
Play, in socialization, 99-100
Pluralism, 316
Political institutions, see State
Polyandry, 416

Polygyny, 416
Population, age composition, 573
 birth control, 563-564, 579-582
 composition, 572-575
 death dip, 567-569
 determinants of size, 560-566
 and ecology, 556-558, 587-589
 emigration, 569
 explosion, 556-558
 fecundity, 561
 fertility, 560-564
 food supply, 577-579
 immigration, 569
 Malthus theory of, 576-577
 mortality, 564-569
 pyramids, 573-575
 sex composition, 572
 spatial distribution, 570-572
 in United States, 559-575
 world growth, 576-582
 zero growth, 562-563
Position, 114
Poverty, combating, 512-514
 conceptions of, 512-514
 culture of, 67-69, 267
 defined, 10
 and education, 536-537
 ghetto living, 8-10
 non-sociological views of, 8
 sociological views of, 9-10
 and work, 488
Power, authority, 502-504
 Black, 138, 311, 321
 colonialism, 308-310, 497
 defined, 257
 and deviance, 205-207
 elite thesis, 504-507, 508-509
 and force, 315
 hierarchies, 257-259
 pluralist thesis, 507-509
 in United States, 504-509
Prejudice, changing, 28-30
 and cities, 611-613
 colonialism, 308-310
 combating, 28-30
 defined, 296
 discrimination, 296-298
 institutional racism, 299-302
 toward Jews, 28-30
 responses to, 318-322
 and social unity, 310-318
 sources of, 302-310
Preoperational period, 90
Presentation rituals, 263

Subject Index

Priests, 135-136
Primary groups, defined, 153
  degree of, 155-156
  facilitated by, 153
  functions of, 153-155
  importance of, 156-158
  among troops, 156-158
Principle of legitimacy, 407
Prisoners of war, 149
Privilege, 257, 259-261
Production, 481
Professional fence, 196-197
Propinquity, 422
Protestant Ethic, 462-470, 496
Psychoanalytic theory, 336-337
Public, conceptions of social problems, 238-241
  defined, 236
  phases in, 237-238
Public opinion, 19-20, 237-238

Questionnaires, 19-20, 26-27

Race, 293
Racism, colonialism, 308-310
  competition in, 304-306
  discrimination, 296-298
  ethnocentrism, 294
  institutional, 299-302
  power in, 308-310
  prejudice, 296-298
  responses to, 318-322
  and social unity, 310-318
  sources of, 302-310
  in South Africa, 312-314
  split-labor market, 304-306
Rape, 353
Rationality, 62
Reference groups, 161-164, 297
Regions, 122
Rehabilitation, 198-200
Reinforcement, 338-339
Relative deprivation, 320-321
Religion, and church, 453-455, 461-462
  civil, 444-445
  as collective behavior, 245
  countercultural, 473-474
  and Communism, 443-444
  and cults, 458-459
  defined, 441
  and denominations, 458
  dysfunctions of, 374
  functions of, 374, 447-453

humanistic, 443-445
and magic, 445-447
and nationalism, 444-445
Protestant Ethic, 462-470
and sects, 455-457
secular, 443-444
secularization, 472-473
social change, 471-475
social class, 277
types of structures, 453-462
Research, analysis, 30-31
  controlled experiments in, 27-30
  descriptive, 22
  ethics in, 31-32
  exploratory, 22
  hypothesis, defined, 21
  interviews, 25-26
  observation in, 22-24
  participant observation, 22-24
  questionnaires, 19-20, 26-27
  selecting problems, 21-22
  use of available data, 27
Resistance, 398-399
Rights, 115
Riots, see Crowd
Rituals, 263, 567-569
Role, adolescent, 138-140
  ambiguity, 136-140
  androgynous, 356-358
  childcare, 346-348
  chiropracter, 136-137
  compartmentalization, 133
  conflict, 127-133
  defined, 111-114
  emergent, 136-137
  gender, 328-343
  hierarchy of obligations, 133
  and identity, 122-125
  and impression management, 120-122
  nurse, 114-116
  physician, 131-132
  and social structure, 116
  strain, 127-140
Role-making, 117-119
Role-taking, 117-119
Role-set, 114-116, 131
Role strain, 127-140
Romantic love, 417-419, 420-421

Schemas, 88-89
Science, applied, 35-37
  assumptions of, 10-11
  characteristics of, 10-12

competition in, 387-389
critical science orientation, 37-38
diffusion of, 392-394
ethics in, 31-32
and facts, 11
pursuit of objectivity, 8-10
and research, 19-32
and subjectivity, 8-12
Secondary groups, 155
Sect, Black Muslims, 459-461
  critique of typology, 461-462
  defined, 455-457
  emergence of, 459-461
Sector theory, cities, 604
Secularization, religious, 472-473
Segregation, 316-317, 606
Self, appraisals, 94-97
  conceptions, 94
  defined, 92
  development, 97-106
  face-saving, 126
  identity, 122-125
  images, 94
  looking-glass, 93-94
  Mead's theory, 97-100
Self-appraisals, 94-97
Self-conceptions, 94
Self-fulfilling prophecy, 544-546
Self-image, 94
Sensorimotor period, 90
Sex, regulation of, 406-407
Sexism, 345. See also Gender
Significant other, 99-100
Situation, definition of, 51-53
Social category, 152
Social change, cultural lag, 378, 380
  diffusion, 381, 390-394
  directed, 396-398
  economic, 512-517
  education, 547-550
  exponential principle of, 384
  in family, 427-435
  future shock, 378
  and gender roles, 354-358
  individual genius and, 385-386
  innovation, 381-389
  institutional, 376-399
  persistence, 398
  under pressure, 396-398
  rate of, 377-380
  religious, 471-475
  resistance to, 398-399
  reworking, 394-395
  and role ambiguity, 137-138

Subject Index

syncretism, 395
Social class, and caste, 279, 305
   and child-rearing practices, 275-276
   definition, 256
   and education, 539-546
   and family relations, 276
   and health, 274-275
   and mobility, 281-282
   objective approach to, 269
   and political behavior, 278-279
   and religious life, 277
   reputational approach to, 270-274
   significance of, 274-279
   as social category, 273-274
   as social group, 274
   and socialization, 275-276
   Warner, W. Lloyd, 270-274
   see also Stratification
Social exchange theory, 16-17, 423
Social groups, *see* Group
Social interaction, 12
Socialization, anticipatory, 339-340
   Cooley's theory of, 93-94
   defined, 76
   development of self, 97-106
   and education, 524
   environment, 77-89
   and family, 408-409
   and games, 99-100
   and gender roles, 336-341
   heredity, 77-89
   inadequacy of environment, 82-84
   inadequacy of heredity, 84-86
   interplay between heredity and environment, 87-91
   across life span, 102-106
   looking-glass self, 92-94
   Mead's theory of, 97-100
   mechanisms of, 338-340
   nature and nurture, 77-89
   and play, 99-100
   reflected appraisals and, 95-97
   self, 92-106
   self-appraisals, 94-97
Social mobility, caste, 279
   in Czechoslovakia, 282
   defined, 279
   intergenerational, 281-282
   intragenerational, 281
   status attainment process, 283-287
Social movements, anti-war, 217-218, 223
   back-to-basics, 549-550
   Black Power, 138, 311, 321
   civil rights, 137-138, 216, 221, 453
   defined, 243
   determinants of, 219-224
   elements of, 243-248
   exclusion, 305
   expressive, 245
   goals of, 244-245
   ideology of, 222, 245-246
   organization of, 246-247
   reactionary, 244-245
   reform, 244
   and relative deprivation, 320-321
   resistance, 244-245
   revolutionary, 244
   tactics of, 247
   Women's Liberation, 354-356
Social problems, 238-241
Social stratification, *see* Stratification
Social structure, 116, 371-372
Social unity, coercion, 315
   consensus, 311
   functional reciprocity, 312
   polar view of, 310
Sociobiology, 80-81
Sociology, advocacy in, 32-38
   applied, 35-37, 38
   critical science orientation of, 37-38
   defined, 7
   myth of value-free, 35-38
   practical uses of, 32-38
   pursuit of objectivity, 8-10
   and radicalism, 37-38
   and research, 19-32
   and science, 10-11
   subject matter, 12-13
   and theory, 13-19
   value judgments in, 34-38
South Africa, 312-314
Split-labor market, 304-306
State, authority, 502-504
   defined, 497-501
   functions, 499-501
   power in United States, 504-509
Statistical categories, 151-152
Status, 257, 261-263
Stratification, and athletic performance, 25
   approaches to study, 267-274
   conflict theory of, 265-267
   defined, 256
   and education, 539-546
   and family relations, 276
   functionalist theory of, 263-265
   and gender, 345-353
   and health, 274-275
   Marxism, 265-267
   objective approach to, 269
   of occupations, 271
   and political behavior, 278-279
   and religious life, 277
   reputational approach to, 270-274
   self-classification, 269-270
   and self-conceptions, 25
   and socialization, 275-276
   and social mobility, 279-287
   sources of, 263-265
   subjective approach to, 269-270
   in youth groups, 25
Style of life, 262
Subculture, 67-69
Suburbs, 594-598
Success, 60-61
Succession, 655-656
Symbol, defined, 17, 63
   importance of, 64-65, 82-86
   and language, 66-67, 97-100
   and Mead's theory, 17, 97-100
   of status, 261
   and symbolic interaction theory, 17-18
Symbolic interaction theory, 17-18, 98-100, 209-212

Tchambuli, 331
Theory, conflict, 15-16, 205-207, 258, 265-267
   defined, 14
   ethnomethodological, 18-19, 173, 239-241
   social exchange, 16-17, 423
   structure-function, 14-15, 264-265, 371-375
   symbolic interaction, 17-18, 98-100, 209-212
Traditional authority, 503
Tungus, 306-307

Unidentified flying objects, 218-219, 222
Urban centers, concentric circle theory of, 602-603
   crisis of, 599-601
   ecological processes in, 605-608
   industrial-urban center, 593
   metropolitan, 593-594
   multiple nuclei theory of, 604-605
   origins of, 590-593
   patterns of growth, 601-605

preindustrial, 590-593
sector theory of, 604
social consequences of, 608-613
suburbs, 594-598
Wirth's theory of, 608-613

Values, 34-38, 60-63
Voting behavior, 514-517

White-collar crime, 195-196
Women's Liberation, 354-356
Work, and activity, 61
   alienation in, 488-494
   attitudes toward, 61, 487
   and identity, 486
   incentives to, 484-487
   meanings of, 486
   and poor people, 488
   and Protestant Ethic, 462-470

Zero population growth, 562-563

CHAPTER OPENER PHOTO CREDITS

Chapter 1: Shelly Rusten
Chapter 2: Jacques Jangoux/Peter Arnold
Chapter 3: Constantine Manos/Magnum
Chapter 4: Constantine Manos/Magnum
Chapter 5: George W. Gardner
Chapter 6: David Bookbinder/Peter Arnold
Chapter 7: Leif Skoogfors/Woodfin Camp
Chapter 8: Jeff Albertson/Stock, Boston
Chapter 9: Frank Siteman/Stock, Boston
Chapter 10: Paul Fortin/Stock, Boston
Chapter 11: Charles Gatewood
Chapter 12: Rick Smolan
Chapter 13: Elliott Erwitt/Magnum
Chapter 14: Bruce Davidson/Magnum
Chapter 15: J. Berndt/Stock, Boston
Chapter 16: Owen Franken/Stock, Boston
Chapter 17: Inge Morath/Magnum